COASTAL
FISHES
of
SOUTH - EASTERN
AUSTRALIA

COASTAL
FISHES
—————— of ——————
SOUTH - EASTERN
AUSTRALIA

RUDIE H. KUITER

UNIVERSITY OF HAWAII PRESS
HONOLULU

A CHP Production

Produced and published by
Crawford House Press Pty Ltd
PO Box 1484
Bathurst NSW 2795 Australia

Published in the United States of America by
University of Hawaii Press
2840 Kolowalu Street
Honolulu, Hawaii 96822

Designed by David H. Barrett

Library of Congress Cataloguing-in-Publication Data
   Kuiter, Rudolf H. (Rudolf Herman), 1943–
     Coastal fishes of south-eastern Australia / Rudolf H.
     Kuiter
       p.   cm.
     Includes indexes.
     ISBN 0-8248-1523-8
     1. Fishes -- Australia, Southeastern. 2. Fishes --
   Australia, Southeastern -- Classification. 3. Fishes --
   Australia, Southeastern -- Identification. I. Title.
   QL636.K84   1993
   597.09943--dc20   92-32504
                                   CIP

Printed in Hong Kong by Colorcraft Ltd

10 9 8 7 6 5 4 3 2 1

CONTENTS

ACKNOWLEDGEMENTS

Foremost, my special thanks to Alison, wife and dive-buddy, for her continuous support and contributing in many ways to my work.

I would like to thank the numerous people which have been instrumental in bringing about this book, but it would be impossible to name them all. The groundwork for this book dates back to my first interest in marine fishes in 1964, when living in Sydney. In the late 1960s, seeking scientific knowledge and help, it was John Paxton at the Australian Museum who was most helpful. To John I am particularly grateful for giving me lots of time and advice, and for pointing me in the right direction. I thank the numerous ichthyologists who have taught me through correspondence and kindly sent their scientific publications. Special thanks to those individuals who come randomly to mind: Jack Randall, Gerry Allen, Martin Gomon, Doug Hoese, Helen Larson, Barry Russell, Rob Myers, John Glover, Hajime Masuda, Keiichi Matsuura, Hiroshi Senou, Ted Pietsch, David Grobecker, Bruno Conde, Phil Heemstra, Peter Last, Barry Hutchins, Walter Ivantsoff, Howard Choat, Jeffrey Leis, Tony Gill, Stuart Poss, Chuck Dawson, William Smith-Vaniz, Peter Last, Graham Hardy, Malcolm Francis, and Tony Ayling.

I also thank the following people for their logistic support, time and friendship: Lew and Mary Reynolds, John and Kerry-Ann Meredith, Bob and Cathy Reed, Paul Zorn, Terry Brisset, Pang Quang, Roger Steene, Dave and Liz Parer, Helmut Debelius, Tsuneo Nakamura, Takuya Mori, Barry Andrewartha, Belinda Barnes, Ian Head, Dave Pollard, Johan Bell, Scoresby Shepherd, Doug Reilly, Murray McDonald, Barry Bruce, Adrian Newman, Reg Lipson, Malcolm Wells, Ian MacIntosh from the early days, and Frank and Val Russell during my bachelor years, with their typical great Australian hospitality.

A special thanks to those who contributed photographs, who are individually credited with the illustrations.

Finally, I would like to thank the institutions which provided support and invited me on field trips: Australian Museum; NSW State Fisheries; Museum of Victoria; Fisheries and Wildlife, Victoria; South Australian Museum; South Australian Department of Fisheries; Western Australian Museum; Australian Broadcasting Corporation (ABC television); Toba Aquarium, Japan; Manly Marine Land; and Darling Harbour Aquarium, Sydney.

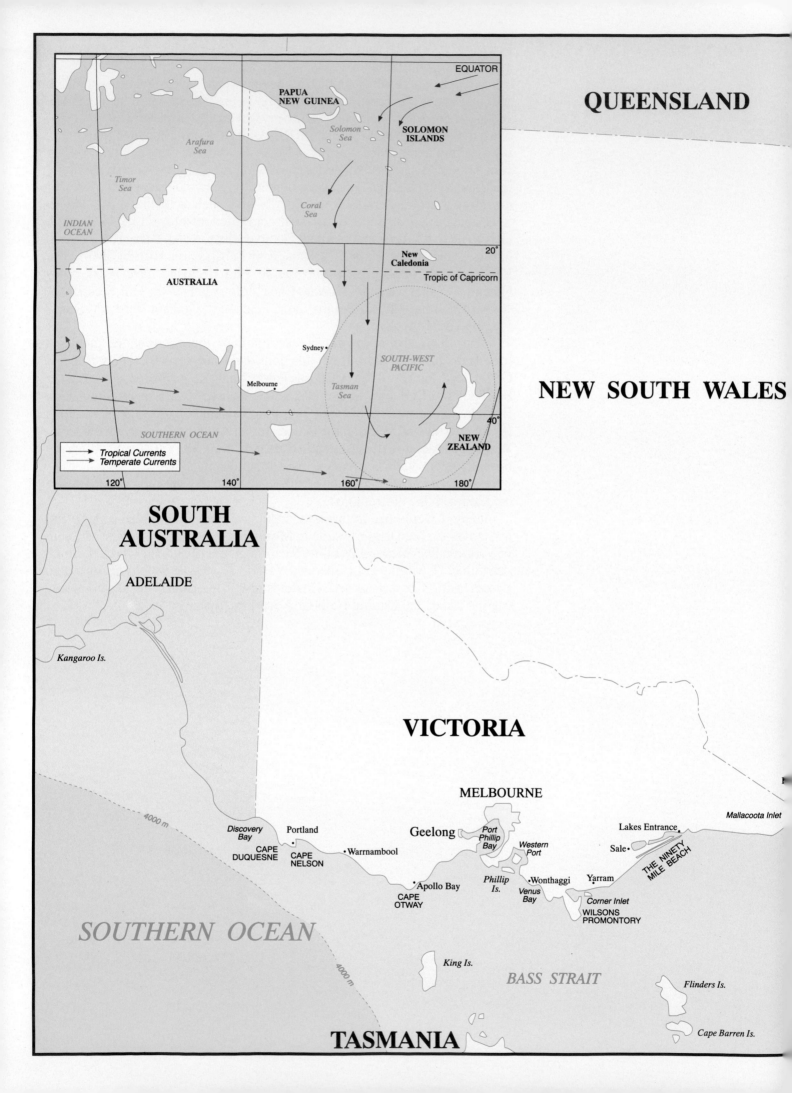

QUEENSLAND

NEW SOUTH WALES

EQUATOR

PAPUA
NEW GUINEA

Solomon
Sea

SOLOMON
ISLANDS

*Arafura
Sea*

*Timor
Sea*

INDIAN
OCEAN

*Coral
Sea*

New
Caledonia

20°

AUSTRALIA

Tropic of Capricorn

Sydney •

SOUTH-WEST
PACIFIC

Melbourne •

*Tasman
Sea*

SOUTHERN   OCEAN

40°

NEW
ZEALAND

→ Tropical Currents
→ Temperate Currents

120°   140°   160°   180°

SOUTH
AUSTRALIA

ADELAIDE

Kangaroo Is.

VICTORIA

MELBOURNE

Mallacoota Inlet

4000 m

Geelong

*Port
Phillip
Bay*

Lakes Entrance

*Discovery
Bay*

Portland

*Western
Port*

Sale •

CAPE
DUQUESNE

CAPE
NELSON

• Warrnambool

*Phillip
Is.*

• Wonthaggi

Yarram •

THE NINETY
MILE BEACH

• Apollo Bay

*Venus
Bay*

Corner Inlet

CAPE
OTWAY

WILSONS
PROMONTORY

SOUTHERN OCEAN

King Is.

BASS STRAIT

Flinders Is.

4000 m

TASMANIA

Cape Barren Is.

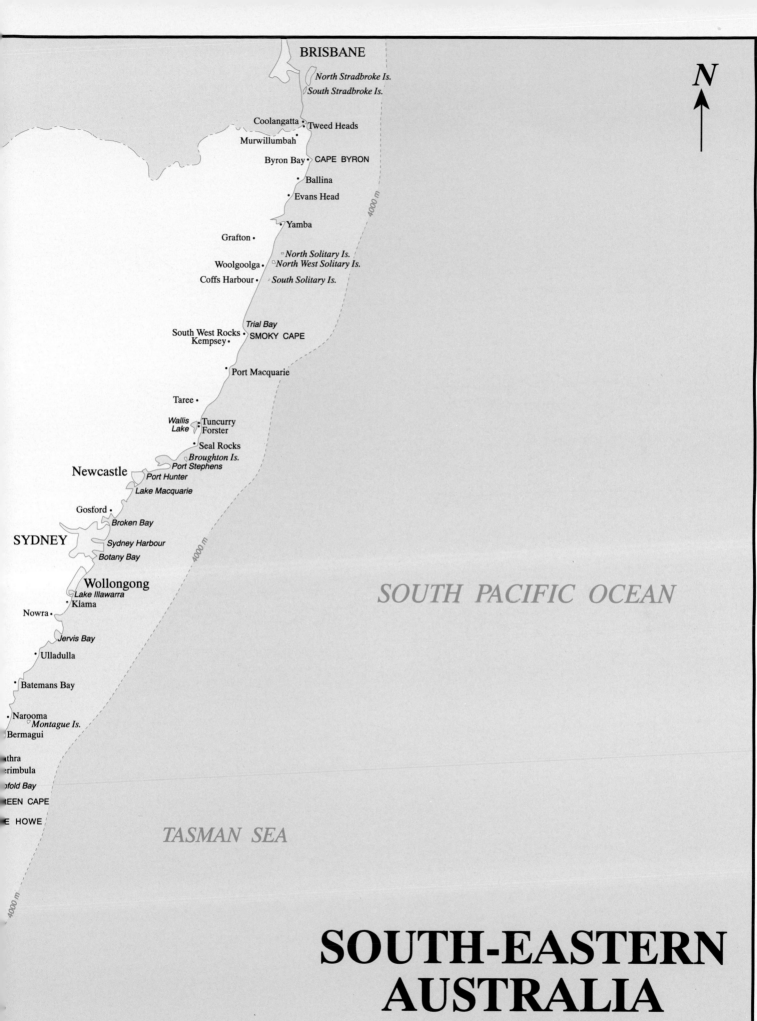

BRISBANE

North Stradbroke Is.
South Stradbroke Is.

Coolangatta • • Tweed Heads
Murwillumbah •
Byron Bay • CAPE BYRON
• Ballina
• Evans Head
• Yamba
Grafton •
□ *North Solitary Is.*
Woolgoolga • □ *North West Solitary Is.*
Coffs Harbour • *South Solitary Is.*

Trial Bay
South West Rocks • SMOKY CAPE
Kempsey •

• Port Macquarie

Taree •

Wallis Lake • Tuncurry
Forster
• Seal Rocks
Broughton Is.
Port Stephens
Newcastle • Port Hunter
Lake Macquarie

Gosford •
Broken Bay
SYDNEY *Sydney Harbour*
Botany Bay

Wollongong
Lake Illawarra
Kiama
Nowra •

Jervis Bay
• Ulladulla

• Batemans Bay

• Narooma
Montague Is.
Bermagui

athra
erimbula
fold Bay
EEN CAPE
E HOWE

4000 m

SOUTH PACIFIC OCEAN

TASMAN SEA

N

SOUTH-EASTERN AUSTRALIA

Scale = 1:5 500 000

PICTORIAL GUIDE TO FAMILIES

The following outline drawings represent typical members of most of the families included in this book. The scientific name of the family is indicated beneath the relevant picture, and the number of the page on which the family will be found is included in parentheses.

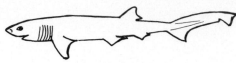

Hexanchidae (p. 2)

Heterodontidae (p. 3)

Brachaeluridae (p. 7)

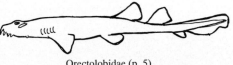

Orectolobidae (p. 5)

Parascyllidae (p. 7)

Scyliorhinidae (p. 8)

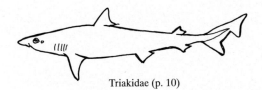

Triakidae (p. 10)

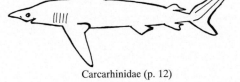

Carcarhinidae (p. 12)

Sphyrnidae (p. 11)

Lamnidae (p. 14)

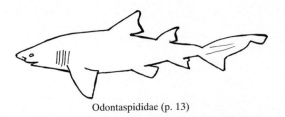

Odontaspididae (p. 13)

Callorhinchidae (p. 24)

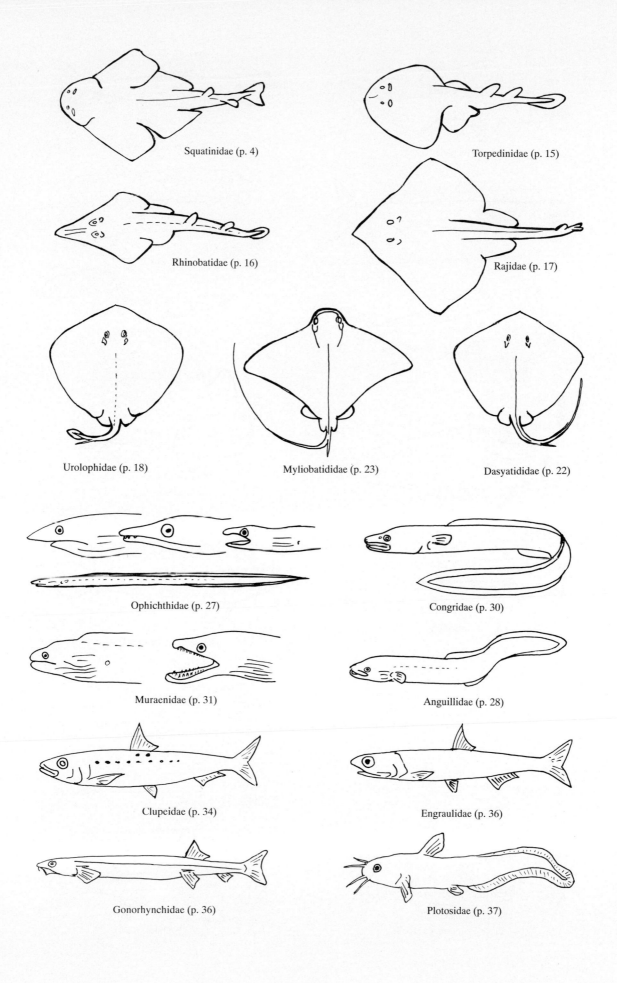

Squatinidae (p. 4)

Torpedinidae (p. 15)

Rhinobatidae (p. 16)

Rajidae (p. 17)

Urolophidae (p. 18)

Myliobatididae (p. 23)

Dasyatididae (p. 22)

Ophichthidae (p. 27)

Congridae (p. 30)

Muraenidae (p. 31)

Anguillidae (p. 28)

Clupeidae (p. 34)

Engraulidae (p. 36)

Gonorhynchidae (p. 36)

Plotosidae (p. 37)

Aulopidae (p. 39)

Synodontidae (p. 40)

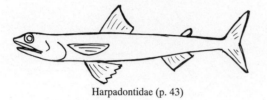

Harpadontidae (p. 43)

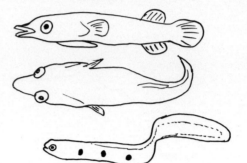

Gobiesocidae (p. 52)

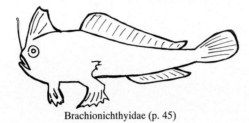

Brachionichthyidae (p. 45)

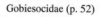

Antennariidae (p. 46)

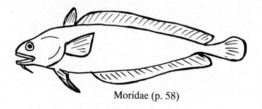

Moridae (p. 58)

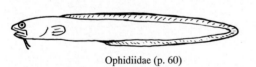

Ophidiidae (p. 60)

Batrachoididae (p. 44)

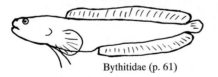

Bythitidae (p. 61)

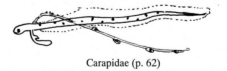

Carapidae (p. 62)

Hemiramphidae (p. 63)

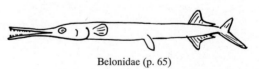

Belonidae (p. 65)

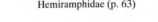

Atherinidae (p. 66)

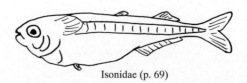

Isonidae (p. 69)

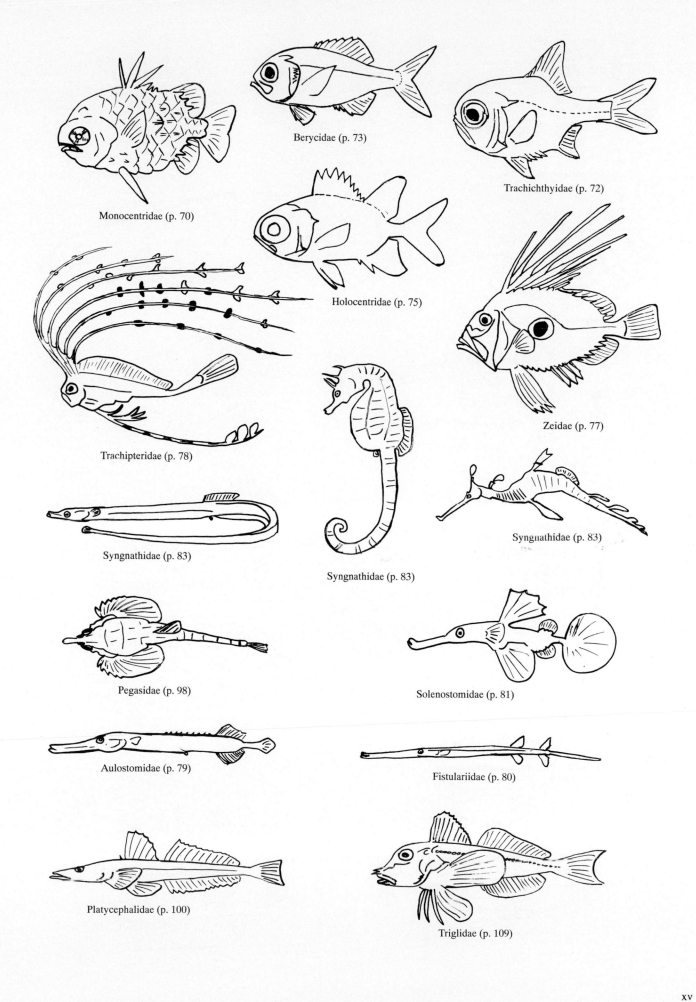

Monocentridae (p. 70)

Berycidae (p. 73)

Trachichthyidae (p. 72)

Holocentridae (p. 75)

Zeidae (p. 77)

Trachipteridae (p. 78)

Syngnathidae (p. 83)

Syngnathidae (p. 83)

Syngnathidae (p. 83)

Pegasidae (p. 98)

Solenostomidae (p. 81)

Aulostomidae (p. 79)

Fistulariidae (p. 80)

Platycephalidae (p. 100)

Triglidae (p. 109)

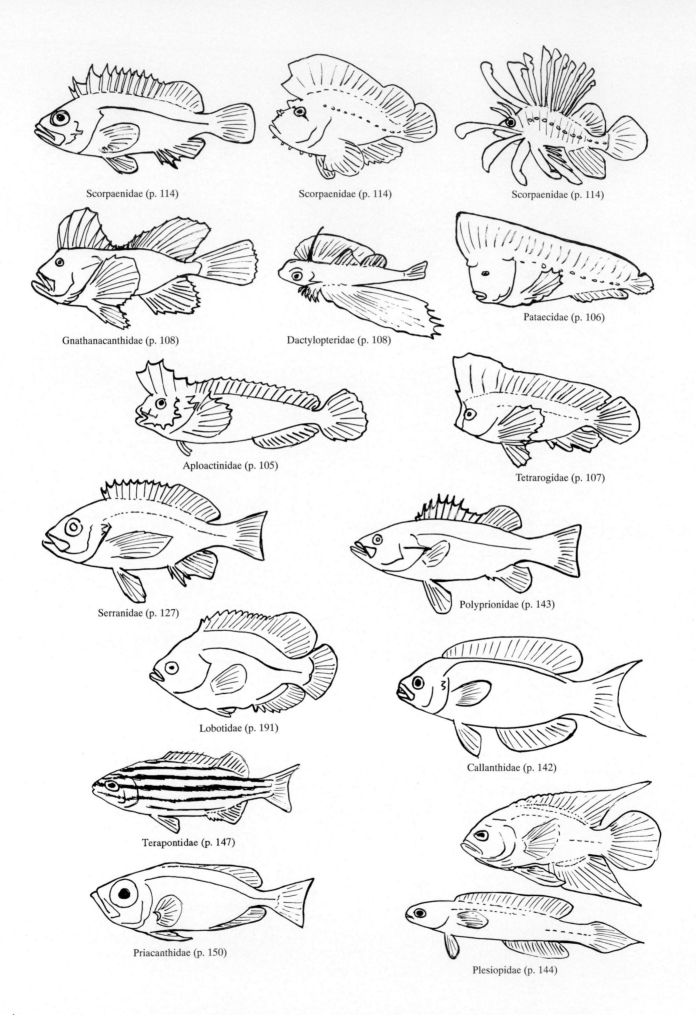

Scorpaenidae (p. 114)

Scorpaenidae (p. 114)

Scorpaenidae (p. 114)

Gnathanacanthidae (p. 108)

Dactylopteridae (p. 108)

Pataecidae (p. 106)

Aploactinidae (p. 105)

Tetrarogidae (p. 107)

Serranidae (p. 127)

Polyprionidae (p. 143)

Lobotidae (p. 191)

Callanthidae (p. 142)

Terapontidae (p. 147)

Priacanthidae (p. 150)

Plesiopidae (p. 144)

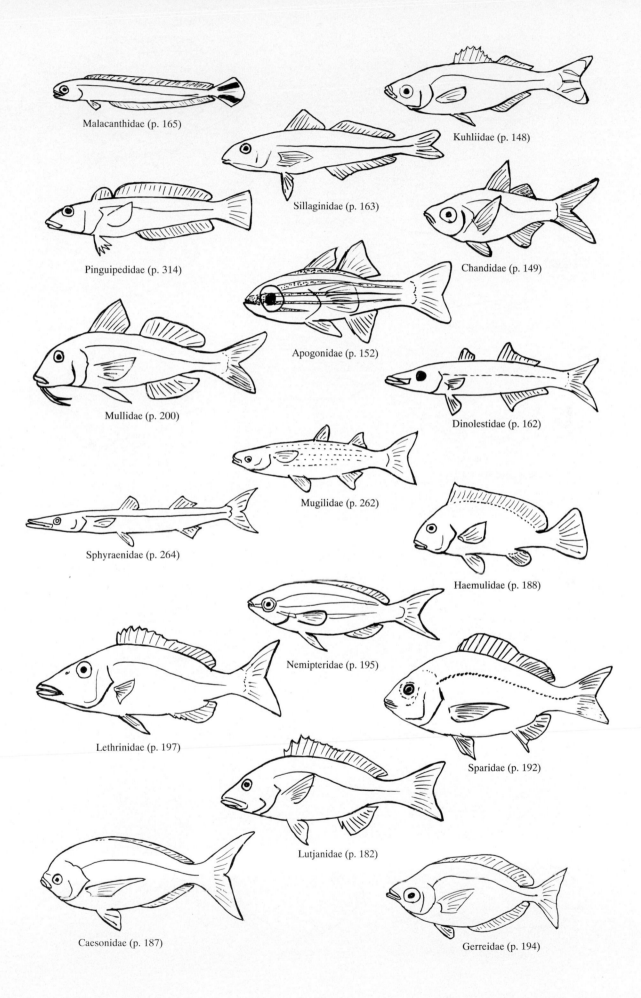

Malacanthidae (p. 165)

Kuhliidae (p. 148)

Sillaginidae (p. 163)

Pinguipedidae (p. 314)

Chandidae (p. 149)

Apogonidae (p. 152)

Mullidae (p. 200)

Dinolestidae (p. 162)

Mugilidae (p. 262)

Sphyraenidae (p. 264)

Haemulidae (p. 188)

Nemipteridae (p. 195)

Lethrinidae (p. 197)

Sparidae (p. 192)

Lutjanidae (p. 182)

Caesonidae (p. 187)

Gerreidae (p. 194)

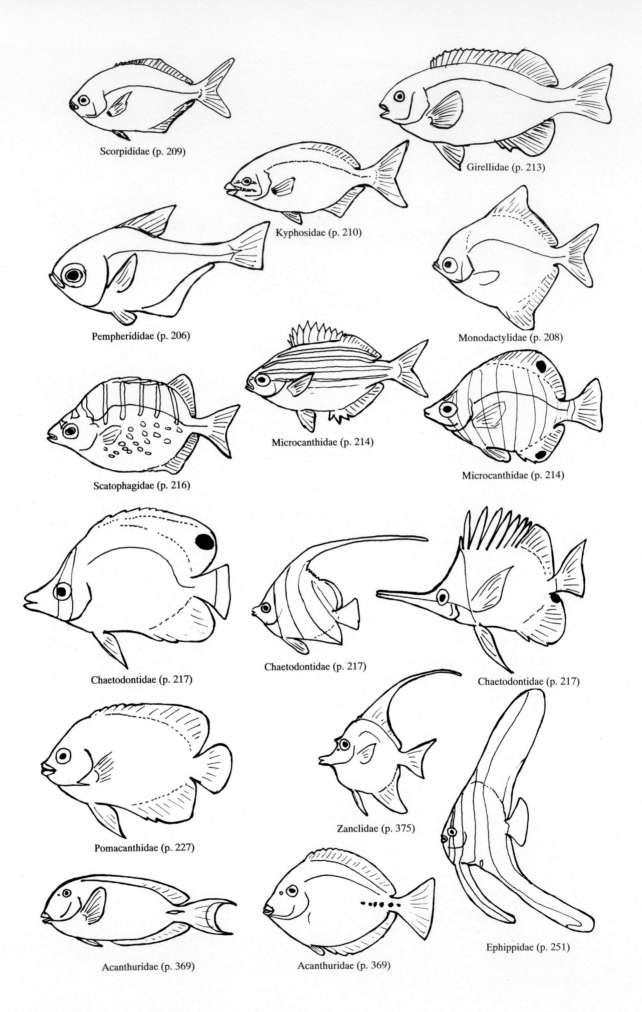

Scorpididae (p. 209)

Girellidae (p. 213)

Kyphosidae (p. 210)

Pempherididae (p. 206)

Monodactylidae (p. 208)

Scatophagidae (p. 216)

Microcanthidae (p. 214)

Microcanthidae (p. 214)

Chaetodontidae (p. 217)

Chaetodontidae (p. 217)

Chaetodontidae (p. 217)

Pomacanthidae (p. 227)

Zanclidae (p. 375)

Ephippidae (p. 251)

Acanthuridae (p. 369)

Acanthuridae (p. 369)

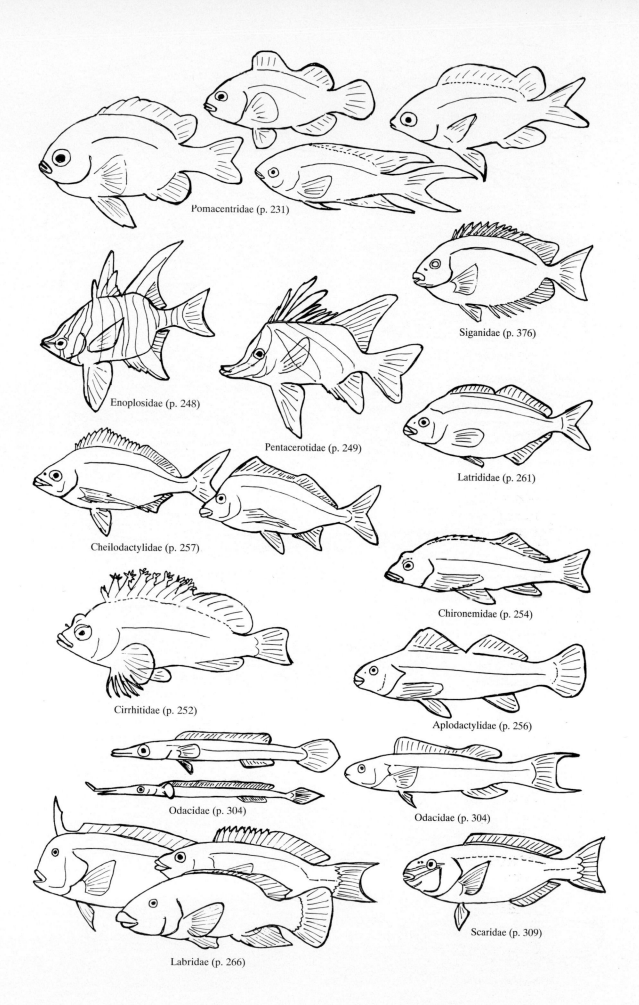

Pomacentridae (p. 231)

Siganidae (p. 376)

Enoplosidae (p. 248)

Pentacerotidae (p. 249)

Latrididae (p. 261)

Cheilodactylidae (p. 257)

Chironemidae (p. 254)

Cirrhitidae (p. 252)

Aplodactylidae (p. 256)

Odacidae (p. 304)

Odacidae (p. 304)

Labridae (p. 266)

Scaridae (p. 309)

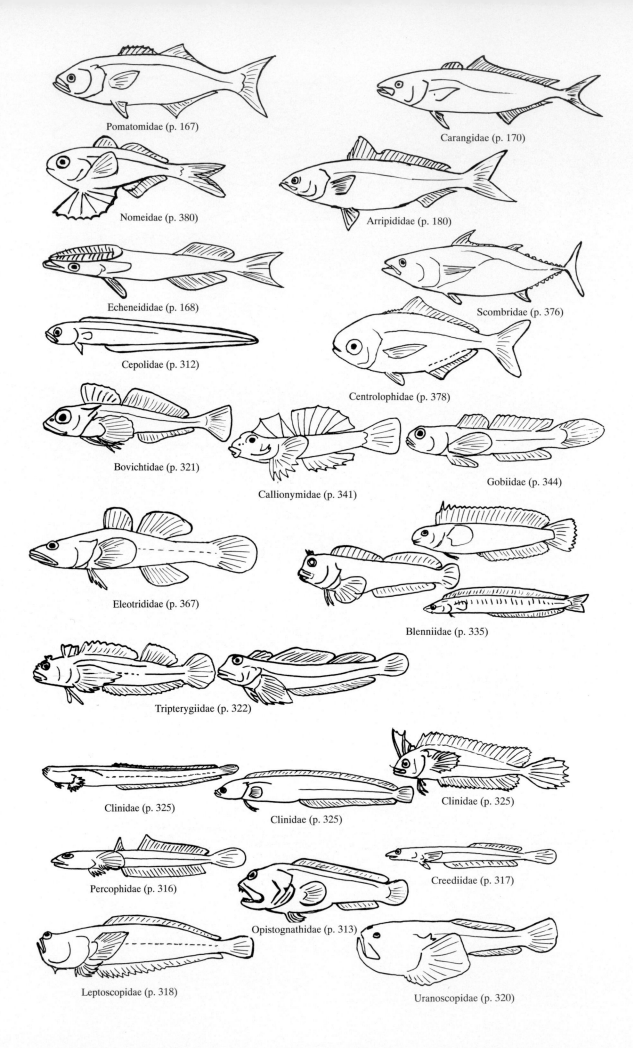

Pomatomidae (p. 167)

Carangidae (p. 170)

Nomeidae (p. 380)

Arripididae (p. 180)

Echeneididae (p. 168)

Scombridae (p. 376)

Cepolidae (p. 312)

Centrolophidae (p. 378)

Bovichtidae (p. 321)

Callionymidae (p. 341)

Gobiidae (p. 344)

Eleotrididae (p. 367)

Blenniidae (p. 335)

Tripterygiidae (p. 322)

Clinidae (p. 325)

Clinidae (p. 325)

Clinidae (p. 325)

Percophidae (p. 316)

Creediidae (p. 317)

Opistognathidae (p. 313)

Leptoscopidae (p. 318)

Uranoscopidae (p. 320)

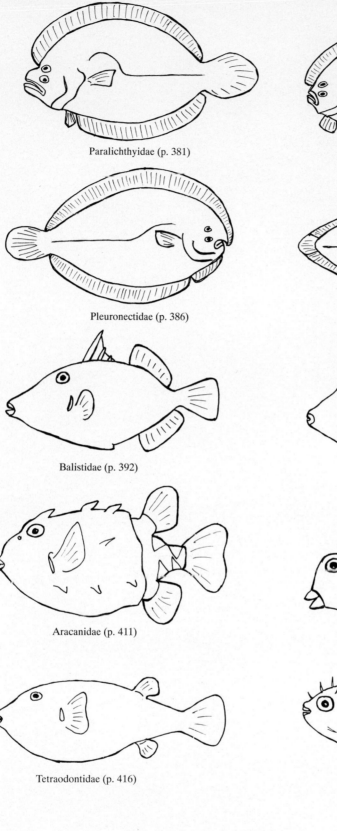

Paralichthyidae (p. 381)

Bothidae (p. 383)

Pleuronectidae (p. 386)

Soleidae (p. 388)

Balistidae (p. 392)

Monacanthidae (p. 397)

Aracanidae (p. 411)

Ostraciidae (p. 413)

Tetraodontidae (p. 416)

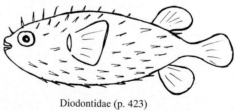

Diodontidae (p. 423)

INTRODUCTION

Australia's south-east coast is part of the south-west Pacific, an area which approximately ranges from the Coral Sea off Queensland to Tasmania's east coast and includes the New Zealand area. A basin, more than 5 km deep, the Tasman Basin, lays between the coast of Australia from southern Queensland to eastern Tasmania and New Zealand, extended by the Norfolk Rise as far as Brisbane. The sea over this area is known as the Tasman Sea. In the south it is influenced by the southern circumpolar current, and on the east coast of Australia by currents originating further north, generally referred to as the East Australian Current. These circumstances cause some instability with regard to the species make-up of the fauna in the region. The majority of Australian fishes have pelagic stages and may get dispersed over large areas, often well beyond their breeding range. On the east coast there is the gradual change from tropical in the north to temperate in the south, and the range of species in the area often fluctuates north or south. In addition, there are numerous expatriates which float into areas as eggs or larvae, and although the majority are from the north, some originate from south-western waters. Most tropical species can not survive the colder waters in the south, particularly inshore where, compared to offshore, temperatures are generally lower by a few degrees. New South Wales has a few islands along the south coast to support tropical species, and the only island away from inshore conditions is Montague Island, but it is too far south to sustain populations over long periods. Although many species reach adult sizes there and spawn occasionally, at different times, sometimes after several years, cold up-wellings wipe out the tropical species.

Habitats vary greatly along the coast, with numerous small to large bays along the entire New South Wales and eastern Victorian coast and Bass Strait, with sandy beaches, shallow and deep lagoons or estuaries, and from tropical coral habitats in the north to temperate weedy or seagrass beds in the south. The entire coastal area is rich in fish species, and recreational fishing is part of life for those people living near the coast. In addition, the east coast is well known for the

(Opposite) The leafy seadragon is one of the most spectacular of all fishes and is unique to southern Australian waters.

The author photographing a small fish on the reef while a school of snapper swim past.

Photo: Alison Kuiter

A long-spined sea urchin, *Diadema palmeri*, photographed at Montague Island at 30 m depth. The east Australian fauna shares many invertebrates like this sea urchin and fishes with northern New Zealand.

many excellent dive sites with extremely rich and diverse reef life including sponge gardens, kelp reefs, sea-whip walls, and numerous fishes. Fishes are like birds in the forest, and divers are increasingly becoming interested in looking at or photographing the various species. Just like the birds, some are obvious while others are secretive and difficult to see. The birds are well covered by many excellent books, however with fishes it is a different story. The most recent comprehensive illustrated publication on the New South Wales area was in 1927 by McCulloch, titled *Fishes and Fish-like Animals of NSW*. A book on Victorian sea fishes never eventuated. Since that time numerous changes and additions were published in scientific papers. The aim of this book is the fill the vacuum.

About the Book

As the primary purpose of this book is to allow the user to identify certain species of fish, it has been designed to accommodate various people with different levels of knowledge about fish. The terminology has been kept as simple as possible, and only the external features are used in keys. For those who have little knowledge of fish features, photographs speak for themselves, and in a way similar to a situation where a specimen is not at hand. It may be difficult to identify a fish by its features, apart from colour and shape, from a photograph. Much more difficult is trying to identify a species from memory, especially if it moves about quickly and there is no time to see any unusual features. In many cases it is necessary to recognise the family in which it belongs. Many species have various stages which can differ dramatically in colour and shape between juvenile and adult or between sexes, and some are extremely variable. Photographs are provided of different stages and extreme colour-forms of the more difficult species. The majority of species were photographed in their natural habitat except some, virtually impossible to photograph while diving, which were collected and placed in an aquarium to obtain their normal living colour. Using the pictorial guide to the families with its outline drawings, the reader will be able to narrow a species down to a small group. Knowing or learning the terminology from the external features shown in the diagrams makes the keys usable as well. Individual species write-ups give the external meristics and features of use in identification not easily observed in the illustrations. Additional information on size, distribution and behaviour is supplied where known. Much of the behavioural information is based on the author's observations.

All fishes presented in this book belong at the highest level in the superclass Pisces, which basically encompasses those which have jaws, usually well-

Sponges and basketstars occur commonly in southern Australian waters in depths of 25 m or more where kelp can no longer grow because of lack of light.

(Top) The rugged south Victorian coast near Port McDonald showing the effect of the ocean swell.

(Bottom) Sugarloaf Point seen from Seal Rocks village, a small holiday and fishing spot popular with divers in New South Wales. It is close to the continental shelf and has a great variety of fish species.

developed eyes, and paired fins present (though these features may be degenerated in a few cases). They are in two major groups: the class Chondrichthyes, the cartilaginous fishes comprising the sharks and rays, and; the Osteichthyes, the bony fishes comprising a great variety including eels and those species generally referred to as "fishes". General information about the classes and a key to the next level down, the orders, are provided within. The same procedure is repeated in each order for the next level down, the families. Keys at family level are not provided as the space it would take is not warranted by the value of the exercise. Having determined the family from the provided higher-level keys, the pictures of the species within the family would undoubtedly beat any key in time, except where a specimen has been preserved for a considerable length of time, for which this book has not been designed. Classification of fishes at all levels at this stage in time is unstable. Every author has a different view and may or may not adopt work by others, resulting in every book, including this one, adapting differently to information available. The approach in this book has been simplification and uniformity where possible, and some logical input to accommodate the majority of those interested in fishes which have no access to a microscope, x-ray machine or other expensive equipment. The description of individual species, however, includes various features such as type of scales, fin and element counts and so on, which would need a microscope to determine, but with many small species is sometimes the only way to separate or identify them.

Common Names

There are no official rules in the use of common names, but it seems logical to maintain those used locally even though it may be misleading as to the type of

Sandstone reefs of Victorian estuaries are covered by kelp on top but the sides are eroded by wave action and sea urchins grinding their own hollows for shelter. Eventually the caves become large and home for numerous sea urchins.

fish. For example, the Blue Groper is really a wrasse, not a groper (spelt grouper elsewhere). Australian names for certain families usually differ from those used elsewhere, and often find their way into Australian publications. In this book Australian names have been given preference. In some cases compromises had to be made where names doubled for different species, or where a general name for a group was applied to parrotfishes on the south coast and to wrasses elsewhere, while true parrotfishes are a distinct group of tropical species. A wide-ranging species may be known under a number of different names from state to state, and even from one fishing place to another, and it is very difficult to pick the right name unless it is available from early publications such as those by McCulloch, Whitley, Stead, Munro or Grant, who were the major authors using common names. In some cases the early spearfishing records were of use. A large number of species included in this book were never blessed with a common name and are here named for the first time. In each case, the naming is because of certain characters, a habitat or locality, or after a particular person.

Scientific Names

The starting point for our biological nomenclature is 1758, with the publication of the tenth edition of Carl Linnaeus' *Systema Natura*. From that time fishes were named by scientists who gave them a Latin name and described the various features that distinguished the fishes from others. Many species were named up to 200 years ago and, as one can imagine, communication in the early days was rather slow. Consequently many scientists were unaware of what everybody else was doing at the same time. Obtaining a specimen of an unknown fish often resulted in a quick description of the new species. As a result, sometimes the

(Top) A red gorgonian off Kiama, New South Wales.

(Bottom) The New South Wales coast has many reefs which are rich with colourful invertebrates such as seastars, sponges and gorgonians. This brickstar, *Asterodiscides truncatus*, was photographed off Bermagui.

(Opposite) A glasseye, *Priacanthus blochii*, feeding on zooplankton, tiny mysids, which are sucked into the large mouth and strained from the water by the numerous gill rakers (which look like combs along the gill arches).

same species was described over and over again. The Sargassum Anglerfish probably tops the list with at least 20 different names assigned to six different genera. Normally the first published name applies, but there may be complications as the name may already exist. An insect or something else may have been described prior to the date the fish was named, and with the same name as used for the fish's genus, or as in many cases, the species may have been thought to belong in a particular already known genus when it should have been given a new generic status. In the case of the Sargassum Anglerfish, its first name appeared as *Lophius histrio* Linnaeus, 1758. Several species were classified in the same genus, which was incorrect as these species were generically different. It was not until 1813, after the use of several other incorrect generic names, that the genus was recognised by Fischer as being distinct – *Histrio*. In many case the same species is described from different sexes and as they are often collected together they are usually described in the same paper, from one page to the other, in which case the priority page rules regardless of sex. This is particularly the case with wrasses (Labridae), where the male is often so different in colour patterns from the female it is difficult to imagine a close relationship unless studying the particular species underwater. In the last decade, many species once thought to be different were found by underwater observation to be sexual forms of the same species. In addition, juveniles can differ greatly from adults and many juveniles were grown in aquariums to determine their identity, some taking about four years. Numerous tropical larvae settle along the New South Wales coast and photographs of such stages have been included, and although adults of these species are generally rare they have been included as well.

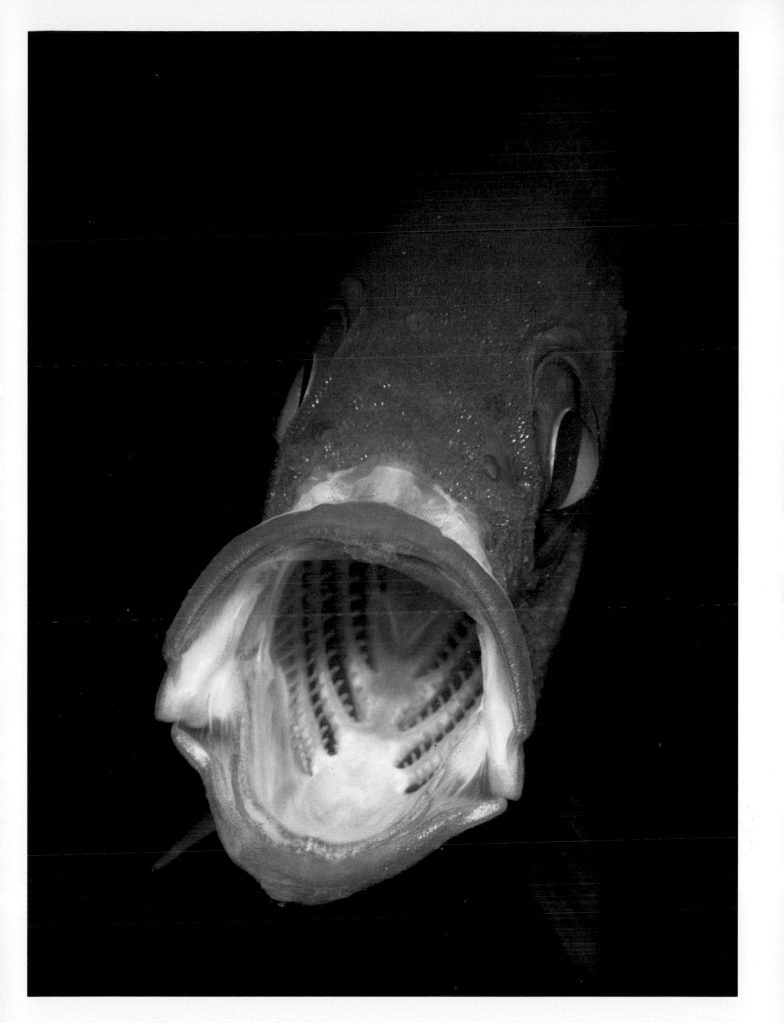

Count and Measurement Methods

Features which are in numbers and are countable, such as fin elements or scale rows, are presented in formulas to simplify descriptions and are known as meristic values. Fin formulas begin with the first letter of the type of fin, thus dorsal D, anal A, caudal C, pectoral P and ventral V. The letter is followed by the number of elements. Counts are in the direction of head to tail. The number of fin spines is given in Roman numerals and the number of soft rays in Arabic numerals, thus a dorsal fin with 10 spines and 14 rays is presented as D X,14. If the fin is in separate parts and the division is in the spinous part with one spine in the second part it is presented as IX+I,14. Similarly, if the anal fin has three spines and seven rays, it is presented as A III,7. Pectoral fin counts include all developed rays excluding rudimentary rays. Caudal fin rays include only branched and segmented rays, known as principal rays, excluding preceding small and simple rays. Divided rays sharing a common base are counted as 1, except when the base is covered by scales and the rays appear to be separate. Scale counts are usually along the lateral line and given as LL followed by the number of scales along this line to the point where the body ends and the caudal fin begins (the end of the hypural), even though several scales may follow beyond. The lateral line may be interrupted and the parts are presented in separate counts, for example LL 15+7. Some species have an upper lateral line (ULL) and lower lateral line (LLL). Tiny additional scales (auxiliary scales) which are sometimes present are not included in the count. Sometimes a lateral line is absent and when scales are counted they are presented in a lateral scale row (LSR), counting the vertical of least obliquely angled rows from pectoral fin base to caudal fin base. The length given is the total length from the tip of the snout to the end of the tail. Soft flexible parts such as fleshy barbels or fin filaments are not included in the measurement. Forked fins are pushed together and measured to the tips. Measurements are based on local specimens, often recorded larger elsewhere, and where possible on captured material. The actual description for each species may vary from on to the other, as features which are diagnostic to a family or species are mainly given and obvious features seen in the illustrations are not repeated. Some are specifically pointed out to determine the identity of or distinguish between similar species.

EXTERNAL FEATURES OF FISHES

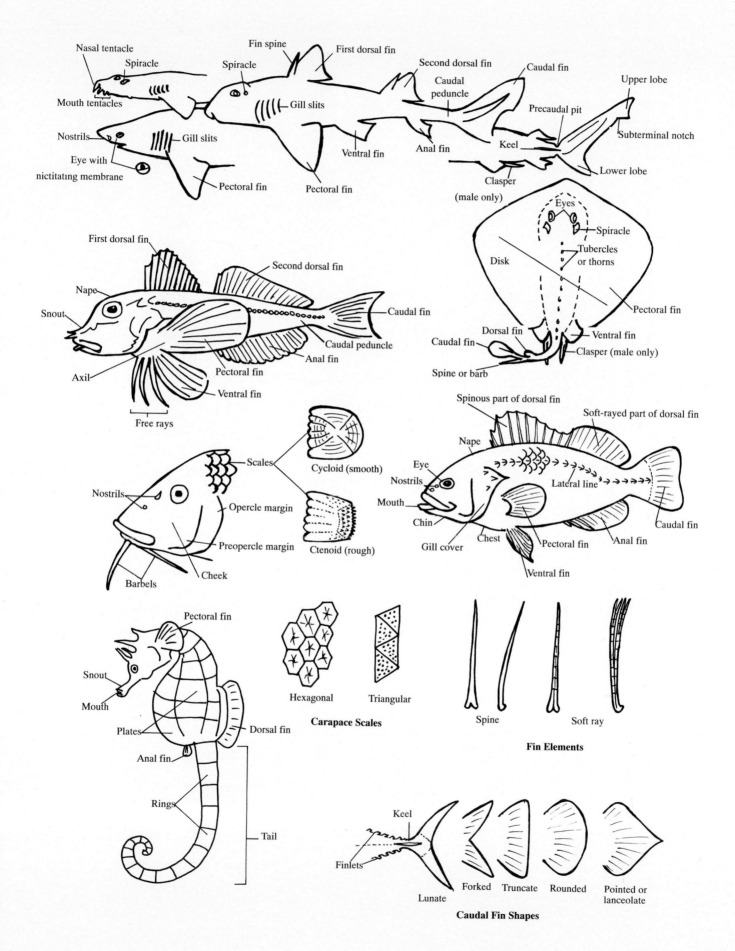

Nasal tentacle
Spiracle
Mouth tentacles
Nostrils
Eye with nictitating membrane
Pectoral fin
Spiracle
Fin spine
First dorsal fin
Gill slits
Gill slits
Pectoral fin
Pectoral fin
Ventral fin
Second dorsal fin
Caudal peduncle
Anal fin
Keel
Clasper (male only)
Caudal fin
Upper lobe
Precaudal pit
Subterminal notch
Lower lobe

First dorsal fin
Nape
Snout
Axil
Pectoral fin
Ventral fin
Free rays
Second dorsal fin
Caudal fin
Caudal peduncle
Anal fin

Eyes
Spiracle
Disk
Tubercles or thorns
Pectoral fin
Dorsal fin
Caudal fin
Spine or barb
Ventral fin
Clasper (male only)

Scales
Nostrils
Opercle margin
Preopercle margin
Barbels
Cheek
Cycloid (smooth)
Ctenoid (rough)

Spinous part of dorsal fin
Nape
Eye
Nostrils
Mouth
Chin
Gill cover
Chest
Ventral fin
Pectoral fin
Lateral line
Anal fin
Caudal fin
Soft-rayed part of dorsal fin

Pectoral fin
Snout
Mouth
Plates
Anal fin
Rings
Tail
Dorsal fin

Hexagonal
Triangular
Carapace Scales

Spine
Soft ray
Fin Elements

Keel
Finlets
Lunate
Forked
Truncate
Rounded
Pointed or lanceolate
Caudal Fin Shapes

THE CARTILAGINOUS FISHES

CLASS CHONDRICHTHYES

This group comprises sharks, rays, and ghost sharks. Shared features are a more or less hardened cartilaginous skeleton and internal fertilisation. Males have paired organs on the inside of the ventral fins (claspers) to transmit sperm. Primarily marine fishes, a few have adapted fully to fresh water. They are divided into two major groups: the sharks and rays, Subclass Elasmobranchii, with the upper jaw suspended from the skull and five to seven paired gill openings, and; ghost sharks, Subclass Holocephali, with the upper jaw fused to the skull and only one paired gill opening.

SHARKS AND RAYS

A highly diverse group, organised in 14 orders, and by far the most successful of the cartilaginous fishes, comprising at least 43 families and more than 750 species. They are readily recognisable with five to seven paired gill openings directly to the anterior. Other features are a unique blood type, and upper jaw slung from the skull. Sharks primarily differ from rays in having pectoral fins separate from the sides of the head. In rays, these are fused to the side of the head over the gills. Sharks, Superorder Squalomorphea, are arranged in eight orders, and rays, Superorder Batoidea, in six orders.

Sharks: About 350 species occur worldwide, primarily oceanic and widespread in tropical to temperate zones. Some coastal species enter fresh water and can live there for some time. Each species has distinctive types of teeth, which is useful in taxonomy. Some sharks have a movable inner eyelid, called a nictitating eyelid, and a small opening posterior to the eye called a spiracle. The various orders can be determined with Key 1.

All orders have representatives and many families in Australian waters. Most sharks are covered with tiny teeth-like scales called denticles. There are various types with single or multiple recurving spines, making the skin rough when stroking from tail to head and the skin is sometimes used as sandpaper. Denticles do not grow and larger new ones continually replace the old ones. Similarly, teeth are replaced by new ones forming behind existing ones and moving forward. In some species the replacement rate has been measured at about two weeks. Sharks vary greatly in size. The largest species, also the largest of all fishes, is the plankton-eating giant *Rhiniodon typus*, the Whale Shark. The largest measured specimen was 12.65 m long and weighed 21.5 tonnes, but the species probably attains 18 m. Some of the deepwater species attain only about 25 cm, and may mature at about 15 cm. The majority of species are predators, feeding on other sharks, rays, fishes and various other animals. The planktivorous are the largest, feeding in relatively shallow water. The rarely captured Megamouth, *Megachasma*

pelagios, known from only four specimens (one of which washed up in Western Australia), has a very large mouth to strain the water column down deep, where planktonic animals or open water fishes are low in numbers and spread out. Many species are streamlined, fast swimming, and capable of travelling great distances. The blue sharks, *Prionace glauca*, are thought to be among the fastest, reaching almost 40 kmh, and a tagged specimen travelled almost 6,000 km. Some species are sluggish but usually capable of bursts of speed, and there are various benthic species which lay on the substrate and are slow swimmers. Fertilisation is always internal, and reproduction is in three different modes: laying eggs (oviparous), live-bearing (viviparous), and young hatching from eggs within the mother (ovoviviparous).

Rays: An estimated 450 to 500 species occur worldwide. They are usually benthic and primarily marine, though some enter fresh water and about 30 species are fully adapted to fresh water. The group includes

KEY 1: *The Sharks*

1. Dorsal fins one; six to seven paired gill slits .... HEXANCHIFORMES (p. 2)

   Dorsal fins two; five paired gills 2

2. Anal fin present 3

   Anal fin absent 6

3. Dorsal fins preceded by a spine .... HETERODONTIFORMES (p. 3)

   Dorsal fins without spines 4

4. Mouth distinctly in front of eyes .... ORECTOLOBIFORMES (p. 5)

   Mouth posteriorly below eyes 5

5. Nictitating eyelids present .... CARCHARHINIFORMES (p. 8)

   Nictitating eyelids absent .... LAMNIFORMES (p. 13)

6. Mouth at front; ray-like .... SQUATINIFORMES (p. 4)

   Mouth underneath head; not ray-like 7

7. Snout produced, saw-like .... PRISTIOPHORIFORMES

   Snout not produced .... SQUALIFORMES

stingrays, manta rays, eagle rays, stingarees, skates and sawfishes. The batoids are placed in six orders. Characters used in taxonomy are the various shapes, dorsally or ventrally viewed, type of snout, presence of electric organs, type of tail, and number of paired gill openings. The various orders with representatives in Australia can be determined with Key 2 (not included the Hexatrygoniformes which have six paired gill openings, comprising two species from African and Chinese seas).

The sawfishes, shovelnose rays and fiddler rays are in some ways similar to sharks. The others, typically 'ray-like', have greatly depressed bodies virtually surrounded by the large and greatly expanded pectoral fins which form a disc. Viewed from the top, the shape varies from almost circular to diamond-shaped, and some are wider than long with a wing-like appearance. Mouth and gills are underneath. Tails range from thorny and thick to extremely long and whip-like, and a large number of species possess a venomous spine. The electric rays have a ray-like disc but the tail is more shark-like, with a large caudal fin and the presence of one or two dorsal fins. These fishes possess electric organs which are used to stun prey or for defensive purposes, and probably employ electric fields to detect prey buried in the substrate. Rays vary greatly in size. The smallest, a dwarf electric ray, is just 10 cm fully grown. The largest in length are the sawfishes, reaching at least 7.3 m, and in width the mantas at 7 m. Mantas are planktivorous, often feeding on the surface near reefs, and sometimes jumping into the air. Most others are bottom dwellers, feeding on a variety of invertebrates. The wing-like rays can swim extremely fast, particularly the eagle rays, whilst the slender species such as fiddler rays are sluggish and will not move much even when handled. They are well represented in Australian waters, with nine families and many species endemic in southern areas.

GHOST SHARKS

The ghost sharks or Chimaeras are a worldwide tropical to temperate group comprising three families. The majority of species live very deep, some to at least 2,600 m. They are strictly marine and in Australia only one species is found in shallow water, entering estuarine bays. The other representatives of this group feature bodies which taper strongly to a point or whip-like tail, a tall sail-like first dorsal fin preceded by a usually venomous spine, a following low, long-based second dorsal fin, and long and sometimes very broad pectoral fins. Some have a long projecting pointed snout. The included family, comprising a single genus and a few species occurring in temperate waters of the southern hemisphere, is the most peculiar. The snout is elongated with an unusually shaped projection used for digging in sand for molluscs. Like the other members in the group, it is oviparous, producing spindle-shaped eggs with marginal flanges. Species range in size from about 1 to 1.5 m.

FRILLED, SIXGILL AND SEVENGILL SHARKS
ORDER HEXANCHIFORMES

Represented by two families. Chlamydoselachidae, the frilled sharks, are monotypic and considered very primitive. They feature eel-like bodies and a terminal mouth, numerous rows of incurving long tricuspid teeth, and six gill slits almost encircling the head ventrally. They are found only in very deep water, and several specimens have been trawled from 600 to 800 m off the east coast. This family is not included here. Hexanchidae comes in two genera, sixgill and sevengill sharks, which feature more shark-like bodies, with the mouth underneath the head, and six or seven paired lateral gill slits.

SIXGILL AND SEVENGILL SHARKS
FAMILY HEXANCHIDAE

A small family of primarily deep-water sharks, comprising three genera and four species. In possessing six or seven instead of five pairs of gill slits they are readily distinguished from most other sharks. Other features include a single posteriorly placed dorsal fin, a heterocercal caudal fin with long upper lobe, and blade-like comb-shaped teeth in the lower jaw. Adults range in size from about 2 m to almost 5 m. They are ovoviviparous, and litter sizes range from about 10 to 100 in small to large individuals respectively. Broadly distributed in tropical to temperate waters, they are mostly found deep near the bottom, but a few species occasionally come inshore. Although no attacks in the wild are known, these sharks should be regarded as potentially dangerous as they are aggressive when caught or in captivity. Only one species regularly enters southern coastal waters.

KEY 2: *The Rays*

1. Elongate; posteriorly shark-like 2
   Broad, disc-like, not shark-like 3
2. Snout greatly produced, saw-like ....PRISTIDIFORMES
   Snout not greatly produced .....................................RHINOBATIFORMES (p. 16)
3. Caudal fin large, electric organs present .................TORPEDINIFORMES (p. 15)
   Caudal fin small or absent, electric organs absent 4
4. Tail with series of enlarged denticles or thorns ....RAJIFORMES (p. 17)
   Tail mostly smooth, slender often whip-like ......MYLIOBATIDIFORMES (p. 18)

SEVENGILL SHARK
Notorynchus cepedianus (Peron, 1807)

Body long, cylindrical, tapering posteriorly from reach of pectoral fins. Head broad; snout short, broadly rounded. Lower jaw with six rows of large comb-like serrated teeth, with four to seven angled cusps, much smaller and less serrate in upper. Seven gill openings on lower sides of head. Dorsal fin near tail with anal fin below posterior half; ventral fins reach to below dorsal fin origin. Pectoral fins low, horizontal, behind gill openings. Pale grey, shaded above; numerous scattered black and white spots dorsally. Widespread in temperate waters in both hemispheres; in Australian waters from central New South Wales to the Great Australian Bight, including Tasmania. Shallow coastal bays and estuaries to at least 200 m. Apparently includes rays and other sharks in its diet. Known to give birth to as many as 82 young. Attains 3 m. Known also as Tasmanian Tiger Shark. A monotypic genus. Potentially dangerous and may attack when provoked. Reported to attack divers in large display tanks.

BULLHEAD SHARKS
ORDER
HETERODONTIFORMES

Represented by a single family. See below.

PORT JACKSON SHARKS
FAMILY HETERODONTIDAE

A small Indo-Pacific family comprising a single genus with eight species distributed in subtropical and temperate seas. They have a robust blunt head and are also known as bullhead sharks. Other features are two dorsal fins, each headed by a stout, sometimes venomous spine, completely lateral gill slits, and a caudal fin with a large upper lobe and distinct sub-terminal notch. Teeth are similar in both jaws, those in the front with sharp cusps, and in the rear molariform with blunt, rounded cusps. Males have large claspers. The female deposits eggs in reef cracks, though some eggs have long tendrils which anchor to weeds. The egg casings have distinctive spiral flanges. About 15 eggs are produced and young about 15 to 20 cm

long hatch after about 10 months. Port Jackson sharks are slow moving and docile, and feed primarily on benthic invertebrates. They are reef dwellers, often found resting on the substrate, and are mostly active at night. Although not dangerous, they should be handled carefully because of the dorsal spines, and may bite. They range in size from about 60 cm to 1.5 m. Of the three Australian species, one is restricted to the tropics and two are found in south-eastern coastal waters.

PORT JACKSON SHARK
Heterodontus portusjacksoni (Meyer, 1793)

Body tapers to slender tail. Head squarish, blunt; low ridges above eyes to snout; mouth low. Gills laterally in front of and above

Heterodontus portusjacksoni Adult ▲ Juv. ▼

pectoral fins. Dorsal fins triangular, each headed by a large strong spine. Grey to brown, distinct dark harness-like pattern on body. Widespread in southern Australian waters, from southern Queensland to similar latitude on the west coast, including Tasmania; also known from New Zealand. Coastal reefs and rocky estuaries to offshore to at least 250 m. Nocturnal; congregates in caves during the day. Attains 1.6 m. One of the best-known sharks from tagging programs on the east coast. Migrates to breeding areas; travel distances up to 850 km recorded.

CRESTED PORT JACKSON SHARK
Heterodontus galeatus (Günther, 1879)

Body tapers to slender tail. Head squarish, blunt; high ridges above eyes to snout, particularly tall in juveniles; mouth low. Gills laterally in front of and above pectoral fins. Dorsal fins triangular, each headed by a large strong spine. Grey to brown; distinct dark blotched pattern on body. Only known from the east coast, south at least to Montague Island. Coastal reefs, occasionally in rocky estuaries, usually in 20 m or more. Observed singly, generally rare; probably more common in deep water. Egg cases with tendrils up to 2 m long. Attains 1.5 m.

Heterodontus galeatus   Adult ▼ Juv. ▲

ANGELSHARKS, SAND DEVILS AND MONK SHARKS
ORDER SQUATINIFORMES

Represented by a single family. See below.

ANGELSHARKS
FAMILY SQUATINIDAE

A broadly distributed family comprising a single genus with 13 known species. They are benthic sharks with flattened bodies and laterally expanded fins. The anal fin is absent. Angelsharks superficially resemble rays, but their fins are not attached to the head. Gill slits are small, with five pairs ventrally to the side. The head is broadly rounded with small disguised eyes – the spiracles behind the eyes are obvious instead. The snout is often spinous or with fringed nostrils, and is large in some species. There are similar small, sharp, cusped teeth in both jaws. The two small spineless dorsal fins are situated on the tail. Angelsharks are ovoviviparous, having about 10 young per litter at about 30 cm length. Males have large claspers. They are usually white below and sandy-coloured above, and some have large slightly darker ocelli or a mixture of dark and light spots, typical for sand-burrowing fishes. Adult sizes range from about 50 cm to 2 m. Diet consists primarily of benthic invertebrates or fishes. The angelsharks are represented in Australia by two endemic species, one of which is commonly found in shallow coastal waters.

ANGELSHARK
Squatina australis Regan, 1906

Body greatly depressed, widened by large pectoral fins, outline diamond-shaped; snout broadly rounded; tail smooth, stout with equally spaced dorsal fins to caudal fin. Nostrils with large fleshy flaps. Eyes small, well disguised, followed by distinct spiracles. Gill slits small, close together, ventrally on sides of head. Lower lobe of caudal fin larger than upper. White below, sandy-grey to brown above, numerous pale spots. Widespread south coast from central New South Wales to Shark bay, including Tasmania. Shallow to at least 130 m; usually buried in sandy patches near reefs. Extremely well camouflaged; usually discovered accidentally by divers. Not aggressive, but can cause serious wounds if provoked. Fast, and can bite those holding the tail. Attains at least 1.5 m.

CARPETSHARKS
ORDER ORECTOLOBIFORMES

Represented by seven families, all of which have species in Australian waters. They can be determined with Key 3.

Of these families, three have representatives in southern coastal waters and are included here.

1.	Teeth minute, over 300 bands ....RHINIODONTIDAE	
	Nothing like above 2	
2.	Tail about half total length ....STEGOSTOMATIDAE	
	Tail much less than half total length 3	
3.	Many dermal flaps on mouth, large nasally ...................ORECTOLOBIDAE (p. 5)	
	Dermal flaps absent...4	
4.	Nasal tentacle long ....BRACHAELURIDAE (p. 7)	
	Nasal tentacle short 5	
5.	Ventral fins well ahead of dorsal fins ...........................PARASCYLLIDAE (p. 7)	
	Ventral fins about below first dorsal fin .................................HEMISCYLLIDAE	

KEY 3: *The Carpetsharks*

WOBBEGONGS
FAMILY ORECTOLOBIDAE

A small west Pacific family, comprising three genera, two of which are monotypic, and at least seven species, distributed in tropical to temperate waters. Only one genus, *Orectolobus*, occurs in southern waters. This genus comprises at least five species, some of which presently share the same name. Wobbegongs are benthic sharks with flattened bodies broadened by large pectoral fins, but to a lesser extent than the similar angelsharks from which they are readily separated by the presence of an anal fin. The broad flattened head usually features numerous dermal flaps and long barbels on the snout. Dorsal colouration is brownish with various patterns of spots and rings, for which they are often referred to as carpetsharks. Some reach a large size, in excess of 3 m, and can be considered dangerous. Although seemingly sluggish, they can move surprisingly swiftly, and should never be handled (or speared) underwater as they can easily bite their own tail. They are very unpredictable – seemingly dead specimens out of the water may strike a long time after being landed – and also known for robbing spearfishermen of their stringed-up catch. Wobbegongs may attack large prey, screwing up their entire body to tear the victim apart. They are extremely tough, muscular species, occurring in very shallow to deep water, from estuaries to offshore. These sharks are commercially fished, reputed as excellent to eat, and the skin is used for leather in many countries. Of the three species of this genus currently recognised in Australia, two occur commonly in southern coastal waters.

Spotted Wobbegong (*Orectolobus maculatus*)   Juv.

SPOTTED WOBBEGONG
Orectolobus maculatus (Bonnaterre, 1788)

Head greatly flattened, broad. Body broad behind head, tapering to long tail; covered in tough skin. Snout broadly rounded with long leafy skin flaps, some branched, along sides and front. None between nasal tentacles which are long, feeler-like, branched halfway. Eyes small, camouflaged, followed by larger, more obvious spiracles. Dorsal fins set over posterior half of body; anal fin origin posterior to and below end of second dorsal fin, close to caudal fin, seemingly replacing lower lobe. Upper lobe of caudal fin very long. Greenish-brown to light brown or grey; large dark saddles, numerous small white spots forming small circles. East coast from southern Queensland to eastern Victoria. Records from elsewhere appear to be based on other species. Similar species on the west coast appears to be undescribed. Commonly inhabits estuarine waters, but also offshore; recorded to 100 m. Usually sleeps on sand or rocks during the day. Potentially dangerous. Attains 3.2 m.

Orectolobus maculatus   Offshore colouration ▲   Inshore colouration ▼

ORNATE WOBBEGONG
Orectolobus ornatus (De Vis, 1883)

Head greatly flattened, broad. Body broad behind head, tapering to long tail; covered in tough skin. Snout broadly rounded with long leafy skin flaps, some branched, along sides and front. None between nasal tentacles which are long, feeler-like, branched halfway. Eyes small, camouflaged, followed by larger, more obvious spiracles. Dorsal fins set over posterior half of body; anal fin origin posterior to and below end of second dorsal fin, close to caudal fin, seemingly replacing lower lobe. Upper lobe of caudal fin very long. Golden-brown with broad dark areas, somewhat banded below, moderate-sized bluish-grey spots dorsally, usually series of dark spots along fin margins. Broadly distributed along entire Australian coast; reported from Papua New Guinea. Often misidentified as *O. maculatus*. Coastal inshore reefs, offshore islands to at least 50 m. Appears to prefer clear-water reefs, sometimes congregating in small numbers. Potentially dangerous. Attains 3 m.

BLINDSHARKS
FAMILY BRACHAELURIDAE

A very small family, only known from eastern Australia, comprising two genera, each with one species. The blindsharks are benthic sharks, closely related to Orectolobidae and sometimes placed within that family. The head is somewhat depressed, the body thick, snout rounded and each nostril has a long tentacle. Spiracles are small and round, about eye size, placed slightly lower than and behind the eyes. Gill slits are small and partly above the pectoral fins. The dorsal fins are posteriorly placed and the anal fin is near the caudal fin, replacing its lower lobe. The caudal fin has an upper lobe only, which is very elongate. They are small, dull-coloured species reaching about 1 m. Adults are plain dark above, pale below, and the young vary from black to spotted or banded patterns. Blindsharks are secretive, hiding during the day in deep ledges, but move about at night on shallow coastal reefs and seagrass beds feeding on a variety of invertebrates. The Blue-Grey Carpetshark, *Heteroscyllium colcloughi* Ogilby, 1908, is only known from a few southern Queensland specimens and probably ranges into New South Wales. It differs from the included species in colour, reported as dusky-fawn with white spots, and yellow below, and the position of the anal fin is further forward, partly below the second dorsal fin.

BLINDSHARK
Brachaelurus waddi (Bloch and Schneider, 1801)

Body thick; head slightly depressed, flat above, upper profile straight to rounded snout, broad from dorsal view. Long tentacle on each nostril. Eyes with thick eyelids, closed in bright light or when brought to surface. Spiracles small, round, behind and lower than eyes. Dorsal fin over posterior half; anal fin behind and below second dorsal fin. Uniformly black to various shades of brown, sometimes with indistinct broad bands and some pale spotting. Queensland to southern New South Wales, usually in relatively shallow coastal waters. Young among weeds in high-energy surge zones. Adults in caves or ledges during the day. Viviparous; young about 15 cm. Harmless species, attaining a little more than 1 m.

Brachaelurus waddi

COLLARED CATSHARKS
FAMILY PARASCYLLIDAE

A small west Pacific family, comprising two genera: *Parascyllium* confined to southern Australian waters, and *Cirrhoscyllium* confined to southeastern Asia. They are benthic sharks, resembling catsharks of the family Scylliorhinidae, but differ in having distinct nasal barbels, a groove joining the nostrils to the mouth, and a mouth which does not reach to below the eyes. Collared catsharks are very slender sharks with a small head, slightly compressed; ventral, dorsal and anal fins alternate in position along the posterior body and tail. The caudal fin consists of a long upper lobe, notched near the tip. They are nocturnal, hiding in reefs during the day; the young hide under rocks. Some species occur in very shallow depths of only a few metres, while others are mainly known from trawls in excess of 100 m. They are harmless species, and the largest is less than 1 m maximum. Of the three species, two occur regularly in shallow coastal waters. *P. collare* Ramsay and Ogilby, 1888, is mainly known from trawls.

VARIED CATSHARK
Parascyllium variolatum (Dumeril, 1835)

Body long, rounded, head slightly compressed. Nostril barbel short. Smoothly rounded ridge over eyes. Very small spiracles behind eyes. Gill slits small, positioned laterally, partly above pectoral fins. Dorsal fins about equal in size, set over posterior part of body. Ventral fins in front of and below first dorsal fin; anal fin just anteriorly below second dorsal fin, reaching to below centre. Grey to brownish; broad dark band with light speckles around back of head; indistinct dark saddles and light spots an body. Distinct dark spots on fins. Widespread south coast, including Tasmania. Shallow reef and seagrass in reef areas, hiding in reef during the day. Small juveniles under rocks or solid objects in shallow depths. Adults in 3-180 m, sometimes entering lobster pots. Common in Victoria. Attains almost 1 m.

Parascyllium variolatum

RUSTY CATSHARK
Parascyllium ferrugineum McCulloch, 1911

Body long, rounded, head slightly compressed. Nostril barbel short. Smoothly rounded ridge over eyes. Very small spiracles behind eyes. Gill slits small, positioned laterally, partly above pectoral fins. Dorsal fins about equal in size, set over posterior part of body. Ventral fins in front of and below first dorsal fin; anal fin just anteriorly below second dorsal fin, reaching to below origin. Greyish to brownish above with broad, slightly darker saddles, but distinct dark spots dorsally all over body, fins. Widespread south coast, including northern Tasmania and eastern Victoria. Rocky, heavily vegetated reefs, deeper seagrass beds with mixed reefs. Recorded from 5-55 m, but usually deeper; mostly known from trawls. Attains 80 cm.

GROUND SHARKS
ORDER CARCHARHINIFORMES

Represented by eight families, five of which have species in Australian waters. They can be determined with Key 4.

Of these families, four have representatives in southern coastal waters and are included here.

1.	Snout greatly extended laterally, hammer-shaped with eyes at ends ....SPHYRNIDAE (p. 11)
	Snout not extended laterally, pointed 2
2.	First dorsal fin above or posterior to ventral fins ...........SCYLIORHINIDAE (p. 8)
	First dorsal fin anterior to ventral fins 3
3.	Precaudal pits absent (distinct depressions above and below fin origin); eyes usually oval ....TRIAKIDAE (p. 10)
	Precaudal pits present, eyes usually round 4
4.	First dorsal fin more than twice height of second ......CARCHARHINIDAE (p. 12)
	First dorsal fin slightly larger than second ................................HEMIGALEIDAE

KEY 4: *The Ground Sharks*

CATSHARKS
FAMILY SCYLIORHINIDAE

A large family of small shark species, comprising 15 genera and about 90 species, and the most diverse among sharks. Their mouth is posteriorly placed below the eyes. The snout is pointed and of variable length, and some are very elongate. Fins are similarly positioned among the species but there is great variation in sizes. Dorsal fins are small to rather tall, and the caudal fin has a long to very long upper lobe with a distinct notch near its end. The majority of the species are poorly known, occurring in very deep water, and some species are known only from a few specimens. Few species are observed in their natural habitat, as those in shallow depths are very secretive, and are probably venturing away from a normally much deeper habitat. The three species included here are also best known from deep water, but were photographed in relatively shallow depths. No doubt other species will enter shallower depths at times, and eight species are known from the south coast.

SPOTTED CATSHARK
Asymbolis analis (Ogilby, 1885)

Body long, rounded, head flattened with pointed snout. Gill slits lateral, just in front of pectoral fins. No ridge over eyes; generally streamlined, smooth. Dorsal fins placed over posterior half, second slightly smaller than first and near caudal fin. Anal fin with moderately long base, just anterior to and below second dorsal fin. Ventral fins just anterior to first dorsal fin. Pale grey above with faint slightly darker saddles, edged with dark spots. Widespread in southern waters; known from New South Wales to the west coast, commonly found in Tasmania. Reported from deep water to about 180 m, but this may represent an undescribed species. Usually much shallower, about 10 m; rarely deeper than 60 m. Specimens observed were near or among reef on sand. Attains 90 cm. This genus comprises four or five species, only two of which are described; both are included here.

GULF CATSHARK
Asymbolis vincenti (Zietz, 1908)

Body long, rounded, head flattened with pointed snout. Gill slits positioned laterally, just in front of pectoral fins. No ridge over eyes; generally streamlined, smooth. Dorsal fins placed over posterior half, second slightly smaller than first and near caudal fin. Anal fin with moderately long base, just anterior to and below second dorsal fin. Ventral fins just anterior to first dorsal fin. Grey above, mottled with brown and light spots, some faint saddles; pale below. Widespread south coast, including Tasmania. Mixed reef and seagrass habitat, sometimes shallow in a few metres, but usually recorded deeper, between 130-220 m. Attains 60 cm.

SPOTTED SWELLSHARK
Cephaloscyllium laticeps (Dumeril, 1853)

Body long, rounded, stout anteriorly, thickened centrally; head flattened, snout pointed. Gill slits positioned laterally, just in front of pectoral fins. No ridge over eyes; generally streamlined, smooth. Dorsal fins placed over posterior half, second slightly smaller than first and near caudal fin. Anal fin has moderately short base, directly opposite second dorsal fin. Ventral fins just anterior to and reaching almost to end of first dorsal fin. Grey and brown above, mottled with irregular blotching, pale below. Widespread in southern waters. Mostly caught in deep water to 650 m, but occasionally observed in shallow depths; often enters lobster pots. Landed or disturbed specimens inflate their stomach to increase size and deter predators. Eggs oval-shaped with transverse ridges. Largest representative of the family; attains 1.5 m.

Photograph: Peter Boyle

SCHOOL AND GUMMY SHARKS
FAMILY TRIAKIDAE

A moderately large family, comprising nine genera and about 35 species. It is closely related to Carcharhinidae, and included in that family by some authors. The Triakidae are small to medium-sized sharks, not exceeding 2 m, also known as dogfishes and houndsharks. They feature streamlined bodies, and usually long snouts, often with nasal barbels. The mouth is angular or arched, and the teeth are blade-like or with cusps. Eyes are oval and eyelids present. Fins are usually of moderate size, none greatly enlarged. Pectoral, dorsal and ventral fins alternate in position along the body; the anal fin is about below the second dorsal fin. The caudal fin is large with a long upper lobe, distinctly notched, and the lower lobe is sometimes large, giving a double-tailed appearance. These sharks are viviparous or ovoviviparous; litters are of up to about 50 which measure about 30 cm at birth. Mostly demersal species, they swim just above the substrate feeding on a variety of invertebrates and fishes. They are found in various depths, from shallow estuaries to deep offshore to at least 500 m. Many species are of commercial importance, some occurring in great abundance. In Australia the family is represented by three genera with one species each, all three in the area but one confined to deep water.

GUMMY SHARK
Mustelus antarcticus Günther, 1870

Body streamlined; caudal peduncle long, smooth; head slightly flattened; snout long, bluntly pointed. Eyes oval, small spiracles behind. Teeth flattened, smooth, with primary cusps. Gill slits laterally on head, partly above pectoral fins. Dorsal fins widely separate, first slightly larger, its origin just beyond reach of pectoral fins. Anal fin below posterior part of second dorsal fin. Ventral fins below middle of space between dorsal fins. Caudal fin with long, distinctly notched upper lobe, lower lobe small. Grey to brown above, usually with many or numerous small white spots; pale below. Confined to southern Australian waters from southern Queensland to similar latitude on the west coast, including Tasmania. Almost identical species in New Zealand. Estuaries and coastal waters, ranging to 300 m; usually less than 80 m. Litter usually about 15 but sometimes much higher; young to 30 cm at birth. Attains 1.8 m. This genus comprises about 25 species, several commercially fished. Important commercial species in southern waters, its flesh sold as flake.

SCHOOL SHARK
Galeorhinus galeus (Linneaus, 1758)

Body streamlined; caudal peduncle long, smooth; head conical; snout long, pointed. Eyes oval, small spiracles behind. Teeth flattened, serrated, with primary cusps. Gill slits laterally on head, partly above pectoral fins. Dorsal fins widely separate, first distinctly larger, its origin just beyond reach of pectoral fins. Anal fin below posterior part of second dorsal fin. Ventral fins below middle of space between dorsal fins. Caudal fin has long, distinctly notched upper lobe; lower lobe large, extending to notch to a large square cut-out. Uniformly slate grey to brownish above, shading to pale below. Single widespread species recognised, found primarily in temperate areas of all oceans. In Australia from southern Queensland to a similar latitude on the west coast, including Tasmania. Juveniles in estuaries, bays; adults to at least 500 m. Ovoviviparous; about 28 young average, between 30-35 cm at birth. Adults attain 1.8 m.

Mustelus antarcticus ▲

Galeorhinus galeus ▼

HAMMERHEAD SHARKS
FAMILY SPHYRNIDAE

A peculiar family of sharks comprising two genera, one of which is monotypic, and nine species. This family is easily recognised by the greatly laterally extended snout with smell and sight sensors on the lateral edges. Dorsally viewed, their T-shaped head, particularly that of *Euspryra blochii* or the Wing-Head Shark, in which the width of the head is about half length of the body, must rate them as the most unusual of all sharks. Apart from the head, they are similar to whaler sharks, Carcharhinidae, with their large dorsal, caudal and ventral fins, small remaining fins and smooth caudal peduncle. Teeth are oblique with minute serrations, and slightly larger in the upper jaw. Hammerheads are moderate to large sharks, with adults ranging from 1 to 6 m. Most species swim near or on surface waters. They are oceanic travellers, some coming inshore, and a few are found in moderate depths. Some school in particular areas, possibly for mating purposes. None are considered dangerous or known to attack, however large specimens should be treated with respect, particularly if mating is likely to take place. They are viviparous, having about 20 to 30 pups per litter which range in size to 50 cm when born. Of the three Australian species, only one is known from southern coastal waters. The widespread tropical species *Sphyrna lewini* may range into New South Wales. It is distinguished from the included species in having an indent, as opposed to rounded edge, on the snout.

SMOOTH HAMMERHEAD
Sphyrna zygaena (Linneaus, 1758)

Typical hammerhead-shaped front; eyes and other sensory probes laterally placed. Head greatly flattened anteriorly; anteriorly expanded to its unusual shape. Snout at anterior-most point rounded, separating it from similar species which are indented centrally on the snout. Teeth with finely serrated cusps. Gill slits laterally on head, last ones just above pectoral fins. Dorsal fins differ greatly in size; first large, tall; second small, similar-sized anal fin opposite. Ventral fins large, similar size to first dorsal fin. Anal fin with greatly enlarged upper lobe; notched near tip, lower lobe pointed. Grey to blackish or brownish above, pale below. Primarily oceanic, widespread tropical to temperate waters, occasionally inshore, often on the suface with dorsal and caudal fins exposed. Mostly in southern Australian waters. Viviparous; about 30 young at about 55 cm at birth. Adults at least 3 m; reported to 4 m.

Sphyrna zygaena Dorsal view ▲ Anterior ventral view ▼

WHALER SHARKS
FAMILY CARCHARHINIDAE

A large family of small to large sharks, comprising 12 genera and about 50 species. Whaler sharks have streamlined bodies thickened at the dorsal fin position. They include some of the fastest and best distance travelers, and the well-known Tiger Shark. Their snout is broadly rounded, pointed from lateral view (often sharply so) and long. The mouth is well back below the head, and the eyes are usually above the anterior end with a well-developed eyelid. Gill slits are laterally on the sides of the head, the last above the pectoral fins. A large first dorsal fin is anterior to the centre of the body, originating above the posterior pectoral fin flaps. The caudal fin has a long tall upper lobe, notched near the tip. Pectoral fins are long. The remaining fins are small and of similar size. The second dorsal and anal fins are about opposite, their posterior tips nearly at the caudal fin. Ventral fins are closely anterior to the anal fin. Colours are typical for pelagic fishes; blue, grey or bronze above, shaded above and light below. Species are sometimes typified by black or white fin tips or faint banding on the sides of the body. Whaler sharks are mostly found in open water habitat. Some species school, and some are coastal and can live in fresh water for a considerably long time. Oceanic species can travel over great distances. A tagged *Prionace glauca* swam 6,000 km. It is also considered the fastest shark, measured at speeds from 35 km/h to almost 40 km/h. Most species are potentially dangerous but not aggressive unless provoked. A few are unpredictable and may attack. In Australia the Tiger Shark and whaler sharks are responsible for most attacks in tropical and sub-tropical waters. The included three species are moderately common in southern coastal waters, but underwater sightings are often only made by spearfishers.

TIGER SHARK
Galeocerdo cuvier (Lesueur, 1822)

Body streamlined, thick and heavy anteriorly, tapers to narrow caudal peduncle. Head flattened; snout short, bluntly rounded. Eyes oval, spiracle tiny. Mouth large, wide; coarsely serrated cockscomb-shaped teeth with a single cusp in jaws. Gill slits positioned laterally, last ones over pectoral fins. Caudal peduncle with lateral keels. Tall first dorsal fin anterior to centre of back. Caudal fin very large, upper lobe sickle-like, ending in tapering tip. Pectoral fins long, falcate. Other fins small, of similar size; anal fin below second dorsal fin; ventral fins with small space anteriorly. Grey above, pale below; young with distinct dark spots forming striped pattern above, fading with age. Mostly found in all tropical and subtropical seas, occasionally straying to temperate waters. Mostly in reef areas adjacent to deep water but comes close inshore. Responsible for many attacks; second to the Great White Shark. Litters vary from about 10 to 80; young measure up to 70 cm when born. Adults attain 5.5 m; possibly to 7 m. Monotypic genus.

BRONZE WHALER
Carcharhinus brachyurus (Günther, 1870)

Body streamlined, thickened anteriorly, tapers to strong caudal peduncle without keels. Head conical; snout long, pointed. Eyes round, no spiracle. Mouth large, wide; finely serrated, triangular, outward curving teeth in upper jaw, lower teeth more slender and erect. Gill slits positioned laterally, last ones over pectoral fins. Tall first dorsal fin anterior to centre of back. Caudal fin very large, upper lobe sickle-like, with small notch near tip. Pectoral fins very long, anterior margin almost straight. Other fins small, of similar size; anal fin below second dorsal fin, slightly anteriorly; ventral fins with small space anteriorly. Golden-brown above, shading to cream below. Worldwide in temperate to subtropical zones. Coastal reefs, bays, usually in pairs or small aggregations. Feed primarily on fish near the bottom, but responsible for various attacks along beaches and in estuaries. Viviparous; about 16 young around 60-70 cm when born. Reaches almost 3 m. Large genus with about 30 species, 21 of which are recorded from Australian seas.

Photograph: Elizabeth Parer-Cook

Galeocerdo cuvier ▲

Carcharhinus brachyurus ▼

BLACK WHALER
Carcharhinus obscurus (Lesueur, 1818)

Body streamlined, thickened anteriorly, tapers to strong caudal peduncle without keels. Head conical; snout long, pointed. Eyes round, no spiracle. Mouth large, wide; finely serrated, broadly triangular, outward curving teeth in upper jaw, lower teeth more slender and erect. Gill slits positioned laterally, last ones over pectoral fins. Tall first dorsal fin anterior to centre of back. Caudal fin very large, upper lobe sickle-like with small notch near tip. Pectoral fins very long, anterior margin almost straight. Other fins small, of similar size; anal fin below second dorsal fin, slightly posterior; ventral fins with small space anteriorly. Dark grey above shading to pale below; tips, margins of largest fins sometimes black. Widespread tropical to temperate seas. Mostly continental coastlines, inshore in surf, deeper waters to 400 m. Feeds near bottom. Litters to about 15, measuring about 70 cm. Adults to 3.6 m.

MACKEREL SHARKS
ORDER LAMNIFORMES

Represented by seven families, six of which have species in Australian waters. They can be determined with Key 5.

Of the six families mentioned, two have representatives in southern coastal waters, and are included here.

1.	Jaws greatly projecting; snout projecting, very depressed and long; overhanging mouth ....MITSUKURINIDAE
	Jaws not projecting; snout rounded or bluntly pointed 2
2.	Teeth minute in 100+ rows 3
	Teeth moderately large in low number of rows 4
3.	Mouth terminal...MEGACHASMIDAE
	Mouth not terminal ....CETORHINIDAE
4.	Caudal fin about body length ....ALOPIIDAE
	Caudal fin much shorter than body length 5
5.	Caudal fin lunate; peduncle keels present ....LAMNIDAE (p. 14)
	Caudal fin heterocercal; peduncle keels absent ..........ODONTASPIDIDAE (p. 13)

KEY 5: *The Mackerel Sharks*

GREY NURSE SHARKS
FAMILY ODONTASPIDIDAE

A small, globally distributed family comprising two genera and about four species. There is some confusion about generic classification. The grey nurses are large sharks with an impressive fierce appearance, as their teeth are well exposed. Their mouth, particularly in large specimens, appears to be small in proportion to their body. They used to be blamed for shark attacks in Australia which were no doubt caused by other species. Species are heavy-bodied, and have two large dorsal fins with an anal fin situated below the interspace. A very large caudal fin has its upper lobe greatly produced and is notched near the tip. Grey nurse sharks are large species – adults are about 3 to 4 m long. They are found in very shallow surf zones as well as deep; a species known from only one specimen was taken between 600 and 1,000 m. Only one species is regularly observed in southern coastal waters.

Grey Nurse Shark (*Carcharias taurus*)

13

GREY NURSE SHARK
Carcharias taurus Rafinesque, 1810

Adults heavy-bodied, taper anteriorly to bluntly pointed snout, and from first dorsal fin gradually to deep caudal peduncle. Mouth greatly rounded below head; long lanceolate teeth, with cusp on each side, in both jaws. Eyes situated above mouth; spiracles minute, just behind eye. Gill slits positioned laterally, close together, anterior to pectoral fins. Dorsal, ventral, anal fins of similar size, alternating in postion along posterior half of body. Caudal fin very large, upper lobe greatly produced. Grey to brownish-grey, shading from dark above to light below, often with scattered dark spots or blotches on sides. Broadly distributed in tropical and subtropical waters; in Australia from northern Queensland along the southern coasts to the north-west coast. Absent in Tasmania, rare in the Bass Strait region. Usually small aggregations resident at reefs in 20-40 m, but sometimes hunting salmon or mullet along surf beaches. Regularly observed by divers in New South Wales. Non-aggressive, mostly moving about sluggishly but can suddenly take off in a burst of great speed, the tail creating a loud clap. Protected on the east coast. Spearfishing, popular before the camera took over, reduced their numbers greatly but the species now appears to be making a great comeback. Only one young produced per uterus; the other unfertilised eggs or smaller embryos are eaten. About 1 m long when born. Adults can reach almost 4 m. Second species in this genus only known from the northern Indian Ocean.

MAKO AND POINTER SHARKS
FAMILY LAMNIDAE

This family, comprising three genera and five species, includes some of the

Carcharias taurus

largest and fastest predatory sharks, including the Great White Shark or White Pointer. Heavy but streamlined sharks, they have one or two keels along the sides of the caudal peduncle, a cone-shaped pointed snout, and long gill slits. Fins are either large or small; the first dorsal fin is tall and centrally placed, the very small second dorsal fin is nearest the tail, and they have a very large lunate caudal fin. The long pectoral fins, and small ventral and anal fins small, are posteriorly placed. These sharks have typical pelagic colouration, usually white below with shading above, variably grey, blue or bronze. They are primarily oceanic, open water species, with a broad distribution and, except for the Great White Shark, are rarely seen inshore. From tagging programs, some species are known to travel great distances. The greatest distance recorded in Australia is about 2,000 km for a mako. As with other fast pelagic fishes, such

Carcharodon carcharias

as tuna, they generate body heat and may be several degrees warmer than surrounding waters. All are considered very dangerous and unpredictable. Some feed on fish alone, others on any kind of animal dead or alive. They are viviparous; the young feed on eggs and other embryos within the mother. The largest species, most feared by humans, is included here.

GREAT WHITE SHARK
Carcharodon carcharias (Linneaus, 1758)

Body streamlined, rounded, heavy centrally, smoothly curving, tapering to snout and tail. Mouth very large; teeth broad, triangular, serrated, usually smooth-edged in young. Eyes round, without eyelid; spiracle minute, often not visible. Gill slits long, positioned laterally in front of pectoral fins. Very large first dorsal, caudal and pectoral fins; first dorsal centrally placed. Small second dorsal and anal fins about opposite, close to tail. Long lateral keel extends over caudal peduncle. Pale to dark grey or blue-grey above, white below. Reported from all oceans, usually in shelf regions of cool seas. In Australia mostly in southern waters, commonly around Tasmania and Victorian coasts, sometimes entering shallow bays. Responsible for numerous attacks on people, swimming or on surfboards, and even boats. Hooked specimens may jump into the boat, or become so angry that they attack the boat after being cut loose; may persist until it sinks. Will eat just about anything. Items found in their stomach include human remains, scuba tanks, dogs, turtles, seals, goats, even pumpkins. South Australian populations thought to be declining; protective measures considered. Accepted record for the largest specimen captured is 6.4 m and 3,312 kg, however a 9 m monster was reported from Azores, 1978.

Photograph: Barry Andrewartha

14

ELECTRIC RAYS
ORDER TORPEDINIFORMES

Represented by a single family. See below.

NUMBFISHES
FAMILY TORPEDINIDAE

A small family which can be divided in four distinct groups, regarded by some authors as separate families, comprising about 10 genera and some 40 species. The numbfishes are globally distributed in tropical and temperate seas. Their discs are rounded, soft and flabby, thick at the body, and have smooth skin. Dorsally, they have small eyes with moderate-sized spiracles behind. Ventrally, they have a small broadly arched mouth, both jaws with small similar-sized teeth, and there are five pairs of gill slits. A pair of large kidney-shaped electric organs on the sides of the head are capable of producing the same as man-made electricity, which can result in a powerful shock. The tail is thick and robust; there are usually one or two dorsal fins present. The caudal fin is often large. Ventral fins direct follow the disc. They are viviparous and bear small litters. Numbfishes are benthic, usually burying in sand or mud, and live in estuaries, close inshore to very deep offshore. They are small to medium-sized – the smallest at about 10 cm fully grown is also the smallest of all cartilaginous fishes – and grow to about 2 m. Of the four Australian species, two occur in southern coastal waters.

NUMBFISH
Hypnos monopterygium (Shaw and Nodder, 1795)

Soft, flabby, rounded disc formed by head and greatly expanded pectoral fins. Broadly rounded ventral fins follow forming second, smaller disc. Eyes minute, followed by moderate-sized spiracles, granulations around opening. Underside with anteriorly arched mouth, opening to large size; numerous small slender tricuspidate teeth in jaws; five paired gill slits follow mouth. Electric organs large. Tail very short with two dorsal fins and similar-sized caudal fin closely together. Colour above highly variable from grey or light-brown to black or dark brown; yellowish below. Southern waters, from southern Queensland to Shark Bay, rare in Victoria, absent from Tasmanian waters. Shallow muddy estuaries to deep offshore; recorded to 220 m. Usually buried, moving about at night. Feeds on comparatively large fish which are stunned and eaten whole. Attacks prey in pouncing fashion, wraps its body around victim held below. Attains 60 cm. A monotypic genus.

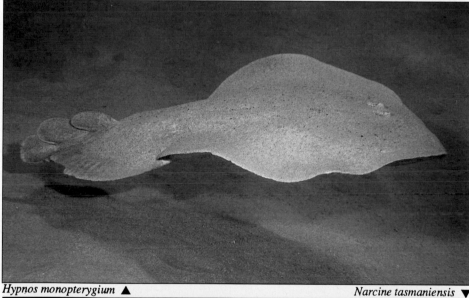

Hypnos monopterygium ▲

Narcine tasmaniensis ▼

TASMANIAN NUMBFISH
Narcine tasmaniensis Richardson, 1840

Soft, flabby, ovate disc formed by head and greatly expanded pectoral fins. Broadly rounded ventral fins follow forming second, smaller disc. Body thick, skin smooth. Eyes small, followed by moderate-sized spiracles, smooth around opening. Underside with transverse mouth; numerous small slender wedge-shaped or single-cusp teeth in jaws; five paired gill slits follow mouth. Electric organs small. Tail very long with two similar-sized dorsal fins and larger caudal fin spaced equally to dorsal fin base length. Pale to dark brown above, whitish below. Only known from south-eastern Australia, ranging New South Wales to Tasmania. Muddy coastal areas to at least 100 m; commonly taken in scallop dredges. Feeds on crustaceans, probably small fishes. Attains 46 cm.

GUITARFISHES
ORDER RHINOBATIFORMES

Represented by a single family. See below.

SHOVELNOSE RAYS
FAMILY RHINOBATIDAE

A moderate-sized tropical to subtropical family of shark-like rays, comprising about eight genera and 50 species worldwide. Their body is thick and elongate, and the head usually greatly depressed; the united pectoral fins to head and trunk are not greatly expanded. The pectoral fin usually forms a narrow, elongated, often pointed disc, mostly shorter than the tail. The tail section has two similar-sized prominent dorsal fins. The ventral fin is below the first dorsal fin in *Rhina* and *Rhynchobatus*, and anteriorly placed in other genera. The caudal fin is usually moderately large. Ovoviviparous or viviparous, the shovelnose rays have small litters, and their egg capsules contain two to eight embryos. They are benthic fishes, and some species bury in sand when resting. These rays enter estuaries, mostly inshore, and a few are found in deep water. Adults vary in size from about 40 cm to 3 m. They feed primarily on benthic invertebrates. There are five genera and 14 species in Australian waters, four of which occur in south-eastern coastal waters.

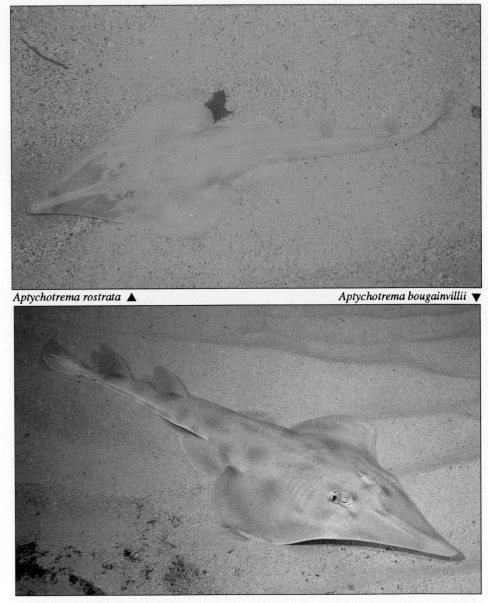

Aptychotrema rostrata ▲   *Aptychotrema bougainvillii* ▼

LONG-SNOUT SHOVELNOSE RAY
Aptychotrema rostrata (Shaw and Nodder, 1794)

Body depressed, tapering posteriorly; lateral ridged skin-folds past ventral fins. Disc wedge-shaped; snout long, triangularly pointed. Distance from eyes to snout-tip four times distance between spiracles. Dorsally, eyes raised, facing laterally, followed closely by spiracles; series of small thorns along dorsal midline from eyes to second dorsal fin. Ventrally, mouth moderately arched, small equal-sized teeth in both jaws, five pairs of gill slits. Dorsal fins prominent, widely separate, posteriorly placed, well back from ventral fins. Caudal fin with well developed upper lobe. Plain, pale sandy to brownish, snout often darker. Eastern Australia, Queensland to eastern Bass Strait. Inshore on fine sand in shallow quiet bays to at least 60 m deep offshore. Attains 1.2 m. Australian genus comprising three species, two of which are included here.

SHORT-SNOUT SHOVELNOSE RAY
Aptychotrema bougainvillii (Müller and Henle, 1841)

Body depressed, tapering posteriorly; lateral ridged skin-folds past ventral fins. Disc wedge-shaped; snout moderately long, triangularly pointed. Distance from eyes to snout-tip three times distance between spiracles. Dorsally, eyes raised, facing laterally, followed closely by spiracles; series of small thorns along dorsal midline from eyes to second dorsal fin. Ventrally, mouth strongly arched, small equal-sized teeth in both jaws, five pairs of gill slits. Dorsal fins prominent, widely separate, posteriorly placed, well back from ventral fins. Caudal fin with well developed upper lobe. Brown to brownish-grey, dark diffused blotches dorsally on body and fins. Southern Queensland and New South Wales, coastal sandy flats; buried, usually 20 m deep or more. Attains 1 m. Very similar to the Southern Shovelnose Ray, *Aptychotrema vincentiana* Haacke, 1885, which is generally darker blotched.

FIDDLER RAY
Trygonorrhina fasciata Müller and Henle, 1841

Body depressed, tapering posteriorly, lateral ridged skin-folds past ventral fins. Disc broadly wedge-shaped; snout rounded, ending bluntly pointed. Dorsally, eyes raised, facing laterally, followed closely by spiracles; series of small thorns along dorsal midline from eyes to second dorsal fin. Ventrally, mouth slightly arched, minute equal-sized teeth in both jaws, five pairs of gill slits. Dorsal fins prominent, widely separate, posteriorly placed, well back from ventral fins. Caudal fin with well-developed upper lobe. Distinctly banded dorsally, light below. Pattern on head diagnostic for this species. East coast, primarily New South Wales, ranging into Queensland and probably eastern Victoria. Inshore, coastal bays, seagrass areas; shallow to at least 120 m. Attains 1.2 m. Australian genus with at least two species, included here; third doubtful, may be mutant form of the following species.

SOUTHERN FIDDLER RAY
Trygonorrhina guaneria Whitley, 1932

Body depressed, tapering posteriorly, lateral ridged skin-folds past ventral fins. Disc broadly wedge-shaped, snout rounded, ending bluntly pointed. Dorsally, eyes raised, facing laterally, followed closely by spiracles; series of small thorns along dorsal midline from eyes to second dorsal fin. Ventrally, mouth slightly arched, minute equal-sized teeth in both jaws, five pairs of gill slits. Dorsal fins prominent, widely separate, posteriorly placed, well back from ventral fins. Caudal fin with well-developed upper lobe. Distinctly banded dorsally, light below. Pattern on head diagnostic for this species. South coast, eastern Bass Strait to south-west coast; shallow seagrass estuaries to offshore; recorded to 50 m. Attains 1.2 m.

SKATES
ORDER RAJIFORMES

The largest group of batoids with possibly several families. Present classification is in a poor state, and only one family is treated here.

SKATES
FAMILY RAJIDAE

A very large family, globally distributed from tropical waters to the coldest seas, with at least 15 genera and more than 200 species. Although their ancestors were shark-like, modern skates show little resemblance to sharks and are ray-like. Body and head are greatly flattened, and extend laterally with the pectoral fins forming a wide disc. The snout is usually pointed, and in some species is greatly projecting and firm. Dorsally, the eyes are slightly raised, facing laterally, and are followed closely by spiracles. Ventrally, there is a small straight mouth with nostril just in front of its corners, nasal flaps expand to overlap the mouth, and there are five pairs of gill slits. The tail varies from thick and robust to thin and feeble. It has lateral folds, usually two small dorsal fins, a longitudinal series of thorns and a pair of slender electric organs. Ventral fins have expanded lateral lobes, sometimes separated from the posterior lobes. About 35 species are known from Australian waters. Skates are benthic, and the majority are restricted to very deep waters in excess of 100 m, particularly in tropical waters. Several species enter shallow depths in Tasmania; only one species occurs in shallow coastal areas on the mainland.

WHITLEY'S SKATE
Raja whitleyi Iredale, 1938

Disc about as wide as long, straight from lateral tips to snout; tail rounded. Snout firm, extremely pointed, angle less than square. Dorsal surface rough with granulations; small thorns variably present from between orbitals to tail. Ventral surface similarly granulated. Tail with one to three series of thorns, regularly spaced granulations, two small close-set dorsal fins, sometimes joined, tiny caudal fin entirely dorsally. Ventral fins deeply incised; claspers long, reaching halfway along tail. Grey to grey-brown to almost black, with irregularly placed white flecks. Only known from south-eastern waters; ranges from southern New South Wales to South Australia, including Tasmania. Commonly enters shallow estuaries, but also recorded to 170 m offshore. Attains 1.7 m, at least 50 kg. Australia's largest skate. This genus is also the most numerous with over 100 species, 24 of which are known from Australia.

EAGLE RAYS, STINGRAYS, STINGAREES AND MANTAS
ORDER MYLIOBATIDIFORMES

Represented by five families, all of which have species in Australian waters. They can be determined with Key 6.

Of these families, three have representatives in southern coastal waters.

1.	Head protruding from disc	2
	Head not protruding from disc	3
2.	Mouth with a pair of large protruding flaps	MOBULIDAE
	Mouth without protruding flaps	MYLIOBATIDIDAE (p. 23)
3.	Tail with small caudal fin	UROLOPHIDAE (p. 18)
	Tail without caudal fin	4
4.	Tail thick near body, usually longer than disc	DASYATIDIDAE (p. 22)
	Tail slender, less than half of disc length	GYMNURIDAE

KEY 6: *Eagle Rays, Stingrays, Stingarees and Mantas*

STINGAREES
FAMILY UROLOPHIDAE

A moderate-sized family, primarily subtropical and temperate, comprising three genera and about 40 species. All genera and about half the species are found in Australian waters. Many species are similar and easily misidentified without examining specimens, and a large number appear to be undescribed. Sometimes two species have a single name applied. Stingarees differ from all other related families in possessing a small caudal fin. The tail is not whip-like, as in many other rays, and carries one or two venomous spines. In addition, a small dorsal fin may be present (variable within a species). Discs are greatly flattened, usually rounded and the width is not greatly different from the length. Dorsally, they have slightly raised, laterally facing eyes, with broad spiracles below and behind. Ventrally, there is a very slightly arched mouth with large nostrils in front of its corners, connected by a groove, numerous small teeth arranged in oblique rows, and the mouth is followed by five pairs of gill slits. Stingarees are mostly smallish rays, the largest about 80 cm long. They are viviparous with small litters. Benthic, fast-moving species, they are usually buried in sand or mud when resting. They may be active either day or night, and feed primarily on a variety of invertebrates. Potentionally dangerous because of venomous spines, stingarees may attack by swimming backwards (they can swim just as fast that way as forwards) to spear an enemy when cornered or provoked. Human victims are usually hospitalised. At least two genera and 10 species occur in southern coastal waters and are included here.

Sparsely-Spotted Stingaree
(*Urolophus paucimaculatus*)

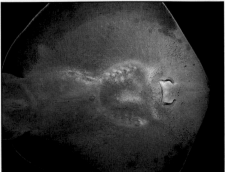

SPOTTED STINGAREE
Urolophus gigas Scott, 1954

Disc about round in young, oval in adults, slightly longer than wide, broadest at gill slits level; snout tip fleshy, blunt, not extended. Tail short, rounded in cross-section, with small dorsal fin and short, deep caudal fin. Dorsally, small eyes with large spiracles below and behind, skin smooth. Ventrally, mouth small, nine to 12 papillae present; internasal flaps broad, followed by five pairs of gill slits. Dark brown to black, irregular whitish spots and rings above, pale with dark margins below. South coast only, Bass Strait to Albany. Coastal bays, estuaries, shallow to at least 35 m. Sandy patches in seagrass areas and near reefs on sand. Attains at least 70 cm. Not aggressive. This genus comprises at least seven species in southern waters, several of which are undescribed; six are included here.

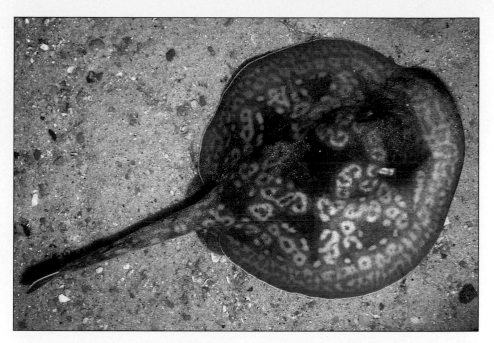

SPARSELY-SPOTTED STINGAREE
Urolophus paucimaculatus Dixon, 1969

Disc about round in young, slightly wider than long, broadest at gill slits level; snout tip fleshy, blunt, pointed but not extended. Tail moderately elongate, lateral skin-folds present, rounded in cross-section, with small dorsal fin and short, deep caudal fin. Dorsally, small eyes with large spiracles below and behind, skin smooth. Ventrally, mouth small, fleshy, five to six mostly bifurcate papillae present; internasal flaps broad, bell-shaped, followed by five pairs of gill slits. Pale grey or brown above with or without distinct large pale spots, usually two to four dark-edged; whitish below with dark margins. Restricted to southern waters from New South Wales to Perth, including Tasmania. Particularly common in shallow waters in the southern part of its range. Muddy and sandy parts of bays and estuaries. May attack with little provocation. Responsible for most accidents with rays in southern waters. Deeper in the northern part of its range, to about 150 m. Attains at least 40 cm.

SANDY-BACK STINGAREE
Urolophus bucculentus Macleay, 1884

Disc slightly wider than long, broadest at gill slits level, angled at snout; anterior margins almost straight before rounding laterally; snout fleshy, slightly expanded. Tail depressed, rather short, lateral skin-folds present; small dorsal fin usually present; caudal fin broadly lanceolate. Dorsally, small eyes with large spiracles below and behind, skin smooth. Ventrally, mouth of moderate size, 14 to 16 papillae present; internasal flap broad with narrowly fringed posterior edge, followed by five pairs of gill slits. Dorsally brown to almost black, often with lighter spots and reticulations; ventrally white. East coast, ranging from southern Queensland to Tasmania. Mostly on the continental shelf in 60-300 m; sometimes relatively shallow at Montague Island, about 25 m. Attains at least 80 cm; the largest stingaree.

Urolophus paucimaculatus ▲

Urolophus bucculentus ▼

GREENBACK STINGAREE
Urolophus viridis McCulloch, 1916

Disc slightly wider than long, broadest at gill slits level, angled at snout; anterior margins almost straight before rounding laterally; snout fleshy, slightly expanded. Tail depressed anteriorly, long; narrow lateral skin-folds present; small dorsal fin usually absent; caudal fin broadly lanceolate. Dorsally, small eyes with large spiracles below and behind, skin smooth. Ventrally, mouth of moderate size, four to six papillae present; internasal flap broad with small-lobed posterior edge, followed by five pairs of gill slits. Dorsally greyish-green to olive-green, sometimes a few darker scattered spots present; ventrally mostly white. East coast, ranging from New South Wales to Tasmania, and to western Bass Strait. Usually deep, 80-200 m; sometimes relatively shallow at Montague Island, about 25 m. Attains 43 cm.

YELLOW-BACK STINGAREE
Urolophus sufflavus Whitley, 1929

Disc barely wider than long, broadest at gill slits level, broadly rounding laterally; snout fleshy, slightly expanded. Tail slender, moderately long, depressed laterally; lateral skin-folds and small dorsal fin absent; caudal fin broadly lanceolate. Dorsally, small eyes with large spiracles below and behind, skin smooth. Ventrally, mouth of moderate size; internasal flap broad, followed by five pairs of gill slits. Dorsally uniformly sandy grey-brown to ochre-yellow; ventrally white. East coast, ranging from southern Queensland to New South Wales. Coastal sandy bays to at least 200 m. Shallow-water specimens are sandy-coloured, usually misidentified. Similar species with mid-dorsal stripe appears to be undescribed. Attains 40 cm.

CROSS-BACK STINGAREE
Urolophus cruciatus (Lacepède, 1804)

Disc longer than wide, broadest at gill slits level, broadly rounded laterally; snout rounded, fleshy. Tail rounded in cross-section, short; lateral skin-folds absent; small dorsal fin sometimes present in juveniles; caudal fin broadly lanceolate. Dorsally, small eyes with large spiracles below and behind, skin smooth. Ventrally, mouth small, four to six papillae present; internasal flap broad, followed by five pairs of gill slits. Distinctly marked dorsally, which combined with short tail readily identifies this species. South-east coast, southern New South Wales to Tasmania. Only trawled in southern New South Wales; rarely seen in less than 25 m in Victoria. Common in shallow Tasmanian waters where it enters estuaries. Attains 50 cm. New South Wales records need to be verified.

BANDED STINGAREE
Trygonoptera sp 1

Disc slightly wider than long, broadest at gill slits level, angled at snout; anterior margins almost straight before rounding laterally; snout fleshy, not expanded. Tail depressed, rather long; lateral skin-folds present; small dorsal fin usually present; long caudal fin broadly lanceolate. Dorsally, small eyes with large spiracles below and behind, skin smooth. Ventrally, mouth of moderate size, four to six papillae present nostrils with broad flattened lobes; internasal flap broad, narrowly fringed on posterior edge, followed by five pairs of gill slits. Dorsally grey to brown, distinct dark pattern; ventrally white. Only known from southern New South Wales, Jervis Bay to Bermagui, no doubt ranging further. Sand flats near reefs, usually deeper than 15 m. Common species, often identified as *Urolophus cruciatus*, appears to be undescribed. Attains 40 cm. This genus comprises about six species; can be separated from *Urolophus* by the presence of broad flat lobes on the posteriolateral border of the nostrils.

Trygonoptera sp 1 ▲

Trygonoptera testacea ▼

COMMON STINGAREE
Trygonoptera testacea Müller and Henle, 1841

Disc slightly wider than long, broadest at gill slits level, angled at snout; anterior margins almost straight before rounding laterally; snout fleshy, not expanded. Tail depressed, rather long; lateral skin-folds present; small dorsal fin usually present; long caudal fin broadly lanceolate. Dorsally, small eyes with large spiracles below and behind, skin smooth. Ventrally, mouth of moderate size, four to six papillae present, nostrils with broad flattened lobes; internasal flap broad, narrowly fringed on posterior edge, followed by five pairs of gill slits. Dorsally light to dark brown, often dark shading below eyes; ventrally and along tail fold white; caudal fin sometimes black with white. East coast, ranging from southern Queensland to New South Wales. Estuaries and coastal bays to about 40 m. Usually sandy to muddy or silty habitat. Attains 45 cm.

WESTERN STINGAREE
Trygonoptera mucosa (Whitley, 1939)

Disc slightly wider than long, broadest at gill slits level, broadly rounding laterally and over snout; snout fleshy, not expanded. Tail depressed anteriorly, rather long; lateral skin-folds and small dorsal fin absent; broadly lanceolate caudal fin. Dorsally, small eyes with large spiracles below and behind, skin smooth. Ventrally, mouth of moderate size, about seven papillae present, nostrils with broad flattened lobes; internasal flap broad, narrowly fringed on posterior edge, followed by five pairs of gill slits. Dorsally grey to black and various browns, occasionally with lighter blotches; ventrally white or yellowish. South coast, ranging from Port Phillip Bay to Geralton on the west coast, not recorded from Tasmania. Shallow coastal bays and estuaries, often muddy habitat. Attains 45 cm.

EASTERN STINGAREE
Trygonoptera sp 2

Disc slightly wider than long, broadest at gill slits level, broadly rounding laterally and over snout; snout fleshy, not expanded. Tail depressed anteriorly, rather long; lateral skinfolds and small dorsal fin absent; broadly lanceolate caudal fin. Dorsally, small eyes with large spiracles below and behind, skin smooth. Ventrally, mouth of moderate size, about seven papillae present; nostrils with broad flattened lobes; internasal flap broad, narrowly fringed on posterior edge, followed by five pairs of gill slits. Uniformly pale brown to black dorsally; cream or white ventrally. East coast, southern New South Wales and eastern Victoria. Reaches at least 75 cm.

STINGRAYS
FAMILY DASYATIDIDAE

A moderately large family in need of revision, comprising about five genera and perhaps about 40 to 50 species worldwide. The tail is usually very long and whip-like, and the disc at least as wide as long, up to twice as wide in some species. The large species are easily separated from other large rays which have anteriorly protruding heads. Heads are usually raised slightly with eyes viewing laterally. Discs are broadly rounded, usually anteriorly, and laterally angular in the large species, but more rounded in smaller species. Species of stingray vary in adult size from about 30 cm to almost 3 m wide. The upper surface of the disc and tail is either naked or with small tubercles, thorns or denticles. The tail is equipped with one or more venomous spines and some have one or more fleshy folds; fins are absent and the tail ends in a long, flexible rod-like section. Stingrays are benthic, feeding on various invertebrates for which they dig, often leaving large impressions in the sand. They are mostly observed moving slowly, but are capable of moving very fast, and large specimens in particular are potentially dangerous. There are reported fatal accidents. They sometimes bring their tail up and point it forward as a warning, and when doing so should not be approached as they may attack. At least two genera with three species are encountered in southern coastal waters.

SMOOTH STINGRAY
Dasyatis brevicaudata (Hutton, 1875)

Disc quadrangular, slightly wider than long, pointed anteriorly at tip, lateral ends rounded. Head slightly elevated; eyes facing laterally, large spiracles below and behind. Tail long, just exceeding length of disc when intact; spines about halfway, skin-folds along lower sides. Mouth with lateral papillae at each corner and transverse series of five; teeth small, in numerous oblique rows; mouth followed by five paired gill slits. Generally smooth; adults with randomly arranged tubercles posteriorly on tail. Dorsally black, usually a series of white flecks near body outline; ventrally white, broad dark margins. Widely reported from southern hemisphere temperate zones. In Australia, from northern New South Wales to the west coast, including Tasmania. Most common in coastal inshore waters, but enters estuaries; recorded to 170 m. Largest of all stingrays, reaching 4.3 m length, 2.1 m disc width, and more than 300 kg. This genus is thought to contain many species, several of which occur in Australia; two are included here. A third, *Dasyatis fluviorum* Ogilby, 1908, occurs in estuaries; brown above, very long tail.

Dasyatis brevicaudata

BLACK STINGRAY
Dasyatis thetidis Waite, 1899

Disc quadrangular, slightly wider than long, pointed anteriorly at tip, lateral ends rounded. Head slightly elevated; eyes face laterally, large spiracles below and behind. Tail long, about one-and-a-half times length of disc when intact; spines about halfway, skin-folds along lower sides. Mouth with lateral papillae at each corner and transverse series of five; teeth small, in numerous oblique rows; mouth followed by five paired gill slits. Generally smooth; adults with large tubercles mid-dorsally becoming prickles on tail. Dorsally black, white below. Broadly distributed in temperate waters of the southern hemisphere. In Australia, northern New South Wales to the south-west coast, including Tasmania. Inshore, well up in estuaries; offshore to 100 m. Attains 3.3 m length, 1.8 m width, and more than 200 kg.

BLUE-SPOTTED STINGRAY
Dasyatis kuhlii (Müller and Henle, 1841)

Disc quadrangular, slightly wider than long, pointed anteriorly at tip, lateral ends rounded. Head slightly elevated; eyes face laterally, large spiracles below and behind. Tail about double disc-length, skin-folds above and below. Mouth with lateral papillae at each corner and transverse series of five; teeth small, in numerous oblique rows; mouth followed with five paired gill slits. Generally smooth; adults have randomly arranged tubercles on dorsal midline. Variable, usually grey to brownish with pale or dark spots, tail distinctly banded. Tropical Indo-Pacific; on the east coast reported to Sydney Harbour. In the tropics normally on deep coastal mud slopes. Attains 45 cm disc width, and about 70 cm total length.

EAGLE RAYS
FAMILY MYLIOBATIDIDAE

A tropical to temperate family of mostly large rays, comprising five genera and about 25 species worldwide. The eagle ray's disc is very angular, the pectoral fins wing-like, the head raised with eyes on the sides, just anterior to disc, and the snout strongly protruding from the disc. The tail is slender and at least as long as the disc. It is whip-like with a prominent dorsal fin at the base, followed by a single spine. The mouth has strong crushing teeth in a pavement-like arrangement, usually in several rows, and is followed by five pairs of gill slits. Some species are large, with a disc width of 3 m possible. Eagle rays are benthic feeders, excavating sand for molluscs and other invertebrates with water drawn through their particularly large spiracles and jetted through their mouth. They are often found near reefs and swimming at any level in the water column. Extremely fast swimmers, these fishes are capable of leaping high into the air. They often swim in small loose aggregations, sometimes migrating in enormous schools. Although not as dangerous as stingrays with the position of their spine, they should be treated with respect because of their size and powerful jaws. Only one species is found in southern waters.

EAGLE RAY
Myliobatis australis Macleay, 1881

Disc greatly angular, kite-shaped, width much greater than length. Head raised, eyes and spiracle on sides, thickly ridged over eyes. Protruding snout flat, rounded, joined to pectoral fins. Skin smooth; small spines sometimes along dorsal midline in adults. Tail long, thin, much longer than disc when intact; small dorsal fin above posterior margin of ventral fins, followed by one or two barbed spines. Jaws with flat teeth arranged in pavement pattern in about 12 series, seven transverse rows, flanked by smaller plates. Dorsally olive-green, various patterns of greyish-blue blotches or streaks; ventrally cream or white. Temperate Australian species, ranging from New South Wales to the south-west coast and Tasmania. Coastal bays, estuaries to offshore; recorded to 240 m. Often in small aggregations near reefs. Viviparous, litters small, about three to seven. Attains 2 m, disc to 1.2 m across. This genus has about 10 species distributed worldwide.

GHOST SHARKS
ORDER CHIMAERIFORMES

Represented by three families, all of which have species in Australian waters. They can be determined with Key 7.

Of this group, only one is represented with a single species in southern coastal waters.

ELEPHANT FISHES
FAMILY CALLORHINCHIDAE

A small family comprising a single genus and four described species, however some descriptions may apply to the same species as they look remarkably similar. Elephant fishes are restricted to temperate zones in the southern hemisphere off Australia, New Zealand, southern Africa and South America. Unusual fishes, they are shark-like in appearance with similar fins, but a single paired gill opening and no spiracle. Their skin is smooth, and the snout is produced in a fleshy trunk-like proboscis. Fins are distinctive and, like related families, the first dorsal fin is preceded by a

1.	Caudal fin raised, dorsal fins widely separate .... CALLORHINCHIDAE (p. 24)
	Caudal fin horizontal, dorsal fins continuous or close 2
2.	Snout long and sharply pointed .... RHINOCHIMAERIDAE
	Snout short and bluntly pointed .... CHIMAERIDAE

KEY 7: *The Ghost Sharks*

Photograph: Bill and Peter Boyle   *Callorhinchus milii*

venomous spine. They are benthic fishes, probing sand flats for molluscs and other invertebrates. Elephant fishes are the only member of this order which enter shallow bays or estuaries. They are oviparous; their egg capsules are spindle-shaped with broad marginal flanges. Elephant fishes are commercially fished for in some areas. A single species is known from Australia.

ELEPHANT FISH
Callorhinchus milii Bory de St Vincent, 1823

Sides compressed; snout elongated, trunk-like, flattened, hoe-shaped. Skin smooth, soft, scales only on claspers; several irregular sensory canals on head; lateral canal behind head irregularly wavy. Dorsal fins widely separate, first headed by a long spine containing a venom gland, second elevated anteriorly. Caudal fin heterocercal, shark-like, lower lobe preceded by a short-based long anal fin, appearing as part of the caudal fin. Pectoral fins large, wing-shaped, set low just behind head. Ventral fins angular anteriorly, males with claspers. Shiny silvery-grey all over, sometimes dark markings on body or fin margins. Southern Australian waters from central New South Wales to south-west coast, including Tasmania, and also in New Zealand. Enters shallow sandy estuaries and inshore, usually on deep sand banks; recorded to 200 m. Shy, occasionally sighted by divers. Feed on a variety of invertebates for which they probe the sand. Egg capsules large, yellow-brown, measuring about 25 cm long, 10 cm wide, with marginal flanges; take about six to eight months to hatch. Attains 1.2 m.

THE BONY FISHES
CLASS OSTEICHTHYES

This group encompasses all fishes with bony skeletons. They feature a single gill opening on each side of the head, or in one family at the throat, and except for a few viviparous species, the majority are oviparous. They are divided in two major groups: the lungfishes and coelacanths, Subclass Sarcopterygii, which have lobed fins, and other fishes, Subclass Actinopterygii, which have rayed fins. Only the latter is represented here.

THE RAYED-FINNED FISHES

The rayed-finned fishes represent an enormous assembly of vertebrate animals. With an estimated 20,000 species worldwide including freshwater and marine they are by far the largest and most diverse group. They range in size from a tiny 10 mm fully-grown goby to the 5 m marlin, and can be found from man-made waterholes to the deepest oceans. Many can live in either fresh or highly saline (much higher than seawater) environments and enter without acclimatisation. In Australia this group is poorly represented in freshwater environments with about 180 species, most of which adapted from marine environments and are probably survivors from Gondwanaland times. The marine fishes, however, are well represented with about 3,500 species. These are either of southern origin, coming with Australia as it parted from Gondwanaland, or of northern origin, tropical species which came from northern waters as Australia came close enough to receive larval fishes from tropical zones. During ice ages fauna migrated north or south to suitable conditions, which created some diversity in species. Those staying in touch with little-changing conditions remained similar or identical to their original form. Those staying behind or caught in a changing environment either successfully adapted and changed, becoming a different species, or dropped out if the change was too quick. Fishes which had pelagic stages were dispersed over wider areas and were most successful. Those which built nests and raised young, and now exist in more stable areas, probably suffered the most, however a few species with completely benthic development of offspring have survived. All of these are endemic species and have tropical relatives, at family level, which have a pelagic stage.

The representatives of the rayed-finned fishes in south-eastern coastal waters included here are arranged in 20 orders, some of which are difficult to categorise as many similar species can belong in different orders. They can be determined with Key 8 (overleaf). NOTE: some orders are repeated several times to catch some of the unusual characters within a group.

Of these groups, the Perciformes is by far the largest. This order comprises about 150 families including the most numerous ones, and includes about one-third of all the species. They are diverse in shapes, sizes and numerous features, but none show specialisation to the degree seen in Syngnathiformes or Scorpaeniformes and some doubt exists about the inclusion of certain families. Many families are in need of revision, and their interrelationships need to be investigated. The majority of species have overlapping scales, well-developed fins and fin spines present. The largest families included are the gobies, wrasses, basses and damselfishes. The large pelagic fishes such as tuna and marlin are also included. In all, 71 families with species in south-eastern coastal waters are included here. The next largest group, the Scorpaeniformes, which includes the flatheads, gurnards and scorpionfishes, has eight families in this book. The Tetraodontiformes, which includes pufferfishes and leatherjackets, is represented with six families, and the next largest group, the Syngnathiformes, which includes the pipefishes and seahorses, is represented with five. The eels, Anguilliformes, have four families represented, and the remainder are represented with one to three families, which are often highly specialised or members of primarily deepwater dwelling groups.

Kelp reef at Montague Island shelters many fishes, including planktivores feeding in the currents

1. Both eyes on one lateral side ....PLEURONECTIFORMES (p. 381)

   An eye on each side, or eyes dorsally 2

2. Ventral fins absent 3

   Ventral fins present 4

3. Gill openings as lateral slits; jaws with six or eight frontal canines or teeth fused into plates;

   body covered with tiny prickly scales or encased with plates; first dorsal spine with lockable

   spines when present ....TETRAODONTIFORMES (p. 392)

   Snout tubular with mouth at tip; body partially covered with bony plates and rings ......................SYNGNATHIFORMES (p. 79)

   Body very long, cylindrical; typical eels ....ANGUILLIFORMES (p. 27)

   Body slender; long snout with fleshy extension from upper lip; wrasse-like (in part, ODACIDAE,

   one species only) ....PERCIFORMES (p. 122)

   Body very compressed; dorsal fin over entire back; pectoral fins large (in part, PATACIDAE

   only) ....SCORPAENIFORMES (p. 100)

   Transparent; first dorsal spine with long trailing filament ....OPHIDIIFORMES (p. 60)

4. Dorsal and ventral fins as large lockable spines; bony scales, plate-like with a short spine

   (in part) ....BERYCIFORMES (p. 70)

   Eyes very large; scales large; preopercle and opercle margins strongly serrate or spinous;

   ventral fins with seven rays; anal fin with four spines (in part) ....BERYCIFORMES (p. 70)

   Eyes very large; head with bony ridges; series of scutes along belly, saw-like ......................................BERYCIFORMES (p. 70)

   Head with spined ridges; pungent fin spines..SCORPAENIFORMES (p. 100)

   Ventral fins with one spine and five soft rays, placed approximately below pectoral fin bases;

   anal fin headed by three spines; dorsal fin with a distinct spinous and soft-rayed section,

   separate or joined ....PERCIFORMES (p. 122)

   Body very compressed; mouth large and greatly protrusible, tubular when extended ....ZEIFORMES (p. 77)

   Body very depressed, encased in bony plates; bony rostrum projecting at snout (in part,

   PEGASIDAE) ....SYNGNATHIFORMES (p. 79)

   Long tubular snout with small mouth at tip ....SYNGNATHIFORMES (p. 79)

   First dorsal spine modified into luring apparatus ....LOPHIIFORMES (p. 45)

   Ventral fins modified to a sucking disc, sometimes reduced; body eel-like; scales absent ..............GOBIESOCIFORMES (p. 52)

   Tail eel-like; paired barbels around snout ....SILURIFORMES (p. 37)

   Head broad and depressed, bony, covered with thick skin; three to five strong spines on opercle;

   three lateral-lines along sides of body, lower two indistinct..BATRACHOIDIFORMES (p. 44)

   Body elongate; adipose dorsal fin present ....AULOPIFORMES (p. 39)

   Head broad; single barbel on chin ....GADIFORMES (p. 58)

   Pair of slender single-rayed ventral fins below head, branched and feeler- like; tail eel-like;

   some with separate caudal fin ....OPHIDIIFORMES (p. 60)

   Body eel-like; caudal fin forked; mouth inferior; jaws without teeth ......................................GONORHYNCHIFORMES (p. 36)

   Dorsal and ventral fins with long trailing filaments; body very compressed; anal fin absent..................LAMPRIFORMES (p. 78)

   Body slender; lower or both jaws greatly produced; silvery; caudal fin large ....BELONIFORMES (p. 63)

   Subcylindrical bodies with silvery, loosely attached cycloid scales; fin spines absent; a single

   short-based dorsal fin about centrally placed ....CLUPEIFORMES (p. 34)

   Body slender, silvery; eyes large; scales large and deciduous; distinct silvery band laterally .............ATHERINIFORMES (p. 66)

   Other than combined characters above ....PERCIFORMES (p. 122)

KEY 8: *The Rayed-Finned Fishes*

EELS
ORDER ANGUILLIFORMES

Represented by about 16 families, four of which have species in south-eastern coastal waters. They can be determined with Key 9.

1.	Body ending in a pointed tip, or reduced fin	OPHICHTHIDAE (p. 27)
	Body ending in confluent median fins	2
2.	Pectoral fins absent, lips not thick	MURAENIDAE (p. 31)
	Pectoral fins present, lips thick	3
3.	Jaws with bands of fine teeth laterally	ANGUILLIDAE (p. 28)
	Jaws with two rows of small conical teeth	CONGRIDAE (p. 30)

KEY 9: *The Eels*

SNAKE AND WORM-EELS
FAMILY OPHICHTHIDAE

A very large family of marine eels, comprising over 50 genera and 250 species worldwide. They are highly diverse and have moderately robust to extremely long tubular bodies. The head is usually sharply pointed and their body often ends in a strong pointed tail. Their body is mostly rounded in cross-section, though some are slightly compressed, usually posteriorly. They are covered with tough, tight, smooth skin. The mouth is variably inferior, in some species to great a extent, and moderate to large. There is usually a smallish eye above the mouth, and in some species it is almost above the end of the lower jaw tip. The small restricted gill openings are usually low, and run from mid-laterally to ventrally. Pectoral fins are present in some species. Dorsal and anal fins are low and confluent with the caudal fin when it is present. These eels display various colour patterns from uniformly pale to spotted or conspicuously banded. Usually they are buried in sand or mud and are rarely sighted during the day. A few banded species move about in the open, usually in shallow coastal areas, and resemble sea snakes. Most species feed on fishes and crustaceans. Adult size varies greatly between species, ranging from about 20 cm to 2.5 m. About 16 genera and 35 species are recognised in Australian waters, but because of their secretive habits additional species can be expected.

Although about six species occur in south-eastern coastal waters, only two are occasionally observed and are included here.

GIANT SNAKE EEL
Ophisurus serpens (Linnaeus, 1758)

Body extremely long, very robust, ending in bony pointed tip; smooth skin. Distinct lateral line arched high on head, then straight, consisting of close-set pores. Head pointed, mouth with slender jaws, lower slightly shorter than snout; large fangs on vomer, series of canines along intermaxillary. Eyes small, laterally and almost centrally above mouth. Small but prominent lateral pectoral fins just behind gill openings. Dorsal and anal fins present, low and long; dorsal fin origin just posterior to pectoral fins; anal fin origin behind anus, situated about one-third total length from head; both fins end on bony tail end. Juveniles silvery, greyish dorsally, darkening with age to greenish-grey or brown above, pale below. Recorded from subtropical and temperate waters worldwide; in Australia from southern Queensland and the west coast at similar latitude, to Tasmania. Shallow estuaries to deep offshore in soft sand or mud; usually buried with only head exposed. Feeds on fish at dusk, probably at night, striking from below at great speed without completely leaving the substrate. Buries with ease, either forwards or backwards. Large adults are extremely powerful, should be left alone. One person speared a large specimen with only a hand spear. The person almost lost the spear when the eel pulled it completely into the sand; the spear was so badly twisted it could no longer be used. Specimens over 2 m commonly observed in the Sydney area; reported to 2.5 m. Genus presently thought to be monotypic.

Ophisurus serpens   Adult ▼   Juv. ▲

SHORT-HEAD WORM-EEL
Muraenichthys breviceps Günther, 1876

Body extremely long, very robust, ending in pointed tip; smooth skin. Distinct lateral line arched high on head, then straight, consisting of close-set pores. Head pointed, mouth with slender jaws, lower slightly shorter than snout; several irregular rows of sharp conical teeth in jaws and vomer. Eyes small, laterally and almost centrally above mouth. Small lateral gill openings. Dorsal, anal and caudal fins present, low and long; dorsal fin origin at vertical about one-third from gill openings to anus; anal fin origin behind anus, situated about one-third total length from head; both fins end confluent with reduced caudal fin. Greenish-grey or brown above, pale below. Occurs along entire south coast, Tasmania, also New Zealand. Commonly encountered in shallow sandy estuaries. Buries in the sand, but out at night and often on overcast days, moving through weeds and low reef in search of prey. Based on limited observations, appears to feed primarily on shrimps. Attains 60 cm. Broadly distributed genus comprising about 20 species worldwide, six of which are found in Australia.

Muraenichthys breviceps   Close-up of specimen about to devour snapping shrimp ▼

FRESHWATER EELS
FAMILY ANGUILLIDAE

A small family of eels comprising one genus and 16 species worldwide. Despite their common name, they spend their early stages in marine environments, entering freshwater systems as juveniles. They return to the sea to spawn, often migrating over great distances to specific breeding grounds, even travelling overland in damp conditions. The larvae are transparent, greatly compressed, leaf-like, and are called leptocephali (all true eels have this stage). Freshwater eels have two additional stages. The transparent but cylindrical glass eel migrates to fresh water where it becomes the pigmented elver. The elver migrates up rivers and resembles the adult. Adults are elongate with muscular, robust and powerful bodies. They have tiny embedded eliptical scales and a complete lateral line consisting of small pores. Fins are entirely soft-rayed. The dorsal fin is continuous with the caudal and anal fins, and freshwater eels have small, prominent, rounded pectoral fins. The mouth is large and horizontal with bands of fine teeth in the jaws. These eels are usually dull coloured as adults, grey, greenish or brown to black, sometimes spotted, and usually pale below. Adults are aggressive predators, mostly nocturnal, feeding on other fish, but take numerous other kinds of creatures in freshwater systems, and may attack large prey. Some species attain a large size, to 1.8 m and a weight of 20 kg. They are excellent to eat, and in many countries are an important culture industry. The two species in Victoria produce about 200 tonnes per year, nearly all of which is exported to Europe and South-East Asia where they are considered a delicacy.

SHORT-FIN EEL
Anguilla australis Richardson, 1841

P 15-19. Other fin rays numerous. Body slender, tubular; smooth, slimy with tiny embedded scales. Moderate-sized horizontal

A. australis Juv. (marine) ▲ Adult (freshwater) ▼

mouth reaches to below posterior edge of eye; fine teeth in broad bands in sides of jaws, a short patch on vomer. Lateral line straight, consisting of small pores. Dorsal fin continuous with broadly rounded caudal and anal fins. Dorsal and anal fin origins about opposite. Small but prominent rounded pectoral fins mid-laterally with small gill opening anteriorly at base. Leptocephali and glass eels transparent. Elvers darkening from above, becoming uniformly grey to black above in dark environments; greenish or olive-brownish in clear water; large individuals with some dark spots, lighter below. Broadly distributed in south-eastern waters, from southern Queensland to South Australia, north

and east Tasmanian coasts, ranging to New Zealand waters. Habitat of adults primarily still freshwater systems, but individuals of various sizes can be found in coastal marine waters. Sheltered coastal bays reaching inland without a freshwater feed sometimes trap individuals where they appear to survive quite well. Occasionally large adults are observed, possibly in process of migration, but it appears some adults retire in the marine environment. Aging individuals in New Zealand suggests that females reach 35 and males 24 years of age, but the greatest number of years spent in freshwater is 10 years less for both sexes. Little is known about the duration at sea as adults, but juveniles may take two to three years to reach their destiny. Leptocephali are present in open oceans all year. Their breeding ground is thought to be in the Coral Sea, near New Caledonia. Females much larger than males; migrating females range from about 50 cm to 1.1 m, males from 35-60 cm.

LONG-FIN EEL
Anguilla reinhardtii Steindachner, 1867

P 16-20. Other fin rays numerous. Body slender, tubular; smooth, slimy with tiny embedded scales. Moderate-sized horizontal mouth reaches just beyond posterior edge of eye; fine teeth in broad bands in sides of jaws, a patch of similar length on vomer. Lateral line straight, consisting of small pores. Dorsal fin continuous with broadly rounded caudal and anal fins. Dorsal fin origin well in front of anal fin origin. Small but prominent rounded pectoral fins mid-laterally with small gill opening anteriorly at base. Leptocephali and glass eels transparent. Elvers darkening from above, becoming grey, greenish or olive-brownish above with distinct dark spots or blotching. Broadly distributed from northern Queensland to Port Phillip Bay; also in New Caledonia and Lord Howe Island. Habitat of adults primarily flowing freshwater systems, but individuals of various sizes can be found in coastal marine waters. An aggressive carnivorous predator, sometimes attacking large prey. Specimens documented range to 2 m, but some individuals restrained from migration have been reported to 3 m, taking ducks as prey. Migrating adults have been reported to move downstream in daylight hours; become bright silvery, losing the spots. Adults observed in marine environment appear to be no different in colouration to non-migrating adults in freshwater. Some specimens have been observed in the same spot for a considerable length of time. Leptocephali of this species have been reported present in open oceans from October to March.

Anguilla reinhardtii Large individual (freshwater) ▲ Large individual (marine) ▼

CONGER EELS
FAMILY CONGRIDAE

A large family of marine eels comprising about 40 genera and 150 species, distributed worldwide in tropical and temperate seas. They feature elongate, muscular and very powerful rounded bodies with smooth skin. A single dorsal fin originates close to and above the gill opening, and is continuous with the caudal and anal fins. Pectoral fins are present and are usually pointed with the upper rays longest. The lateral line is distinct, and straight along the sides. The mouth is moderately to very large and powerful, and the jaws are subequal (or the upper slightly longer) with bands of small teeth. The gill openings are slit-like, extending low ventrally. Conger eels are usually drab coloured, grey to black, and pale whitish below. Adults range in size from 10 cm to 3 m, and the heaviest known, weighing 114.5 kg, was caught off Iceland. Most live in muddy or silty grounds, from shallow estuaries to depths of several kilometres, where they are thought to spawn in mid-winter. The shallow-water species hide during the day and move about at night hunting for prey consisting of fishes or cephalopods, and probably a large variety of other invertebrates. Seventeen species are recognised in Australia, two of which are found along the south-east coast. They are good to eat, but handling these fishes can be hazardous

SOUTHERN CONGER
Conger verreauxi Haup, 1856

D 331-347. A 238-265. C 9. P 17-18. Young elongate; large adults very robust, compressed posteriorly. Lateral line with 40 to 44 pores, originating with about five in front of and above pectoral fins, ending before anus vertical. Mouth large with thick fleshy lips; jaws with small conical teeth in two rows, some additional anteriorly. Gill opening large, immediately in front of pectoral fin base. Dorsal fin originates short of gill opening, near vertical of pectoral fin tips, continuous with caudal and anal fins. Pectoral fins prominent, slightly pointed above. Dark grey to bluish-black above, gradually shading lighter to pale below the head and body; sometimes some dark scribbles anteriorly. Juveniles with dark margins on fins. Southern waters of Australia and New Zealand; recorded from Victoria and Tasmania. Coastal reefs, estuaries to deep offshore. Sometimes seen in holes in reefs or at night. Attains 2 m. This genus comprises 15 species; two of the three Australian species are included here.

EASTERN CONGER
Conger wilsoni (Bloch and Schneider, 1801)

D 294-330. A 220-240. C 9. P 15-17. Young slender, snake-like; large adults very robust, compressed posteriorly. Lateral line with 37 to 40 pores, originating with about five in front of and above pectoral fins, ending before anus vertical. Mouth large with thick fleshy lips; jaws with small conical teeth in two rows, some additional anteriorly. Gill opening large, immediately in front of pectoral fin base. Dorsal fin originates well short of pectoral fin tips, continuous with caudal and anal fins. Pectoral fins prominent, slightly pointed above. Dark grey to brownish-black above, gradually shading lighter to pale below the head and body. Young pale grey with dark fin margins. Widespread in southern subtropical seas; reported from east and west Australia, northern New Zealand, South Africa, and possibly northern hemisphere. Coastal bays and estuaries in muddy habitat in reef or under solid objects on mud. Out at night. Usually less than 1 m, but reported to 1.5 m.

Conger verreauxi ▲

Conger wilsoni ▼

MORAY EELS
FAMILY MURAENIDAE

A large family of marine eels comprising at least 10 genera and well over 100 species (200 according to some authors), distributed worldwide in all tropical and subtropical seas. They feature muscular, robust, posteriorly compressed bodies, with tough thick skin; a single median fin is present, usually originating dorsally before the gill opening and continuing around the tail to the anus. The mouth is up to a moderately large size. Teeth are variable between genera, ranging from small pointed conical to molariform or long depressible fangs – venomous in a few species – on the jaws and usually on the vomer in single or several rows. The lateral line is reduced to a series of pores originating before the gill opening; the head pores are obvious. Gill openings are reduced to a small hole mid-laterally behind the head. Most species have distinct colouration consisting of spots and stripes, often with complicated patterns which are usually typical for a species. Morays are mostly reef dwellers, living secretively in holes and crevices. They are usually observed with only the head exposed, however a few species move about on reefs in the open hunting for food. They feed on a variety of invertebrates and some species feed on fish. Although generally not aggressive, the larger species can inflict serious and painful wounds. Some have relatively poor eyesight and rely more on smell, often coming towards a diver to investigate. Sometimes they congregate in certain areas, apparently to spawn, and in such areas they are known to attack divers. The transparent oceanic larvae are more robust than other eels and have a rounded tail. Some species settle at about 50 mm length, and are very slender. Adults range in size from about 30 cm to 2 m. The number of species is greatly reduced from tropical to temperate seas. In the Sydney area there are four local coastal species. A few tropical species expatriate occasionally to the area, but are known only as juveniles. Several more species occur at Seal Rocks, north of Sydney, and the number rapidly increases near the Queensland border. Of the six species included here, two are tropical species regularly found further south.

Green Moray (*Gymnothorax prasinus*)

GREEN MORAY
Gymnothorax prasinus (Richardson, 1848)

Head, body compressed, greatly posteriorly. Young slender, progressively thickening with age. Skin thick, wrinkled with long folds in various places. Snout narrow, bluntly rounded with projecting long tubed nostrils. Posterior nostrils dorsally above eyes with short upward tubes. Series of pores along both jaws, over snout. Head greatly swollen behind eyes. Mouth large; teeth in single series in jaws, prominent, sharp, followed with two or three median depressible fans in upper jaw, usually one large, and short series on vomer. Low fleshy dorsal fin originates well in front of gill opening. Yellowish-brown to bright green. Nostrils and head pores surrounded by black. Widespread southern waters, from southern Queensland to Shark Bay to northern Tasmania, and New Zealand. Rare on the south coast between eastern Victoria and South Australia. Known from sightings in

Port Phillip Bay. Mostly on coastal reefs but also into muddy estuaries and moderately deep offshore. Juveniles settle at about 40 mm. Attains almost 1 m. A large genus, comprising about 120 species worldwide, about 30 of which are found in Australian waters.

Gymnothorax cribroris ▲

SIEVE-PATTERNED MORAY
Gymnothorax cribroris Whitley, 1932

Head, body compressed, greatly posteriorly. Skin thick, wrinkled with minute criss-cross folds, large long folds over gills. Snout narrow, bluntly rounded with projecting long tubed nostrils. Posterior nostrils dorsally above eyes as a large pore. Series of pores along both jaws, over snout. Head slightly swollen behind eyes. Mouth large; teeth in a single series in jaws, prominent, sharp, two rows on vomer. Fleshy, moderately tall dorsal fin originates well in front of gill openings. Variable from pale to dark brown; irregular paler spots, form a dark mosaic pattern anteriorly which darkens progressively posteriorly. Eastern Australia from Queensland to New South Wales. Silty habitat, coastal reefs and harbours; secretive, in reef and under solid objects on sand or mud. Occurs commonly in Sydney Harbour. Attains at least 45 cm; doubtfully reported to 75 cm.

WHITE-SPECKLED MORAY
Gymnothorax eurostus (Abbott, 1860)

Head, body compressed, greatly posteriorly. Skin thick, mostly smooth, with long shallow folds over gills. Snout narrow, bluntly rounded with projecting long tubed nostrils. Posterior nostrils dorsally above eyes as a large pore. Series of pores along both jaws, over snout. Head gradually swollen behind eyes. Mouth large; teeth in a single and double series in jaws, prominent, sharp. Fleshy, moderately tall dorsal fin originates well in front of gill opening. Variable from pale yellowish to dark brown. Dark forms with small white spots all over, dense anteriorly with some larger darks spots which become less numerous posteriorly. Spots very large in young and pale forms. Widespread Indo-Pacific in subtropical zones. On the east coast from central Queensland to Seal Rocks, New South Wales. Coral reefs and clear coastal waters among boulders. Attains 80 cm; usually to 60 cm.

Gymnothorax eurostus ▼

SAW-TOOTH MORAY
Gymnothorax prionodon Ogilby, 1895

Head, body compressed, greatly posteriorly. Skin thick, wrinkled with minute vertical folds, large long folds over gills. Snout narrow, bluntly rounded with projecting long tubed nostrils. Posterior nostrils dorsally above eyes as a large pore. Series of pores along both jaws, over snout. Head greatly swollen behind eyes. Mouth large; teeth in single series in jaws, prominent, sharp, with following serrated edge. Low fleshy dorsal fin originates well in front of gill opening. Variable from pale greenish-brown to dark brown; small white spots anteriorly in adults, progressively increasing in size to large on tail. Gill opening black; some dark streaks on throat. Appears to be restricted to New South Wales, northern New Zealand, and Japan. Coastal reefs; recorded from harbours, but seems more common offshore at islands, usually fairly deep; at Montague Island in about 25 m or more. Rocky, boulder slopes and ledges, sometimes out in the open. Recorded to 1 m in New Zealand. Records from Queensland probably based on the similar *G. nudivomer* (Playfair and Günther, 1867).

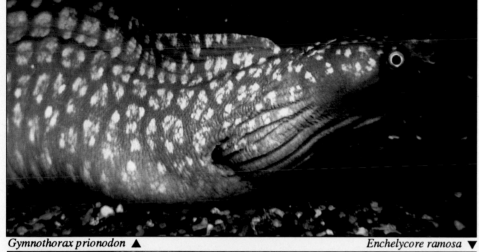

Gymnothorax prionodon ▲

MOSAIC MORAY
Enchelycore ramosa (Griffin, 1926)

Head, body compressed, greatly posteriorly. Skin thick, mostly smooth with large long folds over gills. Snout narrow, slightly elongated, bluntly rounded with projecting long tubed nostrils. Posterior nostrils dorsally anterior to eyes as a large pore. Series of pores along both jaws, over snout. Head slightly swollen behind eyes. Mouth large with hooked jaws and series of prominent, sharp teeth, numerous with many very long, some recurving. Fleshy, moderately tall dorsal fin originates well in front of gill opening. Pale yellow with variable dark patterns, distinctly mosaic in juveniles, becoming diffused and more spotted with age. Subtropical to temperate south Pacific, New South Wales to Eastern Island. Seal Rocks to Montague Island, usually in coastal rocky outcrops or islands among rocky boulders. Recorded in New Zealand to 1.5 m. Small Pacific genus comprising about 10 species.

Enchelycore ramosa ▼

Enchelycore ramosa Juv.

WHITE-EYED MORAY
Siderea thyrsoidea (Richardson, 1845)

Head, body compressed, greatly posteriorly. Skin thick, wrinkled with minute criss-cross folds, large long folds over gills. Snout narrow, bluntly rounded with projecting long tubed nostrils. Posterior nostrils dorsally above eyes as a large pore. Series of pores along both jaws, over snout. Head slightly swollen behind eyes. Mouth large; teeth all conical in one and two rows in jaws. Fleshy, moderately tall dorsal fin originates well in front of gill opening. Variable from pale grey to slightly brownish, with distinct white eye. Widespread tropical west to central Pacific; juveniles commonly south to Sydney. Coastal rocky outcrops in ledges and among boulders. Recorded to 65 cm, but usually to 40 cm. A small genus comprising three species.

HERRINGS AND SARDINES
ORDER CLUPEIFORMES

Represented by about four families, two of which have species in south-eastern coastal waters. They can be separated using Key 10.

1. Snout projecting; eyes above front of mouth ....ENGRAULIDAE (p. 36)

    Snout not projecting; eyes above end of mouth ....CLUPEIDAE (p. 34)

KEY 10: *The Herrings and Sardines*

PILCHARDS
FAMILY CLUPEIDAE

A large family of small fishes, comprising about 65 genera and 180 species. Distributed worldwide, they constitute an important food source for predators, and are probably the greatest single group exploited by commercial fisheries. This family comprises the herrings, sardines and pilchards, all silvery fishes with large weakly attached cycloid scales. They occur in schools inshore and offshore. Some schooling juveniles enter estuaries, but adults are usually in coastal bays or offshore. The lateral line is indistinct or absent. Other features are usually a large mouth, distensible jaws with a single row of tiny teeth, and numerous elongated gill rakers. Fins are entirely soft-rayed, and mostly short-based. A single dorsal fin is centrally placed with ventral fins on the abdomen below it. The pectoral fins are low, behind the head and almost ventrally placed. The anal fin is close to the caudal fin, and the latter is forked. Their diet consists of tiny zooplankton filtered from the water with the long gill rakers. A few species have adapted to fresh water. Most species are small, the largest being about 25 cm. Presently 15 genera and 32 species are recognised in Australian waters; four species are commonly found in southern waters.

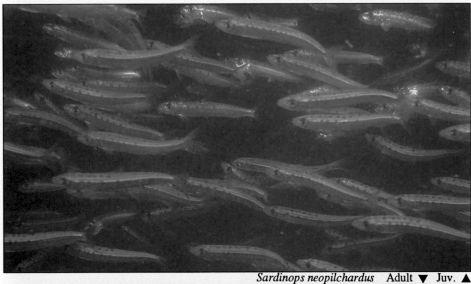

Sardinops neopilchardus Adult ▼ Juv. ▲

PILCHARD
Sardinops neopilchardus (Steindachner, 1879)

D 17-20. A 16-20. C 19. P 17-18. V 8-9. LSR 44-50. Young very slender with almost cylindrical bodies; deepen centrally with age, become more oval in cross-section. Scales cycloid, moderately small, weakly attached on body. Eyes moderately large, headed by transparent adipose tissue to halfway on snout, forming evenly curved head profile. Dorsal fin short with anterior rays longest, centrally placed on back; ventral fins abdominal below. Caudal fin distinctly forked. Anal fin posteriorly near caudal fin. Pectoral fins low, just behind head. Bluish or greenish above, silvery below; series of evenly spaced dark spots along upper sides. Widespread in southern waters from central Queensland and similar latidude on the west coast, and also in New Zealand. Adults school in coastal waters, juveniles enter estuaries. Attains 25 cm. Small genus with five temperate species.

SANDY SPRAT
Hyperlophus vittatus (Castelnau, 1875)

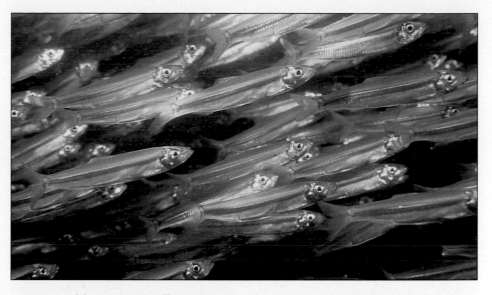

D 15-17. A 17-20. C 19. P 14-15. V 7. LSR 42-45. Body compressed, deepest centrally, covered with moderately small, weakly attached cycloid scales; compressed ventrally and anterior to dorsal fin into a serrate ridge. Eyes moderately large, with a narrow strip of transparent adipose tissue behind and in front, forming evenly curved head profile. Dorsal fin short with anterior rays longest, centrally placed on back; ventral fins abdominal, anteriorly below. Caudal fin distinctly forked. Anal fin posteriorly near caudal fin. Pectoral fins low, just behind head. Juveniles transparent; adults pale brownish with a silver band along sides. Widespread in southern waters from southern Queensland and west coast at similar latidude to Bass Strait, schooling in coastal bays and estuaries. Attains 10 cm. Australian endemic genus comprising two species. The other very similar species, Transparent Sandy Sprat, *H. translucidus* McCulloch, 1917, has deciduous scales and can be identified by anal fin origin just below last dorsal fin ray; occurs from southern Queensland to Botany Bay.

BLUE SPRAT
Spratelloides robustus Ogilby, 1897

D 11-13. A 9-12. C 17. P 13. V 8. LSR 38-45. Body flattened on sides, evenly tapering over posterior half to moderately slender caudal peduncle; covered with weakly attached cycloid scales. Eyes moderately large, headed by short transparent adipose tissue on snout, forming evenly curved head profile. Dorsal fin short with anterior rays longest, centrally placed on back; ventral fins abdominal below posterior end. Caudal fin distinctly forked. Anal fin posteriorly near caudal fin. Pectoral fins low, just behind head. Steel-blue above, shiny silvery-blue on sides, silvery-white below. Widespread in southern waters, subtropical to Tasmania. Commonly occurs in estuaries and coastal bays in large schools, actively feeding at night. Attains 12 cm. Small genus comprising four west Pacific species. Two of the three Australian species are tropical.

SOUTHERN HERRING
Herklotsichthys castelnaui (Ogilby, 1897)

D 16-18. A 17-21. C 19. P 14-15. V 7. LSR 44-45. Body compressed, deepest centrally, covered with moderately small, weakly attached cycloid scales. Eyes moderately large, narrow strip of transparent adipose tissue behind and in front forms evenly curved head profile. Dorsal fin short, anterior rays longest, central on back; ventral fins abdominal below. Caudal fin distinctly forked. Anal fin posteriorly near caudal fin. Pectoral fins low, just behind head. Silvery, thin dusky black tips in adults. East coast from central Queensland to southern New South Wales. Primarily in estuaries, usually in large schools near the sea entrance feeding near the surface. Attains 20 cm.

ANCHOVIES
FAMILY ENGRAULIDAE

A moderately large family comprising about 16 genera and 140 species worldwide. Small, to about 20 cm, but commercially important fishes, anchovies often occur in enormously large and dense schools. Elongate silvery fishes, they have subcylindrical bodies covered with moderately large, weakly attached cycloid scales. A blunt snout protrudes over a very large mouth. The teeth are minute and the fins entirely soft-rayed. Feeding fishes swim fast with the mouth fully extended to filter zooplankton from the water with their numerous long slender gill rakers. The anchovies are mostly coastal fishes in shallow depths, though sometimes found to 200 m, and commonly enter large coastal estuaries in the tidal channels. In Australia, four genera and 19 species are recognised, only one of which is found in southern waters.

AUSTRALIAN ANCHOVY
Engraulis australis (White, 1790)

D 13-16. A 17-19. C 19. P 14-16. V 7. LSR 40-41. Body slightly compressed, dorsal profile almost straight; covered with moderate-sized cycloid scales. Snout pointed, rounded at tip, protruding in front of mouth. Mouth low, extremely large; single series of minute teeth in jaws. Dorsal fin short-based, centrally placed on back; anterior rays longest with progressively shorter rays following. Ventral fins small, placed midway on belly, just anterior to dorsal fin origin. Anal fin short-based, placed about midway between dorsal and anal fins. Pectoral fins low, ventrally placed, just behind head. Bluish-green above, silvery-white below. Fins clear. Southern waters from Heron Island to Swan river, including Lord Howe Island, and also in New Zealand. School in coastal and offshore waters in large numbers, entering large estuaries such as Port Phillip Bay. Attains 15 cm. There is some confusion about the number of species of this antitropical genus which either comprises several or a single widespread species.

BEAKED SALMONS
ORDER GONORHYNCHIFORMES

Represented by four families, only one of which is represented, with a single species, in south-eastern coastal waters. See below.

BEAKED SALMONS
FAMILY GONORYNCHIDAE

A small family comprising a single genus with up to about seven species. Several presently recognised as good species are probably synonymous. The family is widespread and antitropical in both hemispheres of the Indo-Pacific. Also known as sandfishes, these peculiar fishes have cylindrical elongated bodies with somewhat flattened sides. They have a barbel, long and hair-like, on the mouth situated under the head. The mouth is small and protrusible, and the jaws lack teeth. Except for the pectoral fins near the head, all fins are placed in the posterior half of the body. Scales are small and roughly ctenoid. Pale sandy-coloured fishes, beaked salmons usually have distinct dark markings on their fins. They feed on small benthic invertebrates, usually in the dark, and bury in the sand during the day; consequently they are rarely seen except during night dives. Attaining about 60 cm, these fishes are considered quite edible, however there are contradictory opinions.

BEAKED SALMON
Gonorynchus greyi (Richardson, 1845)

D 12-13. A 10. C 19. P 10. V 9. LL 172-178. Body very elongate, rectangular in cross-section, shallow and thick, tapering to shallow caudal peduncle; covered with firmly attached tiny scales; lateral line straight. Head small, conical; mouth positioned ventrally with fleshy lips, single narrow medial barbel below. Jaws without teeth; patch of small teeth on roof and floor of mouth. Single short-based dorsal fin placed much closer to caudal fin than head. Small ventral fins placed below; anal fin about halfway to caudal fin. Sandy-coloured fishes; pale grey fins and some dark, blackish fin-tips. Widespread in southern waters; recorded from southern Queensland to Rottnest Island. Shallow sandy estuaries to deep offshore. Attains 50 cm.

Photograph: Graham Edgar

Engraulis australis ▼   *Gonorynchus greyi* ▲

CATFISHES
ORDER SILURIFORMES

Represented by perhaps 25 families, primarily freshwater, only one of which has species in south-eastern coastal waters. See below.

EEL-TAIL CATFISHES
FAMILY PLOTOSIDAE

A tropical Indo-Pacific family, comprising about eight genera and 40 species, about half of which are confined to freshwater systems in Australia and New Guinea. They differ from the worldwide Ariidae, the fork-tailed catfishes (which as their common name suggests have a forked caudal fin), in having an elongated body tapering to an eel-like tail. The Australian marine representatives feature five pairs of barbels around the mouth, and have prominent venomous spines heading their dorsal and pectoral fins. The remainder of their fins are soft-rayed. The dorsal fin is in two parts, the first short-based, the second long-based with numerous rays and continuous with the caudal and anal fins. The skin is smooth and slimy, and the lateral line consists of pores. The marine species are usually estuarine or inhabit coastal reefs, some entering freshwater. They have a dentritic organ, thought to function as a salt regulator, protruding from the anus; it is usually absent in freshwater species. Some freshwater species attain a large size, to 1.4 m, and the largest marine species attain about 60 cm. Diet consists of various invertebrates or fishes. In Australia 16 species are recognised, two of which are in south-eastern marine waters and are included here.

Striped Catfish *(Plotosus lineatus)*

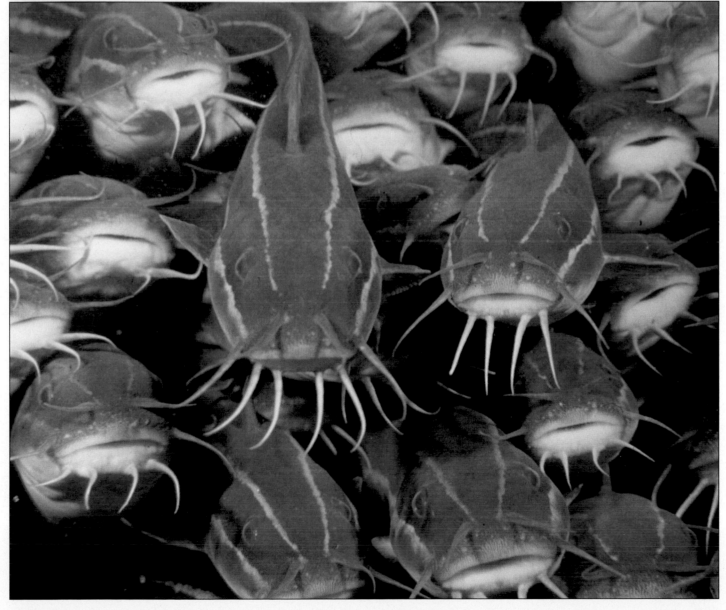

ESTUARY CATFISH
Cnidoglanis macrocephala (Valenciennes, 1840)

D I,4+102-129. A 95-112. C 6-9. P I,9. V 9-12. Body thick anteriorly, tapering over long posterior section to a point; covered with slimy skin. Lateral line in a series of pores with smooth curve above pectoral fins, then straight. Head large, slightly depressed. Mouth rather small; lips thick, fleshy; jaws with patch of short canines anteriorly, surrounded by four pairs of long fleshy barbels. Fifth pair of barbels above snout. Eyes small, positioned dorsally, covered by skin. Short-based first dorsal fin headed by serrate spine, closely followed by long-based section, continuous with caudal and anal fins. Small paddle-like ventral fins place posteriorly near anus. Pectoral fins much larger than ventral fins, paddle-like, adjacent to gill openings. Dentritic organ large, fleshy. Mottled brownish or yellowish. Widespread in southern waters from southern Queensland to Abrolhos Islands, but becoming rare in Victorian and Tasmanian waters. Rocky estuaries, silty coastal bays. Usually solitary, in ledges or under solid objects on mud. Attains 60 cm. Monotypic genus. Reputed as excellent to eat, however special care should be taken in handling these fishes as a stab from the fin spines is extremely painful, and future repeats may be fatal.

STRIPED CATFISH
Plotosus lineatus (Thunberg, 1787)

D I,4+94-115. A 75-82. C 9-11. P I,9-13. V 10-13. Body thick anteriorly, tapering over long posterior section to a point; covered with slimy skin. Lateral line in a series of pores with smooth curve above pectoral fins, then straight. Head large, slightly depressed. Mouth rather small; lips thick, fleshy; jaws with patch of short canines anteriorly, surrounded by four pairs of long fleshy barbels. Fifth pair of barbels above snout. Eyes small, positioned dorsally, covered by skin. Short-based first dorsal fin headed by serrate spine, closely followed by long-based section, continuous with caudal and anal fins. Small paddle-like ventral fins place posteriorly near anus. Pectoral fins much larger than ventral fins, paddle-like, adjacent to gill openings. Dentritic organ well developed. Distinctly coloured; black stripes as juveniles, newly settled juveniles all black, large adults with less distinct stripes. Widespread tropical Indo-Pacific; on the east coast commonly south to central New South Wales. Coastal waters and estuaries, in small aggregations, occasionally solitary but tiny juveniles in closely packed groups of numerous individuals shaping into single bodies of various shapes; seemingly mimic sticks, coconuts or other land-originated matter in coastal regions. Schooling becomes less tight with age; larger juveniles

in large loose schools, however with potential danger quickly get together. Feed primarily on benthic vertebrates and algaes. Attains 35 cm. Small genus comprising five species, one of which lives in fresh water.

GRINNERS
ORDER AULOPIFORMES

Represented by about 15 families, three of which have species in south-eastern coastal waters (Key 11).

SERGEANT BAKERS
FAMILY AULOPIDAE

A small worldwide family comprising a single genus and about 10 species, several of which are not yet described. Sergeant bakers are mostly very deepwater species living on the continental shelf in tropical and temperate seas. They are salmon-like fishes with a large head and jaws, and moderate sized ctenoid scales. Fins are entirely soft-rayed. The dorsal fin is large, elevated anteriorly, and often has a long filamentous ray. The caudal fin is distinctly forked and large. Anal, ventral and pectoral fins are moderately large. These fishes are usually pale pearly below with reddish blotches dorsally and on their sides. Benthic fishes, they are usually perched on their ventral fins on low reefs or sand near reefs. They feed on a variety of swimming invertebrates and other fishes. Of the three species recorded from Australia, one is commonly found in relatively shallow depths, and is featured here.

Aulopus purpurissatus Male ▲ Female ▼

SERGEANT BAKER
Aulopus purpurissatus Richardson, 1843

D 19-22. A 12-14. C 35 (approximately). P 11. V 8-9. LL 49-51. Long posteriorly tapering body, slightly compressed centrally; moderate-sized ctenoid scales. Lateral line almost straight from origin to centres of caudal fin base. Mouth large, jaws with several rows of sharp fine teeth. Eye placed dorsally above end of mouth. Dorsal fin in two parts; first large, centrally placed, anterior rays longest, several becoming filamentous in males and exceptionally long. Last rays almost reach small adipose fin, situated slightly closer to caudal fin than end of first dorsal fin base. Anal fin with moderate length base, situated directly below space between dorsal fins. Ventral fins broad with thick rays, situated below dorsal fin origin. Pectoral fins centrally on sides, just in front of and above ventral fins. Pale whitish to pinkish below, light to dark greenish or purplish above; usually pale reddish to dark saddle-like patches above, and in a series along sides. Australian species, ranging in southern waters from southern Queensland and Shark Bay to northern Tasmania. Mostly found on rocky boulder reefs with rich invertebrate growth; from inshore ocean bays to depths of 250 m. Often caught on fishing lines and considered good eating. Attains 60 cm.

LIZARDFISHES
FAMILY SYNODONTIDAE

A moderate-sized family, primarily tropical, comprising two genera, one monotypic and cosmopolitan, and the other with about 35 species variously distributed worldwide. Lizardfishes are elongate fishes, almost torpedo-shaped, some tapering posteriorly to the caudal fin; they are covered with moderate-sized cycloid scales. The mouth is exceptionally large with a series of sharp, moderate-sized, needle-like teeth along the entire jaws. Their eyes are moderately large, laterally placed, and centrally above the mouth. Fins are comprised entirely of soft rays. The dorsal fin is short-based, elevated anteriorly, and placed centrally on the back. It is followed by a small, posteriorly placed adipose fin. The anal fin is small, and opposite the adipose fin. The caudal fin is distinctly forked, and the pectoral fin is small and placed mid-laterally just behind the head. Lizardfishes have large ventral fins with nine rays. Many species are similarly marked, typically with a series of small blotches mid-laterally along their sides, and a series of bars over the posterior half of the body. Colour is variable and depends, within a species, on depth or habitat. They are smallish fishes, to about 25 cm. Voracious predators, they strike fast at fishes and shrimps which are often larger than might be expected given the lizardfish's size. They are found in various habitats, usually near reefs, some on open sand near reefs, and others taking vantage points on reefs themselves. Both genera are known from Australian waters. Fourteen species are recorded, at least five of which range to southern waters and are included here.

Variegated Lizardfish (*Synodus variegatus*)

TWO-SPOT LIZARDFISH
Synodus dermatogenys Fowler, 1912

D 11-13. A 8-10. C 19. P 11-13. V 8. LL 59-62. Body almost circular in cross-section, covered by moderate-sized cycloid scales extending over most of head, small on top. Lateral line almost straight, five and a half scale-rows above. Prominent, slender, needle-like teeth in single series along entire jaws. Dorsal fin short-based, slightly elevated anteriorly, centrally placed on back; followed by very small adipose fin, positioned closest to caudal fin. Anal fin short-based, placed below adipose fin. Caudal fin deeply forked. Pectoral fin placed mid-laterally just behind head. Ventral fins with long rays, their origin well posterior to and below pectoral bases. Pale brownish-grey; bluish-grey stripe along upper sides, two dark spots on upper snout. Broadly distributed in the tropical Indo-Pacific; on the east coast commonly south to the Sydney area. Coastal sand flats and slopes, usually near reefs; readily buries in the sand. Attains 22 cm.

VARIEGATED LIZARDFISH
Synodus variegatus (Lacepède, 1803)

D 12-14. A 8-10. C 19. P 12-13. V 8. LL 61-63. Body almost circular in cross-section, covered with moderate-sized cycloid scales extending over most of head, small on top. Lateral line almost straight, five and a half scale-rows above. Prominent, slender, needle-like teeth in single series along entire jaws. Dorsal fin short-based, slightly elevated anteriorly, centrally placed on back; followed by very small adipose fin, positioned closest to caudal fin. Anal fin short-based, placed below adipose fin. Caudal fin deeply forked. Pectoral fin placed mid-laterally just behind head. Ventral fins with long rays, their origin well posterior to and below pectoral bases. Usually pale; dark grey to bright red banding dorsally, longitudinal series of red blotches with another series of pale blotches immediately below. Widespread tropical Indo-Pacific, commonly to the Sydney area. Shallow coastal reef slopes; in the Sydney area mostly in silty areas on rubble substrates. Attains 25 cm.

TAIL-BLOTCH LIZARDFISH
Synodus jaculum Russell and Cressey, 1979

D 11-13. A 8-10. C 19. P 12-13. V 8. LL 59-62. Body almost circular in cross-section, covered with moderate-sized cycloid scales extending over most of head, small on top. Lateral line almost straight, five and a half scale-rows above. Prominent, slender, needle-like teeth in single series along entire jaws. Dorsal fin short-based, slightly elevated anteriorly, centrally placed on back; followed by very small adipose fin, positioned closest to caudal fin. Anal fin short-based, placed below adipose fin. Caudal fin deeply forked. Pectoral fin placed mid-laterally just behind head. Ventral fins with long rays, their origin well posterior to and below pectoral bases. Variable from very pale on sand to very dark on reefs; black blotch on caudal peduncle readily identifies this species. Widespread tropical Indo-Pacific, on the east coast south to Montague Island. Shallow reef flats, commonly in 3 m, to deep sand flats, at least 30 m. Often in pairs or small aggregations; has the unusual habit (for the family) of regularly swimming high above the substrate. Attains 20 cm.

EAR-SPOT LIZARDFISH
Synodus similis McCulloch, 1921

D 11-13. A 8-10. C 19. P 11-13. V 8. LL 59-62. Body almost circular in cross-section, covered with moderate-sized cycloid scales extending over most of head, small on top. Lateral line almost straight, five and a half scale-rows above. Prominent, slender, needle-like teeth in single series along entire jaws. Dorsal fin short-based, slightly elevated anteriorly, centrally placed on back; followed by very small adipose fin, positioned closest to caudal fin. Anal fin short-based, placed below adipose fin. Caudal fin deeply forked. Pectoral fin placed mid-laterally just behind head. Ventral fins with long rays, their origin well posterior to and below pectoral bases. Pale, several distinct black spots on upper opercle; also more slender than other similar species. Widespread tropical Indo-Pacific. On the east coast south to Montague Island. Sand flats, slightly sloping and bay-like into reefs; usually fairly deep, 20 m or more. Typically on the substrate with head raised. Attains 20 cm.

PAINTED LIZARDFISH
Trachinocephalus myops (Forster, 1801)

D 11-14. A 13-18. C 19. P 11-13. V 8. LL 51-61. Body almost circular in cross-section, covered with moderate-sized cycloid scales extending over most of head, small on top. Lateral line almost straight, three and a half scale-rows above. Mouth very oblique; prominent, slender, needle-like, teeth in single series along entire jaws. Dorsal fin tall but short-based, elevated anteriorly, centrally placed on back; followed by very small adipose fin, positioned closest to caudal fin. Anal fin long-based, placed below adipose fin, reaching near deeply forked caudal fin. Pectoral fin placed mid-laterally just behind head. Ventral fins with long rays, their origin well posterior to and below pectoral bases. Very pale; alternating blue and yellow longitudinal stripes dorsally. Extremely widespread geographically in tropical waters and in sand habitat from subtidal zones to at least 200 m. Estuarine as well as offshore. Rarely exposed, usually buried in sand with only eyes showing. Usually in loose aggregations; sometimes courting specimens swim above the substrate. South to Bermagui where numerous adults were observed at Horseshoe Bay in about 3 m of water. Attains 30 cm.

SAURIES
FAMILY HARPADONTIDAE

A small tropical family comprising two genera and 14 species. Slender, moderately large-scaled fishes, the sauries feature a large mouth set with numerous rows of needle-like and close-set teeth in the jaws. Other features are a small, centrally placed, spineless dorsal fin, a small adipose fin on the back above the anal fin, and cycloid scales. Their ventral fins, with one feeble spine and eight rays, are typical and readily separate this family from the superficially similar Synodontidae, which in addition has only a single row of teeth in each jaw. The genera *Saurida* was previously placed in Synodontidae. Generally, they are dull-coloured fishes, greyish with dark blotches. They partly bury themselves leaving only their back exposed in the substrate. Sauries are usually in muddy or soft bottom habitat and most species are deepwater dwellers. Small to medium-sized

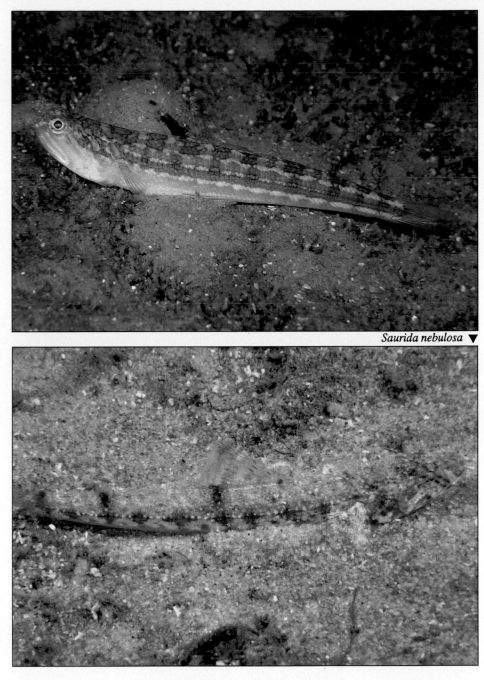

Saurida nebulosa ▼

fishes, they reach about 70 cm. They are voracious predators taking rather large prey with great speed. The sauries are also known as grinners, whilst the fishes in Harpodon are known as bombay ducks. Only one bombay duck and eight sauries are known from Australian waters, but only one saury is moderately common to coastal New South Wales.

BLOTCHED SAURY
Saurida nebulosa Valenciennes, 1849

D 10-11. A 9-10. C 19. P 11-13. V I,8. LL 50-52. Body slender, almost circular in cross-section; covered with moderate-sized cycloid scales extending over most of head, smaller on top of head. Lateral line almost straight. Moderately large eyes placed centrally above very large mouth. Prominent needle-like teeth in broad bands along entire jaws. Small dorsal fin, elevated anteriorly, placed centrally on back, followed by posteriorly placed small adipose fin with small anal fin below. Caudal fin forked. Pectoral fins small, placed mid-laterally just behind head. Ventral fins long, positioned about below pectoral fin bases. Greyish-brown; dark, broad, indistinct saddle-like markings above. Widespread tropical west Pacific, ranging south to central New South Wales. Usually in estuaries or coastal bays; well camouflaged, concealed when buried in sand or mud. Attains 16 cm. Circumtropical genus comprises about 10 species. In New South Wales this species was confused with the similar *S. gracilis* (Quoy and Gaimard, 1824) which occurs in more tropical waters, including Queensland.

FROGFISHES
ORDER
BATRACHOIDIFORMES

Represented by a single family with species occurring in south-eastern coastal waters. See below.

FROGFISHES
FAMILY BATRACHOIDIDAE

A moderate-sized family comprising 18 genera and about 46 species, with only two of the genera and eight species in Australian waters. Frogfishes are smooth-skinned, large and round-headed fishes. Their mouth is broad with bands of small sharp teeth in the jaws. They usually have numerous fleshy papillae along various parts of the head, and often large tentacles above the eyes. They have some prominent or small spines on the opercles, and a series of large mucus pores and sensory pores on the head. The gill opening is slit-like and positioned vertically on the pectoral base. The dorsal fin is in two parts – a small spinous part covered in thick skin with three possibly venomous spines, followed by a large and long-based soft-rayed section. The pectoral fins are broad and rounded. Frogfishes are usually dark, blackish blotched or marbled brown, and sometimes greenish. Juveniles are more distinct, often with broad cross-banding. They are found in various habitats from muddy estuaries to deep offshore reefs, usually under rocks or in deep ledges, making burrows in the sand below. Eggs are large and deposited on the ceiling in their nests. Hatching young move into narrow ledges or below rocks in the vicinity. Frogfishes can make loud croaking noises with their swim-bladder. They feed on a variety of invertebrates, and prey is swallowed whole. The expandable stomach can accomodate anything which fits through the mouth. They are primarily tropical species, and only one frogfish is common in New South Wales, with a second Queensland species ranging further south.

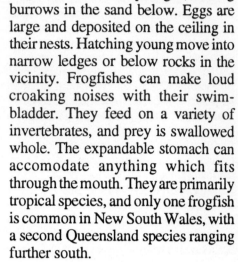

EASTERN FROGFISH
Batrachomoeus dubius (Shaw, 1790)

D III,19-20. A 16-17. C 13-15. P 22-23. V I,2. Head with simple tentacles, larger with fringed margins above eyes. Eyes elevated; interorbital broad, slightly concave. Gill slit over pectoral fin base. Pair of diverging spines on upper edge of opercle. Dorsal fin spines short, in thick skin which extends to base of large, tall, long-based soft-rayed section; last rays almost fully attached to caudal peduncle. Anal fin with much shorter rays, opposite posterior two-thirds of soft-rayed dorsal fin. Pectoral fin rounded, very large, its width equal to body depth. Caudal fin slightly smaller, rounded. Ventral fin slender, fleshy with hidden first spine. Variable, pale greyish to dark bluish-grey; dark fine mottling to large blotching. Juveniles banded. Coastal central New South Wales to southern Queensland. Primarily in silty habitat, commonly found in Sydney Harbour, from subtidal to at least 150 m. Attains 30 cm. A similar species on the west coast. Small Australian genus comprising five species.

Batrachomoeus dubius   Anterior view ▲ Lateral view ▼

SCULPTURED FROGFISH
Halophryne queenslandiae (De Vis, 1882)

D III,20. A 16-17. C 14. P 22-23. V I,2. Head with multi-lobed tentacles, large with coarsely long-fringed margins above eyes; some series along body, particularly long along lateral line. Eyes elevated; interorbital broad, slightly convex. Head with skin-ridges, sometimes forming intersecting patterns, in some specimens extending over entire upper sides. Gill slit over pectoral fin base. Pair of prominent spines, widely separate, on posterior edges of opercle. Dorsal fin spines short, in thick skin which extends to base of large, tall, long-based soft-rayed section; last rays almost fully attached to caudal peduncle. Anal fin with much shorter rays, opposite posterior two-thirds of soft-rayed dorsal fin. Pectoral fin rounded, very large, its width equal to body depth. Caudal fin slightly smaller, rounded. Ventral fin long, slender, fleshy with hidden first spine. Pale brownish with darker blotches. Large individuals usually with bright orange mark just below spinous dorsal fin. Primarily a Queensland species, extending into New South Wales. Although recorded from estuaries, it seems more common offshore at islands, in clear waters among rocks and sand in 20 m or more. Attains 30 cm.

Halophryne queenslandiae   Anterior view ▲   Lateral view ▼

ANGLERFISHES
ORDER LOPHIIFORMES

Represented by 16 families, two of which have species in south-eastern coastal waters (Key 12).

HANDFISHES
FAMILY
BRACHIONICHTHYIDAE

A small family of peculiar little fishes restricted to Australian waters and most of which occur in Tasmania. They feature a tough velvety skin with tiny spinules or a smooth warty surface. The paired fins are hand-like and the pectoral fins arm-like and extended from the body. The dorsal fin is in three

1.	Body elongate; dorsal fin above eye .... BRACHIONICHTHYIDAE (p. 45)
	Body short; spine with thick skin above eye .... ANTENNNARIIDAE (p. 46)

KEY 12: *The Anglerfishes*

parts, headed by a luring apparatus formed from the first dorsal spine. This consists of a rod, called the illicium, and bait, called the esca. The second part of the dorsal fin is anteriorly placed, originates in front of the eyes, and has two spines with a following angular membrane. The third part is long-based and over most of the back. The anal fin is similar to, but shorter than and opposite, the posterior part of the dorsal fin. The caudal peduncle is distinct with a moderate-sized caudal fin. The mouth is small with tiny teeth in each jaw. Gill openings are small and pore-like, and positioned above and behind the pectoral fins.

Handfishes are benthic and move about slowly, walking on the paired fins, but when nescessary can swim well. The function of the luring apparatus is not clear; most species feed on crustaceans or worms and various other invertebrates. Sometimes the lure is lowered in front and held down; perhaps it creates a smell to attract prey. They live in quiet bays and deep in sponge areas where some species are trawled. Presently one genus is recognised; most species appear to be undescribed with many discovered only recently. About six species are known, two of which are in mainland waters, and one is included here.

AUSTRALIAN HANDFISH
Brachionichthys sp

D I+II,17-18. A 9-10. C 9. V I,4. Body elongated posteriorly, tapering evenly to caudal fin. Skin entirely covered with tiny spinules; variably with fleshy filaments, one rather large and leafy, curiously placed dorsally on arm part of pectoral fins. Illicium long, slender with small oval esca. Pale, slightly darker above, with yellowish or orange longitudinal spots and streaks. Most widespread species in the family, ranging from southern Queensland to South Australia and Tasmania. Rarely seen in the shallows; usually in 40-100 m. Attains 8 cm. This species previously confused with *B. hirsutus* (Lacepède, 1804) which is restricted to Tasmania, occurring commonly in the south. Several other species are trawled off eastern Victoria, all apparently undescribed except *B. verrucosus* (McCulloch and Waite, 1918), also found off the south coast to South Australia where it is recorded from relatively shallow depths in the gulfs.

Brachionichthys sp. Anterior view ▲ Lateral view ▼

ANGLERFISHES
FAMILY ANTENNARIIDAE

A family of specialised predatory fishes comprising 12 genera and 41 species worldwide. Anglerfishes are unique in having a greatly enlarged third dorsal spine, and usually a modified first dorsal fin spine serving as a luring apparatus. The lure consists of a rod or stalk, the illicium, and the bait, the esca. The latter varies greatly between genera, the shapes usually mimicking worms or other invertebrates, and even other fishes. When in use, the lures are even given a movement to copy their model in trying to trick possible prey for an easy strike. The anglerfish is well equipped with a large mouth and a highly expandable stomach to accommodate any prey which fits through the throat. It often sucks up its prey whole, a procedure taking a few milliseconds.

These mostly small fishes, the largest about 30 cm, live in shallow depths to about 300 m. Short-bodied and globose, they primarily feed on other fishes. They have recurving teeth, only for holding, which are small and villiform and in several irregular rows in the jaws. Some species are among the most variable in colour of all fishes – in overall colour virtually every shade except blue – from jet black to bright red, yellow and to a lesser degree green. Various patterns may occur, but when present these are usually consistent with regards to position on body, head or fins, and may be diagnostic for certain species. Colours usually serve as mimicry of their environment, which may be a sponge or algae habitat, however the bright colours of some juveniles suggest the warning colours of poisonous flatworms or nudibranchs. Other features include leg- or hand-like pectoral and ventral fins, used for walking or holding, and a restricted tube-like gill opening, which in some species is used for propulsion when they are moving about without haste; otherwise fins are used. Skin is flexible, from smooth with cutaneous filaments to covered with close-set dermal spinules, bifurcate to simple, depending on genus. Many of the tropical species have pelagic eggs produced in a mucus raft, and several species show parental care, the female guarding the eggs. The temperate Australian species hide egg masses in hollows of rocks and the female covers them with her side. Hatching young drop onto the substrate and crawl out of sight into the nearest crack. All genera have representatives in Australian waters; six of these are found in coastal south-eastern waters. Only one species is considered a tropical expatriate.

PAINTED ANGLERFISH
Antennarius pictus (Shaw and Nodder, 1794)

D I+I+I,12-13. A 6-7. C 9. P 10-11. V 5. Skin covered with tiny dermal spinules, extends over second and third dorsal spines. Dorsal fin in four parts; first the illicium with esca, followed closely by much shorter second spine, about half length, with thin following membrane from tip to base of large third spine. Soft-rayed section long-based, ending clearly separate from caudal fin. Anal fin short-based, opposite posterior part of dorsal fin. Illicium arises on tip of snout; esca consists of broad, laterally compressed appendage with several smaller slender appendages arising from base. Pectoral fins prominent, arm-like. Ventral fins jugular. Extremely variable in colour. Known overall colours range from bright red, yellow, greenish, white, brown and black, with or without saddle-like banding dorsally; often three spots in caudal fin. Tips or outer margins of pectoral fins usually distinctly white. Widespread tropical Indo-Pacific; adults common to the Sydney area. Coastal bays and deep estuaries, usually in or next to sponges. Attains 16 cm. Cosmopolitan tropical genus comprising 24 species in six species-groups. Photographs show various colour-forms.

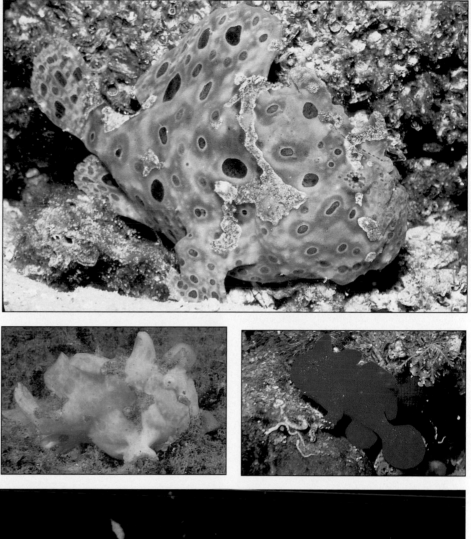

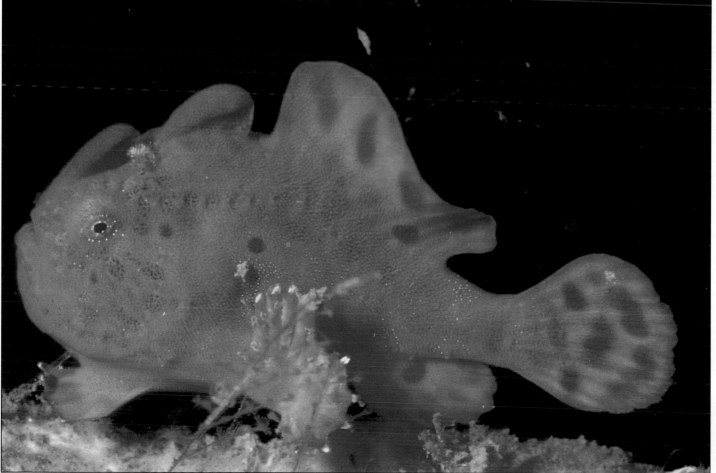

STRIPED ANGLERFISH
Antennarius striatus (Shaw and Nodder, 1794)

D I+I+I,11-12. A 7. C 9. P 9-12. V 5. Skin covered with tiny dermal spinules, extends over second and third dorsal spines. Dorsal fin in four parts; first illicium with esca, followed closely by slightly shorter second spine and large third spine. Soft-rayed section long-based, ending clearly separate from caudal fin. Anal fin short-based, opposite posterior part of dorsal fin. Illicium arises on snout tip; esca consists of two to seven elongate cylindrical worm-like appendages (usually three in the Sydney area), each with small secondary filaments. Pectoral fins prominent, arm-like. Ventral fins jugular. Extremely variable, usually soft-coloured, orange, yellow, brown, white, green; variable striped patterns from a few lines or spots to densely striped; sometimes completely black. Colour can change in a matter of days when removed from habitat; completely black specimen placed in aquarium changed to grey with thin black stripes. Widespread virtually all tropical seas. Shallow rocky estuaries, recorded to more than 200 m. In the Sydney area, most common in sponge areas, usually positioned against the sides or in depressions in the substrate. Attains 20 cm. Almost identical species, *A. hispidus* (Bloch and Schneider, 1829), featuring different esca consisting of oval tuft with numerous slender filaments, also occurs in the Sydney area, but mostly known from trawls; rare in coastal areas. Photographs show various colour-forms.

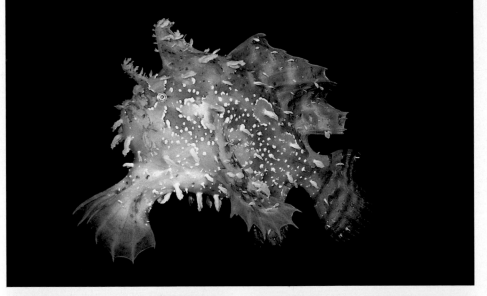

SARGASSUM ANGLERFISH
Histrio histrio (Linnaeus, 1758)

D I+I+I,12. A 7. C 9. P 10. V 5. Skin covered with tiny, rounded, close-set papillae, extends over second and third dorsal spines. Larger leaf-like appendages variously scattered along dorsal spines, head, belly, sides. Dorsal fin in four parts; first the illicium with esca, followed by large second and third spine. Soft-rayed section long-based, ending clearly separate from caudal fin. Anal fin short-based, opposite posterior part of dorsal fin. Illicium arises on tip of snout; esca consists of oval-shaped appendage with numerous parallel folds and cluster of short filaments from base. Pectoral fins large, arm-like. Ventral fins jugular. Usually pale to dark yellowish-brown, with highly variable pattern of dark and white spots and lines. All tropical oceans except east Pacific, often ranging into temperate seas. Pelagic, swims among floating weeds; particularly common in sargassum rafts. Juveniles often drift with weeds into the Sydney beaches with onshore winds; may reach south to Victoria. Attains 15 cm. Monotypic genus. Since its original description this species was redescribed under at least 20 different names in six different genera. Photographs show various colour-forms.

TASSELLED ANGLERFISH
Rhycherus filamentosus (Castelnau, 1872)

D I+I+I,12-13. A 7-8. C 9. P 9-11. V 5. Eyes protrude laterally from surface. Skin covered everywhere with close-set, long, tapering cutaneous appendages. Dorsal fin in four parts; first the illicium with esca, followed closely by two long skin-covered spines, third spine twice as long as second. Soft-rayed section tall, long-based, ending clearly separate from caudal fin. Anal fin short-based, opposite posterior part of dorsal fin. Illicium very long, arises on tip of snout; esca consists of pair of tapering worm-like appendages. Pectoral fins prominent, arm-like. Ventral fins jugular. Brownish to reddish above with dark blotches or stripes. South coast from the Bass Straight area to South Australia. Reasonably common on shallow weed-covered reef to about 60 m. Usually in cracks or small hollows along ledges. Victorian specimens congregate in October on shallow reefs to spawn. Females usually much larger than males, in addition greatly swollen with eggs; usually surrounded by up to four males from which they choose a mate. Egg mass consists of numerous single-egg strings attached to a gel disc about 30 mm in diameter. Disc laid first, followed rapidly by long strings of eggs, each on a long sticky double filament. As the male releases sperm, the female fans the eggs vigorously with caudal fin and posterior sides, trying to spread them out into the back of the cave; male is expelled during this process. Sticky threads entangle themselves with surrounding growth on rocks, forming strong loops. Female then covers the eggs completely with her side. Egg mass large, containing about 5,000 eggs, each about 5 mm in diameter. Young hatch with bulbous yolk after about 30 days, sink rapidly to the bottom, quickly crawl into cracks. Large species; attains 23 cm. Second and only other species in the genus occurs in south-western waters.

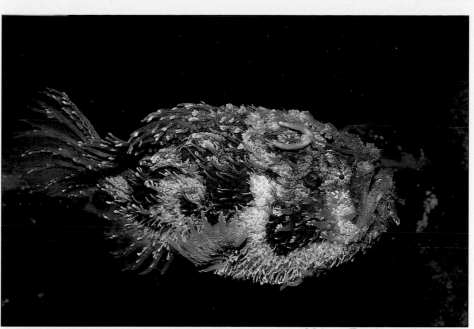

Male ▲ Female guarding eggs ▼

Hatchling, a few weeks old ▼

Eggs, about 5 weeks old

49

ROUGH ANGLERFISH
Kuiterichthys furcipilis (Cuvier, 1817)

D I+I+I,12-14. A 7-8. C 9. P 8-10. V 5. Close-set bifurcate spinules cover body skin, which extends over second and third dorsal spines. Dorsal fin in four parts; first illicium with esca, then long second and third spines of about equal length. Long-based soft-rayed section ends well separate from caudal fin. Anal fin short-based, opposite posterior part of dorsal fin. Illicium long, naked, arises on snout tip; esca large, consists of variable number of small, and some larger, slender appendages arising from base. Pectoral fins prominent, arm-like. Ventral fins jugular. Pinkish or brownish, various dark patchy bands; large round dark spot often distinct on about centre of soft dorsal fin base. Southern waters from central New South Wales to south Western Australia, including Tasmania. Recorded from 9-240 m but rarely seen in shallows; often taken in scallop dredges in Tasmania. Attains 15 cm. Monotypic genus, but may contain another undescribed species.

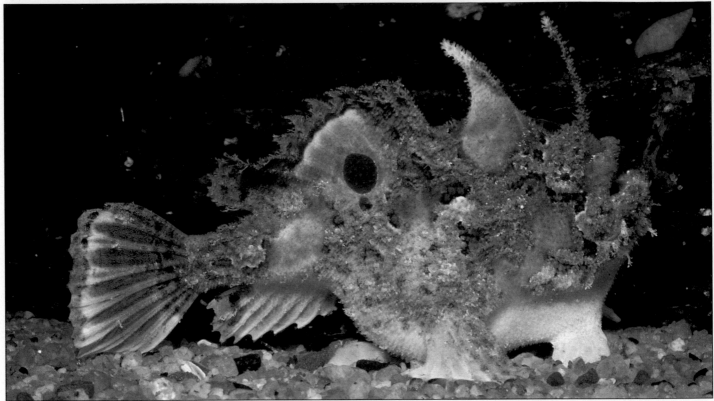

SMOOTH ANGLERFISH
Phyllophryne scortea (McCulloch and Waite, 1918)

D I+I+I,15-16. A 7-9. C 9. P 10-12. V 5. Skin mostly naked except for tiny dermal spinules with each pore in the lateral-line system; extends over second and third dorsal spines. Dorsal fin in four parts; first the illicium with esca, followed closely by about equally long second spine, with the third, slightly longer spine placed high on the steep head-profile. Very long-based soft-rayed section ends separate from caudal fin, but connected by a low membrane. Anal fin with long rays, short-based, about one-third of soft dorsal fin section, and opposite its posterior part. Illicium arises on tip of snout; esca consists of a broad oval shaped appendage with about six filaments on posterior margin. Pectoral fins prominent, arm-like. Ventral fins jugular. Extremely variable in colour; all colours except bright red or blue. Mostly bright orange, yellow, green, jet black; some broad elongate blotches variously present. Entire south coast, including Tasmania. Shallow rocky estuaries to about 45 m. Usually hiding under rocks or other hard objects. Attains 10 cm. Monotypic genus. Esca appears to mimic an amphipod; used to attract sand gobies which feed on these small crustaceans. Photographs show different colour-forms.

PRICKLY ANGLERFISH
Echinophryne crassispina McCulloch and Waite, 1918

D I+I+I,15-16. A 8-9. C 9. P 10-11. V 5. Skin covered with close-set tiny bifurcate spinules, extends over second and third dorsal spines. Dorsal fin in four parts; first the illicium with esca, followed closely by similar length second spine and large third spine. Soft-rayed section very long-based, ending clearly separate from caudal fin. Anal fin very short-based, opposite posterior part of dorsal fin. Illicium thick, covered with close-set dermal spinules, arises on tip of snout; esca totally reduced to thin appendage. Pectoral fins prominent, arm-like. Ventral fins jugular. Reddish-brown to brick red; some darker shading above. Southern waters, recorded from Jervis Bay to the Recherche Archipelago, including northern Tasmania. Shallow protected bays, rocky reefs, to about 20 m. Attains 7 cm. Small genus, comprising three species, two of which are included here. The third, *E. mitchelli* (Morton, 1897), appears to be restricted to deep Tasmanian and Victorian waters; only known from some preserved specimens. Reproductive strategies similar to *Rhycherus*.

SPONGE ANGLERFISH
Echinophryne reynoldsi Pietsch and Kuiter, 1984

D I+I+I,15-16. A 8-9. C 9. P 10. V 5. Skin covered with close-set tiny bifurcate spinules, extends over second and third dorsal spines. Dorsal fin in four parts; first the illicium with esca, followed closely by short second spine and large, mostly embedded third spine. Soft-rayed section very long-based, ending clearly separate from caudal fin. Anal fin large but short-based, opposite posterior part of dorsal fin. Illicium thick, covered with close-set dermal spinules, arises on tip of snout; esca totally reduced to thin appendage. Pectoral fins prominent, arm-like. Ventral fins jugular. Yellow to orange-brown, paler below; sometimes has large circular spots, only slightly darker than surrounding on sides; juveniles usually with broad purplish-brown margin along soft dorsal fin. South coast from Western Port Bay to Lucky Bay, Western Australia. Secretive, in sponges in cave overhangs or large exposed sponges; known from 3-20 m. Attains about 80 mm.

Echinophryne reynoldsi Juv.

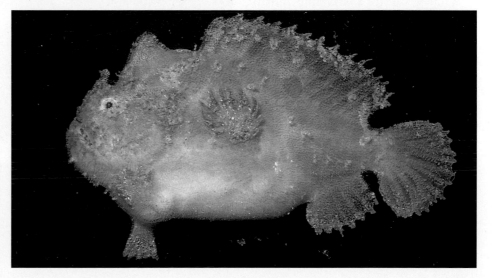

51

RODLESS ANGLERFISH
Histiophryne cryptacantha (Weber, 1913)

D I+I+I,13-16. A 6-9. C 9. P 8-9. V 5. Skin poorly covered with tiny spinules which are sometimes absent; extends over second and third dorsal spines. Dorsal fin in four parts; first the illicium with esca, followed closely by mostly embedded second spine and third spine. Soft-rayed section very long-based, ending clearly separate from caudal fin. Anal fin very short-based, opposite posterior part of dorsal fin. Illicium short; esca tiny, folded into groove, nearly always hidden, on midline of snout anterior to eyes. Pectoral fins prominent, arm-like. Ventral fins small, jugular. Variable, usually pale beige to yellow with some greenish blotches; some specimens with close-set small ocelli all over look like a sponge or ascidian. Broadly distributed in the west Pacific; recorded from entire south coast except Tasmania. Shallow, a few metres to over 100 m. Attains 9 cm. This genus contains only two species, one of which is commonly found on the south coast. A few specimens were found with eggs and recorded as males, but from observations of other species are probably females.

CLINGFISHES
ORDER GOBIESOCIFORMES

Represented by a single family comprising subfamilies, one of which is included here. See below.

CLINGFISHES
FAMILY GOBIESOCIDAE

A large family containing mostly small to very small fishes, many of which are yet to be discovered and described. Presently 33 genera and over 100 species are recognised, however the total number will probably increase markedly in the future. Relationships with other fishes and within the family are not clear and are presently under study. They are characterised by a large ventral sucking-disc formed in part by the union of the ventral fins, however a few specialised species possess only a degenerated rudimentary disc, or it is now absent. Other features are greatly

Undescribed genus and species (Genus 1 sp. 1)   Ventral view

depressed bodies, often broad anteriorly, tapering to a narrow caudal peduncle and to a pointed or rounded snout, spines on the opercle, and a slimy coat instead of scales. Many species are similar and, because small, difficult to identify. Characters are also few and usually simple. Characters used are the size and position of the sucking-disc, spines on the head, the general shape of the body or head, colour pattern and habitat, and adult body size. Australia's south coast contains numerous genera and species, most of which until now appear to be undescribed. Included here are seven genera and 11 species, many of which are under investigation. Some are not yet consigned to either a genus or a species.

COMMON SHORE-EEL
Alabes dorsalis (Richardson, 1845)

C 7-8. Rays only present in caudal fin. Body eel-like, rounded anteriorly, increasingly compressed posteriorly, with slimy coat. Mouth small; lips thick, fleshy; jaws with single row of small teeth. Gill opening positioned ventrally as small slit, tiny ventral fins and vestigial sucking disk immediately behind. Dorsal fin low, gradually arising from centre, continuing with caudal and anal fins. Pectoral fins absent. Colour extremely variable from brown to green to orange, often bright; with or without spots or ocelli in series along sides. Widespread in southern waters; recorded north to southern Queensland. Apparently once common in Sydney rockpools, but now rare north of Victoria. Intertidal, under rocks to about 10 m; very common in Port Phillip and Western Port Bays. Attains 12 cm. Of the four south coast species, three occur in eastern waters. The two other species included here lack ventral fins completely, live among weeds, and are difficult to tell apart. See species descriptions.

Alabes dorsalis ▲

Alabes hoesei Male ▼

PYGMY SHORE-EEL
Alabes parvulus (McCulloch, 1909)

C 7-8. Rays only present in caudal fin. Body eel-like, rounded anteriorly, increasingly compressed posteriorly, with slimy coat. Most of posterior part greatly prehensile. Mouth small; lips thick, fleshy; jaws with single row of small teeth. Gill opening positioned ventrally as very small slit, lacking ventral fins behind. Dorsal fin low, gradually arising well posterior from centre and posteriorly from above anus, continuing with caudal and anal fins. Pectoral fins absent. Colour variable, usually brownish or purplish, depending on weed inhabited. Widespread along south coast from about Sydney to Perth and Tasmania. Coastal reefs; seems to prefer dense brown weeds; usually in small aggregations in 3-6 m. Attains 5 cm. Most similar to the following species, *A. hoesei*, which is usually more estuarine, lives in lighter-coloured weeds. Differs in having pair of sensory pores behind the eye, compared with one in *hoesei*, only visible after preservation. Dorsal origin may be useful in live specimens as it is anterior to the anus in the following species.

Alabes parvulus Juv.

DWARF SHORE-EEL
Alabes hoesei Springer and Fraser, 1976

C 7-8. Rays only present in caudal fin. Body eel-like, rounded anteriorly, increasingly compressed posteriorly, with slimy coat. Most of posterior part greatly prehensile. Mouth small; lips thick, fleshy; jaws with single row of small teeth. Gill opening positioned ventrally as very small slit, lacking ventral fins behind. Dorsal fin low, gradually arising well posterior from centre and anteriorly from above anus, continuing with caudal and anal fins. Pectoral fins absent. Colour variable, usually greenish, depending on weeds it lives among; young transparent. Widespread in southern waters, from about Sydney to Recherche Archipelago and Tasmania. Shallow reefs in pale brownish weeds and seagrasses, from intertidal to a few metres down. Attains 45 mm.

Alabes hoesei Juv.

GRASS CLINGFISH
Genus 1, sp 1

D 7-11. A 9-13. C 10-12. P 20-22. V I,4. Slender, slightly depressed anteriorly, with small caudal peduncle. Snout sharply pointed. Mouth small, lips narrow; jaws with small conical teeth, lower jaw slightly shorter than upper. Large lateral gill openings. Single dorsal fin posteriorly near caudal fin, tall in males, with similar anal fin opposite. Caudal and pectoral fins rounded. Ventral fins united into small, double sucking-disc, posterior half with fleshy edge. Green or reddish-brown, depending on type of weed it associates with; band of small dark spots along sides. Known from southern New South Wales to western Victoria and Tasmania. Similar species in south-western waters may be identical. Commonly found in shallow seagrass beds and flat surfaced weeds to about 20 m. Small endemic genus with two or three species, all undescribed.

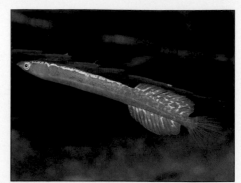

Genus 1, sp 1   Adults ▼   Displaying male ▲

LITTLE CLINGFISH
Parvicrepis parvipinnis (Waite, 1906)

D 3-5. A 4-6. C 10-12. P 18-23. V I,4. Slender, slightly depressed at broad area anteriorly; caudal peduncle small. Snout pointed, shorter than wide. Mouth small, lips narrow; jaws with small conical teeth, lower jaw slightly shorter than upper. Large lateral gill openings. Single short-based dorsal fin posteriorly, twice its base length from caudal fin, with similar anal fin opposite. Caudal and pectoral fins rounded. Ventral fins united into small, double sucking-disc, posterior half with fleshy lobes. Various shades of green, from yellowish or brownish to dark green, usually with some darker spotting. Recorded from just north of Sydney to south-west coast, and to southern Tasmania. Shallow weed and seagrass reefs, mostly intertidal. Attains 30 mm. Small endemic genus comprising three species, two of which are undescribed and all included here.

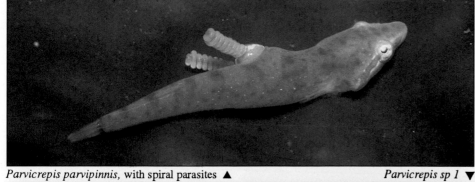

Parvicrepis parvipinnis, with spiral parasites ▲

Parvicrepis sp 1 ▼

LONG-SNOUT CLINGFISH
Parvicrepis sp 1

D 4-6. A 5-7. C 10-12. P 20-22. V I,4. Slender, slightly depressed at broad area anteriorly; caudal peduncle small. Snout pointed, longer than wide. Mouth small, lips narrow; jaws with small conical teeth, lower jaw slightly shorter than upper. Large lateral gill openings. Single short-based dorsal fin posteriorly, twice its base length from caudal fin, with similar anal fin opposite. Caudal and pectoral fins rounded. Ventral fins united into small, double sucking-disc, posterior half with fleshy lobes. Various shades of green, from yellowish or brownish to dark green, usually with some darker fine spotting and some blotching. South coast from Victoria and Tasmania to south-west coast. Shallow weed and seagrass reefs, usually from 1-5 m. Attains 50 mm. Undescribed species.

OBSCURE LITTLE CLINGFISH
Parvicrepis sp 2

D 3-5. A 4-5. C 10-12. P 19-20. V I,4. Slender, slightly depressed at broad area anteriorly; caudal peduncle small. Snout bluntly rounded, shorter than wide. Mouth small, lips narrow; jaws with small conical teeth, lower jaw slightly shorter than upper. Large lateral gill openings. Single short-based dorsal fin posteriorly, twice its base length from caudal fin, with similar anal fin opposite. Caudal and pectoral fins rounded. Ventral fins united into small, double sucking-disc, posterior half with fleshy lobes. Various shades of green, from greyish or brownish to dark green, usually with some indistinct darker broad banding dorsally. South coast from Victoria and Tasmania to south-west coast. Shallow weed and seagrass reefs, usually from 1-5 m. Attains 30 mm. Undescribed species.

KELP CLINGFISH
Genus 2, sp 1

D 3-4. A 4-5. C 10-12. P 19-21. V I,4. Slender, slightly broad and depressed anteriorly and at head; caudal peduncle prominent. Snout bluntly rounded, shorter than wide. Mouth small, lips narrow; jaws with small conical teeth, lower jaw slightly shorter than upper. Large lateral gill openings. Strong hidden spine on sides of head. Single short-based dorsal fin distant from caudal fin, with similar anal fin opposite. Caudal and pectoral fins rounded. Ventral fins united into moderate-sized double sucking-disc, posterior half with fleshy fringe. Pale semitransparent greenish with microscopic spots; several brown-orange spots irregular on back and in broad yellow-orange stripe along sides of head. Only known from a few specimens from the Sydney area and Wilson's Promontory, living on kelp, *Ecklonia radiata*. Specimens from Tasmania and Western Australia differ in colour but may also represent this species. Largest specimen 34 mm. Undescribed genus comprising possibly four or more species, all restricted to southern Australian waters.

WESTERN CLEANER-CLINGFISH
Cochleoceps bicolor Hutchins, 1991

D 5-6. A 5-6. C 11-12. P 21-26. V I,4. Body rather thick, slightly depressed at broad area anteriorly; caudal peduncle moderately long. Snout bluntly rounded, shorter than wide. Mouth small; lips narrow, fleshy; jaws of equal length with small conical teeth. Large lateral gill openings. Single short-based dorsal fin posteriorly near caudal fin, with similar anal fin opposite. Caudal and pectoral fins rounded. Ventral fins united into moderate-sized double sucking-disc, posterior half with fleshy fringe. Yellow to orange, densely covered with dark to bright red spots, usually very red in deep water. Shallow water specimens often with narrow blue dashes or lines dorsally and across sides. Southern waters from Port Phillip Bay to south-west coast. Moderately shallow to at least 40 m; usually associates with sponges or ascidians. Regularly observed cleaning other fishes, probably feeding on small parasites. Attains 70 mm. Similar species in eastern and southern Tasmania has larger oval spots over the back and no blue scribbles or lines. Small genus comprising four or five species, most of which are known cleanerfishes, only two of which are described.

Genus 2, sp 1 ▲   *Cochleoceps bicolor* ▼

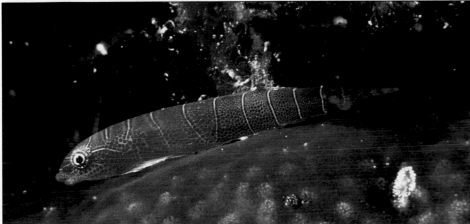

EASTERN CLEANER-CLINGFISH
Cochleoceps orientalis Hutchins, 1991

D 5-6. A 4-6. C 10-12. P 21-24. V I,4. Body rather thick, slightly depressed at broad area anteriorly; caudal peduncle moderately long. Snout bluntly rounded, shorter than wide. Mouth small; lips narrow, fleshy; jaws of equal length with small conical teeth. Large lateral gill openings. Single short-based dorsal fin posteriorly near caudal fin, with similar anal fin opposite. Caudal and pectoral fins rounded. Ventral fins united into moderate-sized double sucking-disc, posterior half with fleshy fringe. Greenish-yellow to orange with small scattered dark spots to larger red spots, variable in density; irridescent blue dashes or lines dorsally and across sides over head, body. East coast, all of New South Wales and eastern Victoria. Adults usually on kelp, *Ecklonia radiata*, on which they deposit their eggs, which are guarded by the male, although the female is often present as well. Often on ascidians or sponges in deep water, probably depositing eggs on algae nearby. In 3-40 m. Attains 55 mm. Fishes which are most often observed being cleaned include boxfishes, porcupinefishes and morwongs.

Cochleoceps orientalis Male ▲ Guarding eggs laid on eklonia fronds ▼

EASTERN CLINGFISH
Aspasmogaster costata (Ogilby, 1885)

D 8-9. A 6-8. C 10-12. P 21-25. V I,4. Body rather thick, slightly depressed at broad area anteriorly; caudal peduncle short. Snout tapers to rounded front, about as long as wide. Mouth small; prominent lips curl over sides of lower jaw and across snout; jaws with small conical teeth, lower jaw slightly shorter than upper. Large lateral gill openings. Single short-based dorsal fin posteriorly near caudal fin, with similar anal fin opposite. Caudal and pectoral fins rounded. Ventral fins united into moderate-sized double sucking-disc, posterior half with fleshy margin. Pinkish with irregular dark banding dorsally on body, more defined on head. East coast, New South Wales to Western Port. Secretive, under rocks, often behind sea urchins. Attains 50 mm. Small genus comprising four southern Australian species, three of which are found in south-eastern waters.

TASMANIAN CLINGFISH
Aspasmogaster tasmaniensis (Günther, 1861)

D 8-10. A 7-9. C 10-12. P 24-26. V I,4. Body rather thick, slightly depressed at broad

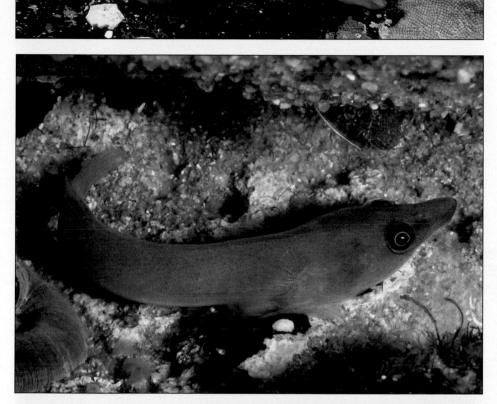

area anteriorly; caudal peduncle short. Snout pointed, tapers to narrow rounded front, slightly longer than wide. Mouth small; prominent lips curl over sides of lower jaw and across snout; jaws with small conical teeth, lower jaw just shorter than upper. Large lateral gill openings. Single short-based dorsal fin posteriorly near caudal fin, with similar anal fin opposite. Caudal and pectoral fins rounded. Ventral fins united into moderate-sized double sucking-disc, posterior half with fleshy margin. Variable colour, pinkish to brownish or greenish, usually with distinct regular dark bands across back and head. South coast from Victoria and Tasmania to the west. Shallow coastal and rocky estuaries, often under rocks. Attains 8 cm.

SMOOTH-SNOUT CLINGFISH
Aspasmogaster liorhyncha Briggs, 1955

D 6-8. A 6-7. C 10-12. P 20-23. V I,4. Body rather thick, slightly depressed at broad area anteriorly; caudal peduncle short. Snout pointed, tapers to narrow rounded front, slightly longer than wide. Mouth small; moderate-sized lips curl over sides of lower jaw, but not across snout; jaws with small conical teeth, lower jaw just shorter than upper. Large lateral gill openings. Single short-based dorsal fin posteriorly near caudal fin, with similar anal fin opposite. Caudal and pectoral fins rounded. Ventral fins united into moderate-sized double sucking-disc, posterior half with fleshy margin. Variable colour, usually plain greenish to dusky brown, often with numerous small dark spots. Widespread in southern waters from New South Wales to Western Australia and Tasmania. Shallow coastal reefs, usually in ledges with sea-urchins. Attains 45 mm.

BROAD CLINGFISH
Creocele cardinalis (Ramsay, 1882)

D 9-10. A 6-8. C 10-12. P 17-20. V I,4. Body rather thick, slightly depressed at broad area anteriorly, tapers to short, compressed caudal peduncle. Snout short with rounded front, shorter than wide. Mouth small; jaws with small conical teeth, lower jaw just shorter than upper. Large lateral gill openings. Hidden strong spine on sides of head. Single short-based dorsal fin posteriorly near caudal fin, with similar anal fin opposite. Caudal and pectoral fins rounded. Ventral fins united into moderate-sized double sucking-disc, posterior half with fleshy margin. Variable colour, usually brownish with dark spots which form bands in young. Known from the Bass Strait area to South Australia. Intertidal to subtidal reefs in rocky weed areas; secretive, under rocks. Attains 75 mm.

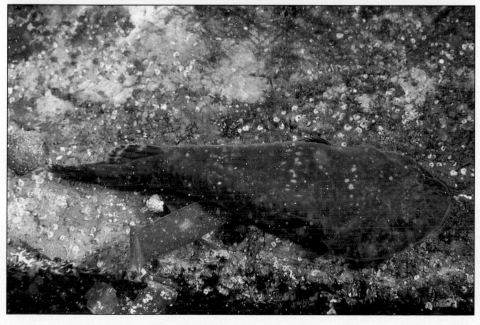

CODS
ORDER GADIFORMES

Represented by eight families, only one of which has species in southern coastal waters. See below.

BEARDIES
FAMILY MORIDAE

The beardies, also known as deepsea cods and rock cods, are a large world-wide family comprising about 15 genera and an estimated 70 species. They are primarily deepwater species but a few inhabit shallow coastal reefs. Soft-bodied fishes, the beardies are poster-iorly elongated and taper to a narrow caudal peduncle. Their scales are small and cycloid, and they have a single continuous lateral line. A chin barbel is often present and ventral fins are reduced, often with greatly extended feeler-like tips. Fins consist entirely of soft rays. The dorsal fin is usually long-based, and variously divided or separated into up to three parts; the first rays are sometimes produced into a filament. The shallow-water species usually feature a dorsal fin in two parts, deeply notched or just separate with a short-based first part and long-based second part. The anal fin is sim-ilar to and opposite the second dorsal fin and not attached by membranes to the short caudal peduncle. In Australia 12 genera and 24 species are recog-nised, five of which are known from shallow south-eastern waters. Various records are based on misidentifications and some of the species recorded from shallow depths may be restricted to deep water. There is some doubt as to whether certain species are identical with populations in New Zealand.

LARGE-TOOTH BEARDY
Lotella rhacina (Bloch and Schneider, 1801)

D 5-8+47-64. A 42-56. C 24. P 22-25. V 8. Body slightly compressed posteriorly, tapers to very small caudal peduncle; covered with tiny cycloid scales, about 230 rows along lateral line. Head moderately large, broad; chin barbel prominent. Dorsal fin in two parts; first short-based, rounded at the top, closely followed by long-based part. Anal fin similar and opposite, its origin distinctly posterior to dorsal division. Ventral fins with long tips, positioned just anterior to pectoral fins. Caudal fin distinctly rounded. Yellowish-grey to reddish-brown; distinct white margin on dorsal, anal and caudal fin readily identifies this species. Broadly distributed in southern waters from northern New South Wales and the west coast at similar latitude, to Tasmania and New Zealand. Coastal bays to offshore reefs, usually in caves in 10-90 m. Attains 50 cm. Small west Pacific genus comprising two or three species.

SLENDER BEARDY
Lotella schuetta Steindachner, 1866

D 5-6+57-61. A 51-55. C 24. P 20-23. V 9. Body slightly compressed posteriorly, tapers to very small caudal peduncle; covered with tiny cycloid scales, about 140 rows along lateral line. Head moderately large, broad; chin barbel prominent. Dorsal fin in two parts; first short-based, rounded at the top, closely followed by long-based part. Anal fin similar and opposite, its origin well posterior, about below tenth ray of second dorsal fin. Ventral fins with long tips, positioned just anterior to pectoral fins. Caudal fin distinctly rounded. Pale to dark brown. East coast, quiet coastal bays and estuaries, usually silty habitat. Attains 25 cm. A closely related species, *L. phycis* (Temminck and Schlegel), occurs in Japan.

FINE-TOOTH BEARDY
Eeyorius hutchinsi Paulin, 1986

D 6+52-58. A 43-48. C 24. P 24-25. V 4. Body slightly compressed posteriorly, tapers to very small caudal peduncle; covered with tiny cycloid scales, about 230 rows along lateral line, extending over head and onto unpaired fin bases. Head moderately large, broad; chin barbel prominent. Dorsal fin in two parts; first short-based, rounded at the top, closely followed by long-based part. Anal fin similar and opposite, its origin distinctly posterior to dorsal division. Ventral fins with long tips, positioned just anterior to pectoral fins. Caudal fin distinctly rounded. Uniform brown with yellowish dusky unpaired fins. Widespread south coast from Bass Strait to south-west coast, usually in shallow bays; secretive, in rocky ledges. Small species attaining about 20 cm. Monotypic genus, separated from the similar *Lotella* by its uniformly fine teeth.

BEARDED ROCK-COD
Pseudophycis barbata Günther, 1862

D 9-11+53-63. A 47-63. C 24. P 21-28. V 5-6. Body thick centrally, slightly compressed posteriorly, tapers to very small caudal peduncle; covered with tiny cycloid scales, about 130 rows along lateral line. Head moderately large, broad; chin barbel small. Dorsal fin in two parts; first short-based, rounded at the top, closely followed by long-based part. Anal fin similar and opposite, mirror image of second part. Ventral fins with long tips, positioned well anterior to pectoral fins, their tips just reaching below the base. Caudal fin distinctly rounded. Pale uniformly grey to motley reddish-brown, with or without dark fin margins; sometimes a dark blotch on

Eeyorius hutchinsi ▼

Pseudophycis barbata ▼

pectoral fin base. Widespread in southern waters from southern New South Wales to Rottnest Island, and New Zealand. Coastal reefs and rocky estuaries; only shallow in the most southern parts of its range. Recorded between 1 m and 300 m. Small Australian-New Zealand genus with three or four species.

This species often identified as *P. bachus* (Bloch and Schneider, 1801), especially when black blotch present on pectoral fin base. However, that species has dark blotch just above pectoral fin base and distinctly truncate caudal fin. Seems restricted to deep water in Australia or may represent a different species.

BASTARD RED COD
Pseudophycis breviuscula (Richardson, 1846)

D 8-11+42-60. A 46-68. C 24. P 19-27. V 5-6. Body thick centrally, slightly compressed posteriorly, tapers to very small caudal peduncle; covered with tiny cycloid scales, about 85 rows along lateral line. Head moderately large, broad; chin barbel moderately long. Dorsal fin in two parts; first short-based, rounded at the top, closely followed by long-based part. Anal fin similar and opposite, mirror image of second part. Ventral fins with long tips, positioned well-anterior to pectoral fins, their tips just reaching below the base. Caudal fin distinctly rounded. Plain reddish-brown, slightly paler below, often with broad dark margins along unpaired fins. South coast from southern New South Wales to the Recherche Archipelago, and New Zealand. Shallow protected bays; secretive, in rocky reefs. Attains about 22 cm. As with preceding species, often identified as *P. bachus* because of reddish colouration.

CUSK EELS
ORDER OPHIDIIFORMES

Uncertain groups comprising about four families, three of which are included here (Key 13).

LINGS
FAMILY OPHIDIIDAE

A large worldwide family with nearly 50 genera and well over 150 species. Small to medium fishes, the lings are benthic, mostly living in deep to extremely deep waters; only a few occur in shallow depths. They have long, posteriorly tapering, slimy bodies, and are eel-like with tiny cycloid scales. Their gill openings are large. The mouth is usually large with small to moderate pointed teeth in the jaws and variously on the vomer and palatines. The eyes are moderately small to very small. Dorsal and anal fins are continuous with the caudal fin; the dorsal fin is over most of the body. The pectoral fins are moderately small and rounded. The ventral fins are reduced to feeler-like filaments, often placed far forward below the head and absent in some

1.	Ventral fins placed below eyes	OPHIDIIDAE (p. 60)
	Ventral fins well posterior to and below eyes	2
2.	Anal fin well back from dorsal fin origin	BYTHITIDAE (p. 61)
	Anal fin just back from dorsal fin origin	CARAPIDAE (p. 62)

KEY 13: *The Cusk Eels*

Genypterus tigerinus

species. Many of the larger species are commercially trawled and are important in some areas. About 25 species are known from Australian seas, several of which are unidentified. Only two species are known from shallow water, one of which is included here.

ROCK LING
Genypterus tigerinus Klunzinger, 1872

D 144-157. A 107-117. C 9. P 21-22. V 1. Body compressed, tapers evenly to caudal fin; covered with minute embedded cycloid scales extending over most of head. Lateral line almost straight along upper sides. Dorsal fin from just behind head, continuous with caudal and anal fin, of uniform height. Pectoral fins small, rounded. Ventral fins with single ray, divided at base, long in part, situated below front of eyes. Juveniles pale with blackish irregular markings; median fins black with narrow white margin. Large adults almost uniformly black with white ventral fins. Widespread in southern waters from central New South Wales to south Western Australia, including Tasmania. Coastal bays and estuaries in 3-60 m. Juveniles often in seagrass areas under objects; occur in very shallow depths until large individuals of about 50 cm. Adults move away from inshore, usually live in burrows under rocks in 15 m or more. Attains 1.2 m and 9 kg. Small, temperate southern hemisphere genus comprising about five species.

BLINDFISHES
FAMILY BYTHITIDAE

A large family of small secretive fishes comprising 28 genera and several hundred species, many of which are undescribed. The blind fishes have only recently been separated from Ophidiidae on the basis of being viviparous and the males having copulatory structures anterior to the anal fin. They are often referred to as live-bearing brotulas, however brotulas refers to the Ophidiidae. The blind fishes are moderately elongated with single long-based fins dorsally and ventrally which are either confluent or continuous with the caudal fin. The pectoral fins are rounded and sometimes have an extended fleshy base. The ventral fins are simple, comprising a single filamentous ray each. These fishes have slimy skin; their scales are small and cycloid, and absent in a few species. Their eyes are often tiny, pinhead size and sometimes skin-coloured; though vision may be poor, none of the species appear to be totally blind. Most species are shallow coral or rocky reef dwellers, usually less than 10 cm maximum size, however some of the deepwater dwellers reach a maximum size of 70 cm or more. Presently about seven genera and 20 species are known from Australian waters; two species are relatively common in shallow waters and are are included here.

Dermatopsis macrodon ▲

Ogilbya sp ▼

EASTERN YELLOW BLINDFISH
Dermatopsis macrodon Ogilby, 1896

D 71-80. A 45-57. C 14. P 20-23. V 1. Body soft, slightly compressed, covered with tiny cycloid scales. Lateral line indistinct, consists of small fleshy tubes between scales; high along sides above pectoral fin, descends to continue along mid-body. Mouth large, slightly oblique, with row of small teeth in jaws; lower jaw slightly larger, depressible. Head with various small sensory pores and papillae. Dorsal fin long-based, originates above pectoral fin bases, almost confluent with caudal and anal fins. Anal fin origin about below centre of dorsal fin. Ventral fins long, feeler-like. Pale yellow to brown or orange. Only known from the east coast. Originally described from Maroubra; appears to be common in the Sydney area, possibly ranging to eastern Victoria. Similar, more elongate species, *Dermatopsis multiradiatus* McCulloch and Waite, 1918, found in south-western waters. Shallow protected bays; secretive, in rocky ledges or under rocks. Shallow, usually in less than 10 m. Attains 10 cm. Small genus comprising three species distributed in Australian-New Zealand waters.

SOUTHERN PIGMY BLINDFISH
Ogilbya sp

D 97-106. A 70-78. C 14. P 24. V 1. Body soft, slightly compressed, covered with tiny cycloid scales. Lateral-line indistinct, consists of small fleshy tubes between scales; high along sides above pectoral fin, descends to continue along mid-body. Mouth large, slightly oblique, with row of small teeth in jaws; lower jaw slightly larger, depressible. Head with various small sensory pores, papillae; lips, chin sculptured with flaps and pores. Large horizontal spine on upper opercle. Dorsal fin long-based, originates above pectoral fin bases, almost confluent with caudal and anal fins. Anal fin origin about below centre of dorsal fin. Ventral fins long, feeler-like. Uniformly orange to brown. South coast from Port Phillip Bay to south Western Australia. Shallow protected coastal reefs and estuaries. Secretive, in rocky ledges, under rocks, often in muddy habitat; to about 25 m. Appears to be an undescribed species; sometimes identified as *Monothrix polylepis* Ogilby, 1897, a New South Wales species.

PEARLFISHES
FAMILY CARAPIDAE

A small family of secretive fishes, many species of which are only known from a few specimens, comprising about six genera and perhaps 30 species worldwide. Small fishes up to about 20 cm, the pearlfishes are eel-shaped with a low fin dorsally and ventrally along the entire body posterior from pectoral fin. Ventral fins are greatly reduced or absent. Scales are absent and the body is mostly translucent. The gill-opening is extensive, and the anus is located just posterior to the throat. Where known, adults associate within the body cavity of various invertebrates such as echinoderms, bivalves and sponges, and some are apparently parasitic. Juveniles are pelagic, swimming near the surface, usually amid zooplankton on which they feed, and feature a peculiar long predorsal filament from the head known as the vexillum. These specimens are actually referred to as vexillifer larvae. The vexillum has a series of regularly spaced skin flaps with a dark spot in the centre. Some species have black spots in the body with the same spacing. When approached by the author, the species with the body spots retreated backwards and looked very much like the small chained salps which have dark internal parts, so no doubt the spots are some form of mimicry. Another species without black spots on the body was collected in a plastic bag, and this specimen sought refuge by flattening itself against the surface. In addition, the vexillum floated away. The very transparent fish was thought to be lost and searching for it seemed hopeless. However, to the author's surprise, it was found ... in the bag. Unfortunately, the filament was lost during this process. Obviously these fishes have several tricks to escape predators, the latter comparable to a lizard or gecko sacrificing its wriggling tail, or a squid leaving a cloud of dark ink. The pearlfish quickly becomes transparent and shoots away, leaving the predator with very little and surviving. These fishes are of great interest to scientists and with so few specimens known from the south-east coast donations to museums would be very much appreciated. The two species found in larval form in New South Wales are probably the following.

MESSMATE FISH
Echiodon rendahli (Whitley, 1941)

Adults live in sponges at 40-250 m. About 120 rays in both dorsal and anal fins; 15 pectoral rays. Large, about-horizontal mouth, reaches beyond eye; pair of canines in each jaw. Ventral fins absent; caudal fin often breaks away when collected. Juveniles virtually clear with black internal spots, reflective golden parts with angle of light. Adults yellowish-brown with dark specks on head. External intestine dusky. Originally described from Sydney Harbour, however likely to be widespread. Recorded from northern New South Wales to Tasmania and New Zealand. Specimen in photograph came from Bare Island, Botany Bay, and measured about 8 cm. Adults to 15 cm are known. Genus thought to contain about 12 species variously distributed around the world, only two from Australian waters. Until larval and adult stages are connected the total number maybe considerably less. With the way larval forms are distributed it can be expected that each species is wide-ranging.

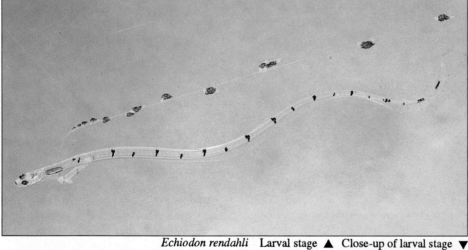

Echiodon rendahli   Larval stage ▲   Close-up of larval stage ▼

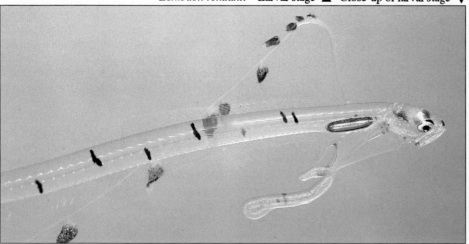

PEARLFISH
Carapus homei (Richardson, 1846)

Adults live inside echinoderms. Fin rays uncountable; larvae have additional long filament on tail. Adults translucent bluish or reddish anteriorly, developing dark bars with age. Head with silver spot on opercle, silvery band of spots along sides. Recorded from most of the tropical Indo-Pacific. Specimen in photograph is from Montague Island; measured about 10 cm without filament on tail. Has been recorded once from Tasmanian waters. Known to 20 cm. This genus thought to contain about 15 species and presently under study.

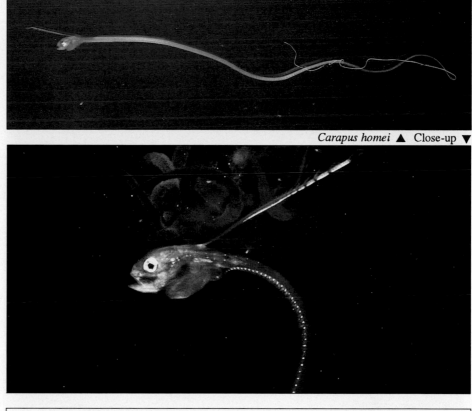

Carapus homei ▲ Close-up ▼

NEEDLEFISHES
ORDER BELONIFORMES

Represented by five families, two of which are included here (Key 14).

GARFISHES
FAMILY HEMIRAMPHIDAE

A moderate-sized family of surface fishes, comprising about 12 genera and 80 species worldwide. The garfishes are primarily tropical marine, but some species have adapted to fresh

| 1. | Both jaws elongated | BELONIDAE (p. 65) |
| | Only lower jaw elongated | HEMIRAMPHIDAE (p. 63) |

KEY 14: *The Needlefishes*

water and some occur in subtropical to temperate zones. Slender fishes with compressed bodies, they are characterised by having a greatly extended lower jaw, beak-like in most species, with a short and triangular upper jaw. The jaws have several rows of small unicuspid or tricuspid teeth. Fins are entirely soft-rayed. The pectoral fins are placed forward and high on the sides; other fins, including the ventral fins, are very posterior and abdominal, placed close to the anal fin, and the separation is much less than the anal fin base length. The scales are moderately large and semi-deciduous. Garfishes are mostly shiny silvery fishes. They are easily disturbed by light, jumping on the surface when people use lights in the dark. Although they do not reach large sizes, the flesh is regarded as excellent to eat and garfishes are popularly fished for in Australian waters. They school in coastal bays and some species in estuaries. Their diet consists of a variety of algae or invertebrate matter or a combination, but all eat zooplankton when it is available. Garfish eggs have sticky filaments and quickly attach to floating matter, however some species are thought to be viviparous. Presently seven genera and 18 species are recognised from Australian waters. Only two species are considered common on the south and east coast, with some tropical expatriates ranging south.

Dussumier's Garfish (*Hyporhamphus dussumieri*)

SOUTHERN GARFISH
Hyporhamphus melanochir Valenciennes, 1846

D 15-18. A 17-20. C 15. P 11-13. V 6. LL 52-57. Body compressed with flat sides; head flattened above, triangular in cross-section. Large cycloid scales cover body, smaller on lateral line along lower sides, extend over most of head, including some on upper jaw. Mouth about horizontal; bands of tiny teeth, many tricuspid, in jaws. Pectoral fins triangular, set high on sides. Other fins positioned posteriorly; dorsal and anal fins about opposite, elevated anteriorly. Ventral fins abdominal, near anal fin, distance about equal to anal fin base. Caudal fin forked, lower lobe longest. Shiny silvery on sides, greenish above; posterior fins dusky or reddish. Widespread along south coast from southern New South Wales to southern Western Australia, including Tasmania. Schools in bays and estuaries over seagrass areas. Attains 50 cm and 0.6 kg. Popular angling fish, also commercially caught. Large, primarily tropical genus comprising about 35 species.

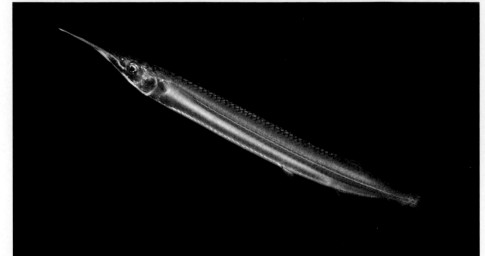

Hyporhamphus melanochir ▲

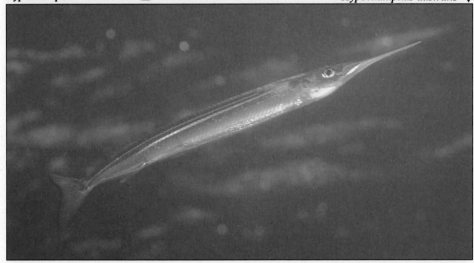

Hyporhamphus australis ▼

EASTERN GARFISH
Hyporhamphus australis (Steindachner, 1866)

D 15-16. A 17-18. C 15. P 11-12. V 6. LL 58-60. Body compressed with flat sides; head flattened above, triangular in cross-section. Large cycloid scales cover body, smaller on lateral line along lower sides, extend over most of head, including some on upper jaw. Mouth about horizontal; bands of tiny teeth, many tricuspid, in jaws. Pectoral fins triangular, set high on sides. Other fins positioned posteriorly; dorsal and anal fins about opposite, elevated anteriorly. Ventral fins abdominal, near anal fin, distance about equal to anal fin base. Caudal fin forked, lower lobe longest. Shiny silvery on sides, greenish above; ventral and pectoral fins with dark tips. East coast from eastern Victoria to southern Queensland. Coastal rocky outcrops and estuaries over seagrasses. Attains 45 cm.

DUSSUMIER'S GARFISH
Hyporhamphus dussumieri (Valenciennes, 1846)

D 15-17. A 15-17. C 15. P 11-12. V 6. LL 51-54. Body compressed with flat sides; head flattened above, triangular in cross-section. Large cycloid scales cover body, smaller on lateral line along lower sides, extend over most of head, including some on upper jaw. Mouth about horizontal; bands of tiny teeth, many tricuspid, in jaws. Pectoral fins triangular, set high on sides. Other fins positioned posteriorly; dorsal and anal fins about opposite, latter slightly posterior. Ventral fins abdominal, near anal fin, distance about equal to anal fin base. Caudal fin forked, lower lobe longest. Shiny silvery on sides, greenish-olive to bluish above. Widespread tropical Indo-Pacific, on the east coast ranging to New South Wales. Clear coastal reefs and lagoons in small to large schools. Attains 25 cm.

LONGTOMS
FAMILY BELONIDAE

A family of surface fishes, comprising about 10 genera and more than 30 species worldwide. Longtoms have very slender, slightly compressed, almost tubular bodies. Their jaws are extremely elongated with numerous needle-like teeth for which they are also known as needlefishes. Juveniles have short jaws which elongate with age; the lower lengthens ahead of the upper. Fins are entirely soft-rayed and except for the pectoral fins are placed well back on the body. Ventral fins are placed near the end of the abdomen, and the moderately long-based dorsal and anal fins are usually elevated anteriorly. Longtoms are mostly silvery and greyish or greenish above. They range greatly in size; some of the small freshwater species attain about 10 cm, whilst the larger marine species attain 1.3 m and a weight of 5.2 kg. The larger species are good to eat, despite their green bones. Most live in offshore surface waters but some enter estuaries and coastal bays, hunting other fishes in small packs or schools. When hunted themselves by large predators they leap over the surface, coming almost vertically out of the water with skips from the caudal fin providing the speed. The author observed a dolphin following its leaping victim for almost 100 m but in the end the longtom fell, seemingly exhausted, into the chaser's mouth. Leaping longtoms are potentially dangerous, especially to people fishing at night with lights, and their spear-like beaks have caused fatalities. In Australia four genera and 11 species are known, many of which range to subtropical waters and some to temperate waters. Only two species are coastal in south-eastern waters and are included here.

SLENDER LONGTOM
Strongylura leiura (Bleeker, 1851)

D 18-22. A 22-26. P 11-12. V 6. LL 185-200. Body compressed; caudal peduncle cylindrical to slightly depressed; covered with tiny, somewhat deciduous scales. Lateral line low on body. Both jaws greatly produced with an inner row of large and outer row of small slender teeth. Dorsal and anal fins positioned posteriorly on body; dorsal origin above seventh or eighth ray; both fins elevated anteriorly. Ventral fins abdominal, positioned posteriorly; distance from anal fin less than fin base length. Caudal fin truncate, centre slightly convex in adults. Silvery sides, greenish above. Dorsal and anal fin yellowish with brownish tips. Dark bar halfway along posterior part of head to eye. Single widespread tropical species presently recognised, ranging south to eastern Victoria. South-eastern Australian form, however, is slightly different in colour and has marginally higher fin counts. Attains 90 cm. Large tropical genus with at least 14 species, however revision seems needed.

STOUT LONGTOM
Tylosurus gavialoides (Castelnau, 1873)

D 20-22. A 19-23. P 14-16. V 6. LL 400 (approximately). Body and caudal peduncle sub-cylindrical, covered with minute, somewhat deciduous scales. Lateral line low on body. Both jaws greatly produced with an inner row of short strong teeth, reduced in outer row. Dorsal and anal fins positioned posteriorly on body; dorsal origin slightly anterior to anal fin origin; both fins elevated anteriorly. Ventral fins abdominal, positioned posteriorly; distance from anal fin less than the fin base length. Caudal fin truncate, centre slightly emarginate in adults. Silvery sides, greenish above; snout and fins dusky in adults. Coastal tropical Australian waters, ranging south to Victoria. Coastal reefs and estuaries, usually in moderately large schools. Attains 1.3 m and 5 kg.

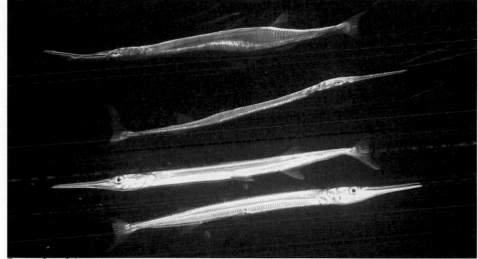

Strongylura leiura ▲   *Tylosurus gavialoides* ▼

65

SILVERSIDES
ORDER ATHERINIFORMES

Represented by about six families, presently not well defined, two of which are included here (Key 15).

| 1. | Body very compressed, ventrally keeled ....ISONIDAE (p. 69) |
| | Body not much compressed, no ventral keel ....ATHERINIDAE (p. 66) |

KEY 15: *The Silversides*

HARDYHEADS
FAMILY ATHERINIDAE

A family of small fishes, also known as silversides, baitfish or greybacks, and presently under revision. The family is thought to contain well over 100 species in more than 10 genera worldwide. Hardyheads are silvery fishes with a broad reflective lateral stripe from the pectoral to the caudal fin. They have slender, slightly compressed bodies with small to moderate-sized cycloid scales. Their eyes are large to very large. Fins are mostly small with short bases. The dorsal fin is in two well separated parts. The ventral fins are about opposite the first dorsal fin, and the anal fin about opposite the second dorsal fin. The caudal fin is forked. Schooling fishes, the hardyheads are usually in great numbers in shallow estuaries. Some species have adapted to fresh water. There are 11 genera in Australia, five of which are known from southern coastal waters. Although of no commercial value, these fishes form an important part of the food-chain of many large commercial species, and are used for bait.

Small-Scale Hardyhead (*Atherinason hepsetoides*)

SMALL-SCALE HARDYHEAD
Atherinason hepsetoides (Richardson, 1843)

D V-X+I,9-13. A I,11-14. C 17. P 13-16. V I,5. LL 58-83. Body slightly compressed, sides flattened; covered with moderately small cycloid scales. Dorsal fins widely separate, first at centre of back, second similar to and opposite anal fin. Ventral fins abdominal, placed just anterior to and below first dorsal fin. Pectoral fins high on upper sides. Mouth slightly oblique; teeth in jaws minute or absent. Silvery, greyish above, scales above lateral stripe with dusky edges. Recorded from Sydney to Spencer Gulf, but primarily a Bass Strait species; particularly common in the upper reaches of Port Phillip Bay. Usually in very large schools, swimming closely packed near the substrate, feeding on mysids or zooplankton near the surface at night. Shallow shores of estuaries in 1-4 m, however recorded to 30 m in coastal bays. Attains 9 cm. Monotypic genus.

SILVERFISH
Leptatherina presbyteroides (Richardson, 1843)

D VI-VIII+I,9-13. A I,10-15. C 17. P 12-15. V I,5. LL 40-47. Body slightly compressed, sides flattened; covered with moderately large cycloid scales. Dorsal fins widely separate, first at centre of back, second similar to and opposite anal fin. Ventral fins abdominal, placed just anterior to and below first dorsal fin. Pectoral fins high on upper sides. Mouth slightly oblique; teeth in jaws minute. Silvery, greyish above, scales above lateral stripe with dusky edges. Some iridescent speckling on back, green area internally behind eyes. Widespread in southern waters from southern New South Wales to Abrolhos Islands, including Tasmania. Common schooling species in coastal bays and clear-water estuaries. Shallow sandy or seagrass areas. Attains 11 cm. Only other species in genus restricted to south-west coast.

SMALL-MOUTH HARDYHEAD
Atherinosoma microstoma (Günther, 1861)

D V-IX+I,8-11. A I,8-13. C 17. P 12-16. V I,5. LL 36-41. Body slightly compressed, sides flattened; covered with moderately large cycloid scales. Dorsal fins widely separate, first at centre of back, second high anteriorly, similar to and opposite anal fin. Ventral fins abdominal, placed just anterior to and below first dorsal fin. Pectoral fins high on upper sides. Mouth slightly oblique; teeth small. Silvery, pale greenish or yellowish internally; scales above lateral stripe with dusky edges. Iridescent green to golden area internally behind eyes. South-east coast from central New South Wales to South Australia,

Leptatherina presbyteroides ▲   *Atherinosoma microstoma* ▼

including Tasmania. Shallow coastal bays, estuaries and lakes ranging from pure fresh to salinities in excess of seawater. Attains 10 cm. Genus may be monotypic as second species, occurring in south-western waters, presently regarded as doubtfully distinct; further studies may show it to be a geographical variation only.

PIKE-HEAD HARDYHEAD
Kestratherina esox (Klunzinger, 1872)

D V-VIII+I,9-12. A I,11-13. C 17. P 12-14. V I,5. LL 43-48. Body slightly compressed, sides flattened; covered with moderately large cycloid scales. Dorsal fins widely separate, first at centre of back, second similar to and opposite anal fin. Ventral fins very small, abdominal, placed just below first dorsal fin origin. Pectoral fins high on upper sides. Mouth slightly oblique; teeth in jaws minute. Silvery, greenish or brownish above; scales above lateral stripe with dusky edges. South coast from Western Port to Spencer Gulf, and to southern Tasmania where most common. Shallow seagrass bays, usually less than 1 m. Schooling species, primarily feeding on crustaceans but also small fishes. Attains 15 cm. This genus comprises two species, both included here.

SHORT-SNOUT HARDYHEAD
Kestratherina brevirostris Pavlov *et al*, 1988

D VIII-X+I,10-12. A I,12-14. C 17. P 12-14. V I,5. LL 46-49. Body slightly compressed, sides flattened; covered with moderately large cycloid scales. Dorsal fins widely separate, first at centre of back, second elevated anteriorly, similar to and opposite anal fin. Ventral fins abdominal, placed just anterior to and below first dorsal fin. Pectoral fins high on upper sides. Mouth slightly oblique; teeth in jaws small but distinct. Silvery, greenish or brownish above; scales above lateral stripe with dusky edges. South coast from Western Port to South Australia, incuding Tasmania. Mainly in sheltered coastal bays and clear marine estuaries. Small schools in rocky, sandy vegetated areas. Attains 10 cm.

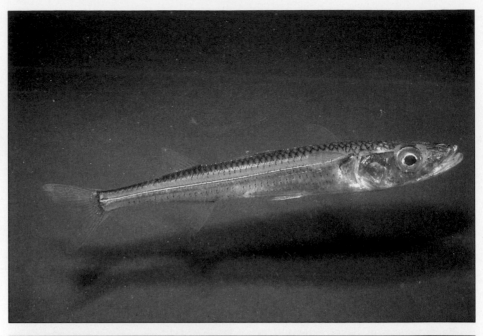

OGILBY'S HARDYHEAD
Atherinomorus ogilbyi (Whitley, 1930)

D V-VII+I,8-10. A I,12-15. C 17. P 15-18. V I,5. LL 38-44. Body slightly compressed, sides flattened; covered with moderately large cycloid scales. Dorsal fins widely separate, first just posterior to centre of back, second elevated anteriorly, similar to and slightly posteriorly above anal fin. Ventral fins abdominal, placed well anterior to and below first dorsal fin. Pectoral fins high on upper sides. Mouth oblique. Silvery, greenish above. Tropical Australia, on the east coast south to Narooma. Coastal estuaries, schooling in rocky entrances and under jetties. Attains 12 cm. Tropical Indo-Pacific genus comprising about 10 species. Of the four Australian species, only this species known from subtropical waters.

SURFSARDINES
FAMILY ISONIDAE

A small Indo-Pacific family comprising a single genus and about five species of tiny fishes. They are similar and closely related to the Atherinidae, and feature greatly compressed bodies with a deep keel-like convex belly, deepening with age, and taper evenly from ventral to caudal fins. They have a bluntly rounded head with an oblique mouth, and minute teeth in jaws. Their scales are very small, and absent on the front part of the body. The pectoral fins are placed very high and anteriorly on body and have a greatly angular base. The dorsal fin is in two low parts, with the tiny first part placed about centrally on the back. The anal fin is long-based, greatly exceeding the length of the second dorsal fin anteriorly. The ventral fins are tiny and abdominal, and the caudal fin is forked with rounded corners. Surf sardines are silvery fishes; they are small, not exceeding 10 cm. They are usually in large schools in foaming surf waters along rocky shores, feeding on surface zooplankton. Only one species is known from Australian waters.

FLOWER OF THE WAVE
Iso rhothophilus (Ogilby, 1895)

D III-IV+I,10-17. A I,20-28. C 17. P 13-16. V I,5. LL 49 (approximately). Body very compressed, dorsal profile almost straight, ventral profile deep and broadly convex at ventral fin, then straight to shallow caudal peduncle. Scales small, somewhat deciduous; lateral line indistinct, seemingly consisting of several parallel sensory lines. Dorsal fins separate; minute first dorsal fin about centrally placed above anus. Anal fin long-based; much shorter-based second dorsal fin opposite posteriorly. Ventral fins tiny. Shiny, silvery with a very reflective band from pectoral fin bases to caudal fin base. Some greenish reflective areas depending on angle of light. Widespread west Pacific, south to eastern Victoria, and north to Japan, and also on the west coast to Fremantle. Usually in large, dense schools in surf around rocky outcrops or islands. Attains 75 mm.

Iso rhothophilus

SAWBELLIES
ORDER BERYCIFORMES

Represented by about six families, four of which are included here. They can be determined with Key 16.

1.	Large lockable dorsal and ventral fin spines ..............MONOCENTRIDAE (p. 70)
	Not as above 2
2.	Three anal fin spines ....TRACHICHTHYIDAE (p. 72)
	Four anal fin spines 3
3.	Dorsal fin with 10 or more tall spines ........................HOLOCENTRIDAE (p. 75)
	Dorsal fin with seven or less spines ....BERYCIDAE (p. 73)

KEY 16: *The Sawbellies*

PINEAPPLEFISHES
FAMILY MONOCENTRIDAE

This small family comprises two genera and three species restricted to warm temperate waters of the Indo-Pacific. Two species are found in Australian waters, and one is endemic. The pineapplefish's body is covered with strong plate-like scales armed with curving spines; large solid spines in the dorsal and ventral fins can be locked in an outward position or folded partly into grooves. There is a prominent light organ on each side of the lower jaw. The light is produced by bacteria living symbiotically on a patch of skin. The bacteria are already present in the smallest known juveniles (20 mm). Pineapplefishes are nocturnal fishes found during the day in caves and ledges on coastal reefs and in harbours. They feed at night, primarily on small shrimps, leaving the reef and usually swimming in the open over sand, using the light organs to locate prey. They are often in small aggregations in caves during the day, but each goes its own way at night. They occur in a broad depth range from very shallow estuaries to at least 250 m. A lateral line is present but indistinct. Pineapplefishes are popular aquarium fishes which are easily maintained.

Pineapplefishes (*Cleidopus gloriamaris*) Juveniles congregating in a cave during the day

PINEAPPLEFISH
Cleidopus gloriamaris De Vis, 1882

D V-VII,12-13. A 11-12. P 14. V I,3. LSR 15. Body with six large-scaled longitudinal rows; 11 scales along midline of body, four on caudal peduncle, the last of which are often very small. Each scale has large flattened recurving spine, becoming very broad along ventral-most row. Fin spines lockable in outward position. Dorsal fin with four prominent free spines, the middle two longest; particularly large spine in ventral fin. Slightly variable in colour from pale yellow to yellow-orange. Light organ produces green light in juveniles but becomes more reddish with age because of an overgrowing filter. East coast from southern Queensland to southern New South Wales and separate population on the south-west coast. Juveniles in estuaries; adults in deeper water offshore to 250 m. Attains 25 cm. Also known as Knightfish. Western population was described as a subspecies; it has 10 scales along body midline and smaller spines; probably deserves species status. Pineapplefish in captivity will accept a great variety of food but may have to learn to recognise some foods offered. Readily accepted are mysids, tiny swimming shrimp-like crustaceans which school on sand near reef or in caves; can be collected and put in aquarium live. Frozen mysids will be accepted as well; by mixing other kinds of food they soon learn to be fed. Ideally small live shrimps are provided on which they can feed in the dark. Competition from faster fish can cause problems when feeding frozen food. This species can live for about 10 years in private aquariums. Unaggressive; best kept in small groups in large tanks.

Cleidopus gloriamaris   Adult ▼   Tiny juv., already has light organs ▲

JAPANESE PINEAPPLEFISH
Monocentrus japonicus (Houttuyn, 1782)

D V-VII,10-12. A 9-11. P 13-15. V I,2-3. LSR 13-16. Body with six large-scaled longitudinal rows; nine to 10 scales along midline of body, four to six on caudal peduncle, the last few of which are often very small. Each scale has large flattened recurving spine, becoming very broad along ventral-most row. Fin spines lockable in outward position. Dorsal fin with four prominent free spines, the middle two longest. Ventral fins with particularly large spine. Slightly variable in colour from pale to darker yellow. Widespread tropical Indo-Pacific from Japan to east Africa, New Zealand and New South Wales, but only commonly known from Japan. Adults usually deep along rocky reefs in 10-200 m; juveniles often very shallow, trawled in warmer parts of their range. A juvenile was collected in Botany Bay from 3 m. Attains 16 cm. This genus comprises at least two species; *M. reedi* Schultz, 1956, occurs off Chile.

ROUGHIES
FAMILY TRACHICHTHYIDAE

The roughies, or sawbellies, are a globally distributed family of mostly deepwater fishes. Currently seven genera are recognised, comprising an estimated 32 species. These fishes have a compressed, often deep body, a bony head, and a series of scales with a keel-like ridge ventrally along the belly. They are small to medium-sized fishes and some are commercially trawled in very deep water; for example, the Orange Roughy between 500 and 1,000 m. Some species are known to produce loud low frequency noises, drum-like or clicking, and the recently described Golden Roughy, *Aulotrachichthys pulsator* Gomon and Kuiter, 1987, from South Australia was named for the noise it can produce. Shallow-water species are found in caves and ledges during the day; they move out at night to feed. Roughies are usually in small aggregations in estuarine rocky reefs as well as offshore habitats to fairly deep reefs. Some deepwater species occur in large schools. Their diet consists of invertebrates, primarily shrimps. A few species occur in shallow water, three of these on the south-east coast.

Paratrachichthys sp ▲

SANDPAPERFISH
Paratrachichthys sp

D V, 13. A III, 10. P 12-14. V I, 6. LL 48-52. Body covered with firmly attached small ctenoid scales; lateral line nearly straight. A few small scales on preopercle. Anus situated between ventral fins; a series of 11 to 16 scutes on belly. Mouth large, oblique. Spinous section of dorsal fin small with short spines. Few small spines on various protruding ridges on head; large spine on lower corner of preopercle. Variable in colour with depth; reddish or brown to greenish-yellow. Widespread along south coast from about Sydney to Perth, including Tasmania. Rocky reefs, in caves during the day; usually in small aggregations, in depths ranging from 30-220 m. Only known in the shallower part of its range in Tasmania and Victoria. Attains 25 cm. Previously confused with a New Zealand species; presently undescribed. Small genus comprising three species, one in Australian waters.

Optivus elongatus   Extremes of colour variation ▲ ▼

SLENDER ROUGHY
Optivus elongatus (Günther, 1859)

D IV, 11. A III, 9-10. P 10-12. V I, 6. LL 26. Body covered with firmly attached small ctenoid scales; lateral line nearly straight. A few small scales on preopercle. Anus situated just ahead of anal fin; a series of 11 to 12 strong scutes on belly. Mouth large, oblique. Spinous section of dorsal fin small with very short spines; soft-rayed section situated over centre of body. Strong spines at upper corner of opercle and lower corner of preopercle. Eye large, anterior on head. Brown to grey, darker above; sometimes with golden sides. East coast from southern Queensland to east Victoria, with stragglers to Port Phillip Bay, Lord Howe Island, and New Zealand. Coastal estuarine reefs to offshore reefs in 3-50 m. Attains 12 cm. Sometimes called Violet Roughy. A similar species found on the south-west coast is undescribed at this stage. Small genus comprising three species, two known from Australia. Photographs show extremes of colour variation.

ROUGHY
Trachichthys australis Shaw and Nodder, 1799

D III, 11-12. A III, 9-10. P 13. V I,6. LL 63. Body covered with firmly attached small ctenoid scales; lateral line with slight curve from origin to below dorsal fin. Anus situated just ahead of anal fin; a series of 11 to 12 strong scutes on belly. Spinous section of dorsal fin small with very short spines; soft-rayed section situated over centre of body. Large strong spines at upper corner of opercle and lower corner of preopercle. Eye large, anterior on head. Mouth large, oblique. Variable brown to reddish-brown; small juveniles black with large white blotches. Southern half of Australia, including Tasmania. Estuarine and coastal to offshore rocky reefs in 2-40 m; adults usually in deeper water. In ledges in small aggregations during the day. Attains 18 cm. A small juvenile kept in an aquarium took two years to attain adult size. Can produce a milky skin toxin from scaled areas when distressed. A captured specimen held in the hand under water vibrated strongly and the milky substance slowly rose from the sides. Monotypic genus.

Trachichthys australis   Adult ▼ Juv. (45 mm) ▲

Trachichthys australis   Juv. (10 mm)

NANNYGAI AND RED SNAPPER
FAMILY BERYCIDAE

Although this family is small, representatives are found worldwide with the exception of the east Pacific. It comprises two genera, of which *Beryx*, with two species, is a deepwater dweller. It is widespread, known only from trawls and long-lines, and is not included here. In Australia, members of this genus are known as Alfonsinos (deepwater), Nannygai and Red Snapper. The other genus, *Centroberyx*, contains about seven species with representatives found in the cooler parts of the Indo-Pacific – Japan, Africa, New Zealand and Australia. Berycids are predominantly red. Other diagnostic characters include a deeply forked caudal fin, usually four spines in the anal fin, moderately large ctenoid scales, and their very perch-like appearance. Most species occur in large schools, feeding mid-water on zooplankton. They are medium-sized fishes and some are of commercial importance. Of the four Australian species, three occur in our area.

Nannygai (*Centroberyx affinis*)

NANNYGAI
Centroberyx affinis (Günther, 1859)

D VII,11-12. A IV,12. C 19. P 13. V I,7. LL 41-44. Distinctly ctenoid moderate-sized scales cover body and part of head. Lateral line straight, with seven scales above to dorsal origin. Opercle and preopercle margins coarsely serrated. Eyes very large, placed anteriorly on head. Mouth large, oblique. Dorsal fin headed by short spines, followed by markedly and progressively longer spines, then long soft rays progressively decreasing in length; anal fin similar and opposite. Caudal fin forked, large, proportionally larger in adults. Bright red from deep water; fins orange to red. Shallow-water specimens silvery-blue to red, usually darker dorsally. Confined to south-eastern Australia from New South Wales to western Bass Strait, and New Zealand. Occurs to about 150 m. Mid-water feeders, often occurring in large schools. Juveniles also in large schools in estuaries such as Botany Bay. Attains about 40 cm. Commercially important in New South Wales, eastern Victoria. Also known as Golden Snapper, King Snapper, Redfish, Koarea (New Zealand). Records west of Victoria are misidentifications of *C. australis* Hutchins, 1987, which has distinct yellow eyes.

RED SNAPPER
Centroberyx gerrardi (Günther, 1887)

D VI,13. A IV,12-13. C 19. P 13. V I,7. LL 36-39. Distinctly ctenoid moderate-sized scales cover body and part of head. Lateral line straight, with seven scales above to dorsal origin. Opercle and preopercle margins coarsely serrated. Eye very large, placed anteriorly on head. Mouth large, oblique. Dorsal fin headed by short spines, followed by markedly and progressively longer spines, then long soft rays progressively decreasing in length; anal fin similar and opposite. Caudal fin forked, large. South coast, common in South Australia and south Western Australia, extending occasionally to Port Phillip Bay. Shallow coastal rocky reefs, usually solitary in caves, to offshore to about 300 m. Attains 46 cm. Also known as Bight Redfish, King Snapper.

SWALLOWTAIL
Centroberyx lineatus (Cuvier, 1829)

D VI,14. A IV,14. C 19. P 14. V I,7. LL 49-51. Moderately small, distinctly ctenoid scales cover body and part of head. Lateral line straight, with seven scales above to dorsal origin. Opercle and preopercle margins coarsely serrated. Eye very large, placed anteriorly on head. Mouth large, oblique. Dorsal fin headed by short spines, followed by markedly and progressively longer spines, then long soft rays progressively decreasing in length; anal fin similar and opposite. Caudal fin forked, large. South coast, common in South Australia and south Western Australia, extending through Bass Strait to southern New South Wales. Shallow rocky reefs, often swimming well above substrate or under jetties; to at least 300 m. Only known in New South Wales from populations off Bermagui in 20-25 m, swimming in separate schools from the more common Nannygai on the same reefs. Attains 36 cm.

Centroberyx gerrardi ▲

Centroberyx lineatus ▼

SQUIRRELFISHES
FAMILY HOLOCENTRIDAE

A large, globally distributed tropical family with two distinct subfamilies: the Holocentrinae, which has a prominent spine on the lower corner of the preopercle, and Myripristinae in which the preopercle spine is very small. Holocentrinae comprises three genera: *Holocentrus*, restricted to the Atlantic, *Sargocentron* and *Neoniphon*. Myripristinae comprises five genera, some of which are monotypic and restricted to the Atlantic or deep water; only the largest genus, *Myripristis*, with about 25 species, is commonly encountered on shallow reefs. In all, there are nearly 70 species of Holocentridae. The squirrelfishes are medium-sized fishes with oblong to ovate and moderately compressed bodies, coarsely serrated scales and spiny heads. The dorsal fin has a large spinous section and is divided or deeply notched. The ventral fin has one spine and seven rays, and the anal fin has four spines, of which the first two are small and the third is very prominent in most species. Generally nocturnal fishes, they retire to reefs during the day. Adults often gather in large schools in caves; the young are usually very secretive and deep inside reefs. The four species included here are only known from juveniles in the Sydney area but because of their secretive nature are probably more common than they seem. Small specimens are ideal for the home aquarium. In the wild they feed on crabs and shrimps, but may eat smaller fishes in captivity. They accept all kinds of food but favour small shrimps, preferably live. Various individuals or different species can be kept together and are not aggressive. Most species attain a moderate size, but in small aquariums their growth is retarded and they usually stay small. They often live for many years, becoming very friendly. Avoid handling, especially contact with the large head-spine in some species, which is venomous.

Sargocentron diadema   Adult ▲   Juv. (Sydney Harbour) ▼

CROWN SQUIRRELFISH
Sargocentron diadema (Lacepède, 1802)

D XI,12-14. A IV,8-10. C 17. P 13-15. V I,7. LL 46-50. Body covered with moderately large, coarsely ctenoid scales, smaller dorsally and on thorax. Opercle scales spiny; preopercle serrate, moderate spine on lower corner. Dorsal fin has large, evenly arched spinous section, lowering to near body before short-based soft-rayed section with long rays; longest ray equal to or longer than its base or longest spine. Third spine on anal fin very large. Distinctly coloured; little variation with growth; readily identified by pattern of dorsal fin. Widespread tropical Indo-Pacific from New South Wales to Japan and to east Africa; juveniles south to Sydney. Shallow reefs, in lagoons with coral outcrops and slopes; to 30 m. Juveniles in Sydney from rocky boulder slopes from the harbour near the ocean in 3-10 m. Attains 17 cm. This genus comprises about 25 species, five of which are found in the Atlantic; at least three species expatriate to southern reefs and are included here.

SAMURAI SQUIRRELFISH
Sargocentron ittodai (Jordan and Fowler, 1903).

D XI,13-14. A IV,8-10. C 17. P 14-15. V I,7. LL 43-47. Body covered with moderately large, coarsely ctenoid scales, smaller dorsally and on thorax. Opercle scales spiny; preopercle serrate, moderate spine on lower corner. Dorsal fin with large, evenly arched spinous section, lowering to near body before short-based soft-rayed section with long rays; longest ray equal to or longer than its base or longest spine. Third spine on anal fin very large. Distinctly coloured; little variation with growth; small juveniles lighter and pinkish; readily identified by pattern on dorsal fin. Widespread tropical Indo-Pacific from New South Wales to Japan and to east Africa; juveniles south to Sydney. Outer reef lagoons and slopes, usually with outcrops from 15-40 m. Juveniles in the Sydney area in protected coastal reefs in narrow ledges behind sea-urchins; 10-20 m. Attains 20 cm.

RED-STRIPED SQUIRRELFISH
Sargocentron rubrum (Forsskål, 1775)

D XI,12-14. A IV,8-10. C 17. P 13-15. V I,7. LL 34-38. Body covered with moderately large, coarsely ctenoid scales, smaller dorsally and on thorax. Opercle scales spiny; preopercle serrate, moderate spine on lower corner. Dorsal fin with large, evenly arched spinous section, lowering to near body before short-based soft-rayed section with long rays; longest ray equal to or longer than its base or longest spine. Third spine on anal fin very large. Distinctly coloured; little variation with growth; red to blackish-red bands. Widespread tropical Indo-Pacific from New South Wales to southern Japan, and to east Africa and Red Sea; juveniles to the Sydney area. Coastal shallow reefs with small caves; usually in small aggregations; to about 15 m. Juveniles in Sydney Harbour in rocky ledges in silty areas such as Parsley Bay. Attains 25 cm.

Sargocentron rubrum ▲

Myripristis murdjan ▼

CRIMSON SQUIRRELFISH
Myripristis murdjan (Forsskål, 1775)

D XI,13-15. A IV,11-13. C 17. P 14-16. V I,7. LL 27-32. Body covered with moderately large, coarsely ctenoid scales, smaller dorsally and on thorax. Opercle spiny posteriorly; preopercle finely serrate, no prominent spine on lower corner. Dorsal fin with large, evenly arched spinous section, lowering to near body before short-based soft-rayed section with long rays; longest ray equal to or longer than its base or longest spine. Third spine on anal fin very large. Little variation with growth; several similar species. Widespread tropical Indo-Pacific, New South Wales to southern Japan, and to east Africa and Red Sea. Coastal reef slopes; secretive, in caves and ledges, often in ship wrecks; to at least 50 m. Attains 25 cm. Large genus with more than 20 species; *M. murdjan* the only species of the genus in southern water but the most common squirrelfish juvenile in Sydney Harbour. Also called soldierfishes because many drift in cave entrances like soldiers on guard.

DORIES
ORDER ZEIFORMES

Represented by about five families, one of which is included here. See below.

DORIES
FAMILY ZEIDAE

A small, globally distributed family comprising five genera and nine species; some species are widely distributed, one globally. Dories are deepwater fishes commonly trawled in 100 to 300 m. They are oval and compressed with a large protrusible mouth. Their scales are small or rudimentary when present. The dorsal and ventral fins are often very large with extended rays. Predatory fishes, the dories hunt alone or in small to large aggregations. They swim above the substrate in the vicinity of small schooling fishes. Medium-sized fishes, they are often regarded as some of the best food-fish. Only two species venture into shallower depths in southern waters and are included here.

JOHN DORY
Zeus faber Linnaeus, 1758

D X,21-24. A IV-V,20-25. C 13. P 12-15. V I,6-7. Scales small, cycloid to rudimentary; lateral line on upper sides, follows contour of back anteriorly to midline posteriorly. Bases of soft-rayed sections of dorsal and anal fins with three to nine bucklers; 12 to 27 keeled scutes ventrally between ventral and anal fin. Large bony head; very large mouth, oblique, tube-like when extended. Large spinous sections in dorsal and anal fins, continuous with soft rays in dorsal fin, separate in anal fin. Ventral fins small, paddle-like, placed high on sides. Juveniles with very large dorsal and ventral fins, similar to batfishes. Variable from dark brown as juveniles to silvery-bronze as adults. Usually large dark blotch on sides, variable in size and surrounding colours. Widespread in temperate seas of the Pacific and Atlantic. Most common in 60-400 m but in southern waters from 5-150 m, regularly observed by divers. Attains 66 cm. Only one of the two species in this genus occurs in Australian waters. Important commercial species; fetches a high market price.

Zeus faber ▲

Cyttus australis ▼

SILVER DORY
Cyttus australis (Richardson, 1843)

D VIII-IX,27-30. A II,28-31. C 13. P 11. V I,6. LL 77-88. Tiny cycloid scales cover body; lateral line along upper sides, follows contour of back. Dorsal and anal fin bases with low sheaths of large scales in two rows. Ventral scutes anterior to ventral fins in double row. Head large, bony; mouth large, oblique, greatly protrusible. Dorsal spines long, continuous with soft rays; anal fin spines very short, separate from soft rays. Pectoral fins very small, placed high above ventral fins. Juveniles silver, becoming rosy as adults. South coast from southern New South Wales to south Western Australia. Mainly on continental shelf to 350 m. Enters shallow depths in Tasmania; small aggregations occur in sheltered coastal bays in 10-30 m. Attains 40 cm. This genus comprises three species, one of which is included here.

VELIFERS AND RIBBONFISHES
ORDER LAMPRIFORMES

A difficult group with uncertain relationships. Only one representative with one species included here. See below.

RIBBONFISHES
FAMILY TRACHIPTERIDAE

This small family comprises three genera and an undetermined number of species. About 30 species have been named but most have been named several times, sometimes for different stages. There are perhaps less than 10 species. Adults are rarely seen deepwater pelagics. Only the juveniles of one species are regularly seen as they drift into shallow bays and harbours. Transparent with trailing long filaments, they have the appearance of a stinger-type planktonic invertebrate. Adults are extremely compressed, elongate fishes, tapering gradually from the head to the caudal fin. Fins consist entirely of soft rays. The long-based dorsal fin has numerous rays; it originates over the interorbital and is usually crest-like above the head and continuous to the caudal fin. There is no anal fin. The ventral fins are filamentous in the young and become proportionally shorter in adults but remain moderately long and slender. Adults are silvery with some darker blotches, and may have bright red fins. Some species become very large, up to several metres in length.

SCALLOPED RIBBONFISH
Zu cristatus (Bonelli, 1820)

D 120-150. P 10-12. V 5-7. LL 99-106. Tiny, very deciduous scales in adults only. First six dorsal rays in young greatly extended into narrow ribbon filaments with small evenly spaced broad flaps; several ventral fin rays similar. Juveniles have very compressed bodies with step-like profile ventrally. Body silver with blue shine, golden-black markings. Most juveniles observed were about 10 cm long, in clear coastal bays in shallow depths of a few metres; specimens have been collected from Sydney Harbour. This genus comprises two species but only this one known from Australian waters. Appears to be widespread with global distribution, as specimens have been recorded from the Pacific and Atlantic Oceans, Mediterranean Sea and east Africa. Adult attains about 1.2 m.

Zu cristatus Close-up of body

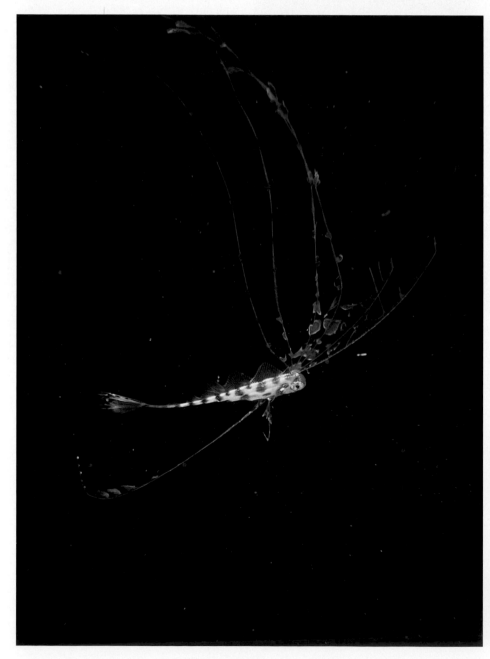

SEAHORSES AND PIPEFISHES
ORDER SYNGNATHIFORMES

Represented by seven families, six of which have species in southern waters. The primarily deepwater member, Macrorhamphosidae, is included in Key 17 as juveniles may get trapped in large harbours.

1.	Head and body greatly depressed; projecting bony rostrum, mouth below and well back from tip ....PEGASIDAE (p. 98)
	Not depressed, usually compressed; mouth at tip of tubular snout 2
2.	Ventral fins absent ....SYNGNATHIDAE (p. 83)
	Ventral fins present 3
3.	Ventral fins large ....SOLENOSTOMIDAE (p. 81)
	Ventral fins small 4
4.	Caudal fin middle rays filamentous, long ......................FISTULARIIDAE (p. 80)
	Caudal fin without filament 5
5.	First dorsal fin with large spine ................................MACRORHAMPHOSIDAE
	Dorsal fin headed by a series of low, separate spines .... AULOSTOMIDAE (p. 79)

KEY 17: *The Seahorses and Pipefishes*

TRUMPETFISHES
FAMILY AULOSTOMIDAE

This family comprises only one genus and two species, divided between Atlantic and Indo-Pacific seas. The trumpetfish's body is very elongate and slightly compressed. The head is compressed and the snout tubular and produced. The dorsal fin has evenly spaced short spines, each separate with a small triangular membrane following. The soft-rayed part of the dorsal fin is similar to and opposite the anal fin, and is posteriorly placed well back on the body near the caudal fin. The ventral fins are well back, about halfway along the body. The caudal fin is small and lanceolate. Cunning predators, trumpetfishes position themselves vertically along objects or ride on the backs of other fishes to get close to prey, which consists primarily of other fishes. The Indo-Pacific species is wide-ranging in tropical seas and expatriates to the south coast.

TRUMPETFISH
Aulostomus chinensis (Linnaeus, 1766)

D VIII-XII,23-27. A 26-29. P 17. V 6. LSR 350 (approximately). Body covered with tiny ctenoid scales. Ventral fin very small, just reaching anus, entirely soft-rayed. Fleshy barbel on chin. Several bony plates dorsally immediately behind head. Colour variable between juvenile and adult, and between individuals; from longitudinal bands to vertical banding, can quickly change colour. Xanthic form common in some areas. Widespread tropical Indo-Pacific from New South Wales to southern Japan, well into the Pacific and to east Africa, but not recorded from the Red Sea. South to Montague Island where specimens up to about 25 cm long have been observed. Juveniles in seagrass and soft coral areas. Adults from shallow reef flats to drop-offs, from coastal waters to outer reefs; mostly solitary, sometimes loosely in pairs. Attains 60 cm; doubtfully recorded to 90 cm.

Aulostomus chinensis   Typical colour-form ▲   Xanthic form ▼

FLUTEMOUTHS
FAMILY FISTULARIIDAE

The flutemouths are a single genus family comprising four species, distributed globally in tropical and warm-temperate seas. They are similar fishes with a long tubular body, long, slightly compressed head and an extremely long snout with a relatively small mouth at the end. The middle pair of rays in the caudal fin is greatly produced as an extremely long filament and the connecting membrane is large in juveniles. Excluding the filament, the caudal fin is forked and an enlarged version is formed anteriorly by the opposite dorsal and anal fins, along about one-third of the body. The ventral fin is small, well back from the head, and just ahead of the anus. Fin spines are absent. Flutemouths are found from coastal to offshore reefs to deep continental shelf depths. Their young enter estuaries. These fishes swim close to the bottom, singly or in small aggregations, hunting small fishes as their main food source. They are large fishes, some reaching 2 m in length.

ROUGH FLUTEMOUTH
Fistularia petimba Lacepède, 1803

D 14-16. A 14-15. P 15-17. V 6. Dorsal midline has embedded elongate plates in vicinity of dorsal fin. Lateral line ossified posteriorly, ends in retrorse spine. Interorbital slightly concave, without longitudinal ridges. Upper ridges on snout distinctly separate, parallel. Eye large with round pupil. Colour variable with depth; shallow-water specimens pale, greenish-grey; deepwater specimens brownish-red, dark above, light below. Distinct banding at night. Young with diffused spotting and mottling on back, indistinct banding. Widespread tropical to warm-temperate Indo-Pacific from east Africa to east Pacific, including Australia's south coast. Coastal, from inshore to deep outer reefs; to at least 200 m. Juveniles commonly in estuaries, often in muddy environments; young adults in coastal bays. Attains nearly 2 m.

SMOOTH FLUTEMOUTH
Fistularia commersonii Rüppell, 1838

D 15-17. A 14-16. P 14-16. No embedded elongate plates on dorsal midline or spine posteriorly on lateral line. Interorbital flat with longitudinal ridges. Upper ridges on snout close together, just anterior to orbital, diverging to near end of snout then converging to tip. Eye very large, pupil anteriorly elongated. Greenish-grey to brownish; adults with thin blue lines or dashes dorsally. Widespread tropical Indo-Pacific from east Africa to east Pacific; on the east coast of Australia south to at least Montague Island, but absent on the south coast. Common in seagrass beds in Queensland, and coastal reef slopes. Attains about 1.5 m. The two species included here are very similar; live specimens difficult to identify, especially juveniles. Smooth Flutemouth more slender, develops blue lines along back, has larger eye with more elongate pupil.

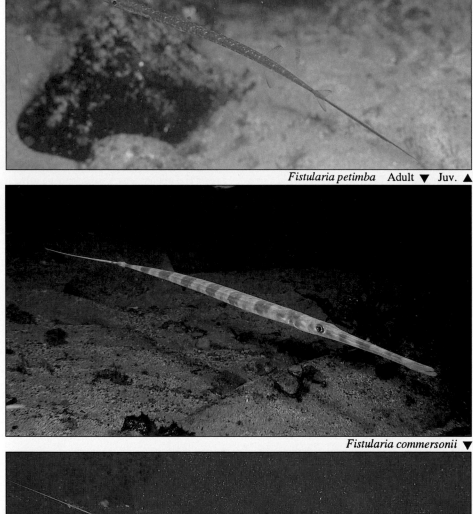

Fistularia petimba   Adult ▼ Juv. ▲

Fistularia commersonii ▼

GHOSTPIPEFISHES
FAMILY SOLENOSTOMIDAE

A small family closely related to Syngnathidae, the true pipefishes, and comprising a single genus with at least three species. The names applied to the species here are tentative as further studies are required to confirm their true identity. The ghost pipefishes are a tropical family distributed in the west Pacific and Indian Ocean, and some species are widespread. They have short compressed bodies encased in bony plates, two separate dorsal fins, a large anal fin similar to and opposite the second dorsal fin, and a large ventral fin. In the female the ventral fin is enlarged and hooked onto the body to form a pouch for holding eggs. It appears the ghost pipefishes have a prolonged larval stage, and settling juveniles are almost adult size. Settling specimens are almost transparent but quickly transform to adult colours and are virtually ready to breed. Young adults are more slender than older specimens which, as they grow, deepen at the caudal peduncle, the body between the dorsal and ventral fins and in the snout. Such changes have led to the various forms being described as different species. The three species presently recognised all occur in Australian waters; two range to the south-east coast. These small delicate fishes are not suited for the aquarium. Attempts to keep them are usually unsuccessful and only a specially prepared aquarium will have good results. Several specimens can be kept together, but without any other fish, crustaceans or invertebrates with stinging tentacles. They feed on mysids and readily spawn in such set-ups, but only live for a few months.

Ornate Ghostpipefish (*Solenostomus paradoxus*)

ORNATE GHOSTPIPEFISH
Solenostomus paradoxus (Pallas, 1770)

D V,19-20. A 19-20. P 25-28. V 7. C 15-16. Five plates between dorsal fin and interorbital; 27 rings posterior to dorsal fin, with small recurving spines on lateral corners. Dorsal fin spines feeble, membranes incised. Caudal fin and ventral fins similarly incised, small membranes on tips. Several pairs of longer membranes on first and last dorsal spines and variously distributed on caudal fin and body; most numerous on snout. Caudal peduncle always long, slender. Extremely variable from red, white or yellow blotching on segments, to almost totally black. Widespread tropical species found throughout the west Pacific from southern Japan and New South Wales to east Africa and the Red Sea. Coastal reefs with rock faces or coral dropoffs; float vertically near the bottom. Common species, but easily overlooked. Specimens observed in 3-25 m, usually solitary. In the Sydney area primarily in pursuit of mysids. Attains about 10 cm. *S. leptosomus* Tanaka, 1908, considered a synonym.

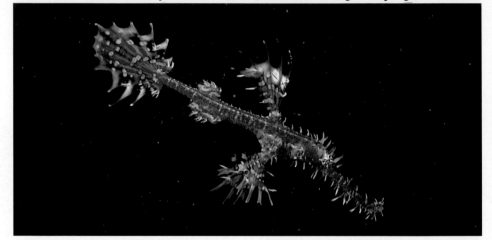

Solenostomus paradoxus   Adult ▼   Transitional stage from pelagic to benthic ▲

ROBUST GHOSTPIPEFISH
Solenostomus cyanopterus Bleeker, 1854

D V,18-20. A 18-20. P 25-27. V 7. C 16. Five plates between dorsal fin and interorbital; 25 rings posterior to dorsal fin, with small recurving spines on lateral corners. Dorsal fin spines feeble, membranes not incised. Caudal fin membranes not, or only slightly, incised. No elaborate elongate skin membranes over body but a few on snout. Caudal peducle always present but deepens with age; caudal fin enlarges over caudal peduncle and deepens. Body deepens at first dorsal and ventral fin section; depth here is always much greater than depth of second dorsal and anal fins section. Variable from green to brownish-red, or blackish. West Pacific from southern New South Wales to southern Japan. Common in seagrass beds but very well camouflaged. Also on deeper coastal reefs in 15-25 m; usually reddish-brown or blackish there. Attains 15 cm. *Solenichthys raceki* Whitley, 1955, a synonym. Third species, *S. armatus* Weber, 1913, known from a few specimens only; specimens photographed in Sydney waters probably represent this species. Very similar to *S. cyanopterus*, but adults slender with distinct caudal peduncle.

PIPEFISHES AND SEAHORSES
FAMILY SYNGNATHIDAE

The family Syngnathidae comprises some of the most interesting fishes in both behaviour and appearance, including the most unusual such as seahorses and seadragons. This large family comprises more than 50 genera and well over 200 species, distributed globally in all but the coldest seas. Some occur in fresh water, and more than half are recorded from Australian waters. They are mostly slender fishes and their bodies are encased in bony plates arranged in series of rings. They have a small oblique mouth at the end of a tubular snout. Their gills are enclosed, with a small pore-like opening above the opercle. Ventral fins are absent, as are teeth in the jaws. The anal and caudal fins may be very small or lacking in certain species, depending on their stage. The tail is prehensile in some species. Most species live on shallow reefs or in seagrass beds, feeding primarily on small crustaceans which are sucked up with the long snout. They are found in a broad range of depths; some species occur as shallow as the intertidal zone in protected bays, and some species are trawled offshore in more than 400 m. There is also a broad range of sizes, with some species maturing at about 25 mm and the largest species exceeding 65 cm. Their reproduction method is unique. Males incubate the eggs in a pouch, or ventrally on the tail or belly, with or without a skin cover. Hatchlings are often well advanced and may already resemble their parents. More details, if available, are given under species accounts. They are well represented in southern waters and 20 genera comprising 28 species are included here.

Half-Banded Pipefish (*Mitotichthys semistriatus*)

UPSIDE DOWN PIPEFISH
Heraldia nocturna Paxton, 1975

R 16-19+13-16. D 23-27. P 18-22. A 4. C 11. Body with prominent ridges dorsally and laterally. Caudal fin very large with incised membranes. Anal fin large for pipefish. Male has brood area along full length of belly, without pouch or skin-flaps. Skin raises slightly on each egg when deposited by female, leaving shallow pockets which disappear soon after hatching. Two distinct colour-forms; east coast, dark brown to black with or without a few pale blotches; south coast, yellow-brown with dark and light markings. Only known from southern waters; Seal Rocks, New South Wales to Jervis Bay and from Port Phillip Bay to south Western Australia. Secretive during the day, in low and deep ledges in rocky reef; usually in pairs, swimming on ceiling upside down. Sheltered bays, ocean side of large estuaries, shallow reefs; to about 20 m. Attains 10 cm. Single species recognised, but comprises two distinct forms, east coast and south coast; apart from colour they differ in counts and measurements. East coast form has fewer trunk and tail rings, 16-17 versus 18-19 and 13-15 versus 14-16 respectively, and proportionally larger caudal fin.

Heraldia nocturna Male with eggs, south coast form ▲ Male with eggs, east coast form ▼

Histiogamphelus briggsii Males ▲ Female ▼

BRIGGS' PIPEFISH
Histiogamphelus briggsii McCulloch, 1914

R 20-22+33-37. D 24-28. A 3. P 11-14. C 10. Snout slightly crested. Females deep-bodied compared to male. Male with tail pouch, its skin-flaps overlapping. Caudal fin large in small juveniles, similar to *Heraldia*. Variable from almost black to brown and orange; sometimes two-tone with posterior half of body very pale. East and south coast; from Seal Rocks, New South Wales to Robe, South Australia and northern Tasmania. Singly or in small aggregations; usually on clean sand off ocean beaches near reefs where loose matter under which they hide tends to accumulate. Feed on mysids, usually present in such areas, and other small crustaceans off the debris. In 3-20 m. Attains 25 cm. Only other species in this genus restricted to south-western waters.

Histiogamphelus briggsii Tiny juv.

RING-BACKED PIPEFISH
Stipecampus cristatus (McCulloch and Waite, 1918)

R 19-21+39-42. D 26-30. A 3-4. P 10-13. C 8. Snout slightly crested. Male and female similar in shape; male with tail pouch, consisting of large overlapping flaps. Flaps held wide open during courtship, which begins with male circling female. They then rise vertically, ventrally together, up to about 1-2 m above bottom for exchange of eggs. Incubating period about four weeks. Fifty to 100 young approximately 20 mm long when hatching. Pelagic, swimming to light in aquarium. Monotypic genus only known from Bass Strait to South Australia. Enters Port Phillip Bay in September, often in large numbers, apparently for breeding purposes. Usually in very sparse seagrass on clean sand in 3-15 m; probably deep offshore in Bass Strait. Attains 24 cm.

Stipecampus cristatus   Adults ▼   Hatchling ▲

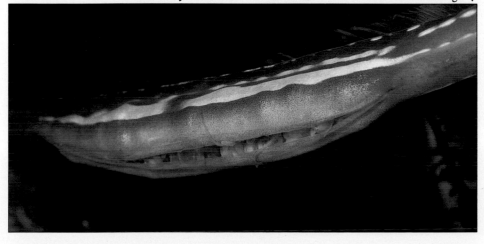

Mitotichthys semistriatus   Female ▲   Pouch of male with hatchlings ▼

HALF-BANDED PIPEFISH
Mitotichthys semistriatus (Kaup, 1856)

R 19-20+46-50. D 36-40. A 2-3. P 12-14. C 10. Female much deeper-bodied than male, compressed. Male with tail pouch consisting of broad overlapping skin-flaps which are distinctly striped to break up outline of pouch when loaded with eggs. Female initiates courtship, brightly marked with blue spots on sides. Distinct species with broad stripes on head; usually green or brownish depending on environment. Usually in small aggregations among tall eelgrass in very shallow water, 1-3 m. Only known from the Bass Strait area, Port Phillip Bay, Western Port and north eastern Tasmania. Attains 25 cm; smallest known brooding male 14 cm. Australian endemic genus comprising four species, two of which are found in south-eastern waters.

MOLLISON'S PIPEFISH
Mitotichthys mollisoni (Scott, 1955)

R 20+44-46. D 28-35. A 2-3. P 13. C 10. Female deep-bodied compared to male. Male with tail pouch consisting of broad overlapping skin-flaps. Little known about behaviour of this species, but very similar to *M. semistriatus*. Orange-brown; female with blue markings. Thin longitudinal line through eye only distinct marking on male. Only known from holotype until 1988, when three specimens found in Port Phillip Bay. Caudal fin appears to have paired rays; at first glance seems to have only five rays, however when fin spread on fresh specimens it was found there are 10 rays. This probably accounts for Scott's count of six. His pectoral fin ray count of 18 seems to be an error for 13. Only known from the type at 46 m off south-eastern Tasmania, and in Port Phillip Bay from about 7 m. Latter were among sparse brown weeds attached to low reef on sand. Largest specimen, female, 22 cm.

Mitotichthys mollisoni   Male ▲   Female ▼

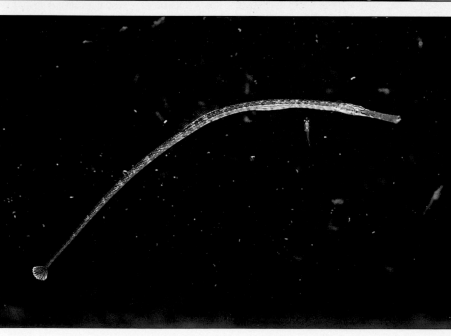

KNIFE-SNOUT PIPEFISH
Hypselognathus rostratus (Waite and Hale, 1921)

R 24-25+41-44. D 30-35. A 3-4. P 12-14. C 10. Very slender, rather plain species, characterised by deep compressed snout. Nothing known about brooding males; generally rare species, with a few specimens in collections. Known from dredge and trawl samples off Victoria, South Australia, northern Tasmania. One specimen observed at Victor Harbour, on the bottom in 10 m. Several specimens observed and photographed in Port Phillip Bay, floating almost vertically with head upwards near surface; probably drifted in from Bass Strait with the big tides, as numerous forms of oceanic plankton were present at the same time. Although juvenile, some specimens were reasonably large, about 20 cm long. Largest known specimen 31 cm.

DEEP-BODY PIPEFISH
Kaupus costatus (Waite and Hale, 1921)

R 16-18+35-38. D 30-36. A 3-4. P 9-11. C 9-10. Female much deeper-bodied than male. Male with tail pouch which consists of broad overlapping skin-flaps and seems greatly expandable. Variable in general colouration from green to brown; female ornamented with bright red bars which are used for display when courting male. Known from isolated populations at Corner Inlet (Victoria), Flinders Island (Tasmania) and several places in South Australia. Very habitat specific; quiet seagrass beds in silty, yet clear-water environments. It lives secretly in seagrass; usually found in drag-nets. Often in small aggregations of mixed sex in the intertidal zone to about 3 m. Attains 14 cm. Monotypic genus endemic to Australia.

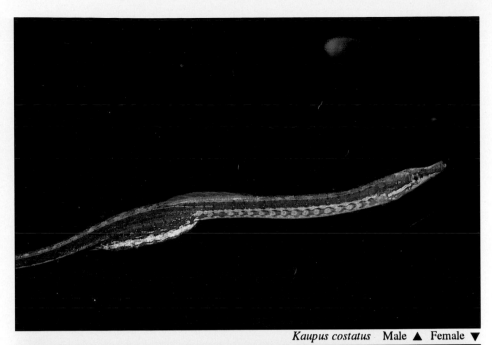

Kaupus costatus   Male ▲   Female ▼

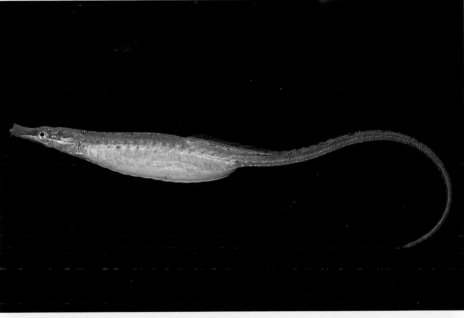

TIGER PIPEFISH
Filicampus tigris (Castelnau, 1879)

R 17-20+34-38. D 24-27. A 4. P 14-16. C 8. Male and female similar, difficult to tell apart unless male has brood in pouch along tail. Juveniles usually have leafy appendages above eyes. Small appendages spaced dorsally over body. Little variation in colour; some specimens with more blue than others. Only known on the east coast from Sydney to Moreton Bay, South Australia's Spender Gulf, and Western Australia from Shark Bay to Broome. Usually found lying low on the substrate in estuaries, on rubble-sand or mud with sparse plant life. Fairly common in Sydney Harbour in the coves near the heads; found in shallows to at least 30 m. Attains 30 cm. Monotypic genus endemic to Australian waters.

GIRDLED PIPEFISH
Festucalex cinctus (Ramsay, 1882)

R 16-18+36-39. D 21-28. A 4. P 12-14. C 10. Males and females very similar; body, head rather smooth without spines or prominent ridges. Some leafy appendages over back. Male's pouch on tail, not obvious unless with brood. Variable in colour; usually dark, grey or brown-orange; rare pale form. Usually orange on opercle. Endemic to Australia; New South Wales, Queensland, Northern Territory, although latter and specimens from northern Queensland slightly different, may represent another species. Fairly common in Sydney Harbour, usually on rubble-covered sand with a little plant growth or sponges, in 10-20 m. Other specimens known from trawls to 30 m. Attains 16 cm. This genus comprises at least six species distributed throughout the tropical Indo-Pacific.

Festucalex cinctus   Usual colour-form ▲   Rare pale form ▼

MOTHER-OF-PEARL PIPEFISH
Vanacampus margaritifer (Peters, 1869)

R 18-20+34-38. D 22-26. A 3-4. P 10-12. C 10. Ridges low, not well defined on body. Males and females similar; males have pouch with large overlapping skin-flaps on tail. Usually pale to dark grey with numerous spots; most distinct marking a series of pale dashes along ventral ridges along tail. Widespread south coast from southern Queensland to south Western Australia. Usually shallow estuaries on sandy low reefs with little vegetation; sometimes in seagrasses; to about 10 m. Attains 16 cm. Endemic Australian genus comprising four species, most of which are found in estuaries; one species, only known from Kangaroo Island and Spencer Gulf, not included here.

LONG-SNOUT PIPEFISH
Vanacampus poecilolaemus (Peters, 1869)

R 18-20+44-51. D 25-31. A 3-4. P 11-14. C 10. Ridges low, not well defined on body. Males and females similar; males have pouch with large overlapping skin-flaps on tail. Usually brownish with indistinct barring and spotting; similar to other species and best identified by long snout. Recorded widespread from the south coast but occurrence now restricted to various isolated populations due to habitat restrictions. Records range from Bass Strait, Tasmania to south Western Australia. Still common in American River, Kangaroo Island. Shallow seagrass beds in quiet, silty, clear-water areas, to about 10 m. Attains 28 cm.

PORT PHILLIP PIPEFISH
Vanacampus phillipi (Lucas, 1891)

R 17-20+38-46. D 22-29. A 3-4. P 9-12. C 10. Ridges low, not well defined on body. Males and females similar; males have pouch with large overlapping skin-flaps on tail. Usually brownish with indistinct barring and spotting; similar to other species and best identified by blue bars on sides which become most evident in larger specimens. Widespread south coast, southern New South Wales to south Western Australia and Tasmania. Commonly found among various brown or green weeds in low reefs on sand in shallow estuaries and protected bays. From intertidal to at least 25 m. Attains 20 cm.

PUG-NOSE PIPEFISH
Pugnaso curtirostris (Castelau, 1872)

R 17-19+41-44. D 21-25. A 2-3. P 8-11. C 10. Body smooth; ridges low on head, not well defined. Female and male similar; male has pouch with large overlapping skin-flaps under tail. Very slender, snout short. Motley colours, often with whitish diffused patches above, orange below; a series of orange blotches along lower sides. South coast from the Bass Strait area to south Western Australia, common in Western Port. Shallow seagrass beds and weeds on low reef on sand, in estuaries and protected bays; to about 10 m. Attains 15 cm. Australian endemic monotypic genus, closely related to *Vanacampus*.

SAWTOOTH PIPEFISH
Maroubra perserrata Whitley, 1948

R 16-17+26-29. D 23-27. A 4. P 17-19. C 10. Principal body ridges elevated, areas between concave; ridge on each ring terminates in prominent distal spine. Male and female show no difference; difficult to sex unless male carries eggs. Pouch absent; eggs attached externally along ventral area on trunk. Australian endemic, widespread in southern waters, from Byron Bay to Rottnest Island and to south-eastern Tasmania. Typically lives in narrow rock crevices usually rich with various forms of invertebrates such as shrimps and sponges or sea-urchins. Common along semi-protected ocean reefs in 5-25 m, but also in rocky estuaries in 3-15 m. Occurs in pairs or small aggregations. Small species; attains 85 mm. Only other species in this genus endemic to Japan.

Trachyramphus bicoarctatus   Usual brown colour-form ▲   Yellow colour variation ▼

STICK PIPEFISH
Trachyrhamphus bicoarctatus (Bleeker, 1857)

R 21-24+55-63. D 24-32. A 4. P 15-19. C 9. Body very elongate, rather smooth. Pouch of male along tail, has large overlapping skin-flaps. Ventral caudal fin ray unusually thickened, usually longer than others. Head slightly angled from gradual curve downward in anterior trunk area. Widespread tropical Indo-Pacific from Sydney to southern Japan, and to east Africa and Red Sea. In current areas of quiet bays and deep estuaries, on sand and mud flats with sparse invertebrate or plant life; in shallows to at least 40 m. Has unusual posture, "standing" on posterior part of tail, facing current. Anchors in the substrate with tail, using the modified lower fin ray. Feeds on zooplankton drifting along the substrate. Attains 40 cm. Genus comprises three species, all tropical Indo-Pacific.

SMOOTH PIPEFISH
Lissocampus caudalis Waite and Hale, 1921

R 12-14+51-60. D 13-14. A 3-4. P 5-6. C 10. Body ridges very low, indistinct. Snout dorsal ridge slightly elevated in large specimens. Pouch of male on tail section, has large overlapping skin-flaps. Australian endemic from the Bass Strait region to south Western Australia. Secretive, extremely well camouflaged species; mimics various weeds and seagrasses, including exposed seagrass roots. Often with small outcrops of rock and weeds on sand; nearly always in pairs. Colour can range from brown to orange, purple or whitish, or combinations of these in bands. Coastal waters, including rock pools and sometimes in floating weeds; to at least 10 m. Attains 10 cm. Genus comprises five species, one restricted to the Red Sea, one to New Zealand, others to Australian waters.

Lissocampus caudalis   Male ▲ Female ▼

JAVELIN PIPEFISH
Lissocampus runa (Whitley, 1931)

R 13-14+45-49. D 13-15. A 3-4. P 6-7. C 10. Body ridges very low, indistinct. Snout dorsal ridge not elevated, snout concave above. Pouch of male on tail section has large overlapping skin-flaps. Australian endemic from the Sydney area to south Western Australia, and to north-eastern Tasmania. Secretive, extremely well camouflaged species; mimics various weeds. Reported from rock pools and shallow reefs but author was unable to locate specimens in Victoria; instead, specimens were located at Bicheno, eastern Tasmania, among algae in 20 m. Attains 10 cm.

RED PIPEFISH

Notiocampus ruber (Ramsay and Ogilby, 1886)

R 18-19+48-49. D 11-13. A 0. P 0. C 6-7. Body extremely slender, smooth. Fins greatly reduced; lacks anal fin; adults lack pectoral fin. Mature males unknown. Only known from a few specimens from Sydney Harbour and various south coast locations, including Tasmania and south Western Australia, from 5-20 m. Specimen in photograph found at Bicheno, Tasmania, in 20 m among a large piece of dense filamentous red algae on a rock face. Moved in snake-like fashion, was lost and found several times in the process of photographing it. Attains 17 cm. Monotypic Australian endemic genus. Presently known from only eight specimens.

HAIRY PIPEFISH

Urocampus carinirostris Castelnau, 1872

R 7-10+49-59. D 13-15. A 2. P 13-15. C 10. Males have convex snout ridge, large pouch with overlapping skin-flaps under tail; snout ridge slightly concave in females. Body has leafy appendages, often numerous, depending on habitat. Widespread along most of Australia's coasts and to Papua New Guinea. Mostly occurs in estuaries in tall eelgrasses, often in lower reaches of rivers. Also observed off Sydney Harbour beaches among long stringy algaes on low reef on sand to about 5 m. Small species; attains 10 cm. Genus comprises two species; second restricted to semi-tropical north-western Pacific.

Urocampus carinirostris   Juv.

Urocampus carinirostris   Adult males, specimen on right with eggs in pouch

BRUSHTAIL PIPEFISH
Leptoichthys fistularius Kaup, 1853

R 22-28+18-24. D 33-41. A 5. P 20-23. C 11. Slender species; snout very long; mouth distinctly oblique. Caudal fin large, more or less lanceolate. Brood pouch of male on trunk has pouch plates but folds absent. Bright green to greenish-brown; large specimens have electric blue on snout. South coast from north-eastern Tasmania to south Western Australia. Adults in tall dense seagrass in 3-20 m. Small juveniles sometimes observed swimming well above the substrate along reef slopes, sometimes in small aggregations, perhaps in the process of finding a suitable place to settle. Largest known pipefish; attains 65 cm. Monotypic genus endemic to Australian waters.

Leptoichthys fistularius ▲ Close-up of head ▼

SPOTTED PIPEFISH
Stigmatopora argus (Richardson, 1840)

R 16-23+78-91. D 37-64. A 4. P 13-18. Male very slender with large, well sealed pouch along tail. Female very wide-bodied, expandable when displaying to male. No caudal fin; tail prehensile. Snout very long, slender; mouth small. Common south coast species from the Sydney area to Tasmania and south Western Australia. Mostly in small to large aggregations among tall eelgrasses in estuaries. Sometimes in floating weeds. Juveniles float near surface attached to bits of seagrass or weeds. Attains 27 cm. This genus comprises three species restricted to Australian and New Zealand waters; each has one endemic species, third is found in both.

Stigmatopora argus Male ▲ Female ▼

93

WIDE-BODY PIPEFISH
Stigmatopora nigra Kaup, 1856

R 16-19+67-79. D 35-47. A 4. P 11-16. C 0. Male very slender with large, well sealed pouch along tail. Female very wide-bodied, expandable when displaying to male. No caudal fin; tail prehensile. Snout very long, slender; mouth small. Common south coast species from southern Queensland to Tasmania and south Western Australia, and New Zealand. Mostly in small to large aggregations; found in seagrasses and various weed habitats on rocky reefs, unattached weeds moved by currents over sand, or floating weeds. One of the most abundant species in estuaries along the south coast. Attains 16 cm.

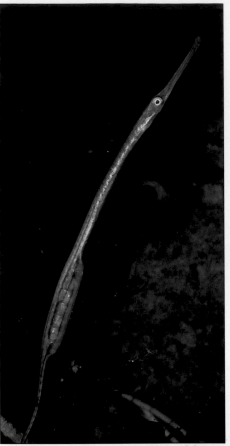

Stigmatopora nigra   Male ▲

Stigmatopora nigra   Female courting male

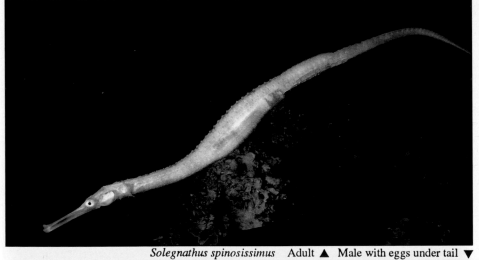

Solegnathus spinosissimus   Adult ▲   Male with eggs under tail ▼

SPINY PIPEHORSE
Solegnathus spinosissimus Günther, 1870

R 24-27+51-59. D 34-42. A 4. P 23-26. Gill membrane with spinous platelets; body surface with spiny ridges. Females slightly deeper-bodied than males. Male carries eggs externally over large section below tail; skin forms shallow cup for each egg during deposition; cups gradually disappear after eggs hatch. Tail prehensile, but mainly over posterior part. Yellowish-orange. South-eastern Australia, from southern Queensland to Bass Strait and southern Tasmania, and New Zealand. Deepwater species, often washed up after storms, mostly known from trawls. Depth range from 3-400 m, but only known in southern Tasmania in shallow depths of the Derwent River. Attains almost 50 cm. Indo-Pacific genus comprising five species distributed in west Pacific and west Australia. Known as Spiny Sea Dragon in New Zealand.

WEEDY SEADRAGON
Phyllopteryx taeniolatus (Lacepède, 1804)

R 17-18+31-37. D 27-34. A 4-5. P 20-23. Body unusually shaped, somewhat undulating vertically; spines dorsally and ventrally on head, large leaf-like appendages at tips. Head slightly angled down with long snout. Large females become very deep, compressed on trunk compared with males, which deepen to much lesser degree. Breeding season early summer; one brood per season. Males carry eggs externally below tail; skin forms cup on each egg during deposition. Incubation time about eight weeks; up to about 250 young hatch. Hatching period about six days; young distributed over wide area during this period. Young stay close to substrate near weeds, begin feeding on tiny mysids after about two days when yolk used. At the same time certain features, in particular the longer snout, develop. Young grow rapidly at first; measure 25 mm at birth, triple size in three weeks. Some mature in one year, but usually breed in second year when fully grown. Widespread south coast from about the Sydney area to south Western Australia, and to southern Tasmania. In the south in shallow estuaries to deep offshore reefs from 1-50 m; on the east coast usually deeper, 10-50 m. Usually along reefs with kelp, along the edge on sand, feeding on mysids and other small crustaceans. Attains 45 cm. Monotypic genus endemic to Australian waters. Also known as Common Seadragon.

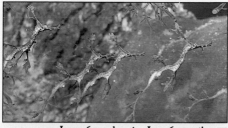

Juvs. 6 weeks ▲ Juv. 6 months ▼

Male with eggs ▲ Female ▼

LEAFY SEADRAGON
Phycodurus eques (Günther, 1865)

R 18+41-44. D 34-38. A 4. P 19-21. Body vertically undulating; large spines along ridges, particularly numerous ventrally. Elaborate leaf-like appendages on bony stalks in various places, singly on head, paired on trunk and tail. Head angled with large horizontal protrusion between eyes, very long snout. Pectoral and dorsal fins very large. Restricted south coast distribution; mainly known from South Australia and south Western Australia where common in a few localities. Recently discovered off Victorian coast near Anglesea but has been reported as far as Wilson's Promontory to the east. In South Australia it occurs on kelp reef in 4-30 m or more. In Western Australia usually deeper than 20 m; in Victoria apparently deeper, about 30 m, but at Anglesea in about 6-10 m. Usually occurs over sand patches close to reefs with kelp, feeding on mysids and other crustaceans. One of the most spectacular examples of camouflage which works two ways; predators do not recognise it as a fish, prey not worried by a piece of "floating weed". Divers, too, usually swim past, often find it by accident. Sometimes the fish carries a large, very obvious isopod crustacean; on several occasions divers have wondered what the isopod was doing on a piece of weed. Only upon investigation did they discover the seadragon as the "weed" swam away. Reproductive strategy similar to Weedy Seadragon, but males with eggs usually found in deeper water. This truly spectacular fish is the only one in the genus. Australian endemic. Attains 35 cm.

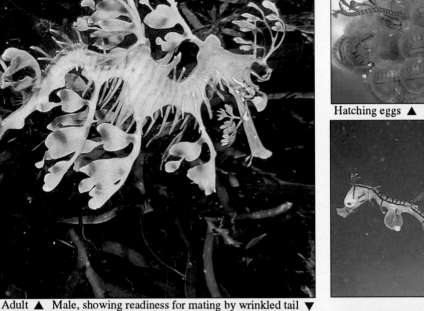

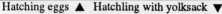

Hatching eggs ▲   Hatchling with yolksack ▼

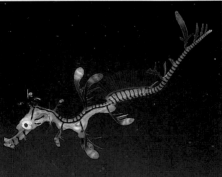

Adult ▲   Male, showing readiness for mating by wrinkled tail ▼

Juv. 2 days ▲   Juv. 4 weeks, 90 mm ▼

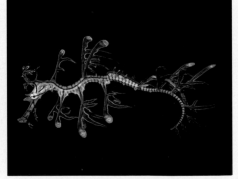

BIG-BELLY SEAHORSE
Hippocampus abdominalis Lesson, 1827

R 11-13+44-49. D 26-31. A 4. P 14-17. Vertical posture with angled-down head; tail long, prehensile. Trunk broad, expanded ventrally in adults; male with sack-like pouch below. With or without long filaments on head or body. Variable from brown or orange to yellow and grey, usually matching habitat. Widespread south-eastern Australia from New South Wales to South Australia and Tasmania, and also in New Zealand. Adults in harbours and protected coastal bays or deep with sponges. Often under jetties, attached to the holdfast of kelp. Young pelagic, floating attached to bits of seagrass or weed; up to several centimetres long before settling. Adults move into certain areas in spring for breeding purposes; in Port Phillip Bay their numbers increase greatly in some areas. One of the largest seahorses; attains 25 cm. This genus comprises numerous but many very similar species; badly in need of revision. Worldwide in tropical to warm-temperate seas; perhaps 25 species, about nine in Australian waters.

Hippocampus abdominalis Male, with inflated pouch, displaying to female ▲

SHORT-HEAD SEAHORSE
Hippocampus breviceps Peters, 1870

R 11+38-42. D 19-22. A 4. P 14-15. Vertical posture with angled-down head; tail long, prehensile. Trunk broad, expanded ventrally in adults; male with sack-like pouch below. Usually with numerous long filaments on head and along back ridges. Top of head pointed. Variable from brown or orange to yellow and grey, usually matching habitat. Widespread south coast from southern New South Wales, Lancelin, Western Australia, and Tasmania. Particularly common in Port Phillip Bay where they occur in small to large aggregations in weed patches attached to rocks on sand, mostly in sargassum weeds. Breeds on monthly cycle throughout summer; produces 50 to 100 young in single or combined brood from several females. Small species, attains 15 cm; usually about 12 cm. Closely related species in Japan, southern Africa.

Hippocampus breviceps Male giving birth

Hippocampus breviceps Pair, male with large pouch ▲

WHITE'S SEAHORSE
Hippocampus whitei Bleeker, 1855

R 11+33-36. D 16-17. A 4. P 15-16. Vertical posture with angled-down head; tail long, prehensile. Trunk only slightly expanded ventrally in adults; male with sack-like pouch below. Head pointed with knob-like coronet. Small filaments sometimes present on head. Ridges raised with blunt knobs on rings. Variable in colour, usually plain from dull grey to dusky yellow, sometimes with pale saddle-like markings or scribbled and finely spotted pattern. Australian endemic from southern Queensland to southern Victoria; recorded from South Australia; possibly in Spencer Gulf. Doubtfully recorded from Victoria; perhaps ranges to eastern Victoria, but records probably based on juvenile Short-Head Seahorse, which virtually fit the descriptions of White's Seahorse in some literature. Common in Sydney Harbour with broad-leaf seagrasses and on holdfast of kelp under jetties; to about 20 m. Attains 20 cm.

Hippocampus whitei   Male with young ▲ Female ▼

Hippocampus whitei   Juv.

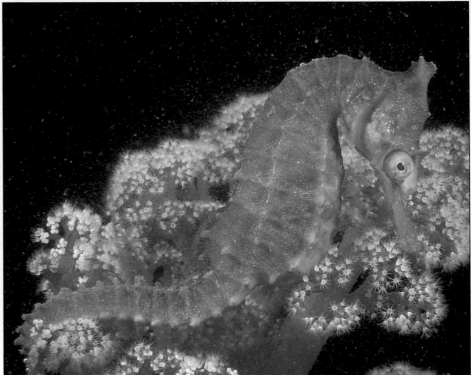

SEAMOTHS
FAMILY PEGASIDAE

A small Indo-Pacific family of small curious fishes, comprising two genera and five species. The dwarf genus, *Eurypegasus*, contains two species, one a Hawaiian endemic, and one widespread. The other genus, *Pegasus*, has three species; one is restricted to southern Australian waters, one is widespread and the third is only known from an area from Sri Lanka to southern Japan. Seamoths are small benthic fishes with horny, depressed bodies and large horizontal-held pectoral fins. They crawl on the bottom with the ventral and pectoral fins. They have a produced rostrum, and an inferior, downward protrusible, tube-like mouth. The gill openings are restricted to small posterior openings facing upward. The body is encased in rigid bony plates and the tail is encircled by bony rings. The ventral fin elements, including the spine, are combined into two pairs of slender structures used for walking. Eggs and larvae are pelagic and small juveniles may float into tidal pools. The seamoths' diet consists primarily of tiny crustaceans and other small invertebrates.

LITTLE DRAGONFISH
Eurypegasus draconis (Linnaeus, 1766)

D 5. A 5. P 10-12. V I,2. C 8. Three body rings. Eight tail rings. Carapace thick, broad. Rostrum variable; usually fairly broad, with lateral hook-like serrations. Tail slender, flexible. Colour highly variable, matches surroundings, capable of quick changes. Mimics bits of surrounding debris such as pieces of broken shell. Widespread tropical Indo-Pacific, from southern Japan to Sydney and to east Africa and Red Sea. Sheltered coastal bays on fine sand with sparse rubble. Extremely well camouflaged; partly buries when resting. Specimens in Sydney were found in depths ranging from 3-15 m. Aquarium specimens regularly discarded their outer layer of skin in one complete piece, apparently to prevent accumulation of epibiotic growths such as algae, hydroids and other organisms. Small species reaching only about 8 cm.

SCULPTURED SEAMOTH
Pegasus lancifer Kaup, 1861

D 5. A 5. P 16-19. V I,3. C 8. Three body rings. Fourteen tail rings. Carapace depressed, broad. Rostrum variable, from short in juveniles to long and slender in adults; with lateral hook-like serrations. Tail slender, flexible; posterior seven rings fused together, with lateral retrorse spines. Colour highly variable, matching surroundings, capable of quick changes, but usually pale sandy in most areas. Males with additional colours on pectoral fins. South coast only from the Bass Strait area and Tasmania to south Western Australia. Shallow sand flats in the vicinity of seagrass beds to deep water, at least 50 m. Breeding populations move into Port Phillip Bay in early spring; large numbers pair in certain shallow sandy bays. Males display with ornamented pectoral fin, turning it vertical to face female. Spawning involves swimming upwards, ventrally together, to several metres from the substrate. They quickly dart back after the release of eggs and sperm, which floats to the surface. These activities are mainly towards dusk on high tides. Attains 12 cm.

SLENDER SEAMOTH
Pegasus volitans Linnaeus, 1758

D 5. A 5. P 10-12. V I,2. C 8. Three body rings. Twelve tail rings. Carapace depressed, slender in adults. Rostrum variable, from short in juveniles to long and slender in adults; with lateral hook-like serrations. Tail slender, flexible; posterior three rings fused together, with lateral retrorse spines. Colour highly variable from pale sandy in most areas to almost black, matching surroundings, capable of quick changes. Widespread tropical west Pacific and Indian Ocean; known south to Bermagui on the east coast. Shallow sandy bays and estuaries in the vicinity of seagrass beds, often in current prone areas. Usually shallow, about 3-6 m, but recorded to 75 m. Large adults common in Moreton Bay tidal channels, on rubble in open seagrass patches. Attains 14 cm.

Pegasus lancifer   Adult ▲   Male displaying to female ▼

Pegasus volitans   Light form ▲   Dark form ▼

SCORPIONFISHES AND FLATHEADS
ORDER SCORPAENIFORMES

Represented by about 20 families, eight of which have species in south-eastern coastal waters and are included here. They can be determined with Key 18.

1.	Dorsal fin origin above or in front of eyes 2
	Dorsal fin origin well posterior to and above eyes 5
2.	Ventral fins absent ....PATAECIDAE (p. 106)
	Ventral fins present 3
3.	Dorsal fin deeply notched in centre ..............GNATHANACANTHIDAE (p. 108)
	Dorsal fin without distinct notch 4
4.	Lateral line prominent; scales tiny, embedded ............TETRAROGIDAE (p. 107)
	Lateral line hidden; scales small, with skin-covered spines, velvety to touch ....APLOACTINIDAE (p. 105)
5.	Head greatly depressed; ventral fins reach past pectoral fins ....PLATYCEPHALIDAE (p. 100)
	Head not greatly depressed; pectoral fins reach past ventral fins 6
6.	Dorsal fin continuous; long-based spinous part ............SCORPAENIDAE (p. 114)
	Dorsal fin distinctly in two parts; short-based spinous part 7
7.	Pectoral fins reach caudal peduncle ......................DACTYLOPTERIDAE (p. 108)
	Pectoral fins reach halfway along body .... TRIGLIDAE (p. 109)

KEY 18: *The Scorpionfishes and Flatheads*

FLATHEADS
FAMILY PLATYCEPHALIDAE

As the name suggests, flatheads are fishes with greatly depressed heads. This large, primarily Indo-Pacific family comprises numerous small tropical species and a number of large warm-temperate species which are of commercial importance. Of the estimated 18 genera and 60 species, 12 genera and 44 species are recognised in Australian waters. They are well represented in southern waters, including the largest species, some exceeding 1 m in length. Their heads bear sharp bony ridges and are frequently armed with large pungent spines. The body is usually less depressed than the head and is covered with small ctenoid scales. Fins feature strong slender spines, and the first dorsal fin spine is typically tiny, partly embedded and detached from the fin. The majority of species lack a swim bladder and live on sand substrates, either buried to some extent or just resting on the fins, swimming short distances when active. A few species venture far up estuaries but most occur on deeper coastal sand flats and some are mainly known from trawls to about 150 m. Their diet consists of small fishes, crustaceans and in some areas they prey heavily on small sand-dwelling squid; they appear to be opportunistic feeders during day or night. Included here are 12 species but it is likely that some of the northern species range to southern waters on occasion. They are of commercial importance and are sought after by both the professional and amateur fisherman.

Mud Flathead (*Suggrundus jugosus*)

ROCK FLATHEAD
Thysanophrys cirronasus (Richardson, 1848)

D VIII-IX,11-12. A 11. C 15. P 19-21. V I,5. LL 51-55. Body elongate, slightly compressed; head very large, greatly depressed with several raised ridges bearing strong spines. Eye large with well-developed ocular flap consisting of finely branched sections. Mouth large; villiform teeth in bands on jaws, vomer, palatines. Preopercle with two to three short stout angled spines, others on opercle. Scales small, finely ctenoid; lateral-line scales enlarged. Swim bladder absent. Highly variable from pale brown to purple with darker saddle-like markings. Fins with narrow streaks. Southern waters from southern Queensland to Lancelin, Western Australia, but not recorded from the Bass Strait area. Lives among rocky and weedy reefs on sand patches. Attains 35 cm. Indo-Pacific genus comprising seven species, four of which are found in Australian waters; one ranges to southern waters.

Thysanophrys cirronasus Juv.

MUD FLATHEAD
Suggrundus jugosus (McCulloch, 1914)

D VIII-IX,11. A 11. C 15. P 17-18. V I,5. LL 54. Body, head greatly compressed; spinous and serrated ridges on head. Body covered with small ctenoid scales. Lateral line with spine on first 16 scales. Upper preopercle spine much longer than lower. Eye large with curtain-line, thinly branched ocular flap. Mouth large; villiform teeth in bands on jaws, vomer, palatines. Pale brownish-grey to dusky with variable mottling. Southern Queensland to Botany Bay. Muddy estuaries; buried during the day, active at night; in 3-30 m. Attains 25 cm. This genus comprises mainly tropical species, about five of which occur in Australian waters.

TIGER FLATHEAD
Neoplatycephalus richardsoni (Castelnau, 1872)

D VIII-IX,14. A 14. C 15. P 19-20. V I,5. LL 64-74. Body elongate, slightly depressed. Head large, depressed, with several low, almost spineless ridges. Eyes large with small ocular flap. Mouth large; strong canines on jaws, palatines, vomer. Strong, angled preopercle spines. Body and most of head covered with small, finely ctenoid scales. Lateral-line scales slightly enlarged, about 84

Suggrundus jugosus ▲   *Neoplatycephalus richardsoni* ▼

scale rows above. Swim bladder present. Variable grey-brown with series of dark blotches or bands; small orange spots all over. South-eastern Australia from New South Wales to Tasmania and Victoria through Bass Strait. Usually offshore in 30-160 m. Attains 60 cm. Important commercial species in Victoria. This genus comprises large-toothed species; the three known species are confined to southern waters.

101

TOOTHY FLATHEAD

Neoplatycephalus aurimaculatus Knapp, 1987

D VIII-IX,14. A 13-15. C 15. P 16-20. V I,5. LL 75-80. Body elongate, slightly depressed. Head large, depressed, with several low, almost spineless ridges. Eyes large with long ocular flap. Mouth large; strong canines on jaws, palatines, vomer. Strong, angled preopercle spines. Body and most of head covered with small, finely ctenoid scales. Lateral-line scales slightly enlarged, about 95 scale rows above. Swim bladder absent. Sandy-coloured; small yellow to orange spots all over, some larger whitish spots above; sometimes has dark blotching. Restricted to the south coast from Bass Strait and Tasmania to South Australia. Occurs in sandy bays and coastal waters in 10-160 m. Attains 55 cm. Often mistaken for Tiger Flathead; also known as Yellow-Finned Flathead.

LONG-SPINE FLATHEAD

Platycephalus longispinis Macleay, 1884

D VII-IX,14. A 14. C 15. P 20-21. V I,5. LL 75. Body elongate, slightly depressed. Head large, depressed, with several low, almost spineless ridges. Eyes large with small rounded ocular flap. Mouth large; small pointed teeth on jaws, small conical teeth on palatines. Strong, angled preopercle spines, lower two or three times as long as upper, and longer than interorbital width. Body and most of head covered with small, finely ctenoid scales. Lateral-line scales slightly enlarged, about 100 scale rows above. Swim bladder absent. Sandy-coloured, finely marbled; small pale spots all over back, a series of slightly larger spots spaced beside dorsal fins. East coast from New South Wales to eastern Victoria; second population, apparently this species, found in south Western Australia. Common in southern New South Wales near rocky reefs on sand flats in about 15-20 m, often in loose aggregations. Mainly on clean sand, including estuaries, from 3-75 m. Recorded to 38 cm, but usually to about 30 cm. One of the smallest species of the southern representatives of this speciose genus, eight of which are included here.

Platycephalus longispinis ▲   *Platycephalus arenarius* ▼

FLAG-TAIL FLATHEAD

Platycephalus arenarius Ramsay and Ogilby, 1886

D VII,13-14. A 13-14. C 15. P 19-20. V I,5. LL 74-76. Body elongate, slightly depressed. Head large, depressed, with several low, almost spineless ridges. Eyes large with small rounded ocular flap. Mouth large; small pointed teeth on jaws, small conical ones on palatines. Strong, angled preopercle spines, lower distinctly longer than upper. Body and most of head covered with small, finely ctenoid scales. Lateral-line scales slightly enlarged, about 100 scale rows above. Swim bladder absent. Sandy-coloured; distinctly marked caudal fin readily identifies this species. Tropical Australia to Indonesia; south to Bermagui, New South Wales. Estuaries and coastal bays on clean sand; adults in 5-60 m. Young in large schools over shallow sand banks; adults in loose aggregations, usually in deeper part of their range. Attains 45 cm.

BLUE-SPOTTED FLATHEAD
Platycephalus caeruleopunctatus
McCulloch, 1922

D VIII-IX,14. A 14. C 15. P 19-21. V I,5. LL 82-87. Body elongate, slightly depressed. Head large, depressed, with several low, almost spineless ridges. Eyes large with small rounded ocular flap. Mouth large; small pointed teeth and small canines anteriorly on jaws, small conical teeth on palatines. Strong, angled preopercle spines, lower distinctly longer than upper. Body and most of head covered with small, finely ctenoid scales. Lateral-line scales slightly enlarged, about 115 scale rows above. Swim bladder absent. Sandy-coloured with small, pale blue spots; distinctly marked caudal fin readily identifies this species. East coast from southern Queensland to eastern Victoria, south to Lakes Entrance. Coastal bays and estuaries to offshore sand flats in 5-100 m. Attains 45 cm.

YANK FLATHEAD
Platycephalus speculator Klunzinger, 1872

D VIII-IX,13-14. A 14. C 15. P 19-21. V I,5. LL 80. Body elongate, slightly depressed. Head large, depressed, with several low, almost spineless ridges. Eyes large with broad, rounded ocular flap. Mouth large; small pointed teeth on jaws, in one or two rows on vomer, in single row on each palatine. Strong, angled preopercle spines, lower distinctly longer than upper. Body and most of head covered with small, finely ctenoid scales. Lateral-line scales slightly enlarged, about 95 scale rows above. Swim bladder absent. Sandy-coloured; distinctly marked caudal fin readily identifies this species; adults sometimes very dark, sometimes confused with Dusky Flathead. South coast from eastern Bass Strait and Tasmania to Kalbarri, Western Australia. Estuaries, inshore coastal bays, beaches; large adults often just beyond surf waves, to about 30 m. Attains 90 cm and 8 kg.

Platycephalus bassensis   Adult ▼ Juv. ▲

SAND FLATHEAD
Platycephalus bassensis Cuvier, 1829

D VIII-IX,14. A 14. C 15. P 19-20. V I,5. LL 70. Body elongate, slightly depressed. Head large, depressed, with several low, almost spineless ridges. Eyes large with small, rounded ocular flap. Mouth large; small pointed teeth on jaws, broad patch on vomer, narrow row on each palatine. Strong, angled preopercle spines, lower distinctly longer than upper. Body and most of head covered with small, finely ctenoid scales. Lateral-line scales slightly enlarged, about 100 scale rows above. Swim bladder absent. Sandy-coloured, often with broad dark bands; distinctly marked caudal fin readily identifies this species. South-eastern Australia, from central New South Wales, Tasmania to eastern South Australia. Shallow coastal sand flats and estuaries to about 100 m. Attains 46 cm.

103

DUSKY FLATHEAD
Platycephalus fuscus Cuvier, 1829

D VIII-IX,13-14. A 13-14. C 15. P 19-20. V I,5. LL 95. Body elongate, slightly depressed. Head large, depressed, with several low, almost spineless ridges. Eyes large with small, rounded ocular flap. Mouth large; small pointed teeth on jaws, broad patch on vomer, narrow row on each palatine. Strong, angled preopercle spines, lower distinctly longer than upper. Body and most of head covered with small, finely ctenoid scales. Lateral-line scales slightly enlarged, about 120 scale rows above. Swim bladder absent. Sandy-coloured, variable pale to very dark with small spots. Distinct markings on pectoral fins and caudal fin readily identify this species. East coast from southern Queensland to eastern Victoria, south to Lakes Entrance. Estuaries to offshore to 25 m, but most common in shallow depths, in quiet beach corners and mud flats in estuaries. Largest of all flatheads; attains 1.2 m and 15 kg.

Platycephalus fuscus Offshore form ▲ Estuarine form ▼

MARBLED FLATHEAD
Platycephalus marmoratus Stead, 1908

D VIII,13. A 13. C 15. P 19-20. V I,5. LL 65. Body elongate, slightly depressed. Head large, depressed, with several low, almost spineless ridges. Eyes large with large, rounded ocular flap. Mouth large; small, pointed teeth on jaws, broad patch on vomer, narrow row on each palatine. Strong, angled preopercle spines, lower distinctly longer than upper. Body and most of head covered with small, finely ctenoid scales. Lateral-line scales enlarged, about 85 scale rows above. Swim bladder absent. Sandy-coloured, variable but distinct dark and light markings above. East coast from Queensland to southern New South Wales. Coastal bays to deep offshore reefs. On sand near low rocky reefs or on rubble; usually deep, 20-80 m, but juveniles as shallow as 3 m in Sydney Harbour on rubbly white sand. Attains 45 cm.

Platycephalus marmoratus ▼

Platycephalus marmoratus Juv.

GRASS FLATHEAD
Platycephalus laevigatus Cuvier, 1829

D IX,14-15. A 14-15. C 15. P 18-21. V I,5. LL 85-90. Body elongate, only slightly depressed; caudal peduncle long. Head rather small, only slightly compressed. Mouth large; small, pointed teeth in broad bands in each jaw. Preopercle spines of moderate size, lower shorter than upper. Body and most of head, to eyes, covered with tiny ctenoid scales; lateral-line scales of similar size to adjacent ones. Swim bladder absent. Variable pale greenish with banding to very dark dusky all over. Juveniles strongly banded. Southern Australian waters from New South Wales to Geographe Bay, Western Australia, including Tasmania. Weed-covered reefs and in seagrass beds to 20 m. Unlike most flatheads, this species rarely buries in sand and sleeps under overhanging weeds. Attains 50 cm. Provisionally placed in this genus; may warrant its own.

VELVETFISHES
FAMILY APLOACTINIDAE

The velvetfishes are a highly diverse family, as the estimated 25 species assigned to about 17 genera show. Most are distributed in the tropical to temperate west Pacific. Velvetfishes are unusual looking fishes with prickly scales and large thick fins. The dorsal fin originates above or in front of the eyes; the first three to five rays are somewhat separate from the rest and elevated in adults. They are secretive species, well camouflaged, sometimes partly buried in the substrate, hiding under rocks or in sponges. Some species are rarely seen and known only from a few records, however some of these records come from widely separate areas, indicating a broad geographical range. With some species, adults are known from only two or three specimens, but larval specimens are regularly collected in plankton sampling, indicating the difficulty in finding or collecting adults. Only one species is commonly observed in southern waters. A second species, known from juvenile specimens in the

Aploactisoma milesii   Adult ▲ Juv. ▼

Sydney area, is included. Diet consists primarily of shrimps or similar crustaceans.

VELVETFISH
Aploactisoma milesii (Richardson, 1850)

D XIII-XV,12-16. A I,9-12. C 13. P 10-11. V 1,2. LL 10-14. Body rather slender, slightly compressed. Head, mouth of moderate size; small conical teeth in jaws. Blunt spines on preopercle margin; prominent ridges on opercle, each ending in blunt spine. Scales with outward pointing spines; all spines, including those on head, covered in thick skin, giving knob-like appearance. Dorsal fin originates just ahead of orbital, almost confluent with caudal fin, leaving small gap. Pectoral fin large, rounded; incised membranes in upper part. Highly variable from grey or creamy to dark purple-brown and red patches. Southern waters from Sydney to Shark Bay, including Tasmania. Common species in rocky estuaries, hiding under rocks or buried partly in sand among rocks. Shallow protected reefs to sponge reef in deeper parts of estuaries; 3-30m. Attains 20 cm. Monotypic genus endemic to Australian waters.

MOSSBACK VELVETFISH
Paraploactis trachyderma Bleeker, 1856

D XIII,10-11. A I,10-11. C 13-14. P 12-14. V I,2. LL 13. Body fairly deep just behind head, tapering to caudal peduncle, slightly compressed. Head large with steep profile; prominent spines on preopercle edge; opercle corner covered with thick skin. Scales with outward pointing spines, covered with skin. Lateral-line scales with leafy appendages. Dorsal fin originates on top of head, just behind vertical of posterior margin of eye; has short spines, first three somewhat separate from the rest. Pectoral fin large, broadly rounded. Variable in colour from very dark, dusky brown, with variable yellow to orange markings which are most elaborate in large specimens from sponge areas. East coast from central Queensland to Sydney. Mainly known from southern Queensland where occasionally trawled with prawns. Estuaries to offshore in 10-50 m. This genus comprises several tropical species endemic to Australian waters. Recorded from South Australia, but probably based on specimens in museum collections which are *Kanekonia queenslandica*.

Paraploactis trachyderma Adult ▼ Juv. ▲

PROWFISHES
FAMILY PATAECIDAE

A small family of unusual looking fishes comprising three monotypic genera and confined to southern Australian waters. They are compressed fishes with a high dorsal fin over the entire back that, without being attached, is confluent with the caudal fin. They lack ventral fins and instead of scales have a tough, sometimes lumpy skin. The outer layer of skin is regularly shed in a complete piece to get rid of epibiotic growth such as algae or bryazoas. These extremely well camouflaged fishes live in sponge areas of rocky reefs, among boulders or in crevices, including shallow estuaries with suitable habitats. Most specimens are known from trawls to about 80 m. Their diet consists primarily of shrimps and other crustaceans.

RED INDIANFISH
Pataecus fronto Richardson, 1844

D XXII-XXV,14-17. A IX-XI,4-7. C 10. P 8. Ventral fins absent. Body deep anteriorly, tapering to narrow caudal peduncle; very tall dorsal fin originates above steep forehead, extends to caudal fin. Head large; mouth oblique, prominent; band of minute teeth in each jaw. Pectoral fin large, positioned low on body, reaches anus. Head with oblique ridges, lacking sharp spines; skin smooth. Lateral line indistinct with 14 to 27 minute pores. Colour variable from brown to orange or red, sometimes with diffused dark blotches dorsally. Southern waters from southern Queensland to eastern Victoria and south-west Australia to Exmouth Gulf. Coastal and offshore reefs in 20-80 m. Not often seen by divers due to excellent camouflage; the few that have been observed were in areas with similar-coloured sponges. Attains 25 cm.

WARTY PROWFISH
Aetapcus maculatus (Günther, 1861)

D XVIII-XXII,12-13. A IV-IX,3-5. C 9. P 8. Ventral fins absent. Body deep anteriorly, tapering to narrow caudal peduncle; very tall dorsal fin originates above steep forehead, extends to caudal fin. Head large; mouth oblique, prominent; band of minute teeth in each jaw. Pectoral fin large, positioned low on body, reaches anus. Head with oblique ridges, lacking sharp spines; skin smooth, becoming lumpy in adults. Lateral line indistinct with eight to 20 minute pores. Variable from brown to orange or pale whitish to yellow, with dark blotches. South coast from Bass Strait and Tasmania to Shark Bay. Coastal reefs and rocky estuaries in shallow sponge crevices or among large boulders in kelp areas. Shallow to deep channels in estuaries and deeper in protected coastal bays; 3-30 m. Attains 22 cm.

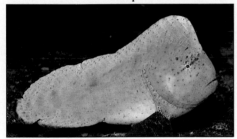

Aetapcus maculatus Juv.

WASPFISHES
FAMILY TETRAROGIDAE

A little-known family of small fishes, included in Scorpaenidae by many authors, comprising an estimated 15 genera with about 40 species that primarily occur in the tropical Indo-Pacific. Superficially they are similar to the velvetfishes and prowfishes, mainly because of the large and similarly positioned dorsal fin. Although small, some species only reaching about 40 mm in total length, they could be considered dangerous, with many possessing highly venomous spines. They are benthic fishes with tiny embedded scales on the body. The dorsal fins originate on top of the head and are confluent with the caudal fin; in some species these fins are partly joint. Many species are observed on dusk and seem most active at night, hiding during the day. They feed on small shrimps and other crustaceans, and some probably feed on other fishes.

Ablabys taenionotus Adult ▲ Juv. ▼

Only one species ranges south to the Sydney area and is included here, however other species could possibly expatriate into southern areas.

LEAF FISH
Ablabys taenionotus (Cuvier, 1829)

D XVII,8. A III,4 (last ray branched to base). C 13-14. P 12. V I,5. LL 27-29. Body fairly elongate, compressed. Head not large but as high as greatest body depth. Body with tiny embedded scales; lateral line prominent with tubed scales. Dorsal fin elongated over first few rays in large adults; following rays subequal, as long as caudal fin rays, following confluently with membrane connecting basally. Variably brownish, but usually distinctly white over forehead from dorsal fin down over orbital and mouth. Variable dark

scribbled lines or blotches in large adults. West Pacific from New South Wales to southern Japan, south to the Sydney area. Shallow estuaries and reef flats to about 20 m. As with many cryptic species, mostly observed on dusk when out to feed. In Sydney, most specimens were observed in late afternoon or on night dives in areas near the heads, in the open on sand in the vicinity of rocky reefs and seagrass beds. Specimens to about 10 cm found in Sydney Harbour, but known to reach 15 cm. Also known as Cockatoo Fish.

RED VELVETFISH
FAMILY GNATHANACANTHIDAE

This monotypic family is similar and closely related to the prowfishes, but possesses large ventral fins and has a deeply notched dorsal fin. The ends of the dorsal and anal fins and the inside of the ventral fins are connected to the body by a membrane. Scales are absent and the skin is covered with fleshy projections in adults. The skin is tough but highly flexible and continuous with the fins. Like the scorpionfishes, the spines in the dorsal fin are venomous. This unusual species is endemic to southern Australian waters. NOTE: although the last two rays in the dorsal and anal fin have a common base, they are counted as separate rays because the thick skin can hide this fact. Also, because of the thick skin, small spines are easily missed.

RED VELVETFISH
Gnathanacanthus goetzeei Bleeker, 1855

D XIII,9-10. A III,8-9. C 12. P 11. V I,5. Body fairly deep, very compressed. Head very large, almost half body size; preopercle ends high on body. Mouth large; jaws strong, band of minute teeth in each. Lateral line present with 15 to 23 small pores, high along sides. Dorsal fin originates above eyes, strongly arched over first seven spines; eighth spine very short, followed by rapidly and progressively lengthening spines and soft rays, which reverse trend at fourth soft ray, resulting in similarly shaped second part. Anal fin similar shape to and opposite second dorsal fin part. Pectoral fin large, rounded. Ventral fins large, reaching as far as anus, attached to belly along the inside by membrane as continuation of fin. Juvenile distinctly different from adult, changing at about 60 mm to brownish with less distinct spotting. Adults brown to red with motley pattern. Widespread along south coast from Wilson's Promontory and Tasmania to south Western Australia. Secretive; in kelp-covered reef in shallow coastal bays to at least 30 m. Although fairly common in some localities, rarely seen during the day. Feed at night on shrimps. Attains 30 cm.

Gnathanacanthus goetzeei   Adult ▼ Juv. ▲

FLYING GURNARDS
FAMILY DACTYLOPTERIDAE

The flying gurnards are a small family of benthic fishes comprising two genera and seven species which occur in tropical to warm-temperate seas. The monotypic *Dactylopterus* is restricted to the Atlantic and the six species of *Dactyloptena* are Indo-Pacific; four are recorded from Australia, but only one ranges to southern waters. They feature very large pectoral fins, almost forming a circle from head to tail when spread. They are used for display but also to scare off possible predators by suddenly spreading the fins to look much larger. Juveniles have additional large eye-like markings and with the fins spread the face image is a good bluff for defense. With the fins folded along side they are well camouflaged and rest on the bottom that way for most of the day. Most activities are on dusk; they hunt small fishes and crustaceans and can move surprisingly fast. When disturbed by a diver during the day they seem to have a "waking-up" period, or perhaps it is a bluffing technique. The fins are spread out and the fish begins to swim away relatively slowly. Suddenly, though, the pectoral fins are withdrawn along the sides and with a great burst of speed the fish is usually out of sight within a few seconds. Juveniles make interesting aquarium fishes, but their seemingly small mouth can eat a fair-sized fish, thus they should be kept with fishes of at least their own size.

FLYING GURNARD
Dactyloptena orientalis (Cuvier, 1829)

D IX,8. A 6-7. C 10. P 32-34. V I,4. LL 47. Head almost square with flattened sides, similar above and below, blunt, bony with long preopercle spine. Body elongate, tapering gradually from squarish head to caudal peduncle; covered with ctenoid scales. Dorsal fin in several parts; first spine long, separate, well ahead of next spine which is also separate, but short and positioned just in front of joint five-spined section. Small separate spine heads soft-rayed section. Front part of pectoral fin finger-like; used in conjunction with ventral fins to walk along substrate. This species is the most widespread and only common shallow-water species; ranges in the west Pacific from New South Wales to southern Japan and to east Africa. Estuaries and quiet coastal bays to deepwater sand flats and slopes. Recorded south to off Tathra; fairly common in Sydney Harbour on clean sand flats with sparse algae and rubble in 3-10 m, but trawled to 100 m. Attains 32 cm.

Dactyloptena orientalis   Adult ▼   Juv. ▲

GURNARDS
FAMILY TRIGLIDAE

The gurnards are a large family of benthic fishes comprising an estimated 13 genera and 120 species and found in all oceans. In Australia eight genera and 33 species are in collections. They are well represented in southern waters and eight species range to coastal waters. The body is covered with small ctenoid scales, or more or less embedded cycloid rudimentary ones, and the head is distinctly armoured with bony plates. The pectoral fin is large to very large and rounded, with the lower three rays free and thickened.

The pectoral fins are usually brilliantly coloured on the insides and are spread horizontally with the colours upwards for display or startling a possible predator. Small juveniles often have additional large false eyes on the fins. During the day the shallow-water species partly bury in the sand and are well camouflaged. They become very active on dusk, hunting small bottom-dwelling fishes, crustaceans and other substrate invertebrates. The enlarged lower pectoral fin rays are used for walking but also for probing the substrate for prey. On the mainland most species are restricted to deep water and only a few species can be observed by divers, but in Tasmania several species venture into divable depths; they are otherwise only known from trawls. A few of the larger species are of commercial importance, the largest reaching about 1 m. When handled, these fishes often produce grunting noises. Most of the species turn bright red when captured.

Eastern Spiny Gurnard (*Lepidotrigla pleuracanthica*)

RED GURNARD
Chelidonichthys kumu (Lesson, 1826)

D VIII-IX,15-16. A 14-15. C 11. P 14. V I,5. LL 62-65. Moderate-sized bony head with almost triangular profile; fairly smooth, with a few small retrorse spines along posterior margins. Eyes of moderate size; slighty depressed interorbital not elevated. Mouth moderately small, horizontal; band of granular teeth in each jaw. Body, except anterior ventral area, covered with tiny, embedded cycloid scales in approximately 110 to 120 diagonal rows. Lateral line with slightly enlarged spineless scales. Dorsal fin bases with enlarged scales in row of 22 to 23 thorn-like bucklers along sides. Dorsal fins separate; large pectoral and ventral fins reach to anal fin. Lower three pectoral rays thickened, free. Grey-brown to brownish-red above, pale below. Inside of pectoral fin greenish-grey with blue; black blotch in juveniles. Southern hemisphere, reported from Africa, New Zealand and probably South America; in Australia from southern Queensland to Shark Bay, and Tasmania. Similar species in Japan and China Sea. Adults usually deep, 80-200 m; juveniles enter shallow estuaries, occur on sand along coastal beaches. Attains 50 cm. Indo-Pacific genus with about seven species, one of which occurs in Australian waters.

Chelidonichthys kumu Juv.

LITTLE RED GURNARD
Lepidotrigla grandis Ogilby, 1910

D IX,15-16. A 15. C II. P 14. V I,5. LL 60-64. Head small but prominent, rectangular in cross-section. Eyes large, elevated on head; interorbital depressed. Mouth moderately small, horizontal; band of granular teeth in each jaw. Preopercle with serrated ridge, ending in low spine. Body, except anterior ventral area, covered with moderate-sized ctenoid scales. Lateral line with enlarged scales. Dorsal fin bases with row of enlarged scales, thorn-like bucklers, along each side. Pectoral fins moderate, reaching to below third dorsal ray; lower three rays thick, free. Reddish-brown above, pale below. Inside of pectoral fin greenish-grey with blue spots and margin, dark spot near base. East coast from Queensland to central New South Wales; slightly different form from north-western Australia. Usually deep offshore, but occasionally in coastal bays on sand near reefs in 10 m. Attains 18 cm. Large genus presently comprises about 40 species worldwide in tropical to warm-temperate seas. Further studies may recognise this group in other genera. About 18 species in Australian waters, six of which range to south-eastern areas.

DEEPWATER GURNARD
Lepidotrigla mulhalli Macleay, 1884

D IX,14-15. A 15. C 11. P 14. V I,5. LL 54-60. Head small but prominent, rectangular in cross-section. Eyes large, interorbital depressed; head profile steep, rounded; snout with strong projecting spines. Mouth moderately small, horizontal; band of granular teeth in each jaw. Preopercle with serrated ridge, ending in low spine. Body, except anterior ventral area, covered with small, firmly attached, ctenoid scales. Lateral line with slightly enlarged spineless scales. Dorsal fin bases with row of enlarged scales, thorn-like bucklers, along each side. Pectoral fins moderate, reaching to below second dorsal fin; lower three rays thick, free. Pink to red above, pale below. Inside of pectoral fin distinctly marked; diffused red blotch on first dorsal fin. South-eastern Australia from central New South Wales to Tasmania and western Bass Strait. Offshore on sand in 10-200 m; usually in deeper part of range. Attains 20 cm.

BUTTERFLY GURNARD
Lepidotrigla vanessa (Richardson, 1839)

D X-XI,16-17. A 16-17. C 11. P 14. V I,5. LL 64-69. Head small but prominent, rectangular in cross-section. Eyes large, interorbital depressed; head profile slightly concave on snout; snout with short projecting spines. Mouth moderately small, horizontal; band of granular teeth in each jaw. Preopercle with serrated ridge, ending in low spine. Body, except anterior ventral area, covered with small, firmly attached, ctenoid scales. Lateral line with slightly enlarged spineless scales. Dorsal fin bases with row of enlarged scales, thorn-like bucklers, along each side. Pectoral fins moderate, reaching to below second dorsal fin; lower three rays thick, free. Pale pink or reddish above with darker red blotches. Inside of pectoral fin distinctly marked; dark blotch on dorsal fin. Southern waters from central New South Wales, Tasmania to south Western Australia. Coastal to offshore sand flats to at least 100 m. Juveniles occasionally in estuaries in shallow sand flats. Attains 25 cm.

Lepidoptrigla vanessa　Day colouration ▲　Night colouration ▼

MINOR GURNARD
Lepidotrigla modesta Waite, 1899

D IX,15-16. A 16. C 11. P 14. V I,5. LL 58-62. Head small but prominent, rectangular in cross-section. Eyes large, interorbital depressed; head profile concave on snout; snout with short projecting spines. Mouth moderately small, horizontal; band of granular teeth in each jaw. Preopercle with serrated ridge, ending in low spine. Body, except anterior ventral area, covered with small, weakly attached, cycloid scales. Lateral line with enlarged scales, spineless, but with distinctly branched pores. Dorsal fin bases with row of enlarged scales, thorn-like bucklers, along each side. Pectoral fins moderate, reaching to below origin of second dorsal fin; lower three rays thick, free. Reddish above, pale below; inner surface of pectoral fin unusually marked with ash-grey, orange and blue. South-east coast from central New South Wales to Tasmania and western Bass Strait. Coastal to offshore sand flats in 20-200 m. Attains 20 cm.

Lepidotrigla modesta   Day colouration ▲   Night colouration ▼

Lepidotrigla pleuracanthica   Adult ▼   Juv. ▲

EASTERN SPINY GURNARD
Lepidotrigla pleuracanthica (Richardson, 1845)

D VIII-IX,14-15. A 14-15. C 11. P 14. V I,5. LL 60-64. Head small but prominent, rectangular in cross-section. Eyes large, interorbital depressed; head profile slightly concave on snout. Mouth moderately small, horizontal; band of granular teeth in each jaw. Preopercle with serrated ridge, ending in low spine. Body, except anterior ventral area, covered with small, firmly attached, ctenoid scales. Lateral line with greatly enlarged scales, each with several prominent spines. Dorsal fins with row of enlarged scales, thorn-like bucklers, along each side. Pectoral fins moderate, reaching to below second dorsal fin; lower three rays thick, free. Membranes between anterior dorsal fin spines incised from shorter to longer spine, from tip to next spine at height of shorter spine; membranes between inner rays of pectoral fins distinctly incised. Pink to red above; distinctly marked pectoral and first dorsal fins. East coast, from southern Queensland to southern New South Wales, probably extending to eastern Victoria. Shallow coastal reefs and estuaries to offshore to about 50 m. Attains 20 cm. Often confused with similar Southern Spiny Gurnard which differs in being not as red, having white instead of yellow below black dorsal fin spot, pale blue rather than dark blue pectoral fin margins, and membranes between spines of dorsal fin being continuous over tips instead of incised anteriorly.

SOUTHERN SPINY GURNARD
Lepidotrigla papilio (Cuvier, 1829)

D VIII-IX,13-15. A 13-15. C 11. P 14. V I,5. LL 54-60. Head small but prominent, rectangular in cross-section. Eyes large, interorbital depressed; head profile slightly concave on snout. Mouth moderately small, horizontal; band of granular teeth in each jaw. Preopercle with serrated ridge, ending in low spine. Body, except anterior ventral area, covered with small, firmly attached, ctenoid scales. Lateral line with greatly enlarged scales, each with several prominent spines. Dorsal fins with row of enlarged scales, thorn-like bucklers, along each side. Pectoral fins moderate, reaching to below second dorsal fin; lower three rays thick, free. Membranes between anterior dorsal fin spines continuous over tips of spines; membranes between inner rays of pectoral fins not distinctly incised. Greyish-brown with reddish mottling above, pale below. First dorsal fin with almost round white-edged black spot; juveniles with distinct ocellus on each pectoral fin, still evident in adolescents. South coast from Bass Strait, Tasmania to south Western Australia. Shallow coastal bays and estuaries to 50 m. Attains 20 cm.

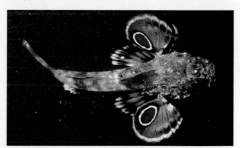

Lepidotrigla papilio   Adult ▼ Small juv. ▲

Photograph (below): Malcolm Wells

LATCHET
Pterygotrigla polyommata (Richardson, 1839)

D VII-VIII,12. A 12. C 11. P 15. V I,5. LL 63-70. Moderate-sized head rectangular in cross-section. Eyes large, interorbital sharply depressed; head profile slightly concave on snout. Mouth moderately small, horizontal; band of granular teeth in each jaw; prominent rostral spines. Opercle ends with long spine; preopercle with several long spines. Body, except anterior ventral area, covered with tiny, somewhat embedded, cycloid scales in approximately 110 to 120 diagonal rows. Lateral line has enlarged scales without spines. Dorsal fins with row of enlarged scales, bony bucklers, along each side. Pectoral fins large, reaching to below posterior part of second dorsal fin; lower three rays thick, free. Reddish above, silvery below, with some diffused reddish blotches. Pectoral fin distinctly marked with blue and yellow; large ocellus in juveniles. Southern waters from central New South Wales to Perth and Tasmania. Usually deep on muddy and sandy substrates in 35-200 m, but occasionally ventures into shallow estuaries in southern Tasmania. Attains 50 cm. Indo-Pacific genus comprising about six species, three of which occur in Australian waters, two in southern waters. *P. picta*, commonly trawled off New South Wales, restricted to deep water, the shallowest about 120 m, thus not included here.

113

SCORPIONFISHES
FAMILY SCORPAENIDAE

A family of spiny fishes, as the name suggests, and a complicated group with about 10 subfamilies, three of which are of importance here: Pteroinae, the lionfishes; Scorpaeninae, the rockcods, and; Sebastininae, the gurnard perches. The lionfishes are tropical fishes with very long dorsal spines and great pectoral fins which often reach past the anal fin. Some expatriate to southern waters, but few reach adult size south of the Sydney area. The rockcods are a diverse group comprising 12 genera, seven of which are included here. They are widely distributed in all but the coldest seas. They have spiny heads and are mostly substrate-hugging and very well camouflaged fishes. The gurnard perches are more perch-like in appearance, are less spinous on the head, and readily swim above the substrate in similar fashion to some of the serranids. The south coast species are mostly of medium size, 30 to 40 cm, and a few are small, reaching about 15 to 20 cm. All possess venomous spines, a sting producing extreme pain followed by numbness, but none of the southern species are known to have caused fatalities. If stung, the victim should immerse the wound in very hot water to kill the venom and instantly relieve the pain. Despite their appearance most species are excellent food fishes and some species are of commercial value on the south coast.

LIONFISH
Pterois volitans (Linnaeus, 1758)

D XIII,10-11. A III,6-7. P 14-16. V I,5. LL 27-30. LSR 90-120. Body covered with small cycloid scales. Lateral line with pored scales. Dorsal spines very long, usually much longer than greatest body depth. Pectoral fins with unbranched rays extended well beyond membranes; reach past anal fin. Tentacle above eye highly variable in length, shape; long in juveniles, usually broad; leaf-like in adults, but occasionally absent. Variable from reddish-brown to black bands; fins with variable sized spots or banding. Sometimes totally black in estuaries. Widespread tropical Indo-Pacific from broadly the west Pacific to east Africa and Red Sea; ranges into warm-temperate zones; adults are known as far south as Montague Island. Occurs from shallow estuaries to deep offshore reefs, often under jetties or in shipwrecks. In the Sydney area, the tiny 20 mm juveniles live in narrow crevices behind sea-urchins. Feeds primarily on fishes which it sometimes corners with spread pectoral fins. Attains 30 cm. This genus comprises seven species, two of which range into southern waters. Long fin rays and unbranched pectoral rays diagnostic characteristics. Also known as Devilfishes, Turkeyfishes or Firefishes.

Pterois volitans Adult ▼

Tiny juvenile ▲

SPOTFIN LIONFISH
Pterois antennata (Bloch, 1787)

D XII-XIII,11-12. A III,6. P 16-17. V I,5. LL 26. LSR 50-54. Body covered with small, mostly ctenoid scales. Lateral line with pored scales. Dorsal spines very long, usually much longer than greatest body depth. Pectoral fins with unbranched rays, extended well beyond membranes; reach past anal fin. Tentacle above eye usually long. Banding usually pale to dark brown with variable width; pectoral fin rays white to gold. Widespread tropical Indo-Pacific, broadly from west Pacific to east Africa, and south to the Sydney area. Coastal to offshore reefs from shallow reef flats to deep slopes in coral heads; to about 50 m. Sydney juveniles usually in pale sponges, fairly deep, 10-25 m. Attains 20 cm.

Pterois antennata Tiny juv.

ZEBRA LIONFISH
Dendrochirus zebra (Cuvier, 1829)

D XIII,10-11. A III,6-7. P 16-17. V I,5. LL 45-55. Body covered with small mostly ctenoid scales. Lateral line with pored scales. Dorsal spines very long; longest usually equal to or slightly longer than greatest body depth. Pectoral fins with unbranched rays extended well beyond membrane in young; become variably branched in adults, extended parts may be reduced to slight points. Tentacle above eye usually long. Slightly variable from pale to dark reddish-brown; fins pale to brown with white spots; large dark to bluish spot inside pectoral fin near base. Widespread tropical Indo-Pacific from central Pacific to east Africa and Red Sea, southern Japan and southern New South Wales. Coastal reefs and lagoons, in large coral heads; shallow to fairly deep water, about 60 m. Small juveniles in the Sydney area settle among boulder reefs in large estuaries near ocean. Attains 20 cm. This genus comprises about six species; differs only slightly from *Pterois* in having shorter rays and divided pectoral fin rays in adults. Juveniles can not be separated using these characters.

Dendrochirus zebra Tiny juv.

DWARF LIONFISH
Dendrochirus brachypterus (Cuvier, 1829)

D XIII,9-10. A III,5-6. P 17-18. V I,5. LL 40-45. Body covered with small mostly ctenoid scales. Lateral line with pored scales. Dorsal spines long; longest usually equal to or slightly shorter than greatest body depth. Pectoral fins with branched rays, only slightly extended beyond membrane in young. Tentacle above eye usually short; small leafy appendages on head, often dorsally on body and along lateral line. Banding variable from very distinct to none at all. Pectoral fins usually with distinct spotted bands. Extremely variable from red to brown or dark purplish-brown. Widespread tropical Indo-Pacific, broadly in the west Pacific from southern New South Wales to southern Japan, and to east Africa and Red Sea. Coastal reefs and estuaries, often in silty environments. Most common in Sydney Harbour and Botany Bay, in sponge areas in 15-20 m. Small juveniles settle on outcrops on sand or in crevices with sea-urchins in shallow rocky reefs. Attains 15 cm; usually about 12 cm.

D. brachypterus   Adult ▼   Tiny juvs. ▲

PAPER FISH
Taenionotus triacanthus Lacepède, 1802

D XII,10-11. A III,5-6. P 14-15. V I,5. Body covered with small prickly scales; lateral line indistinct. Body very depressed; large sailfin-like dorsal fin attached by short membrane to caudal fin. Bearded with small leafy appendages, sometimes along lateral line. Extremely variable in colour, matching sponges, algae; from white, green, brown, red, various spotting. Settling juveniles about 20 mm long, semi-transparent, smooth skin. Widespread tropical Indo-Pacific throughout most of the Pacific to east Africa and Red Sea. Although common in many areas, so well camouflaged that many discoveries accidental. Juveniles in Sydney have been found in various habitats in quiet coastal bays and Sydney Harbour near the heads, in 3-10 m. On coral reefs, usually on shallow reef crests and slopes with sparse vegetation or sponges; recorded from trawls to 135 m. Attains 10 cm. Monotypic genus with interesting behaviour in common with temperate scorpaenoid fishes, Patacidae, which rock sideways as pushed by swell.

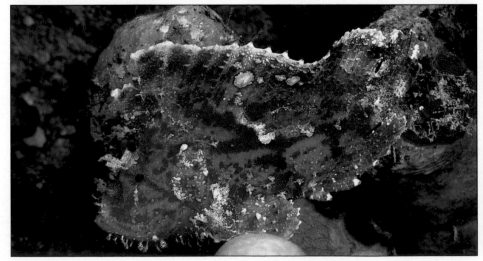

T. triacanthus   Juv. ▼   Newly settled juv. ▲

GOBLINFISH
Glyptauchen panduratus (Richardson, 1850)

D XVI-XVIII,6-7. A III,5-6. P 13-15. V I,5. C 12. LL 27-29. Body covered with tiny scales; head naked, lateral line distinct. Acute spines on head, below eye and preopercle margin. Dorsal fin very large; consists of long spinous section followed by short, elevated soft-rayed section. Adults with deeply and broadly excavated nape. Large, broad, long pectoral fins reach almost to posteriorly positioned anal fin. Variable in colour; able to change quickly to match environment but mainly black and white. Widespread south coast, from Sydney to Perth and Tasmania. Coastal reefs and rocky estuaries, under rock slabs, in crevices, shallow to at least 60 m. Feeds on crustaceans. Attains 20 cm. Monotypic genus closely related to *Gymnapistes*; previously thought to be related to stonefishes because of unusually shaped head. Endemic to Australia.

Glyptauchen panduratus   Adult ▲   Close-up of head ▼

COBBLER
Gymnapistes marmoratus (Cuvier, 1829)

D XII-XIII,8-9. A III,5-6. C 12. P 11-12. V I,5. LL 23-31. Body and head without scales, except for lateral line. Dorsal fin with incised membranes from tip backwards; originates above posterior margin of preopercle. Large retrorse spine on each side of snout below eye; can be moved sideways, locked in position. Slight differences in juvenile to adult with blotches becoming diffused in adults. South coast from Sydney to Perth, including Tasmania. Mainly estuarine, sometime aggregating in large schools of several hundred individuals, possibly for spawning or migration to spawning grounds. Juveniles among seagrasses. Mostly active at night; hides in weeds during day. Feeds on shrimps and other crustaceans. Attains 22 cm. Monotypic Australian endemic genus; easily confused with Fortesque, however latter has scales. Also called Soldierfish.

Gymnapistes marmoratus ▼

Gymnapistes marmoratus   Juv.

FORTESQUE
Centropogon australis (White, 1790)

D XVI,8-9. A III,5-6. C 12. P 14-15. V I,5. LL 25-28. LSR 50 (approximately). Body covered with small embedded ctenoid scales. Lateral line distinct, smoothly curved, following contour of back. Large horizontal spine below eye, extending well over preopercle margin; several more along margin below. Dorsal fin has long pungent spines originating near posterior edge of orbital. Pectoral fin large, reaching halfway along body. Colour dusky grey-brown to white with dark, near-black blotches; juveniles motley. East coast, southern Queensland to eastern Victoria. Estuaries, sheltered bays. Often in large aggregations in harbours in silty or muddy environments along rocky reefs on rubble in deeper parts of tidal channels; to 30 m. Small juveniles in tide pools, sandbank channels. Attains 14 cm. This genus comprises two species, one restricted to the west coast and not included here. *C. marmoratus* Günther, 1862, a synonym.

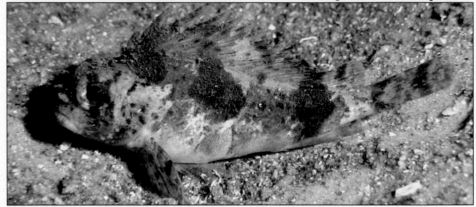

C. australis Normal colouration ▲ Colour variation, sometimes regarded as different species ▼

LITTLE SCORPIONFISH
Maxillicosta scabriceps Whitley, 1935

D XIII,6-8. A III,5. C 10-12. P 21-24. V I,5. LL 28-33. LSR 40-45. Body covered with small ctenoid scales which extend onto most of head. Upper ridges of eyes with well-developed, separate spines. Interorbital deep.

Dorsal fin with tall, strongly arched spinous section; deep notch almost separates soft-rayed section. Pectoral fin large, reaching to anal fin. Pale sandy with variable dark markings forming indistinct saddles. South coast from Western Port to Exmouth Gulf. Shallow coastal bays and estuaries. Buries in sand during day with only eyes exposed. Usually in sparse seagrass beds or in vicinity of weedy rocks from 2-40 m. Attains 12 cm. South Pacific genus comprising five species, three of which are found in Australian waters; two range to south-eastern areas.

WHITLEY'S SCORPIONFISH
Maxillicosta whitleyi Eschmeyer and Poss, 1976

D XIII,7. A III,5. C 10-12. P 21-23. V I,5. LL 28-33. LSR 40-45. Body covered with small ctenoid scales which extend onto most of head. Upper ridges of eyes with poorly developed, separate spines. Interorbital shallow. Dorsal fin with tall, strongly arched spinous section; deep notch almost separates soft-rayed section. Pectoral fin large, reaching to anal fin. Pale sandy with variable dusky-brown markings forming indistinct saddles; white below. South coast from southern Queensland to the eastern end of the Great Australian Bight. Coastal offshore and deep sand-channels in estuaries, in 20-140 m. Usually on sand slopes in small aggregations; buried during day, sits on sand at night. Attains 10 cm.

Maxillicosta scabriceps ▲

Maxillicosta whitleyi ▼

PYGMY ROCKCOD
Scorpaenodes scaber Ramsay and Ogilby, 1885

D XIII,9. A III,5. C 14. P 17-19. V I,5. LSR 25-27 (diagonal rows, about 45 irregular vertical rows). Body covered with small ctenoid scales which extend to opercle, preopercle, cheek; tiny scales on fin bases. Lateral line almost straight, distinct with spaced pores. Series of retrorse spine dorsally on head; small leaf-like appendages in series dorsally and along outside of mouth. Dorsal fin with evenly arched spinous section. Pectoral fin large, reaching to anus. Variable brownish-red or pink to bright red with darker blotching. East coast from southern Queensland to southern New South Wales, probably to eastern Victoria, Lord Howe Island and northern New Zealand. Estuary reefs to offshore reef habitats. Usually in caves, often upside down on ceilings of large overhangs, from 3 m to at least 30 m. Attains 12 cm. Large genus with undetermined number of species throughout tropical Indo-Pacific. Many very similar species; this species commonly confused with *S. littoralis* from northern Pacific. Similar species found in Western Australia, Easter Island area, southern Africa, all seemingly belonging in the "scaber complex".

Scorpaenodes scaber ▲

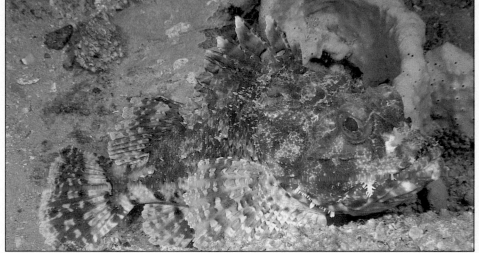

Scorpaena cardinalis ▼

RED ROCKCOD
Scorpaena cardinalis Richardson, 1842

D XII,9-10. A III,5. C 13. P 16-17. V I,5. LL 23-25. LSR 48-55. Body covered with small, slightly ctenoid scales which become cycloid towards thorax; thorax has some embedded scales, is naked anteriorly. Small spines dorsally on head and along horizontal ridge below eye; larger spines on posterior margin of preopercle. Head large, becoming bulbous in very large specimens. Dorsal fin with arched spinous section, deeply notched just ahead of soft-rayed section. Pectoral fin large, broadly rounded. Extremely variable from dull grey-brown to bright red, with or without black blotch on outer margin of spinous section of dorsal fin between sixth and tenth spines. Medium-sized black spots on belly and thorax usually identify this species. Widespread along east coast from southern Queensland to eastern Victoria; abundant in southern New South Wales, and also in New Zealand. Shallow estuaries to deep offshore on rocky reefs. Large genus as presently defined; widely distributed in tropical to temperate waters. Attains 40 cm. Highly diverse; some species may be assigned to genera pending further studies. Many similar species in south Pacific with close relatives in northern Pacific, including some 30 species assigned to *Scorpaenopsis*, three of which are included here.

COOK'S ROCKCOD
Scorpaena cookii Günther, 1875

D XII,9-10. A III,5. C 13. P 17-18. V I,5. LSR 65-70. Body covered with small, slightly ctenoid scales which become cycloid towards thorax, becoming embedded anteriorly. Small spines dorsally on head and along horizontal ridge below eye; larger spines on posterior margin of preopercle. Head large, becoming bulbous in very large specimens. Dorsal fin with arched spinous section, deeply notched just ahead of soft-rayed section. Pectoral fin large, broadly rounded. Extremely variable from dull grey-brown to reddish-brown; usually has numerous small black spots all over. Mainly known from Lord Howe Island, Kermadec Islands and New Zealand; rare in New South Wales. Shallow lagoons to at least 50 m. Offshore reefs in New South Wales, usually fairly deep. Attains 60 cm.

SOUTHERN ROCKCOD
Scorpaena papillosa (Bloch and Schneider, 1801)

D XII,9-10. A III,5. C 13. P 15-16. V I,5. LL 23. LSR 43-47. Body covered with small, slightly ctenoid scales which become cycloid towards thorax. Moderate-sized spines dorsally on head and along horizontal ridge below eye; larger spines on posterior margin of preopercle. Dorsal fin has arched spinous section; deeply notched just ahead of soft-rayed section. Pectoral fin large, broadly rounded. Extremely variable from dull purplish-brown to bright red; with or without black blotch on outer margin of spinous section of dorsal fin between seventh and ninth spines. Widespread in southern waters, from Sydney to south Western Australia, including Tasmania, and in New Zealand. Shallow estuaries from muddy environments to offshore reefs in kelp reef. Sometimes buries in mud; in 3-50 m. Attains 30 cm.

Scorpaena papillosa Adult ▼ Juv. ▲

Neosebastes scorpaenoides ▼

RUDDY GURNARD PERCH
Neosebastes scorpaenoides Guichenot, 1867

D XIII,8. A III,5. C 15. P 20. V I,5. LL 42. LSR 76. Small ctenoid scales cover body, head, except very narrow strip dorsally on head and at base of dorsal fin. Lateral line has short curve at origin, then straight to caudal fin. Head with small spines; most distinct five spines on each preopercle. Anterior dorsal fin spines long; fin deeply notched just ahead of short-based soft-rayed section. Pectoral fins large, reaching to anal fin. Body shapes, fin sizes change gradually with age; large specimens have proportionally smaller fins, larger head with steep front. Highly variable from very pale with little blotching to reddish with dark saddle-like markings. South coast from southern New South Wales to South Australia and Tasmania. Most common in the Bass Strait area from shallow estuaries to deep offshore reefs, to about 140 m. Rocky reefs, particularly sponge areas, on sandy patches. Attains 40 cm. Only representative of genus in shallow south-eastern waters; the six other species occur in other areas or very deep, only known from trawls.

Helicolenus percoides ▼

SEA PERCH
Helicolenus percoides (Richardson, 1842)

D XII,12-13. A III,5. C 13. P 18-20. V I,5. LL 28-30. LSR 58-65. Small ctenoid scales cover body, most of head. Lateral line straight except for small curve at origin. Several sharp spines on posterior margins of preopercle, upper opercle; a series of small spines dorsally on head. Eyes rather large, not elevated above head profile. Spinous section of dorsal fin deeply incised; third spine longest followed by progressively and gradually shorter spines, to slight notch ahead of soft-rayed section. Variable from brown to bright red, depending on depth. Eastern Australia, probably restricted to southern New South Wales to southern Tasmania, and New Zealand. Usually deep rocky reefs, 30-800 m. Attains 45 cm. Commercially important species trawled off New South Wales and Tasmania; rarely seen by divers.

RED GURNARD PERCH
Helicolenus alporti (Castelnau, 1873)

D XII,11-12. A III,5. C 13. P 18-20. V I,5. LL 27-30 LSR 58-65. Small ctenoid scales cover body, most of head. Lateral line straight except for small curve at origin. Several sharp spines on posterior margins of preopercle, upper opercle; a series of small spines dorsally on head. Eyes rather large, not elevated above head profile. Spinous section of dorsal fin deeply incised; third spine longest, followed by progressively shorter spines to deep notch ahead of soft-rayed section. Variable from brown to bright red, depending on depth. Eastern Australia, probably restricted to area from southern New South Wales to southern Tasmania. Usually deep rocky reefs, however recorded in Tasmania as shallow as 10 m. Attains 40 cm. Large genus globally represented in tropical deep and cool-temperate seas. Several similar species in our waters need to be studied, two of which are included here.

FALSE KELPFISH
Sebastiscus marmoratus (Cuvier, 1829)

D XII,10-12. A III,5. C 13. P 17-19. V I,5. LL 49-54. Small ctenoid scales cover body, most of head. Lateral line straight except for small angle at caudal peduncle. Several sharp spines on posterior margins of preopercle, upper opercle; a series of small spines dorsally on head. Eyes rather large, not elevated above head profile. Spinous section of dorsal fin slightly incised; third spine longest, followed by progressively and gradually shorter spines to slight notch ahead of soft-rayed section. Variable from brown to bright red, depending on depth. Eastern Australia, but only known from Sydney Harbour, and southern Japan to the Philippines. Attains 30 cm. Genus mainly known from the northern Pacific. Australian specimens possibly introduced from ships, however this species looks remarkably similar to common kelpfishes (*Chironemus spp*) and could go unnoticed by divers.

PERCH-LIKES
ORDER PERCIFORMES

Represented by about 150 families, 71 of which have species in southern coastal waters. Because of the large number of similar families, a single key to the entire order becomes increasingly unusable. Instead, readily separable families with diagnostic characteristics are listed first, then groups keyed. For quick identification check in the following order.

1.	Pair of prominent barbels on chin .... MULLIDAE (p. 200)
2.	Ventral fins with an inner and outer spine .... SIGANIDAE (p. 376)
3.	Broad sucking disc on top of head .... ECHENEIDAE (p. 168)
4.	One or more lateral spines on caudal peduncle .... ACANTHURIDAE (p. 369)
5.	Single tall dorsal fin above pectoral fins .... PEMPHERIDIDAE (p. 206)
6.	Two very tall dorsal fins .... ENOPLOSIDAE (p. 248)
7.	Series of finlets behind dorsal and anal fins .... SCOMBRIDAE (p. 376)

KEY 19: *Single Characteristics*

SINGLE CHARACTERISTICS
See Key 19.

1.	Widely separate short-based dorsal fins; teeth minute or absent .... MUGILIDAE (p. 262)
2.	Widely separate short-based dorsal fins; teeth large, sharp .... SPHYRAENIDAE (p. 264)
3.	Body eel-like; median fins continuous, reddish .... CEPOLIDAE (p. 312)
	Same, but with broad longitudinal stripes .... CLINIDAE (p. 325)

KEY 20: *Combined Characteristics*

COMBINED CHARACTERISTICS
See Key 20.

1-3.	Smallish, elongated reef and sand species.
4.	Compressed, rounded to deeply oval reef species.
5.	Perch-like species; moderately compressed, elongate-oval.
6.	Slender to moderately elongate reef species.
7.	Pelagic species; streamlined, usually shiny and silvery.

KEY 21: *Groups*

GROUPS
See Key 21.

1.	Ventral fins separate, not connected by membrane; second dorsal fin base shorter than caudal peduncle .... ELEOTRIDAE (p. 367)
	Ventral fins usually united, fully or at bases by membrane; if not, second dorsal fin base longer than caudal peduncle 2
2.	Eyes laterally placed, not raised .... MICRODESMIDAE (p. 363)
	Eyes dorsally placed, usually raised .... GOBIIDAE (p. 344)

KEY 22: *Group 1*

GROUP 1
Small goby-like fishes; elongate, without lateral line; sandy or weedy coloured; sand and reef-dwelling; scales present; fin spines flexible; head bluntly rounded; two dorsal fins; ventral fins separate or united to form cup-like disc. See Key 22.

GROUP 2

Small blenny-like fishes; moderately elongate to very elongate, usually with lateral line; camouflaged, weedy or distinctly coloured; ventral fins usually slender with a few finger-like rays, and clearly in front of pectoral fins; slimy, naked with small embedded scales, or scaled; pectoral fins often large with lower rays thickened. See Key 23.

GROUP 3

Sand-dwelling species; usually sandy-coloured; eyes dorsally placed, often very small; body elongate to very elongate, either depressed or compressed. See Key 24.

1. Scales absent; dorsal fin mostly soft-rayed 2

   Scales present; dorsal fin mostly spinous 3

2. Head triangular; large spine at opercle edge ....BOVICHTIDAE (p. 321)

   Head pointed; large hooked spine at propercle ..........CALLIONYMIDAE (p. 341)

   Head rounded; no large spine on sides of head ....BLENNIIDAE (p. 335)

3. Dorsal fin usually clearly in three parts .....................TRIPTERYGIIDAE (p. 322)

   Dorsal fin usually continuous, often elevated

       anteriorly and divided between third and

       fourth spine ....CLINIDAE (p. 325)

KEY 23: *Group 2*

1. Mouth vertically across very large head; upward-

       facing eyes well spaced ....URANOSCOPIDAE (p. 320)

   Mouth not vertical; head not particularly large;

       eyes close together 2

2. Dorsal fin without spines 3

   Dorsal fin spines present 4

3. Snout rounded; lips densely fringed ...........................LEPTOSCOPIDAE (p. 318)

   Snout pointed; lips plain ....CREEDIIDAE (p. 317)

4. Dorsal fin spinous to about centre .........................OPISTOGNATHIDAE (p. 313)

   Spinous part of dorsal fin short 5

5. Anal fin headed by two spines ....BOVICHTIDAE (p. 321)

   Anal fin without spines 6

6. Dorsal fins continuous or just divided ..........................PINGUIPEDIDAE (p. 314)

   Dorsal fins clearly separate 7

7. Large hooked spine at preopercle ...............................CALLIONYMIDAE (p. 341)

   No large spine at preopercle ....PERCOPHIDAE (p. 316)

KEY 24: *Group 3*

Sergeant Baker (*Aulopus purpurissatus*), family Aulopidae, and Australian Mados (*Atypichthys strigatus*), family Microcanthidae

GROUP 4

Colourful reef species; body compressed and round to deeply oval shaped. See Key 25.

1. Anal fin headed by two spines ..................................POMACENTRIDAE (p. 231)
   Anal fin headed by three spines 2
   Anal fin headed by four spines ................................SCATOPHAGIDAE (p. 216)

2. Dorsal fin in two tall parts (except in tiny specimens) .....ENOPLOSIDAE (p. 248)
   Dorsal fin continuous 3

3. Caudal peduncle with one or more lateral spines ........ACANTHURIDAE (p. 369)
   Caudal peduncle without spines 4

4. Head encased with bony plates ..............................PENTACEROTIDAE (p. 249)
   Head not as above, usually scaly 5

5. Ventral fins absent or minute ................................MONODACTYLIDAE (p. 208)
   Ventral fins present, normally developed 6

6. Dorsal, anal and ventral fins tall and long ....EPHIPPIDAE (p. 251)
   Dorsal, anal and ventral fins not all tall and long 7

7. Dorsal fin with extremely long ribbon-like filament;
      caudal fin lunate ....ZANCLIDAE (p. 375)
   Dorsal fin without extremely long filament or,
      if present, caudal fin truncate or rounded 8

8. Opercle with prominent spine at angle .....................POMACANTHIDAE (p. 227)
   Opercle without prominent spine at angle..9

9. Ventral fins placed below pectoral fin bases ..........CHAETODONTIDAE (p. 217)
   Ventral fins placed posteriorly to below pectoral
      fin bases ....MICROCANTHIDAE (p. 214)

KEY 25: *Group 4*

Species *Dascyllus aruanus*, *trimaculatus* and *reticulatus* (family Pomacentridae) often mix; *reticulatus* only ranges to the Solitary Islands.

GROUP 5

Perch-like species; body moderately compressed, elongate-oval shaped; one or two dorsal fins, continuous to deeply notched, first part spinous, second soft-rayed, similar base length; small to large. See Key 26.

1. Anal fin headed by one spine .... DINOLESTIDAE (p. 162)
   Anal fin headed by two spines 2
   Anal fin headed by three spines 3
2. Second dorsal fin similar to anal fin, base short .... APOGONIDAE (p. 152)
   Second dorsal fin unlike anal fin, base long .... SCIAENIDAE (p. 199)
3. Opercle horizontal ridge ends in spine .... POLYPRIONIDAE (p. 143)
   Opercle ends in two sharp spines .... TERAPONTIDAE (p. 147)
   Opercle with two flat spines 4
   Opercle with three flat spines .... SERRANIDAE (p. 127)
   Opercle without horizontal ridge or flat spines 7
4. Lateral line runs near dorsal fin base .... CALLANTHIIDAE
   Lateral line runs well below dorsal fin base 5
5. Dorsal fin with shallow notch .... KUHLIIDAE (p. 148)
   Dorsal fin divided or notched to base 6
6. Caudal fin forked .... CHANDIDAE (p. 149)
   Caudal fin rounded .... SERRANIDAE (GRAMMISTINAE) (p. 127)
7. Lateral line in two distinct sections .... PLESIOPIDAE (p. 144)
   Lateral line complete 8
8. Pectoral fins rounded or pointed in centre 9
   Pectoral fins with pointed upper corner 14
9. Pectoral fins small, without extended rays 10
   Pectoral fins fairly large, usually extended lower
      rays 12
10. Anal fin base shorter than longest soft ray .... APLODACTYLIDAE (p. 256)
    Anal fin base longer than longest spine 11
11. Caudal fin rounded .... LOBOTIDAE (p. 191)
    Caudal fin forked .... LATRIDIDAE (p. 261)
12. Ventral fins reach past pectoral fins .... CHIRONEMIDAE (p. 254)
    Pectoral fins reach past ventral fins 13
13. Dorsal fin spines with tufts .... CIRRHITIDAE (p. 252)
    Dorsal fin spines without tufts .... CHEILODACTYLIDAE (p. 257)
14. Scales cycloid, weakly attached .... GERREIDAE (p. 194)
    Scales weakly to coarsely ctenoid, firmly attached 15
15. Caudal fin truncate to rounded 16
    Caudal fin forked 17
16. Second anal fin spine enlarged in adults; caudal
       fin strongly rounded in juveniles .... HAEMULIDAE (p. 188)
    Second anal fin spine not enlarged; caudal fin
       marginally rounded in juveniles .... LUTJANIDAE (p. 182)
17. Head profile steep, snout short .... SPARIDAE (p. 192)
    Head profile moderately steep, snout long .... LETHRINIDAE (p. 197)
    Head profile not steep 18
18. Lateral line curving, high along sides .... NEMIPTERIDAE (p. 195)
    Lateral line about straight, just above body midline .... CAESIONIDAE (p. 187)

KEY 26: *Group 5*

GROUP 6

Plain and coloured reef species: slender to elongated. See Key 27.

1.	Dorsal fin in two parts of similar height 2
	Dorsal fins continous, spinous and soft-rayed parts joined 5
2.	Anal fin headed by one spine; two long barbels on chin ....MULLIDAE (p. 200)
	Anal fin headed by two or three spines; no barbels on chin 3
3.	Head rounded; lateral line absent; teeth minute ....MUGILIDAE (p. 262)
	Head pointed; lateral line present; teeth prominent 4
4.	Dorsal fins widely separate; teeth large ........................SPHYRAENIDAE (p. 264)
	Dorsal fins close together; teeth small ........................SILLAGINIDAE (p. 163)
5.	Anal fin headed by two spines 6
	Anal fin headed by three spines 7
6.	Body very elongate ........................MALACANTHIDAE (p. 165)
	Body not very elongate ........................POMACENTRIDAE (p. 231)
7.	Jaws with bands or one row of small incisiform teeth 8
	Jaws with conical, molariform teeth, or fused, beak-like 10
8.	Body deep, greatly compressed; caudal fin deeply forked ....SCORPIDIDAE (p. 209)
	Body very oblong, thick, caudal fin shallowly forked 9
9.	Jaws with single row of incisiform teeth ....KYPHOSIDAE (p. 210)
	Jaws with several rows of tricuspid teeth ....GIRELLIDAE (p. 213)
10.	Jaws with individual conical or molariform teeth ....LABRIDAE (p. 266)
	Jaws with fused teeth 11
11.	Teeth mostly fused, but with recognisable tips ....ODACIDAE (p. 304)
	Teeth completely fused, no recognisable tips ....SCARIDAE (p. 309)

KEY 27: *Group 6*

GROUP 7

Pelagic species; streamlined; usually shiny and silvery, bluish or greenish, shaded above to pale below. See Key 28.

1.	Long series of finlets following dorsal and anal fins; several lateral keels on caudal peduncle ....SCOMBRIDAE (p. 376)
	Without the above 2
2.	Scales minute, cycloid, often difficult to see 3
	Scales small to moderate-sized, distinct 5
3.	Head broad, depressed; caudal fin truncate to lunate 4
	Head not broad, depressed; caudal fin forked ....CARANGIDAE (p. 170)
4.	Head with large sucker disc above ........................ECHENEIDIDAE (p. 168)
	Head without sucker disc ........................RACHYCENTRIDAE (p. 169)
5.	Anal fin base short, below posterior half of second dorsal fin ....ARRIPIDIDAE (p. 180)
	Anal fin base about as long as second dorsal fin base 6
6.	Dorsal fin continuous ........................CENTROLOPHIDAE (p. 378)
	Dorsal fin divided in two parts 7
7.	Ventral fins attached by membrane to belly ....NOMEIDAE (p. 380)
	Ventral fins free ....POMATOMIDAE (p. 167)

KEY 28: *Group 7*

ROCKCODS AND SEAPERCHES
FAMILY SERRANIDAE

The Serranidae is a highly diverse family as presently defined, with several major groups, some of which will probably be raised to family status. In all there are nearly 50 genera and well over 400 species distributed worldwide. Thirty-six species are presented here, including tropical expatriates which range to south-eastern waters. They are assigned here to various subfamilies: Epinephelinae, comprising *Epinephelus, Cephalopholis, Variola, Chromileptis*; Centrogenysinae, comprising *Trachypoma, Acanthistius*; Hypoplectrodinae, comprising *Hypoplectrodes, Othos*; Anthiinae, comprising *Caprodon, Caesioperca, Pseudanthias*; Grammistinae with *Aulocephalus*, and; Diploprioninae with *Diploprion*. Even within these groups there are diverse assemblages of fishes, varying in size, shape and behaviour. The Epinephelinae are the large rockcods, gropers or coral-trouts, which have tiny scales, an indistinct lateral line, 24 vertebrae and a rounded or emarginate caudal fin (except in *Variola*, in which it is lunate). Most of the larger species are of commercial importance, reaching 1 to 2 m. Being home-ranging on reefs, some are vulnerable to spearfishing, causing the decline of species in certain areas. The similar Centrogenysinae feature more dorsal fin spines, a short-based elevated soft-rayed section, subequal jaws, distinct lateral line, and usually a very large second anal fin spine. The Hypoplectrodinae are coarsely scaled and have a long soft-rayed section in the dorsal fin, its base about equal to the base of the spinous portion. The dorsal fin is distinctly notched at the last spine. The eyes are large and bulging, and placed high on head. The Anthiinae comprises two groups, the small tropical species and the larger temperate or deepwater forms. They feature small to moderate-sized ctenoid scales, and large eyes placed laterally and anteriorly on the head. The dorsal fin has subequal rays over almost its entire length, often with certain rays elongated in males of the smaller species. The caudal fin is deeply emarginate to greatly lunate. Males are often brightly coloured and entirely different from females. The Grammistinae and Diploprioninae have a slimy skin which contains a toxin. All serranids are carnivorous; the Athiinae usually feed in schools in open water on zooplankton, and others are benthic feeders, taking various invertebrates and other fishes. Some of the reef dwellers are secretive or nocturnal and live deep in caves.

STRAWBERRY COD
Trachypoma macracanthus Günther, 1859

D XII,13-14. A III,6. P 16-17. V I,5. LL 48-50. LSR 90-97. Small scales cover body and head, except maxilla and mandible. Distinct lateral line, smoothly curved, follows contour of back. Eye very large, placed high on head. Anterior nostril with frilled tentacle. Mouth large, reaching to below middle of eye; band of villiform in each jaw, on vomer and palatines. Opercle with three strong spines, angular flap. Posterior margin of preopercle serrate with three to four strong antrorse spines below. Dorsal fin with long-based spinous section, notched over last few spines. Anal fin short-based with very long second spine; originates below last dorsal fin spines. Caudal and pectoral fins rounded. Brownish-orange to red, sometimes with irregular blotched pattern; tiny white spots all over. New South Wales and the Lord Howe Island, Norfolk Island regions to northern New Zealand, and Kermadec Islands. Rocky estuaries to clear coastal waters in shallow protected waters to about 20 m. Usually in boulder reefs, perched in similar fashion to scorpaenid fishes, or in caves. Attains 40 cm. Monotypic genus. Also known as Pacific Perch, and in New Zealand as Toadstool Grouper.

Trachypoma macracanthus Adult ▼ Juv. ▲

EASTERN WIRRAH
Acanthistius ocellatus (Günther, 1859)

D XIII,15-16. A III,8-9. P 19-21. V I,5. LL 58-67. LSR 90-110. Small scales cover body and head, except snout and preorbital. Lateral line smoothly curved, follows contour of back. Eye large in juveniles, becoming proportionally smaller in larger fish, placed high on head. Mouth large reaching to below posterior edge of eyes; band of filiform teeth in each jaw (outer row enlarged with conical teeth), on vomer and palatines. Opercle with three strong spines; middle spine long, close to lower small spine. Dorsal fin notched over last few spines. Anal fin similar to and opposite soft-rayed section of dorsal fin; second spine largest. Pectoral fin rounded; caudal fin with rounded corners. Dusky yellow to greenish; small dark spots, usually blue-centred, over body, head and onto fins. Juveniles with indistinct banding, spots proportionally larger. East coast from southern Queensland to northern Tasmania and eastern Bass Strait, and Lord Howe Island. Wide-ranging habitats, from shallow rocky estuaries to offshore to at least 100 m. Juveniles often in tide pools. Adults mainly in caves. Attains 45 cm. This genus widespread in southern hemisphere with about eight species, mostly in temperate waters; five species known from Australian waters. Included here are two east coast species; two of the others restricted to the west coast. Superficially very similar to *Epinephelus* but readily separated in having XIII versus XI dorsal spines and round pupil as opposed to egg-shaped.

STRIATED WIRRAH
Acanthistius paxtoni Hutchins and Kuiter, 1982

D XIII,15. A III,8. P 18-19. V I,5. LL 51-53. LSR 110-115. Small scales cover body and head, except snout and preorbital. Lateral line smoothly curved, follows contour of back. Eyes moderately large, placed high on head. Mouth large, reaching to below posterior edge of eyes; band of filiform teeth in each jaw (outer row enlarged with conical teeth), on vomer and palatines. Opercle with three strong spines; middle spine long, closest to small lower one. Dorsal fin notched over last few spines. Anal fin similar to and opposite soft-rayed section of dorsal fin; second spine largest. Pectoral and caudal fins rounded. Broadly banded, has additional wavy orange lines and spots. Only known from Sydney Harbour and Seal Rocks, New South Wales. Probably a deepwater species which may also be very secretive. Known from 20 m and 64 m. Attains 30 cm.

ORANGE-SPOTTED COD
Cephalopholis sonnerati (Valenciennes, 1828)

D IX,14-16. A III,9. P 18-20. V I,5. LL 66-67. LSR 115-140. Very small scales cover body and head. Lateral line with large smooth curve from origin, over middle of body, to caudal peduncle. Jaws with bands of teeth; inner row in lower jaw depressible; anterior row in upper jaw long, slender; pairs of canines anteriorly. Preopercle rounded, finely serrate; three spines on opercle, centre spine closest to lower spine. Pectorals and posterior fins rounded. Colour highly variable with size. Very small juveniles black with blue head, broad white margin on caudal fin; change to brown with increasing red spotting, then bright red as adults. Widespread tropical Indo-Pacific from broadly the west Pacific to east Africa; juveniles south to Sydney. Coastal slopes with outcrops on rubble-mud habitat. 10-150 m; adults usually in deeper part of range. Only known in Sydney from tiny juveniles off Clovelly in 20 m. Attains 65 cm. Indo-Pacific genus with about 20 species. Adults also known as Tomato Cod.

Acanthistius ocellatus ▲

Acanthistius paxtoni ▼

Cephalopholis sonnerati ▼

Cephalopholis sonnerati Juv.

BARRAMUNDI COD
Chromileptes altivelis (Valenciennes, 1828)

D X,17-19. A III,10. P 17-18. V I,5. LL 53-55. LSR 74-140. Scales very small, cycloid. Lateral line smoothly curved following contour of dorsal profile. Preopercle broadly rounded, serrated. Opercle with two small spines. Head profile markedly concave dorsally just behind eye, except in very small juveniles; snout pointed. Fins large with rounded posterior parts. Juveniles distinctly spotted; become grey to reddish-brown as adults with proportionally smaller, more numerous spots. Widespread tropical Indo-Pacific, broadly west Pacific to east Africa; juveniles south to Sydney. Coastal reefs, lagoons and deep, somewhat silty slopes to at least 40 m. Sydney juveniles very small (about 30 mm long); known from muddy bays on rocky outcrops. Attains 70 cm. Monotypic genus.

PURPLE ROCKCOD
Epinephelus cyanopodus (Richardson, 1846)

D XI,16-17. A III,8. P 18-20. V I,5. LL 65-75. LSR 120-150. Small ctenoid scales cover body, cycloid on head. Lower jaw projects strongly. Jaws with narrow bands of teeth, pairs of anterior canines in each. Opercle with pointed flap, three equally spaced spines; centre spine longest. Preopercle angular, coarsely serrated at angle. Dorsal fin with shallow notch in centre; membranes not deeply incised between spines. Anal fin spines long, third slightly longer than second. Small juvenile dark blue with orange tail, changing to light grey-blue with numerous tiny spots; somewhat larger spots scattered all over large adults. Widespread tropical west to central Pacific; juveniles south to the Sydney area. Coastal reefs and large silty lagoons on outcrops with caves. Shallow to at least 150 m. Juveniles in Sydney; mainly in silty or muddy areas with rocky outcrops or junk in the harbour. Attains 75 cm. Large worldwide genus with about 100 species, 13 of which are included here.

SCRIBBLED ROCKCOD
Epinephelus undulatostriatus (Peters, 1867)

D XI,15-16. A III,8. P 17-18. V I,5. LL 48-56. LSR 96-110. Small, mostly ctenoid scales cover body, cycloid on head; tiny scales on maxilla. Lateral line indistinct, smoothly curved, follows contour of dorsal profile. Jaws with bands of fine teeth; anterior canines small. Opercle with moderate subequal spines. Preopercle angular, coarsely serrated at angle. Dorsal fin slightly notched in centre; mem-

Epinephelus cyanopodus ▲   *Epinephelus undulatostriatus* ▼

branes incised between spines. Anal fin spines large; second and third subequal but second is strongest. Small juveniles strongly striped; stripes become fine and numerous on adults, breaking up into spotted lines. Southern Queensland to Batemans Bay, New South Wales. Coastal reefs and deep estuaries in 10-70 m. Adults occur in Sydney Harbour; pair was known to live in ship wreck in 20 m. Attains 40 cm. Also known as Maori Cod.

HONEYCOMB COD
Epinephelus merra Bloch, 1793

D XI,15-17. A III,8. P 16-18. V I,5. LL 48-52. LSR 100-114. Small, mostly ctenoid scales cover body, cycloid on head; very small scales on maxilla. Lateral line indistinct, smoothly curved, following contour of dorsal profile. Jaws with bands of fine teeth; anterior canines small. Preopercle angular, coarsely serrated at angle. Dorsal fin without notch in centre; membranes incised between spines. Anal fin spines large; second is strongest. Variable pale to brown with close-set hexagonal brown blotches. Widespread tropical Indo-Pacific, to southern Japan and east Africa; south nearly to Sydney as adults. Shallow reef flats and lagoons in corals, and protected slopes to 50 m. Small species; attains 28 cm.

LONG-FINNED COD
Epinephelus quoyanus (Valenciennes, 1830)

D XI,16-18. A III,8. P 17-19. V I,5. LL 48-51. LSR 95-110. Small, mostly ctenoid scales cover body, cycloid on head; very small scales on maxilla. Lateral line indistinct, smoothly curved, following contour of dorsal profile. Jaws with bands of fine teeth; anterior canines moderate. Preopercle angular, coarsely serrated at angle. Dorsal fin without notch in centre; membranes incised between spines. Anal fin spines large; second is strongest. Pectoral fin large; ventral fins long, sometimes reaching anus. Pale to brownish with close-set, round to hexagonal, brown to black spots. Widespread west Pacific and eastern Indian Ocean; south nearly to Sydney as adults. Shallow to deep coastal and estuarine reefs, 10-30 m. Attains 35 cm.

CORAL ROCKCOD
Epinephelus corallicola (Valenciennes, 1828)

D XI,15-16. A III,8. P 18-20. V I,5. LL 54-63. LSR 80-110. Small, mostly ctenoid scales cover body, cycloid on head; very small scales on maxilla. Lateral line indistinct, smoothly curved, following contour of dorsal profile. Jaws with bands of fine teeth; anterior canines moderate. Preopercle angular, slightly enlarged serrations at angle. Dorsal fin without notch in centre; membranes incised between spines. Anal fin spines large; second is strongest. Pectoral fin, posterior ends of dorsal and anal fins, and caudal fin rounded. Pale grey to brownish with small black spots all over. Western Pacific from New South Wales to the Philippines; south to near Sydney as adult. Secretive; coastal reefs, often in silty or rocky estuaries in crevices and large corals, to 30 m. Only attains about 32 cm.

MARBLED ROCKCOD
Epinephelus maculatus (Bloch, 1790)

D XI,15-17. A III,8. P 17-18. V I,5. LL 48-51. LSR 103-120. Small, mostly ctenoid scales cover body, cycloid on head; very small scales on maxilla. Lateral line indistinct, smoothly curved, follows contour of dorsal profile. Jaws with bands of fine teeth; anterior canines moderate. Preopercle angular, enlarged serrations at angle. Dorsal fin without notch in centre, fairly high at third

Epinephelus maculatus Adult ▼ Juv. ▲

and fourth spine; membranes incised between spines. Anal fin spines large; second is strongest. Pectoral fin, posterior ends of dorsal and anal fins, and caudal fin rounded. Juveniles jet black with white blotches and spots, becoming small spotted with alternating dark and light saddles along back. Broadly west Pacific from southern Japan to New South Wales, east to Marshall Islands and Samoa. Mostly in large lagoons with large coral outcrops. Juveniles in Sydney in coastal bays or rocky estuaries to 15 m. Attains 50 cm.

Epinephelus caeruleopunctatus ▼

SMALL-SPOTTED COD
Epinephelus caeruleopunctatus (Bloch, 1790)

D XI,15-17. A III,8. P 17-19. V I,5. LL 51-61. LSR 86-106. Small, mostly ctenoid scales cover body, cycloid on head; very small scales on maxilla. Lateral line indistinct, smoothly curved, following contour of dorsal profile. Jaws with bands of fine teeth; anterior canines moderate. Preopercle angular, enlarged serrations at angle. Dorsal fin without notch in centre; membranes incised between spines. Anal fin spines large; second is strongest. Pectoral fin, posterior ends of dorsal and anal fins, and caudal fin rounded. Variable pale to dark-grey or brown, scattered white spots of various sizes, dark blotches. Widespread tropical Indo-Pacific from New South Wales to Japan, and to east Africa. Secretive; shallow clear-water reefs in protected coastal waters to 20 m. Attains 60 cm.

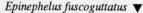

Epinephelus fuscoguttatus ▼

FLOWERY COD
Epinephelus fuscoguttatus (Forsskål, 1775)

D XI,14-15. A III,8. P 18-20. V I,5. LL 52-58. LSR 102-115. Small, mostly ctenoid scales cover body and head; partly ctenoid in juveniles; very small scales on maxilla. Lateral line indistinct, smoothly curved, follows contour of dorsal profile. Jaws with bands of fine teeth; anterior canines moderate. Preopercle angular, slightly enlarged serrations at angle. Dorsal fin with slight notch in centre; membranes incised between spines. Anal fin spines large; second is strongest. Pectoral fin, posterior ends of dorsal and anal fins, and caudal fin rounded. Variable brownish or dusky yellow, with series of irregular dark blotches, darker above. Widespread tropical Indo-Pacific, west and central Pacific to east Africa. Coastal reefs and mangrove areas to deep slopes to 60 m. Secretive, wary, usually about just before dark. Attains 95 cm.

QUEENSLAND GROPER
Epinephelus lanceolatus (Bloch, 1790)

D XI,14-16. A III,8. P. 18-19. V I,5. LL 53-67. LSR 89-110. Small, mostly cycloid scales cover body and head; partly ctenoid in juveniles; very small scales on maxilla. Lateral line with branched tubes, indistinct in adults; smoothly curved, follows contour of dorsal profile. Jaws with bands of fine teeth; anterior canines small. Preopercle angular, coarse serrations at angle. Dorsal fin changes with age; juveniles with subequal spines and rays over middle section; spines become proportionally shorter in large adults, posterior-most spine longest. Anal fin spines large; second is strongest. Pectoral fin, posterior ends of dorsal and anal fins, and caudal fin rounded. Juveniles with large blotched and banded pattern, becoming mottled and spotted to evenly dark grey to brownish. Widespread tropical Indo-Pacific from New South Wales to Japan and east Africa. A few specimens also known from South Australia. Along outer reefs in large lagoons and slopes to at least 50 m. Reported to 3 m and about 400 kg, making it one of the largest of all bony fishes, and the largest on reefs.

ESTUARY COD
Epinephelus malabaricus (Schneider, 1801)

D XI,14-16. A III,8. P 18-20. V I,5. LL 54-64. LSR 102-117. Small, mostly cycloid scales cover body and head, partly ctenoid on body; very small scales on maxilla. Lateral line without tubes, indistinct in adults; smoothly curved, follows contour of dorsal profile. Jaws with bands of fine teeth; anterior canines small. Preopercle angular, three to five coarse enlarged serrae at angle. Dorsal fin membranes incised between spines. Anal fin spines large; second is strongest. Pectoral fin, posterior ends of dorsal and anal fins, and caudal fin rounded. Juveniles distinctly banded; bands become diffused in adults which are additionally densely covered with small black spots. Widespread tropical Indo-Pacific, from New South Wales to southern Japan, east Africa and Red Sea. Coastal waters, estuaries, often near river outlets. Attains about 1 m. Previously confused with *E. suillus* (= *coioides*) which lives in coral reefs and grows much larger, attaining 1.7 m.

BLACK COD
Epinephelus daemelii (Günther, 1876)

D XI,14. A III,8. P 18. V I,5. LL 66-75. LSR 110-130. Small, mostly cycloid scales cover body and head, partly ctenoid on body in young; very small scales on maxilla. Lateral line without tubes, indistinct in adults; smoothly curved, follows contour of dorsal profile. Jaws with bands of fine teeth; anterior canines small. Preopercle angular, slightly enlarged serrae at angle. Dorsal fin membranes incised between spines. Anal fin spines large; second is strongest. Pectoral fin, posterior ends of dorsal and anal fins, and caudal fin rounded. Colour highly variable, can change quickly from totally black to blotched or distinctly banded pattern. Usually black in estuaries, banded in clear-water reefs. East coast from southern Queensland to eastern Victoria and to the Lord Howe Island and northern New Zealand region. Shallow rocky estuaries to deep offshore in caves; home ranging. Mostly active on dusk and at night. Attains 1.2 m.

Epinephelus daemelii Adult ▼ Juv. ▲

CONVICT COD
Epinephelus octofasciatus Griffin, 1926

D XI,14. A III,9-10. P 17. V I,5. LL 62. LSR 107. Small, mostly cycloid scales cover body and head, partly ctenoid on body in young; very small scales on maxilla. Lateral line without tubes, indistinct in adults; smoothly curved, follows contour of dorsal profile. Jaws with bands of fine teeth; anterior canines small. Preopercle angular, slightly enlarged serrae at angle. Dorsal fin membranes incised between spines; spines moderately long and subequal from third, becoming slightly notched over last few spines in adults. Anal fin spines large; second is strongest. Pectoral fin, posterior ends of dorsal and anal fins, and caudal fin rounded. Distinctly banded; adults becoming more brownish on interspaces. Only known from New South Wales to eastern Bass Strait and New Zealand; possibly widespread temperate southern Pacific, southern Africa; probably identical to similar form in temperate northern Pacific. Adults deepwater, caught on long-lines; juveniles in harbours and protected bays with rocky outcrops on sand; 10-150 m. Attains at least 60 cm. Northern Pacific form occurs in Japan sympatrically with similar *E. septemfasciatus* which is more elongate. Dark bands on *E. septemfasciatus* arranged differently below first two dorsal spines and there is an extra band on body near caudal peduncle; commonly found in shallower depths. *E. ergastularius* a synonym.

Epinephelus octofasciatus Juvs.

133

RED-BARRED COD
Epinephelus fasciatus (Forsskål, 1775)

D XI,15-17. A III,8. P 17-19. V I,5. LL 50-62. LSR 87-120. Small, mostly ctenoid scales cover body, cycloid on head; very small scales on maxilla. Lateral line indistinct, smoothly curved, following contour of dorsal profile. Jaws with bands of fine teeth; anterior canines moderate. Preopercle angular, enlarged serrations at angle. Dorsal fin without notch in centre, membranes incised between spines. Anal fin spines large; second is strongest. Pectoral fin, posterior ends of dorsal and anal fins, and caudal fin rounded. Variable from banded to pale; upper part of head dark; several geographical variations. Widespread tropical Indo-Pacific from New South Wales to Japan and Micronesia, to east Africa; adults south to Seal Rocks, New South Wales. Reef crests and slopes, clear coastal reefs from very shallow to at least 150 m. Attains 35 cm.

Epinephelus fasciatus ▲

Variola louti ▼

Othos dentex ▼

LYRE-TAIL COD
Variola louti (Forsskål, 1775)

D XI,13-15. A III,8. P 16-19. V I,5. LL 64-78. LSR 113-135. Small, mostly ctenoid scales cover body, cycloid on head; very small scales on maxilla. Lateral line indistinct, smoothly curved, following contour of dorsal profile. Jaws with bands of fine teeth; anterior canines prominent. Preopercle angular, without enlarged serrations at angle. Dorsal fin without notch in centre; membranes incised between spines, but only slightly with first few spines. Anal fin spines small; third is longest. Posterior ends of dorsal and anal fins angular, becoming pointed in adults. Caudal fin lunate with long tips in adults. Juvenile with distinct colour pattern, changing gradually to all orange with small blue spots all over. Widespread tropical Indo-Pacific, New South Wales to Japan, east Africa and Red Sea. Shallow coastal reef flats, outer reef crests and slopes from very shallow to at least 100 m. Juveniles secretive, in rubble areas. Attains 80 cm. Genus comprises two species, both recorded from tropical Australian waters.

Variola louti Juv.

HARLEQUIN FISH
Othos dentex (Cuvier, 1828)

D X,18-19. A III,8-9. C 17. P 15. V I,5. LL 81-87. LSR 95-115. Small ctenoid scales cover body and fin bases, smallest on thorax; smaller scales on cheeks, opercle. Opercle ends with pointed flap and three spines. Posterior margin of preopercle finely serrate, with three to four enlarged serrae below. Eyes large, close together, high on head. Mouth large; jaws have bands of villiform teeth, with very large anterior canines laterally in lower jaw; fine teeth on vomer, palatines. Bases of spinous and soft-rayed dorsal fin sections about equal; fin notched over last spines. Spines shorter than long posterior soft rays in adults. Anal fin short-based with long soft rays. Caudal fin rounded. Colours highly variable; pink, green, brown and red forms; usually has large yellow spots below, blue spots above. Only known from the south coast; common in South and south Western Australia, ranging east to Port Phillip Bay. Shallow rocky reefs to at least 30 m. Inquisitive species, found mainly in cave and large boulder areas. Attains 76 cm. Monotypic genus endemic to Australian waters.

BANDED SEAPERCH
Hypoplectrodes nigroruber (Cuvier, 1828)

D X,16-18. A III,8. C 17. P 13-14. V I,5. LL 55-58. LSR 60-65. Small ctenoid scales cover body and fin bases, smallest on thorax; smaller scales on cheeks, opercle. Lateral line smoothly curved, high along upper sides. Opercle ends with upward-angled pointed flap halfway between axil and dorsal fin origin, with two large spines and small embedded spine above. Preopercle serrate posteriorly; three large antrorse spines below. Head large with straight dorsal profile. Eyes large, close together, high on head, well above dorsal profile. Mouth large, oblique; lower jaw ends in front of upper with mouth closed; band of villiform teeth in each jaw, with single or paired anterior canines; small teeth on vomer, palatines. Bases of spinous and soft-rayed dorsal fin sections about equal; fin notched over last spines. Spinous section deeply incised; posterior part of soft-rayed section has longest rays in adults. Anal fin short-based with long soft rays. Caudal fin rounded. Colours highly variable; pink, green, brown and red forms, but bands usually black. Young with white stripe from tip of snout to dorsal fin. Widespread south coast from northern New South Wales to Houtman Abrolhos, and northern Tasmania. Shallow coastal reefs and estuaries to at least 30 m; in caves and crevices but not secretive. Attains 30 cm. South Pacific subtropical and temperate genus comprising about 12 species. Until recently most species were placed in *Ellerkeldia*.

Hypoplectrodes nigroruber   Adult ▼   Juv. ▲

BLACK-BANDED SEAPERCH
Hypoplectrodes annulatus (Günther, 1859)

D X,17-18. A III,7. C 17. P 15-16. V I,5. LL 43-48. LSR 53-55. Moderate-sized, coarsely ctenoid scales cover body and fin bases; also on cheeks, opercle. Lateral line smoothly curved, along upper sides. Opercle ends with angular flap which has three spines, middle one at corner largest. Preopercle strongly serrate posteriorly; three large antrorse spines below. Head large with straight dorsal profile. Eyes large, high on head, slightly above dorsal profile. Mouth large, oblique; lower jaw subequal to upper with mouth closed; band of villiform teeth in each jaw, with single or paired anterior canines; small teeth on vomer, palatines. Spinous section of dorsal fin not deeply incised; soft-rayed section taller with subequal rays. Anal fin short-based with long soft rays and very large second spine. Pale to dusky yellow with distinct bands. East coast from southern Queensland to Wilson's Promontory. Coastal reefs and estuaries in caves, usually upside down, in 10-100 m. Attains 30 cm.

HALF-BANDED SEAPERCH
Hypoplectrodes maccullochi Whitley, 1929

D X,21. A III,8. C 17. P 16-17. V I,5. LL 46-48. Moderate-sized ctenoid scales cover body and fin bases; somewhat smaller on cheeks, opercle. Lateral line smoothly curved, along upper sides. Opercle ends with angular flap which has three strong spines; upper small, middle one at corner largest. Preopercle strongly serrate posteriorly; three large antrorse spines below. Head large with straight dorsal profile. Eyes large, high on head, not above dorsal profile. Mouth large, oblique; lower jaw subequal to upper with mouth closed; band of villiform teeth in each jaw, with single or paired anterior canines; small teeth on vomer, palatines. Spinous section of dorsal fin not deeply incised, has low central notch; soft-rayed section taller with subequal rays. Anal fin short-based with long soft rays and very large second spine. Pale pink to brown-red with indistinct banding. East coast from northern New South Wales to eastern Tasmania. Shallow coastal and estuarine rocky reefs to at least 50 m. Particularly common in sponge areas, sometimes in loose aggregations. Attains 20 cm.

JAMESON'S SEAPERCH
Hypoplectrodes jamesoni (Ogilby, 1908)

D X,20. A III,8. C 17. P 16. V I,5. LL 38-40. Moderate-sized ctenoid scales cover body and fin bases; somewhat smaller on cheeks, opercle. Lateral line smoothly curved, along upper sides. Opercle ends with angular flap which has three moderate spines; upper small, middle one at corner largest. Preopercle strongly serrate posteriorly; three moderate-sized antrorse spines below. Head large with straight dorsal profile. Eyes large, high on head, not above dorsal profile. Mouth large, oblique; lower jaw subequal to upper with mouth closed; band of villiform teeth in each jaw, with single or paired anterior canines; small teeth on vomer and palatines. Spinous section of dorsal fin not deeply incised, has low central notch; soft-rayed section taller with subequal rays. Anal fin short-based with long soft rays and very large second spine. Variable brownish-grey, sometime violet tinged. Southern Queensland to Sydney. Estuarine species, usually in sponges in 10-30 m. Attains 12 cm.

LONG-FINNED PERCH
Caprodon longimanus (Günther, 1859)

D X,19-20. A III,8. P 17-18. V I,5. LL 63-65. LSR 68-75. Ctenoid scales cover body and head, including maxilla, and extend greatly onto unpaired fins. Mouth oblique; jaws with bands of villiform teeth, a few anterior canine-like; broad bands of fine teeth on vomer, palatines. Posterior margin of preopercle finely serrate to angle. Opercle ends in three flat spines. Dorsal fin with subequal spines and soft rays over almost entire fin; spinous section incised. Pectoral fin pointed; longest rays much longer than head. Caudal fin deeply emarginate. Variable from pink as juveniles to added yellow and dark blotches in males. New South Wales, Crowdy Head to Montague Island, Kermadec Islands and New Zealand. Usually deep, taken on line in Australia, but may rise to 10 m to feed, usually in schools. Attains 43 cm. Small Indo-Pacific genus with two species in Australia, one of which is included here. Known in New Zealand as Pink Maomao.

Hypoplectrodes jamesoni ▲   *Caprodon longimanus* ▼

BARBER PERCH
Caesioperca rasor (Richardson, 1839)

D X-XI,19-22. A III,9-10. P 14-15. V I,5. LL 49-55. LSR 54-60. Ctenoid scales cover body and head, including maxilla, and extend onto unpaired fins as broad sheaths. Mouth oblique; jaws with bands of villiform teeth, a few anterior canine-like; broad bands of fine teeth on vomer, palatines. Posterior margin of preopercle finely serrate to angle. Opercle ends in two strong spines. Dorsal fin with subequal spines and soft rays over almost entire fin; spinous section shallowly incised. Pectoral fin pointed; longest rays much longer than head. Caudal fin deeply emarginate. Juveniles with black head, becoming pink, then changes, with dark central blotch and blue markings in males. South coast, Bass Strait and Tasmania to Albany. Juveniles shallow, in estuaries; adults usually in schools feeding on zooplankton in 10-100 m. Attains 25 cm.

Caesioperca rasor   Male ▲ Female ▼

Caesioperca rasor   Juv.

Caesioperca lepidoptera   Adult ▼ Juv. ▲

BUTTERFLY PERCH
Caesioperca lepidoptera (Bloch and Schneider, 1801)

D X,19-21. A III,9-10. P 16. V I,5. LL 54-65. LSR 65-70. Ctenoid scales cover body and head, including maxilla, and extend onto unpaired fins as broad sheaths. Mouth oblique; jaws with bands of villiform teeth, a few anterior canine-like; broad bands of fine teeth on vomer, palatines. Posterior margin of preopercle finely serrate to angle. Opercle ends in two strong spines. Dorsal fin with subequal spines and soft rays over almost entire fin; spinous section incised. Pectoral fin pointed; longest rays about as long as head. Caudal fin deeply emarginate. Usually pinkish with dark blotch on side, but unusual forms may occur; sometimes dark blotch on side absent, pectoral fin yellow, dark pigmentation present on head or posterior part of body. Some specimens observed were normal on one side, abnormal on other. Common in southern waters from central New South Wales to Albany, including Tasmania, and the New Zealand area. Often in cloud-like schools feeding well above the substrate, otherwise in rocky boulder reefs and caves. Shallow in southern range, but usually deep, to 100 m, in northern parts. Attains 30 cm.

RED SEAPERCH
Pseudanthias cooperi (Regan, 1902)

D X,15-17. A III,7-8. P 18-20. V I,5. LL 48-52. Small ctenoid scales cover body and head, except upper snout and lips. Distinct lateral line, smoothly curved along upper sides to caudal fin. Opercle with three flat spines, middle one largest. Preopercle margin serrated. Jaws with bands of filiform teeth, broad anteriorly, outer row enlarged and canine-like, larger canine anteriorly on sides. Vomer with patch and palatines with bands of villiform teeth. Caudal fin and ventral posterior corners of dorsal and anal fins become very pointed or elongated in males. Juveniles and females plain red, lighter below, developing vertical dark red bar. Males variable silvery-grey to red, can quickly change during display. Widespread tropical Indo-Pacifc, broadly throughout west Pacific to east Africa and Red Sea. Juveniles commonly south to Montague Island. Coastal and offshore reefs; juveniles enter clear rocky estuaries. Boulder reefs and drop-offs in crevices and caves, in small aggregations; 5-60 m. Attains 12 cm. Large tropical Indo-Pacific genus of small fishes, typically colourful; males often develop long fin elements. Several subgenera; in all, an estimated 35 species, six of which are included here.

Pseudanthias cooperi Adult ▼ Juv. ▲

PINK SEAPERCH
Pseudanthias hypselosoma (Bleeker, 1856)

D X,16. A III,7-8. P 18-20. V I,5. LL 44-46. Small ctenoid scales cover body and head, except upper snout and lips. Distinct lateral line, smoothly curved along upper sides to caudal fin. Opercle with three flat spines, middle one largest. Preopercle margin serrated. Jaws with bands of filiform teeth, broad anteriorly, outer row enlarged and canine-like, larger canine anteriorly on sides. Vomer with patch and palatines with bands of villiform teeth. Caudal fin truncate; males with short filaments at tips and posterior part of dorsal fin. Variable pale to darker pink; juveniles with red tips and narrow margin on caudal fin; males change during display to have pale forehead, red caudal fin. Widespread tropical west Pacific, from New South Wales to southern Japan; particularly common in Indonesia where they occur in large aggregations with coral heads. Juveniles south to Montague Island. Shallow in equatorial waters but deep in cooler areas, 3-50 m; usually on slopes with outcrops. Juveniles in crevices along drop-offs. Attains 12 cm.

Pseudanthias hypselosoma ▼

Pseudanthias hypselosoma Juv.

LILAC-TIPPED SEAPERCH
Pseudanthias rubrizonatus (Randall, 1983)

D X,16. A III,7. P 18-20. V I,5. LL 42-47. Small ctenoid scales cover body and head, except upper snout and lips. Distinct lateral line, smoothly curved along upper sides to caudal fin. Opercle with three flat spines, middle one largest. Preopercle margin serrated. Jaws with bands of filiform teeth, broad anteriorly, outer row enlarged and canine-like, larger canine anteriorly on sides. Vomer with patch and palatines with bands of villiform teeth. Caudal fin emarginate with short filaments at tips, becoming elongate in adults. Variable pale to darker pink; juveniles with red tips and narrow margin on caudal fin; males have broad red bar over middle of body. Uncertain distribution; known from the Philippines and eastern Australia; perhaps identical to similar fish from north-western Australia. Juveniles in the Sydney area in rocky estuaries along rock walls with ledges. Attains 10 cm.

Pseudanthias rubrizonatus Juv.

ORANGE SEAPERCH
Pseudanthias squamipinnis (Peters, 1855)

D X,17-18. A III,6-8. P 16-18. V I,5. LL 40-44. Body and head, except upper snout and lips, covered with small ctenoid scales. Distinct lateral line, smoothly curved along upper sides to caudal fin. Opercle with three flat spines, middle one largest. Preopercle margin serrated, coarse at angle. Jaws with bands of filiform teeth, broad anteriorly, outer row enlarged and canine-like, larger canine anteriorly on sides. Vomer with patch and palatines with bands of villiform teeth. Caudal fin emarginate with short filaments at tips, becoming elongate in adults. Third spine of dorsal fin very elongate in males. Widespread tropical Indo-Pacific, broadly in the west Pacific to east Africa; some geographical variations and possibly several species masquerading under this name. Juveniles commonly south to Montague Island and occasionally reach adult size. Reef crests, slopes and drop-offs, often in large aggregations; mainly shallow to 20 m. Attains 12 cm. Often collected for the aquarium, being the most common seaperch species in the Sydney area, however, like the other species, usually kept with little success. Require excellent water conditions, making ideal specimens for invertebrate aquarium with other small planktivorous fishes such as hulas (*Trachinops spp*). Thrive on live mysids but accept them frozen; also like fine graded pieces of (frozen) squid. Take about two years to grow from tiny juveniles to adults. Several species may be kept together but require space. Usually largest specimen dominates others.

Pseudanthias squamipinnis Male ▲ Female ▼

RED-STRIPE SEAPERCH
Pseudanthias fasciatus (Kamohara, 1954)

D X,16-17. A III,7. P 18. V I,5. LL 41-44. Small ctenoid scales cover body and head, except upper snout and lips. Distinct lateral line, smoothly curved along upper sides to caudal fin. Opercle with three flat spines, middle one largest. Preopercle margin finely serrated. Jaws with bands of filiform teeth, broad anteriorly, outer row enlarged and canine-like, larger canine anteriorly on sides. Vomer with patch and palatines with bands of villiform teeth. Caudal fin emarginate with short filaments at tips, becoming elongate in adults. West Pacifc, southern Japan and eastern Australia, south to Montague Island. Adults in large caves, often upside down near the ceiling, along deep drop-offs, in 30-60 m. Juveniles in 20-30 m, usually in small aggregations. Attains 15 cm.

Pseudanthias fasciatus Juv.

Photograph: Neville Coleman

Pseudanthias pictilis Male ▲ Female ▼

PURPLE-YELLOW SEAPERCH
Pseudanthias pictilis (Randall and Allen, 1978)

D X,15-16. A III,7. P 18-19. V I,5. LL 46-50. Small ctenoid scales cover body and head, except upper snout and lips. Distinct lateral line, smoothly curved along upper sides to caudal fin. Opercle with three flat spines, middle one largest; upper spine poorly developed. Preopercle posterior margin finely serrated, becoming increasingly coarse to angle. Jaws with bands of filiform teeth, broad anteriorly, outer row enlarged and canine-like, larger canine anteriorly on sides. Vomer with patch and palatines with bands of villiform teeth. Caudal fin emarginate with pointed tips; dorsal and anal fins tipped at corners in males. Pink to red with yellow posterior back and caudal fin; male distinct with vertical band and caudal fin markings. East coast from Queensland to Montague Island and Lord Howe Island, and New Caledonia. Juveniles solitary in boulder reefs; adults in small to large aggregations along outer reef slopes to 40 m. Attains 12 cm.

Pseudanthias pictilis Juv.

GOLD-RIBBON COD
Aulacocephalus temmincki Bleeker, 1857

D IX,12. A III,9. P 14-16. V I,5. LL 76-82. LSR 83-87. Body very compressed, covered with small ctenoid scales; small embedded scales extend onto opercle, preopercle. Lateral line with large curve, closely passing dorsal fin. Opercle with three large spines at corner flap, small spine on upper corner. Preopercle serrate at vertical margin, increasingly coarse to angle. Head large; mouth oblique, large, reaching to below eye; bands of villiform teeth in jaws, vomer, palatines. Fin spines short; pectoral and ventral fins rather small. Pale to dark blue; yellow band along back. Widespread tropical, anti-equatorial, Indo-Pacific; known from New South Wales, New Zealand, Japan, Taiwan and various other locations to east Africa. Secretive, along deep rocky drop-offs in crevices, sometimes in loose agregations; 10-70 m. Attains 30 cm. Monotypic genus which belongs in subfamily known as soapfishes.

YELLOW EMPEROR
Diploprion bifasciatum Kuhl and van Hasselt, 1828

D VIII,13-16. A II,12-13. P 17-18. V I,5. LL 80-88. LSR 100-110. Body very compressed, covered with small ctenoid scales; small embedded scales extend onto opercle, preopercle. Lateral line with large curve, closely passing dorsal fin. Opercle with three large spines at corner flap. Preopercle serrate at vertical margin, increasingly coarse to angle. Head large; mouth oblique, large, reaching to below eye; bands of villiform teeth in jaws, vomer, palatines. Dorsal fin deeply notched; longest spines tall, about equal to longest rays. Pectoral and ventral fins long. Anal fin spines short. Pale to bright yellow, body sometimes all black. West Pacific from New South Wales to southern Japan, and east Indian ocean. Coastal reefs and quiet lagoons, enters estuaries and often in isolated outcrops of rock or debris on sand or mud; 5-50 m. Attains 25 cm.

Diploprion bifasciatum Juv.

SPLENDID PERCHES
FAMILY CALLANTHIIDAE

This small family contains only a single genus comprising about eight species, distributed over temperate areas and some in deep tropical waters. They are superficially similar to the anthiid fishes in the Serranidae, and until recently were considered to belong in that group, however they differ in having a lateral line very high over the body, just below the base of the dorsal fin. In addition, the nasal organ is different and a modified row of scales mid-laterally on the body bears a series of pits or grooves. They are generally deepwater fishes, schooling and planktivorous, of which two species occur on the south-east coast but only one occurs in divable depths. Most species are orange or red with yellow fins and are particularly brightly coloured when brought up from deep water.

SPLENDID PERCH
Callanthias australis Ogilby, 1899

D XI,10-12. A III,10-11. C 17. P 18-23. V I,5. LL 34-41. Body moderately elongate and compressed, covered with large, finely ctenoid scales; head small. Lateral line rises steeply from origin to near base of third dorsal fin spine, following profile of back, nearly to base of upper caudal fin lobe. Mouth small, oblique; single row of conical teeth in jaws, several enlarged, forward directed anteriorly. Palatines with or without fine teeth. Opercle with two flat spines dorsally; preopercle margins smooth. Dorsal fin headed by short spines, progressively increasing in size, followed by similarly increasing soft rays without notch. Anal fin long-based, similarly shaped and opposite posterior part of dorsal fin. Caudal fin truncate with long tips, becoming filamentous in adults. Colour variable with size and depth. Juvenile pink; adults bright orange or red with red or yellow fins. South-east coast from central New South Wales to Tasmania and to south Western Australia; also in New Zealand. Offshore reefs in 20-200 m; small to large aggregations. Juveniles sometimes inshore in 10-20 m. Attains 30 cm.

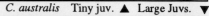

C. australis   Tiny juv. ▲   Large Juvs. ▼

SEA BASSES
FAMILY POLYPRIONIDAE

A small group of fishes which have been assigned to the Serranidae and recently Percichthyidae, the latter a family of primarily freshwater basses of the southern hemisphere. However, the sea basses are now considered to belong in a separate family. The are oceanic fishes which grow quite large, some in excess of 2 m and 300 kg, and are of commercial importance to the long-line fishing industry. Juveniles are pelagic until quite large (about 50 cm) and seek shelter with floating objects. Sea basses are generally large-headed with moderately oblong bodies, tiny scales, short fin spines in adults, and a horizontal ridge on the opercle which ends in a small spine. Eyes are positioned dorsally on the head, and the large mouth reaches to below the eye. Most species are not well known as they live deep and are only occasionally caught; only one species is common in the south-east region. It is occasionally observed by divers, and thus is included here.

HAPUKU
Polyprion oxygeneios (Forster, 1801)

D XI-XII, 12-13. A III,8-9. P 18-19. V I,5. LL 80-95. LSR 140-180. Body and head covered with tiny ctenoid scales which extend onto fin bases. Head large, snout pointed. Eye small, high on head, protruding. Mouth large, oblique; lower jaw protruding; villiform teeth in bands on jaws, and on vomer, palatines, tongue. Opercle with horizontal ridge, ending in spine on angular end. Long-based dorsal fin with low spinous section in adults. Anal fin with three small spines. Caudal fin from rounded in young to truncate in adults. Young with broad irregular banding; adults plain steel-grey, darker above. Southern Australian waters, New South Wales to Western Australia and Tasmania, New Zealand; also reported from Chile. Deep water, 50-400 m; occasionally as shallow as 15 m. Sometimes in caves. Attains 1.5 m and 70 kg. Reputed to be one of the best eating fish in southern waters.

BLUE DEVILS AND HULAFISHES
FAMILY PLESIOPIDAE

Presently comprises six genera and about 20 species, but the relationships of some included genera are not clear and it seems likely that further studies will change this arrangement. The small species in *Assessor* and *Trachinops* are planktivorous and even these are very different to each other, not only morphologically but also biologically. For example, *Assessor* is a known mouth-breeder. Other genera are reef dwellers and have similar body shapes and fin arrangements. They are usually secretive but in some cases are the opposite, being very inquisitive. The species on the south coast are all of southern origin and no tropical species is known to expatriate south. This is probably because of their reproduction strategy, which is known for a few species; *Calloplesiops* has been bred in captivity. Eggs are laid in nest-like spaces in rocks. The hatchlings have a very short pelagic stage and are well advanced compared to other tropical species which are known expatriates down the coast. The southern genera look unlikely to be in the same family, but probably represent the two extremes of the group, and are endemic to these waters. Generally, the body is elongated and the head rounded; the lateral line is in two parts, and the ventral fin has one spine and four rays.

ALISON'S BLUE DEVIL
Paraplesiops alisonae Hoese and Kuiter, 1984

D XI-XII,9-11. A III,9-11. C 17. P 17-18. V I,4. LL 34-38+12-16. LSR 34-38. Body moderately long and shallow compared to other species in genus. Scales of moderate size, ctenoid on body, cycloid on head. First part of lateral line angled upward from origin to just below dorsal fin, continuing to below last soft ray; second part along midline from below soft-rayed section of dorsal fin to caudal fin. Dorsal fin long-based with spinous section clearly longest; membranes between spines deeply incised. Caudal fin large, broadly rounded. Ventral fin long, slender. Colour highly variable, differs between sexes; young and females dark, dusky, faintly banded with blue spots, blue fin margins. Males orange and blue. Only known from the Bass Strait area to South Australia. Secretive, nocturnal, in rocky crevices; 3-30 m. Attains 15 cm. Only species in genus which shows distinct colour differences between sexes; smallest of the five known species. *P. sinclairi* restricted to south Western Australia and not included here.

Paraplesiops alisonae   Male ▲ Female ▼

Paraplesiops alisonae   Tiny juv.

EASTERN BLUE DEVIL
Paraplesiops bleekeri (Günther, 1861)

D XI-XII,1O. A III,9-10. C 17. P 17-18. V I,4. LL 34-40+11-14. LSR 39-45. Body moderately elongate; scales of moderate size, ctenoid on body, cycloid on head. First part of lateral line angled upward from origin to just below dorsal fin, continuing to below last soft ray; second part along midline from below soft-rayed section of dorsal fin to caudal fin. Dorsal fin long-based with spinous section clearly longest; membranes between spines shallowly incised. Caudal fin large, broadly rounded. Ventral fin long, slender. Posterior parts of dorsal and anal fins elongated; when fins spread they overlap, and seem continuous with, caudal fin, giving impression of large body outline. Little variation in colour; typically banded as shown. East coast from southern Queensland to Montague Island. Secretive species, sometimes inquisitive; seems common only south of Sydney to Ulladulla. Shallow in estuaries but deep offshore, 3-30 m. Attains 40 cm. Also known as Blue-Tipped Longfin. One of the most beautiful reef fishes in New South Wales; protected (not to be speared or collected without permit).

Paraplesiops bleekeri   Adult ▼   Juvenile ▲

SOUTHERN BLUE DEVIL
Paraplesiops meleagris (Peters, 1869)

D XI-XII,9-1O. A III,9-11. C 17. P 17-19. V I,4. LL 34-43+12-21. LSR 39-50. NOTE: high element counts in Victoria compared to south-western populations. Body moderately elongate; scales of moderate size, ctenoid on body, cycloid on head. First part of lateral line angled upward from origin to just below dorsal fin, continuing to below last soft ray; second part along midline from below soft-rayed section of dorsal fin to caudal fin. Dorsal fin long-based with spinous section clearly longest; membranes between spines shallowly incised. Caudal fin large, broadly rounded. Ventral fin long, slender. Posterior parts of dorsal and anal fins elongated; when fins spread they overlap, and seem continuous with, caudal fin, giving impression of large body outline. Little variation in colour; typically as shown. South coast from Cape Woolamai, Victoria to Houtman Abrolhos, Western Australia. Shallow rocky reefs to 45 m. Inquisitive species which can be photographed with close-up lenses underwater; a favorite of many in southern waters. Attains 33 cm.

Paraplesiops meleagris   Adult ▼   Juvenile ▲

NORTHERN BLUE DEVIL
Paraplesiops poweri Ogilby, 1908

D XII,9-1O. A III,10. C 17. P 18-20. V I,4. LL 28-32+9-13. LSR 32-38. Body moderately elongate; scales of moderate size, ctenoid on body, cycloid on head. First part of lateral line angled upward from origin to just below dorsal fin, continuing to below last soft ray; second part along midline from below soft-rayed section of dorsal fin to caudal fin. Dorsal fin long-based with spinous section clearly longest; membranes between spines moderately incised. Caudal fin large, broadly rounded. Ventral fin long, slender. Posterior parts of dorsal and anal fins elongated; when fins spread they overlap, and seem continuous with, caudal fin, giving impression of large body outline. Little variation in colour; typically as shown; banding more or less distinct. Southern Queensland to northern New South Wales. Estuarine reefs, in deep ledges; secretive, probably nocturnal. Attains 18 cm.

SOUTHERN HULAFISH
Trachinops caudimaculatus McCoy, 1890

D XIV-XV,16-17. A III,17-19. C 17. P 18. V I,4. LL 45-51+13-18. Body slender, slightly compressed, covered with small ctenoid scales. Head small with cycloid scales. Lateral line angled upwards from origin to straight section just below dorsal fin base, ending just below last ray; second part along midline onto caudal peduncle to caudal fin. Dorsal fin low, long-based with spinous section slightly longer than soft-rayed section. Anal fin similar to, longer than, and opposite soft-rayed section of dorsal fin. Caudal fin rounded in juveniles, becoming pointed in adults; middle rays elongated in some individuals. South coast,

Bass Strait, Tasmania to Investigator Group in Great Australian Bight. Particularly common in southern Tasmania where they school midwater in clouds, feeding on zooplankton.

Coastal reefs and rocky estuaries to 35 m. Attains 15 cm. This genus comprises four similar species, two of which are included here.

EASTERN HULAFISH
Trachinops taeniatus Günther, 1861

D XIV,16-17. A III,19-20. C 17. P 16-17. V I,4. LL 51-57+0-7. Body slender, slightly compressed, covered with small ctenoid scales. Head small with cycloid scales. Lateral line angled upwards from origin to straight section just below dorsal fin base, ending just below last ray. Second part along midline onto caudal peduncle to caudal fin. Dorsal fin low, long-based with spinous section slightly longer than soft-rayed section. Anal fin similar to, longer than, and opposite soft-rayed section of dorsal fin. Caudal fin rounded in juveniles, becoming pointed in adults; very elongated middle rays in some individuals. Southern Queensland to eastern Victoria. Schooling species, in some places filling every hole or crevice available in rocks. Particularly common in southern New South Wales where large schools occupy reefs in about 10-20 m. Attains about 10 cm.

GRUNTERS
FAMILY TERAPONTIDAE

A moderately large family comprising 16 genera and about 40 species. It is particularly well represented in Australia with 13 genera and 30 species. They feature small to moderate-sized ctenoid scales which extend along the dorsal and anal fins in sheaths. They have prominent spines on the opercle, and the preopercle margin is serrate. A single but often deeply notched dorsal fin is present. These typically perch-like fishes are widespread in the tropical Indo-Pacific and in Australia are mostly found inland and in estuaries. Of the nine marine species, two range to south-eastern waters. The freshwater species are usually called grunters, while the marine species are known as trumpeter, perch, thornfish and some of the striped juveniles as tigerfish. The marine species are usually schooling and move over large areas. Small juveniles are often among floating weeds and in tide pools. Some species enter fresh water, both as young and adults. While some of the freshwater species are excellent to eat, the marine species are mainly used as bait-fish. Juveniles are often kept in aquaria and, being very tolerant to water conditions, are easily kept, though rather aggressive.

EASTERN STRIPED TRUMPETER
Pelates sexlineatus (Quoy and Gaimard, 1824)

D XII,10. A III,9. P 13-14. V I,5. LL 64-68. Small ctenoid scales cover body, most of head. Lateral line very slighly curved, parallel to dorsal profile, passing just below line from upper eye to upper caudal peduncle. Lower opercle spine largest, flattened, equal to or just over posterior margin. Posterior margin of preopercle coarsely serrated. Jaws with bands of villiform teeth; two rows in lower jaw, three in upper with outer row enlarged. Vomer and palatines without teeth. Dorsal fin slightly notched in juveniles; first spine sometimes very small, following spines to fourth progressively longer; remaining spines subequal and short compared to longest soft rays. Anal fin spines short, less than half length of longest soft ray. Little colour variation; somewhat brownish in estuaries, silvery-grey in coastal bays. Eastern Australia from southern Queensland to Jervis Bay, New South Wales. Large rocky estuaries and coastal reefs in 6-30 m. In small or large schools. Attains 20 cm. The other member of the genus, similar, widespread tropical Indo-Pacific species, *P. quadrilineatus*, may occur in northern New South Wales; has longer fin spines, usually a large black area in spinous dorsal fin, and extra half stripe between upper stripes, particularly distinct in juveniles. Until recently *P. octolineatus* included in this genus, but this species rather different, having tricuspid teeth, small head; belongs in another genus as *Helotus sexlineatus*.

Pelates sexlineatus   Adult ▼ Juv. ▲

P. quadrilineatus   Juv., tropical species, may range into NSW, often confused with *sexlineatus* ▼

Photograph: G. R. Allen

147

CRESCENT PERCH
Terapon jarbua (Forsskål, 1775)

D XI-XII,9-11. A III,8-10. P 13-14. LL 79-93. Small ctenoid scales cover body, most of head. Lateral line very slighly curved, parallel to dorsal profile, passing just over first line above. Opercle spines prominent; lower horizontal, very large. Posterior margin of preopercle coarsely serrated, large serrae at angle. Jaws with bands of villiform teeth; outer rows enlarged. Vomer and palatines with some deciduous teeth in young, lost with age. Dorsal spine with deep notch; fourth and fifth spine tall. Spines in anal fin prominent. Little variation in colour or from juvenile to adult; distinctly curved stripes readily identify this species. Widespread tropical Indo-Pacific, west Pacific to east Africa. Shallow coastal waters near rivers or in estuaries; enters fresh water. Usually schools in loose groups, swimming close to the substrate. Juveniles south to Sydney, often in tidal pools. Attains 25 cm.

FLAGTAILS
FAMILY KUHLIIDAE

A small family of moderate-sized perch-like fishes of the tropical Indo-Pacific and eastern Atlantic which comprises two genera and about six species. Flagtails are coastal fishes commonly found in estuaries and some enter fresh water. The fishes living permanently in fresh water which are included by some authors – the Australian pygmy perches, *Nannoperca* and allies – belong in Percichthyidae. The widespread Indo-Pacific genus *Kuhlia* is represented in Australia with three species, one of which ranges south and is included here. This genus comprises fishes which typically have distinctly striped caudal fins, elongate-oval shaped bodies with moderate-sized ctenoid scales, and bands of villiform teeth in the jaws, vomer and palatines. Colours may vary within species if in freshwater or marine environments.

OCEAN FLAGTAIL
Kuhlia mugil (Schneider, 1801)

D X,9-11. A III,9-11. P 14. V I,5. LL 50-56. Body moderately elongate, covered with moderate-sized ctenoid scales; scales extend onto head, snout, and onto dorsal and anal fins with narrow sheath. Lateral line almost straight except for smooth curve above pectoral fin. Opercle with two spines, lower largest and just above axil. Preopercle serrate, angular. Dorsal fin short-based; spinous part longest with tall spines and small notch; fifth spine longest. Anal fin originates opposite last dorsal fin spine; has three strong spines, first half length of second. Usually silvery, but sometimes with yellow tinge in harbours. Widespread tropical Indo-Pacific from central New South Wales to Southern Japan and to east Africa. Coastal reefs and harbours, often in turbulent coastal waters; schools near rocks, just below surface. Juveniles sometimes in tide pools. Attains 25 cm. This species has been named several times; *Kuhlia taeniura* a synonym. Also known as Five-Bar Flagtail.

GLASSFISHES
FAMILY CHANDIDAE

A moderately large family of small fishes comprising about eight genera and 40 species, of which three genera and about 14 species are known from Australia. Most species live in coastal freshwater or in brackish estuaries of the tropical west Indo-Pacific from the Indo-Australian region to India. A few are marine species which usually cloud the edges of rocky tidal channels to estuaries in dense schools. These mostly semi-transparent fishes are usually less than 10 cm in maximum size. Two species are commonly encountered when diving in New South Wales harbours. They feature large cycloid scales on the body and head to the snout, a continuous or interrupted lateral line, a steep head profile, and a tall, deeply notched, sometimes separated dorsal fin. The lower opercle and preopercle have a strong spine-like serration at their corners. The dorsal and anal fins have scaly basal sheaths. The mouth is strongly oblique and the teeth are conical, in bands in the jaws, vomer and palatines. NOTE: a tiny procumbent spine just in front of the first, usually very short, dorsal fin spine is not included in the count.

PORT JACKSON GLASSFISH
Ambassis jacksoniensis (Macleay, 1881)

D VIII,9-10. A III,9. P 14. V I,5. LL 27-29. Scales on body large, cycloid; two rows on cheek; preopercle scaled. Lateral line continuous, following contour of back to below end of spinous dorsal fin where it descends to midline, onto caudal peduncle. Dorsal fin short-based with tall spinous section headed by small spine; notched deeply before last spine which heads soft-rayed section. Anal fin headed by small spine followed by two long subequal spines. Silvery transparent, yellowish inside. East coast estuaries from southern Queensland to southern New South Wales. Schools in lakes and along the tidal channels from the sea to estuaries, along breakwaters and under jetties which offer shelter from the strong currents; feeds on zooplankton from near the surface to the substrate. Attains 70 mm.

RAMSAY'S GLASSFISH
Ambassis marianus Günther, 1880

D VII-VIII,9-10. A III,10-11. P 14. V I,5. LL 24-26. Scales on body large, cycloid; two rows on cheek; preopercle scaled. Lateral line interrupted, from below end of spinous dorsal fin to midline. Dorsal fin short-based with tall spinous section headed by small spine; notched deeply before last spine which heads soft-rayed section. Anal fin headed by small spine followed by two long subequal spines. Silvery transparent, somewhat dusky. East coast estuaries from southern Queensland to central New South Wales. Schools in lakes and along the tidal channels from the sea to estuaries, along breakwaters and in under sheltered areas, usually in brackish water. Attains 10 cm.

BIGEYES
FAMILY PRIACANTHIDAE

A small family of distinct-looking fishes comprising four genera and about 17 species distributed worldwide in tropical to subtropical seas. Three genera and eight species are currently recognised in Australia, and three species are known from south-eastern coastal waters. They are known as red bullseyes, goggle-eyes and glass-eyes because of their most obvious feature – the very large eyes. The body is somewhat elongate and compressed, and scales are small. The lateral line is complete and placed high along the fish's sides. The head is large and there is a prominent spine at the angle of the preopercle. The mouth is very oblique and nearly vertical; the jaws, vomer and palatines have numerous rows of small to large conical teeth. Dorsal fin spines are depressible into a groove, and the ventral fins are connected to the belly by a membrane. Nocturnal fishes, the bigeyes are usually reddish-brown to deep red depending on depth. They feed on crustaceans, cephalopods and fishes. Bigeyes are usually solitary, but are known to school in some areas.

SPOTTED BIGEYE
Priacanthus macracanthus Cuvier, 1829

D X,12-14. A III,13-14. P 17-18 . V I,5. LL 66-83. LSR 85-96. Small ctenoid scales cover body, head. Lateral line distinct, curving slightly upwards from origin, then nearly straight to caudal peduncle. Spine at angle of preopercle long, slender; short in small juveniles. Dorsal and anal fin spines subequal to following soft rays. Caudal fin rounded in juveniles, has rounded corners in adults. Colour greatly variable depending on age, time of day, depth. Usually blotchy on body, brown to bright red. Widespread tropical west Pacific, ranging south to eastern Victoria. Juveniles in shallow estuaries, nearly always in soft corals during the day. Adults secretive, in deep rocky ledges; best known from trawls. Juveniles in 3-20 m; adults to at least 100 m. Nocturnal, feeding over sandy or muddy substrates on shrimps. Attains 46 cm.

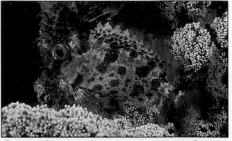

Priacanthus macracanthus   Adult ▼ Juv. ▲

CRESCENT-TAIL BIGEYE
Priacanthus hamrur (Forsskål, 1775)

D X,14-15. A III,14-15. P 17-19. V I,5. LL 75-80. LSR 112-119. Small ctenoid scales cover body, head. Lateral line distinct, curving slightly upwards from origin, then nearly straight to caudal peduncle. Spine at angle of preopercle short and broad in young, seemingly rather undeveloped in adults, with coarse serrae on margin above. Dorsal and anal fin spines subequal to following soft rays; posterior fin parts rounded. Anal fin emarginate in young, deeply lunate in adults. Usually bright red, banded at night or as fright pattern. Widespread tropical Indo-Pacific from Sydney to southern Japan and to east Africa and Red Sea. Coastal reefs and lagoons, solitary or small aggregations in caves or deep crevices; 10-100 m. Attains 45 cm.

GLASSEYE
Priacanthus blochii (Lacepède, 1801)

D X,12-14. A III,13-15. P 17-19. V I,5. LL 69-77. LSR 100-110. Small ctenoid scales cover body, head. Lateral line distinct, with short curve upwards from origin, then nearly straight to caudal peduncle. Spine at angle of preopercle short but prominent in young, seemingly rather undeveloped in adults, with coarse serrae on margin above. Dorsal and anal fin spines subequal to following soft rays; posterior fin parts rounded. Anal fin rounded in young, truncate in adults. Usually bright red when hiding or at night, silvery when in the open during the day; usually a series of dark spots along lateral line. Widespread tropical Indo-Pacific from central New South Wales to southern Japan, and to east Africa and Red Sea. Lagoons and protected outer reefs in 3-30 m, probably ranging deeper. Singly or in small aggregations; sometimes in the open during the day. Attains 30 cm. This species often confused with similar *Heteropriacanthus cruentatus* (Lacepède, 1801), which differs in being slightly deeper bodied, lacking scales on pre-opercle margin. Records from New South Wales need to be verified.

CARDINALFISHES
FAMILY APOGONIDAE

The cardinalfishes are a very large family of small fishes commonly found on coral reefs. A small number occur in temperate waters. Presently some 26 genera containing an estimated 250 species are distributed globally, of which about 20 genera and more than 100 species occur in Australian coastal waters. Many species are undescribed and various problems with similar species need to be solved to determine the number of species more accurately. The majority of species live in shallow coastal waters, occupying caves and crevices during the day and drifting out in the open during the night to feed. A few species live deep on continental slopes and some are restricted to fresh water. Most feed on small invertebrates and a few on small fishes as well, but their large mouth serves an additional purpose – as a brooding chamber. The male incubates the eggs in his mouth. The hatchlings have a pelagic stage and on the east coast a number of tropical species expatriate to the south coast, sometimes greatly outnumbering the local species. Of the 23 species included here, only seven are considered true local south coast species. The shallow tropical species are mostly less than 15 cm in maximum length, and some are as small as 4 cm. Apogons typically have two spines in the anal fin, two usually separate dorsal fins, large eyes, and large scales. The deepwater species are an exception, having small, loosely attached scales. Of the three subfamilies, only Apogoninae is presented here.

Southern Orange-Lined Cardinalfish (*Apogon properuptus*) with Sydney Cardinalfish (*A. limenus*) in the background

SILVER SIPHONFISH
Siphamia roseigaster (Ogilby, 1886)

D VI+I,10. A II,9-10. P 14. V I,5. LL 26. Body compressed with large cycloid to slightly ctenoid scales. Mouth oblique; jaws with narrow bands of villiform teeth, sometimes on vomer, absent on palatines. Dorsal fins separate; first spinous, small, steeply rounded; second with long soft rays headed by spine. Anal fin similar to and opposite second dorsal fin. Tube-like subcutaneous gland along either side of anal fin, continuing over belly. Shiny silvery; sometimes blackish line above base of dorsal and anal fins. East coast only, from central New South Wales to about Gladstone, Queensland. Coastal estuaries in small to large aggregations, usually muddy and rocky habitat. Attains 75 mm. This genus comprises about 20 species, including small tropical species which live among spines of sea-urchins or crown-of-thorns seastars.

LITTLE SIPHONFISH
Siphamia cephalotes (Castelnau, 1875)

D VI+I,8. A II,8. P 12. V I,5. LL 25. Body moderately compressed with large cycloid to slightly ctenoid scales. Mouth oblique; jaws with narrow bands of villiform teeth, others on vomer, palatines. Dorsal fins separate; first spinous, small, steeply pointed at second spine; second headed by spine, soft-rayed section slightly higher. Anal fin similar to and opposite second dorsal fin. Tube-like subcutaneous gland along either side of anal fin, continuing over belly. Variable, greenish or brownish depending on habitat; usually brown in kelp areas, green in seagrass areas. Widespread in southern waters, from northern New South Wales to Shark Bay, Western

Australia and Tasmania. Coastal reefs and estuaries in 1-30 m; usually in small to large aggregations in vicinity of kelp or open spaces in seagrass beds. Attains 50 mm.

HARBOUR CARDINALFISH
Foa brachygramma (Jenkins, 1903)

D VII+I,9. A II,8. P 12. V I,5. LL 9-12. LSR 20. Body moderately compressed with very large cycloid scales. Mouth oblique; jaws with narrow bands of villiform teeth, others on vomer, palatines. Nostrils forward on snout with projecting tubes. Dorsal fins separate; first spinous, small, slightly pointed at third spine; second headed by spine, soft-rayed section subequal in height to first dorsal fin. Anal fin similar to and opposite second dorsal fin. Caudal fin rounded with centre slightly emarginate. Colour variable, usually speckled with faint banding, brownish or dusky. Widespread tropical Indo-Pacific, from central New South Wales to southern Japan, Hawaiian Islands and to east Africa. Quiet coastal bays and rocky estuaries, usually on mud or sand with small weedy outcrops. Attains 50 mm. This genus comprises a few secretive, very similar looking species, some probably undescribed.

VARIEGATED CARDINALFISH
Fowleria variegata (Valenciennes, 1832)

D VII+I,9. A II,8. P 13. LL 10-11. LSR 21. Body moderately compressed with very large cycloid scales. Mouth oblique; jaws with narrow bands of villiform teeth, others on vomer but absent on palatines. Nostrils forward on snout with projecting tubes. Dorsal fins separate; first spinous, small, slightly pointed at third spine; second headed by spine, soft-rayed section rounded, subequal in height to first dorsal fin. Anal fin similar to and opposite second dorsal fin. Caudal fin rounded. Pale to dark brown with variable spotting all over; dark patch on opercle. Widespread tropical Indo-Pacific, from Sydney Harbour to southern Japan and Micronesia, and to the Red Sea. Lagoons and coastal reefs. Shallow reef channels in large rubble pieces or under coral slabs; very secretive. Attains 65 mm. Small genus, about five species, all very secretive during the day; in need of revision.

EASTERN GOBBLEGUTS
Vincentia novaehollandiae (Valenciennes, 1832)

D VII+I,8-9. A II,8-9. P 14-15. LL 24-27. Body oval, compressed, with long caudal peduncle; covered with large ctenoid scales. Lateral line evenly curved with dorsal profile, continuing onto caudal fin. Posterior margin of preopercle serrated, coarse at rounded angle. Mouth large, oblique; jaws, vomer, palatines with narrow bands of villiform teeth. Dorsal fins just separate, tall, somewhat angular. Caudal fin slightly emarginate with rounded corners. Ventral fin large, similar in size to, and opposite first dorsal fin. Coppery-brown with pale or dark speckles. East coast from central New South Wales to southern Queensland and Lord Howe Island. Harbours, estuaries, protected coastal bays in 3-20 m. Secretive, out at night, floating near reefs close to the substrate. Attains 10 cm. Australian temperate genus comprising about five species.

Vincentia novaehollandiae   Adult ▲   Male with brood in mouth ▼

SOUTHERN GOBBLEGUTS
Vincentia conspersa (Klunzinger, 1872)

D VII+I,9-10. A II,8-9. P 14-15. LL 24-27. Body oval, compressed, with long caudal peduncle; covered with large ctenoid scales. Lateral line evenly curved with dorsal profile, continuing onto caudal fin. Posterior margin of preopercle finely serrated, coarse at rounded angle. Mouth large, oblique; jaws, vomer, palatines with narrow bands of villiform teeth. Dorsal fins just separate, tall, somewhat angular. Caudal fin slightly emarginate with rounded corners. Ventral fin large, similar in size to, and opposite first dorsal fin. Variable, dusky grey-brown to brown-red, usually with irregular dark spots; in some areas speckled with whitish spots. South coast from Wilson's Promontory to the east side of the Bight, including Tasmania. Sheltered coastal bays and rocky estuaries, in caves and crevices during the day; 3-30 m. Attains 14 cm.

Vincentia conspersa   Adult ▲   Deepwater form ▼

BULLS-EYE CARDINALFISH
Apogon atripes (Ogilby, 1916)

D VII+I,9. A II,8. P 15. LL 23. Body oval, compressed, with short caudal peduncle; covered with large cycloid scales. Lateral line evenly curved with dorsal profile, continuing onto caudal fin. Posterior margin of preopercle coarsely serrated. Mouth large, oblique; jaws, vomer, palatines with narrow bands of small conical teeth. Dorsal fins just separate, tall, somewhat rounded. Caudal fin slightly rounded with rounded corners. Ventral fins large; larger than and opposite first dorsal fin. Variable from greyish-brown to black. Ocellus above pectoral fin develops from spot in small juveniles. Caudal and pectoral fins clear, other fins usually black. East coast from Queensland to southern New South Wales. Protected coastal bays and estuaries in sponge and soft-coral areas; 6-30 m. Attains 9 cm. Often confused with similar *A. nigripinnis*, from west coast and Indian Ocean, which has LL 27, truncate caudal fin, different colour pattern.

Apogon atripes   Juv.

PLAIN CARDINALFISH
Apogon apogonides (Bleeker, 1856)

D VII+I,9. A II,8. P 14. LL 28. Body elongate, compressed, with long caudal peduncle; covered with large cycloid scales. Lateral line evenly curved with dorsal profile, continuing onto caudal fin. Posterior margin of preopercle finely serrated. Mouth large, oblique; jaws, vomer, palatines with narrow bands of small villiform teeth which are enlarged, caniniform, recurving anteriorly in jaws. Dorsal fins separate, tall, somewhat angular. Caudal fin emarginate with rounded corners. Ventral fins small; slightly smaller than and opposite first dorsal fin. Juveniles very plain without distinct markings; adults with blue lines on head, some blue spotting. Widespread tropical Indo-Pacific from New South Wales to southern Japan and to east Africa; juveniles south to Montague Island. Coastal reef flats and slopes to outer reefs below drop-offs; 3-50 m. Juveniles in small aggregations at front of caves and overhangs. Attains 10 cm.

Apogon apogonides ▲

TAIL-SPOT CARDINALFISH
Apogon cf aureus

D VII+I,9. A II,8. P 14. LL 24. Body elongate, compressed, with long caudal peduncle; covered with large cycloid scales. Lateral line evenly curved with dorsal profile, continuing onto caudal fin. Posterior margin of preopercle finely serrated. Mouth large, oblique; jaws, vomer, palatines with narrow bands of small villiform teeth which are enlarged, caniniform, recurving anteriorly in jaws. Dorsal fins separate, tall, somewhat angular. Caudal fin emarginate with rounded corners. Ventral fins small; slightly smaller than and opposite first dorsal fin. Juveniles very plain with small spot on caudal peduncle; adults with orange and blue markings. Widespread tropical south-west Pacific, south to Montague Island as juvenile. Clear coastal to offshore reefs in 6-30 m. In small to large aggregations over corals. Attains 10 cm. This species appears to be undescribed.

Apogon cf aureus ▼

Apogon aureus ▼

RING-TAIL CARDINALFISH
Apogon aureus (Lacepède, 1802)

D VII+I,9. A II,8. P 14. LL 26. Body elongate, compressed, with long caudal peduncle; covered with large cycloid scales. Lateral line evenly curved with dorsal profile, continuing onto caudal fin. Posterior margin of preopercle finely serrated. Mouth large, oblique; jaws with two to three rows of small villiform teeth, indistinct double rows on vomer, palatines. Dorsal fins separate, tall, somewhat angular; first spine minute. Caudal fin emarginate with rounded corners. Ventral fins about equal in size to and opposite first dorsal fin. Adults distinctly marked with black band on caudal peduncle; develops in small juveniles as a large spot. Widespread tropical Indo-Pacific from central New South Wales to southern Japan and to east Africa and Red Sea. Coastal reef crests and slopes; usually in small to large aggregations near large overhangs. Adults pair within aggregations. Juveniles south to Montague Island in 10-25 m, but usually more shallow on coral reefs. Attains 12 cm.

Apogon aureus Juv.

MOLUCCEN CARDINALFISH
Apogon moluccensis Valenciennes, 1828

D VII+I,9. A II,8. P 14. LL 26. Body moderately elongate, compressed, with long caudal peduncle; covered with large cycloid scales. Lateral line evenly curved with dorsal profile, continuing onto caudal fin. Posterior margin of preopercle finely serrated. Mouth large, oblique; jaws with two to three rows of small villiform teeth, double rows on vomer, palatines. Dorsal fins separate, tall, somewhat angular; first spine minute. Caudal fin emarginate with rounded corners. Ventral fins small; about equal in size to and opposite first dorsal fin. Juveniles variable; usually pale with wide orange-brown stripe; adults plain, brown to dark brown. White spot following base of second dorsal fin usually very distinct. Tropical west Pacific from New South Wales to the Philippines and probably southern Japan. Coastal reefs and lagoons; juveniles known from Sydney Harbour; 3-40 m. Attains 85 mm.

Apogon moluccensis Adult ▼ Juv. ▲

Apogon fraenatus ▼

SPINY-EYE CARDINALFISH
Apogon fraenatus Valenciennes, 1832

D VII+I,8-9. A II,8. P 14-15. LL 24-26. Body elongate, compressed, with long caudal peduncle; covered with large cycloid scales. Lateral line evenly curved with dorsal profile, continuing onto caudal fin. Posterior margin of preopercle finely serrated. Mouth large, oblique; jaws, vomer, palatines with bands of small villiform teeth. Dorsal fins separate, tall, somewhat angular; first spine minute. Caudal fin emarginate with rounded corners. Ventral fins of moderate size, about equal to and opposite first dorsal fin. Juveniles pale, adults more dusky. Widespread tropical Indo-Pacific from New South Wales to southern Japan, to east Africa and Red Sea. Juveniles south to Sydney. Coastal reefs; usually in small aggregations in narrow crevices or large groups in caves during the day; 3-30 m. Attains 10 cm.

STRIPED CARDINALFISH
Apogon fasciatus (Shaw, 1790)

D VII+I,9. A II,8. P 15-16. LL 24-27. Body moderately elongate, compressed, with long caudal peduncle; covered with large cycloid scales. Lateral line evenly curved with dorsal profile, continuing onto caudal fin. Posterior margin of preopercle finely serrated. Mouth large, oblique; jaws, vomer, palatines with bands of small villiform teeth. Dorsal fins separate, tall, somewhat angular; first spine minute. Caudal fin emarginate with rounded corners. Ventral fins of moderate size, about equal to and opposite first dorsal fin. Distinctly striped; thin stripe from snout to caudal fin margin readily identifies this species. Juveniles pale, adults more dusky. East coast from Queensland to southern New South Wales. Coastal muddy bays and estuaries in small to large aggregations, rocky reefs; 6-50 m. Attains 15 cm.

RIFLE CARDINALFISH
Apogon kiensis Jordan & Snyder, 1901

D VI+I,9. A II,8. P 15-16. LL 24-27. Body moderately elongate, compressed, with long caudal peduncle; covered with large cycloid scales. Lateral line evenly curved with dorsal profile, continuing onto caudal fin. Posterior margin of preopercle finely serrated. Mouth large, oblique; jaws, vomer, palatines with bands of small villiform teeth. Dorsal fins separate, tall, somewhat angular; first spine minute. Caudal fin emarginate with rounded corners. Ventral fins of moderate size, about equal to and opposite first dorsal fin. Distinctly striped; broad stripe from snout to caudal fin margin readily identifies this species. Widespread tropical Indo-Pacific, south to Sydney Harbour. In small aggregations in lagoons and estuaries. Attains 8 cm.

A. kiensis   Brooding male, eggs in mouth

BLACK-STRIPED CARDINALFISH
Apogon nigrofasciatus Lachner, 1953

D VII+I,9. A II,8. P 13-14. LL 24-25. Body moderately elongate, compressed, with long caudal peduncle; covered with large cycloid to finely ctenoid scales. Lateral line evenly curved with dorsal profile, continuing onto caudal fin. Posterior margin of preopercle finely serrated. Mouth large, oblique; jaws, vomer, palatines with bands of small villiform teeth. Dorsal fins separate, tall, somewhat angular; first spine minute. Caudal fin emarginate with rounded corners. Ventral fins of moderate size, about equal to and opposite first dorsal fin. Distinctly striped; interspacing white or yellow, variable width, particularly narrow when shadow-like margins of black stripes are black as well. Widespread tropical Indo Pacific, broadly ranging in the west Pacific and to the Red Sea, south to Montague Island. Coastal to outer reef drop-offs and rocky estuaries, in 3-50 m; usually in small aggregations in crevices. Attains 10 cm.

Apogon nigrofasciatus   Yellow-striped form ▼   White-striped form, Montague Island ▲

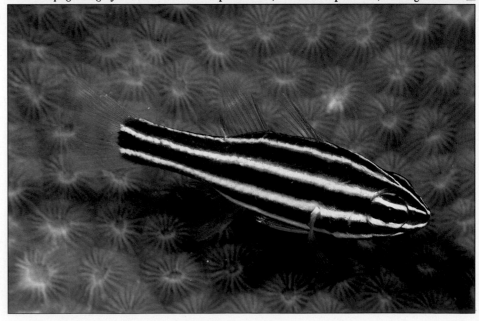

COOK'S CARDINALFISH
Apogon cookii Macleay, 1881

D VII+I,9. A II,8. P 15. LL 24-25. Body moderately elongate, compressed, with long caudal peduncle; covered with large cycloid to finely ctenoid scales. Lateral line evenly curved with dorsal profile, continuing onto caudal fin. Posterior margin of preopercle finely serrated. Mouth large, oblique; jaws, vomer, palatines with bands of small villiform teeth. Dorsal fins separate, tall, somewhat angular; first spine minute. Caudal fin emar-ginate with rounded corners. Ventral fins of moderate size, about equal to and opposite first dorsal fin. Distinctly striped; stripe, from upper orbit to below second dorsal fin origin, and large caudal base spot identify this species from similar ones. Widespread tropical Indo-Pacific from ranging broadly in the west Pacific to east Africa. Very shallow species, usually on reef crests, seagrass beds, slopes with coral pieces; secretive during the day. Attains 10 cm. Uncertain distribution with many records based on other species; juveniles probably south to Sydney.

PEARLY-LINED CARDINALFISH
Apogon taeniophorus Regan, 1905

D VII+I,9. A II,8. P 15. LL 23-24. Body moderately elongate, compressed, with long caudal peduncle; covered with large cycloid to finely ctenoid scales. Lateral line evenly curved with dorsal profile, continuing onto caudal fin. Posterior margin of preopercle finely serrated. Mouth large, oblique; jaws, vomer, palatines with bands of small villiform teeth. Dorsal fins separate, tall, somewhat angular; first spine minute. Caudal fin emarginate with rounded corners. Ventral fins of moderate size, about equal to and opposite first dorsal fin. Distinctly striped; stripe from upper orbit very short. Caudal base spot small. Widespread tropical Indo-Pacific from New South Wales to southern Japan and to east Africa; known from juveniles in Sydney Harbour. Secretive; in narrow crevices in shallow reefs, coastal and rocky estuaries in 2-10 m. Rarely sighted during the day. Attains 10 cm.

Apogon taeniophorus Juv., Sydney Harbour

SYDNEY CARDINALFISH
Apogon limenus Randall and Hoese, 1988

D VII+I,9. A II,8. P 14. LL 24. Body moderately elongate, compressed, with long caudal peduncle; covered with large cycloid to finely ctenoid scales. Lateral line evenly curved with dorsal profile, continuing onto caudal fin. Posterior margin of preopercle finely serrated. Mouth large, oblique; jaws, vomer, palatines with bands of small villiform teeth. Dorsal fins separate, tall, somewhat angular; first spine minute. Caudal fin emarginate with rounded corners. Ventral fins of moderate size, about equal to and opposite first dorsal fin. Distinctly striped; stripe from upper orbit very short. Caudal base spot large. East coast, southern Queensland to southern New South Wales, probably to eastern Victoria. Rocky estuaries to offshore reefs, usually in small aggregations in 1-30 m; usually in 3-15 m. Attains 14 cm.

Apogon limenus Juv.

Apogon cookii ▲

Apogon taeniophorus ▼

Apogon limenus ▼

FOUR-LINE CARDINALFISH
Apogon doederleini Jordan and Snyder, 1901

D VII+I,9. A II,8. P 14-15. LL 25-26. Body moderately elongate, compressed, with long caudal peduncle; covered with large cycloid to finely ctenoid scales. Lateral line evenly curved with dorsal profile, continuing onto caudal fin. Posterior margin of preopercle

Apogon doederleini   Adult ▼ Juv. ▲

finely serrated. Mouth large, oblique; jaws, vomer, palatines with bands of small villiform teeth. Dorsal fins separate, tall, somewhat angular; first spine minute. Caudal fin emarginate with rounded corners. Ventral fins of moderate size, about equal to and opposite first dorsal fin. Distinctly striped; stripes narrow compared to similar species. Widespread west Pacific from Sydney to southern Japan and north-west Australia. Coastal to outer reefs, usually in small aggregations in large crevices; 2-30 m. Juveniles south to Montague Island. Attains 14 cm.

Apogon cf hartzfeldi ▼

WHITE-LINE CARDINALFISH
Apogon cf hartzfeldi

D VII+I,9. A II,8. P 13-14. LL 25-26. Body moderately elongate, compressed, with long caudal peduncle; covered with large cycloid to finely ctenoid scales. Lateral line evenly curved with dorsal profile, continuing onto caudal fin. Posterior margin of preopercle finely serrated. Mouth large, oblique; jaws, vomer, palatines with bands of small villiform teeth. Dorsal fins separate, tall, somewhat angular; first spine minute. Caudal fin emarginate with rounded corners. Ventral fins of moderate size, about equal to and opposite first dorsal fin. Variable with thick and thin stripes, usually yellowish-greenish above. Tropical Australia, south to the Sydney area. Probably in adjacent waters; replaced in Indonesia by similar *A. hartzfeldi*. Coastal and estuarine reefs in 3-30 m; usually solitary. Attains 85 mm.

Apogon properuptus ▼

SOUTHERN ORANGE-LINED CARDINALFISH
Apogon properuptus (Whitley, 1964)

D VII+I,9. A II,8. P 13-14. LL 25-26. Body moderately elongate, compressed, with long caudal peduncle; covered with large cycloid to finely ctenoid scales. Lateral line evenly curved with dorsal profile, continuing onto caudal fin. Posterior margin of preopercle finely serrated. Mouth large, oblique; jaws, vomer with bands of small villiform teeth; teeth indistinct on palatines. Dorsal fins separate, tall, somewhat angular; first spine minute. Caudal fin emarginate with rounded corners. Ventral fins of moderate size, about equal to and opposite first dorsal fin. Colour slightly variable; adults deeper orange. East Australia from southern New South Wales to Lizard Island, Queensland, and New Caledonia. Clear coastal and outer reefs; juveniles in harbours. Among boulder rock and in ledges in 3-30 m; usually in small aggregations. Attains 85 mm. Previously confused with more tropical *A. cyanosoma* which differs in having thin orange stripes.

HALF-BAND CARDINALFISH
Apogon semiornatus Peters, 1876

D VI+I,9. A II,8. P 12-13. LL 25-26. Body moderately elongate, compressed, with long caudal peduncle; covered with large cycloid scales. Lateral line evenly curved with dorsal profile, continuing onto caudal fin. Posterior margin of preopercle finely serrated. Mouth large, oblique; jaws, vomer with bands of small villiform teeth; teeth indistinct on palatines. Dorsal fins separate, tall, somewhat angular; first spine minute. Caudal fin emarginate with rounded corners. Brownish to reddish; juveniles semitransparent. Widespread tropical Indo-Pacific, ranging broadly in the west Pacific, and to east Africa. Juveniles south to Montague Island. Shallow coastal to deep outer reefs. Secretive, in crevices and corals, but common; juveniles in small aggregations in back of caves; observed at 25 m at Montague Island. Attains 75 mm.

LONG-TAIL CARDINALFISH
Apogon coccineus Rüppell, 1838

D VI+I,9. A II,8. P 13-14. LL 24. Body moderately elongate, compressed, with rather long caudal peduncle; covered with large cycloid scales. Lateral line evenly curved with dorsal profile, continuing onto caudal fin. Posterior margin of preopercle finely serrated. Mouth large, oblique; jaws, vomer with bands of small villiform teeth; teeth indistinct on palatines. Dorsal fins separate, tall, somewhat angular; first spine minute. Caudal fin emarginate with rounded corners. Brownish to reddish; juveniles semitranspar-ent. Tropical west Pacific from central New South Wales to southern Japan and Micro-nesia, and east to Rapa. Coastal and rocky estuarine reefs in 3-20 m. Rarely seen during the day; comes out at night and a few specimens known from night-dives in Sydney Harbour. Attains 65 mm.

FIVE-LINE CARDINALFISH
Cheilodipterus quinquelineatus (Cuvier, 1828)

D VI+I,9. A II,8. P 12-13. LL 25-26. Body elongate, compressed, with rather long caudal peduncle; covered with large cycloid scales. Lateral line evenly curved with dorsal profile, continuing onto caudal fin. Posterior margin of preopercle finely serrated. Mouth large, oblique; jaws with narrow bands of villiform teeth interrupted by spaced large canines; vomer, palatines with bands of small villiform teeth. Dorsal fins separate, tall, somewhat angular. Caudal fin deeply emarginate with pointed corners. Distinctly marked; juveniles more yellow on caudal peduncle. Widespread tropical Indo-Pacific from central New South Wales to southern Japan, and to east Africa and Red Sea. Coastal reef crests and slopes from 3-40 m. Small juveniles in Sydney Harbour drift near caves or large kelp, sometimes in small aggregations. Attains 12 cm. Indo-Pacific genus comprising about another five very similar species which need revision.

C. quinquelineatus Adult ▲ Juv. ▼

TIGER CARDINALFISH
Cheilodipterus macrodon Lacepède, 1801

D VI+I,9. A II,8. P 12-13. LL 25-26. Body elongate, compressed, with rather long caudal peduncle; covered with large cycloid scales. Lateral line evenly curved with dorsal profile, continuing onto caudal fin. Posterior margin of preopercle finely serrated. Mouth large, oblique; jaws with narrow bands of conical teeth interrupted by spaced large canines; vomer, palatines with bands of small conical teeth. Dorsal fins separate, tall, somewhat angular. Caudal fin deeply emarginate with pointed corners. Changes from juvenile to adult with additional lines, loss of black caudal base spot. Best separated from similar species by yellow on head of which traces often remain, particularly in iris. West Pacific from Sydney Harbour as juveniles to southern Japan. Coastal reefs and rocky estuaries in 3-30 m. Uncertain distribution because of similar species; probably more widespread.

Cheilodipterus macrodon Juv.

LONGFIN PIKES
FAMILY DINOLESTIDAE

This family comprises a single species confined to Australian waters. The Longfin Pike is a cylindrical fish which is often confused with small species of barracuda or snook of the family Sphyraenidae. Originally this species was placed in the genus *Esox* in which the European pike belongs. At one stage it was included with the Apogonidae from which it differs in having only one anal fin spine and a much greater number of soft rays in both the dorsal and anal fins. The genus was established by Klunzinger in 1872, and interestingly three different authors described this species under different names in the same year.

LONGFIN PIKE
Dinolestes lewini (Griffith, 1834)

D VI-VII,15-19. A I,25-29. C 17. P 16-17. V I,5. LL 64-70. Body long, cylindrical, with small cycloid scales extended over head; caudal peduncle deep. Lateral line virtually straight. Snout pointed, mouth large; single series of small teeth in jaws, several large canines anteriorly. Dorsal fins widely separate; first small, second headed by one or two feeble spines. Anal fin with one spine, its origin opposite origin of second dorsal fin, but base much longer. Caudal fin weakly forked. Silvery-grey in coastal waters, becoming brownish above in estuaries. Widespread southern waters, ranging from central New South Wales to about Perth, and to southern Tasmania. Occurs from shallow seagrass beds to deep offshore reefs to at least 60 m. Usually schools in either small aggregations or very large, sometimes dense schools of thousands of individuals. Attains 50 cm. Not commercially caught, but good eating.

WHITINGS
FAMILY SILLAGINIDAE

The Sillaginidae are a moderate-sized family, widespread in the tropical to temperate Indo-Pacific, comprising three genera and about 25 species. Of these, two genera and almost half the species occur in Australian waters, and six species range into south-eastern waters. Popularly known as whiting in Australia, they are not related to the European whiting (Gadidae). Mostly found in estuaries and coastal waters, these fishes usually school, and feed on sand-dwelling invertebrates, particularly polychaete worms. They feature elongate bodies with a moderate-sized head and pointed snout. Their mouth is small with villiform or fine teeth, and sometimes the outer row is enlarged. Their scales are small and ctenoid. The dorsal fin is in two parts; the first is spinous, and the second long-based and usually headed by one spine. The anal fin is headed by two spines and is similar to and opposite the second dorsal fin. A few species attain a reasonable size for commercial value, but some of the southern species are important as both commercial and sportfishes, the largest reaching 72 cm and 4.8 kg.

KING GEORGE WHITING
Sillaginodes punctatus (Cuvier, 1829)

D XII-XIII+I,25-27. A II,21-24. C 17. P 15-16. V I,5. LL 129-147. Body elongate, slightly compressed, covered by small ctenoid scales extending onto head, becoming cycloid anteriorly. Lateral line with slight curve over pectoral fins. Teeth in jaws small, villiform. Dorsal fin low, in two parts; first with feeble spines, followed closely by second part, long section of soft rays headed by feeble spine. Anal fin long-based, similar to and opposite second dorsal fin. Caudal fin deeply emarginate. Pectoral and ventral fins small. Colour variable with size, habitat; usually greenish-grey above, silvery below with small spots. Widespread in southern waters, ranging to northern New South Wales and Jurien Bay in Western Australia. On sandy areas with seagrass beds in shallow bays and estuaries to coastal bays in 25 m. Feeds on molluscs, worms and particularly shrimps. Attains 72 cm and 4.8 kg. Monotypic genus. Largest species in family. Sought-after sportfish; excellent to eat, of great commercial value. Other names used are Spotted or Australian Whiting.

Sillaginodes punctatus   Adult ▼ Juv. ▲

SILVER WHITING
Sillago bassensis Cuvier, 1829

D XI-XII+I,18-19. A II,18-20. C 17. P 15-16. V I,5. LL 66-73. Body elongate, slightly compressed, covered by small ctenoid scales extending to cheek on head. Lateral line with slight curve over pectoral fins. Jaws with fine teeth. Dorsal fin low, in two parts; first with feeble spines, followed closely by second part, long section of soft rays headed by feeble spine. Anal fin long-based, similar to and opposite second dorsal fin. Caudal fin deeply emarginate. Pectoral and ventral fins small. Pale sandy colour, pinkish above, often with oblique series of rusty spots. South coast from Western Port Bay to southern Western Australia. Quiet coastal bays, usually in schools over open sand; adults in 6-40 m, juveniles often over sandbanks washed by tides. Attains 33 cm, and about 0.4 kg. This genus contains the majority of species, nine of which occur in Australian waters and five are included here.

Sillago bassensis ▲

Sillago flindersi ▼

SCHOOL WHITING
Sillago flindersi McKay, 1985

D XI+I,16-18. A II,18-20. C 17. P 15-16. V I,5. LL 65-69. Body elongate, slightly compressed, covered by small ctenoid scales extending to cheek on head. Lateral line with slight curve over pectoral fins. Jaws with fine teeth. Dorsal fin low, in two parts; first with feeble spines, followed closely by second part, long section of soft rays headed by feeble spine. Anal fin long-based, similar to and opposite second dorsal fin. Caudal fin deeply emarginate. Pectoral and ventral fins small. Pale sandy with oblique rusty stripes in upper half of body, indistinct in juveniles to distinct in adults. South-east coast, from southern Queensland to eastern Tasmania. Coastal bays; juveniles in estuaries on clean sand areas. Adults schooling in 10-170 m; small juveniles on sandbanks and often in gutters on low tides. Attains 32 cm.

Sillago flindersi Newly settling juvs.

BLUE-NOSE WHITING
Sillago ciliata Cuvier, 1829

D XI+I,17-18. A II,15-16. C 17. P 16. V I,5. LL 61-65. Body elongate, slightly compressed, covered by small ctenoid scales extending to cheek on head. Lateral line with slight curve over pectoral fins. Jaws with fine teeth. Dorsal fin low, in two parts; first with feeble spines, followed closely by second part, long section of soft rays headed by feeble spine. Anal fin long-based, similar to and opposite second dorsal fin. Caudal fin deeply emarginate. Pectoral and ventral fins small. Silvery, greyish above, large specimens becoming bluish. Juveniles blotchy along upper sides. East coast from Queensland and New Caledonia to southern New South Wales and Lord Howe Island. Coastal bays and estuaries. Adults usually in 10-30 m beyond surf beaches or bays in small aggregations; juveniles in seagrass areas and sandbanks in tidal areas. Attains 50 cm and 1.25 kg. Important commercial and angling species on the east coast. Called Sand Whiting in Queensland.

TRUMPETER WHITING
Sillago maculata Quoy and Gaimard, 1824

D X-XI+I,19-21. A II,18-21. C 17. P 16-17. V I,5. LL 70-74. Body elongate, slightly compressed, covered by small ctenoid scales extending to cheek on head. Lateral line with slight curve over pectoral fins. Jaws with fine teeth. Dorsal fin low, in two parts; first with feeble spines, followed closely by second part, long section of soft rays headed by feeble spine. Anal fin long-based, similar to and opposite second dorsal fin. Caudal fin deeply emarginate. Pectoral and ventral fins small. Silvery, darker greyish above with dark irregular blotches; black at pectoral fin base. Widespread tropical Australia, south to Narooma, New South Wales and Mandurah, Western Australia. Young in seagrass areas and rocky estuaries, singly or small aggregations; adults in deeper coastal bays on sandy flats to about 30 m. Attains 30 cm. Also known as Winter Whiting in Queensland.

STOUT WHITING
Sillago robusta Stead, 1908

D XI+I,16-18. A II,16-19. C 17. P 17. V I,5. LL 64-70. Body elongate, slightly compressed, covered by small ctenoid scales extending to cheek on head. Lateral line with slight curve from origin, slight descent below middle of second dorsal fin. Jaws with fine teeth. Dorsal fin low, in two parts; first with feeble, mostly subequal spines, followed closely by second part, long section of soft rays headed by feeble spine. Anal fin long-based, similar to and opposite second dorsal fin. Caudal fin deeply emarginate. Pectoral and ventral fins small. Silvery, greyish and yellowish above. Widespread tropical Australia, south to Eden, New South Wales, and Fremantle, Western Australia. Usually in deep offshore waters to about 70 m, but enters estuaries and shallow bays. Attains 27 cm.

TILEFISHES
FAMILY MALACANTHIDAE

A small tropical family with representatives globally, comprising two genera and nine species. The genus *Hoplolatilus*, with the majority of species, is confined to tropical coral reefs. The two Indo-Pacific species of *Malacanthus* are widespread and range into southern waters, and are common-

ly known as blanquillos. These slender fishes are found on sandy reef flats, either solitary or in pairs, swimming typically just above the bottom and dashing over short distances for a quick stop to study surroundings. Burrows are made under rocks on sand and often several are in the vicinity of their feeding range, allowing the fishes to quickly go for cover if there is a potential threat. Adults may build large nesting sites, shifting large quantities of sand. They are distinctly marked with stripes on the body or tail; juveniles differ greatly from adults in some

species. The body is covered with tiny scales and has a long-based dorsal fin over the entire length. The anal fin is similar to and opposite the dorsal fin from the anus on. The opercle has a prominent spine posteriorly. The mouth is almost horizontal and the jaws have villiform teeth, and some small canines anteriorly. There are no teeth on the vomer or palatines. Postlarval stages are large (3-7 cm) when settling, suggesting a prolonged pelagic life.

FLAGTAIL BLANQUILLO
Malacanthus brevirostris Guichenot, 1848

D V,54-57. A I,48-52. P 15-17. LL 166-175. Body very elongate, covered with small ctenoid scales. Small scales on cheek, opercle. Distinct, prominent spine ends opercle. Snout bluntly pointed; jaws with rows of villiform teeth, outer row enlarged. Dorsal fin headed by weak spines which are confluent with soft rays. Caudal fin rounded in juveniles, becoming more truncate in adults. Ventral fins very small. Little variation in colour from juvenile to adult. Settling young very pale, nearly translucent with dark oblique marks in fins. Widespread tropical Indo-Pacific, to southern Japan, east Pacific, and to east Africa and Red Sea; juveniles south to Montague Island. Along margins of quiet coastal reefs on sand, or in sand flats within large reefs. Usually in 6-50 m. Settling juveniles large, 7-9 cm, secretive, under rocks. Feeds primarily on sand-dwelling invertebrates. Recorded to 30 cm, but commonly to 20 cm.

Malacanthus brevirostris　Adult ▼　Juv. ▲

BLUE BLANQUILLO
Malacanthus latovittatus (Lacepède, 1801)

D IV,43-46. A I,38-40. P 16-17. LL 120-130. Body very elongate, covered with small ctenoid scales. Small scales on cheek, opercle. Distinct, prominent spine ends opercle. Snout long, conical; jaws with rows of villiform teeth, outer row enlarged. Dorsal fin headed by weak spines which are confluent with soft rays. Caudal fin rounded in juveniles, becoming more truncate in adults. Ventral fins very small. Juveniles very different from adults in being almost black, except ventrally, with pale stripe dorsally. Widespread tropical Indo-Pacific from eastern Australia to Hawaii, Japan and to east Africa and Red Sea; south to Montague Island as juveniles. Adults usually in pairs on outer reef crests, juveniles on coastal reef slopes; often quite deep, 20-30 m. Attains 40 cm.

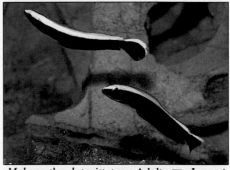

Malacanthus latovittatus　Adults ▼　Juvs. ▲

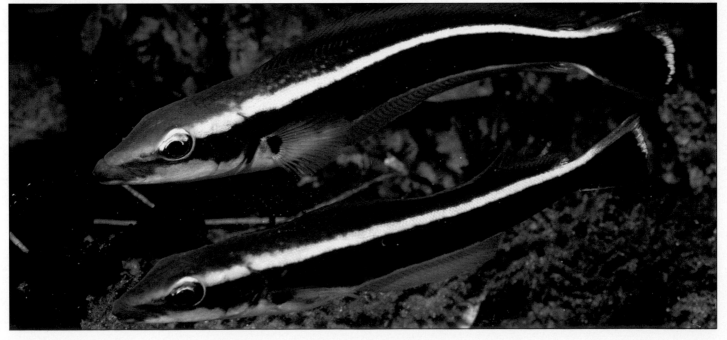

TAILORS
FAMILY POMATOMIDAE

Only a single wide-ranging species is currently recognised in this family, with populations in the Atlantic, southern Indian Ocean and eastern Australia. A pelagic schooling fish, it voraciously hunts smaller pelagic fishes such as pilchards or mullet, and ranges from tropical to warm-temperate seas. The streamlined body covered with smooth scales and the large tail are the ingredient needed for speed and strength, making it an excellent game fish. Known as Bluefish in America and Elf in South Africa.

TAILOR
Pomatomus saltatrix (Linnaeus, 1766)

D VIII-VIX, 23-28. A III,23-27. C 17. P 16-17. V I,5. LL 90-100. Body moderately elongate, compressed, covered by small ctenoid scales. Scales on opercle, preopercle, along bases of second dorsal fin and anal fin. Lateral line slightly curved over pectoral fin, then straight. Mouth oblique; jaws with single series of small, sharp, compressed teeth; additional row of small conical teeth in lower jaw. Dorsal fin divided; first part with short spines, depressible into groove; second headed by one spine, long-based with elevated anterior soft rays. Anal fin with three spines; first two small, usually separate from rest of fin, mostly embedded. Caudal fin large, forked. Pectoral and ventral fins rather small. Slightly variable from steel-grey to bluish above, silvery below. In Australia, recorded in southern waters, north to Fraser Island, Queensland and Onslow, Western Australia. Elsewhere known from America's east coast, Mediterranean, Africa, southern Indian Ocean. Occurs in fast swimming schools in open ocean and along shore; usually close to surface, but observed down to 15 m. Attains at least 1.2 m and 14 kg.

Pomatomus saltatrix   Adult ▲ Dense school ▼

REMORAS
FAMILY ECHENEIDIDAE

A small distinct family, easily recognised by the large sucking-disc dorsally on the head and nape. The family comprises four genera and eight species. All genera and seven species occur in Australian waters; one species is included here. The sucker disc is, in fact, a modified first dorsal fin comprising transverse movable laminae, and is used to attach by suction to other fish, usually sharks or rays. Some remoras are host-specific, however others may attach to almost anything which moves, including ships and divers. Food is obtained when the host is feeding, but parasitic copepods which may attach to the host are taken as well. The remoras feature an elongate body with tiny embedded scales, a depressed head, a greatly protruding lower jaw, and dorsal and anal fins which are like a mirror image of each other, similar and opposite.

SLENDER SUCKERFISH
Echeneis naucrates Linnaeus, 1758

Disc laminae 20-28 pairs. D 31-42. A 30-38. C 17. P 21-24. V I,5. Body very elongate, shallow. Mouth small; lower jaw protruding well in advance of upper jaw; bands of villiform teeth in jaws, patches on vomer and tongue. Disc extending over head and anterior part of trunk, elongate, about two and a half times longer than wide. Scales minute, embedded; lateral line indistinct. Dorsal and anal fins with elevated anterior rays. Caudal fin truncate or slightly emarginate. Pectoral fins high on body, similar to and almost opposite ventral fins. Colour patterns variable from distinctly striped in juveniles to sometimes almost uniform grey in large adults. Occurs in all tropical seas, except east Pacific, and on the east coast south to the Sydney area. Mostly pelagic offshore, but enters coastal and estuarine waters with host. Usually attached to sharks and rays; often swimming free. Attains 1 m. Also known as Shark Remora or Striped Suckerfish.

Echeneis naucrates ▼   Close-up showing sucking-disc ▲

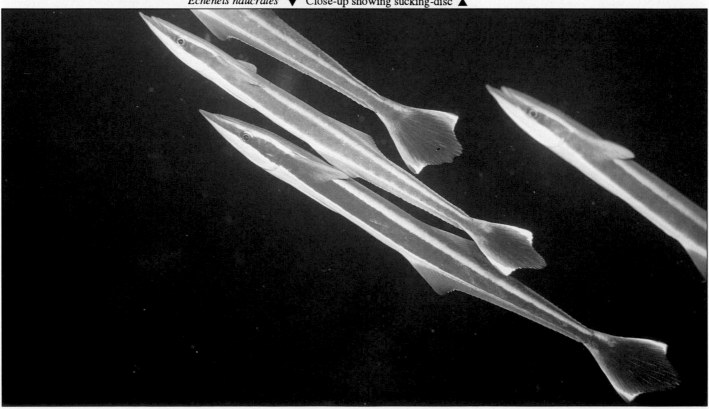

BLACK KINGFISHES
FAMILY RACHYCENTRIDAE

This family contains a single wide-ranging species found in all tropical seas except the east Pacific. A large pelagic species, it attains at least 2 m, and large adults are usually in small aggregations. They occasionally visit reefs and under water have the appearance of a shark. This can be scary for a diver as these fishes are curious and often approach quickly to within close range. Juveniles look similar to the Slender Suckerfish, but lack the sucking-disc and have small spines instead, the second part of their dorsal fin is placed well ahead of the anal fin, and the pectoral fins are positioned low on the body. They feed primarily on crustaceans and are sometimes known as crab-eaters. Elsewhere they are known as Cobia.

BLACK KINGFISH
Rachycentron canadum (Linnaeus, 1766)

D VIII-X,33-36. A II-III,22-28. P 21-22. V I,5. LL >300. Body cylindrical with broad, depressed head. Scales very small, pointed; lateral line almost straight with some irregular shallow curves in anterior part. Mouth moderately large; bands of fine teeth in jaws, minute on palatines, vomer, tongue. Dorsal fin headed by very short spines, without membranes, depressible into groove; has long soft-rayed section headed by one spine and anteriorly elevated. Anal fin similar but shorter based and opposite posterior part of dorsal fin. Caudal fin truncate in juveniles, becoming lunate in adults. Ventral fins small, pectoral fins closely placed above. Juveniles distinctly striped, becoming plain brownish in large adults. In Australia in tropical waters, ranging on the east coast to at least Jervis Bay. Juveniles sometimes singly on coastal reefs; adults usually sighted in small groups of three to six individuals, entering shallow water; observed in 2-3 m. Reported to attain over 2 m and almost 70 kg. Excellent game fish, good eating, but of little commercial value.

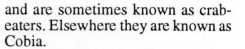
Rachycentron canadum   Adult ▼ Juv ▲

JACKS AND TREVALLIES
FAMILY CARANGIDAE

A large tropical to temperate family comprising approximately 25 genera and 140 species. Many are pelagic and wide-ranging, and some enter brackish water. Many species are food and game fish and in general are of great commercial value. At least 23 species range on the east coast to southern coastal waters, and many are expatriates as either or both juvenile and adult. Many species migrate as adults over great distances, so they may commonly occur in certain areas for only a few months of the year. Many of the postlarval stages come with floating objects or weed rafts, and are taken by the currents to southern waters well beyond their normal range. The species included here are mostly known to range as adults to coastal central New South Wales. The jacks and trevallies are streamlined, fast swimming, usually schooling fishes, with some diversity in shape and size. They have mostly oblong to elongate, compressed bodies, with small to tiny and often embedded cycloid scales, and usually with enlarged spiny scutes posteriorly along the lateral line. They are carnivorous, smaller species feeding on zooplankton, and larger species feeding on other fishes such as pilchards, mullet or herring-type species. The larger species attain about 2 m and about 80 kg.

Yellow-Tail Scad (*Trachurus novaezelandiae*)

170

RAINBOW RUNNER
Elagatis bipinnulata (Quoy and Gaimard, 1825)

D VII,27-30. A II,17-22. C 17. P 19-21. V I,5. LL 100. Body streamlined, elongate, slightly compressed. Scales cycloid, tiny; lateral line with long gradual curves, without scutes. Mouth moderately small, not reaching eye; jaws, vomer, palatines with villiform teeth. Dorsal and anal fins with two detached finlets each; dorsal fin with low spinous section; anal fin headed by two spines, one of which is separate; soft-rayed sections of both dorsal and anal fins only slightly elevated anteriorly. Pectoral and ventral fins pointed, small. Caudal fin deeply forked. Distinctly marked with two longitudinal blue stripes which are particularly bright in juveniles. Circumtropical species, common in coral reef areas, on the east coast ranging south to at least Montague Island. Pelagic schooling species, often in lagoons or moving along drop-offs in surface waters to about 20 m. Attains 1.2 m and about 15 kg. Monotypic genus.

Elagatis bipinnulata ▲   *Naucrates ductor* ▼

PILOT FISH
Naucrates ductor (Linnaeus, 1758)

D V-VI,25-29. A III,15-17. C 17. P 19. V I,5. LL 133-144. Body streamlined, elongate, slightly compressed. Scales cycloid, very small; lateral line with small curve over pectoral fins, without scutes. Mouth moderately small, just reaching eye; jaws with narrow bands of, and vomer and palatines with, villiform teeth. Dorsal fin has low spinous section with spines mostly unconnected in adults; anal fin headed by three spines, two of which are separate, becoming indistinct in adults. Pectoral and ventral fins pointed, small. Caudal fin deeply forked. Distinctly marked with dark cross-bands. Circumtropical, ranging to temperate waters. Pelagic, commonly inshore swimming close to large predators to feed on scraps when prey is taken. Juveniles under floating weeds or objects, sometimes washed into tidal pools. Attains 70 cm. Monotypic genus.

Seriola rivoliana ▼

HIGHFIN AMBERJACK
Seriola rivoliana Valenciennes, 1833

D VII-VIII,27-33. A III,18-22. C 17. P 19-21. V I,5. LL 122-143. Body streamlined, elongate, slightly compressed. Scales cycloid, very small; lateral line with small curve over pectoral fins, without scutes. Mouth of moderate size, reaching below eye; jaws with narrow bands of, and vomer and palatines with, villiform teeth. Dorsal fin with low spinous section, first spine minute; anal fin headed by three spines, two of which are separate, and very small in adults; soft-rayed sections of both dorsal and anal fins steeply elevated anteriorly with long tips. Pectoral and ventral fins pointed, small. Caudal fin deeply forked. Brownish or greenish above, silvery below; young with distinct oblique dark stripe over head through eye, becoming indistinct in some large adults. Circumtropical, ranging to temperate waters. Adults deep, along drop-offs in 30-140 m. Young under floating weed-rafts. Attains 1 m and about 25 kg. Known as Almaco Jack in America. This genus comprises nine species, four of which are found in Australian waters and included here. Large fishes; terrific game, excellent eating.

AMBERJACK
Seriola dumerili (Risso, 1810)

D VII-VIII,32-33. A III,19-22. C 17. P 20-23. V I,5. LL 165-180. Body streamlined, elongate, slightly compressed. Scales cycloid, very small; lateral line with small curve over pectoral fins, without scutes. Mouth of moderate size, reaching below eye; jaws with narrow bands of, and vomer and palatines with, villiform teeth. Dorsal fin with low spinous section, first spine minute in adults; anal fin headed by three spines, two of which are separate, and very small in adults; soft-rayed sections of both dorsal and anal fins steeply elevated anteriorly. Pectoral and ventral fins pointed, small. Caudal fin deeply forked. Bluish or purplish above, silvery below, often with amber stripe from snout to caudal peduncle. Circumtropical, ranging to warm-temperate waters; south to at least Jervis Bay on the east coast. Schooling species along reefs, usually deeper than 20 m; was observed from a submersible at 335 m. Attains almost 2 m and 80 kg.

YELLOW-TAIL KINGFISH
Seriola lalandi Valenciennes, 1833

D VIII,30-37. A III,19-21. C 17. P 20-21. V I,5. LL 161-162. Body streamlined, elongate, slightly compressed. Scales cycloid, very small; lateral line with small curve over pectoral fins, without scutes. Mouth of moderate size, reaching below eye; jaws with narrow bands of, and vomer and palatines with, villiform teeth. Dorsal fin with low spinous section, first spine minute in adults; anal fin headed by three spines, two of which are separate, and very small in adults; soft-rayed sections of both dorsal and anal fins elevated anteriorly. Pectoral and ventral fins pointed, small. Caudal fin deeply forked. Bluish or greenish above, silvery-white below; upper and lower colouration separated by broad yellowish stripe. Small juveniles yellowish with dark vertical bands. Broadly distributed in tropical and warm-temperate seas of the southern hemisphere and northern Pacific. On the east coast ranging south to Tasmania, and Port Phillip Bay. Schooling on coastal reefs, entering estuaries. Attains almost 2 m and 60 kg.

Seriola lalandi   Adult ▼ Juv. ▲

SAMSON FISH
Seriola hippos Günther, 1876

D VIII,22-25. A III,16-17. C 17. P 19-21. V I,5. LL 130. Body streamlined, elongate, slightly compressed. Scales cycloid, very small; lateral line with small curve over pectoral fins, without scutes. Mouth of moderate size, reaching below eye; jaws with narrow bands of, and vomer and palatines with, villiform teeth. Dorsal fin with low spinous section, first spine minute in adults; anal fin headed by three spines, two of which are separate, and very small in adults; soft-rayed sections of both dorsal and anal fins elevated anteriorly. Pectoral and ventral fins pointed, small. Caudal fin deeply forked. Adults greenish above, silvery below. Young yellow with broad vertical bands. South coast, to Moreton Bay on the east coast and Shark Bay on the west coast. Adults on deep reefs to about 70 m, often solitary or in small aggregations. Juveniles under floating objects. Attains 1.5 m and 50 kg.

Seriola hippos Juv.

GOLDEN TREVALLY
Gnathanodon speciosus (Forsskål, 1775)

D VIII,18-21. A III,15-17. C 17. P 20-23. V I,5. LLScutes 15-25. Body oval, compressed; head large, bluntly rounded. Mouth moderately large, lips thick; minute teeth, only present in small juveniles. Scales tiny, cycloid, covering body including thorax; lateral line with long curve over pectoral fin, ends in large scutes over caudal peduncle. Dorsal fin divided; first part with small spines; second headed by spine, soft-rayed with elevated anterior section. Anal fin with three spines, two of which are separate and short; similar to and opposite second dorsal fin. Caudal fin deeply forked; pectoral fin with very long upper rays reaching to straight posterior section on lateral line. Juveniles bright golden with black vertical stripes; adults become silvery with scattered spotting. Widespread tropical Indo-Pacific; juveniles expatriate to the Sydney area on the east coast. Coastal reefs; adults over open sand, juveniles under floating objects or swimming close to large pelagics. Attains 1 m and 15 kg. Monotypic genus.

173

BIG-EYE TREVALLY
Caranx sexfasciatus Quoy and Gaimard, 1825

D VIII-IX,19-21. A III,16-18. C 17. P 22-23. V I,5. LLScutes 28-37. Body oval, compressed; head large, bluntly rounded. Mouth moderately large; jaws with row of strong conical teeth, upper with inner villiform band; vomer, palatines, tongue with villiform teeth. Scales tiny, cycloid, covering body, including thorax; lateral line with long curve over pectoral fin, ends in large scutes over caudal peduncle. Dorsal fin divided; first part with small spines; second soft-rayed, headed by spine, has elevated, pointed anterior section. Anal fin with three spines, two of which are well separate and short; similar to and opposite second dorsal fin. Caudal fin deeply forked; pectoral fin with very long upper rays reaching to straight posterior section on lateral line. Silvery, grey above; juveniles with dark cross-bars. Widespread tropical Indo-Pacific; south to Sydney on the east coast. Adults along deep drop-offs, 30-60 m; juveniles school in estuaries. Attains 85 cm. Genus comprises about 13 species, three of which are included here.

Caranx sexfasciatus ▲　　　　　　　　*Caranx ignobilis* ▼

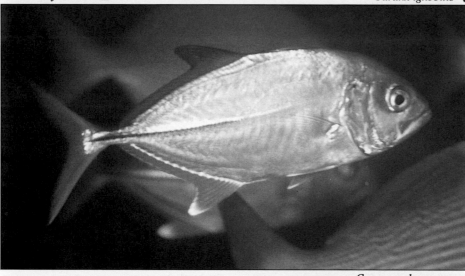

GIANT TREVALLY
Caranx ignobilis (Forsskål, 1775)

D IX,19-21. A III,15-17. C 17. P 20-21. V I,5. LLScutes 30-39. Body oval, compressed; head large, bluntly rounded. Mouth moderately large; jaws with row of small conical teeth, upper with inner villiform band; vomer, palatines, tongue with villiform teeth. Scales tiny, cycloid, covering body; thorax mostly naked; lateral line with long curve over pectoral fin, ends in large scutes over caudal peduncle. Dorsal fin divided; first part with small spines; second soft-rayed, headed by spine, has elevated, pointed anterior section. Anal fin with three spines, two of which are well separate and short; similar to and opposite second dorsal fin. Caudal fin deeply forked; pectoral fin with very long upper rays reaching to straight posterior section on lateral line. Dusky grey above, silvery below; juveniles with yellowish anal and lower caudal fins. Widespread tropical Indo-Pacific; south to the Sydney area on the east coast. Inner reefs, usually deep, 20-40 m, on sand flats and in reef channels. Attains 1.7 m and 62 kg.

BLUE-FIN TREVALLY
Caranx melampygus Cuvier, 1833

D IX,20-25. A III,17-20. C 17. P 20-21. V I,5. LLScutes 30-40. Body oval, compressed; head large, bluntly rounded. Mouth moderately large; jaws with row of small conical teeth, upper with inner villiform band; vomer, palatines, tongue with villiform teeth. Scales tiny, cycloid, covering body and thorax; lateral line with long curve over pectoral fin, ends in large scutes over caudal peduncle. Dorsal fin divided; first part with small spines; second soft-rayed, headed by spine, has elevated, pointed anterior section. Anal fin with three spines, two of which are well separate and short; similar to and opposite second dorsal fin. Caudal fin deeply forked; pectoral fin with very long upper rays reaching to straight posterior section on lateral line. Greyish above, sometimes faintly banded; median fins blue. Widespread tropical Indo-Pacific, on the east coast south to Seal Rocks, New South Wales. Coastal reefs, often solitary along slopes. Attains 70 cm and about 7 kg.

Caranx melampygus ▼

BANDED TREVALLY
Carangoides ferdau (Forsskål, 1775)

D IX,29-33. A III,21-26. C 17. P 21-23. V I,5. LLScutes 21-37. Body oval, compressed; head large, bluntly rounded. Mouth moderately large; jaws with bands of villiform teeth, outer ones enlarged; vomer, palatines, tongue with villiform teeth. Scales tiny, cycloid, covering body; thorax naked ventrally; lateral line with low curve over pectoral fin, ends in large scutes over caudal peduncle. Dorsal fin divided; first part with small spines; second soft-rayed, headed by spine, has elevated, pointed anterior section. Anal fin with three spines, two of which are well separate and short; similar to and opposite second dorsal fin. Caudal fin deeply forked; pectoral fin with very long upper rays reaching to straight posterior section on lateral line. Bluish-green above, mostly greyish with distinct to faint broad banding. Widespread tropical Indo-Pacific, on the east coast south to Bermagui. Coastal reefs, solitary or in small aggregations along deep slopes to 60 m. Attains 70 cm. Large genus, comprising about 20 species, three ranging to southern waters.

BLUE TREVALLY
Carangoides orthogrammus (Jordan and Gilbert, 1882)

D VIII,29-33. A III,26-27. C 17. P 21-23. V I,5. LLScutes 22-30. Body oval, compressed; head large, bluntly rounded. Mouth moderately large; jaws with bands of villiform teeth, outer ones enlarged; vomer, palatines, tongue with villiform teeth. Scales tiny, cycloid, covering body; thorax naked ventrally; lateral line with low curve over pectoral fin, ends in large scutes over caudal peduncle. Dorsal fin divided; first part with small spines; second soft-rayed, headed by spine, has elevated, pointed anterior section. Anal fin with three spines, two of which are well separate and short; similar to and opposite second dorsal fin. Caudal fin deeply forked; pectoral fin with very long upper rays reaching to straight posterior section on lateral line. Bluish-grey with blue fins; some scattered dark spots and a few yellow spots on body. West Pacific, ranging south to Sydney. Coastal reefs, schooling in Queensland, swimming with other fish further south. Attains 60 cm.

LONG-NOSE TREVALLY
Carangoides chrysophrys (Cuvier, 1833)

D IX,19-21. A III,15-16. C 17. P 20. V I,5. LLScutes 17-28. Body oval, compressed; head large, bluntly rounded. Mouth moderately large; jaws with bands of villiform teeth, outer ones enlarged; vomer, palatines, tongue with villiform teeth. Scales tiny, cycloid,

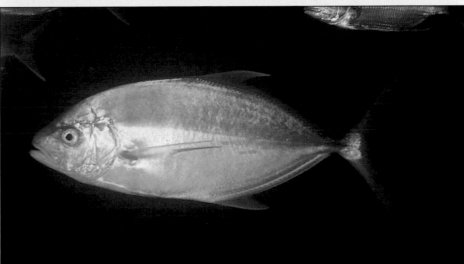

Carangoides orthogrammus ▲   *Carangoides chrysophrys* ▼

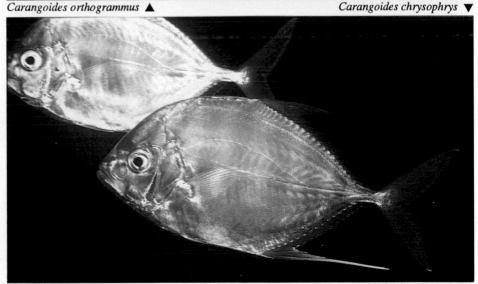

covering body; thorax naked ventrally; lateral line with low curve over pectoral fin, ends in large scutes over caudal peduncle. Dorsal fin divided; first part with small spines; second soft-rayed, headed by spine, has elevated, pointed anterior section, filamented in juveniles. Anal fin with three spines, two of which are well separate and short; similar to and opposite second dorsal fin. Caudal fin deeply forked; pectoral fin with very long upper rays reaching to straight posterior section on lateral line. Shiny silvery, bluish-green above; juveniles broadly banded. West Pacific and Indian Ocean to east Africa. Coastal reefs, in small aggregations; make grunting noises when caught. Attains 60 cm.

WHITE TREVALLY
Pseudocaranx dentex (Bloch and Schneider, 1801)

D IX,25-28. A III,21-24. C 17. P 18-19. V I,5. LLScutes 34-46. Body oval, compressed; head large, bluntly rounded. Mouth moderately large; jaws with bands of villiform teeth, outer ones enlarged; vomer, palatines, tongue with villiform teeth. Scales tiny, cycloid, covering body; thorax naked ventrally; lateral line with low curve over pectoral fin, ends in large scutes over caudal peduncle. Dorsal fins connected by low membrane; first part with small spines; second soft-rayed, headed by spine, has elevated, pointed anterior section, filamented in juveniles. Anal fin with three spines, two of which are well separate and short; similar to and opposite second dorsal fin. Caudal fin deeply forked; pectoral fin with very long upper rays reaching to straight posterior section on lateral line. Silvery-white below, greenish-grey above; juveniles usually with yellow stripe along caudal peduncle. Widespread in all warm-temperate seas; apparently anti-tropical. South coast, extending to southern Queensland. Schools in coastal waters and enters estuaries. Attains 80 cm and 4.5 kg.

Pseudocaranx dentex   Adult ▼ Juv. ▲

SKIPJACK TREVALLY
Pseudocaranx wrighti (Whitley, 1931)

D IX,22-26. A III,19-22. C 17. P 18-19. V I,5. LLScutes 24-35. Body oval, compressed; head large, bluntly rounded. Mouth moderately large; jaws with bands of villiform teeth, outer ones enlarged; vomer, palatines, tongue with villiform teeth. Scales tiny, cycloid, covering body; thorax naked ventrally; lateral line with low curve over pectoral fin, ends in large scutes over caudal peduncle. Dorsal fins connected by low membrane; first part with small spines; second soft-rayed, headed by spine has elevated, pointed anterior section, filamented in juveniles. Anal fin with three spines, two of which are well separate and short; similar to and opposite second dorsal fin. Caudal fin deeply forked; pectoral fin with very long upper rays reaching to straight posterior section on lateral line. Blue-grey, silvery below. South coast from New South Wales to south Western Australia. Schooling, usually in great numbers, mainly in shelf waters to about 30 m. Attains 70 cm.

DIAMOND TREVALLY
Alectis indica (Rüppell, 1830)

D VII,18-19. A III,18-20. C 17. P 18. V I,5. LLScutes 5-12. Body oval, compressed, tapering evenly from midbody posteriorly. Head large, deep; mouth low, protractile; jaws with bands of villiform teeth; vomer, palatines, tongue with villiform teeth. Scales tiny, embedded; lateral line with strongly arched curve over pectoral fin. Dorsal fin spines minute, embedded in adults; soft-rayed section with tall elevated anterior section, produced as long filaments in young. Anal fin mirror image of dorsal fin. Caudal fin deeply forked; pectoral fin with very long upper rays reaching to straight posterior section on lateral line. Shiny silvery, bluish-green above; juveniles broadly banded. Widespread tropical Indo-Pacific; on the east coast south to Wollongong. Coastal reefs, entering estuaries; adults often in large schools. Attains 1.5 m and 20 kg. This genus comprises three species, two of which are included here as expatriates to the region.

THREADFIN TREVALLY
Alectis ciliaris (Bloch, 1787)

D VIII,18-22. A III,18-20. C 17. P 20. V I,5. LLScutes 8-15. Body oval, compressed, tapering evenly from midbody posteriorly. Head large, deep; mouth low, protractile; jaws with bands of villiform teeth; vomer, palatines, tongue with villiform teeth. Scales tiny, embedded; lateral line with strongly arched curve over pectoral fin. Dorsal fin spines minute, embedded in adults; soft-rayed section with tall elevated anterior section, produced as long filaments in young. Anal fin mirror image of dorsal fin. Caudal fin deeply forked; pectoral fin with very long upper rays reaching to straight posterior section on lateral line. Shiny silvery, bluish-green above; juveniles broadly banded. Widespread tropical Indo-Pacific, on the east coast south to Wollongong. Coastal waters and bays. Attains 1 m and 18 kg.

Alectis ciliaris ▼

Alectis ciliaris Juv.

QUEENFISH
Scomberoides lysan (Forsskål, 1775)

D VII-VIII,19-21. A III,17-19. C 17. P 17-18. V I,5. Body elongate, slightly compressed; long tapering posterior section. Mouth moderate-sized; two rows of conical teeth in lower jaw, one row in upper, latter with inner villiform row anteriorly. Skin leathery with small embedded lanceolate scales; lateral line almost straight, slightly curved over pectoral base, without scutes. Dorsal fin with short, almost free spines; soft-rayed section elevated anteriorly, headed by one spine, posterior rays loosely attached. Anal fin with three spines, two of which are well separate and short; similar to and opposite second dorsal fin. Caudal fin deeply forked; pectoral fin small. Silvery, bluish-green above; juveniles with single row, adults with double row of large dark blotches on sides. Widespread tropical Indo-Pacific, ranging to warm-temperate waters; on the east coast south to Sydney. Coastal reefs, young enter estuaries, singly or small groups; usually shallow, but down to 100 m. Attains 70 cm. This genus comprises four species. Possesses venomous spines, particularly on the anal fin, which can cause a painful wound.

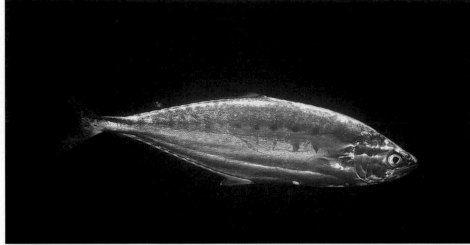

Scomberoides lysan ▲

SNUB-NOSE DART
Trachinotus blochii (Lacepède, 1801)

D VII,18-20. A III,11-18. C 17. P 20. V I,5. Body elongate, oval, slightly compressed; short tapering posterior section. Snout very blunt, mouth small; jaws with small villiform teeth in young. Body and thorax with small scales, head naked; lateral line with long low curve over pectoral base, without scutes. Dorsal fin with short, free spines, connected in juveniles only; soft-rayed section elevated greatly anteriorly, headed by one spine, posterior rays low. Anal fin with three spines, two of which are well separate and short; similar to and opposite second dorsal fin. Caudal fin deeply forked; pectoral fin small. Silvery, bluish-green above; lower anterior parts yellowish. Widespread tropical Indo-Pacific; on the east coast south to Batemans Bay. Coastal reefs, bays, lagoons, usually in small to large aggregations. Attains 65 cm. This genus comprises 19 species.

Trachinotus blochii ▼

YELLOW-TAIL SCAD
Trachurus novaezelandiae Richardson, 1843

D IX,27-33. A III,22-29. C 17. P 21-22. V I,5. LL 67-81. Body elongate, slightly compressed. Mouth moderately small; jaws with with single row of minute teeth. Scales very small, cycloid, covering body and much of head; lateral line with prominent scutes over entire length. Dorsal fin divided; first part with small spines, first spine embedded; second part soft-rayed, headed by spine, has elevated, pointed anterior section. Anal fin with three spines, two of which are well separate and short; similar to and opposite second dorsal fin. Caudal fin deeply forked; pectoral fin with very long upper rays reaching to straight posterior section on lateral line. Yellowish-green above, silvery below. Widespread southern waters to southern Queensland, and New Zealand. Similar "sister" species in Japan. Usually in large schools on coastal reefs. Attains 50 cm. This genus comprises 13 species distributed in all major oceans.

Trachurus novaezelandiae ▼

JACK MACKEREL
Trachurus declivis (Jenyns, 1841)

D IX,29-35. A III,24-29. C 17. P 20-21. V I,5. LL 71-89. Body elongate, slightly compressed. Mouth moderately small; jaws with single row of minute teeth. Scales very small, cycloid, covering body and much of head; lateral line with prominent scutes over entire length. Dorsal fin divided; first part with small spines, first spine embedded; second part soft-rayed, headed by spine, has elevated, pointed anterior section. Anal fin with three spines, two of which are well separate and short; similar to and opposite second dorsal fin. Caudal fin deeply forked; pectoral fin with very long upper rays reaching to straight posterior section on lateral line. Greenish-grey above, silvery below. Southern waters to southern Queensland and also New Zealand. Schools in great numbers, very densely packed, giving impression of large single body. Coastal to offshore on shelf, from surface to 500 m. Attains 50 cm.

SLENDER MACKEREL-SCAD
Decapterus macrosoma Bleeker, 1851

D IX,34-38. A III,28-31. C 17. P 22-23. V I,5. LL 120, scutes 24-28. Body very elongate, slightly compressed. Scales very small; lateral line straight, except for descending section above anus; scutes mainly posteriorly. A few teeth in single row anteriorly in lower jaw, none in upper. Dorsal fin divided; first section short, spinous, angular; second soft-rayed, slightly elevated anteriorly, has one separate finlet, is headed by one spine. Anal fin similar, slightly back from, opposite second dorsal fin; headed by three spines, two of which are well separate. Silvery below,

Decapterus macrosoma ▼

greenish-blue above. Widespread tropical Indo-Pacific, ranging to warm-temperate waters; on the east coast south to Eden. Clear coastal waters to deep offshore, about 150 m. Attains 30 cm. Genus comprises nine species, some very similar, almost unidentifiable from photos taken underwater. Very similar *D. macarellus* recorded south to Norah Head, but usually occurs deeper than 50 m, though could venture into divable depths.

SOUTHERN MACKEREL-SCAD
Decapterus muroadsi (Temminck and Schlegel, 1844)

D IX,32-35. A III,25-28. C 17. P 23-25. V I,5. LL 130, scutes 25-28. Body very elongate, slightly compressed. Scales very small; lateral line straight, except for smoothly descending section above anus; scutes mainly posteriorly. A few teeth in single row anteriorly in lower jaw, none in upper. Dorsal fin divided; first section short, spinous, angular; second soft-rayed, slightly elevated anteriorly, has one separate finlet, is headed by one spine. Anal fin similar, slightly back, opposite second dorsal fin; headed by three spines, two of which are well separate. Silvery below, greenish-blue above, often with golden stripe posteriorly. Widespread tropical west Pacific, on the east coast to southern New South Wales. Shallow coastal bays, enters estuaries, often with *Trachurus* in mixed schools. Attains 20 cm.

AUSTRALIAN SALMONS
FAMILY ARRIPIDIDAE

This small family contains one genus, comprising three species, which is confined to the cooler temperate waters of Australian and New Zealand coasts. These migratory fishes form very large schools, some travelling long distances to spawning grounds. They are strong swimmers and have streamlined bodies. Other features are small ctenoid scales, rough to touch in young, and a moderate-sized mouth with small, pointed teeth in the jaws. They are medium-sized fishes; the smallest species, the Tommy Rough, is widespread in southern waters, and two larger, similar species, the Australian Salmons, have an east and west distribution overlapping in the Tasmanian region where they spawn. They are popular angling species, and are also commercially netted, primarily for canning. The two larger salmon, once considered to be only sub-species, are very similar, slightly differing in colour, but grow to a different maximum size and have different gill-raker counts (60 and 75 cm, 33-40 and 25-31, for east and south coast species respectively). Juveniles of the two species may occur in mixed schools, but separate for migration.

TOMMY ROUGH
Arripis georgiana (Valenciennes, 1831)

D IX,13-14. A III,10. C 17. P 15. V I,5. LL 53-55. Body moderately elongate, slightly compressed. Head rather small; eyes moderately large. Scales small, ctenoid, rough to touch, covering body and head to about eyes. Narrow band of small, pointed teeth in jaws. Lateral line almost straight. Long-based dorsal fin with low notch between spinous and soft-rayed section; spinous part noticeably higher. Anal fin small, opposite posterior part of dorsal fin. Caudal fin deeply forked; pectoral fins small; ventral fins moderately long, reaching halfway to anus. Shiny silvery below, variably darker above, greenish-grey with vertical lines following scale-rows. South coast, ranging north to Sydney on the east, and Garden Island on the west coasts. Occurs in large schools in shallow coastal bays, clear estuaries. Attains 40 cm.

Arripis georgiana

WESTERN AUSTRALIAN SALMON
Arripis truttacea (Johnston, 1882)

D IX,15-19. A III,10. C 17. P 16-17. V I,5. LL 48-52. Body moderately elongate, slightly compressed. Head rather small; eyes moderately small. Narrow band of small, pointed teeth in jaws. Scales small, ctenoid, smooth to touch in adults, covering body and head to about eyes. Lateral line almost straight. Long-based dorsal fin with low notch between spinous and soft-rayed section; spinous part noticeably higher. Anal fin small, opposite posterior part of dorsal fin. Caudal fin deeply forked; pectoral fins small; ventral fins moderately long, reaching halfway to anus. Shiny silvery below, variably darker, usually greyish above; pectoral fins yellowish; juveniles with vertical stripes and series of spots. South coast from Tasmania to Geraldton on the west coast. Juveniles school in coastal bays and estuaries. Adults travel in large schools along shores, often coming through shallows along beaches, appearing as dark patch when viewed from above; to depths of about 30 m. Attains at least 75 cm.

Arripis truttacea   Adults ▼ Juv. ▲

Arripis trutta   Adults ▼ Juvs. ▲

EASTERN AUSTRALIAN SALMON
Arripis trutta (Bloch and Schneider, 1801)

D IX,15-19. A III,10. C 17. P 16-17. V I,5. LL 48-52. Body moderately elongate, slightly compressed. Head rather small; eyes moderately small. Narrow band of small pointed teeth in jaws. Scales small, ctenoid, smooth to touch in adults, covering body and head to about eyes. Lateral line almost straight. Long-based dorsal fin with low notch from spinous to soft-rayed section, spinous part noticeably higher. Anal fin small, opposite posterior part of dorsal fin. Caudal fin deeply forked; pectoral fins small; ventral fins moderately long, reaching half way to anus. Shiny silvery below, variably darker, usually greyish above; pectoral fins yellowish; juveniles with vertical stripes and series of spots. South-east coast from southern Queensland to Tasmania, and also in northern New Zealand and Kermadec Islands. Juveniles school in shallow coastal bays and estuaries; adults move in large schools along shores, feeding on zooplankton and pelagic fishes from surface waters to about 30 m. Attains 60 cm.

CORAL SNAPPERS
FAMILY LUTJANIDAE

A large tropical and subtropical family comprising 17 genera and 103 species. They occur in all seas and a few inhabit fresh water. Of the four subfamilies, three are represented here: the Etelinae with *Aphareus*, Apsilinae with *Paracaesio*, and Lutjaninae with *Lutjanus*. Except for one species, they are expatriates to the south-east coast, and a total of 10 species are presently known from this area. Some of these species are only known from juveniles and no doubt other species will range intermittently to southern waters. Many species are of commercial importance, and for this reason one species was successfully introduced to the Hawaiian region. In Australia, many of the larger species can cause ciguatera poisoning and eating them can be fatal. In general they are reef-dwelling fishes which display no differences between sexes, often school in great numbers, and may feed night or day depending on the species. Many are night-feeding predators and others may live primarily on zooplankton, however in most cases diet changes during growth from juvenile to adult, and with opportunities for food. Some species specialise and possess large canines to capture and hold prey or crush tough invertebrates. Colouration varies within species according to habitat or size; juveniles often look completely different to adults. The coral snappers feature scaly bodies, large eyes and mouths, a single dorsal fin with strong spines and generally moderately large fins.

Blue-Stripe Snapper (*Lutjanus kasmira*)

SMALL-TOOTH JOBFISH
Aphareus furca (Lacepède, 1802)

D X,11. A III,8. P 15-16. V I,5. LL 65-75. Body elongate, compressed, covered with small, weakly ctenoid scales which extend over head to about eyes. Lateral line smoothly curved, following contour of back; scales above lateral line parallel, smaller than those below. Moderate-sized mouth reaches well below eye; minute teeth in jaws. Dorsal fin tallest at second spine, gradually lowering to soft part which ends with pointed or extended posterior rays. Anal fin similar to and opposite soft-rayed section of dorsal fin. Caudal fin deeply forked; pectoral fin with long upper rays, reaching to above anus. Plain, silvery below, greyish-brown above; bright yellow over nape during display. Widespread tropical Indo-Pacific, from central Pacific to east Africa; on the east coast south to Seal Rocks, New South Wales where medium-sized specimens in small schools were observed and photographed. Adults in small aggregations on slopes near deep drop-offs. Juveniles school loosely in shallow coastal bays. Attains 40 cm; commonly to 30 cm. This genus comprises two species; the other species has similar range, but more tropical.

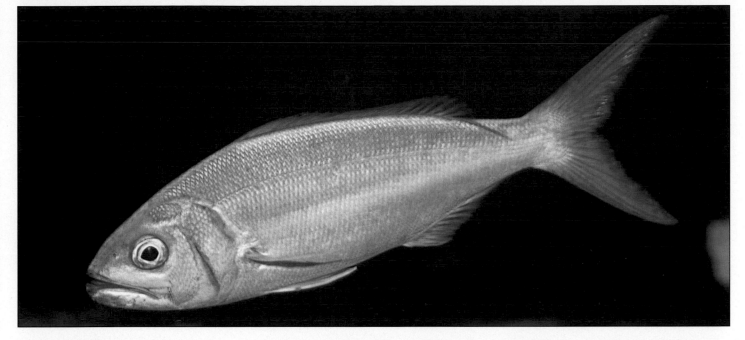

BLUE-STRIPE SNAPPER
Lutjanus kasmira (Forsskål, 1775)

D X,14-15. A III,7-8. P 16-17. V I,5. LL 48-51. Body oval-elongate, compressed, covered with small scales which extend over head to about eyes. Preopercle distinctly notched. Lateral line smoothly curved, following contour of back; scale rows above lateral line rise obliquely and below horizontally. Moderate-sized mouth reaches well below eye; jaws with narrow bands of teeth, outer series enlarged, small canines anteriorly. Dorsal fin with moderately large spines, third and fourth tallest; posterior end pointed. Anal fin similar to and opposite soft-rayed section of dorsal fin. Caudal fin emarginate; upper rays of pectoral fin longest. Typically bright yellow with blue lines, pale below. Widespread tropical Indo-Pacific from central Pacific to east Africa and Red Sea; introduced to Hawaii. Coastal reef slopes in small aggregations and sometimes in large schools; juveniles in harbours. Attains 35 cm; usually to 25 cm. Australian populations differ slightly in colour pattern. Large circumtropical genus comprising 65 species, eight of which expatriate as juveniles to southern waters.

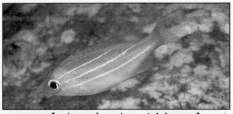

Lutjanus kasmira   Adult ▼ Juv. ▲

183

FIVE-LINE SNAPPER
Lutjanus quinquelineatus (Bloch, 1790)

D X,13-15. A III,8. P 16-17. V I,5. LL 47-49. Body oval-elongate, compressed, covered with small scales which extend over head to about eyes. Preopercle distinctly notched. Lateral line smoothly curved, following contour of back; scale rows above lateral line rise obliquely and below horizontally. Moderate-sized mouth reaches well below eye; jaws with narrow bands of teeth, outer series enlarged, small canines anteriorly. Dorsal fin with moderately large spines, third and fourth tallest; posterior end pointed. Anal fin similar to and opposite soft-rayed section of dorsal fin. Caudal fin emarginate; upper rays of pectoral fin longest, reaching above anal fin. Variably yellow with blue lines; more or less distinct dark blotch below anterior soft rays of dorsal fin, just above lateral line. Widespread tropical Indo-Pacific from broadly the west Pacific to northern Indian Ocean; commonly south to Sydney as juvenile. Coastal reefs and lagoons; juveniles in rocky estuaries in small aggregations. Attains 35 cm; usually to 25 cm.

Lutjanus quinquelineatus　Adult ▼　Juvs. ▲

MOSES PERCH
Lutjanus russelli (Bleeker, 1849)

D X,14-15. A III,8. P 16-17. V I,5. LL 47-50. Body oval-elongate, compressed, covered with small scales which extend over head to about eyes. Preopercle slightly notched. Lateral line smoothly curved, following contour of back; scale rows above lateral line rise obliquely and below horizontally. Moderate-sized mouth reaches well below eye; jaws with narrow bands of teeth, outer series enlarged, small canines anteriorly. Dorsal fin with moderately large spines, second to fifth tallest and subequal; posterior end rounded. Anal fin short-based, similar to and opposite posterior soft-rayed section of dorsal fin. Caudal fin truncate; upper rays of pectoral fin longest. Variable from juvenile to adult. Widespread tropical west Pacific; replaced by different form in Indian Ocean, however co-occurring in Indonesia. Coastal reefs and estuaries; large adults deep offshore, 70-80 m. Attains 45 cm; usually to 35 cm.

Lutjanus russelli　Adult ▼　Juv. ▲

BLACK-SPOT SNAPPER
Lutjanus fulviflammus (Forsskål, 1775)

D X,12-14. A III,7-8. P 15-17. V I,5. LL 45-50. Body oval-elongate, compressed, covered with small scales which extend over head to about eyes. Preopercle slightly notched. Lateral line smoothly curved, following contour of back; scale rows above lateral line rise obliquely and below horizontally. Moderate-sized mouth reaches well below eye; jaws with narrow bands of teeth, outer series enlarged, small canines anteriorly. Dorsal fin with moderately large spines, third and fourth tallest and subequal; posterior end rounded. Anal fin short-based, similar to and opposite posterior soft-rayed section of dorsal fin. Caudal fin emarginate; upper rays of pectoral fin longest. Variable from juvenile to adult. Widespread tropical Indo-Pacific, broadly in the west Pacific, and to east Africa and Red Sea. Juveniles south to Sydney Harbour. Coastal reefs and estuaries in 3-30 m; juveniles enter brackish water. Attains 35 cm.

Lutjanus adetii ▼

Lutjanus fulviflammus Juv.

HUSSAR
Lutjanus adetii (Castelnau, 1873)

D X,14. A III,8. P 17. V I,5. LL 52. Body oval-elongate, compressed, covered with small scales which extend over head to about eyes. Preopercle slightly notched. Lateral line smoothly curved, following contour of back; scale rows above lateral line rise obliquely and below horizontally. Moderate-sized mouth reaches well below eye; jaws with narrow bands of teeth, outer series enlarged, small canines anteriorly. Dorsal fin evenly arched, long-based with moderately large

spines; followed by low, short-based soft-rayed section. Anal fin short-based, with moderately long spines and soft rays. Caudal fin emarginate; upper rays of pectoral fin longest. Small juveniles plain whitish with distinct black caudal peduncle spot, pale yellowish spinous dorsal fin. Longitudinal yellow stripe develops with age; adults become reddish with whitish belly. East coast south to Sydney Harbour, and to New Caledonia. Coastal reefs and estuaries, in lagoons with outcrops, often in large schools. Attains 50 cm; usually 35 cm.

Lutjanus gibbus

PADDLE-TAIL
Lutjanus gibbus (Forsskål, 1775)

D X,13-14. A III,8. P 16-17. V I,5. LL 46-53. Body oval-elongate, compressed, covered with small scales which extend over head to about eyes. Preopercle deeply notched. Lateral line smoothly curved, following contour of back; scale rows above lateral line rise obliquely and below horizontally. Moderate-sized mouth reaches well below eye; jaws with narrow bands of teeth, outer series enlarged, small canines anteriorly. Dorsal fin spinous section with moderately large spines, evenly arched; followed by equal-sized soft-rayed section which ends in broad angle. Anal fin similar to and opposite posterior part of dorsal fin. Caudal fin emarginate with broadly rounded lobes, enlarging with age. Pectoral fin sharply pointed with upper rays longest. Widespread tropical Indo-Pacific from central Pacific to east Africa and Red Sea. Juveniles south to Sydney on the east coast. Coastal reef slopes to 35 m; juveniles in mangroves and seagrass beds. Attains 45 cm.

Lutjanus gibbus Juv.

RED EMPEROR
Lutjanus sebae (Cuvier, 1828)

D XI,15-16. A III,10. P 17. V I,5. LL 48-57. Body oval-elongate, compressed, covered with small scales which extend over head to about eyes. Preopercle distinctly notched. Lateral line smoothly curved, following contour of back; scale rows above lateral line rise obliquely and below in line with above. Moderate-sized mouth reaches well below eye; jaws with narrow bands of teeth, outer series enlarged, small canines anteriorly. Dorsal fin with moderately large spines continuous with soft-rayed section; broadly notched from anterior to posterior ends, becoming shallow with age; angular end. Anal fin similar to and opposite posterior part of dorsal fin. Caudal fin truncate to slightly emarginate. Pectoral fin sharply pointed with upper rays longest. Widespread tropical Indo-Pacific, from west Pacific to east Africa and Red Sea. Coastal sand flats, deep lagoons, usually in small aggregations near outcrops in 10-100 m. Tiny juveniles frequently among sea-urchin spines, occasionally south to Sydney. Large adults mostly red, lose banded pattern. Attains 1 m.

Lutjanus sebae Adult ▼ Juv. ▲

Lutjanus argentimaculatus ▼

Paracaesio xanthura ▼

MANGROVE JACK
Lutjanus argentimaculatus (Forsskål, 1775)

D X,13-14. A III,8-9. P 16-17. V I,5. LL 44-56. Body oval-elongate, compressed, covered with small scales which extend over head to about eyes. Preopercle serrate with shallow but distinct notch. Lateral line smoothly curved, following contour of back; scale rows above lateral line rise obliquely and below horizontal. Moderate-sized mouth reaches well below eye; jaws with narrow bands of teeth, outer series enlarged, small canines anteriorly. Dorsal fin with moderately large spines, continuous with soft-rayed section; broadly notched from anterior to posterior ends in adults; rounded end. Anal fin similar to and opposite posterior part of dorsal fin. Caudal fin truncate to slightly emarginate. Pectoral fin sharply pointed with upper rays longest. Widespread tropical Indo-Pacific, from central Pacific to east Africa and Red Sea; juveniles known from Sydney area. Adults deep offshore to 100 m; juveniles in mangroves and estuaries in lower reaches of freshwater streams. Attains 1.2 m and 16 kg.

Lutjanus argentimaculatus Juv.

SOUTHERN FUSILIER
Paracaesio xanthura (Bleeker, 1869)

D X,10-11. A III,8-9. P 16. V I,5. LL 70-72. Body oval-elongate, compressed, covered with small scales which extend over head to about eyes. Lateral line smoothly curved, following contour of back; scale rows above lateral line parallel and below horizontal. Smallish mouth reaches well below eye; jaws with narrow bands of teeth, outer series enlarged, small canines anteriorly. Dorsal fin with moderately large spines continuous with soft-rayed section, sharply pointed posteriorly. Anal fin similar to and opposite posterior part of dorsal fin. Caudal fin forked. Pectoral fin sharply pointed with upper rays longest. Little variation in colour from juvenile to adult. Widespread tropical Indo-Pacific, from central Pacific to east Africa and Red Sea; adults south to Montague Island. Attains 40 cm. Tropical Indo-Pacific genus comprising six species.

Paracaesio xanthura Juv.

FUSILIERS
FAMILY CAESIONIDAE

This primarily tropical family comprises four genera and 20 species, and although a large number of these occur in Queensland and as adults in northern New South Wales, only a few species are found further south as juveniles. They are closely related to the Lutjanidae but are schooling, planktivorous, smallish fishes, streamlined and often colourful, dominantly blue with yellow stripes, and restricted to the Indo-Pacific region. As most of these fishes are rather small, they have little commercial value; the larger species, attaining about 45 cm, are reputed to be good eating, and the other species are mostly used as bait. On the reefs, these fishes certainly have ornamental value with their bright colours and movement, and large schools commonly patrol the slopes and walls in pursuit of zooplankton. Only two species are known from the Sydney area as juveniles, and others included here occur as adults in northern New South Wales.

ROBUST FUSILIER
Caesio cuning (Bloch, 1791)

D X,14-16. A III,10-12. P 17-20. V I,5. LL 47-51. Body oval-elongate, compressed, covered with small scales which extend over most of head. Lateral line very distinct, smoothly curving with dorsal profile. Mouth small; jaws protrusible with several rows of teeth, outer row enlarged, pairs of canines anteriorly-laterally; minute teeth on vomer, palatines. Median fins rather low, but caudal fin very large, forked. Pectoral fin pointed, upper rays longest. Colour varies slightly except at night, or after death when they become bright red. Several similar species; the others more slender, lack indistinct stripes below eye. Widespread tropical Indo-Pacific, from west Pacific to east Africa and Red Sea. Coastal reefs, lagoons, usually in large schools. Adults south to the Solitary Islands. Attains 45 cm; one of the larger species. This genus comprises eight species, two of which are included here.

GOLD-BANDED FUSILIER
Caesio caerulaurea Lacepède, 1801

D X,14-16. A III,12-13. P 20-22. V I,5. LL 57-65. Body moderately elongate, compressed, covered with small scales which extend over most of head. Lateral line very distinct, smoothly curving with dorsal profile. Mouth small; jaws protrusible with single series of small conical teeth. Median fins rather low; dorsal fin elevated anteriorly; anal fin slightly elevated anteriorly. Caudal fin very large, forked. Pectoral fin pointed, upper rays longest. Colour varies slightly with size; reddish at night. Broadly distributed in the tropical Indo-Pacific; on the east coast south to Sydney as juveniles. Coastal reef slopes and inner reefs, along drop-offs to about 25 m. Attains 35 cm.

Caesio cuning ▲

Caesio caerulaurea ▼

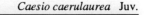
Caesio caerulaurea Juv.

BLACK-TIPPED FUSILIER
Pterocaesio digramma (Bleeker, 1865)

D X,14-16. A III,11-12. P 20-23. V I,5. LL 66-76. Body moderately elongate, compressed, covered with small scales which extend over most of head. Lateral line very distinct, smoothly curving with dorsal profile. Mouth small; jaws protrusible with single series of small conical teeth. Median fins rather low; dorsal fin elevated anteriorly; anal fin slightly elevated anteriorly. Caudal fin very large, forked. Pectoral fin pointed, upper rays longest. Colour slightly different between juveniles and adults. Widespread tropical Indo-Pacific; juveniles south to the Sydney area. Coastal reefs, lagoons, usually in large schools near coral outcrops. Juveniles in the Sydney area with other planktivores such as *Trachinops* in clear coastal waters including the harbour. Attains 30 cm. This genus comprises 10 species broadly distributed in the tropical Indo-Pacific.

Pterocaesio digramma   Adar ▼   Juv. ▲

Pterocaesio chrysozona ▼

YELLOW-BAND FUSILIER
Pterocaesio chrysozona (Cuvier, 1830)

D X-XI,14-16. A III,11-13. P 17-20. V I,5. LL 62-72. Body moderately elongate, compressed, covered with small scales which extend over most of head. Lateral line very distinct, smoothly curving with dorsal profile. Mouth small; jaws protrusible with single series of small conical teeth. Median fins rather low; dorsal fin elevated anteriorly; anal fin slightly elevated anteriorly. Caudal fin very large, forked. Pectoral fin pointed, upper rays longest. Colour slightly different between juveniles and adults; increasingly broader yellow band with age. Widespread tropical Indo-Pacific; on the east coast adults south to the Solitary Islands. Attains 30 cm.

SWEETLIPS
FAMILY HAEMULIDAE

A large family of medium-sized fishes, comprising about 18 genera and an estimated 120 species. It includes two subfamilies: Haemulinae, the estuarine grunters, and Plectorhynchinae, the sweetlips or thick-lipped grunters. Only the latter is represented here, with four species ranging to south-eastern waters. These primarily tropical species are reef dwellers; the larger species, as adults, are usually along deep drop-offs. They are mostly in caves during the day, coming into the open during the night to feed on benthic invertebrates. Juveniles are usually in shallow protected bays or estuaries, with reef or other outcrops on sand or mud. Some species go through various colour stages and young often have proportionally large fins, swimming unusually with an exaggerated twisting of the body. Sweetlips feature smallish ctenoid scales, slightly compressed and somewhat elongated bodies, strong fin spines, a large head, a small mouth with thick lips, and small pointed teeth in the jaws. The species included here occur as adults south to northern New South Wales with juveniles well south as expatriates.

PAINTED SWEETLIPS
Diagramma labiosum Macleay, 1883

D IX-X,22-25. A III,7. P 16-17. V I,5. LL 65. LSR 110-115. Adults deep-bodied anteriorly, tapering to long peduncle; small ctenoid scales. Lateral line smoothly curved, low along upper sides. Juveniles more slender, anterior part of dorsal fin very tall. Dorsal fin base long; first spine small, second spine longest; except in juveniles, fin outline almost straight from anterior to posterior ends. Caudal fin long, round in juveniles, changing to truncate at about 25 cm. Anal fin short-based.

Colour changes dramatically with size; juveniles striped, adults plain. Tropical Indo-Pacific, broadly west Pacific to east Africa and Red Sea. Juveniles in shallow estuaries and lagoons. Adults along slopes and deep lagoons, often in large schools. Attains 1 m. Small genus; until recently thought to be monotypic with single variable species, *D. pictum*. However, two species now recognised and there may be more. *D. pictum* was described from Japan, but several forms there may represent different species; true identity yet to be determined. Most common form which is probably *D. pictum* is spotted as adult, ranges at least to Indonesia, occurring sympatrically with *D. labiosum*. Indian Ocean and Red Sea form very similar to spotted form; may be identical.

Diagramma labiosum Adult ▼ Intermediate stage ▲

Diagramma labiosum Juv.

GOLD-SPOTTED SWEETLIPS
Plectorhinchus flavomaculatus (Ehrenberg, 1830)

D XIII-XIV,20-22. A III,7. P 17. V I,5. LL 60. LSR 90. Body moderately oval-elongate with small ctenoid scales. Lateral line smoothly curved, low along upper sides. Mouth small, lips moderate; jaws with several rows of small teeth, outer row enlarged. Dorsal fin base long; first spine small, followed by slightly arched spinous section and subequal-based soft-rayed section. Caudal fin slightly rounded in juveniles, changing to truncate at early age. Anal fin short-based, second spine large. Colour changes dramatically with size; juveniles with stripes that break up into spots which become more numerous and proportionally smaller with age. Widespread tropical Indo-Pacific; in Australia, adults south to central New South Wales on the east coast and Perth on the west coast. Small juveniles among seagrasses, appear like small lutjanids; adults on protected coastal reefs to about 30 m. Attains 60 cm.

Plectorhinchus flavomaculatus ▼

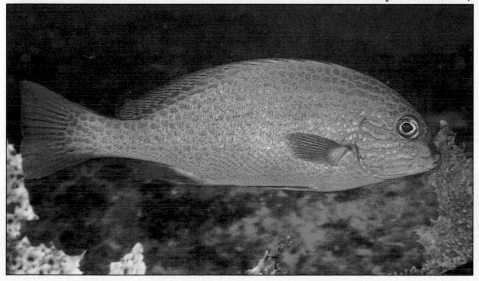

Plectorhinchus flavomaculatus Juv.

MAGPIE SWEETLIPS
Plectorhinchus picus (Cuvier, 1830)

D XII,19-20. A III,7. P 17-18. V I,5. LL 65-70. LSR 120. Body moderately oval-elongate with small ctenoid scales. Lateral line smoothly curved, low along upper sides. Mouth small, lips moderate, thickening with age; jaws with several rows of small teeth, outer row enlarged. Dorsal fin base long; first spine moderate, followed by slightly arched spinous section and subequal-based soft-rayed section. Caudal fin long, rounded, almost lanceolate in juveniles, changing to truncate in adults. Anal fin short-based, second spine large. Colour changes dramatically with size, with broad black markings of juveniles gradually breaking up with age into small spots all over, except ventrally. Widespread tropical Indo-Pacific; on the east coast adults to northern New South Wales on offshore reefs. Juveniles also offshore in 10-30 m, swimming unusually by "waving" caudal fin. Attains 90 cm.

Plectorhinchus picus Adult ▼ Juv. ▲

BROWN SWEETLIPS
Plectorhinchus gibbosus (Lacepède, 1802)

D XIII-XIV,13-18. A III,7-8. P 17. V I,5. LL 49-50. LSR 55-60. Body moderately oval-elongate with moderate-sized ctenoid scales. Lateral line smoothly curved, low along upper sides. Mouth small, lips moderate, becoming very thick with age; jaws with several rows of small teeth, outer row enlarged. Dorsal fin base long; strongly arched spinous section, particularly tall at fourth spine in juveniles, followed by short-based soft-rayed section. Caudal fin rounded in juveniles, changing to truncate in adults. Anal fin short-based, second spine very large. Widespread tropical Indo-Pacific; juveniles at least south to Sydney Harbour on the east coast. Coastal, often muddy reef habitats; juveniles in shallow estuaries, including brackish water. Small specimens float with debris on the surface like leaves, larger juveniles under floating objects or weed rafts. Attains 75 cm. Reported as excellent to eat in Africa, but of poor taste in Queensland; reported to be affected by ciguatera.

Plectorhinchus gibbosus Adult ▼ Juv. ▲

TRIPLE-TAILS
FAMILY LOBOTIDAE

This family contains a single genus and species which is found in all tropical and subtropical seas. Juveniles most commonly occur under sargassum weed rafts after the wet season, mimicking the mangrove leaves commonly in among the weed rafts, and may spend a long time floating over great distances until shallow waters are reached in which to settle. This method of dispersal of young, like many other species floating with sargassum weeds, obviously attributes to the widespread occurrence. The leaf-like juveniles differ in shape and some characters, such as serrations, from the adults and were thought to be different species – even different genera – at one stage. Triple-tails are perch-like fishes with moderate-sized, weakly ctenoid scales and rather deep, compressed bodies. Their posterior fins are covered with small scales and the lateral line is continuous onto the caudal fin (not included in the count, +5).

TRIPLE-TAIL
Lobotes surinamensis (Bloch, 1790)

D XI-XII,15-16. A III,11-12. P 17. V I,5. LL 43-45. Body rather deep, covered with moderate-sized, weakly ctenoid scales which extend over head, except preorbital; smaller scales onto soft-rayed section of dorsal, anal and caudal fins. Head of moderate size; eyes large in juveniles, proportionally smaller in adults, profile becoming very concave above. Preopercle margin serrate in juveniles, becoming finely serrate in adults. Median fins generally large with strong spines. Long-based dorsal fin, slightly notched over posterior spines; soft-rayed section broadly rounded. Anal fin similar to and opposite posterior part of dorsal fin. Caudal fin large, rounded. Juveniles yellowish-brown with dark mottling; adults jet black. Widespread circum-tropical, on the east coast to New South Wales, and doubtfully recorded from eastern Victoria. Mainly coastal waters with young dispersed well offshore; sometimes in brackish waters and may enter lower reaches of streams. Attains 1 m and 15 kg. Reputed as excellent game fish and excellent eating. Sometimes called Jumping Cod.

Lobotes surinamensis   Adult ▼ Juv. ▲

SNAPPER and BREAMS
FAMILY SPARIDAE

A moderately large family with 22 genera and 41 species, most of which occur in southern African waters. In Australia, these fishes are a very important commercial group of medium-sized species, and popular angling fishes in southern waters, particularly the snapper which attains 1.2 m and 20 kg. The larger species occur mostly in subtropical to temperate waters and although the number of species in southern Australian waters is low, they occur in great numbers in some areas. Of the three genera along the southeast coast, two are represented by a single species, and one with two species. They occur mostly over sandy or rubble substrates in the vicinity of reefs, in coastal as well as estuarine waters. They are usually in small aggregations or in large schools when migrating. They feed on a variety of bottom-dwelling invertebrates and small fishes. Bream enter fresh water, feeding on shrimps and insects. They feature strong fin spines, and small to moderately large, slightly ctenoid scales cover the body and head, except the preorbital. The mouth is low and almost horizontal, and the jaws have conical teeth and anterior canines. Mostly silvery fishes, they sometimes have indistinct banding or small blue spots.

BREAM
Acanthopagrus australis (Owen, 1853)

D XI-XII,11-12. A III,8-9. P 14-15. V I,5. LL 43-46. Moderate-sized scales cover body and head except snout, extend onto bases of soft dorsal, anal and caudal fins. Lateral line smoothly curving with contour of back. Jaws with canines anteriorly, followed by bands of smaller teeth, changing to molars posteriorly. Fin spines prominent; dorsal fin with long-based spinous section; second spine in anal fin very large. Caudal fin forked with pointed lobes; pectoral fin large, upper rays longest, reaching to anal fin. Silver, slightly darker above; lower fins often yellow. Juveniles or adults with broad dusky banding at night. East coast from central Queensland to eastern Victoria. Coastal reefs, rocky or muddy estuaries. Usually in small to large schools; silvery in clear coastal waters, darker in estuaries. Attains 65 cm and about 4 kg. Also known as Yellow-Finned Bream; originally known as Black Bream. Wide-ranging genus, to Japan and Africa; two species included here.

SOUTHERN BREAM
Acanthopagrus butcheri (Munro, 1949)

D X-XII,10-13. A III,8-9. P 14-16. V I,5. LL 52-58. Moderate-sized scales cover body and head except snout, extend onto bases of soft dorsal, anal and caudal fins. Lateral line smoothly curving with contour of back. Jaws with canines anteriorly, followed by bands of smaller teeth, changing to molars posteriorly. Fin spines prominent; dorsal fin with long-based spinous section; second spine in anal fin very large. Caudal fin forked with pointed lobes; pectoral fin large, upper rays longest, reaching to anal fin. Silver, slightly darker above, lower fins pale to dusky; dark in fresh water. Southern waters, widespread from eastern Victoria to Shark Bay and Tasmania. Primarily in estuaries, travelling far up rivers, including adults. Schooling species, moving to sea during floods. Juveniles commonly in lower reaches of streams. Attains 60 cm and 3.5 kg.

Acanthopagrus australis ▲

Acanthopagrus butcheri ▼

Acanthropagrus butcheri. Juvs.

TARWHINE
Rhabdosargus sarba (Forsskål, 1775)

D XI,13-14. A III,11. P 15. V I,5. LL 58-63. Moderate-sized scales cover body and head except snout and preopercle flange. Lateral line smoothly curving with contour of back. Jaws with canines anteriorly, followed by bands of smaller teeth, changing to molars posteriorly, last enlarged. Fin spines slender; dorsal fin with subequal-based spinous and soft-rayed sections. Anal fin with small first spine, followed by two long, subequal ones. Caudal fin forked with pointed lobes; pectoral fin large, upper rays longest, reaching to anal fin. Silver with variably thin yellow lines over scale-rows; slightly darker above; lower fins usually yellow. Widespread tropical to subtropical Indo-Pacific; on the east coast to southern New South Wales. Coastal reefs and estuaries. Attains 45 cm and about 1.4 kg. Originally described from Red Sea; Indian

Ocean form, including West Australia, differs from West Pacific form, ranging north to Japan, and may need species recognition. This genus comprises several similar species.

Chrysophrys auratus   Adult ▼   Intermediate stage ▲

SNAPPER
Chrysophrys auratus (Schneider, 1801)

D XII,9-10. A III,8-9. P 15-16. V I,5. LL 52-59. Moderate-sized scales cover body and head posteriorly. Lateral line smoothly curving with contour of back. Jaws with canines anteriorly, followed by bands of smaller teeth, changing to molars posteriorly, last enlarged. Fin spines slender; dorsal fin with subequal-based spinous and soft-rayed sections. Anal fin with small first spine, followed by two long, subequal ones. Caudal fin forked with pointed lobes; pectoral fin large, upper rays longest, reaching to anal fin. Large individuals develop large hump above head, posterior part of body becomes more slender. Silvery-white; darker, pinkish above with small blue spots scattered over upper sides, most obvious in young. Widespread southern half of Australia, and New Zealand. Offshore in 5-200 m; juveniles in more shallow protected bays and estuaries. Attains 1.2 m and 20 kg. One of the best-known food fish in Australia. Also known as Cockneys; Squires refers to young fish, Old Man Snappers to hump-headed individuals. This genus comprises two similar species restricted to warm-temperate waters of the west Pacific, occurring at similar latitudes with one in each hemisphere.

Chrysophrys auratus   Juv.

SILVER BELLIES
FAMILY GERREIDAE

A small mostly tropical family of silvery fishes, comprising seven genera and an estimated 40 species, which is most diverse in American waters. In Australia, silver bellies are represented by three genera and an undetermined number of species, only two of which range into southern waters. They are generally small to medium-sized fishes inhabiting shallow coastal waters and estuaries, usually schooling over sandy areas and feeding on bottom invertebrates. The mouth is greatly protrusible into a downward directed tube, and the eyes are usually large and placed immediately behind the mouth. They are oval-elongate with moderate-sized deciduous cycloid scales, a smallish head and a long-based dorsal fin which is anteriorly elevated in most genera. There are many similar species of silver bellies. They are usually shiny silver with some dusky markings or black tips on their fins; juveniles are generally spotted or have faint dark bars.

Parequula melbournensis Day colouration ▲ Night colouration ▼

MELBOURNE SILVER BELLY
Parequula melbournensis (Castelnau, 1872)

D IX,16-17. A III,17. C 17. P 14-15. V I,5. LL 37-38. Body oval, greatly compressed with slender caudal peduncle; covered with moderate-sized, weakly attached cycloid scales which extend over head. Lateral line smoothly curved, following contour of back; extends onto caudal fin with several scales. Mouth small but greatly protractile; jaws with numerous villiform teeth. Dorsal fin evenly outlined with small spines anteriorly, progressively increasing in size, a trend confluent with soft rays to posterior rounded end. Anal fin long-based, similar to and opposite posterior part of dorsal fin. Caudal fin slightly forked; pectoral fins small. Juveniles shiny silver; large adults ornamented with blue and yellow. South coast from eastern Victoria and Tasmania to Perth. Shallow estuaries to deep offshore, at least 100 m. Usually on sandy or muddy bottom near reefs or seagrass beds. Usually in small aggregations, sometimes schooling deep and trawled in large numbers. Attains 18 cm. Monotypic genus endemic to the south coast.

Gerres subfasciatus Adult ▲ Juvenile ▼

COMMON SILVER BELLY
Gerres subfasciatus Cuvier, 1830

D IX-X,9-11. A III,7. C 17. P 17. V I,5. LL 39-42. Body oval, greatly compressed with moderately deep caudal peduncle; covered with moderate-sized, weakly attached cycloid scales which extend over head. Lateral line with gradual curve, following contour of back; extends onto caudal fin with several scales. Mouth small but greatly protractile; jaws with numerous villiform teeth. Dorsal fin spines elevated anteriorly, notched over remaining spines, followed by longer, sub-equal soft rays. Anal fin short-based, similar to and opposite posterior part of dorsal fin. Caudal fin deeply forked; pectoral fins pointed with long upper rays, reaching anal fin. Adults shiny silvery with dark-tipped dorsal fin;

juveniles olive above with some indistinct dark blotching. Northern half of Australia, south to Wollongong on the east coast, Albany on the west coast; most northern part of range uncertain with several similar species there. Estuaries, harbours, to fairly deep water along shores; usually schools over sandy patches near reefs; 3-40 m. Attains 20 cm. Also known as Silver Biddy; *G. ovatus*, commonly used in literature, a synonym. Most numerous genus in family with about 30 species.

SPINECHEEKS AND WHIPTAILS
FAMILY NEMIPTERIDAE

A moderately large tropical family, comprising five genera and about 64 species. Two of the genera are usually deep, in excess of 40 m, and are excluded here. The other genera are shallow coral reef dwellers, some of which expatriate to southern waters. Two of these genera, with five species, are included here. They are mostly very colourful fishes, with oval to elongate bodies covered with ctenoid scales which extend onto the head. The eyes are large, the mouth is smallish, and the jaws have narrow bands of small teeth, the outer row enlarged. They feature a large single dorsal fin, and a caudal fin often extended with filaments in adults, for which they are often referred to as whiptails. Most species are small and generally regarded as "trash fish" by fishermen. Juveniles are distinctly striped with bright colours, and make excellent aquarium pets; adults are markedly different in colour pattern. Juveniles are mostly solitary and some adults school, usually near reefs. They feed on sand flats, picking off small invertebrates from rubble or filtering them from a mouthful of sand.

Scolopsis monogramma   Adult ▼ Juv. ▲

LATTICE SPINECHEEK
Scolopsis monogramma Cuvier, 1830

D X,9. A III,7. P 18. V I,5. LL 46-49. Body with moderate-sized ctenoid scales extending to above eye and cheek. Lateral line evenly curved, following contour of back. Prominent spine immediately below eye; posterior margin of preopercle serrate, slightly enlarged on lower corner. Jaws with villiform teeth. Dorsal fin long-based, continues with subequal spines, except first short, followed by slightly longer soft rays. Anal fin short-based with subequal spines and rays, except first spine small; positioned below posterior part of dorsal fin. Caudal fin forked to lunate in adults. Pectoral and ventral fins pointed, of similar size, upper or first rays longest. Distinctly marked at different stages; adults variably change colour at will. Widespread west Pacific, central New South Wales to southern Japan. Coastal reef slopes, lagoons; juveniles in estuaries and harbours; 3-50 m. Attains 30 cm. Large genus comprising 17 species, many of which are found in northern waters; two included here.

Scolopsis bilineata ▼

MONOCLE BREAM
Scolopsis bilineata (Bloch, 1793)

D X,9. A III,7-8. P 17. V I,5. LL 44-47. Body with moderate-sized ctenoid scales extending to above eye and cheek. Lateral line evenly curved, following contour of back. Moderate spine immediately below eye; posterior margin of preopercle serrate. Jaws with villiform teeth. Dorsal fin long-based, continues with subequal spines and soft rays, except first short; shallow notch at last spine. Anal fin short-based with third spine and middle ray longest; positioned below posterior part of dorsal fin. Caudal fin deeply emarginate in adults. Pectoral and ventral fins pointed, of similar size with upper or first rays longest. Distinctly marked at different stages; adults variably change colour at will. Widespread west Pacific, central New South Wales to southern Japan. Coastal reef slopes, lagoons; juveniles in clear-water estuaries and harbours; 3-30 m. Attains 20 cm.

Scolopsis bilineata Juv.

PARADISE WHIPTAIL
Pentapodus paradiceus Günther, 1859

D X,9. A III,7. P 17. V I,5. LL 46-48. Body with moderate-sized ctenoid scales extending

Pentapodus paradiceus   Adult ▼ Juv. ▲

Pentapodus sp ▼

to above eye and cheek. Lateral line evenly curved, high along upper sides, following contour of back. No spine below eye; posterior margin of preopercle smooth. Snout pointed, mouth small; jaws with several pairs of small projecting canines. Dorsal fin long-based, continues with subequal spines and soft rays, except first spine slightly shorter. Anal fin short-based with third spine longest, soft rays longer; positioned below posterior part of dorsal fin. Caudal fin deeply emarginate; upper ray with long filament in adults. Pectoral and ventral fins pointed, of similar size with upper or first rays longest. Juveniles with broad longitudinal stripes which break up into multicoloured lines with growth. East coast ranging to Papua New Guinea; juveniles to Sydney Harbour. Coastal reefs and bays, in 3-30 m. Juveniles in estuaries, usually solitary. Attains 20 cm. Genus comprises about eight similarly shaped species, most confined to the west Pacific.

BLUE WHIPTAIL
Pentapodus sp

D X,9. A III,7. P 16-17. V I,5. LL 42-48. Body with moderate-sized ctenoid scales extending to above eye and cheek. Lateral line evenly curved, high along upper sides, following contour of back. No spine below eye; posterior margin of preopercle smooth. Snout pointed, mouth small; jaws with several pairs of small projecting canines. Dorsal fin long-based, continues with subequal spines and soft rays, except first spine slightly shorter. Anal fin short-based with third spine longest, soft rays longer; positioned below posterior part of dorsal fin. Caudal fin emarginate without long lobes. Pectoral and ventral fins pointed, of similar size with upper or first rays longest. Juveniles with broad longitudinal stripes, changing gradually to adult pattern. Tropical eastern Australia to Fiji; juveniles south to Sydney. Usually on deep coastal slopes or lagoons, in small aggregations on open rubble sand or mud. Juveniles in harbours on mud flats. Attains 20 cm.

Pentapodus sp Juv.

JAPANESE WHIPTAIL
Pentapodus nagasakiensis (Tanaka, 1909)

D X,9. A III,7. P 16. V I,5. LL 44-45. Body with moderate-sized ctenoid scales extending to above eye and cheek. Lateral line evenly curved, high along upper sides, following contour of back. No spine below eye; posterior margin of preopercle smooth. Snout pointed, mouth small; jaws with several pairs of small projecting canines. Dorsal fin long-based, continues with subequal spines and soft rays, except first spine slightly shorter. Anal fin short-based with third spine longest, soft rays longer; positioned below posterior part of dorsal fin. Caudal fin without extended lobes. West Pacific, Sydney Harbour and north-west Australia to southern Japan; mainly known from Japan. Small juveniles in Sydney Harbour. Coastal reefs and bays; juveniles on muddy reef; 10-100 m. Attains 20 cm.

EMPERORS AND LARGE-EYE BREAMS
FAMILY LETHRINIDAE

The emperors and large-eye breams are medium-sized fishes, some species reaching 1 m, of commercial importance. They comprise five genera and 39 species which are distributed over the Indo-Pacific, except one that only occurs in the eastern Pacific. The largest genus, *Lethrinus*, has 28 species, followed by *Gymnocranius* with eight species. *Gnathodentex*, *Monotaxis* and *Wattsia* have one species each. These fishes are mainly found on or near tropical reefs and only a few range into warm-temperate waters. Only four species are included here, although some juveniles of other species could expatriate to southern New South Wales waters. The *Lethrinus* species are also known as emperor-sweetlips or emperor-snapper, whilst the remaining genera are mainly known as large-eye breams. They are carnivorous bottom-dwellers, feeding on a variety of invertebrates and small fishes. Some species feed only at night, resting on reefs during the day, but others feed during both periods and may alternate between open sand and reef. Most species, however, feed on or near reefs, either solitary or schooling. The emperors are regarded as first-rate food fish, but some of the large-eyed breams, generally excellent to eat, can be effected by iodine which causes cooking problems. In addition, in some areas these fishes can be affected by ciguatera poisoning.

Gnathodentex aurolineatus   Pale form ▲   Dark form ▼

GOLD-SPOT EMPEROR
Gnathodentex aureolineatus (Lacepède, 1802)

D X,10. A III,8-9. P 15, V I,5. LL 68-74. Scales of moderate size, finely ctenoid. Lateral line smoothly curved, following dorsal profile, five scale-rows above to middle of dorsal fin base. Pectoral fin base naked. Colour variable according to habitat; pale in white sand areas to very dark, lacking stripes, along deep drop-offs. Yellow blotch below soft dorsal fin usually remains prominent in all colour variations. Widespread in the tropical Indo-Pacific from east Africa to the central Pacific. In New South Wales south to Broughton Island. Schooling species, sometimes in very large aggregations of several hundred individuals. Bottom feeder, occurs from reef lagoons to deep drop-offs to depths of about 30 m. Attains about 30 cm. Also known as Gold-Lined Sea Bream or Glow-fish.

LANCER
Lethrinus genivittatus Valenciennes, 1830

D X,9. A III,8. P 13. V I,5. LL 46-47. Scales of moderate size, finely ctenoid. Lateral line smoothly curved, following dorsal profile, four and a half scale-rows above to middle of dorsal fin base. No scales on cheek.

Lethrinus genivittatus   Adult ▼   Juv. ▲

Second dorsal spine distinctly longest of fin. From pale yellow to brown with dark brown to black mottling, highly variable in density. Black blotch below fourth and fifth dorsal spine, just under lateral line; usually distinct, particularly in juveniles, but can be turned off at will. Tropical west-Pacific to the eastern Indian ocean; on the east Australian coast south to Jervis Bay. Shallow coastal reefs and seagrass areas. Juveniles occur commonly in Sydney Harbour and Botany Bay. Attains about 25 cm. *L. nematacanthus* Bleeker, generally used, is a synonym. Also known as Long-Spine Emperor.

GRASS EMPEROR
Lethrinus laticaudis Alleyne and Macley, 1877

D X,9. A III,8. P 13. V I,5. LL 46-48. Scales of moderate size, finely ctenoid. Lateral line smoothly curved, following dorsal profile, five and a half scale-rows above to middle of dorsal fin base. Cheek naked. Pale, yellowish to brown, irregular dark blotches along upper sides. Fins pale yellow to pink. Northern half of Australia to southern Indonesia and New Guinea. South in New South Wales to Bass Point. Juveniles mainly in seagrass beds and mangroves. Adults move to coastal reefs. Important angling species in Queensland. Attains about 56 cm. Large adults also known as Brown Emperor or Brown Sweetlips. *L. fletus* Whitley (1943) a synonym.

Lethrinus laticaudis ▼

SPANGLED EMPEROR
Lethrinus nebulosus (Forsskål, 1775)

D X,9. A III,8. P 13. V I,5. LL 46-48. Scales of moderate size, finely ctenoid. Lateral line smoothly curved, following dorsal profile, five and a half scale-rows above to middle of dorsal fin base. Cheek naked. Usually pale yellow, darker above, with pale blue centre in most scales. Juveniles often with dark irregular bars. Widespread in the tropical Indo-West Pacific from east Africa and the Red Sea to Japan and central New South Wales, and east to Samoa. Found in estuaries and shallow inshore to deep outer reefs. Juveniles usually in large schools. Adults often solitary or in small aggregations. Large species; attains about 95 cm and 10 kg (Grant, 1987). Also known as Yellow Sweetlip.

Lethrinus nebulosus ▼

Lethrinus nebulosus Juv.

JEWFISHES
FAMILY SCIAENIDAE

A large family comprising almost 50 genera and over 100 species found worldwide in tropical shallow seas and estuaries. They are medium to large fishes which are an important food source in some areas. Only a single species occurs in temperate southern Australian waters, and is included here. They are known under a variety of common names, including croakers or drums, as they can produce a range of sounds by means of muscles attached to the gasbladder. Other features include a moderately elongated and somewhat compressed body, a single, usually deeply notched and long-based dorsal fin, and small ctenoid or cycloid scales. The lateral line is continuous to the end of the caudal fin. The mouth is positioned ventrally with rows of small conical teeth, sometimes canines, in jaws. The anal fin is small with two weak spines, and of similar size to the ventral fins. Many species are highly regarded as game fish and for their excellent quality flesh.

JEWFISH
Argyrosomus hololepidotus (Lacepède, 1802)

D XI,26-29. A II,7. C 17. P 18-19. V I,5. LL 46-52. Body moderately deep, elongated posteriorly, slightly compressed; covered with small, finely ctenoid scales which extend to tip of snout; single row of scales along bases of dorsal and anal fins. Lateral line with long smooth curves, to end of caudal fin. Mouth of moderate size; jaws with two series of pointed teeth, outer rows with some irregularly spaced large canines. Dorsal fin deeply notched before last spine, continuing with long-based soft-rayed part. Anal fin small, placed forward, almost below centre of soft-rayed part of dorsal fin. Caudal fin pointed in young, becoming slightly concave in upper half. Shiny silvery to bronze-greenish above; a series of pearly spots along lateral line. Distributed in the southern hemisphere; in Australia along the south coast, north to southern Queensland and Exmouth Gulf. Coastal waters to 150 m, estuaries as shallow as 5 m. Sometimes in large schools. Exciting sportfish, excellent to eat. Attains 2 m; usually to 1.5 m. Also known as Mulloway. Genus comprises five species, variously distributed in the Indo-Pacific and east Atlantic. The similar Teraglin, *Atractoscion aequidens*, caught in deep water off New South Wales and Queensland, is sometimes confused with the Jewfish; differs in having concave caudal fin.

Argyrosomus hololepidotus

199

GOATFISHES
FAMILY MULLIDAE

A moderately large family of small to medium-sized fishes, comprising six genera and about 35 species, globally distributed in tropical to warm-temperate seas. They are most unusual in having two long, strong barbels on the chin, used for digging and sensing prey, and all fins are either pointed or angular. Generally they have elongate to slightly oblong moderately compressed bodies with large, finely ctenoid scales. The mouth is positioned ventrally, is rather large and nearly horizontal, and has variable rows of villiform or conical teeth in the jaws. The dorsal fin is in two parts; the first is spinous and typically steeply triangular, and the second is headed by a spine. The first soft ray is usually long, and is followed by progressively shorter ones, but in some species the last ray is elongated. The caudal fin is typically deeply forked. They are well represented in Australia; on the east coast some 11 species are local or range from tropical waters to southern areas. However, only three species are considered to be of southern origin. Most species school, and on the east coast are mostly in small aggregations, either as juveniles or adults. They seem to favour sheltered coastal bays and harbours in shallow depths, and deep waters offshore. Some of the large southern species are considered good eating, and have some commercial importance. NOTE: Often only X-rays will show that the last two soft rays of the dorsal and anal fins have a common base; unless obvious, they are counted in full.

Yellow-Stripe Goatfish
(*Mulloidichthys vanicolensis*)

YELLOW-STRIPE GOATFISH
Mulloidichthys vanicolensis (Valenciennes, 1831)

D VII+I,8-9. A I,7-8. P 16-17. V I,5. LL 36-42. Body elongate, slightly compressed, covered with large scales which extend onto head, including cheeks. Lateral line with long gradual curves, following contour of back. Opercle rounded, small spine on upper edge. Eye rather large, centrally in upper level of head. Mouth of moderate size, just reaching to below eye; jaws with several rows of villiform teeth. Dorsal fins separated by four scales; first spine minute, second is longest, followed by progressively shorter spines; soft-rayed section headed by one spine. Anal fin almost identical to, with one spine, and opposite second dorsal fin. Caudal fin deeply forked; other fins pointed. Pale to bright yellow. Very widespread tropical Indo-Pacific; on the east coast juveniles to central New South Wales. Schooling species from coastal to outer reefs, usually on slopes in 5-20 m, but recorded to more than 100 m. Mainly feeds at night on sand flats. Attains 30 cm. Genus comprises four species, two of which are included here. *Mulloides*, used by many authors, preoccupied; junior synonym for *Arripis*.

SQUARE-SPOT GOATFISH
Mulloidichthys flavolineatus (Lacepède, 1801)

D VII+I,8-9. A I,7-8. P 16-18. V I,5. LL 34-39. Body elongate, slightly compressed, covered with large scales which extend onto head, including cheeks. Lateral line with long gradual curves, following contour of back. Opercle rounded, small spine on upper edge. Eye moderately large, placed slightly posterior to centre in upper level of head. Mouth of moderate size, clearly not reaching to below eye; jaws with several rows of villiform teeth. Dorsal fins separated by four scales; first spine minute, second is longest, followed by progressively shorter spines; soft-rayed section headed by one spine. Anal fin almost identical to, with one spine, and opposite second dorsal fin. Caudal fin deeply forked; other fins pointed. Pale to yellowish, usually a black spot on sides. Very widespread tropical Indo-Pacific; on the east coast south to Montague Island. Coastal reefs and shallow lagoons to about 30 m. Juveniles in small to large schools on reef flats; large adults often solitary on slopes. Feeds actively during the day. Attains 35 cm. Apart from colour, very similar to Yellow-Stripe Goatfish, but snout longer, mouth terminates well short of eye.

Mulloidichthys flavolineatus Adult ▼ Juvs. ▲

BAR-TAIL GOATFISH
Upeneus tragula Richardson, 1846

D VIII+I,8. A I,7. P 16-18. V I,5. LL 29-30. Body elongate, slightly compressed, covered with large scales which extend onto head, including cheeks and preorbital. Lateral line with long gradual curves, following contour of back. Mouth of moderate size, reaching to below eye; jaws, palatines, vomer with bands of villiform teeth. Dorsal fins separated by six scales; first spine minute, second is longest, followed by progressively shorter spines; soft-rayed section with small scales on anterior part and headed by one spine. Anal fin almost identical to, having one spine and small scales, and opposite second dorsal fin. Caudal fin deeply forked, small scales approaching margin; other fins pointed. Juveniles similar to adults, except fin markings less distinct; oceanic fish more silvery-white. Very widespread tropical Indo-Pacific, on the east coast south to central New South Wales. Coastal reefs, lagoons; juveniles usually in small to large aggregations; adults often solitary. Attains 30 cm. Genus comprises about 12 species, usually small, schooling in large numbers, mostly deep on muddy slopes. At least two species in New South Wales, the second (see photograph) an undetermined species known from New South Wales and southern Queensland, common in Sydney estuaries; grows to about 20 cm.

Upeneus tragula   Photographed in Sydney ▲   *Upeneus sp*   Undetermined species, Sydney ▼

ROUND-SPOT GOATFISH
Parupeneus pleurostigma (Bennett, 1830)

D VIII+I,8-9. A I,6-7. P 15-17. V I,5. LL 28-29. Body elongate, slightly compressed, deepening with age; covered with large scales which extend onto head including cheeks, interorbital. Lateral line with long gradual curves, following contour of back. Snout long; mouth of moderate size, reaching well short to below eye; jaws with strong conical teeth in single row. Dorsal fins separated by three scales; first spine minute, third or fourth is longest, followed by progressively shorter spines; soft-rayed section headed by one spine. Anal fin almost identical to, having one spine, and opposite second dorsal fin. Caudal fin deeply forked, small scales approaching margin; other fins pointed. Juveniles similar to adults, except shape. Very widespread tropical Indo-Pacific; juveniles south to Montague Island. Mainly clear-water reefs, lagoons, slopes; usually in 10-40 m. Attains 30 cm. Large genus comprising about 20 species, some very similar in meristics and colour; others, obviously different in live colour, may be identical in meristics. Juveniles elongate, adults much deeper bodied; eyes noticably smaller proportionally and positioned much higher on head in adults.

Parupeneus pleurostigma   Adult ▲   Juv. ▼

202

BANDED GOATFISH
Parupeneus multifasciatus (Quoy and Gaimard, 1824)

D VIII+I,8-9. A I,6-7. P 15-17. V I,5. LL 28-29. Body elongate, slightly compressed, deepening with age; covered with large scales which extend onto head including cheeks, interorbital. Lateral line with long gradual curves, following contour of back. Snout long; mouth of moderate size, reaching well short to below eye; jaws with strong conical teeth in single row. Dorsal fins separated by three scales; first spine minute, third or fourth is longest, followed by progressively shorter spines; soft-rayed section headed by one spine, last ray extended in adults. Anal fin almost identical to, having one spine, and opposite second dorsal fin. Caudal fin deeply forked, small scales approaching margin; other fins pointed. Juveniles similar to adults, except shape. Widespread tropical Indo-Pacific; juveniles south to the Sydney area. Coastal reefs to outer reef drop-offs; recorded to 140 m. Attains 25 cm.

Parupeneus multifasciatus   Juv.

YELLOW-SADDLE GOATFISH
Parupeneus cyclostomus (Lacepède, 1801)

D VIII+I,8-9. A I,6-7. P 16-17. V I,5. LL 28-29. Body elongate, slightly compressed, deepening with age; covered with large scales which extend onto head including cheeks, interorbital. Lateral line with long gradual curves, following contour of back. Snout long; mouth of moderate size, reaching well short to below eye; jaws with strong conical teeth in single row. Dorsal fins separated by three scales; first spine minute, third or fourth is longest, followed by progressively shorter spines; soft-rayed section headed by one spine. Anal fin almost identical to, having one spine, and opposite second dorsal fin. Caudal fin deeply forked, small scales approaching margin; other fins pointed. Juveniles similar to adults, except shape; xanthic forms common in some areas. Widespread Indo-Pacific; juveniles south to central New South Wales. Various habitats, from coastal lagoons to deep offshore sand flats. Usually adults in pairs; juveniles occur singly and mixed with other kinds of fish, often accompanied by labrids. Attains 40 cm.

Parupeneus cyclostomus   Normal form ▲   Yellow form ▼

HALF-AND-HALF GOATFISH
Parupeneus barberinoides (Bleeker, 1852)

D VIII+I,8-9. A I,6-7. P 14-16. V I,5. LL 28-29. Body moderately elongate, slightly compressed, covered with large scales which extend onto head including cheeks, interorbital. Lateral line with long gradual curves, following contour of back. Snout long, mouth of moderate size, reaching well short to below eye; jaws with strong conical teeth in single row. Dorsal fins separated by three to four scales; first spine minute, third or fourth is longest, followed by progressively shorter spines; soft-rayed section headed by one spine. Anal fin almost identical to, having one spine, and opposite second dorsal fin. Caudal fin deeply forked, small scales approaching margin; other fins pointed. Juveniles similar to adults, including shape. Widespread tropical west Pacific; south to the Sydney area. Juveniles in shallow lagoons and harbours. Adults on deeper coastal reef slopes to about 40 m. Usually solitary. Attains 30 cm, but rarely over 20 cm.

BLACK-SPOT GOATFISH
Parupeneus signatus (Günther, 1867)

D VIII+I,8-9. A I,6-7. P 15-16. V I,5. LL 28-29. Body elongate, slightly compressed, deepening with age; covered with large scales which extend onto head including cheeks, interorbital. Lateral line with long gradual curves, following contour of back. Snout long; mouth of moderate size, reaching well short to below eye; jaws with strong conical teeth in single row. Dorsal fins separated by three to four scales; first spine minute, third or fourth is longest, followed by progressively shorter spines; soft-rayed section headed by one spine. Anal fin almost identical to, having one spine, and opposite second dorsal fin. Caudal fin deeply forked, small scales approaching margin; other fins pointed. Juveniles similar to adults, except more slender, more yellow. Northern half of Australia, extending to Papua New Guinea and northern New Zealand waters. Coastal reefs, estuaries; juveniles in small schools; adults singly or in small aggregations. Attains 50 cm. Often confused with similar *P. spilurus* from Japan and China Seas, and *P. rubescens* from western Indian Ocean and Red Sea.

Parupeneus signatus Juvs.

DIAMOND-SCALED GOATFISH
Parupeneus ciliatus (Lacepède, 1801)

D VIII+I,8-9. A I,6-7. P 15-16. V I,5. LL 28-29. Body elongate, slightly compressed, covered with large scales which extend onto head including cheeks, interorbital. Lateral line with long gradual curves, following contour of back. Snout long; mouth of moderate size, reaching well short to below eye; jaws with strong conical teeth in single row. Dorsal fins separated by three to four scales; first spine minute, third or fourth is longest, followed by progressively shorter spines; soft-rayed section headed by one spine. Anal fin almost identical to, having one spine, and opposite second dorsal fin. Caudal fin deeply forked, small scales approaching margin; other fins pointed. Widespread tropical West-Pacific and east Indian Ocean; replaced by similar *P. porphyreus* in Hawaii. Coastal to outer reefs; adults to the Sydney area. Attains 35 cm.

Parupeneus signatus ▲

Parupeneus ciliatus ▼

BLUE-LINED GOATFISH
Upeneichthys lineatus (Bloch and Schneider, 1801)

D VIII+I,8. A I,6. P 15-16. V I,5. LL 27. Body compressed, covered with large scales which extend onto head and are embedded on cheeks, interorbital. Lateral line slightly curved from origin to below dorsal fin. Snout bluntly angled in lateral profile; mouth small with fleshy lips; jaws with blunt conical teeth in single row, some additional irregular rows anteriorly in large adults. Dorsal fins separated by three to four scales; first spine minute, second or third is longest, followed by progressively shorter spines; soft-rayed section headed by one spine. Anal fin almost identical to, having one spine, and opposite second dorsal fin. Colour extremely variable from pale, almost white, to bright red, and from juvenile to adult with spotting and stripes on head. East coast from southern Queensland to Bermagui. Sheltered bays and harbours, usually in small aggregations on sand in 5-40 m; occasionally trawled to 100 m. Attains 30 cm. Small genus comprising four species, three of which are Australian endemics, one a New Zealand endemic. New Zealand and two south coast species very similar, differing slightly in colour. Latter two overlap in southern New South Wales; apart from colour, southern species has slightly longer snout, lateral line at origin usually straight instead of slightly curved.

U. lineatus   Night colouration ▲   Juvs. ▼

SOUTHERN GOATFISH
Upeneichthys vlamingii (Cuvier, 1829)

D VIII+I,8. A I,6. P 15-16. V I,5. LL 27. Body moderately elongate, compressed, covered with large scales which extend onto head and are embedded on cheeks, interorbital. Lateral line almost straight from origin to below dorsal fin. Snout bluntly angled in lateral profile; mouth small with fleshy lips; jaws with blunt conical teeth in single row, some additional irregular rows anteriorly in large adults. Dorsal fins separated by four to five scales; first spine minute, second or third is longest, followed by progressively shorter spines; soft-rayed section headed by one spine. Anal fin almost identical to, having one spine, and opposite second dorsal fin. Posterior ends of dorsal and anal fins elongate in large individuals. Colour extremely variable between juveniles and adults, and individuals. Pale specimens have black or red stripe; reddish or large adults brightly striped and spotted. Widespread south coast and Tasmania, ranging to southern New South Wales and southern Western Australia. Schooling species, occurring in large numbers in rocky estuaries and sheltered coastal waters to at least 100 m. Attains 35 cm.

U. vlamingii   Night colouration ▲   Juvs. ▼

BULLSEYES
FAMILY PEMPHERIDIDAE

Two genera are currently recognised and both are represented in southern waters. An estimated 20 species are distributed globally in tropical to warm-temperate seas. They are closely related to the silver batfishes and have many features in common. The dorsal and anal fin tips are about opposite over the centre of the body, but the dorsal fin base is short and extends anteriorly, while the anal fin base is long and extends posteriorly. Their bodies are oblong to moderately slender and compressed. The scales are small, either ctenoid or cycloid, and sometimes deciduous. The lateral-line scales may extend to the posterior margin of the caudal fin and are not included in the count. About 10 species of bullseyes occur in Australian waters and four range into south-eastern waters. Small to large schools aggregate near reefs or in large caves during the day and during the night feed well away in open water on zooplankton, usually small crustaceans and cephalopods. Small juveniles are semitransparent, often in very large cloud-like formations along the front of small reefs in coastal estuaries. Bullseyes are small fishes; the largest attains 22 cm.

SLENDER BULLSEYE
Parapriacanthus elongatus (McCulloch, 1911)

D IV-V,9-11. A III,23-27. P 17-18. V I,5. LL 57-68. Scales mostly deciduous, cycloid. Body moderately elongate, very compressed; caudal peduncle slender. Lateral line slightly curved, extending onto caudal fin but not reaching margin. Last dorsal fin ray above first anal fin ray. Eye very large. Mouth large, oblique; a series of small conical teeth in each jaw. Greyish or brownish above with numerous tiny black spots; lighter below. South coast from southern New South Wales to Perth, including Tasmania. Coastal reefs in large schools; usually fairly deep to about 60 m, but occasionally enters rocky coastal estuaries in shallow depths of a few metres. Attains 13 cm.

BLACK-TIPPED BULLSEYE
Pempheris affinis McCulloch, 1911

D V,10-11. A III,38-42. P 16-17. V I,5. LL 60-62. Scales weakly attached, cycloid, slightly extending onto anal fin posteriorly, covering body and head up to snout. Body deep, considerably compressed; caudal peduncle long. Lateral line smoothly curved to below dorsal fin, then straight, extending to caudal fin margin. Eye very large. Mouth large, oblique; band of small conical teeth in each jaw, outermost largest. Golden-yellow on sides, pale greyish above with distinct black fin tips; anal fin with black margin. East coast from southern Queensland to Montague Island. Coastal waters in rocky reefs, ledges and caves during the day. Out at night. In small aggregations to depths of at least 30 m. Attains 15 cm.

SMALL-SCALE BULLSEYE
Pempheris compressa (Shaw, 1790)

D VI,10-11. A III,30-38. P 16-17. V I,5. LL 59-67. Scales adherent, ctenoid, covering body and head except snout. Lateral line slightly curved from origin, extending to caudal fin margin. Eye very large. Mouth large, oblique; band of small conical teeth in each jaw, outermost largest and enlarged in adults. Pale brownish; leading edge of dorsal fin black. Common New South Wales species only ranging from Byron Bay to the south coast. Usually on offshore reefs in large schools, in depths of about 20-30 m. Juveniles on coastal reefs and near entrance of coastal estuaries with rocky reefs. Attains 20 cm.

COMMON BULLSEYE
Pempheris multiradiata Klunzinger, 1879

D V,11-12. A III,32-39. P 16-17. V I,5. LL 42-49. Scales weakly attached, variably cycloid laterally to ctenoid dorsally and ventrally; slightly extend onto anal fin posteriorly; cover body and head up to snout. Body deep, considerably compressed; caudal peduncle long. Lateral line smoothly curved to below dorsal fin, then straight, extending to caudal fin margin. Eye very large. Mouth large, oblique; band of small conical teeth in each jaw, outermost largest. Brown to dark grey with dusky fins. Juveniles pale with black fin tips. Widespread in southern waters from Sydney to Perth and to southern Tasmania. Rocky reefs, in ledges and caves in small to large aggregations during the day; out at night feeding. Shallow coastal bays and harbours to deep offshore reefs; to about 30 m. Attains 22 cm. Very common in southern waters; juveniles sometimes kept in cold-water aquariums. Because of general drab appearance, most collectors do not bother with them, targeting more colourful species, but pempherids are interesting, easy to keep. Juveniles ideal, forming small schools in an aquarium. Despite large mouth they eat relatively small things; eat virtually any kind of food offered. However, collecting these fishes must be done with special care. Shock easily; scales and fins often damaged in the process which can cause disease problems. Small specimens best collected with plastic bag; handling should be minimal; should be transported with plenty of water. Not suitable for tropical aquariums.

Pempheris multiradiata Adult ▼ Juv. ▲

SILVER BATFISHES
FAMILY MONODACTYLIDAE

A small family of tropical fishes comprising three genera and five species. The monotypic *Psettus* occurs in the Atlantic, *Monodactylus*, with two species, is widespread in the Indo-Pacific, and *Schuettea*, with two species, is endemic to southern Australian waters. The silver batfishes are typically deep-bodied and compressed with small silvery deciduous scales which extend onto the median fins and head. The ventral fin is small and becomes rudimentary in some adults. The spines in the dorsal and anal fins are reduced, and the heading soft rays are tall and situated above and below centre of body, giving an overall diamond shape. The mouth is small and oblique, and there are bands of small brush-like teeth in the jaws.

Juveniles are mainly estuarine and some species can live in fresh water. Adults school in coastal bays and large estuaries, feeding on zooplankton, algaes, or almost anything else suspended or floating. The silver batfishes are small fishes, up to 30 cm, but usually to about 20 cm. One species from each of the two Indo-Pacific genera is included here.

EASTERN POMFRED
Schuettea scalaripinnis Steindachner, 1866

D V,28-30. A III,28-30. P16-18. VI,5. LL 49-52. Body moderately deep, covered with small ctenoid scales which extend onto dorsal and anal fins and head. Lateral line almost straight, except small curve at origin. Juveniles silver with yellow fins; adults more yellow or gold along back. Only known from coastal New South Wales to southern Queensland. Schooling species, in coastal bays, protected island coves, deeper part of large estuaries close to sea entrance. Along rocky drop-offs with kelp in 10 to 30 m. Attains 20 cm. Western Pomfred, *S. woodwardi*, occurs at similar latitude in Western Australia.

SILVER BATFISH
Monodactylus argenteus (Linnaeus, 1758)

D VII-VIII,27-31. A III,27-31. P 16-18. V I,2-3. LL 50-65. Body very deep, covered with tiny deciduous scales which extend onto dorsal and anal fins and head. Lateral line with gradual curve from shoulder to caudal peduncle. Juveniles dark, adults silver. Widespread tropical Indo-Pacific from west Pacific to Samoa and to east Africa and Red Sea. Adults south to at least Jervis Bay. Occurs mainly in large coastal estuaries in silty habitats, often in large schools around breakwaters or under jetties. Juveniles in brackish water, sometimes moving into fresh water. Shallow reefs to about 10 m. Attains 25 cm, but usually to 20 cm.

SWEEPS
FAMILY SCORPIDIDAE

This small family comprises two or three genera. The four species of the Australian and New Zealand genus *Scorpis* are restricted to warm temperate waters. They differ from the closely related kyphosids in having smaller scales, more soft rays on the dorsal and anal fins, and deep, compressed bodies. Large individuals become more elongate and the head profile of some species is very similar to the kyphosids. The posterior half of the fish looks symmetrical with the same shaped and sized fins opposite. Colours vary slightly between steel-grey and blue; the young of some species have dusky saddle-like markings. The sweeps are mainly mid-water feeders, taking algae and zooplankton, usually in large schools. The large species are considered good eating. Of the four species, one is restricted to south-western waters and is not included here. The large-spined mados are now placed in Microcanthidae, which has affinities with the scats and butterflyfishes.

SEA SWEEP
Scorpis aequipinnis Richardson, 1848

D IX-X,27-28. A III,25-26. P 18. V I,5. LL 100 (approximately). Small, firmly attached ctenoid scales cover body, head and extend far onto median fins. Spinous section of dorsal fin very low; soft-rayed portion elevated at first few rays; similar-shaped anal fin opposite. Caudal fin long, forked. Mouth small, oblique; jaws with bands of strong teeth, outer enlarged, recurving. Variable silvery-grey to blue, with or without dusky saddles which are most pronounced in juveniles. Shape of body alters with size; small juveniles deep-bodied, adults oblong. Southern waters from southern New South Wales to south Western Australia, including Tasmania. Common species in turbulent coastal waters; juveniles in rocky estuaries and under jetties. Attains 38 cm.

Scorpis aequipinnis   Adult ▼ Juv. ▲

BLUE SWEEP
Scorpis violacea (Hutton, 1873)

D IX-X,27-28. A III,25-26. P 18. V I,5. LL 100 (approximately). Small, firmly attached ctenoid scales cover body, head and extend far onto median fins. Spinous section of dorsal fin very low; soft-rayed portion elevated at first few rays; similar-shaped anal fin opposite. Caudal fin long, forked. Mouth small, oblique; jaws with bands of strong teeth, outer enlarged, recurving. Variable silvery-grey to iridescent blue. Rare in New South Wales; more common at Lord Howe Island, most abundant at the Kermadec Islands and northern New Zealand. Schooling species feeding mid-water on algae and zooplankton. Attains 40 cm.

SILVER SWEEP
Scorpis lineolata Kner, 1865

D IX-X,26-28. A III,27-28. P 17-18. V I,5. LL 87-94. Small, firmly attached ctenoid scales cover body, head and extend far onto median fins. Spinous section of dorsal fin low; spines about half as long as soft rays; soft-rayed portion not elevated at first few rays; similar-shaped anal fin opposite. Caudal fin long, forked. Mouth small, oblique; jaws with bands of strong teeth, outer enlarged, recurving. Variable silvery-grey to greenish-grey above. East coast from southern Queensland to eastern Tasmania and to Port Phillip Bay, Lord Howe Island and northern New Zealand. Particularly common in southern New South Wales where it schools in great numbers. Coastal reefs to 30 m; small juveniles in estuaries and rock pools. Attains 30 cm.

DRUMMERS
FAMILY KYPHOSIDAE

Some authors combine the families Kyphosidae and similar Girellidae in a single family, however the Girellidae feature more dorsal fin spines, and differ considerably in dentition. Thus, they are regarded here as separate families. Kyphosids have small, usually weakly ctenoid scales, covering the body and head, a small mouth with incisor-like teeth in a single row in each jaw, and smaller teeth on the tongue, vomer and palatines. The drummers are a small family comprising three genera, two of which are monotypic and are not included here. The genus *Kyphosus* comprises an estimated eight species which have a global distribution. Kyphosids are primarily tropical reef fishes, commonly found in high-energy zones in shallow coastal waters where they feed on algae and associated invertebrates. They are mostly in large boulder areas where they go for cover. These medium-sized fishes usually occur in large schools. Occasionally they are caught by line fisherman but are considered to be of poor taste, and are reputed in some areas to cause vivid nightmares after consumption. At least six species occur in Australian waters, five of which are included here. Some species have a xanthic form. NOTE: not all lateral-line scales have pores but are included in the count.

210

SOUTHERN SILVER DRUMMER
Kyphosus sydneyanus (Günther, 1886)

D XI,12. A III,10-11. P 16-18. V I,5. LL 55-59. Strongly ctenoid scales cover body, head, and greatly extend onto anal fin and soft-rayed section of dorsal fin. Lateral line with gradual curve anteriorly. Spinous section of dorsal fin evenly arched, its base much longer than base of soft-rayed section. Anal fin similar to and opposite soft-rayed section of dorsal fin. Caudal fin large, slightly lunate with rounded corners. Silvery-grey to dark grey, often with silver streak along sides; darker on upper half. Distinct black spot below axil; black posterior margin on opercle. Caudal fin usually broadly black posteriorly, but fades in large adults. Dorsal, anal, pectoral and ventral fins may be variably black in oceanic waters. Widespread south coast species ranging to Queensland and south Western Australia, but rare in Tasmania and the Bass Strait area. Also in northern New Zealand, Lord Howe and Norfolk Islands. Shallow rocky reefs, coastal bays and harbours to at least 20 m. Attains 75 cm. Known as Dreamfish at Lord Howe Island.

Kyphosus sydneyanus   East coast form ▲   South coast form ▼

Kyphosus sydneyanus Juv.

NORTHERN SILVER DRUMMER
Kyphosus gibsoni Ogilby, 1912

D XI,13. A III,10-11. P 17-18. V I,5. LL 65-70. Strongly ctenoid scales cover body, head, and greatly extend onto anal fin and soft-rayed section of dorsal fin. Lateral line with gradual curve anteriorly. Spinous section of dorsal fin evenly arched, its base slightly longer than base of soft-rayed section. Anal fin similar to and opposite soft-rayed section of dorsal fin. Caudal fin large, slightly lunate with rounded corners. Silvery-grey; scale centres pale, forming indistinct longitudinal lines along scale rows. Caudal fin usually broadly black posteriorly. Tropical Australia, south to Montague Island. Coastal rocky outcrops; in New South Wales sometimes mixed with *K. sydneyanus*, which is very similar but has larger scales and usually a distinct black spot below pectoral fin base. Attains about 50 cm.

Kyphosus gibsoni Juv.

SNUBNOSE DRUMMER
Kyphosus cinerascens (Forsskål, 1775)

D XI,12. A III,11-12. P 18-19. V I,5. LL 65-72. Small ctenoid scales cover body, head. Lateral line with gradual curve to caudal peduncle. Spinous section of dorsal fin low, length of its base about equal to base of soft-rayed portion. Anterior soft ray about twice length of posterior soft ray. Anal fin similar to and opposite soft-rayed section of dorsal fin. Caudal fin large, slightly forked. Silvery-grey with thin longitudinal lines over body scales. Caudal and anal fins and soft-rayed section of dorsal fin mostly dusky. Widespread tropical Indo-Pacific, central New South Wales to southern Japan and to east Africa and Red Sea; common at Lord Howe Island. Usually in large schools, often swimming mid-water. Shallow coastal reefs and lagoons, feeding mainly on algae. Attains at least 50 cm; probably larger in cooler regions.

Kyphosus cinerascens　Adult ▼　Juv. ▲

Kyphosus vaigiensis ▼

BRASSY DRUMMER
Kyphosus vaigiensis (Quoy and Gaimard, 1824)

D X-XI,14-15. A III,12-14. P19-20. V I,5. LL 65-77. Small ctenoid scales cover body, head. Lateral line with gradual curve to below soft dorsal fin, continuing straight to caudal peduncle. Spinous section of dorsal fin slightly arched above height of soft-rayed section; base of spinous section shorter than base of soft-rayed section. Anal fin similar to and opposite soft-rayed section of dorsal fin. Caudal fin large, slightly forked. Pectoral fins rather small. Silvery-grey with brownish longitudinal lines over body scales below lateral line. Widespread tropical Indo-Pacific, from Sydney area to broadly west Pacific and to east Africa and Red Sea. Coastal reef slopes, lagoons. Swims mid-water, often singly or in small aggregations. Coastal to outer reefs in exposed areas. Attains 40 cm.

Kyphosus bigibbus ▼

GREY DRUMMER
Kyphosus bigibbus (Lacepède, 1803)

D XI,11-13. A III,11-13. P18-20. V I,5. LL 65-75. Small ctenoid scales cover body, head. Lateral line with gradual curve to below soft dorsal fin, continuing straight to caudal peduncle. Spinous section of dorsal fin slightly arched above height of soft-rayed section; base of spinous section shorter than base of soft-rayed section. Anal fin similar to and opposite soft-rayed section of dorsal fin. Caudal fin large, slightly forked. Pectoral fins rather small. Pale to dusky grey, usually darker along upper half of body. Sometimes xanthic, uniformly yellow; rare albino forms occur. Widespread tropical Indo-Pacific, seemingly anti-equatorial; from New South Wales south to Montague Island, Lord Howe and Norfolk Island; Kermadec Islands and also to east Africa and Red Sea. Coastal reefs, lagoons. Schools in shallow water in somewhat exposed areas feeding on algae. Large species; attains 75 cm.

BLACKFISHES
FAMILY GIRELLIDAE

This family is closely related to Kyphosidae and Microcanthidae (previously part of Scorpididae) and some authors combine them all, or Girellidae with either one. However, the Girellidae possess a much greater number of dorsal fin spines and differ considerably in dentition. A single genus, *Girella*, is recognised, comprising about 10 species distributed along continental margins of the Pacific and south Western Australia. Most occur at a similar latitude in warm-temperate or subtropical waters. In Australia there are five species, one of which is restricted to south Western Australia and is not included here, and two range to New Zealand waters. They are characterised by oblong bodies and tricuspid teeth in the jaws, and are mostly coastal reef and estuarine fishes. They feed primarily on algae which is bitten off rocks or floating matter. Small juveniles live in the intertidal zone and school in the larger rock pools, and some can cope with low salinities. Despite being primarily vegetarian, they are popular fish with the angler and some species are excellent to eat. These medium-sized fishes can attain about 70 cm.

BLACKFISH
Girella tricuspidata (Quoy and Gaimard, 1824)

D XIV-XVI,11-13. A III,11-12. P 16. V I,5. LL 48-51. Small, adherent ctenoid scales cover body, extend onto head with much smaller scales over part of opercle, cheek, and onto anal and dorsal fin bases in narrow sheaths. Mouth small; outer teeth tricuspid, in several rows in jaws. Caudal fin truncate, slightly emarginate. Bluish-grey in oceanic waters, brownish dorsally in estuaries. Southern Queensland to South Australia and north-eastern Tasmania, and New Zealand. Coastal reefs, in large schools, moving in and out of estuaries during specific times of the year. Shallow to about 20 m. Attains 50 cm. Also known as Luderick and in New Zealand as Parore.

ROCK BLACKFISH
Girella elevata Macleay, 1881

D XIII,14. A III,11-12. P 19. V I,5. LL 48-52. Body covered with small, adherent ctenoid scales, largest laterally; become very small on thorax and extended parts on fins and head; partly over opercle, cheek. Mouth small; outer teeth tricuspid, in single row. Caudal fin truncate. Little variation in colour; usually very dark brown to bluish-black, including fins. East coast from southern Queensland to north-eastern Tasmania; recorded from Lord Howe Island. Secretive during the day, among rocks and hiding in caves and ledges. Coastal to outer reefs from very shallow exposed areas to about 25 m. Attains 60 cm. Also known as Black Drummer.

ZEBRA FISH
Girella zebra (Richardson, 1846)

D XIV,13-15. A III,11. P 17-18. V I,5. LL 72-81. Tiny ctenoid scales cover body, head; minute on thorax and head, not extending onto fins. Mouth small; outer teeth tricuspid, in single row in each jaw. Caudal fin more or less emarginate. Distinctly marked with vertical bands, but sometimes more dusky all over with less distinct bands. Southern waters from southern New South Wales and Tasmania to south Western Australia. Shallow coastal reefs and estuaries in dense vegetated reef. Juveniles in rock pools. Attains 34 cm.

STRIPEYS AND MADO
FAMILY MICROCANTHIDAE

This small subtropical family comprises four genera and five species, distributed in southern waters of Australia and northern New Zealand, and the northern Pacific. They were previously placed in Scorpididae, but fishes of the genus *Scorpis* are close to Kyphosidae. The genera *Neatypus*, *Tilodon* and *Microcanthus* are mono-typic; the latter, however, consist of isolated populations which need to be investigated. *Atypichthys* comprises two species. The close-set brush-like teeth and scalations suggest a close relationship with the butterflyfishes, Chaetodontidae, especially *Tilodon*, which is virtually identical in external characters. They are primarily benthic feeders, taking a variety of small invertebrates, but may school in great numbers when suitable zooplankton is available. Some have been observed cleaning other fishes. They have oval to very deep bodies and the dorsal, anal and ventral fins have strong spines. Scales are small, covering the body, most of the soft-rayed portions of the dorsal and anal fins, and to various degrees forming a scaly sheath along the base of the spinous part of the dorsal fin. Only *Tilodon* reaches an edible size and is reputed to be tasty; the others are small and have no commercial value except as aquarium fishes.

AUSTRALIAN MADO
Atypichthys strigatus (Günther, 1860)

D XI-XII,16. A III,16-17. P 16-18. V I,5. LL 70-78. Small, firmly attached ctenoid scales cover body, head and extend over soft-rayed sections of dorsal and anal fins, almost to margins. Dorsal fin with long spines, evenly arched; fin tallest at fourth to fifth spine. Anal fin spines large, second is longest. Body moderately elongate; caudal fin forked; eye large. Mouth small, oblique; outer row of teeth slightly enlarged. Distinctly coloured with no obvious variations. South-east coast from southern Queensland to eastern Tasmania, extending into Bass Strait and to Lord Howe Island. Schooling species, particularly common on coastal reefs in southern New South Wales. Also commonly found under jetties in harbours and large estuaries. Attains 25 cm; usually to 18 cm.

NEW ZEALAND MADO
Atypichthys latus McCulloch and Waite, 1916

D XI-XII,15. A III,15-16. P 16-18. V I,5. LL 70-78. Small, firmly attached ctenoid scales cover body, head and extend over soft-rayed sections of dorsal and anal fins, almost to margins. Dorsal fin with long spines, evenly arched; fin tallest at fourth to fifth spine. Anal fin spines large, second is longest. Body slightly elongate; caudal fin forked; eye large. Mouth small, oblique; outer row of teeth slightly enlarged. Distinctly coloured with no obvious variations. Occurs commonly around islands off northern New Zealand, Kermadec Islands and Lord Howe Island. Possibly in New South Wales; easily overlooked with the other species so common there. Reefs with caves and overhangs. Solitary or small aggregations, occasionally in large schools. Variable depths from surface to at least 60 m. Attains 25 cm.

STRIPEY
Microcanthus strigatus (Cuvier, 1831)

D XI,16-18. A III,15-16. P 16. V I,5. LL 56-60. Small, firmly attached ctenoid

scales cover body, head and extend over soft-rayed sections of dorsal and anal fins, almost to margins. Dorsal fin with long spines, evenly arched; fin tallest at third and fourth spine. Anal fin spines large, second is longest. Body deep, compressed; caudal fin emarginate; eye large. Head profile concave above eye; mouth small, oblique. Distinctly marked; colour variable from pale to bright yellow. At least three distinct populations. East coast from southern Queensland to southern New South Wales, west coast from Exmouth Gulf to Cape Leeuwin, and from southern Japan to Taiwan and Hawaii. Protected coastal waters and rocky estuaries, in small to large aggregations. Juveniles often in rock pools. Diet consists of invertebrates and algae picked from rocks or suspended matter. Attains 16 cm. Originally described from Japan; Australian forms may be distinct, in which case *M. howensis* Whitley, 1931, applies to the east coast population, and *M. vittatus* (Castelnau, 1873) to the west coast population.

MOONLIGHTER
Tilodon sexfasciatus (Richardson, 1842)

D X,20-21. A III,17-19. P 17. V I,5. LL 75-90. Small, firmly attached ctenoid scales cover body, head and extend over soft-rayed sections of dorsal and anal fins, almost to margins. Dorsal fin with long spines, evenly arched, folding back between scaly sheaths. Anal fin spines large, second is longest. Body very deep, compressed; caudal fin emarginate; eye large. Head profile concave above eye; mouth small, oblique with bands of brush-like teeth in jaws. Juveniles with distinct ocelli in posterior parts of dorsal and anal fins; the latter only in small individuals, common in butterflyfishes. Banded pattern readily identifies this species. South coast from Bass Strait and Tasmania to south Western Australia. Coastal rocky reef in ledges and caves. Large adults more in the open, usually in pairs. Juveniles in estuaries, solitary in small protected coves in very shallow depths. Attains 40 cm.

Microcanthus strigatus ▲

Tilodon sexfasciatus ▼

Tilodon sexfasciatus Juv.

SCATS OR BUTTERFISHES
FAMILY SCATOPHAGIDAE

A small family comprising two genera and three or four species, widespread in the tropical Indo-Pacific. These fishes are primarily estuarine and regularly enter fresh water. Both genera are represented with one species each in Australian waters and both range into southern waters as juveniles.

Diagnostic features are very small ctenoid scales, deep and compressed bodies, and four spines in the anal fin. The spiny fins can inflict painful wounds and are thought to be venomous. The mouth is small and the jaws contain bands of small tricuspid teeth. They are scavengers, eating almost anything, and are usually schooling fishes. Juveniles are often observed from the shore near the entrance of rivers. Young settle in quite brackish water and are sometimes found in rock pools. Small specimens are popular with freshwater aquarists. They are considered of poor taste.

STRIPED SCAT
Selenotoca multifasciata (Richardson, 1846)

D XII,16. A IV,15-16. P 17. V I,5. LL 90 (approximately). Tiny, strongly attached ctenoid scales cover body, head. Lateral line distinct, curved, following back profile. Head small; snout rounded with terminal mouth. Caudal peduncle relatively long and slender with large truncate fin. Pattern of spots and bars variable. Silvery, a little greenish above, lips outlined in black. Known from Shark Bay in the west through northern Australia and Papua New Guinea to central New South Wales, becoming rare in Sydney. Coastal estuaries, river entrances, rock pools. Attains 40 cm. Also known as False Scat and Striped Butterfish.

Selenotoca multifasciata Juv.

SPOTTED SCAT
Scatophagus argus (Linnaeus, 1766)

D XI,16-18. A IV,13-15. P 16. V I,5. LL 85-120. Tiny, strongly attached ctenoid scales cover body, head. Lateral line distinct, curved, following back profile. Head small; snout rounded with terminal mouth. Caudal peduncle short, deep with large truncate to rounded fin. Variable stages with age. Small juveniles black with red first forming bands, then becoming spotted, decreasing to small spots in adults. Widespread tropical west Pacific to eastern Indian Ocean; to southern New South Wales as juveniles. Coastal estuaries and river entrances, mainly in brackish water, including settling juveniles. Attains 35 cm. Also known as Tiger Scat and Spotted Butterfish.

BUTTERFLYFISHES
FAMILY CHAETODONTIDAE

Of all the tropical fishes, the butterflyfishes are probably the most popular with aquarists and divers. This large family comprises 10 genera with about 120 species, most of which are beautifully coloured. The majority of species live on tropical coral reefs, however a few species are of temperate origin. Together with a large number of tropical expatriates, 26 species range into south-eastern waters and are included here. The various genera can be separated by the number of fin elements, but many species are closely related and share identical counts, and are best separated on colour. The main features are: deep, compressed bodies; a pointed to sometimes very elongated snout; small ctenoid scales over the body, head and most of the soft-rayed portions of the dorsal and anal fins, and; strong sheaths along the spinous portion of the dorsal fin. Teeth are typically brush-like, slender and close-set with recurving tips. Fin spines are large and solid and are usually proportionally much larger in juveniles. Larval butterflyfishes are distinct in having bony head-armour and often long serrated spines; this is known as the tholichthys stage. Settling specimens of the genus *Chaetodon* are as small as about 10 mm, not including the caudal fin, but pelagic stages up to 60 mm were reported for this family. Most species occur in shallow depths from 3-30 m, but some juveniles can be found in tidal pools and a number of species are deepwater dwellers ranging to 200 m. Behaviour of species can vary from time of the year to geographical zones within a species. While certain species only occur in pairs in some areas, they may school elsewhere. Their diet consists primarily of small invertebrates and feeding is usually benthic; some species include live corals in their diet and a few are plankton feeders. Sizes vary between genera; *Chaetodon*, with the greatest number of species, also has the greatest size range with the smallest about 10 cm and the largest more than 30 cm.

Brown Butterflyfish (*Chaetodon kleinii*)

THREE-BAND CORALFISH
Chaetodon tricinctus Waite, 1901

D XII,22-23. A III,18-19. P 15. V I,5. LL 53-55. Dorsal and anal fin spines very large, longest spines about equal to longest soft ray; fourth spine longest in dorsal fin, second spine in anal fin. Spines greatly enlarged in small juveniles. Snout moderately short; mouth blunt, rounded; caudal fin slightly rounded. Very little colour change from juvenile to adult or variation between individuals. Juveniles lack ocellus usually found in other species. Common at Lord Howe Island and Norfolk Island regions; rare stragglers in northern New South Wales. Common in rich coral growth in lagoons and shallow reefs to about 10 m. Nibbles on coral polyps which are probably an important part of diet. Attains 18 cm.

LORD HOWE BUTTERFLYFISH
Amphichaetodon howensis (Waite, 1903)

D XII,22-23. A III,21. P 15. V I,5. LL 45-50. Dorsal and anal fin spines very large, longest spines longer than longest soft ray; third spine longest in dorsal fin, second spine in anal fin. Spines greatly enlarged in small juveniles. Snout moderately long, pointed; caudal fin truncate. Very little colour change from juvenile to adult or variation between individuals. Juveniles lack ocellus usually found in other similar species; only newly settled specimens, about 15 mm long, differ slightly in having last body band pale with black spots at top and bottom. East coast from southern New South Wales to southern Queensland, Lord Howe Island and ranging to northern New Zealand. Primarily deep outer-reef dweller from about 20 m to at least 150 m, but occasionally ventures into shallow turbulent water a few metres deep. Juveniles solitary; adults usually in pairs along vertical walls or in large caves. Attains 18 cm. Second species, virtually identical in appearance, occurs in the south-east Pacific.

Amphichaetodon howensis ▲

Amphichaetodon howensis Juv.

Chelmonops truncatus Adult ▲ Juv. ▼

TRUNCATE CORALFISH
Chelmonops truncatus (Kner, 1859)

D XI,26-28. A III,17-20. P 16-17. V I,5. LL 47-50. Dorsal and anal fin spines strong; first short, following spines progressively longer, continuing with several soft rays, then rapidly shortening rays form almost square corner with vertical posterior margin. Anal fin smaller than dorsal fin but with similar shape and opposite. Snout greatly produced, forehead profile steep. Colour variations only slight; juveniles with large ocelli near corner of dorsal fin which remains to near adult size. East coast only, from Jervis Bay to southern Queensland. Protected coastal bays and estuaries, usually in deeper part along steep rocky reefs. Juveniles solitary, adults in pairs. Depth range about 10-70 m. Attains 22 cm. Second species in this genus, *C. curiosus*, restricted to south-western coast. Sometimes called Square Back.

BEAKED CORALFISH
Chelmon rostratus (Linnaeus, 1758)

D IX,28-30. A III,19-21. P 14-15. V I,5. LL 48-55. Dorsal and anal fin spines strong; first short, following spines progressively longer, continuing with several soft rays, then gradually shortening rays form rounded corner with vertical posterior margin. Anal fin smaller than dorsal fin but with similar shape and opposite. Snout greatly produced, forehead profile steep. Distinctly coloured; little variation from juvenile to adult; ocellus proportionally larger in small juveniles. West Pacific from New South Wales to southern Japan; juveniles south to Botany Bay; rare south of Forster. Coastal reefs, lagoons, estuaries. Adults often in pairs. Shallow to about 15 m. Attains 20 cm. The two other species in this genus occur in northern waters; similar *C. marginalis*, lacking middle band, in the northwest, and *C. muelleri*, dusky looking species, from silty northern Australian coastal waters.

OCELLATE CORALFISH
Parachaetodon ocellatus (Cuvier, 1831)

D VI-VII,28-30. A III,18-20. P 14-15. V I,5. LL 39-46. First spines of dorsal and anal fins short, followed by rapidly increasingly longer spines; dorsal fin with following longer soft rays which progressively shorten posteriorly, forming corner at high point. Anal fin rays subequal. Lateral line rather low along upper sides. Slightly variable from brown to orange bands; juvenile has ocellus on caudal peduncle. West Pacific from New South Wales to southern Japan, south to at least Sydney. Coastal bays and estuaries; often in small aggregations in seagrass habitat. Shallow lagoons to deep mudflats in 60 m. Attains 18 cm. Monotypic genus.

HIGHFIN CORALFISH
Coradion altivelus McCulloch, 1916.

D VIII,31-33. A III,20-22. P 14. V I,5. LL 49-50. First spines of dorsal and anal fins short, followed by rapidly increasingly longer spines and long soft-rayed section, forming long rounded fins. Snout produced, forehead profile steep. Slight changes in colour pattern from juvenile to adult; adult more orange, has no ocellus on dorsal fin. West Pacific, northern New South Wales to southern Japan. Common in Moreton Bay; a few juveniles known from Balmoral, Sydney Harbour. Coastal reefs to protected inner reefs, to about 30 m. Attains 15 cm. Genus comprises two other species, similar but with lower fins, which are restricted to more tropical waters of the west Pacific.

BLACK-BACK BUTTERFLYFISH
Chaetodon melannotus Bloch and Schneider, 1801

D XII, 18-20. A III,16-18. P 14-15. V I,5. LL 33-39. Spinous section of dorsal fin slightly arched, highest in centre, followed by subequal soft rays. Posterior margins of dorsal and anal fins rounded; caudal fin rounded at corners. Snout slightly produced; head profile slightly concave over eyes. Juveniles similar to adults, with ocellus on caudal peduncle. Widespread tropical Indo-Pacific from the west to central Pacific to east Africa. Replaced in some areas of Indonesia by similar *C. ocellicaudus*. Juveniles regularly south to the Sydney area. Adults singly or in pairs in rich coral reefs. Sometimes seen in groups of 10 or more, seemingly migrating. Juveniles in harbours on shallow rocky reefs. Adults to about 30 m. Attains 15 cm.

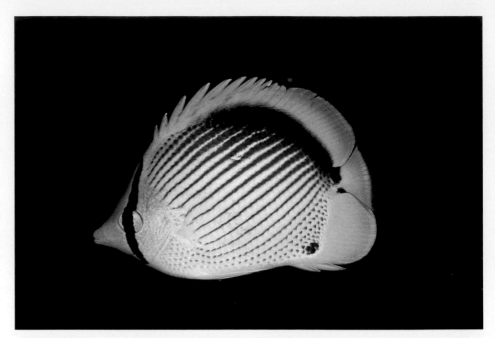

LINED BUTTERFLYFISH
Chaetodon lineolatus Cuvier, 1831

D XII,24-27. A III,20-22. P 15-17. V I,5. LL 26-33. Spinous section of dorsal fin slightly arched in juveniles, highest in centre, followed by subequal soft rays which even out in adults. Posterior margins of dorsal and anal fins rounded; caudal fin rounded at corners. Snout produced; head profile concave over eyes. Juveniles similar to adults; posterior black band reduced to spot on caudal peduncle. Widespread tropical Indo-Pacific from west and central Pacific to east Africa and Red Sea. Best known in New South Wales from warm-water outlet of the power station near Swansea. Coastal to outer reefs, usually shallow on reef crests with deep gutters, to about 30 m. Singly or in pairs on Great Barrier Reef, but schooling in southern Japan. Largest species in family; attains 30 cm.

DOUBLE-SADDLE BUTTERFLYFISH
Chaetodon ulietensis Cuvier, 1831

D XII,22-24. A III,19-21. P 14-15. V I,5. LL 32-37. Spinous section of dorsal fin slightly arched in juveniles, highest in centre, followed by subequal soft rays which even out in adults. Posterior margins of dorsal and anal fins rounded; caudal fin rounded at corners. Snout produced; head profile concave over eyes. Juveniles similar to adults with more pronounced spot on caudal peduncle. Widespread tropical west to central Pacific, south to Sydney; known from small juveniles in Watson's Bay, Sydney Harbour. Coastal reef slopes with rich coral growth. Usually in pairs but in some parts of the Pacific in large schools. Observed to 25 m. Attains 15 cm. Replaced by similar *C. falcula* in the Indian Ocean.

Chaetodon lineolatus ▲

Chaetodon ulietensis ▼

Chaetodon ulietensis Juv.

SADDLED BUTTERFLYFISH
Chaetodon ephippium Cuvier, 1831

D XII-XIV,21-24. A III,20-22. P 15-16. V I,5. LL 33-40. Spinous section of dorsal fin slightly arched in juveniles, highest in centre, followed by subequal soft rays which even out in adults. Posterior margins of dorsal and anal fins rounded in juveniles, caudal fin rounded at corners; large filament trails from top of dorsal fin in adults, and caudal fin has produced corners. Snout produced; head profile concave over eyes. Juveniles similar colour to adults. Widespread tropical west to central Pacific, south to Sydney; known from small juveniles in Watson's Bay, Sydney Harbour. Coastal reef slopes with rich coral growth. Usually in pairs to about 10 m, but commonly observed at 25 m in southern Japan. Attains 23 cm.

Chaetodon ephippium   Juv.

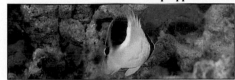

THREADFIN BUTTERFLYFISH
Chaetodon auriga Forsskål, 1775

D XIII,22-25. A III,19-21. P 14-15. V I,5. LL 33-43. Spinous section of dorsal fin slightly arched in juveniles, highest in centre, followed by subequal soft rays which even out in adults. Posterior margins of dorsal and anal fins rounded in juveniles, caudal fin rounded at corners; large filament trails from top of dorsal fin in adults, and caudal fin has produced corners. Snout produced; head profile concave over eyes. Juveniles similar colour to adults. Widespread tropical Indo-Pacific from New South Wales to Japan, central Pacific, and east Africa and Red Sea. Commonly to the Sydney area as juveniles and south to Green Cape. Coastal reefs; juveniles in boulder reef, in protected bays and harbours under jetties. Attains 20 cm.

Chaetodon auriga   Juv.

VAGABOND BUTTERFLYFISH
Chaetodon vagabundus Linnaeus, 1758

D XIII,23-26. A III,19-21. P 15-17. V I,5. LL 31-38. Spinous section of dorsal fin slightly arched in juveniles, highest in centre, followed by subequal soft rays which even out in adults. Posterior margins of dorsal and anal fins rounded; caudal fin rounded at corners.

Chaetodon auriga ▲

Chaetodon vagabundus   Adult ▲ Juv. ▼

Snout produced; head profile concave over eyes. Juveniles similar to adults, with pronounced spot on posterior margin of dorsal fin. Widespread tropical Indo-Pacific from west to central Pacific, and to east Africa. Juveniles commonly south to Sydney, and to southern New South Wales. Shallow coastal rocky to rich coral slopes. Usually in pairs; juveniles solitary. Attains 18 cm.

221

GÜNTHER'S BUTTERFLYFISH
Chaetodon guentheri Ahl, 1913

D XIII,21-22. A III,18. P 14. V I,5. LL 39-40. Spinous section of dorsal fin slightly arched in juveniles, highest in centre, followed by subequal soft rays which even out in adults. Posterior margins of dorsal and anal fins rounded; caudal fin rounded at corners. Snout slightly produced; head profile concave over eyes. Juveniles similar to adults, with pronounced spot on posterior margin of dorsal fin. Widespread tropical west Pacific, ranging well into warm-temperate zones. Reaches near adult size at Montague Island. Mainly outer reefs; juveniles on outer fringes of low reef on sand in 10-30 m. Adults from about 20 m to at least 50 m. Usually very deep near the equator. In small to large aggregations; large adults often well above the substrate cleaning large pelagic fishes; may even approach divers for an inspection. Attains 14 cm.

Chaetodon guentheri Juv.

CITRON BUTTERFLYFISH
Chaetodon citrinellus Cuvier, 1831

D XIV,20-22. A III,16-17. P 13-14. V I,5. LL 36-42. Spinous section of dorsal fin slightly arched in juveniles, highest in centre, followed by subequal soft rays which even out in adults. Posterior margins of dorsal and anal fins rounded; caudal fin rounded at corners. Snout slightly produced; head profile concave over eyes. Juveniles almost identical in colour pattern to adults. Widespread tropical west Pacific and east Indian Oceans. Juveniles commonly south to the Sydney area and as far as Montague Island. Seems to prefer clear-water reefs; one of the more common species off New South Wales islands. Juveniles often share small reef areas; adults regularly school. Mostly shallow, but at Montague Island from 10-25 m. Small species; attains 11 cm.

BROWN BUTTERFLYFISH
Chaetodon kleinii Bloch, 1790

D XIII-XIV,20-23. A III,17-20. P 13-15. V I,5. LL 33-41. Spinous section of dorsal fin slightly arched in juveniles, highest in centre, followed by subequal soft rays which even out in adults. Posterior margins of dorsal and anal fins rounded; caudal fin rounded at corners. Snout slightly produced; head profile concave over eyes. Juveniles almost identical in colour pattern to adults. Widespread tropical Indo-Pacific, New South Wales to Japan, to central Pacific and to east Africa. Juveniles commonly south to the Sydney area and as far as Montague Island. Seems to prefer clear-water reefs; one of the more common species off New South Wales Islands. Juveniles secretive, among rocks, often with sea-urchins. Adults usually in pairs. Mostly shallow, but at Montague Island from 10-25 m. Small species; attains 12 cm.

RACOON BUTTERFLYFISH
Chaetodon lunula (Lacepède, 1803)

D XI-XIII,22-25. A III,17-19. P 15-16. V I,5. LL 35-44. Spinous section of dorsal fin slightly arched in juveniles, highest in centre, followed by subequal soft rays which even out in adults. Posterior margins of dorsal and anal fins rounded; caudal fin rounded at corners. Snout slightly produced; head profile concave over eyes. Juveniles almost identical in colour pattern to adults, with additional spot near posterior margin of dorsal fin. Widespread tropical Indo-Pacific, New South Wales to Japan, to central Pacific and to east Africa. Juveniles south to the Sydney area but not common; usually in silty areas such as Rose Bay, Sydney Harbour. Shallow coastal reefs and lagoons, in pairs and sometimes in small to large aggregations; usually in less than 10 m, but commonly observed at 25 m in Japan. Attains 20 cm.

Chaetodon lunula Juv.

MERTEN'S BUTTERFLYFISH
Chaetodon mertensii Cuvier, 1831

D XII-XIV,21-23. A III,16-17. P 14. V I,5. LL 35-43. First spine of dorsal fin short, followed by subequal spines and soft rays to posterior rounded corner. Anal fin with long second spine, rounded with long rays centrally. Head pointed; terminal mouth small. Caudal fin with sharp corners. Distinct pattern with little change from juvenile to adult. West Pacific, Great Barrier Reef to New South Wales; juveniles south to Sydney and in the north-west Pacific at similar latitude. Several similar species in various parts of tropical Indo-Pacific. Outer reefs, usually from 15-30 m. Juveniles in the Sydney area along margins of low reef near land in 10-20 m, but observed as shallow as 3 m in Long Bay. Attains 12 cm.

Chaetodon mertensii ▲

DUSKY BUTTERFLYFISH
Chaetodon flavirostris Günther, 1873

D XII-XIII,24-27. a III,20-21. P 15-16. V I,5. LL 40-46. Spinous section of dorsal fin slightly arched in juveniles, highest in centre, followed by subequal soft rays which even out in adults. Posterior margins of dorsal and anal fins rounded; caudal fin rounded at corners. Snout slightly produced; head profile concave over eyes. Juveniles similar in colour pattern to adults, with additional spot near posterior margin of dorsal fin; adults with reduced black band on head to nape only, where a hump develops. Widespread tropical south-west Pacific; New South Wales to Pitcairn group. Juveniles in the Sydney area occasionally survive mild winters, can reach near adult size. Coastal reefs; adults usually in pairs; juveniles solitary in rocky estuaries. Attains 20 cm.

Chaetodon flavirostris Adult ▲ Juv. ▼

223

DOT-AND-DASH BUTTERFLYFISH
Chaetodon pelewensis Kner, 1868

D XIII,22-25. A III,17-18. P 14-15. V I,5. LL 39-47. First spine of dorsal fin short, followed by subequal spines and soft rays to posterior rounded corner. Anal fin with large second spine; soft rays subequal, fin rounded. Head profile slightly concave above; snout pointed with small terminal mouth. Distinctly marked with variable pattern of spots forming diagonal stripes. Widespread tropical west Pacific; replaced by closely related *C. punctatofasciatus* in various equatorial areas. Juveniles south to Sydney, secretive, in low small boulder reefs in protected clear-water bays. Shallow to at least 30 m. Attains 10 cm.

TEARDROP BUTTERFLYFISH
Chaetodon unimaculatus Bloch, 1787

D XIII,21-23. A III,18-20. P 14-15. V I,5. LL 38-47. First spine of dorsal fin short, followed by subequal spines and soft rays to posterior rounded corner. Anal fin with large second spine; soft rays subequal to posterior edge, fin rounded. Head profile concave above; snout bluntly pointed with thick-lipped terminal mouth in adults. Some geographical variations. Widespread tropical Indo-Pacific; the illustrated form West Pacific to Hawaii and Polynesia. More yellow form Indian Ocean to east Africa. Juveniles south to Sydney, known from several juveniles near Balmoral Beach. Fairly deep, from 10-30 m, in some areas, but observed swimming over reef flats covered by high tide in Micronesia. Attains 15 cm.

BLUE-DASH BUTTERFLYFISH
Chaetodon plebeius Cuvier, 1831

D XIII-XIV,16-18. A III,14-16. P 15. V I,5. LL 36-41. Spinous section of dorsal fin slightly arched, longest spines in middle, followed by subequal soft rays to rounded posterior part. Anal fin with large second spine; posterior part similar to and opposite dorsal fin. Body more elongate than most other species; head profile almost straight above with slightly pointed snout. Some geographical variations; blue spot reduced or missing in certain areas. Very small juveniles have ocellus on caudal peduncle, then similar to adult. Widespread west Pacific from northern New South Wales to Japan and Fiji. Juveniles south to Broughton Island. Rich coral reefs, shallow lagoons to depths of at least 25 m. Coral dependent as part of diet; small juveniles at Broughton Island live only among branching corals there. Attains 12 cm.

Chaetodon unimaculatus ▲   Chaetodon plebeius ▼

Chaetodon plebeius Juv., Broughton Island

LONG-NOSE BUTTERFLYFISH
Forcipiger flavissimus Jordan and
McGregor, 1898

D XII,22-24. A III,17-18. P 15. V I,5.
LL 74-80. Dorsal fin with long spines,
subequal from third spine to subequal first
soft rays; rays decrease proportionally becoming short near caudal peduncle. Caudal fin
rounded, middle rays very long. Head profile
concave over eye; snout very long with pincer-like mouth. Very widespread in tropical Indo-Pacific, including central American coast.
Juveniles occasionally to Sydney area. Outer-reef fish, usually along deep drop-offs in pairs
or small aggregations. From reef crests, about
3 m, to at least 30 m. Similar species with
longer snout, *F. longirostris*, usually found
deeper, to at least 60 m. Sydney specimens all
fairly large, about 70 mm, which seems to
suggest fairly large tholichthys stage. Attains
22 cm.

REEF BANNERFISH
Heniochus acuminatus (Linnaeus, 1785)

D XI,24-27. A III,17-19. P 15-18. V I,5.
LL 47-54. Greatly extended fourth dorsal fin
spine with long ribbon-like filament, followed
by strong spines slightly decreasing in length,
and large round soft-rayed section. Anal fin
with three strong spines, first half length of
second; soft section long, rounded, equal to or
longer than ventral fin. Widespread tropical
Indo-Pacific from New South Wales to
southern Japan, to the Society Islands and
east Africa. Juveniles to southern New South
Wales. Coastal reefs, large rocky estuaries,
often under jetties. Large adults usually in
pairs along reef slopes and drop-offs to about
30 m. Juveniles often solitary but sometimes
very common under jetties and appear in
loose groups. Attains 25 cm.

Heniochus acuminatus ▲

Heniochus acuminatus Juv.

SCHOOLING BANNERFISH
Heniochus diphreutes Jordan, 1903

D XII,23-25. A III,17-19. P 16-18. V I,5.
LL 46-54. Greatly extended fourth dorsal fin
spine with long ribbon-like filament, followed
by strong spines, slightly decreasing in length,
and large round soft-rayed section. Anal fin
with three strong spines, first half length of
second; soft section long, rounded, shorter
than ventral fin. Widespread tropical Indo-Pacific from New South Wales to southern
Japan, to the Hawaiian Islands and to east
Africa and the Red Sea. Juveniles to southern

New South Wales. Coastal to offshore reefs.
Large adults usually in large schools, well
away from reef slopes, mid-water feeding on
zooplankton; often engage in cleaning pelagic
fishes. Juveniles often in small to large schools
in estuaries; usually on remote outcrops on
muddy substrates in depths of 15-25 m, and
some sheltered coastal bays in 5-20 m. Attains
20 cm.

Heniochus diphreutes Adult ▲ Juv. ▼

MASKED BANNERFISH
Heniochus monoceros Cuvier, 1831

D XII,24-27. A III,18-19. P 16-17. V I,5. LL 58-64. Greatly extended fourth dorsal fin spine with long ribbon-like filament, followed by strong spines slightly decreasing in length without forming notch, and large round soft-rayed section. Anal fin with three strong spines, first half length of second; soft section long, rounded, shorter than ventral fin. Adults with projecting hump on nape, small spine from each orbital. Widespread tropical Indo-Pacific from New South Wales to southern Japan, the Society Islands, and to east Africa. Juveniles south to the Sydney area. Adults often in pairs, mainly along outer reef slopes, moving through ledges, caves, and along bommies, in about 10-20 m. Juveniles from Sydney in protected coastal bays in ledges with sea-urchins. Attains 23 cm.

PENNANT BANNERFISH
Heniochus chrysostomus Cuvier, 1831

D XI-XII,21-22. A III,17-18. P 16. V I,5. LL 57-61. Greatly extended fourth dorsal fin spine with long, broad ribbon-like membrane; followed by progressively but markedly smaller spines forming large notch before taller rounded soft portion of dorsal fin. Anal fin with three strong spines, first half length of second; soft section long, rounded, equal to or longer than ventral fin. Juveniles differ from adults in having distinct ocellus in anal fin. Widespread tropical Indo-Pacific from New South Wales to southern Japan, Hawaii, Tahiti, and to the east Indian Ocean. Juveniles known from Balmoral, Sydney Harbour. Adults usually seen in pairs along deep drop-offs, staying close to the reef in caves and gutters; to at least 30 m. Juveniles solitary, in lagoons and estuaries. Attains 16 cm.

Heniochus chrysostomus Juv.

ANGELFISHES
FAMILY POMACANTHIDAE

This family comprises some of the most beautiful reef fishes, comparable to the butterflyfishes, however they are generally larger and more majestic. They are sought after and highly prized by aquarists, however over-exploitation of species in some areas has led to many European countries banning imports of the entire family. They are closely related to butterflyfishes but are readily separated by possessing a large spine on the lower corner of the preopercle. The seven genera with about 80 species comprises several distinct groups: the larger species, of which *Pomacanthus* reaches 35 cm; the small species, *Centropyge*, known as pygmy angels, some only reaching

about 10 cm, and; the lyre-tailed *Genicanthus*, planktivorous and with a distinct shape. The larger species have the most dramatic and different-coloured juveniles imaginable, not even slightly relating to the adult, and *Genicanthus* has very different colour patterns between sexes. Juveniles of most species live secretly in reefs and are very territorial, particularly with their own kind but also to closely related species. A few, only the lyre-tail and some of the pygmy angels, aggregate in numbers as adults but most fishes in the family are usually solitary or in pairs. They are benthic feeders, except for *Genicanthus*, scraping and biting algae off coral-rock, or feed on sponges

and corals, including the associated invertebrates. This activity seems to take most of the day. These fishes can produce low frequency drum-like or thumping noises, and when produced by the large species the noise is so loud that it can startle a diver. Although primarily from tropical reefs, some species have a more southern distribution and several others are dispersed by currents and expatriate to southern areas. A few species are only known from New South Wales and Lord Howe Island, and together with tropical visitors, the species included here comprise three genera and nine species. NOTE: Lateral scale rows (LSR) are vertical rows from axil to hypural.

Half-Circled Angelfish (*Pomacanthus semicirculatus*), large juvenile

227

BALLINA ANGELFISH
Chaetodontoplus ballinae Whitley,1959

D XIII,18. A III,18. P 16. V I,5. LSR 90 (approximately). Scales very small, strongly ctenoid, posterior margin with numerous ctenii; cover body in irregular rows, head, and fins to outer margins. Lateral line curves evenly along back, following contour. Mouth small; lower jaw more prominent; lips with minute scales; close-set, moveable, flattened, long slender teeth with recurving tips in jaws. Posterior margin of preopercle serrate, large horizontal spine on lower corner. Distinctly coloured; variations not known. Juvenile probably very different. Only two specimens are in the Australian Museum, both collected from deep water in northern New South Wales. Scuba divers have reported seeing this fish on deep dives in several localities off Coffs Harbour. The two specimens are 19 and 20 cm long. Genus comprises an estimated 10 species, distributed mainly in the Indo-Australian Archipelago, ranging northward to Japan.

CONSPICUOUS ANGELFISH
Chaetodontoplus conspicillatus (Waite, 1900)

D XIII,18. A III,18. P 18. V I,5. LSR 125 (approximately). Scales very small, strongly

ctenoid, posterior margin with numerous ctenii; cover body in irregular rows, head, and fins to outer margins. Lateral line curves evenly along back, following contour. Mouth small, lower jaw more prominent; lips with

C. conspicillatus Adult ▼ Juv. ▲

Chaetodontoplus meredithi ▼

minute scales; close-set, moveable, flattened, long slender teeth with recurving tips in jaws. Posterior margin of preopercle serrate, large horizontal spine on lower corner. Distinctly coloured; juvenile very different; newly settled juveniles, about 12 mm long, all black with greenish-white dorsal fin. Southern Queensland to central New South Wales and Lord Howe Island; also occurs in New Caledonia. Adults on outer reefs in depths of 20-40 m. Juveniles in lagoons and, in New South Wales, in harbours and protected bays from 3-10 m; usually in soft-coral areas which grow prolifically in some tidal channels. Attains 25 cm.

YELLOW-FINNED ANGELFISH
Chaetodontoplus meredithi Kuiter, 1990

D XIII,18-19. A III,18-19. P 18. V I,5. LSR 130 (approximately). Scales very small, strongly ctenoid, posterior margin with numerous ctenii; cover body in irregular rows, head, and fins to outer margins. Lateral line curves evenly along back, following contour. Mouth small, lower jaw more prominent; lips with minute scales; close-set, moveable, flattened, long slender teeth with recurving tips in jaws. Posterior margin of preopercle serrate, large horizontal spine on lower corner. Distinctly coloured; juveniles very different from adults. East coast from northern Queensland to central New South Wales; replaced by closely related *C. personifer* on west coast. Adults on deep outer reefs, usually in more than 30 m. Juveniles in harbours, often under deep jetties with prolific sponge growth on which they seem to feed. Attains 30 cm.

Chaetodontoplus meredithi Juv.

HALF-CIRCLED ANGELFISH
Pomacanthus semicirculatus (Cuvier, 1831)

D XIII,20-23. A III,18-22. P 19-21. V I,5. LSR 65-70. Scales small, strongly ctenoid, posterior margins with numerous ctenii; cover body; very small scales cover thorax, head and median fins to outer margins. Lateral line with long smooth curve. Mouth small, lower jaw more prominent; lips with minute scales; close-set, moveable, flattened, long slender

P. semicirculatus Adult ▼ Juv. ▲

teeth with recurving tips in jaws. Posterior margin of preopercle finely serrate, large horizontal spine on lower corner. Fin shape alters with growth; rounded in young; tips produced on posterior extremes of dorsal and anal fins in adults. Distinctly coloured; juvenile completely different from adult. Widespread tropical Indo-Pacific from New South Wales to southern Japan, central Pacific and east Africa and the Red Sea; some geographical variations. Juveniles south to Sydney. Adults usually solitary, in shallow to deep reef crests and slopes to about 30 m. Small juveniles in the Sydney area are secretive, in rocky ledges in shallow coastal bays in 1-3 m. Specimens south to at least Bermagui. Attains 35 cm. Large genus with about 22 species, one of which ranges into southern waters.

KEYHOLE ANGELFISH
Centropyge tibicen (Cuvier, 1831)

D XIV,15-17. A III,17-18. P 16-17. V I,5. LSR 41 (aproximately). Scales strongly ctenoid with longitudinal ridges; moderate-sized laterally on body, becoming smaller on head, fins. Lateral line terminates below end of dorsal fin. Ventral margin of opercle and posterior margin of preopercle coarsely serrate; large horizontal spine on corner of preopercle, small spines on ventral margin. Fins rounded, becoming more angular in adults. Juveniles similar to adults; large adults with yellow and bluish shine. Widespread, often common in tropical Indo-Pacific from New South Wales to southern Japan, east Indian Ocean; juveniles south to Montague Island. Coastal reefs, crests and shallow slopes to about 25 m. Juveniles in narrow ledges in protected bays and rocky estuaries, shallow to about 10 m. Attains 15 cm. Large Indo-Pacific genus with estimated 30 species, five of which range to southern waters.

PEARLY-SCALED ANGELFISH
Centropyge vroliki (Bleeker, 1853)

D XIV,15-16. A III,16-17. P 16-17. V I,5. LSR 45 (approximately). Scales strongly ctenoid with longitudinal ridges; moderate-sized laterally on body, becoming smaller on head, fins. Lateral line terminates below end of dorsal fin. Posterior margin of preopercle coarsely serrate; large horizontal spine on corner of preopercle, small spines on ventral margin. Fins rounded, including in large adults. Juveniles very similar to adults. Widespread tropical west Pacific, from New South Wales to southern Japan and Micronesia; replaced by closely related *C. eibli* in the Indian Ocean. Only known in the Sydney area from a few juveniles at Shelly Beach, Manly. Reef crests and slopes with rich coral growth; shallow to about 25 m. Attains 12 cm.

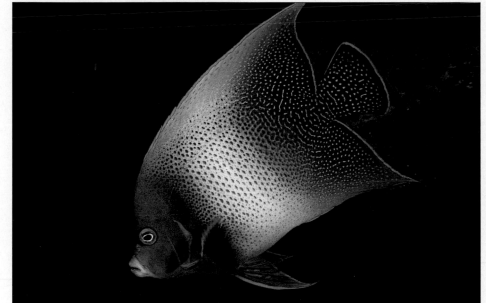

Centropyge tibicen ▼

Centropyge vroliki ▼

CORAL BEAUTY
Centropyge bispinosus (Günther, 1860)

D XIV-XV,16-18. A III,18-20. P 16. V I,5. LSR 43 (approximately). Scales strongly ctenoid with longitudinal ridges; moderate-sized laterally on body, becoming smaller on head, fins. Lateral line terminates below end of dorsal fin. Ventral margin of opercle and posterior margin of preopercle coarsely serrate; large horizontal spine on corner of preopercle, second much smaller spine on ventral margin. Fins rounded at all sizes. Variable species, changing colour and pattern with depth or habitat; from orange or wine-red to blue; barred pattern can be very pronounced to barely visible. Widespread tropical Indo-Pacific, broadly west Pacific to east Africa; juveniles south to Bass Point, New South Wales. Habitat from shallow coastal reef flats to deep lagoons and outer reef slopes to at least 55 m. Secretive, sometimes in small aggregations in coral heads. Juveniles in Sydney rarely seen, sometimes collected accidently from low rocky reef outcrops. Attains 10 cm.

Centropyge bispinosus Normal form ▲ Unusual blue form ▼

Centropyge bicolor ▼

Centropyge flavicauda ▼

BLUE AND GOLD ANGELFISH
Centropyge bicolor (Bloch, 1787)

D XV,16-17. A III,18-19. P 16-17. V I,5. LSR 42 (approximately). Scales strongly ctenoid with longitudinal ridges; moderate-sized laterally on body, becoming smaller on head, fins. Lateral line terminates below end of dorsal fin. Ventral margin of opercle and posterior margin of preopercle coarsely serrate; large horizontal spine on corner of preopercle, small spines on ventral margin. Fins rounded, becoming more angular in adults. Juveniles similar to adults, except shape of fins. Widespread west Pacific from New South Wales to southern Japan; juveniles south to Bermagui. Reef crests, usually in small aggregations in coral heads and dense branching corals, to about 20 m. Juveniles very habitat specific as specimens in Sydney rare but nearly always occur in same spots every season – sheltered coves within exposed ocean shores. Attains 16 cm.

Centropyge bicolor Juv.

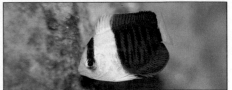

DAMSEL ANGELFISH
Centropyge flavicauda Fraser-Brunner, 1933

D XIV,15-16. A III, 17. P 16. V I,5. LSR 40 (approximately). Scales strongly ctenoid with longitudinal ridges; moderate-sized laterally on body, becoming smaller on head, fins. Lateral line terminates below end of dorsal fin. Ventral margin of opercle and posterior margin of preopercle coarsely serrate; large horizontal spine on corner of preopercle, second much smaller spine on ventral margin. Fins rounded at all sizes. Variable from dark brown to black or blue, with white to yellow tail. Widespread west Pacific to east Indian Ocean from New South Wales to southern Japan, extending east to much of the Pacific. Rubble reef slopes from 6 m to at least 40 m. Easily overlooked; behaves and looks like many common species of damselfish (*Pomacentrus spp*). Juveniles occur regularly in the Watson's Bay area of Sydney Harbour, in rock-piles in shallow water. Attains about 80 mm. Also known as White-Tail Angelfish.

DAMSELFISHES
FAMILY POMACENTRIDAE

Damselfishes or demoiselles are a very large family found particularly in tropical coral reef habitats. Some species occur in such great numbers that they are probably the most numerous fishes in those areas. An estimated 300 species are globally distributed in tropical and subtropical waters, and they are well represented in the coastal waters of south-east Australia with at least 48 species. Many of these are tropical expatriates and it is likely that many more could turn up intermittently in New South Wales, however there are a distinct group of damselfishes restricted to temperate waters of Australia and New Zealand. These are among the larger species, are of southern origin, and live in shallow weeds with prolific algae growth. In general, damselfishes have deep, rounded and compressed bodies, variable to moderately elongate, are covered with ctenoid scales which usually extend onto the fins, and have a small mouth with one or a few rows of small conical to compressed teeth in the jaws. The anal fin has two spines, the first much shorter than the second. Most genera are distinct in shape and other characters, but within a genus many species are similar and have geographical variations. Juveniles are often very different from the adult, but differences between sexes are small and often colour changes only occur during the spawning period. Habitats are nearly always reefs which feature plenty of cover such as small crevices and are close to the food source. Basically, algae feeders occupy the shallow reef flats and planktivores occupy the rocky outcrops. Only a few species do not hole up on reefs but move about over open substrates. This family comprises several specialised groups, including the symbiotic anemonefishes and algae farmers. Most species are small and of no commercial value except as aquarium fishes.

Spawning site of One-Spot Puller
(*Chromis hypsilepis*)

SCALY FIN
Parma victoriae (Günther, 1863)

D XIII,16-17. A II,15-16. P 19-21. V I,5. LL 21-22. Large ctenoid scales cover body, become smaller on thorax, head, fin bases; very small scales extend onto fin membranes. Lateral line evenly curved, following contour of back to below soft dorsal fin. Dorsal fin with long spinous section and short, elevated soft-rayed section. Colour highly variable between juveniles and adults, and between large individuals. South coast, from the Bass Strait area to south Western Australia. Coastal reefs; adults with large boulders or vertical rock faces. Juveniles in coastal estuaries in rocky reefs. Shallow to about 25 m. Attains 30 cm. Genus *Parma* comprises 10 species, two of which are restricted to New Zealand, one to Lord Howe Island waters, and another three to Australia's south-west coast. Species ranging to Lord Howe Island, and five others, are included here. Males clear rock faces for nesting sites; look after deposited eggs, removing debris or interfering invertebrates by picking them up with mouth, dropping them well away from site. They guard eggs from other fishes and fiercely attack those coming a little too close for comfort without regard to size; may even attack divers.

Parma victoriae   Male ▼   Large juv. ▲

Parma victoriae   Juv.

Parma microlepis   Male ▼   Juv. ▲

WHITE-EAR
Parma microlepis Günther, 1862

D XIII,16-18. A II,14-16. P 20-21. LL 23-28. Large ctenoid scales cover body, become smaller on thorax, head, fin bases; very small scales extend onto fin membranes. Lateral line evenly curved, following contour of back to below soft dorsal fin. Dorsal fin with long spinous section and short, elevated soft-rayed section. Colour highly variable between juveniles and adults, and between large individuals. East coast from northern New South Wales to north-eastern Tasmania and into Bass Strait. Shallow coastal reefs and estuaries to at least 30 m. Small juveniles in rock pools, very territorial. Adults in small loose aggregations distributed over reef sections. Egg-guarding males very aggressive, marked with additional white patches on head. Attains 16 cm.

Parma microlepis   Large juv.

Parma unifasciata   Adult ▼   Large juv. ▲

GIRDLED PARMA
Parma unifasciata (Steindachner, 1867)

D XIII,17-19. A II,14-15. P 20-22. V I,5. LL 22-27. Large ctenoid scales cover body, become smaller on thorax, head, fin bases; very small scales extend onto fin membranes. Lateral line evenly curved, following contour of back to below soft dorsal fin. Dorsal fin with long spinous section and short, elevated soft-rayed section. Colour highly variable between juveniles and adults, and between large individuals. East coast from southern Queensland to southern New South Wales. Coastal to offshore reefs, usually in exposed areas and surge zones, among large boulders, from shallow to about 25 m. Juveniles solitary; adults in loose, often large aggregations. Attains 20 cm.

Parma unifasciata   Juv.

Parma oligolepis ▼

BIG-SCALE PARMA
Parma oligolepis Whitley, 1929

D XIII,17-20. A II,13-15. P 20-22. V I,5. LL 22-24. Large ctenoid scales cover body, become smaller on thorax, head, fin bases; very small scales extend onto fin membranes. Lateral line evenly curved, following contour of back to below soft dorsal fin. Dorsal fin with long spinous section and short, elevated soft-rayed section. Colour highly variable between juveniles and adults, and between large individuals. East coast from Cairns, Queensland to central New South Wales; adults rare in Sydney, occasionally in Clovelly Pool. Mainly on exposed offshore rocky reefs and coral-rock reefs with large boulders to about 25 m. Attains 20 cm.

Parma oligolepis   Juv.

Parma polylepis ▼

BANDED PARMA
Parma polylepis Günther, 1862

D XIII,16-19. A II,13-14. P 20-22. V I,5. LL 26-33. Large ctenoid scales cover body, become smaller on thorax, head, fin bases; very small scales extend onto fin membranes. Lateral line evenly curved, following contour of back to below soft dorsal fin. Dorsal fin with long spinous section and short, elevated soft-rayed section. Colour highly variable between juveniles and adults, and between large individuals. Large adults have prominent knob-like lumps above and between eyes. East coast from the Capricorn area, Queensland, to Bass Point, New South Wales, Lord Howe and Norfolk Islands, and New Caledonia. Coastal to offshore reefs in semi-protected bays; shallow to about 20 m. Attains 20 cm.

IMMACULATE DAMSEL
Mecaenichthys immaculatus (Ogilby, 1885)

D XIII,16-17. A II,13-14. P 20-21. V I,5. LL 19. Large ctenoid scales cover body, become smaller on thorax, head, fin bases. Lateral line evenly curved, following contour of back to below soft dorsal fin. Dorsal fin with long spinous section and short, elevated soft-rayed section. Head pointed, eye large. Colour very different between juveniles and adults. East coast only, from southern Queensland to southern New South Wales. Various habitats from rocky estuaries to coastal and offshore reefs. Juveniles share habitat with adults, shallow in protected bays but usually deeper on coastal reefs, to at least 30 m. Attains 15 cm. Monotypic genus, closely related to *Parma*.

Mecaenichthys immaculatus Juv.

BENGAL SERGEANT
Abudefduf bengalensis (Bloch, 1787)

D XIII,14-15. A II,13-15. P 19-20. V I,5. LL 20-21. Large ctenoid scales cover body, become smaller on thorax, head, fin bases; small scales extend onto median fins. Lateral line evenly curved, low along upper sides, to below soft dorsal fin. Dorsal fin with long spinous section and short, elevated soft-rayed section. Head pointed, eye large. Little variation in colour from juvenile to adult. Widespread tropical west Pacific, to southern Japan, and to east Indian Ocean; juveniles south to Sydney. Coastal reefs and estuaries, shallow lagoons and protected bays. Solitary or in small aggregations to about 10 m. Attains 15 cm. Tropical genus comprising 14 species, mostly Indo-Pacific, five of which range into New South Wales. Primarily schooling fishes in very shallow water, most of which exhibit banded patterns, hence common name. Males guards eggs on cleared rock faces, often in large groups with numerous nesting sites close together.

Abudefduf bengalensis ▲   *Abudefduf vaigensis* ▼

SERGEANT MAJOR
Abudefduf vaigiensis (Quoy and Gaimard, 1825)

D XIII,12-13. A II,11-13. P 18-19. V I,5. LL 20-21. Large ctenoid scales cover body, become smaller on thorax, head, fin bases; small scales extend onto median fins. Lateral line evenly curved, low along upper sides, to below soft dorsal fin. Dorsal fin with long

spinous section and short, elevated soft-rayed section. Head pointed, eye large. Little variation in colour from juvenile to adult. Widespread tropical Indo-Pacific, to southern Japan, and to east Africa and Red Sea; juveniles to southern New South Wales. Coastal reefs and estuaries, shallow lagoons and protected bays; often in large schools around jetties or coral outcrops. One of the most common species; attains 15 cm.

SCISSOR-TAIL SERGEANT
Abudefduf sexfasciatus (Lacepède, 1801)

D XIII,12-14. A II,12-14. P 18-19. V I,5. LL 19-21. Large ctenoid scales cover body, become smaller on thorax, head, fin bases; small scales extend onto median fins. Lateral line evenly curved, low along upper sides, to below soft dorsal fin. Dorsal fin with long spinous section and short, elevated soft-rayed section. Head pointed, eye large. Little variation in colour from juvenile to adult. Widespread tropical Indo-Pacific, to southern Japan, and to east Africa and Red Sea; juveniles to central New South Wales. Coastal reefs and estuaries to outer reef slopes. Small to large aggregations to depths of about 10 m. Juveniles in Sydney often mixed with other sergeant juveniles. Attains 15 cm.

Abudefduf sexfasciatus ▲

Abudefduf sordidus ▼

Abudefduf whitleyi ▼

BLACK-SPOT SERGEANT
Abudefduf sordidus (Forsskål, 1775)

D XIII,14-16. A II,14-15. P 19. V I,5. LL 21-23. Large ctenoid scales cover body, become smaller on thorax, head, fin bases; small scales extend onto median fins. Lateral line evenly curved, low along upper sides, to below soft dorsal fin. Dorsal fin with long spinous section and short, elevated soft-rayed section. Head pointed, eye large. Little variation in colour from juvenile to adult. Widespread tropical Indo-Pacific, to southern Japan, Hawaii, and to east Africa; juveniles to southern New South Wales. Coastal reefs, estuaries, sometimes in surge zones; usually just below intertidal zone. Juveniles in rock pools. Attains 17 cm.

Abudefduf sordidus Juv.

WHITLEY'S SERGEANT
Abudefduf whitleyi Allen and Robertson, 1974

D XIII,13. A II,12. P 19-20. V I,5. LL 20-22. Large ctenoid scales cover body, become smaller on thorax, head, fin bases; small scales extend onto median fins. Lateral line evenly curved, low along upper sides, to below soft dorsal fin. Dorsal fin with long spinous section and short, elevated soft-rayed section. Head pointed, eye large. Colour varies from juvenile to adult; males become very colourful. Restricted to Queensland and New Caledonia to central New South Wales; juveniles to Sydney. Shallow on clear-water reefs; deeper at islands off northern New South Wales, to at least 15 m. In small to large schools, feeding mid-water on zooplankton. Attains 15 cm.

Abudefduf whitleyi Juv.

ONE-SPOT PULLER
Chromis hypsilepis (Günther, 1876)

D XIII,13-14. A II,12-13. P 20-21. V I,5. LL 19-20. Large ctenoid scales cover body, become smaller on thorax, head, fin bases; small scales extend onto median fins. Lateral line curving from origin high along upper sides, to below soft dorsal fin. Dorsal fin with long spinous section and short, rounded soft-rayed section. Head pointed, eye large. Juveniles similar to adults. East coast from northern New South Wales to eastern Bass Strait islands, Lord Howe and Norfolk Islands and northern New Zealand. Most common damsel at Montague Island where very large schools congregate in protected coves for spawning activities. Eggs carpeted over rock surfaces, including algae or fixed invertebrates on them; guarded by numerous males. Most common on outgoing reef ridges in current areas between 10-40 m; feed in large schools mid-water on zooplankton. Attains 15 cm. Large genus comprising about 80 species, mostly on tropical coral reefs.

ROBUST PULLER
Chromis chrysura (Bliss, 1883)

D XIII,14-15. A II,13-14. P 19. V I,5. LL 18-19. Large ctenoid scales cover body, become smaller on thorax, head, fin bases; small scales extend onto median fins. Lateral line evenly curved, high along upper sides, to below soft dorsal fin. Dorsal fin with long spinous section and short, rounded soft-rayed section. Body rather deep for genus; head bluntly pointed, eye large. Juveniles similar to adults with additional bright blue markings. Widespread tropical west Pacific to southern Japan, New Caledonia, Coral Sea and Great Barrier Reef; juveniles south to Wattamolla, New South Wales. Outer reef slopes, in small loose aggregations, to 25 m. Juveniles solitary, among low boulder reef in 10-20 m. Attains 16 cm.

Chromis chrysura Juv.

HALF-AND-HALF PULLER
Chromis margaritifer Fowler, 1946

D XII, 12-13. A II,12-13. P 17. V I,5. LL 17-18. Large ctenoid scales cover body, become smaller on thorax, head, fin bases; small scales extend onto median fins. Lateral line evenly curved, high along upper sides, to below soft dorsal fin. Dorsal fin with long spinous section and short, rounded soft-rayed section. Caudal fin with double filaments on tips. Head with blunt snout, eye large. Juveniles similar to adults. Widespread tropical west Pacific from New South Wales to southern Japan and to north Western Australia; juveniles south to Montague Island. Rich coral reef slopes, coastal to outer reefs; solitary or in small aggregations. Juveniles in harbours as well as offshore reefs, from 1 m to at least 25 m. Attains 75 mm.

YELLOW-TAIL PULLER
Chromis flavomaculata Kamohara, 1960

D XIII,12-13. A II,11-13. P 20. V I,5. LL 17-18. Large ctenoid scales cover body, become smaller on thorax, head, fin bases; small scales extend onto median fins. Lateral line with slight upward curve from origin to below dorsal fin, continuing straight to below soft-rayed section. Dorsal fin with long spinous section and short, rounded soft-rayed section. Head pointed, eye large. Juveniles similar to adults. Widespread tropical west Pacific, anti-equatorial, southern Japan and eastern Australia to Coral Sea and Lord Howe Island, and south to Montague Island. Outer reefs, schooling above slopes in 10-45 m. Juveniles solitary, in caves. Attains 12 cm.

SMOKEY PULLER
Chromis fumea Tanaka, 1917

D XIII-XIV,10-12. A II,9-10. P 17-19. V I,5. LL 17-19. Large ctenoid scales cover body, become smaller on thorax, head, fin bases; small scales extend onto median fins. Lateral line with slight upward curve from origin to below dorsal fin, continuing straight to below soft-rayed section. Dorsal fin with long spinous section and short, rounded soft-rayed section. Head pointed, eye large. Juveniles similar to adults. Widespread tropical west Pacific, anti-equatorial; southern Japan, eastern Australia to Lord Howe Island, and northern New Zealand. Uncommon in New South Wales; a few specimens known from Swansea and Sydney; in rocky estuaries along steep slopes in 5-10 m. Attains 9 cm.

WEBER'S PULLER
Chromis weberi Fowler and Bean, 1928

D XIII,11-12. A II,11-12. P 19-20. V I,5. LL 18-19. Large ctenoid scales cover body, become smaller on thorax, head, fin bases; small scales extend onto median fins. Lateral line with slight upward curve from origin to below dorsal fin, continuing straight to below soft-rayed section. Dorsal fin with long spinous section and short, rounded soft-rayed section. Head pointed, eye large. Juveniles similar to adults. Widespread tropical west Pacific, from New South Wales to Japan, far into the Pacific and to east Africa. Outer reef crests and slopes from 6-30 m; in small to large aggregations. Juveniles south to Montague Island, in caves. Attains 12 cm.

237

VANDERBILT'S PULLER
Chromis vanderbilti (Fowler, 1941)

D XII,11. A II,11. P 16-18. V I,5. LL 16-18. Large ctenoid scales cover body, become smaller on thorax, head, fin bases; small scales extend onto median fins. Lateral line slightly curved from origin, continuing straight along upper sides, to below soft dorsal fin. Dorsal fin with long spinous section and short, rounded soft-rayed section. Caudal fin with extended tips. Widespread tropical west Pacific; anti-equatorial with populations in southern Japan to Hawaii, and New South Wales to Queensland, and to Pitcairn group; juveniles south to Sydney. Outer reef crests near drop-offs, in small aggregations. Juveniles in Sydney small, swim well away from rock walls, are easily overlooked. Attains 60 mm.

YELLOW-BACK PULLER
Chromis nitida (Whitley, 1928)

D XIII,11-13. A II,10-11. P 19. V I,5. LL 17-18. Large ctenoid scales cover body, become smaller on thorax, head, fin bases; small scales extend onto median fins. Lateral line with slight upward curve from origin to below dorsal fin, continuing to below soft-rayed section. Dorsal fin with long spinous section and short, rounded soft-rayed section. Head pointed, eye large. Juveniles similar to adults. East coast from central New South Wales to about Cairns, Queensland; juveniles south to Montague Island. Coastal to outer reefs and rocky estuaries. Shallow to about 25 m; usually in small to large aggregations. Attains 90 mm.

YELLOW-TAIL DAMSEL
Neopomacentrus azysron (Bleeker, 1877)

D XIII,11-12. A II,11-12. P 18. V I,5. LL 17-19. Large ctenoid scales cover body, become smaller on thorax, head, fin bases; small scales extend onto median fins. Lateral line with slight upward curve from origin to below dorsal fin, continuing straight to below soft-rayed section. Dorsal fin with long spinous section and short, pointed soft-rayed section. Caudal fin with extended tips. Juveniles similar to adults but fins rounded. Widespread tropical west Pacific, New South Wales to Philippines; juveniles south to Sydney. Shallow coastal reefs and lagoons with large bommies. Attains 75 mm. Genus comprises about 12 species, typically slender, similar to some *Chromis*, often with trailing filaments on dorsal, anal and caudal fin tips. Mostly small, about 80 mm; one species enters fresh water. Small juveniles swim well above or away from substrate, are easily overlooked, but three species known from the Sydney area.

HALF-MOON DAMSEL
Neopomacentrus bankieri (Richardson, 1845)

D XIII,11-12. A II,11-12. P 17. V I,5. LL 19. Large ctenoid scales cover body, become smaller on thorax, head, fin bases; small scales extend onto median fins. Lateral line with slight upward curve from origin to below dorsal fin, continuing straight to below soft-rayed section. Dorsal fin with long spinous section and short, pointed soft-rayed section. Caudal, dorsal and anal fins with extended tips, filamentous in adults. Colour varies with habitat; usually deep orange tail in silty conditions. East coast, from Sydney as juveniles, to Queensland. Coastal estuaries on rocky reefs and under jetties; in small aggregations to about 15 m. Attains 75 mm. Also known as Orange-Tailed Demoiselle.

REGAL DAMSEL
Neopomacentrus cyanomos (Bleeker, 1856)

D XIII,11-12. A II,11-12. P 17. V I,5. LL 17-18. Large ctenoid scales cover body, become smaller on thorax, head, fin bases; small scales extend onto median fins. Lateral line with slight upward curve from origin to below dorsal fin, continuing straight to below soft-rayed section. Dorsal fin with long spinous section and short, pointed soft-rayed section. Caudal, dorsal and anal fins with extended tips which become very long filaments in adults. Widespread west Pacific; some geographical variation. Very common on the Great Barrier Reef; juveniles south to Sydney. Shallow coastal reefs and lagoons to about 15 m; often in large aggregations. Attains 10 cm.

Neopomacentrus cyanomos Juv.

Neopomacentrus cyanomos ▲

Chrysiptera notialis ▼

SOUTHERN DAMSEL
Chrysiptera notialis (Allen, 1975)

D XIII,14-15. A II,15-16. P 16-18. V I,5. LL 16-18. Large ctenoid scales cover body, become smaller on thorax, head, fin bases; small scales extend onto median fins. Lateral line with slight upward curve from origin to below dorsal fin, continuing straight to below soft-rayed section. Dorsal fin with long spinous section and short, pointed soft-rayed section. Caudal, dorsal and anal fins with extended tips. Juveniles deep blue, becoming darker with age. Southern Queensland to Montague Island, New Caledonia and Lord Howe Island. Outer reef habitat with small boulder reefs on sand; usually deep, from 5-45 m. Attains 75 mm. Large tropical Indo-Pacific genus comprising about 25 species, many of which expatriate to the Sydney area; six included here. No doubt other species can be found there.

239

SURGE DAMSEL
Chrysiptera leucopoma (Lesson, 1830)

D XIII,12-13. A II,12-13. P 18-19. V I,5. LL 18-19. Large ctenoid scales cover body, become smaller on thorax, head, fin bases; small scales extend onto median fins. Lateral line with slight upward curve from origin to below dorsal fin, continuing straight to below soft-rayed section. Dorsal fin with long spinous section and short, angled soft-rayed section. Variable as adults, with two distinctly different forms. Widespread tropical west Pacific and adjacent areas; juveniles commonly south to Sydney. Very shallow exposed reef flats with algal growth; rarely deeper than 3 m. Juveniles in Sydney in protected ocean coves, such as Fairy Bower, in 1 or 2 m, on low boulder reefs on sand. Attains 70 mm.

Chrysiptera leucopoma Juv.

YELLOW-FINNED DAMSEL
Chrysiptera flavipinnis (Allen and Robertson, 1974)

D XIII,14-15. A II,13-14. P 17-18. V I,5. LL 15-18. Large ctenoid scales cover body, become smaller on thorax, head, fin bases; small scales extend onto median fins. Lateral line with slight upward curve from origin to below dorsal fin, continuing straight to below soft-rayed section. Dorsal fin with long spinous section and short, angled soft-rayed section. Slight differences from juvenile to adult; juvenile more yellow. East coast to southern Papua New Guinea and Coral Sea, south to Montague Island. Outer reef habitat, in deep lagoons on rubble reefs, or low boulder reefs on sand. About 5-40 m. Attains 70 mm.

STARCK'S DAMSEL
Chrysiptera starcki (Allen, 1973)

D XIII,14. A II,14-15. P 16-17. V I,5. LL 15-16. Large ctenoid scales cover body, become smaller on thorax, head, fin bases; small scales extend onto median fins. Lateral line with slight upward curve from origin to below dorsal fin, continuing straight to below soft-rayed section. Dorsal fin with long spinous section and short, angled soft-rayed section. Distinctly coloured with little variation from juvenile to adult; fins become more pointed with growth. Tropical west Pacific from eastern Australia and New Caledonia to southern Japan; juveniles south to Sydney. Usually in loose aggregations; very deep, in 25 m or more, on low reef on sand, however a small juvenile was collected from Watson's Bay, Sydney Harbour, in 3 m. Attains 70 mm.

PINK DAMSEL
Chrysiptera rex (Snyder, 1909)

D XIII,13-14. A II,11-13. P 16-17. V I,5. LL 16-17. Large ctenoid scales cover body, become smaller on thorax, head, fin bases; small scales extend onto median fins. Lateral line with slight upward curve from origin to below dorsal fin, continuing straight to below soft-rayed section. Dorsal fin with long spinous section and short, angled soft-rayed section. Distinctly coloured; considerable variation from juvenile to adult; fins become more pointed with growth. Widespread tropical west Pacific from eastern Australia and New Caledonia to southern Japan; juveniles south to Sydney. Outer reef lagoons and surge channels in 3-10 m. Juveniles in protected ocean coves. Attains 60 mm.

Chrysiptera rex Juv.

THREE-BAND DAMSEL
Chrysiptera tricincta (Allen and Randall, 1974)

D XIII,11-13. A II,12-14. P 18-19. V I,5. LL 15-17. Large ctenoid scales cover body, become smaller on thorax, head, fin bases; small scales extend onto median fins. Lateral line with slight upward curve from origin to below dorsal fin, following contour of back, to below soft-rayed section. Dorsal fin with long spinous section and short, angled soft-rayed section. Distinctly coloured; considerable variation from juvenile to adult; fins become more pointed with growth. East coast from southern Queensland to Sydney, and to New Caledonia, Fiji and Samoa Islands. With small isolated outcrops on sand in 10-40 m. Juveniles in sandy tidal channels in deep estuaries such as Botany Bay. Attains 60 mm.

HUMBUG DASCYLLUS
Dascyllus aruanus (Linnaeus, 1758)

D XII,12-13. A II,12-13. P 17-18. V I,5. LL 17-18. Large ctenoid scales cover body, become smaller on thorax, head, fin bases; small scales extend onto median fins. Lateral line with slight upward curve from origin to below dorsal fin, following contour of back, to below soft-rayed section. Dorsal fin with long spinous section and short, rounded soft-rayed section. Distinctly coloured; little variation with growth, except very small juveniles (about 10 mm) nearly all black. Widespread tropical Indo-Pacific, from well into the Pacific to east Africa; juveniles south to Sydney. Shallow lagoon and coastal reefs in coral heads; in small to large aggregations depending on hiding space. Juveniles in Sydney with long-spined sea-urchins. Attains 70 mm. Tropical Indo-Pacific genus comprising nine species, two of which range to Sydney as juveniles, and a third as adults to the Solitary Islands, but no juveniles are known further south.

Chrysiptera tricincta ▲

Dascyllus aruanus ▼

THREE-SPOT DASCYLLUS
Dascyllus trimaculatus (Rüppell, 1828)

D XII,15-16. A II,14-15. P 19-20. V I,5. LL 18-19. Large ctenoid scales cover body, become smaller on thorax, head, fin bases; small scales extend onto median fins. Lateral line with slight upward curve from origin to below dorsal fin, following contour of back, to below soft-rayed section. Dorsal fin with long spinous section and short, rounded soft-rayed section. Distinctly coloured; little variation with growth, except adults become greyish or spots become less distinct. Widespread tropical Indo-Pacific, from well into the Pacific to east Africa; juveniles south to Sydney. Shallow lagoon and coastal reefs in coral heads, in small to large aggregations depending on hiding space; also in large anemones. Juveniles in Sydney with long-spined sea-urchins. Attains 12 cm.

Stegastes apicalis   Adult ▼ Juv. ▲

YELLOW-TIPPED GREGORY
Stegastes apicalis (De Vis, 1885)

D XIII,15-16. A II,13-14. P 20. V I,5. LL 19-20. Large ctenoid scales cover body, become smaller on thorax, head, fin bases; small scales extend onto median fins. Lateral line with slight upward curve from origin to below dorsal fin, following contour of back, to below soft-rayed section. Dorsal fin with long spinous section and short, rounded soft-rayed section, becoming angular in adults. North-east coast to Sydney as juveniles. Rubble and sparse coral reef, in lagoons and outer reefs. Juveniles in exposed reefs with narrow ledges and cracks. Attains 14 cm. Genus comprises about 20 mostly rather drab tropical species found in Atlantic and Pacific reefs. At least two species range commonly as juveniles to the Sydney area and are included here.

GOLD-BELLY GREGORY
Stegastes gascoynei (Whitley, 1964)

D XIV,15-16. A II,13-14. P 20-21. V I,5. LL 19-20. Large ctenoid scales cover body, become smaller on thorax, head, fin bases; small scales extend onto median fins. Lateral line with slight upward curve from origin to below dorsal fin, following contour of back, to below soft-rayed section. Dorsal fin with long spinous section and short, rounded soft-rayed section. Juveniles similar to adults, but brighter orange or yellow. Southern Great Barrier Reef and New Caledonia to Lord Howe Island, extending to northern New Zealand and Montague Island. Exposed reef fronts and rocky shores, often in strong surge areas in deeper parts of reefs, to at least 30 m. Juveniles in narrow ledges and cracks with sea-urchins. Attains 14 cm.

Stegastes gascoynei ▼

Stegastes gascoynei Juv.

MULTI-SPINE DAMSEL
Neoglyphidodon polyacanthus (Ogilby, 1889)

D XIV,13-14. A II,14. P 18. V I,5. LL 18-19. Large ctenoid scales cover body, become smaller on thorax, head, fin bases; small scales extend onto median fins. Lateral line with slight upward curve from origin to below dorsal fin, following contour of back, to below soft-rayed section. Dorsal fin with long spinous section and short, elevated, pointed soft-rayed section. Colour changes during growth, becoming dark dorsally with dark area extending down over most of body. Southern Queensland to northern New South Wales and Lord Howe Island. Outer margins of reefs in surge channels and slopes to 30 m. Attains 15 cm. Small tropical Indo-Pacific genus with about 12 species, only one of which ranges to southern waters. Most inhabit rich coral slopes in relatively deep water.

JEWEL DAMSEL
Plectroglyphidodon lacrymatus (Quoy and Gaimard, 1825)

D XII,16-18. A II,13-14. P 19-20. V I,5. LL 18-19. Large ctenoid scales cover body, become smaller on thorax, head, fin bases; small scales extend onto median fins. Lateral line with slight upward curve from origin to below dorsal fin, following contour of back, to below soft-rayed section. Dorsal fin with long spinous section and short, elevated soft-rayed section. Colour changes during growth; become dull as adults, losing large iridescent spots featured in juveniles. Widespread tropical Indo-Pacific, extending to Japan, far into the Pacific and to east Africa, juveniles south to Sydney. Clear-water reefs in gutters and upper edge of drop-offs, to about 10 m. Juveniles in sheltered ocean bays, in shallow low boulder-reefs well above sand level. Attains 10 cm. Small tropical Indo-Pacific genus comprising about 10 species, mostly living in surge zones or exposed outer reefs; two species included here.

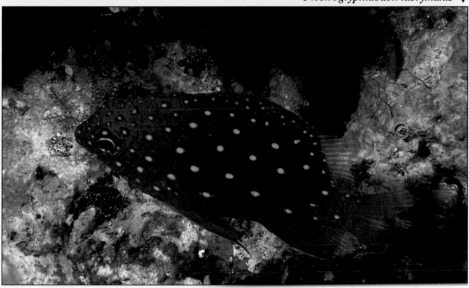

Plectroglyphidodon lacrymatus ▼

WHITE-BAND DAMSEL
Plectroglyphidodon leucozonus (Bleeker, 1859)

D XII,15-16. A II,12-13. P 20-21. V I,5. LL 20. Large ctenoid scales cover body, become smaller on thorax, head, fin bases; small scales extend onto median fins. Lateral line with slight upward curve from origin to below dorsal fin, following contour of back, to below soft-rayed section. Dorsal fin with long spinous section and short, elevated soft-rayed section. Colour changes during growth; become dull as adults, losing distinct band and ocellus featured in juveniles. Widespread tropical Indo-Pacific, extending to Japan, far into the Pacific and to east Africa; juveniles south to Montague Island. Clear-water reefs in gutters and upper edge of drop-offs; rarely deeper than a few metres. Juveniles in sheltered ocean bays, in shallow low boulder-reefs well above sand level, to about 6 m. Attains 10 cm.

AUSTRALIAN DAMSEL
Pomacentrus australis Allen and Robertson, 1973

D XIV,13-14. A II,14-15. P 17-19. V I,5. LL 17-19. Large ctenoid scales cover body, become smaller on thorax, head, fin bases; small scales extend onto median fins. Lateral

Pomacentrus australis Adult ▼ Juv. ▲

Pomacentrus coelestis ▼

Pomacentrus pavo ▼

line with slight upward curve from origin to below dorsal fin, following contour of back, to below soft-rayed section. Dorsal fin with long spinous section and short, elevated soft-rayed section. Colour changes during growth; become dull as adults, losing iridescent blue featured in juveniles. Southern Queensland to southern New South Wales; adults to Sydney Harbour. Coastal reefs and harbours, often muddy or silty reefs in Sydney Harbour in 3-20 m. Attains 10 cm. Large tropical Indo-Pacific genus with about 50 species, eight of which are included here, but possibly more expatriate to southern waters.

BLUE DAMSEL
Pomacentrus coelestis Jordan and Starks, 1901

D XIII,13-15. A II,14-15. P 17-18. V I,5. LL 17-18. Large ctenoid scales cover body, become smaller on thorax, head, fin bases; small scales extend onto median fins. Lateral line with slight upward curve from origin to below dorsal fin, following contour of back, to below soft-rayed section. Dorsal fin with long spinous section and short, elevated soft-rayed section. Colour changes little with growth. Widespread tropical west Pacific and far into the Pacific, to southern New South Wales. Coastal to outer reefs, shallow crest or slopes on coral reefs, usually in small aggregations to about 10 m; juveniles on southern reefs, on low boulder reefs to 25 m. Attains 85 mm. Most common tropical damsel in Sydney; first recruitment about first week of year. Also known as Neon Damsel.

AZURE DAMSEL
Pomacentrus pavo (Bloch, 1787)

D XIII,13-14. A II,12-14. P 17. V I,5. LL 16-17. Large ctenoid scales cover body, become smaller on thorax, head, fin bases; small scales extend onto median fins. Lateral line with slight upward curve from origin to below dorsal fin, following contour of back, to below soft-rayed section. Dorsal fin with long spinous section and short, elevated soft-rayed section; posterior parts of dorsal, anal and caudal fins form tips in adults. Colour changes little with growth. Widespread tropical west Pacific and far into the Pacific; juveniles occasionally south to Sydney. Lagoons and coastal reef slopes, often in large schools around outcrops or steep bommies; to about 30 m. Attains 10 cm. Also known as Sapphire Damsel.

BLUE-SCRIBBLED DAMSEL
Pomacentrus nagasakiensis Tanaka, 1909

D XIII,15-16. A II,15-16. P 18-19. V I,5.
LL 17-19. Large ctenoid scales cover body,
become smaller on thorax, head, fin bases;
small scales extend onto median fins. Lateral
line with slight upward curve from origin to
below dorsal fin, following contour of back,
to below soft-rayed section. Dorsal fin with
long spinous section and short, elevated soft-
rayed section; posterior parts of dorsal, anal
and caudal fins form tips in adults. Colour
changes little with growth. Widespread
tropical west Pacific from New South Wales
to Japan; juveniles to the Sydney area. Coastal
reefs and deep lagoons, usually in small
aggregations with large soft corals in 10-
40 m. Attains 10 cm.

WHITE-TAIL DAMSEL
Pomacentrus chrysurus Cuvier, 1830

D XIII,14-16. A II,15-16. P 18. V I,5.
LL 18-19. Large ctenoid scales cover body,
become smaller on thorax, head, fin bases;
small scales extend onto median fins. Lateral
line with slight upward curve from origin to
below dorsal fin, following contour of back,
to below soft-rayed section. Dorsal fin with
long spinous section and short, elevated soft-
rayed section; posterior parts of dorsal, anal
and caudal fins rounded. Juvenile similar to
adult; ocellus lost in large specimens. East
coast to Papua New Guinea, Solomon Islands,
New Caledonia and south to the Sydney area.
Few specimens known from Sydney Harbour.
Shallow reefs, outcrops in lagoons and rocky
boulder slopes in Sydney Harbour to 5 m.
Attains 85 mm.

WARD'S DAMSEL
Pomacentrus wardi Whitley, 1927

D XIII,15-16. A II,15-16. P 18-19. V I,5.
LL 18-19. Large ctenoid scales cover body,
become smaller on thorax, head, fin bases;
small scales extend onto median fins. Lateral
line with slight upward curve from origin to
below dorsal fin, following contour of back,
to below soft-rayed section. Dorsal fin with
long spinous section and short, elevated soft-
rayed section; posterior parts of dorsal, anal
and caudal fins rounded. Juvenile similar to
adult; large specimens lose ocellus, are generally darker. East coast, mainly common in the
Capricorn area; south to Sydney. Lagoons
and reef slopes to 20 m; rocky boulder slopes
to 5 m in Sydney Harbour. Attains 10 cm.

FIRE DAMSEL
Pomacentrus bankanensis Bleeker, 1853

D XIII,15-16. A II,15-16. P 18. V I,5. LL 17-19. Large ctenoid scales cover body, become smaller on thorax, head, fin bases; small scales extend onto median fins. Lateral line with slight upward curve from origin to below dorsal fin, following contour of back, to below soft-rayed section. Dorsal fin with long spinous section and short, elevated soft-rayed section; posterior parts of dorsal, anal and caudal fins rounded. Juvenile similar to adult but brighter; large specimens lose ocellus, are generally darker. Widespread tropical west Pacific, to Japan and into Pacific; juveniles south to the Sydney area. Shallow reef crests and slopes to about 10 m. Juveniles in Sydney in protected coastal bays among small boulder reefs on sand. Attains 85 mm.

AMBON DAMSEL
Pomacentrus amboinensis Bleeker, 1868

D XIII,14-16. A II,14-16. P 17. V I,5. LL 16-17. Body covered with large ctenoid scales, becoming smaller on thorax, head, fin bases; small scales extend onto median fins. Lateral line with slight upward curve from origin to below dorsal fin, following contour of back, to below soft-rayed section. Dorsal fin with long spinous section and short soft-rayed section; posterior parts of dorsal and anal fins rounded in young, becoming pointed in adults. Variable pale to bright yellow. Ocellus present at all stages. Widespread tropical west Pacific, south to the Sydney area as juvenile. Usually in small aggregations on sheltered reefs from very shallow to about 20 m. Attains 10 cm.

ROAMING DAMSEL
Pristotis jerdoni (Day, 1873)

D XIII,12-13. A II,12-14. P 17-18. V I,5. LL 19-20. Large ctenoid scales cover body, become smaller on thorax, head, fin bases; small scales extend onto median fins. Lateral line with slight upward curve from origin to below dorsal fin, following contour of back, to below soft-rayed section. Dorsal fin with long spinous section and short soft-rayed section; posterior parts of dorsal, anal and caudal fins rounded in juveniles, becoming pointed in adults. Widespread tropical Indo-Pacific, west Pacific from Sydney to southern Japan and to east Africa. Adults over open sand in small aggregations, moving over wide area in 5-40 m. Utilise empty shells, partly burying them, for nesting sites which are usually far away from reefs, guarded by male. Juveniles in small aggregations with small outcrops on sand. Attains 12 cm.

Pristotis jerdoni Juv.

BLUE-LIP ANEMONEFISH
Amphiprion latezonatus Waite, 1900

D XI,15-16. A II,12-14. P 19-20. V I,5. LL 34-36. Small ctenoid scales cover body, become smaller on thorax, head, fin bases; small scales extend onto median fins. Lateral line evenly curved, following contour of back, to below end of soft-rayed section. Spinous section of dorsal fin slightly longer than soft-rayed section; shallow notch in centre of fin. Juveniles similar to adults but white bands narrower, colour of caudal fin differs. Only known from northern New South Wales to southern Queensland, and the Lord Howe Island region. Offshore islands in 15-45 m. Attains 15 cm. Anemonefishes or clownfishes have a strong relationship with sea-anemones, sheltering among tentacles without getting stung. These tropical Indo-Pacific fishes comprises 26 species, one of which is placed in a separate genus; three species included here.

Amphiprion latezonatus Juv.

BROWN ANEMONEFISH
Amphiprion akindynos Allen, 1972

D X,15-17. A II,13-14. P 19-20. V I,5. LL 31-40. Small ctenoid scales cover body, become smaller on thorax, head, fin bases; small scales extend onto median fins. Lateral line evenly curved, following contour of back, to below end of soft-rayed section. Spinous section of dorsal fin slightly longer than soft-rayed section; shallow notch in centre of fin. Juveniles similar to adults but with additional white bands on caudal peduncle, adults vary from pale to dark brown. Common Great Barrier Reef species, south to the Solitary Islands; in shallow lagoons and reef slopes to 30 m. Attains 12 cm.

BLACK ANEMONEFISH
Amphiprion melanopus Bleeker, 1852

D X,16-18. A II,13-14. P 18-19. V I,5. LL 34-42. Small ctenoid scales cover body, become smaller on thorax, head, fin bases; small scales extend onto median fins. Lateral line evenly curved, following contour of back, to below end of soft-rayed section. Spinous section of dorsal fin slightly longer than soft-rayed section; shallow notch in centre of fin. Juveniles similar to adults but with additional white bands on body, no black on sides. Queensland, south to the Solitary Islands, and eastern Indonesia to Melanesia. Usually on shallow reef flats prone to current, with anemones in deep corals to about 10 m. Usually deep at the Solitary Islands, 20-30 m, because of anemone habitat. Attains 12 cm.

247

OLD WIFES
FAMILY ENOPLOSIDAE

This family contains a single species which is an Australian endemic. It resembles the boarfishes (Pentacerotidae) as an adult because of the large dorsal and anal fins, but post-larvae and small juveniles are teraponid-like. Adults are also similar to banjosids which are closely related to teraponids. Further studies of larval fishes may show a clearer relationship with other families than the present clasification.

OLD WIFE
Enoplosus armatus (White, 1790)

DIX,14-15. A III,14015. P 13-14. V I,5. LL 56-60. Scales ctenoid, small, cover body and head, extend in scaly sheaths onto anal and dorsal fins. Lateral line highly elevated below spinous dorsal fin. Large spines in dorsal and anal fins very robust. Colour varies little from silver-white to brown with black stripes. Common in southern waters ranging into southern Queensland. Post-larvae settle in seagrass beds and large algae on rocks.

Small juveniles usually solitary, often under jetties, form schools at later stages. Adults solitary, in pairs, or may form schools of hundreds of individuals. While juveniles inhabit estuaries, adults occur in a wide variety of habitats, including estuaries and shallow coastal reefs to at least 90 m. In Victoria, tiny juveniles appear in early spring, suggesting winter breeding winter. Attains 25 cm. Reputed as good eating, but should be handled with care; possesses sharp spines on head and dorsal and anal fins. In addition, dorsal fin spines contain poison, can cause severe pain.

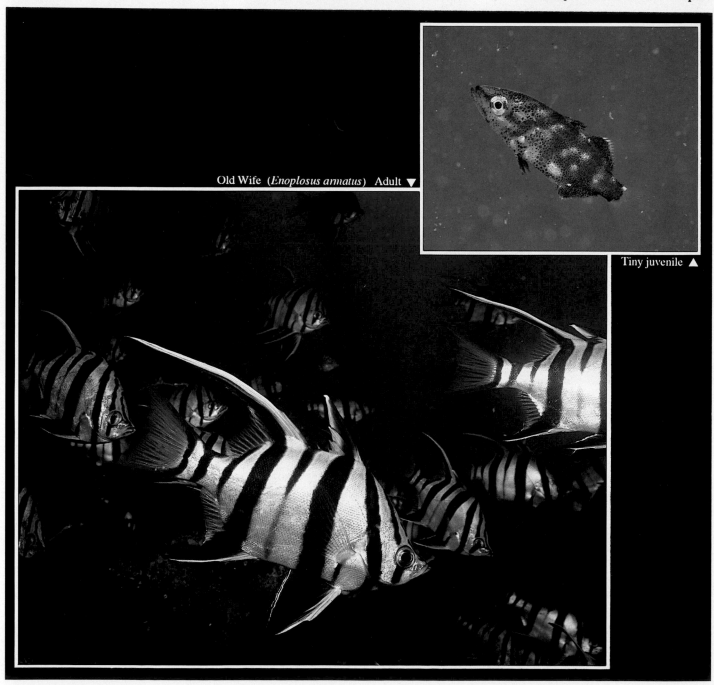

Old Wife (*Enoplosus armatus*) Adult ▼

Tiny juvenile ▲

BOARFISHES
FAMILY PENTACEROTIDAE

This family of temperate fishes comprises eight genera and 13 species, occurring in all oceans but most diverse in the Pacific. *Pentaceros* and *Pseudopentaceros* have three species each, *Paristiopterus* has two species, and *Histiopterus, Evistias, Pentaceropsis, Parazanclistius* and *Zanclistius* have one species each. All species feature strong spines and heads encased with rough striated bony plates. Some features, such as extended fin rays and elongation of the mouth, are greatly developed in certain species with increasing body size. Some juveniles have tall fins which reduce during growth. All genera occur in Australian waters but some are restricted to very deep water. Four species, each from a different genus, are found in shallow water in south-eastern Australia and are included here. Juveniles are rarely seen and appear to be solitary. Adults usually occur in pairs or small aggregations, mostly close to reefs with large caves in which they rest. The species are distinctly marked with broad stripes, but juveniles are very different and are usually covered in moderate-sized spots. They feed on a variety of invertebrates which are probed with the long snout from the sea bed. The larger species, attaining 1m and 12 kg, are reputed to be excellent food fish. They should be handled with care as some species possess venomous spines.

STRIPED BOARFISH
Evistias acutirostris (Temminck and Schlegel, 1844)

D IV-V,26-28. A III-IV,11-14. P 16-18. V I,5. LL 58-77. Small ctenoid scales cover body, extend along bases of dorsal and anal fins; large patch of scales on cheek. Lateral line strongly arched above pectoral fin. Dorsal fin tall in juveniles, reducing in size with growth. Brush-like patch of short barbels under front of mouth. Distinct colouration readily identifies this species. Occurs at Lord Howe Island and northern New Zealand islands, and also in Japan and Hawaii. Lives fairly deep, to several hundred metres, but occasionally observed as shallow as about 30 m. Rocky reef with caves, in pairs or small aggregations. Attains 65 cm.

Photograph: Malcolm Francis

GIANT BOARFISH
Paristiopterus labiosus (Günther, 1871)

D VII,16-18. A II,8-10. P 16-18. V I,5. LL 85-96. Small ctenoid scales cover body; large patch on cheek. Lateral line curved above pectoral fin, then straight to caudal peduncle. Long-based dorsal fin with long third spine followed by progressively shorter spines. Juveniles moderately deep-bodied, becoming more elongate as adults. Distinctly banded as juveniles and adult females; males with yellow spotting. Occurs from Tasmania to northern New South Wales, into Bass Strait, and New Zealand. Usually deep, to nearly 200 m, but occasionally ventures into shallower depths; has been observed in Port Phillip Bay in 15 m. Lives primarily over open sand and mud; adults in pairs, large juveniles were observed in small to large aggregations. Attains 1 m. Reputed to be tasty.

LONG-SNOUT BOARFISH
Pentaceropsis recurvirostris (Richardson, 1845)

D X-XI,14-15. A III,10-11. P 16-18. V I,5. LL 78-85. Small ctenoid scales cover body; large patch on cheek. Scaly sheaths along bases of soft dorsal and anal fins. Lateral line with large curve over pectoral fin to near caudal peduncle. Long-based dorsal fin with widely separated spines; very tall in juveniles, reduces with growth except long third and fourth spine. Adults distinctly banded; juveniles white with moderate-sized black spots. Common south coast species, ranging to central New South Wales (Botany Bay). Adults have been observed in very shallow depths of a few metres in Port Phillip Bay, but venture to 260 m. Rocky reefs, often under overhangs; solitary, pairs or small aggregations. Attains 50 cm.

SHORT BOARFISH
Parazanclistius hutchinsi Hardy, 1983

D VI,25-27. A III,13-14. P 16-18. V I,5. C 17. LL 66-72. Small ctenoid scales cover body, cheek. Lateral line highly curved above pectoral fin. Deep-bodied; dorsal fin tall, sail-like. Forehead distinctly shaped with deeply concave snout. Pectoral fin very long, almost reaching caudal peduncle. Rare temperate species on the south coast, primarily known from south Western Australia, and a single specimen each from the York Peninsula and Port Philip Bay. Deep offshore but occasionally entering shallow depths. Attains 33 cm.

Photograph: W.L. Boyle

LONG-FIN BOARFISH
Zanclistius elevatus (Ramsay and Ogilby, 1889)

D V-VII,25-29. A III,12-17. P 15-17. V I,5. LL 55-65. Small ctenoid scales cover body, cheek. Lateral line highly curved above pectoral fin. Deep-bodied; dorsal fin with long extended rays. Forehead distinctly shaped with bony crest above eyes. Temperate species, known from the south coast to central New South Wales, and New Zealand. Usually occurs in depths from 30-500 m; not often seen by divers in Australia. Occasionally along rocky drop-offs, feeding from crevices on a variety of invertebrates. Small species, attains 30 cm. Also known as One-Spot Boarfish.

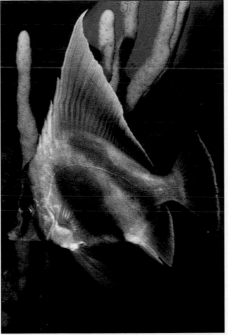

Photograph: B.C. Russell

BATFISHES
FAMILY EPHIPPIDAE

A small family comprising several genera of which one, *Platax,* is commonly encountered in the Indo-Pacific. Others are confined to deep water or Atlantic seas. The genus comprises at least four species, one of which is wide-ranging and included here. Batfishes are deep-bodied fishes with high fins which can be extremely tall, particularly in juveniles. They feature small ctenoid scales which extend well onto the fins and head, a small terminal mouth, and brush-like tricuspid teeth. Juveniles of some species settle in estuaries and are very fast growing. Small specimens are often collected for the home aquarium, but quickly outgrow this. The batfishes' diet consists of algae and a variety of invertebrates. The largest species attains at least 60 cm. They are also known as spadefishes in some countries.

LONGFIN BATFISH
Platax teira (Forsskål, 1775)

D V-VI,28-34. A III,22-28. P 16-18. V I,5. LL 48-53. Juveniles with extremely long dorsal, anal and ventral fins, almost double body height in small individuals. Although fins become proportionally smaller with increasing size, fins in adults still large with long vertical posterior edge. Colour varies from reddish-brown in small juveniles to grey-brown with various shades of dark banding. Often confused with similar Round-Faced Batfish, *P. orbicularis*, but this has generally narrow bands and *teira* usually has black blotch in lower part of band behind pectoral fin. Very widespread in most of the tropical Indo-Pacific; south to at least Sydney in New South Wales; on the west coast large adults are known from Geographe Bay. Small juveniles float near surface mimicking floating leaf; may drift in currents for several weeks with weeds or other objects. Schools of large juveniles often under sargassum rafts. Adults deep, usually rarely seen in less than 20 m. Attains at least 60 cm.

Platax teira Adult

Platax teira Tiny juv.

HAWKFISHES
FAMILY CIRRHITIDAE

The hawkfishes are a family of tropical fishes of which only a few range into warm-temperate seas. Nine genera and 35 species are known and are mostly distributed in the Indo-Pacific. Only three species occur in the Atlantic. Several species included here are tropical expatriates which settle in New South Wales, well beyond the normal breeding range, during the summer months. These small fishes hug the bottom, resting on the thickened lower rays of the pectoral fins, but unlike most bottom dwellers they are very active, restlessly moving their positions. Only one species, which feeds on zooplankton, swims regularly. Small tufts of filaments on the tips of the dorsal fin spines characterise these fishes. Most species live in shallow water, on reef crests and strong surge zones. Some are territorial and a few can be found in loose aggregations. They feed on small invertebrates and fishes. Most species do well in captivity but the territorial species can be aggressive toward other occupants. Fortunately these are usually less colourful, thus not so popular. Most species are less than 10 cm long but some attain 26 cm.

Photograph: Adrian Newman

SPLENDID HAWKFISH
Cirrhitus splendens (Ogilby, 1889)

D X,12. A III,6. P 14. V I,5. LL 43. Moderate-sized cycloid scales on body, markedly smaller on chest and cheek; four scale-rows above middle of lateral line. Large pectoral fins, longest rays reaching anus. First soft ray of dorsal fin extended. Eyes large, elevated. Distinctly coloured; red spots on head, further markings on body. Mainly known from Lord Howe Island but a few specimens have been observed at islands off northern New South Wales, thus appear to be confined to offshore and clear-water conditions. Large species; attains 20 cm.

BLOTCHED HAWKFISH
Cirrhitichthys aprinus (Cuvier, 1829)

D X,12. A III,6. P 15. V I,5. LL 41-45. Moderate-sized cycloid scales cover body, most of head; three scale-rows above middle of lateral line. Large pectoral fin with extended lower rays. First soft ray in dorsal fin extended. Preopercle margin coarsely serrate. Colour pattern with variable large blotches often joining, forming bars in some populations. Widespread in the west Pacific from central New South Wales to south-eastern Japan near Tokyo. Mainly on coastal reefs and rocky estuaries, usually with sponges. Attains 12 cm in colder part of range, but much smaller, to about 9 cm, in equatorial waters.

CORAL HAWKFISH
Cirrhitichthys falco Randall, 1963

D X,12. A III,6. P 14. V I,5. LL 42-45. Moderate-sized cycloid scales cover body, most of head. Large scales on cheek, opercle; three scale-rows above middle of lateral line. Large pectoral fins with extended, thickened lower rays. Membranes of spinous section of dorsal fin deeply incised. Preopercle margin coarsely serrate. Colour varies slightly between habitats; pale specimens from white sand reefs, darker colouration on deeper reefs. Tropical species of the west Pacific and Micronesia; expatriate juveniles range south to the Sydney area. Shallow coral reefs to about 45 m. Attains 65 mm.

Cirrhitichthys falco Juv.

SPOTTED HAWKFISH
Cirrhitichthys oxycephalus (Bleeker, 1855)

D X,12-13. A III,6. P 14. V I,5. LL 41-45. Moderate-sized cycloid scales cover body, most of head. Large scales on cheek, opercle; three scale-rows above middle of lateral line. Large pectoral fins with extended, thickened lower rays. First soft ray of dorsal fin extended. Preopercle margin coarsely serrate. Colouration varies from dark to light to suit various habitats. Basically blotched with violet sheen. Widespread tropical species throughout the west Pacific and west to east Africa. Juveniles south to the Sydney area. Mainly clear-water reefs to 40 m. Attains 9 cm.

Cirrhitichthys oxycephalus Juv.

LYRE-TAIL HAWKFISH
Cyprinocirrhites polyactis (Bleeker, 1875)

D X,16-17. A III,6. P 14. V I,5. LL 47-49. Moderate-sized cycloid scales cover body, most of head. Large scales on cheek; three scale-rows above middle of lateral line. Large pectoral fins with extended lower rays, longest reaching anal fin soft rays. First soft ray of dorsal fin extended. Caudal fin lunate, tips greatly extented into filaments. Preopercle margin coarsely serrate. Colour varies from light to dark brown. Tropical species ranging into warm-temperate areas. West Pacific to east Africa. Coastal to outer reefs, usually on deep slopes from 20-50 m. Feeds well above bottom on zooplankton; superficially resembles anthiids. Attains 10 cm.

FRECKLED HAWKFISH
Paracirrhites forsteri (Schneider, 1801)

D X,11. A III,6. P 14. V I,5. LL 45-49. Moderate-sized cycloid scales cover body, most of head. Large scales on cheek; five scale rows above middle of lateral line. Ventral and pectoral fins small. Preopercle margin finely serrate. Colour highly variable; appears to have different colour phases during growth. Young black to red above, pale white below. Sometimes all dark with yellowish tail; adults with additional spotting on head. Abundant species in most of the tropical Pacific ranging to east Africa, Hawaii and Polynesia, and islands of northern New South Wales. Mainly outer reef slopes, perched among outermost coral branches. Attains 20 cm.

KELPFISHES
FAMILY CHIRONEMIDAE

A small family of temperate southern hemisphere fishes with representatives in Australia, New Zealand and South American seas. It comprises two genera; four species occur in Australian and New Zealand waters, three of which are found in south-eastern seas. They feature a distinct head profile and the tips of the dorsal fin spines have a variable number of filaments, forming tufts in some species. The membranes between the dorsal fin spines are often deeply incised. The kelpfishes are closely related to the tropical hawkfishes and their behaviour is very similar – closely hugging the substrate and restlessly moving about. Some species occupy strong surge zones, wedging themselves in the rocks during the wash. Generally, all species are in kelp and weed areas, mostly very shallow to about 20 m where the larger weeds usually decline. Their diet consists of small invertebrates which are taken from the weeds or rocks. Some species are secretive and although common in some areas they are not often seen. Others occur in exposed areas in large but loose aggregations. The larger species can reach a length of about 40 cm, but generally they are of small size and poor taste.

TASSELLED KELPFISH
Chironemus georgianus Cuvier, 1829

D XV-XVI,15-18. A III,7. P 14. V I,5. LL 47-48. Moderate-sized cycloid scales cover body, decreasing in size to small on thorax; markedly smaller scales on most of head to cheeks. Lateral line virtually straight from shoulder, along middle of caudal peduncle, to last scale on caudal fin. Base of spinous section of dorsal fin much longer than base of soft-rayed section. Tips of spines with dense tufts. Lower part of pectoral fin with extended rays. Mouth small, reaching well short of eye. Pale whitish to brown with variable dark blotching. Small white spot at origin of opercle. Known from the south coast only, Bass Strait to Western Australia. Small, secretive species living among weeds. Attains 20 cm. Also known as Western Kelpfish.

KELPFISH
Chironemus marmoratus Günther, 1860

D XIV-XV,16-18. A III,6-8. P 15. V I,5. LL 55-58. Moderate-sized cycloid scales cover body, decreasing in size to small on thorax; markedly smaller scales on most of head to cheeks. Lateral line virtually straight from shoulder, along middle of caudal peduncle, to last scale on caudal fin. Bases of spinous and soft-rayed section of dorsal fin of about equal length. Tips of spines without dense tufts. Pectoral fin large with extended lower rays. Mouth small, reaching well short of eye. Light to dark grey with dark blotches; pale spot on most body scales. Eastern Australia, from northern New South Wales to Tasmania, and New Zealand. Coastal surge zones, often in large aggregations loosely distributed over certain reefs. Intertidal to about 20 m depth. Attains 40 cm. Also known as Large Kelpfish, Eastern Kelpfish and in New Zealand as Hiwihiwi.

SILVER SPOT
Threpterius maculosus Richardson, 1850

D XIV,18-19. A III,8. P 14. V I,5. LL 58-60. Moderate-sized cycloid scales cover body, opercle. Lateral line straight from shoulder to caudal fin. Spinous section of dorsal fin with deeply incised membranes; tips of spines with dense tufts. Pectoral fin large with greatly extended rays in lower half. Mouth large, reaching below and past centre of eye. Eye large. Variable from grey to green to reddish-brown with dark patches along back. Distinct silver spot at tip of opercle. South coast from Bass Strait to Western Australia and New Zealand. Secretive, in shallow rocky reefs with dense algae cover. Attains 35 cm.

SEACARPS
FAMILY APLODACTYLIDAE

A small family of temperate fishes of the southern hemisphere with representatives in Australia, New Zealand and South American seas. It comprises two genera and five species of which four are known from Australian and New Zealand waters, and two are included here. The fourth species is restricted to south-western Australian waters. They have elongate and robust bodies with small cycloid scales. The dorsal fin base is long with spinous and soft-rayed sections of equal length. The anal fin base is very short and the pectoral fins are large, about equal to the size of the head, and positioned well forward. Sea carps are medium-sized fishes, reaching up to 65 cm in length, which feed on algae and weeds. Usually they are found in small to large aggregations in coastal surge zones and tidal current areas of large estuaries, feeding on suspended weeds going past. Most of their time is spent resting on the bottom and they only swim to grab food. Sloppy swimmers, they curiously keep the dorsal fin raised during the exercise. Although these fishes reach a fair size they are generally regarded as poor tasting.

SOUTHERN SEACARP
Aplodactylus arctidens (Richardson, 1839)

D XVII,17. A III,6. P 14. V I,5. LL 101-103. Body covered with small cycloid scales which extend onto dorsal fin base as narrow sheath. Patches of small scales on cheek. Lateral line virtually straight from shoulder to caudal fin. Dorsal fin tall in two similar angular parts forming angles at third spine and first soft ray. Anal and ventral fin rays longer than their short bases. Pectoral fin large, middle rays at least equal to head length. Head profile smoothly rounded. Variable from grey to greenish-brown with variable blotches and scribbles. Common Bass Strait species ranging to southern Tasmania and eastern South Australia (replaced by similar species westwards), and New Zealand. Weedy reef slopes, usually to about 15 m but ventures to about 40 m. Attains 65 cm. Also known as Marblefish.

ROCK CALE
Crinodus lophodon Günther, 1859

D XVI-XVII,21. A II-III,6-7. P 14-16. V I,5. LL 66-70. Body covered with small cycloid scales which extend onto dorsal fin base as long narrow sheath. Lateral line with gradual curve following contour of back. Tall dorsal fin with small notch in centre. Anal fin long, short-based; ventral fin long, slender. Pectoral fin large with thickened lower rays. Head small, snout blunt, mouth angled downwards. Variable from grey to bluish-black, lighter mottling on body, light spots in fins. Juveniles with distinct ear-mark. East Australia only, from southern Queensland to Victoria. Shallow exposed rocky shores, aggregating in high-energy zone, just below foaming surface to depths of about 10 m. Feeds on either loose or attached weeds and algae. Attains 35 cm. Also called Cocky, Cockatoo Fish or Joey.

Crinodus lophodon   Adult ▼   Small juv. ▲

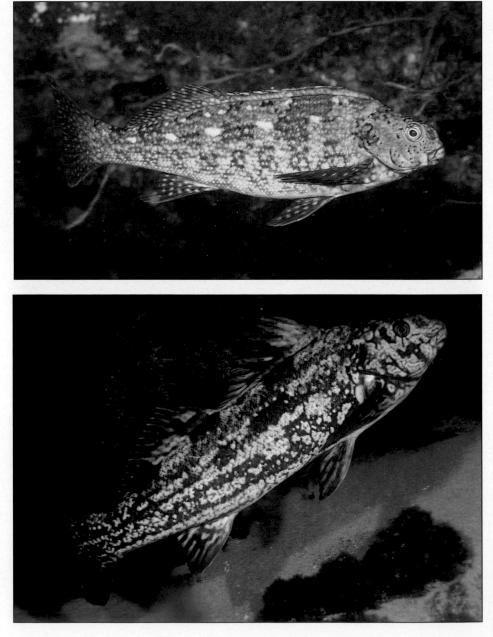

MORWONGS
FAMILY
CHEILODACTYLIDAE

This family is essentially anti-tropical with species distributed along the northern and southern hemispheres, at similar latitudes, between tropical and cool-temperate zones of the Indo-West Pacific. There are four genera and approximately 20 species of which Australia has the greatest number of species. Three genera are present in Australian waters: *Cheilodactylus* with 10 species, *Nemadactylus* with three species and *Dactylophora* with one species. Most species have large rubbery lips, long elongated pectoral fin rays and a forked tail. The dorsal fin is often elevated and they are distinctly coloured. They are reef and bottom dwellers, feeding on worms and small invertebrates which are filtered through the gills from randomly-taken mouthfuls of sand or matter scraped from

rocks. These fishes are often seen resting on the bottom, using the pectoral fins to stabilise. The long pectoral fin rays are often used to attend to irritations on the body and tail. Eggs and larvae are pelagic and newly settled juveniles are silvery, extremely thin and deep-bodied. This is known as the "paper stage". Aquarium-kept specimens would hide until becoming patterned which took about one week. Several species have been observed at this stage and are about 45-60 mm long. Juveniles and adults can be found in various habitats from shallow coastal reefs to deep offshore water. Most species occur on reefs to about 60 m, but those of the genus *Nemadactylus* go much deeper and one species is commercially trawled to 400 m. Whilst the latter may occur in large schools,

most species are in small, loose aggregations. They are good to eat, except *Dactylophora* which is also the largest, reaching 1.2 m in length.

PAINTED MORWONG
Cheilodactylus ephippium McCulloch and Waite, 1916

D XVII,32. A III,8. P 13. V I,5. LL 65. Scales cycloid, moderate-sized on body, small and embedded on head. Lateral line slightly curved after origin, becoming almost straight over most of posterior part. Lower pectoral rays slightly extended. Pair of small knob-like protrusions in front of eyes. Distinct colouration with banding and spots. Mainly known from Lord Howe Island, Norfolk Island, Kermadec Islands, islands off New Zealand and occasionally New South Wales. Usually in small aggregations where common. This species prefers offshore habitats, inhabits lagoons and reefs to 60 m. Attains 55 cm. Known in New Zealand as Painted Moki.

Photograph: Adrian Newman

257

RED MORWONG
Cheilodactylus fuscus Castelnau, 1879

D XVII,32. A III,8. P 13. V I,5. LL 60.
Scales cycloid, moderate-sized on body, small
and embedded on head. Lateral line slightly
curved after origin, becoming almost straight
over most of posterior part. Lower pectoral
rays slightly extended. Pairs of horn-like
protrusions in front of eyes and immediately
above lips. Pale to dark brown; banding can
be put on at will. Particularly common in New
South Wales, but ranges into southern
Queensland and eastern Victoria, and also
north-eastern New Zealand. Juveniles on
coastal reefs among algae. Adults occur in
small to large aggregations on exposed rocky
reefs to about 30 m. Attains 65 cm.

Cheilodactylus fuscus Juv.

MAGPIE PERCH
Cheilodactylus nigripes Richardson, 1850

D XVIII-XIX,25-28. A III,9-10. P 13.
V I,5. LL 63-69. Scales cycloid, moderate-
sized on body, small on head. Lateral line
slightly curved after origin, high along sides,
becoming straight over posterior part. Lower
pectoral rays extended. Pairs of horn-like
protrusions in front of eyes and immediately
above lips. Distinctly banded, but large adults
can change colour quickly by losing second
band. Southern New South Wales to southern
West Australia, rare south of Bass Straight;
northern New Zealand. Shallow rocky reef to
about 60 m. Juveniles often under jetties.
Adults usually in small, loose aggregations.
Attains 40 cm.

Cheilodactylus nigripes Juv.

Cheilodactylus nigripes ▲   *Cheilodactylus spectabilis* ▼

BANDED MORWONG
Cheilodactylus spectabilis (Hutton, 1872)

D XVII-XVIII,26-27. A III,8. P 14-15.
V I,5. LL 48-54. Scales cycloid, distinct,
moderate-sized on body. Lateral line slightly
curved, following contour of back. No obvious
protrusions on forehead or extended rays on
pectoral fin. Dorsal fin low with notch between
spinous and soft-rayed sections. Banding
variable to almost indistinguishable, particularly in large adults. Most abundant in
Tasmania and New Zealand's north island,
extending to Seal Rocks, New South Wales;

rare in eastern South Australia. Shallow reef
with sand patches to about 50 m. Large species,
recorded to 1 m and 15 kg. Examination of
otoliths in large specimens in New Zealand
suggest an age of about 60 years. Called Red
Moki in New Zealand.

258

CRESTED MORWONG
Cheilodactylus vestitus (Castelnau, 1878)

D XVI-XVII,32-35. A III,8-9. LL 58-65. Scales cycloid, moderate-sized on body, small on head. Lateral line rises little from origin, curves smoothly to straight on most of posterior part. First three dorsal spines short, followed by tall fourth spine with progressively shortening spines to long low dorsal fin. Lower part of pectoral fin with extended rays. Pairs of knob-like protrusions in front of eyes and immediately above lips. Distinct pattern with little variation. Occurs from central New South Wales well into tropical waters of the Great Barrier Reef and New Caledonia, and Lord Howe Island. Shallow estuaries, inshore and offshore reefs to about 20 m. Solitary or in small aggregations. Attains about 35 cm. Similar species in Japan, Hawaii and West Australia, of which latter is Magpie Morwong, *C. gibbosus.*

Cheilodactylus vestitus Juv.

Dactylophora nigricans Adult ▲ Intermediate stage ▼

DUSKY MORWONG
Dactylophora nigricans (Richardson, 1850)

D XV-XVI,24-26. A III,9-10. P 14. V I,5. LL 45-55. Scales cycloid, moderate sized on body, small and embedded on head. Lateral line with gradual curve in juveniles, almost straight in adults. Small juveniles have second lateral line from origin to middle of body, ending above anus. Body from deep in small juveniles to elongate in large adults. Lower part of pectoral fin with extended rays. Grey or green with variable spotting and blotches. South coast only, from Bass Straight to West Australia. Juveniles among weeds, seagrasses. Adults with seagrass beds and rocky outcrops to about 30 m. Attains 1.2 m. Not favoured for eating. Also known as Strongfish.

Dactylophora nigricans Juv.

BLUE MORWONG
Nemadactylus douglasi (Hector, 1875)

D XVII-XVIII,27-28. A III,16-17. P 15. V I,5. LL 47-55. Scales cycloid, moderate-sized on body, small on nape and below pectoral fin. Lateral line with gradual curve along upper sides. Lower five rays of pectoral fin greatly extended, uppermost reaching to above middle of anal fin; remaining part of fin pointed with upper rays longest. Grey to blue, upper part darkened with yellow or brown. In the vicinity of rocky reefs over sand. Usually seen in small aggregations, but said to school in deep water where commercially trawled in about 100 m. Southern Queensland to Tasmania, and New Zealand where they are known as Porae. Attains 70 cm. Also known as Rubberlip Morwong or Grey Morwong.

Nemadactylus douglasi ▲

Nemadactylus macropterus ▼

JACKASS MORWONG
Nemadactylus macropterus (Schneider, 1801)

D XVII-XVIII,25-28. A III,14-15. P 14-15. V I,5. LL 59-60. Scales cycloid, moderate-sized on body, small on nape. Lateral line with gradual curve along upper sides. Lower six rays of pectoral fin strong; uppermost greatly extended, reaching to above middle of anal fin. Spinous section of dorsal fin tall; fifth and sixth spine longest. Adult distinctly coloured with black bar over nape; juveniles may be plain with faint brown bars on sides. Juveniles in deep parts of estuaries; adults generally deep to about 400 m, but occasionally seen by divers in about 25 m. Southern waters from New South Wales to West Australia, and New Zealand where it is known as Tarakihi. Attains 70 cm.

QUEEN SNAPPER
Nemadactylus valenciennesi (Whitley, 1937)

D XVII,30-31. A III,17-19. P 15. V I,5. LL 64-68. Scales cycloid, moderate-sized on body, small on nape. Lateral line with gradual curve along upper sides. Lower six rays extended; uppermost greatly extended, reaching to above middle of anal fin. Dorsal fin long-based, low with elevation over fifth and sixth spines. Juveniles deep-bodied; adults become elongate. Young blue with yellow stripes, dark blotch in middle of body. During growth blotch and stripes fade on body, distinct yellow lined pattern radiates around eyes. Inshore rocky reefs to deep offshore, to 240 m. South coast from West Australia into Bass Staight to Wilson's Promentory. Attains 90 cm. Also called Blue Morwong (Southern).

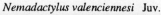

Nemadactylus valenciennesi ▼

Nemadactylus valenciennesi Juv.

TRUMPETERS
FAMILY LATRIDIDAE

A small family of cold-temperate fishes restricted to Australia, New Zealand and South America. Of the three genera, *Latridopsis* has two species, *Latris* one species and *Mendosoma* one or two. These fishes are similar to morwongs, but have a more perch-like appearance with the deeply notched dorsal fin and small pectoral fins. The number of fin elements is high and scales are small and numerous. Bodies are moderately compressed, and the protruding mouth extended in *Mendosoma*. Trumpeters are reef and bottom dwellers feeding on a variety of invertebrates, except *Mendosoma* which feeds on zooplankton. Most are schooling fishes, occurring in small aggregations to large schools of hundreds of individuals. Like the morwongs, the post-larvae is known as the paper-fish, and the juveniles of some species retain this appearance to about 15 cm length. The larger species are regarded as excellent table fish, especially *Latris* which reaches 1.2 m. Several species are of commercial importance in Australia and New Zealand.

BASTARD TRUMPETER
Latridopsis forsteri (Castelnau, 1872)

D XVII,38-40. A III,32-35. P 18. V I,5. LL 115-120. Small cycloid scales cover body, much of tail. Small embedded scales on head. Lateral line smoothly curved to mid-body, then straight. Fins small, low; deep notch in centre of dorsal fin; caudal fin forked. Body compressed, tapering to narrow caudal peduncle. Silvery-grey with various shades of brown along back. Caudal fin of adults with distinct black margin at posterior edge. Common species in Tasmania ranging north to Sydney and west to eastern South Australia. Shallow coastal waters to about 60 m. Solitary or in small aggregations, but migrates in very large schools. Usually on sand near or among reefs, feeding on various invertebrates. Attains 65 cm. Also known as Silver Trumpeter and in New Zealand as Copper Moki.

Latridopsis forsteri ▲

Latris lineata ▼

Latridopsis forsteri Juv.

STRIPED TRUMPETER
Latris lineata (Schneider, 1801)

D XVIII,34-36. A III,31-32. P 18. V I,5. LL 114. Small cycloid scales cover body, much of tail. Small embedded scales on head. Lateral line virtually straight. Dorsal fin moderate-sized with deep notch in middle; base of spinous section straight. Ventral and pectoral fins small. Pale dusky green or yellow above with distinct dark longitudinal bands; silvery below. Variable spotting on head. Tasmania to southern New South Wales and eastern South Australia, and New Zealand. Generally deepwater species to 300 m, but juveniles often in very shallow coastal water. Feeds on large invertebrates; in New Zealand has been observed feeding on zooplankton consisting of crustaceans. Regarded as one of the best food fish. Attains 1.2 m. Also known as Tasmanian Trumpeter or Stripey and in New Zealand as Trumpeter or Kohikohi.

MULLETS
FAMILY MUGILIDAE

A large family with approximately 13 genera containing an estimated 70 species. They are distributed in estuaries and all but the coldest seas, and some species enter fresh water. Mullets have moderately elongate bodies, a broad depressed head and two widely separated dorsal fins which are of similar size. The mouth is small and terminal. The jaws are usually with or without loosely attached teeth in one group, and firmly attached more rigid teeth in another. These groups are regarded as subfamilies. Scales can be cycloid or ctenoid and vary in size from moderate to large. There are often greatly enlarged scales on the head. A lateral line is absent, but all species have scales with a groove or pit. The first ray in the second dorsal fin is often mistaken for a spine. Some species are of commercial importance in various parts of the world. Only the larger species are commercially fished in Australia. Most species occur in large schools along the coast and migrate to spawn, some into estuaries and others out to sea. They feed by taking materials out of rocks or mud, either pre-filtered through the gills or swallowed. Sometimes large quantities of nutriment-rich mud are swallowed for treatment with the specially adapted stomach, which has a muscular portion similar to the gizzard of a bird. There are four local species on the south-east coast, and two tropical species range to central New South Wales.

YELLOW-EYE MULLET
Aldrichetta forsteri (Valenciennes, 1836)

D IV,10. A III,12. P 14-15. V I,5. LSR 54-58. Body covered with small, weakly ctenoid scales; several scale rows on cheek. Mouth small, terminal; bands of strong canine teeth in each jaw. First dorsal fin centrally placed. Anal fin origin well ahead of second dorsal fin origin. Pectoral fin nearly reaches first dorsal fin. Varies from silver to brownish along top, usually associated with environment. Fishes in clear ocean waters silvery with little darkening dorsally. Brownish in fresh water. Eye distinctly yellow. Common species in southern waters from Tasmania to central New South Wales and Western Australia, and New Zealand. Mainly in estuaries, where it breeds and occurs in all sizes. Ventures into fresh water; large schools may travel coastal bays. Of commercial importance in some states. Attains 40 cm.

Aldrichetta forsteri　Adults ▼　Juvs. ▲

FLAT-TAIL MULLET
Liza argentea (Quoy and Gaimard, 1825)

D IV,10. A III,10. P 16. V I,5. LSR 35-38. Body covered with moderate-sized cycloid scales; head with slightly larger scales. Most body scales have horizontal sensory tube, creating lined pattern. Mouth small, terminal; close-set row of slender monocuspid teeth in edge of lips, three or four rows of bicuspid teeth in inner side of lips. First dorsal fin placed back from centre of body. Anal fin base slightly longer than and opposite second dorsal fin base. Silvery with grey upper sides; brownish dorsally. Gold spot on upper corner of opercle. Reported from all states except Tasmania. Coastal waters and estuaries, usually in large schools. Attains 30 cm. Also known as Tiger Mullet and Jumping Mullet.

SEA MULLET
Mugil cephalus Linnaeus, 1758

D IV,9. A III,8. P 16-17. V I,5. LSR 38-42. Body covered with moderate-sized scales, cycloid in young, becoming weakly ctenoid in adults. Several rows of large scales on opercle, cheek. Mouth small, terminal; close-set row of slender monocuspid teeth in te edge of lips, three or four rows of bicuspid teeth in inner side of lips. Eye covered with verticle adipose eyelids, except for area across pupil. First dorsal fin centrally placed. Second dorsal fin opposite and similar in shape and size to anal fin. Silvery with grey to olive backs, becoming darker in estuaries. Widely distributed in the Pacific, Indian and southern Atlantic oceans. Occurs along entire coast of Australia in estuaries; large schools migrate along ocean beaches. Spawns offshore and young move into estuaries. Small schools of juveniles enter rivers; adults occasionally venture up rivers as well. Adults often seen feeding on algae-covered rocks, on which they pounce for short periods when on the move. Most important commercial species; attains 75 cm.

SAND MULLET
Myxus elongatus Günther, 1861

D IV,9-10. A III,9. P 16. V I,5. LSR 43-46. Body covered with moderate-sized cycloid scales. Head with moderate-sized scales, five rows on cheeks. Mouth small, terminal; single row of close-set incisor teeth in jaws. First dorsal fin centrally placed. Anal fin base longer, placed more forward than second dorsal fin base. Grey to olive-green above, silvery below. Distinct black axil-spot and yellow spot on upper opercle close together. Southern Australian waters to Queensland, West Australia and also at Lord Howe Island. Mostly shallow in coastal bays but also in estuaries and harbours. In small to large schools over sandy flats. Small species; average size about 25 cm but attains 35 cm. Flat-Tail Mullet or young Sea Mullet sometimes confused with this species, but easily separated by anal fin ray count.

WARTY-LIP MULLET
Crenimugil crenilabrus (Forsskål, 1775)

D IV,9. A III,9. P 16-17. V I,5. LSR 38-41. Body covered with distinctly pitted moderate-sized scales. Several rows of large scales on opercle, cheek. Adipose eyelid absent. Mouth small, terminal; fleshy lips, notched and papillate, lower folded outwards. First dorsal fin centrally placed. Second dorsal fin opposite and similar in shape and size to anal fin. Pectoral fins sharply pointed, reaching to below dorsal fin origin. Silvery with grey longitudinal lines along scale rows; slightly darker, sometimes greenish above. Widespread tropical Indo-Pacific, on the east coast to central New South Wales. Clear coastal reefs, usually roaming in large schools over shallow sandy slopes. Attains 40 cm.

FRINGE-LIP MULLET
Crenimugil labiosus (Valenciennes, 1836)

D IV,9. A III,9. P 16-17. V I,5. LSR 34-36. Body covered with slightly grooved moderate-sized scales. Several rows of large scales on opercle, cheek. Adipose eyelid absent. Mouth small, terminal; fleshy lips, upper notched with a few rows of papillae, with obsolete lateral papillate. First dorsal fin centrally placed. Second dorsal fin opposite and similar in shape and size to anal fin. Pectoral fins sharply pointed, reaching well short of and below dorsal fin origin. Shiny silvery sides, variable greenish to olive above. Queensland species, occasionally ranging south to the Sydney area. Coastal schooling species. Attains 35 cm.

Striped Sea-Pike (*Sphyraena obtusata*), schooling ▼

BARRACUDAS
FAMILY SPHYRAENIDAE

Barracudas are primarily of tropical seas. The family comprises one genus and about 20 globally distributed species, a few of which range into warm-temperate waters. Some species are large, reaching more than 1 m in length – the Great Barracuda attains over 2 m. They are fierce predators, feeding mainly on other fishes and squid. They hunt alone or in groups, and some of the smaller species hunt in close-packed schools. Their bodies are streamlined and the large mouth is equipped with powerful jaws and sabre-like teeth. Most of the hunting is done during dawn and dusk, though they appear to patrol the reefs looking to take advantage of any opportunity for an easy feed which comes along. In Australia, the smaller species, about 30 cm, are usually called sea pikes. Of the eight species found in Australian waters, two occur on the south coast and are included here.

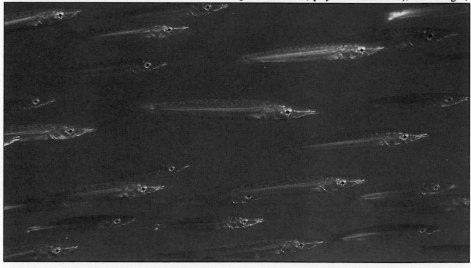

264

SNOOK
Sphyraena novaehollandiae Günther, 1860

D VI,I,9. A II,9-10. P 13. V I,5. LL 125-135. Body covered with tiny cycloid scales. Lateral line almost straight, with 10 to 12 scales above to dorsal fin origin. Pectoral fin situated well forward, nearly halfway between ventral fin and eye. Body very elongate, cylindrical; head pointed, mouth large. Lower jaw protruding; teeth prominent, flattened, distinctly pointed; enlarged anterior canines often in lower jaw. Greenish-grey above, silvery below. Fins pale yellowish or greenish. Confined to southern Australian waters from southern Victoria and Tasmania to south Western Australia. Numerous records from other places, including New Zealand, Africa, Micronesia and so on, refer to closely related species. Shallow depths in vicinity of reefs; enters large estuaries. Attains 1 m. Excellent to eat, commercially important. Also known as Short-Finned Sea Pike.

STRIPED SEA PIKE
Sphyraena obtusata Cuvier, 1829

D V,I,9. A II,9. P 13-15. V I,5. LL 85-96. Body covered with small cycloid scales. Lateral line almost straight, with seven to eight scales above to dorsal fin origin. Pectoral fin just in advance of ventral fin, their tips reaching about equal vertical. Body elongate, cylindrical; head pointed, mouth large. Lower jaw protruding; teeth prominent, flattened, distinctly pointed; enlarged anterior canines often in lower jaw. Yellowish or greenish-grey above, silvery below; two longitudinal stripes over sides. Uncertain distribution with several similar tropical species. Originally described from Sydney Harbour; occurs at least in southern Queensland, southern Western Australia, and rare in South Australia. Usually in small agregations near substrate; young in large schools mid-water. In coastal bays, large estuaries. Attains 30 cm.

WRASSES
FAMILY LABRIDAE

The wrasses make up one of the most speciose families of the Indo-Pacific and occur in all but the coldest seas. Studies are in progress to determine the subfamily levels of this most diverse group, which comprises more than 60 genera and an estimated 400 species. Although the majority of species occur on tropical reefs, 32 genera and 85 species range into south-eastern waters and of these, the true local species are the dominant fishes on the reefs here. More than half these species are tropical and expatriate far south during summer months, but few of them survive the colder water in the winter. The species included here have elongate to very elongate bodies, a terminal mouth, usually with thick lips,

and protruding canine teeth. Cycloid scales cover the body and often most of the head. The lateral line is continuous or interrupted, depending on the tribe. There are usually various and distinct colour-forms within species between juvenile and sexes. Juveniles are usually female first and adults are referred to as the initial phase (IP); as males derive from females this form could represent either sex. Fully developed males usually become very colourful and very different from the IP, and are referred to as the terminal phase (TP). Most males dominate a harem-like group of females and are territorial toward other males. If the male disappears the most dominant, usually largest, female takes over and

changes sex. They are mostly benthic feeders, taking a great variety of invertebrates but also some small fishes. A few are specialised plankton-feeders or pick parasites from other fishes. All species are diurnal and retire by either burying in the sand or wedging themselves into crevices. They are primarily shallow reef dwellers, but a few species are adapted to open sand and rubble and are trawled in depths in excess of 100 m. The following species appear in the order of the tentative subfamilies Hypsigeniinae, Cheilininae and Julidinae and similar species are grouped together. Because of the large family, further general information is found with the first species of each genus.

Courting Snake-Skin Wrasses (*Eupetrichthys angustipes*)

WESTERN BLUE GROPER
Achoerodus gouldii (Richardson, 1843)

D XI,11. A III,11. P 16-18. V I,5. LL 33-37. Moderate-sized cycloid scales cover body, bases of dorsal and anal fins, extend onto head, including cheeks. Lateral line smoothly curved; seven to seven and a half scale-rows above lateral line to dorsal fin origin. Lips fleshy, thick, becoming very large in adults with upper lip well out in front. Eye reduces in size proportionally during growth, becoming very small in large adults. Colour variable between blue and green. Eye always blue; last third of pectoral fin and posterior margin of caudal fin distinctly whitish. Primarily south-west coast species, occasionally ranging as far as Port Phillip Bay. Rocky reefs; large adults roam over wide area from shallow to about 40 m. Juveniles in estuaries and sheltered bays in sea grasses and weeds, moving out with increasing size. Attains 1.6 m. Protected from spearfishing in various areas of South Australia. This genus comprises two species, confined to southern Australian waters.

Achoerodus gouldii   Male ▲ Female ▼

Achoerodus viridis   Male ▲ Female ▼

EASTERN BLUE GROPER
Achoerodus viridis (Steindachner, 1866)

D XI,10-11. A III,10-11. P 16-18. V I,5. LL 41-45. Moderate-sized cycloid scales cover body, bases of dorsal and anal fins, extend onto head, including cheeks. Lateral line smoothly curved; nine to 10.5 scale-rows above lateral line to dorsal fin origin. Lips fleshy, thick, becoming very large in adults with upper lip well out in front. Eye reduces in size proportionally during growth, becoming very small in large adults. Variable between grey or blue and reddish-brown; small juveniles green. Blue stripes from eye in juveniles become scribbles in adults. Eastern Australia ranging from southern Queensland to Wilson's Promontory. Rocky reefs; large adults roam over wide area from shallow to about 40 m. Juveniles mainly in seagrass beds in large estuaries, moving out with increasing size. Attains 1.2 m. Totally protected in New South Wales.

Achoerodus viridis   Juv.

267

PIGFISH
Bodianus unimaculatus (Günther, 1862)

D XII,11. A III,12. P 17-18. V I,5. LL 32-33. Moderate-sized cycloid scales cover body, bases of dorsal and anal fins, extend onto head, including cheeks. Lateral line smoothly curved; five scale-rows above lateral line to dorsal fin origin. Juvenile pinkish-white with thin longitudinal lines over centre of scales, reddish bands from eye over head, followed by long dashes along midline and upper sides. Larger specimens become reddish above; dashes decrease in size, fade away in males. Eastern Australia from southern Queensland to Victoria, and New Zealand. Generally in deep water in Australia; caught on fishing lines in depths in excess of 50 m but occasionally observed by divers in about 30 m. Offshore on deep reefs or islands. Attains 45 cm. Previously confused with similar species: *B. vulpinus*, a West Australian endemic, and *B. oxycephalus* from Japan. Other similar species at Easter Island and Hawaii. Known as Red Pigfish in New Zealand.

Bodianus unimaculatus　Male ▼　Female ▲

Photograph: Malcolm Francis

Bodianus frenchii ▼

FOXFISH
Bodianus frenchii (Klunzinger, 1880)

D XII,10. A III,11. P 16-17. V I,5. LL 34-38. Moderate-sized cycloid scales cover body, bases of dorsal and anal fins, extend onto head, including cheeks. Lateral line smoothly curved; six scale-rows above lateral line to dorsal fin origin. Eyes moderately large in juveniles, becoming proportionally smaller in adults. Varies from brown to bright red; usually pale under head. Small juveniles dark brown with three yellow bands. Large black spot around pectoral fin base retained in all but larger adults. This primarily south-western species expatriates through Bass Strait; sightings of juveniles in southern New South Wales not uncommon. Oceanic reefs in 10-40 m, usually in caves. Attains 45 cm. This genus comprises about 35 species, primarily tropical; seven species are included here; commonly known as pigfishes and hogfishes.

Bodianus frenchii　Juv.

GOLDEN-SPOT PIGFISH
Bodianus perditio (Quoy and Gaimard, 1835)

D XII-XIII,10. A III,12. P 17. V I,5. LL 33-35. Moderate-sized cycloid scales cover body, bases of dorsal and anal fins, extend onto head to above orbital and cheeks. Lateral line smoothly curved; seven scale-rows above lateral line to dorsal fin origin. Juveniles have distinct colouration; change to adult gradual. Appears to have anti-equatorial distribution; in Australia from southern Queensland to central New South Wales and at a similar latitude in southern Japan; also in Western Australia and east Africa. However, known from trawling off north-western Australia and may occur elsewhere in deep tropical waters. Juveniles often in rocky estuaries in New South Wales. Adults in 10-40 m along deep rocky slopes on offshore reefs or islands. Attains 40 cm. Indian Ocean populations differ slightly in colour, considered to be geographical variation.

Bodianus perditio Juv.

CORAL HOGFISH
Bodianus axillaris (Bennett, 1835)

D XII,9-10. A III,11-12. P 15-17. LL 29-31. Moderate-sized cycloid scales extend on head to about nostrils, and well onto dorsal and anal fin bases up to three scales high. Very distinct juvenile; IP jet black with large white spots. Dramatic change from IP to TP completed in about one week, resulting in totally different looking fish; head darkish with colour extending to halfway along body; tail pale, some large black spots in fins, on axil. Widespread tropical Indo-Pacific from the central Pacific to east Africa. Ranges into warm-temperate waters of Japan and Australia; in New South Wales south to Montague Island. Rocky reefs, in caves and ledges from shallow reef crest to deep drop-offs. Juveniles usually fairly deep, often observed picking parasites off other fishes. Attains 20 cm.

Bodianus axillaris Juv.

Bodianus axillaris   Terminal phase ▲   Transitional stage ▼

BLACKBELT HOGFISH
Bodianus mesothorax (Schneider, 1801)

D XII,9-10. A III,11-12. P 16. V I,5. LL 30-32. Moderately large cycloid scales cover body and head to above orbit and cheeks, extend onto dorsal and anal fin bases. In many aspects similar to Coral Hogfish, but juvenile not quite black, spots yellow, transformation to adult pattern takes place at earlier stage. Tropical west Pacific, including Micronesia, and eastern Indian Ocean. Juveniles expatriate as far south as Sydney. Mostly found in clear outer reef waters in rich coral growth, but just as common on silty coastal reefs in some areas such as Indonesia. Shallow, from about 5-40 m. Attains 20 cm.

Bodianus mesothorax   Terminal phase ▲   Transitional stage ▼

Bodianus mesothorax   Juv

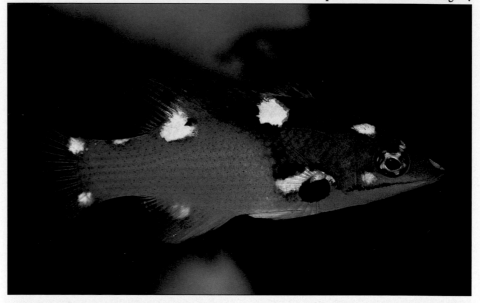

DIANA'S HOGFISH
Bodianus diana (Lacepède, 1801)

D XII,9-10. A III,10-12. P 15-17. V I,5. LL 30-31. Moderately large cycloid scales cover body and head to above orbit and cheeks, extend onto dorsal and anal fin bases. Variable from light to dark brown. Juveniles with longitudinal series of small white spots which elongate with growth, eventually drop out ventrally upwards. Widespread tropical Indo-Pacific from Red Sea, east Africa to Japan, Micronesia, Tonga and New South Wales as far south as Montague Island. Outer reefs in rich coral growth, particularly soft corals, from shallow reef flats to 40 m. Juveniles usually deep in about 20-30 m, in soft corals or swimming upside down on ceiling under large overhangs, sometimes in small aggregations. Attains 20 cm.

Bodianus diana   Juv.

STRIPED HOGFISH

Bodianus izuensis Araga and Yoshino, 1975

D XII, 9-10. A III,12. P 16-17. V I,5. LL 32. Moderately large cycloid scales cover body, extend slightly over head and cheeks, but not onto dorsal and anal fin bases. Slender, torpedo-shaped species. Distinct stripes become paler and more reddish in adults. Anti-equatorial distribution; only known from the west Pacific from a few locations in Japan, New Caledonia and New South Wales. Occurs deep on rocky reefs in Japan, in 30-50 m. Only a few juvenile specimens have been found in Sydney Harbour and Botany Bay. Very small specimens, about 15 mm long, swim over muddy flats well out in the open; appear to mimic juvenile *Pentapodus spp* which occur in same area and have similar pattern at same size. Juveniles from about 25 mm stay close to rock-faces, quickly hide in crevices for cover. Attains 10 cm.

Bodianus izuensis ▲

Bodianus izuensis Juv.

VENUS TUSKFISH

Choerodon venustus (De Vis, 1884)

D XIII,7. A III,9. P 15-16. V I,5. LL 27-28. Large cycloid scales cover body, extend onto caudal fin and opercles; small patch of scales on lower part of cheek. Lateral line smoothly curved, high along sides; two to two and a half scales above middle of lateral line to dorsal fin base. Eye large in juveniles, becoming proportionally much smaller in large adults. Mouth terminal, lips not protruding; two pairs of prominent anterior canines in lower jaw. Pale to dark brown or reddish. Adults with small spot in each scale on posterior part of body and over back and belly. Mainly known from southern Queensland; ranges into New South Wales and a few specimens are known from Sydney Harbour. Coastal reefs to about 40m; juveniles in rocky kelp estuaries. Attains 50 cm. There are about 25 tuskfish species, distributed in the tropical Indo-Pacific; common name derived from enlarged canines.

Choerodon venustus ▼

Choerodon cephalotes ▼

GRASS TUSKFISH

Choerodon cephalotes (Castelnau, 1875)

D XIII,7. A III,10. P 18-19. V I,5. LL 26-29. Large cycloid scales cover body, extend onto caudal fin and opercles; small patch of scales on lower part of cheek. Lateral line smoothly curved, high along sides; three to three and a half scales above middle of lateral line to dorsal fin base. Eye large in juveniles; becomes proportionally much smaller in large adults. Mouth terminal, lips not protruding; two pairs of prominent anterior canines in lower jaw. Young adult shown. Diagnostic short blue stripes develop across forehead and snout with growth, thickening with age; interspaces become thin lines in large males. Coastal, in shallow weed zones of northern Australia, ranging to Indonesia; juveniles south to Sydney Harbour. Attains 38 cm.

HALF-AND-HALF WRASSE
Hemigymnus melapterus (Bloch, 1791)

DIX,11. A III,11. P14. V I,5. LL 25. Large cycloid scales cover body. Narrow band of small scales below and behind eye. Lateral line slightly curved at shoulder, curved downward below soft dorsal fin to horizontal section along caudal peduncle. Lips thick, fleshy; lower incised, forming two lobes. Single pairs of strong canines in each jaw. Small juveniles, adolescents and adults each have distinct colour pattern. Large adults mainly green with blue margin on each body scale, blue scribbles on head. Widespread tropical Indo-Pacific from west and central Pacific to east Africa. Juveniles south to Sydney. Coastal reefs and lagoons to about 40 m. Attains 50 cm. Genus comprises two species, widespread in the tropical Indo-Pacific. Feeds on variety of invertebrates filtered from mouthfuls of sand.

Hemigymnus melapterus Juv.

BANDED THICKLIP
Hemigymnus fasciatus (Bloch, 1792)

DIX,11. A III,11. P14. V I,5. LL 25. Large cycloid scales cover body. Narrow band of small scales below and behind eye. Lateral line slightly curved at shoulder, curved downward below soft dorsal fin to horizontal section along caudal peduncle. Lips thick, fleshy; lower incised, forming two lobes. Single pairs of strong canines in each jaw. Small juveniles similar to those of other species of this genus, but pale vertical lines all narrow. Widespread tropical Indo-Pacific from west and central Pacific to east Africa. Juveniles south to Sydney. Outer reefs, shallow to about 40 m in lagoons and on rubble slopes. Attains 30 cm.

Hemigymnus fasciatus Juv.

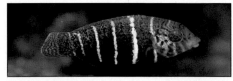

Hemigymnus fasciatus ▲

Pseudolabrus guentheri Adult ▲ Juv. ▼

GÜNTHER'S WRASSE
Pseudolabrus guentheri Bleeker, 1862

D IX,11. A III,10. P 13. V I,5. LL 25-26. Large cycloid scales cover body; somewhat smaller on thorax, extend into narrow sheath along dorsal and anal fin bases, and onto caudal fin. Small scales below and behind eye. Lateral line descends abruptly below end of dorsal fin. Mouth small, terminal with moderately fleshy lips; enlarged anterior canines in both jaws. Variable from green to brown; no great differences between stages or sexes. Eastern Australia from Lindeman Island to Montague Island. Shallow reefs to 20 m, usually in weed or algae habitat. Small species; attains about 18 cm. One species of this genus occurs in Japan, but remaining eight distributed along south Pacific and south Western Australia; three species included here.

LUCULENTUS WRASSE
Pseudolabrus luculentus (Richardson, 1848)

D IX,11. A III,10. P 13. V I,5. LL 25-26. Large cycloid scales cover body; somewhat smaller on thorax, extend into narrow sheath along dorsal and anal fin bases, and onto caudal fin. Small scales below and behind eye. Lateral line descends abruptly below end of dorsal fin. Mouth small, terminal with moderately fleshy lips; enlarged anterior canines in both jaws. Grey-brown to orange or brown-red; males with alternating dark and light saddles along base of dorsal fin. Eastern Australia from the Solitary Islands to Montague Island, Lord Howe, Norfolk and Kermadec Islands, and islands off northeastern New Zealand. Rocky drop-offs and slopes in about 10-50 m. Attains 20 cm. Known in New Zealand as Orange Wrasse.

Pseudolabrus luculentus   Male ▲   Initial phase ▼

Pseudolabrus luculentus   Juv.

ROSY WRASSE
Pseudolabrus psittaculus (Richardson, 1840)

D IX,11. A III,10. P 13. V I,5. LL 25-26. Large cycloid scales cover body; somewhat smaller on thorax, not extending onto dorsal and anal fin bases. Small scales below and behind eye. Lateral line descends abruptly below end of dorsal fin. Mouth small, terminal with moderately fleshy lips; enlarged anterior canines in both jaws. Usually pinkish or reddish with yellow. South coast ranging to New South Wales and King George Sound, Western Australia; usually deep from about 30-200 m except in the Bass Strait area. In Port Phillip Bay as shallow as a few metres. Rocky reefs with caves or crevices. Attains 23 cm. Similar species, *P. miles*, occurs in New Zealand.

Pseudolabris psittaculus ▼

Pseudolabris psittaculus   Juv.

Hybrid, *Notolabrus fucicola* x *N. tetricus* ▼

PURPLE WRASSE
Notolabrus fucicola (Richardson, 1840)

D IX,11. A III,10. P 14. V I,5. LL 25-26.
Large cycloid scales cover body; somewhat
smaller on thorax, not extending onto dorsal
and anal fin bases. Small scales below and
behind eye. Lateral line descends abruptly
below end of dorsal fin. Mouth small, terminal
with moderately fleshy lips; enlarged anterior
canines in both jaws. Dark grey or brown with
purple sheen, pale saddles along back. Little
variation between stages; juveniles greenish.
Widespread in south-eastern Australia from
southern New South Wales to southern
Tasmania and South Australia; common in
New Zealand. In shallow kelp habitat to deep
rocky reefs; reported to 90 m. Attains 45 cm.
This genus only recently created (Russell,
1988) for seven species, previously in
Pseudolabrus, which are restricted to south-
eastern Australian and New Zealand waters.
Medium-sized fishes, dominant on temperate
reefs. Also known as Yellow-Saddled Wrasse
and in New Zealand as Banded Wrasse. In
Australia hybrids of *N. fucicola* and *N. tetricus*
are known from southern New South Wales
and Tasmania, while in New Zealand a hybrid
of *N. fucicola* and *N. inscriptus* was reported
by Ayling (1980).

CRIMSON-BANDED WRASSE
Notolabrus gymnogenis (Günther, 1862)

D IX,11. A III,10. P 14. V I,5. LL 25-26.
Large cycloid scales cover body; much smaller
on thorax, not extending onto dorsal and anal
fin bases. Small scales below and behind eye.
Lateral line descends abruptly below end of
dorsal fin. Mouth small, terminal with
moderately fleshy lips; enlarged anterior
canines in both jaws. Distinct colour-forms
between sexes; juveniles similar to IP.
Shallow-water specimens brownish; deepwater specimens to red-brown. Southern
Queensland to Victoria and a few records
from Lord Howe Island. Rocky reefs from
about 5-40 m. Attains 40 cm.

Notolabrus gymnogenis Juv.

Notolabrus gymnogenis   Male ▲ Initial phase ▼

INSCRIBED WRASSE
Notolabrus inscriptus (Richardson, 1848)

D IX,11. A III,10. P 14. V I,5. LL 25-26. Large cycloid scales cover body; much smaller on thorax, not extending onto dorsal and anal fin bases. Small scales below and behind eye. Lateral line descends abruptly below end of dorsal fin. Mouth small, terminal with moderately fleshy lips; enlarged anterior canines in both jaws. Distinct colour-forms between sexes; large males plain blue-green; juveniles similar to IP. Common at Lord Howe, Norfolk and Kermadec Islands, ranging to New Zealand; rare in southern New South Wales. Rocky reefs in weedy habitats to about 30 m. Attains 50 cm. Know in New Zealand as Green Wrasse.

Notolabrus inscriptus Juv.

Notolabrus tetricus Male ▲ Initial phase ▼

BLUE-THROAT WRASSE
Notolabrus tetricus (Richardson, 1840)

D IX,11. A III,10. P 14. V I,5. LL 25-26. Large cycloid scales cover body; much smaller on thorax, not extending onto dorsal and anal fin bases. Small scales below and behind eye. Lateral line descends abruptly below end of dorsal fin. Mouth small, terminal with moderately fleshy lips; enlarged anterior canines in both jaws. Distinct colour-forms between sexes; large males plain with broad bands; juveniles similar to IP. South-eastern Australia from southern New South Wales to South Australia, including Tasmania. Juveniles in shallow rocky weed habitat, in coastal bays and rocky estuaries. Adults on deeper reefs commonly to 40 m, but largest known specimen, 60 cm long, trawled in about 160 m off north-eastern Tasmania; normally blackish body colour was reddish-brown.

Notolabrus tetricus Juv.

Pictilabrus laticlavius Male ▲ Initial phase ▼

Austrolabrus maculatus Male ▲ Initial phase ▼

SENATOR WRASSE
Pictilabrus laticlavius (Richardson, 1839)

D IX,11. A III,10. P 13. V I,5. LL 25-26. Large cycloid scales cover body; much smaller on thorax, not extending onto dorsal and anal fin bases. Small scales below and behind eye. Lateral line descends abruptly below end of dorsal fin. Mouth small, terminal with moderately fleshy lips; enlarged anterior canines in both jaws. Colour varies with habitat; brown or reddish in red-algae dominated areas, greenish in other habitats. Widespread in southern waters from northern New South Wales to Western Australia, and to southern Tasmania. Mainly in weeds on rocky reefs to about 30 m. Attains 30 cm. Second species recently described in this genus, restricted to south Western Australia.

Pictilabrus laticlavius Juv.

BLACK-SPOTTED WRASSE
Austrolabrus maculatus (Macleay, 1881)

D IX,11. A III,10. P 13. V I,5. LL 25. Large cycloid scales cover body; much smaller on thorax, extending onto dorsal and anal fins in scaly sheets, well extended onto caudal fin. Lateral line descends abruptly below end of dorsal fin. Small scales on cheek below and behind eye. Mouth small, terminal with moderately fleshy lips; enlarged canines in both jaws. Pinkish-brown to yellow-brown; large IPs have distinct black spots over back; TP yellow ventrally. Monotypic genus found only in southern Australian waters in two separate populations: eastern population from central to southern New South Wales, western population from Kangaroo Island to south Western Australia. Slight colour differences between populations; western form lives in shallow depths, mostly between 3-20 m, while eastern form rarely found in less than 15 m and down to 40 m. Eastern form usually in sponge areas, just beyond algae zone on rocky rubble reefs. Attains 20 cm.

PRETTY POLLY
Dotalabrus aurantiacus (Castelnau, 1872)

D IX,11. A III,10. P 12. V I,5. LL 25-26. Large cycloid scales cover body, extend onto head, including cheeks. Lateral line with three to four scale rows above, descends abruptly below end of dorsal fin. Mouth small, terminal with moderately fleshy lips; pairs of enlarged canines in each jaw. Colour highly variable between young and adults, and individuals. Basic colours from green to black to orange, usually associated with colours of weed or depth. Lives in seagrass beds and all kinds of large weeds on rock. Usually shallow but observed in 30 m in clear-water areas where weeds can survive at such depths. South coast only, from Bass Strait to south Western Australia,. and eastern Tasmania. Attains 14 cm. Also known as Castelnau's Wrasse. Has unusual swimming habit, bobbing up and down in almost vertical position with head just above weed. Second and only other species in this genus occurs in south Western Australia.

Normal form ▲ Dark form ▼

Green form ▲ Juv. ▼

SNAKE-SKIN WRASSE
Eupetrichthys angustipes Ramsay and Ogilby, 1888

D IX,12. A III,10. P 13. V I,5. LL 25. Large cycloid scales extend onto head, including cheeks. Lateral line with two scale-rows above, descends abruptly below end of dorsal fin. Mouth small, terminal with moderately fleshy lips; enlarged anterior canines in each jaw; additional enlarged canine posteriorly in upper jaw near corners of mouth. Variable from grey to brown or greenish with broad darker banding. Common in New South Wales and south Western Australia, but occurs in various locations of South Australia and Victoria, including Bass Strait islands. Shallow coastal bays to deep offshore reefs, to at least 40 m. Rock rubble reefs with sand patches. Attains about 15 cm, except in Victoria where it appears to grow much larger (20 cm).

Eupetrichthys angustipes   Male ▲ Initial phase ▼

Eupetrichthys angustipes Juv.

Suezichthys arquatus   Male ▲ Initial phase ▼

PAINTED RAINBOW WRASSE
Suezichthys arquatus Russell, 1985

D IX,11. A III,10. P 13-14. V I,5. LL 25-26. Large cycloid scales extend onto head, including cheeks. Lateral line with two and a half scale-rows above, descends abruptly below end of dorsal fin. Mouth small, terminal with moderately fleshy lips; enlarged anterior canines in each jaw; additional enlarged canine posteriorly in upper jaw near corners of mouth. Little colour variation; usually reddish in deep water. Distinct colour differences between sexes; males brightly coloured. Widespread in New South Wales and southern Queensland; also from New Caledonia, Lord Howe and Norfolk Islands, and northern New Zealand. Rocky reefs from shallow estuaries to deep offshore to at least 50 m. Attains 14 cm. Almost identical species recently discovered in Japan brought total species in this genus to 11; primarily anti-tropical distribution from the east Pacific to the west Indian oceans. Of similar size; many of the IPs look remarkably similar.

CRIMSON CLEANER WRASSE
Suezichthys aylingi Russell, 1985

D IX,11. A III,10. P 13-14. V I,5. LL 25-26. Large cycloid scales extend onto head, including cheeks. Lateral line with one and a half scale-rows above, descends abruptly below end of dorsal fin. Mouth small, terminal with moderately fleshy lips; enlarged anterior canines in each jaw; additional enlarged canine posteriorly in upper jaw at corners of mouth. Little colour variation; usually bright red in deep water. Distinct colour differences between sexes; males more brightly coloured. Eastern Australia from Seal Rocks, New South Wales to south-eastern Tasmania, and northern New Zealand. Common at Montague Island and deep coastal reefs off southern New South Wales. Adults usually beyond 20 m. Regularly observed picking parasites off other fishes. Attains 12 cm.

Suezichthys aylingi   Male ▲   Initial phase ▼

Suezichthys devisi ▼

Leptojulis cyanopleura ▼

GRACILIS WRASSE
Suezichthys devisi Whitley, 1941

D IX,11. A III,10. P 13-14. V I,5. LL 25-26. Large cycloid scales extend onto head, including cheeks. Lateral line with one and a half scale-rows above, descends abruptly below end of dorsal fin. Mouth small, terminal with moderately fleshy lips; enlarged anterior canines in each jaw; additional enlarged canine posteriorly in upper jaw near corners of mouth. Small juveniles with distinct black spot on caudal peduncle, otherwise similar to IP. TP differs only slightly with more colour in general and in caudal fin. Eastern Australia from Heron Island to Jervis Bay. Coastal bays, estuaries, on sand near reefs in 5 m to at least 30 m. Attains 14 cm. Very similar to *S. gracilis* from Japan, which differs in having longer snout, black spot on dorsal fin between first and second spine, generally banded pattern, no distinct black axil spot.

Suezichthys devisi   Juv.

BLUE-SPOT WRASSE
Leptojulis cyanopleura (Bleeker, 1853).

D IX,11. A III,11. P 13. V I,5. LL 27. Body covered with large ctenoid scales; head naked except nape with small scales. Lateral line with four scale-rows above to dorsal fin origin, descends abruptly below end of dorsal fin. Mouth small, terminal with pairs of large anterior canines in jaws; adults have large posterior canine in upper jaw at corners of mouth. Males become ornamented with blue and gold; large metallic blue blotch behind pectoral fin, immediately below lateral line. Tropical west Pacific, Philippines to central New South Wales, Solomon Islands and Sri Lanka. Only as juveniles in the Sydney area, sometimes in small aggregations, mixed with *Trachinops*. Rocky and coral reefs on rubble slopes. Usually in small aggregations feeding on zooplankton, often with other planktivores of similar size. Attains 13 cm. Small genus comprising three species.

Leptojulis cyanopleura   Juvs.

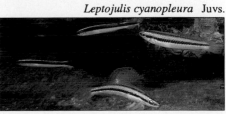

279

ORANGE-LINE WRASSE
Halichoeres hartzfeldi (Bleeker, 1852)

D IX,11. A III,11. P 13. V I,5. LL 27. Large cycloid scales cover body; much smaller scales on thorax; head only has some small embedded

Halichoeres hartzfeldi Adult ▼ Juvs. ▲

scales on sides of nape to orbital. Lateral line with four and a half scales to dorsal fin origin, descends below end of dorsal fin to continue along caudal peduncle. Mouth small, terminal with enlarged anterior canines; adults have enlarged posterior canine in upper jaw at corner of mouth. Juvenile stage similar to IP. Additional patterns in TP. Widespread west Pacific from southern Japan to New South Wales, south to Montague Island. Rocky and coral rubble reefs, in harbours, deep lagoons or coastal slopes. Juveniles in small aggregations. Attains 18 cm. *Halichoeres* presently

the most numerous wrasse genus, but further studies may show that several synonymised genera are valid. Small tropical species found in all seas, some ranging into warm-temperate waters; eight species included here.

YELLOW WRASSE
Halichoeres chrysus Randall, 1980

D IX,12. A III,12. P 13. V I,5. LL 27. Large cycloid scales cover body; much smaller scales on thorax; head only has some small embedded scales on sides of nape to orbital. Lateral line with four and a half scales to dorsal fin origin, descends below end of dorsal fin to continue along caudal peduncle. Mouth small, terminal with enlarged anterior canines; adults have an enlarged posterior canine in upper jaw at corner of mouth. Juvenile stage similar to IP. Additional patterns in TP. Widespread west Pacific from southern Japan to New South Wales, south to Montague Island. Rubble slopes and drop-offs. Shallow to 30 m on tropical reefs, but usually only in deeper part of range in southern waters, possibly because of habitat away from large weeds or kelp, where they occur along edges of reefs and sand. Attains 12 cm.

Halichoeres chrysus Juv.

Halichoeres chrysus ▼

Halichoeres biocellatus ▼

FALSE-EYED WRASSE
Halichoeres biocellatus Schultz, 1960

D IX,12. A III,12. P 13. V I,5. LL 27. Large cycloid scales cover body; much smaller scales on thorax; head only has some small embedded scales on sides of nape to orbital. Lateral line with two and a half scales to dorsal fin origin, descends below end of dorsal fin to continue along caudal peduncle. Mouth small, terminal with enlarged anterior canines; adults have enlarged posterior canine in upper jaw at corner of mouth. Juvenile stage similar to IP. Ocelli lost in TP. Widespread west Pacific from southern Japan to New South Wales, south to Montague Island. Rubble slopes, drop-offs. Shallow to 30 m on tropical reefs, but usually only in deeper part of range in southern waters, possibly because of habitat away from large weeds or kelp, where they occur along edges of reefs and sand. Attains 10 cm. In New South Wales very small juveniles, about 15 mm, often found together with *H. chrysus*.

Halichoeres biocellatus Juv.

HALF-GREY WRASSE
Halichoeres prosopeion (Bleeker, 1853)

D IX,12. A III,12. P 13. V I,5. LL 27. Large cycloid scales cover body; much smaller scales on thorax; head only has some small embedded scales on sides of nape to orbital. Lateral line with two and a half scales to dorsal fin origin, descends below end of dorsal fin along three scales to continue along caudal peduncle. Mouth small, terminal with enlarged anterior canines. Juvenile stage distinctly marked with black stripes which are absent in adults. West Pacific from southern Japan to New South Wales and to central Pacific. Rare in New South Wales, but juveniles known from Sydney. Coastal reef slopes and deep rubble slopes in lagoons to at least 40 m. Attains 12 cm.

Halichoeres prosopeion Juv.

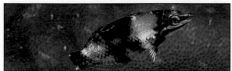

CHECKERBOARD WRASSE
Halichoeres hortulanus (Lacepède, 1801)

D IX,11. A III,11. P 14. V I,5. LL 26. Large cycloid scales cover body; much smaller scales on thorax; head only has some small embedded scales on sides of nape to orbital. Patch of small scales behind eye, opercle; small scales basally along dorsal and anal fins. Lateral line with three and a half scales to dorsal fin origin, descends below end of dorsal fin along three scales to continue along caudal peduncle. Mouth small, terminal with enlarged anterior canines. Juveniles white with dark markings, change gradually during growth to adult patterns. Widespread tropical Indo-Pacific to south Africa, Japan and central Pacific. Juveniles commonly expatriate to the Sydney area. Coastal rubble reefs on sand patches. Shallow to about 40 m. Attains 24 cm.

Halichoeres hortulanus Juv.

DUSKY WRASSE
Halichoeres marginatus Rüppell, 1835

D IX,13-14. A III,12-13. P 14-15. V I,5. LL 27-28. Large cycloid scales cover body; much smaller scales on thorax; head only has some small embedded scales on sides of nape to orbital; small scales basally along dorsal and anal fins. Lateral line with three and a half scales to dorsal fin origin, descends below end of dorsal fin along three scales to continue along caudal peduncle. Mouth small, terminal with enlarged anterior canines. Dull as juvenile and IP but TP with bright colours. Widespread tropical Indo-Pacific from west and central Pacific to east Africa and the Red Sea. Juveniles commonly expatriate to the Sydney area. Coastal reefs from shallow reef flats and slopes to about 30 m. Small juveniles in crevices, often with sea-urchins. Attains 17 cm.

Halichoeres hortulanus ▲

Halichoeres marginatus Male ▲ Juv. ▼

CLOUDED WRASSE

Halichoeres nebulosus (Valenciennes, 1839)

D IX,11. A III,11. P 14. V I,5. LL 27. Large cycloid scales cover body; much smaller scales on thorax; head only has some small embedded scales on sides of nape to orbital; small scales basally along dorsal and anal fins. Lateral line with three and a half scales to dorsal fin origin, descends below end of dorsal fin along three scales to continue along caudal peduncle. Mouth small, terminal with enlarged anterior canines. No great colour differences between stages; male without pink belly and ocellus. Widespread tropical Indo-Pacific from west Pacific to east Africa. Adults south to the Sydney area. Rocky reef slopes, usually 5-20 m, but shallow to 1 m on coral reefs; may venture to 40 m. Attains 11 cm.

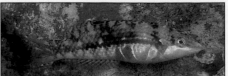

Halichoeres nebulosus Juv.

Halichoeres nebulosus Male ▲   *Halichoeres margaritaceus* ▼

PEARLY WRASSE

Halichoeres margaritaceus (Valenciennes, 1839)

D IX,11. A III,11. P 13. V I,5. LL 27. Large cycloid scales cover body; much smaller scales on thorax; head only has some small embedded scales on sides of nape to orbital; small scales basally along dorsal and anal fins. Lateral line with three and a half scales to dorsal fin origin, descends below end of dorsal fin along three scales to continue along caudal peduncle. Mouth small, terminal with enlarged anterior canines. No great colour differences between stages; male without pink belly and ocellus. Widespread tropical west to central Pacific and eastern Indian Ocean. Adults south to the Sydney area. Shallow weedy habitat, reef flats, rocky shores, usually not deeper than about 5 m. Attains 12 cm.

CHOAT'S WRASSE

Macropharyngodon choati Randall, 1978

D IX,11. A III,11. P 13. V I,5. LL 27. Body scales large, thin, cycloid, becoming small on thorax; most anterior ventral part of thorax naked. Head naked except for several rows of small scales on sides of nape. Lateral line with gradual curve, descends downward below end of dorsal fin over a few scales only. Mouth small, terminal; lips not fleshy; large projecting anterior canines in jaws and posteriorly in upper jaw at corner of mouth, the latter particularly large in TP. Distinctly coloured; juvenile pattern gradually changes to adult. Great Barrier Reef to central New South Wales, and New Caledonia. Lagoons to deep drop-offs to about 35 m. Tiny juveniles 12 mm long collected in Sydney from isolated patches of seagrass on sand. Attains 10 cm. Genus comprises 10 colourful species, similarly sized, widespread in tropical Indo-Pacific; four range into New South Wales.

Macropharyngodon choati Male ▼

Macropharyngodon choati Juv.

KUITER'S WRASSE
Macropharyngodon kuiteri Randall, 1978

D IX,12. A III,12. P 12. V I,5. LL 27. Body scales large, thin, cycloid, becoming small on thorax; most anterior ventral part naked. Head naked except for several rows of small scales on sides of nape. Lateral line with gradual curve, descends downward below end of dorsal fin over a few scales only. Mouth small, terminal; lips not fleshy; large projecting anterior canines in jaws and posteriorly in upper jaw at corner of mouth, the latter particularly large in TP. Distinctly coloured; juvenile pattern gradually changes to adult. Southern Great Barrier Reef to Montague Island, and New Caledonia. Adults deep along bottom of drop-offs. Juveniles along edge of rocky reefs near sand with weeds, in 10-30 m. Attains 10 cm.

Macropharyngodon kuiteri   Male ▲   Initial phase ▼

M. kuiteri   Tiny juv. (18.3 mm SL)

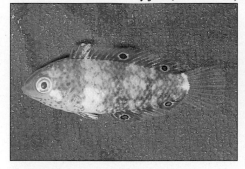

LEOPARD WRASSE
Macropharyngodon meleagris
(Valenciennes, 1839)

D IX,11. A III,11. P 12. V I,5. LL 27. Body scales large, thin, cycloid, becoming small on thorax; most anterior ventral part naked. Head naked except for several rows of small scales on sides of nape. Lateral line with gradual curve, descends downward below end of dorsal fin over a few scales only. Mouth small, terminal; lips not fleshy; large projecting anterior canines in jaws and posteriorly in upper jaw at corner of mouth, the latter particularly large in TP. Distinctly coloured; juvenile pattern gradually changes to adult. Widespread tropical west Pacific, but replaced by similar *M. ornatus* in Indonesia. Juveniles to southern New South Wales. Coastal to outer reefs from shallow reef flats to 30 m. Largest species in genus; attains 14 cm.

Macropharyngodon meleagris   Male ▼

Macropharyngodon meleagris   Juv.

283

BLACK LEOPARD WRASSE
Macropharyngodon negrosensis Herre, 1932

D IX,11. A III,11. P 12. V I,5. LL 27. Body scales large, thin, cycloid, becoming small on thorax; most anterior ventral part naked. Head naked except several rows of small scales on sides of nape. Lateral line with gradual curve, descends downward below end of dorsal fin over a few scales only. Mouth small, terminal; lips not fleshy; large projecting anterior canines in jaws and posteriorly in upper jaw at corner of mouth, the latter particularly large in TP. Distinctly coloured; juvenile pattern gradually changes to adult. Widespread tropical west Pacific to southern Japan and south to Montague Island. Generally deeper than other species, along coastal reefs. Juveniles in Sydney along outer edges of reefs near sand, often two or three together, in 10-25 m. Attains 12 cm.

Macropharyngodon negrosensis   Male ▲

Macropharyngodon negrosensis Juv.

RED-SPOT WRASSE
Stethojulis bandanensis (Bleeker, 1851)

D IX,11. A III,11. P 14. V I,5. LL 26. Large cycloid scales on body, somewhat enlarged on thorax. Head naked; no scales along dorsal and anal fin bases. Lateral line with gradual curve from shoulder, with one and a half scale rows above; descends below end of dorsal fin over two scales to caudal peduncle. Mouth small, terminal, no fleshy lips; anterior canines slightly enlarged, projecting. Juvenile similar to IP but TP has completely different colour pattern. Widespread tropical west Pacific; replaced by similar species in Hawaii and Indian Ocean. Adults south to Montague Island. Shallow reef flats and rubble slopes. Attains 14 cm. This genus comprises nine species; TP typically very different from IP with blue stripes; torpedo-shaped bodies, first anal fin spine minute. Distributed in tropical Indo-Pacific. Usually in small aggregations but in Japan *S. terina* observed in fast-moving, densely packed schools of several hundred individuals.

Stethojulis bandanensis   Male ▲   Initial phase ▼

CUT-RIBBON WRASSE
Stethojulis interrupta (Bleeker, 1851)

D IX,11. A III,11. P 13. V I,5. LL 26. Large cycloid scales on body, somewhat enlarged on thorax. Head naked; no scales along dorsal and anal fin bases. Lateral line with gradual curve from shoulder, with one and a half scale rows above; descends below end of dorsal fin over two scales to caudal peduncle. Mouth small, terminal, no fleshy lips; anterior canines slightly enlarged, projecting. Juvenile similar to IP but TP has completely different colour pattern. Widespread tropical west Pacific; replaced in Japan by closely related *S. terina*. Adults commonly south to Montague Island, usually in small aggregations. Coastal reefs and harbours to shallow offshore reefs. Usually shallow to 15 m. Attains 12 cm.

Stethojulis interrupta Male ▲ Young male still showing some colour from initial phase ▼

Stethojulis interrupta Initial phase

SILVER-STREAKED WRASSE
Stethojulis strigiventer (Bennett, 1832)

D IX,11. A III,11. P 15. V I,5. LL 26. Large cycloid scales on body, somewhat enlarged on thorax. Head naked; no scales along dorsal and anal fin bases. Lateral line with gradual curve from shoulder, with one and a half scale rows above; descends below end of dorsal fin over two scales to caudal peduncle. Mouth small, terminal, no fleshy lips; anterior canines slightly enlarged, projecting. Juvenile similar to IP but TP has completely different colour pattern. Widespread tropical west Pacific, including Micronesia, southern Japan and south to central New South Wales. Coastal reefs and lagoons in weed habitat to about 5 m; rarely deeper. Attains 14 cm.

Stethojulis strigiventer Male following goatfish (*Parupeneus barberinoides*) ▲ Initial phase ▼

Stethojulis strigiventer Tiny juv.

BLUE-RIBBON WRASSE
Stethojulis trilineata (Bloch and Schneider, 1801)

D IX,11. A III,11. P 13. V I,5. LL 26. Large cycloid scales on body, somewhat enlarged on thorax. Head naked; no scales along dorsal and anal fin bases. Lateral line with gradual curve from shoulder, with two and a half scale rows above; descends below end of dorsal fin over two scales to caudal peduncle. Mouth small, terminal, no fleshy lips; anterior canines slightly enlarged, projecting. Juvenile similar to IP but TP has completely different colour pattern. Widespread tropical west Pacific, but mainly along outer reefs; only known from islands in New South Wales; south to Montague Island. Attains 14 cm.

Stethojulis trilineata   Male above female during courtship ▲

CLEANER WRASSE
Labroides dimidiatus (Valenciennes, 1839)

D IX,10. A III,10. P 13. V I,5. LL 52-54. Small cycloid scales cover body and head except snout, interorbital and anterior ventral part of body. Lateral line with four to five scale rows above; gradual downward curve below end of dorsal fin to caudal peduncle. Mouth small, terminal; projecting anterior canines in jaws, upper ones recurved. Distinctly coloured; only small differences between sexes. Widespread tropical west Pacific from southern New South Wales to Japan and Micronesia, and to the Red Sea and east Africa. Rocky and coral reefs from estuaries to offshore reefs. Shallow to about 20 m. Attains 10 cm; usually much smaller. This genus comprises five small species distributed over most of the tropical Indo-Pacific. Specialised feeders, picking parasites off or attending to wounds of other fishes. Individuals choose strategic point on reef, often cave or elevated part of reef, to which other fishes come for service. Such places are called cleaning stations. Juveniles usually solitary, but adults may work in pairs or small aggregations with one male in charge. Large predators common customers. They assist by spreading fins and opening mouth to allow wrasses to clean teeth and gill-rakers, often by swimming through mouth and gills. Unfamiliar or new visiters greeted with up-and-down dance-like motion which appears to assure safety of Cleaner Wrasse. Interestingly, temperate species respond to tropical stragglers in the same way as tropical species.

Labroides dimidiatus Tiny juv.

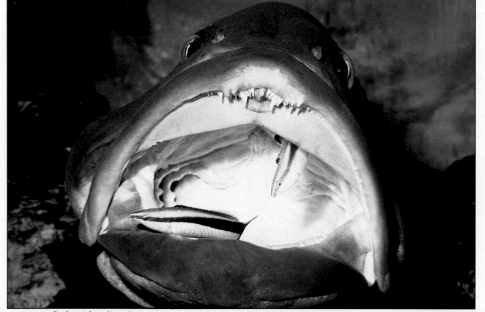

Labroides dimidiatus   Inspecting mouth of large grouper ▲   Inspecting author's fins ▼

TWO-TONE WRASSE
Thalassoma amblycephalum (Bleeker, 1856)

D VIII,13. A III,10-11. P 14. V I,5. LL 26. Body scales large, cycloid, slightly smaller on thorax. Lateral line with three to three and a half scales above, descends below end of

Thalassoma amblycephalum   Male ▼ Juv. ▲

Thalassoma lunare ▼

Thalassoma lutescens ▼

dorsal fin over one scale to caudal peduncle section. Mouth small, terminal; anterior teeth largest as slightly projecting canines. Dorsal fin low; caudal fin lunate with produced lobes in adults. Colour differs greatly between IP and TP. Common widespread species of tropical west to central Pacific from southern New South Wales to southern Japan. Coastal to outer reefs, shallow lagoons to rubble slopes to about 25 m. At Montague Island juveniles often in small aggregations of about 10 individuals; along ledges with sea-urchins in about 20 m. Attains 14 cm. Species of *Thalassoma* occur in all tropical seas; of the 15 or 16 species, eight are included here;

some of these rare, but occur as adults south to about central New South Wales. These fishes typically have complex colour patterns, elongate bodies with rounded heads, and actively swim with the pectoral fins in paddling fashion. Mostly small species; largest attain about 35 cm.

MOON WRASSE
Thalassoma lunare (Linnaeus, 1758)

D VIII,13. A III,11. P 15. V I,5. LL 26. Body scales large, cycloid, slightly smaller on thorax. Lateral line with two to two and a half scales above, descends below end of dorsal fin over one scale to caudal peduncle section. Mouth small, terminal; anterior teeth largest as slightly projecting canines. Dorsal fin low; caudal fin lunate with produced lobes in adults. Colour differs slightly between IP and TP. Common widespread species of the tropical west to central Pacific from southern New South Wales to southern Japan, and to the Red Sea and east Africa. Coastal to outer reefs, in estuaries and lagoons to 30 m. Juveniles often in small aggregations. Attains 22 cm.

Thalassoma lunare Juv.

YELLOW MOON WRASSE
Thalassoma lutescens (Lay and Bennett, 1839)

D VIII,13. A III,11. P 16. V I,5. LL 26. Body scales large, cycloid, slightly smaller on thorax. Lateral line with two to two and a half scales above, descends below end of dorsal fin over one scale to caudal peduncle section. Mouth small, terminal, anterior teeth largest as slightly projecting canines. Dorsal fin low; caudal fin lunate with produced lobes in adults. Colour differs slightly between IP and TP. Tropical west Pacific from central New South Wales to southern Japan, Hawaii, Rapa and east Indian Ocean. Most common towards cooler part of range. Outer reefs in lagoons and slopes to 30 m. Attains 25 cm.

Thalassoma lutescens Juv.

SIX-BAR WRASSE
Thalassoma hardwicke (Bennett, 1830)

D VIII,13. A III,11. P 16. V I,5. LL 26.
Body scales large, cycloid, slightly smaller
on thorax. Lateral line with two to two and a
half scales above, descends below end of
dorsal fin over one scale to caudal peduncle
section. Mouth small, terminal; anterior teeth
largest as slightly projecting canines. Dorsal
fin low; caudal fin lunate with produced lobes
in adults. Colour differs slightly between IP
and TP. Tropical west Pacific from northern
New South Wales to southern Japan, to east
Africa. Juveniles south to Sydney. Mainly
along outer reefs near drop-offs and lagoons,
shallow to about 15 m. Attains 20 cm.

Thalassoma hardwicke Juv.

SURGE WRASSE
Thalassoma purpureum (Forsskål, 1775)

D VIII,13. A III,11. P 16. V I,5. LL 26.
Body scales large, cycloid, slightly smaller
on thorax. Lateral line with three to three and
a half scales above, descends below end of
dorsal fin over one scale to caudal peduncle
section. Mouth small, terminal; anterior teeth
largest as slightly projecting canines. Dorsal
fin low; caudal fin lunate without produced
lobes in adults. Colour differs substantially
from IP to TP; large males green to dark blue
ventrally. Widespread in the tropical west
and central to south Pacific from Japan and
Hawaii to Easter Island, and to the Red Sea
and east Africa. Rare in New South Wales,
restricted to offshore islands; mainly outer
reefs in very shallow depths, usually surge
zones. Largest species in genus; attains
36 cm.

JANSEN'S WRASSE
Thalassoma janseni (Bleeker, 1856)

D VIII,13. A III,11. P 15. V I,5. LL 26.
Body scales large, cycloid, slightly smaller
on thorax. Lateral line with three to three and
a half scales above, descends below end of
dorsal fin over one scale to caudal peduncle
section. Mouth small, terminal; anterior teeth
largest as slightly projecting canines. Dorsal
fin low; caudal fin lunate with produced lobes
in adults. Colour differs slightly between IP
and TP; male more colourful. Tropical west
Pacific from northern New South Wales to

Thalassoma purpureum   Male ▲   Initial phase ▼

Thalassoma janseni   Adult ▲   Juv. ▼

southern Japan and Micronesia, and Indian
Ocean to the Maldives. Juveniles south to
Sydney. Outer reef lagoons and slopes to
about 20 m. Attains 20 cm. East Australian
fish has different colour pattern compared to
elsewhere; name used here only tentative as it
may represent new species.

GREEN-BARRED WRASSE
Thalassoma trilobatum (Lacepède, 1801)

D VIII,13. A III,11. P 16. V I,5. LL 26. Body scales large, cycloid, slightly smaller on thorax. Lateral line with two to two and a half scales above, descends below end of dorsal fin over one scale to caudal peduncle section. Mouth small, terminal; anterior teeth largest as slightly projecting canines. Dorsal fin low; caudal fin lunate without produced lobes in adults. Colour differs substantially from IP to TP; IPs of Ladder Wrasse and Surge Wrasse remarkably similar. Widespread tropical Indo-Pacific from southern Japan to New South Wales and Tonga, and to east Africa. Exposed reefs, just below surge zone usually to about 5 m, venturing to 10 m at most. Attains 27 cm.

Thalassoma trilobatum   Male ▲ Initial phase ▼

Thalassoma trilobatum   Tiny juv. (23 mm SL)

RED-RIBBON WRASSE
Thalassoma quinquevittatum (Lay and Bennett, 1839)

D VIII,13. A III,11. P 16. V I,5. LL 26. Body scales large, cycloid, slightly smaller on thorax. Lateral line with two to two and a half scales above, descends below end of dorsal fin over one scale to caudal peduncle section. Mouth small, terminal; anterior teeth largest as slightly projecting canines. Dorsal fin low; caudal fin lunate without produced lobes in adults. Colour differs slightly between IP and TP; males more colourful. Widespread tropical Indo-Pacific, from New South Wales to southern Japan, Micronesia, and to east Africa. Adult observed at Seal Rocks, New South Wales. Coastal to outer reef crests; shallow to about 10 m. Attains 15 cm.

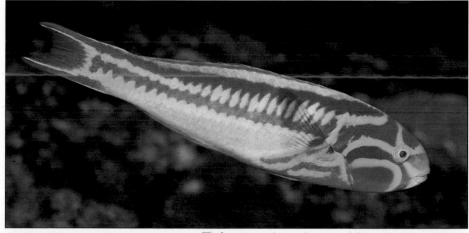

Thalassoma quinquevittatum   Male ▲ Initial phase ▼

DIAMOND WRASSE
Anampses caeruleopunctatus Rüppell, 1828

D IX,12. A III,12. P 13. V I,5. LL 27. Body covered with thin but large cycloid scales, slightly smaller on thorax and sides of nape. Mid-region of nape scaleless; head naked. Lateral line nearly straight from origin to second last ray; descends over one scale to continue along caudal peduncle. Mouth small, terminal with moderately fleshy lips; pairs of forward projecting teeth in jaws, upper chisel-like and up-curving, lower rounded and down-curving. Several colour-forms from small juvenile to TP. Widespread tropical Indo-Pacific from central New South Wales to southern Japan and Micronesia, and to the Red Sea and east Africa. Juveniles commonly south to Montague Island. Reef crest and rubble slopes from 1-30 m. Attains 30 cm. Indo-Pacific genus with 13 species of which five are included here; typified by chisel-like teeth. Several small juveniles swim in unusual way with head down, body twisting.

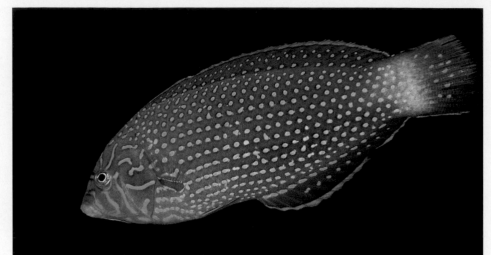

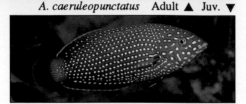

A. caeruleopunctatus Adult ▲ Juv. ▼

ELEGANS WRASSE
Anampses elegans Ogilby, 1889

D IX,12. A III,12. P 13. V I,5. LL 27. Body covered with thin but large cycloid scales, slightly smaller on thorax and sides of nape. Mid-region of nape scaleless; head naked. Lateral line nearly straight from origin to second last ray, descends over one scale to continue along caudal peduncle. Mouth small, terminal with moderately fleshy lips; pairs of forward projecting teeth in jaws, upper chisel-like and up-curving, lower rounded and down-curving. Several colour-forms from small juvenile to TP. Central to southern New South Wales, Lord Howe Island and northern New Zealand. Juveniles in weeds in coastal bays and harbours. Large juveniles in small aggregations on coastal rocky reefs; adults usually deeper to about 30 m. Attains 30 cm.

Anampses elegans Adult ▼ Juv. ▲

BLUE-TAIL WRASSE
Anampses femininus Randall, 1972

D IX,12. A III,12. P 13. V I,5. LL 27. Body covered with thin but large cycloid scales, slightly smaller on thorax and sides of nape. Mid-region of nape scaleless; head naked. Lateral line nearly straight from origin to second last ray, descends over one scale to continue along caudal peduncle. Mouth small, terminal with moderately fleshy lips; pairs of forward projecting teeth in jaws, upper chisel-like and up-curving, lower rounded and down-curving. Similar colour-forms from small juvenile to TP. South Pacific from most of New South Wales, Lord Howe Island to Eastern Island. Outer reefs in small aggregations, usually in at least 10-40 m. Small juveniles secretive, in weeds; larger specimens quickly dive into kelp for cover. Juvenile similar to IP. Attains 12 cm.

Anampses femininus Male ▼

Anampses femininus Juvs.

OLIVE-GREEN WRASSE
Anampses geographicus Valenciennes, 1839

D IX,12. A III,12. P 13. V I,5. LL 48-50. Body covered with small cycloid scales, slightly smaller on thorax and sides of nape. Mid-region of nape scaleless; head naked. Lateral line nearly straight from origin to fourth last ray, descends over one scale to continue along caudal peduncle. Mouth small, terminal with moderately fleshy lips; pairs of forward projecting teeth in jaws, upper chisel-like and up-curving, lower rounded and down-curving. Similar colour-forms from small juvenile to TP. Widespread tropical Indo-Pacific from New South Wales to southern Japan and Micronesia, to Fiji, and west to Mauritius. Reef crests and slopes in algae and soft coral habitat. Attains 16 cm.

Anampses geographicus Juv.

Anampses geographicus Male ▲

BLACK-BACK WRASSE
Anampses neoguinaicus Bleeker, 1878

D IX,12. A III,12. P 13. V I,5. LL 27. Body covered with thin but large cycloid scales, slightly smaller on thorax and sides of nape. Mid-region of nape scaleless; head naked. Lateral line nearly straight from origin to second last ray, descends over one scale to continue along caudal peduncle. Mouth small, terminal with moderately fleshy lips; pairs of forward projecting teeth in jaws, upper chisel-like and up-curving, lower rounded and down-curving. Similar colour-forms from small juvenile to TP. Known from certain locations of the west Pacific, Great Barrier Reef, southern Japan to Taiwan, and New Caledonia; juveniles south to Montague Island (with corals). Outer reef lagoons and rubble slopes with rich coral growth. Attains 12 cm.

Anampses neoguinaicus Juv.

CANDY WRASSE
Pseudojuloides cerasinus (Snyder, 1904)

D IX,12. A III,12. P 13. V I,5. LL 27. Large cycloid scales cover body, much smaller on thorax and nape; head naked. Lateral line almost straight, four scales above to dorsal fin origin; descends abruptly below fifth-last dorsal fin ray to continuing portion along caudal peduncle. Body very elongate; snout pointed; mouth small, terminal with fleshy lips. Anterior canines projecting, well devel-oped, upper slightly out-curving. Dramatic colour differences between sexes. Developing male kept in aquarium took less than one week to completely change from the plain IP to TP colouration. Only widespread species, from the tropical west Pacific to Hawaii and various other Pacific locations to east Africa. Adults south to Montague Island. Deep offshore reefs, usually beyond 20 m, known from 60 m. Usually sparse reefs with sponges or algae below drop-offs. Attains 12 cm. Little-known genus with about 10 species; most are deep dwelling for labrids; distributed throughout the tropical Indo-Pacific; two included here. Mostly very elongate with small caudal fin. Behaviour, particularly feeding, similar to *Anampses* species.

Pseudojuloides cerasinus   Male ▼ Juv. ▲

LONG GREEN WRASSE
Pseudojuloides elongatus Ayling and Russell, 1977

D IX,12. A III,12. P 12. V I,5. LL 27. Large cycloid scales cover body, much smaller on thorax and nape; head naked. Lateral line almost straight, with three scales above to dorsal fin origin; descends abruptly below fifth-last dorsal fin ray to continuing portion along caudal peduncle. Body very elongate; snout pointed; mouth small, terminal with fleshy lips. Anterior canines projecting, well developed, upper slightly out-curving; large adults with additional large canine tooth at corners of mouth. Variable from brown to green depending on environment. TP with additional colours. Disjunct distribution with three separate populations: east Australia and New Zealand, west Australian coast, and Japan. In New South Wales, known from the Solitary Islands to Montague Island, including Sydney Harbour. Mainly in kelp areas, secretive, in small to large aggregations; usually one male present. Mostly shallow, depending on weeds or kelp, ranging from 2-25 m. Attains 15 cm. Japanese population may represent another species; TP markedly differently coloured and they seem slightly deeper bodied.

Pseudojuloides elongatus   Male ▼ Juv. ▲

SMALL-SPOTTED WRASSE
Cirrhilabrus punctatus Randall and Kuiter, 1989

D XI,9. III,9. P 14-16. V I,5. LL 16-18+6-9. Large cycloid scales cover body and head,

Cirrhilabrus punctatus   Adult ▼   Juv. ▲

Pteragogus enneacanthus ▼

Cheilinus bimaculatus ▼

except snout and interorbital; a series of large elongated scales extend onto bases of dorsal and anal fins. Lateral line interrupted; first part high on sides with two scales to dorsal fin origin, second part along middle of caudal peduncle. Grey or pinkish-brown to green; small spot on each body scale. Small juveniles dark brown with conspicuous white nose. Eastern Australia to Papua New Guinea and Fiji, south to Montague Island. Rubble reefs, from shallow lagoons and harbours to deeper reefs offshore to about 35 m. Attains 10 cm. *Cirrhilabrus* comprises about 35 small species, most of which are recently described,

some not yet named. Feed on zooplankton, often well above reefs, usually in large aggregations. Juveniles secretive, among rubble and rocks. They feature a curious double pupil which enables them to recognise tiny planktonic animals on which they feed.

COCKEREL WRASSE
Pteragogus enneacanthus (Bleeker, 1852)

D IX,11. A III,9. P 13. V I,5. LL 23-24. Body slightly compressed, covered with large cycloid scales which extend on head to cheeks. Lateral line continuous, smoothly curved along upper sides following body contour to midline, then straight along caudal peduncle. First two dorsal spines distinctly longer in adults, extended filaments from tips. Colour extremely variable between habitats; individuals can change quickly to match surroundings. Brown-red in deep water; green or pale brown in shallow vegetation habitats. Widespread tropical west Pacific, reaching south to Sydney Harbour. Various habitats from shallow algae reefs to deep offshore on soft bottom with sponges and hydroid colonies. Attains about 15 cm. This genus comprises about five species variously distributed from the western Indian Ocean and Red Sea to the central Pacific, only one of which ranges to New South Wales. Mostly small, secretive species, usually hiding among dense weeds. *P. amboinensis* (Bleeker, 1856) junior synonym based on female.

TWO-SPOT MAORI WRASSE
Cheilinus bimaculatus Valenciennes, 1840

D IX,9-11. A III,8. P 12-13. V I,5. LL 14-16+5-7. Large cycloid scales cover body and head, except snout and base of dorsal fin. Lateral line interrupted; first part smoothly curved high along sides, second part straight, along midline of caudal peduncle. Widespread tropical Indo-Pacific from west Pacific to east Africa. Commonly ranging into warm-temperate zones of Japan and Australia; on the east coast adults as far south as Montague Island. Rubble reefs with algae or weeds in shallow lagoons to 100 m where it lives in sponge habitats. Small species; attains 15 cm. Most widespread species of *Cheilinus* and the only one of the 15 species distributed in the tropical Indo-Pacific which tolerates cooler conditions. Also smallest species in genus, most others averaging 30-40 cm; giant Hump-Headed Maori Wrasse largest at 2.3 m.

Cheilinus bimaculatus   Juv.

ORIENTAL WRASSE
Cheilinus orientalis Günther, 1862

D IX,10. A III,8. P 12. V I,5. LL 13-14+7-8. Body covered with large cycloid scales extending onto base of dorsal fin and over head to snout. Lateral line interrupted, first part smoothly curved high along sides, second part straight, along midline of caudal peduncle. Juveniles with distinct ocelli posteriorly along body midline. Adults variable from pale reddish-brown. Widespread tropical west Pacific, ranging south to Sydney Harbour. From outer reef lagoons to deep slopes with rich growth of corals or other invertebrates. Recorded to 70 m. Juveniles usually among crinoids. Attains 15 cm.

Cheilinus orientalis Juv.

NEW CALEDONIAN WRASSE
Cheilinus sp.

Description of this species in preparation by Dr Martin Gomon (Museum of Victoria) who is revising the genus. Meristic data will be available after publication of the description. Distinctly marked; variable from pale brown to bright red; black posterior margin on caudal fin. Little-known species, presently only known from New Caledonia and single 60 mm specimen from Sydney Harbour which was collected from an algae habitat in 4 m. Attains about 20 cm.

KEELHEAD WRASSE
Xyrichtys jacksoniensis (Ramsay, 1881)

D II,VII,12. A III,12. P 12. A I,5. LL 22+6. Body covered with large cycloid scales, slightly smaller on thorax. Vertical patch of small scales below eye. Lateral line in two parts; first portion to end of dorsal fin, second portion continuous below along caudal peduncle. Mouth terminal without fleshy lips; pair of long anterior canines in each jaw. First two dorsal fin spines separate from others by double normal space between spines, connected by membrane, very long in small juveniles (more than 25 mm). Body and head compressed, dorsally elevated in adults; snout almost vertical, thin keel-like anteriorly; eyes placed high on head. Juveniles extremely variable from black through brown or green to pale sandy colour with various banded patterns. Known from Sydney Harbour and a few trawled specimens off New South Wales. Attains 24 cm. Genus in need of revision;

Cheilinus sp. ▲   *Xyrichtys jacksoniensis* ▼

X. jacksoniensis Various juv. colour-forms ▼

comprises an estimated 25 species of which six are found in the Atlantic; remainder found in the Indo-Pacific, of which two are included here. Tropical sand-dwellers, often in the open well away from reefs, quickly diving into sand if danger approaches. A few occur in relatively shallow water, some only as juveniles.

LEAF WRASSE
Xyrichtys dea Temminck and Schlegel, 1846

D II,VII,12. A III,12. P 12. A I,5. LL 22+6. Body covered with large cycloid scales, slightly smaller on thorax. Vertical patch of small scales below eye. Lateral line in two parts; first portion to end of dorsal fin, second portion continuous below, along caudal peduncle. Mouth terminal without fleshy lips; pair of long anterior canines in each jaw. First two dorsal fin spines separate from others by about four times normal space between spines, very long in juveniles up to about 10 cm; not connected by membrane in larger juveniles, adults. Body and head compressed, dorsally elevated in adults; snout almost vertical, thin keel-like anteriorly; eyes placed high on head. Juveniles extremely variable from black through brown or green to pale sandy colour. Widespread tropical Indo-Pacific, including Red Sea, east Africa, Hawaii and from central New South Wales to southern Japan. Juveniles south to Montague Island; in vicinity of rocky reefs with small outcrops or weeds on sand flats or gradual slopes in about 5-25 m. Adults usually deep to more than 100 m. Attains 36 cm.

SEAGRASS WRASSE
Novaculichthys macrolepidotus (Bloch, 1791)

D IX,12-14. A III,12-14. P 12. V I,5. LL 20+6-9. Body covered with large cycloid scales. Head naked except for patch of small scales below eye. Lateral line interrupted; first portion with two scale-rows above to below about fifth last dorsal fin ray, lower portion along caudal peduncle, beginning and end of interrupted part overlapping at a vertical. Mouth terminal without fleshy lips; anterior canines in each jaw. Varies between brown and green, associated with habitat. Tropical west Pacific to west Indian Ocean and Red Sea. Rare in New South Wales; known from Seal Rocks. Shallow seagrasses in lagoons and protected bays to a few metres depth. Attains 14 cm. Small genus with three Indo-Pacific species; two included here.

REINDEER WRASSE
Novaculichthys taeniourus (Lacepède, 1801)

D IX,12-13. A III,12-13. P 13. LL 19-20+6. Body covered with large cycloid scales. Head naked except for row of small scales below eye. Lateral line interrupted; first portion with two scale-rows above to below about fifth last dorsal fin ray, lower portion along caudal peduncle, beginning and end of interrupted part at a vertical. Mouth terminal without fleshy lips; anterior canines in each jaw. First and second dorsal fin spines greatly produced in juveniles. Juvenile and adult with different colour patterns. Widespread tropical Indo-Pacific, west Pacific from southern Japan, Micronesia to northern New South Wales and to the Red Sea and east Africa. New South Wales offshore reefs and islands, to Broughton Island as juveniles. Sparse reefs on sand with tall algaes. Common on tropical coral reef flats. Attains 30 cm. Also known as Rockmover Wrasse or Dragon Wrasse.

Novaculichthys macrolepidotus ▲   *Novaculichthys taeniourus* ▼

RAZOR WRASSE
Cymolutes torquatus Valenciennes, 1840

D IX,13. A II,12. P 11-13. V I,5. LL 90 (approximately). Body covered with very small cycloid scales; head naked. Lateral line high along upper sides to below end of dorsal fin, descends abruptly to continue along caudal peduncle. Body compressed, head profile fairly steep. Mouth terminal without fleshy lips; pair of long anterior canines in each jaw. Greenish with variable mottling in young; adults with diagonal lines. Widespread tropical Indo-Pacific from New South Wales to southern Japan and to east Africa. Juveniles south to Sydney Harbour; secretive, in seagrasses and green weeds on sand. Adults in open patches but wary. Probably more common than it seems. Attains 20 cm. This genus comprises two or three similar species.

Cymolutes torquatus Adult ▼ Juv. ▲

MAORI WRASSE
Ophthalmolepis lineolata (Valenciennes, 1838)

D IX,12-13. A III,13. P 14. V I,5. LL 52-56. Body covered with small cycloid scales; head naked. Lateral line slightly curved at origin, four to five scale rows above, descends abruptly below fourth last dorsal fin ray to section along caudal peduncle. Mouth small, terminal; a series of strong teeth in each jaw, anterior pairs enlarged, projecting forward with recurved tips. Colour differs slightly between different stages and sexes; males gain bright blue lines or scribbles on head. Southern waters, except Tasmania; southern Queensland to south Western Australia. Coastal bays to offshore reefs, often in loose aggregations. Shallow to at least 60 m. Attains 40 cm. Monotypic genus.

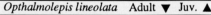

Opthalmolepis lineolata Adult ▼ Juv. ▲

Coris picta Juv. ▲

COMB WRASSE
Coris picta (Bloch and Schneider, 1801)

D IX,12. A III,12. P 14. V I,5. LL 79-83. Body covered with very small cycloid scales; head naked. Lateral line gradually curving from origin to below fifth and sixth dorsal fin spines, continues straight to below last few rays, then descends abruptly to caudal peduncle section. Mouth small, terminal, without fleshy lips; anterior teeth in each jaw canine-like, slightly recurving. Differences in colour between stages or sexes only slight. Male pattern used for display or territorial disputes only temporary, can change either way in a few seconds. Only known from eastern Australia from southern Queensland to northern Victoria, Lord Howe Island, and New Zealand. Coastal to offshore reefs along rocks over sand. Juveniles enter harbours or rocky estuaries. More common on offshore reefs where they occur in large aggregations. Juveniles regularly observed picking parasites off other fishes; sometimes adult-sized fishes clean other fishes; usually in small to large aggregations. Attains 24 cm. Closely related to *C. musume* in Japan. This genus comprises an estimated 20 species, one of which is in the eastern Atlantic, the others distributed throughout the tropical Indo-Pacific. Diverse genus with sizes ranging from about 10 cm to 1 m. With the exception of a few, they have very different-coloured juveniles, and are strikingly marked or coloured. Eight species, including several tropical expatriates, known from New South Wales and included here.

Coris picta Male ▲ Initial phase ▼

Coris pictoides ▼

PIXIE CORIS
Coris pictoides Randall and Kuiter, 1982

D IX,12. A III,12. P 14. V I,5. LL 48-51. Body covered with small cycloid scales; head naked. Lateral line gradually curves from origin to below fifth and sixth dorsal fin spines, continues straight to below last few rays, then descends abruptly to caudal peduncle section. Mouth small, terminal, without fleshy lips; anterior teeth in each jaw canine-like, slightly recurving. Differences in colour between stages or sexes only slight. West Pacific from New South Wales to the Philippines and north-west Australia. One small specimen known from Clovelly, Sydney, at 20 m. Usually deep, 30 m or more, along coastal slopes and inner reefs. Attains 12 cm.

Coris pictoides Juv.

YELLOW-LINED CORIS
Coris aurilineata Randall and Kuiter, 1982

D IX,12. A III,12. P 14. V I,5. LL 48-51. Body covered with small cycloid scales; head naked. Lateral line gradually curves from origin to below fifth and sixth dorsal fin spines, continues straight to below last few rays, then descends abruptly to caudal peduncle section. Mouth small, terminal, without fleshy lips; anterior teeth in each jaw canine-like, slightly recurving. Differences in colour between stages or sexes only slight. Coastal eastern Australia from Keppel Island to Bass Point, New South Wales. Rocky reefs with algae growth. Usually shallow, 3-10 m, in small loose aggregations. Attains 14 cm.

Coris aurilineata Juv.

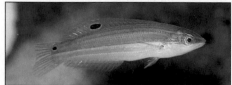

DOUBLE HEADER
Coris bulbifrons Randall and Kuiter, 1982

D IX,12. A III,12. P 14. V I,5. LL 61-66. Body covered with small cycloid scales; head naked. Lateral line gradually curves from origin to below fifth and sixth dorsal fin spines, continues straight to below last few rays, then descends abruptly to caudal peduncle section. Mouth small, terminal, without fleshy lips; anterior teeth in each jaw canine-like, slightly recurving. Juveniles with distinct colour pattern to about 20 cm, then become more like adults; differences in further stages or sexes only slight, but fleshy hump above eyes becomes very large in males. Only known from Lord Howe Island region and central New South Wales. Common in lagoon at Lord Howe Island which has depth of 8 m. Outside the reef to about 20 m. Usually in groups with large male in charge. Attains at least 1m. Reported to 1.4 m. Largest *Coris*.

Coris bulbifrons Adult ▼ Juv. ▲

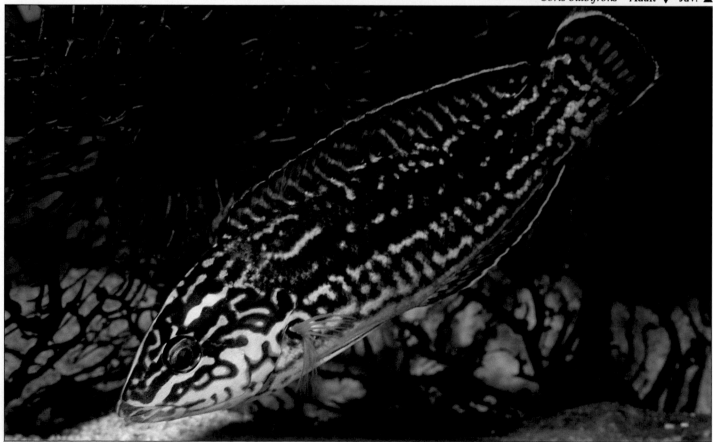

PINK-LINED CORIS
Coris dorsomacula Fowler, 1908

D IX,12. A III,12. P 13. V I,5. LL 50-55. Body covered with small cycloid scales; head naked. Lateral line gradually curves from origin to below fifth and sixth dorsal fin spines, continues straight to below last few rays, then descends abruptly to caudal peduncle section. Mouth small, terminal, without fleshy lips; anterior teeth in each jaw canine-like, slightly recurving. Juveniles plain; colour pattern becomes increasingly complex during growth. Widespread tropical west Pacific, ranging into warm-temperate zones. Adults from Japan, near Tokyo to southern New South Wales. Rubble reef slopes and low algae reef on sand from about 10-40 m. Small juveniles secretive, in algae. Attains 22 cm.

Coris dorsomacula Juv.

Coris dorsomacula Male ▲ Initial phase ▼

VARIEGATED RAINBOWFISH
Coris batuensis (Bleeker, 1856)

D IX,11. A III,11. P 13-15. V I,5. LL 51-54. Body covered with small cycloid scales, head naked. Lateral line gradually curves from origin to below fifth and sixth dorsal fin spines, continues straight to below last few rays where it descends abruptly to caudal peduncle section. Mouth small, terminal, without fleshy lips; anterior teeth in each jaw canine-like, slightly recurving. Variable from greenish to pale sandy. Juveniles with several ocelli in the dorsal fin which fade with age. Widespread tropical Indo-Pacific; replaced by closely related *C. variegata* (Rüppell) in the Red Sea. In Australia, south to Sydney Harbour. Attains 18 cm. *C. schroederi* (Bleeker) junior synonym.

Coris batuensis Male ▼

Coris batuensis Juv.

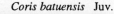

KING WRASSE
Coris sandageri (Hector, 1884)

D IX,12. A III,12. P 14. V I,5. LL 88-95. Body covered with very small cycloid scales; head naked. Lateral line gradually curves from origin to below fifth and sixth dorsal fin spines, continues straight to below last few rays, then descends abruptly to caudal peduncle section. Mouth small, terminal, without fleshy lips; anterior teeth in each jaw canine-like, slightly recurving. Small juveniles, IP and TP considerably different in colour. Central New South Wales to northern Victoria, and New Zealand. Coastal and offshore reefs near weed-covered rocks and sand. Usually in small aggregations of IP over deep sand-slopes from 20-40 m with large TP nearby. Attains 45 cm.

Coris sandageri Male ▼ Initial phase ▲

Coris sandageri Juv.

CLOWN CORIS
Coris aygula Lacepède, 1801

D IX,12. A III,12. P 14. V I,5. LL 63-65. Body covered with very small cycloid scales; head naked. Lateral line gradually curves from origin to below fifth and sixth dorsal fin spines, continues straight to below last few rays, then descends abruptly to caudal peduncle section. Mouth small, terminal, without fleshy lips; anterior teeth in each jaw canine-like, slightly recurving. Small juveniles, IP and TP considerably different in colour. Tropical west Pacific from central New South Wales to southern Japan, Micronesia, Rapa and west to the Red Sea and east Africa. Juveniles south to Bass Point; in shallow coastal bays among small rocks on sand near reefs. Adults along coastal reef-fringes to about 30 m. Attains 60 cm. Records of much larger fish probably based on Lord Howe Island Double Header.

Coris aygula Male ▲ Initial phase ▼

Coris aygula Juv.

GAIMARD'S WRASSE
Coris gaimard (Quoy and Gaimard, 1824)

D IX,12. A III,12. P 13. V I,5. LL 70-75. Body covered with very small cycloid scales; head naked. Lateral line gradually curves from origin to below fifth and sixth dorsal fin spines, continues straight to below last few rays, then descends abruptly to caudal peduncle section. Mouth small, terminal, without fleshy lips; anterior teeth in each jaw canine-like, slightly recurving. Small juveniles, IP and TP considerably different in colour. Tropical west Pacific from central New South Wales to Southern Japan, Micronesia and east Indian Ocean. Mainly with rubble reef sections, shallow outer reef flats and slopes; to at least 50 m. Attains 35 cm.

Coris gaimard Male ▲ Initial phase ▼

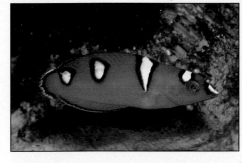

Coris gaimard Juv.

PINK WRASSE
Pseudocoris yamashiroi (Schmidt, 1930)

D IX,12. A III,12. P 13. V I,5. LL 70-72. Body covered with very small cycloid scales; head naked. Lateral line gradually curves from origin to below last few rays, then descends abruptly to caudal peduncle section. Mouth small, terminal, without fleshy lips; teeth small, anterior-most largest and slightly projecting. Little variation in colour from juvenile to IP. Widespread tropical west Pacific from central New South Wales to southern Japan; juveniles south to Montague Island. Common shallow-water species in Indonesia on coastal slopes and reef flats to about 10 m. Usually deep on the Great Barrier Reef from 20-40 m. Juveniles at Montague Island in small aggregations along bottom of drop-offs in at least 15 m. Attains 15 cm. This genus closely related to *Coris* but the four or five known species are planktivorous, usually feeding well above reefs in small to large aggregations or mixed with other species mid-water.

Pseudocoris yamashiroi Juv.

RINGED WRASSE
Hologymnosus annulatus (Lacepède, 1801)

D IX,12. A III,12. P 13. V I,5. LL 110 (approximately). Body covered with tiny cycloid scales which extend over head to above orbital; head then naked. Lateral line high along sides with about eight scale-rows above to about fourth-last dorsal fin ray; descends abruptly to continue along caudal peduncle. Mouth small, terminal; pairs of projecting canines in each jaw. Various colour variations during growth and between sexes. Widespread in the tropical west Pacific and to west Indian Ocean. Juveniles south to Montague Island. Rubble reef flats and slopes. Found in small aggregations; often mixed with other species of same genus. Attains 36 cm. Small genus containing four Indo-Pacific species; three included here. Slender fishes with very small scales.

Hologymnosus annulatus   Adult ▼   Juv. ▲

NARROW-BANDED WRASSE
Hologymnosus doliatus (Lacepède, 1801)

D IX,12. A III,12. P 13. V I,5. LL 105 (approximately). Body covered with tiny cycloid scales which extend over head to above orbital; head then naked. Lateral line high along sides with about eight scale rows above to about fourth-last dorsal fin ray; descends abruptly to continue along caudal peduncle. Mouth small, terminal; pairs of projecting canines in each jaw. Various colour variations during growth and between sexes. Widespread in the tropical west Pacific and to west Indian Ocean. Juveniles south to Montague Island. Rubble reef flats and slopes. Found in small aggregations; often mixed with other species of same genus. Attains 36 cm.

Hologymnosus doliatus   Adult ▼   Juv. ▲

PALE SLENDER WRASSE
Hologymnosus longipes (Günther, 1862)

D IX,12. A III,12. P 13. V I,5. LL 98 (approximately). Body covered with tiny cycloid scales which extend over head to above orbital; head then naked. Lateral line high along sides with about eight scale rows above to about fourth-last dorsal fin ray; descends abruptly to continue along caudal peduncle. Mouth small, terminal; pairs of projecting canines in each jaw. Various colour variations during growth and between sexes. Only known from the tropical south-west Pacific, on outer reefs and islands. Juveniles south to Montague Island. Rubble reef flats and slopes. Found in small aggregations; often mixed with other species of same genus. Attains 30 cm. Similar species with identical juvenile stage is found in the tropical north-west Pacific.

CIGAR WRASSE
Cheilio inermis (Forsskål, 1775)

D IX,12-14. A III,11-12. P 12-13. V I,5. LL 45-59. Body covered with small, diamond-shaped cycloid scales, smaller on thorax; head naked except for small scales over small area in front of and below eyes. Lateral line along upper side, gradually curving down about halfway to continue along midline and caudal peduncle. Body very slender; long pointed head. Mouth moderately large; small teeth, anterior-most enlarged, in jaws. Colour varies little between stages, but sometimes a bright yellow form. Widespread tropical Indo-Pacific from west Pacific to Hawaii, Japan to New South Wales and west to the Red Sea and south Africa. Seagrass and weed areas, or soft corals on some reefs. In Sydney Harbour, observed in kelp. Attains 48 cm. Single Indo-Pacific genus which seems to have much in common with species of next family, temperate Odacidae.

CALES AND WEED-WHITINGS
FAMILY ODACIDAE

This wrasse-like family of temperate fishes is restricted to Australian and New Zealand waters. With four genera and 12 species they are well represented in these waters, inhabiting the sea-grasses and kelp or other weed-covered reefs. They differ from the closely related Labridae mainly in internal features, teeth which are more or less fused and have cutting edges, and a ventral fin which has only four rays or is absent altogether. Like the wrasses, they display dramatic changes in colour during growth and between sexes, and males, deriving from females, dominate a number of females. The bright colours displayed by males are mostly restricted to fins and only show when they are erected, thus with fins relaxed they remain camouflaged. Being primarily associated with the vegetation on reefs and sand restricts them to shallow coastal reefs and estuaries, where they are commonly observed in often large aggregations over shallow seagrass beds. A few species venture to deeper waters to the limit of the kelp range, about 25 m. Most species feed on various invertebrate species which are picked off the weeds or substrate, and a few feed on algaes or weed as well. Some of the smaller species have been observed cleaning other fishes and also feed on swimming mysids. Small juveniles are very secretive and extremely well camouflaged, often mimicking the seagrass or weed they live in. Some adults, too, mimic the seagrass and line up with the general flow of the leaves. Sizes range from about 10-45 cm. All of the 10 species endemic to Australia are included here. The remaining two species are New Zealand endemics.

BLUE WEED-WHITING
Haletta semifasciata (Valenciennes, 1840)

D XVII-XVIII,12-13. A III,10-12. P 14-16. V 1,4. LL 50-57. Small cycloid scales cover body, extend over nape to above posterior margin of preopercle. Opercle mostly scaled; cheek with patch of scales below and behind eye. Lateral line gradually curves down, continues along midline of body. Head pointed; snout moderately long; mouth with thickened lips; teeth in jaws mostly fused but with recognisable tips. Fins rounded. Colour of juveniles variable, matching weeds; green to reddish-brown, usually with whitish-silvery streak on sides. Adults grey to blue. Entire south coast from Sydney to Houtman Abrolhos, and northern to south-eastern Tasmania. Shallow seagrass beds to about 15 m. Attains 35 cm. Monotypic genus.

Haletta semifasciata   Male ▲   Initial phase ▼

Haletta semifasciata   Juv.

LITTLE ROCK-WHITING
Neoodax balteatus (Valenciennes, 1840)

D XV-XVII,11-14. A II-III,11-14. P 13-16. V I,4. LL 33-38. Moderate-sized cycloid scales cover body, most of opercle. Narrow vertical patch of scales behind eye. Lateral line with short gradual curve down, continues along midline of body. Head pointed; snout moderately long, mouth half its length; teeth in jaws mostly fused but with recognisable tips. Fins rounded. Variable between green and brown. Entire south coast from just north of Sydney to Cockburn Sound, and all of Tasmania. Seagrass beds as well as rocky reefs with little vegetation. Usually in small to large aggregations in seagrasses, solitary or two or three together on rocky reefs. Shallow to about 20 m. Attains about 16 cm. Monotypic genus.

Neoodax balteatus Juvs.

SHARP-NOSE ROCK-WHITING
Siphonognathus caninus (Scott, 1976)

D XV-XVI,11-13. A III,10-12. P 13-14. V I,4. LL 41-49. Moderate-sized cycloid scales cover body, most of opercle. Narrow vertical patch of scales behind eye. Lateral line with short gradual curve down, continues along midline of body. Head pointed; snout moderately long, mouth half its length; teeth in jaws mostly fused but with recognisable tips. First three or four first dorsal fin spines long, followed by progressively shorter ones, last few very short but increasing in length; soft-rayed portion only slightly lower than tall spinous part. Green or brown; TP with gaudy colours in fins, blue lines on body which "turn on" during display. Rocky vegetated reefs, usually deeper than other species. Commonly observed at 30 m at Wilson's Promontory. Mostly common in South and Western Australia to Rottnest Island but extends with seemingly isolated populations east to Wilson's Promontory. Attains 12 cm. This genus contains six species, all included here.

Siphonognathus caninus Male ▲ Initial phase ▼

LONG-RAY WEED-WHITING
Siphonognathus radiatus (Quoy and Gaimard, 1834)

D XVII-XX,11-13. A III,9-11. P 12-14. V I,4. LL 38-42. Moderate-sized cycloid scales cover body, extend over nape to interorbital and most of opercle; band down behind eye to cheek. Lateral line with short gradual curve down, continues along midline of body. Head pointed; snout moderately long, mouth slightly more than half its length; teeth in jaws mostly fused but with recognisable tips. Large TPs have extended fin rays heading dorsal and ventral fins, and centrally in caudal fin, which becomes pointed. Usually bright green but occasionally brown on rocky reefs; juveniles with white streak on sides. Mainly secretive, in shallow seagrass beds to about 10 m. Attains 20 cm.

Siphonognathus radiatus   Male ▲   Initial phase ▼

Siphonognathus radiatus Juv.

LONG-TAIL WEED-WHITING
Siphonognathus tanyourus Gomon and Paxton, 1985

D XVI-XVIII,10-12. A III,8-11. P 11-14. V I,4. LL 35-38. Moderate-sized cycloid scales cover body, extend over nape to interorbital, most of opercle; band down behind eye to cheek. Lateral line with short gradual curve down, continues along midline of body. Head pointed; snout moderately long, mouth slightly more than half its length; teeth in jaws mostly fused but with recognisable tips. Long caudal peduncle. Mostly greenish; juveniles with narrow white streak on sides. Little-known species; south coast from Wilson's Promontory to Lucky Bay, south Western Australia. Coastal shallow high-energy zones to about 15 m. Attains 13 cm.

LONG-NOSE WEED-WHITING
Siphonognathus beddomei (Johnston, 1885)

D XIX-XX,11-13. A III,8-10. P 13-15. V I,4. LL 38-45. Moderate-sized cycloid scales cover body, extend over nape to above opercle; a few scales on upper opercle; small vertical patch of scales behind eye. Lateral line with short gradual curve down, continues along midline of body. Body very slender; head pointed; snout very long, mouth about half its length; teeth in jaws mostly fused but with recognisable tips. Males with iridescent blue lines. Juveniles and IP with ocellus in upper part of caudal fin. South coast, including Tasmania, from Wilson's Promontory to Perth. Coastal reefs, usually in small to large aggregations swimming above kelp. Feeds among weed as well as zooplankton; occasionally observed cleaning other fishes. To about 15 m. Attains 14 cm. Also known as Pigmy Rock Whiting.

Siphonognathus beddomei Male ▲ Initial phase ▼

Siphonognathus attenuatus ▼

Siphonognathus argyrophanes ▼

SHORT-NOSE WEED-WHITING
Siphonognathus attenuatus (Ogilby, 1897)

D XIX-XXI,14-16. A III,7-8. P 13-15. V I,4. LL 38-45. Moderate-sized cycloid scales cover body, extend over nape to above opercle and down over much of opercle; small vertical patch of scales behind eye. Lateral line with short gradual curve down, continues along midline of body. Body very long, slender; head pointed; snout moderately long (short compared to body length), mouth about half its length; teeth in jaws mostly fused but with a few tiny recognisable tips. Caudal fin large, lanceolate. Little variation in colour. Distinct eye-like ocellus in centre of caudal fin; real eye not obvious as seems to swim backwards; predators which usually go for the head are fooled by the disguise. South coast from Wilson's Promontory to Rottnest Island and eastern Tasmania. Usually in 10-25 m, along edges of low reefs, outcrops on sand, or open patches in deep seagrass beds. Usually in small aggregations. Attains 13 cm. Also known as Slender Rock Whiting.

Siphonognathus attenuatus Schooling juvs.

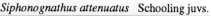

TUBEMOUTH
Siphonognathus argyrophanes Richardson, 1858

D XXII-XXVII,19-22. A 0-II,11-13, P 11-13. V 0,0 (absent). LL 96-108. Small cycloid scales cover body to above opercle; scales extend down opercle to membrane; small vertical patch of scales behind eye. Body extremely long, slender; snout very long; caudal fin long, pointed. Fleshy filament extends forward on upper lip. Mouth about one-third of snout length; teeth mostly fused, beak-like edge anteriorly. Brownish to green. Entire south coast from Bass Strait to Perth, but in many isolated populations, probably due to habitat requirements. In South Australia, where common, usually in broad-leafed and very long seagrasses in which it lives secretly. Juveniles in particular not often seen unless in nets dragged through seagrass. Attains 45 cm.

S. argyrophanes Close-up of head

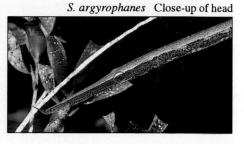

HERRING CALE
Odax cyanomelas (Richardson, 1850)

D XVI-XVIII,9-11. A II-III,9-11. P 12-13. V I,4. LL 47-54. Small cycloid scales cover body; head naked except for small patch on upper opercle. Lateral line indistinct with large gradual curve to midline of body. Body slender with long caudal peduncle. Snout rounded, short. Mouth almost to below edge of eye; teeth totally fused, serrated edge. Dorsal fin with long spinous portion; first three spines long, followed by progressively shorter ones; soft-rayed section short-based and above similar-shaped anal fin. Caudal fin large, becomes lunate with long tips in TP. Colours between yellow-brown to greyish green, males bluish-black. Widest ranging species in southern waters, to northern New South Wales, Houtman Abrolhos and southern Tasmania. Particularly common in surge zones with large kelp, often in large loose aggregations. From intertidal to 30 m. Attains 40 cm. This genus contains three species, one of which is found in New Zealand.

Odax cyanomelas Juv.

Odax cyanomelas   Male ▲   Initial phase ▼

RAINBOW CALE
Odax acroptilus (Richardson, 1846)

D XIV-XVI,8-10. A III,11-12. P 14-15. V I,4. LL 30-32. Large cycloid scales cover body, extend down over posterior part of opercle; large patch of embedded scales below eye. Lateral line gradually descends to midline along body. Body moderately deep; head bluntly pointed to rounded. Mouth almost to below edge of eye; teeth totally fused, beak-like with serrated edges. Dorsal fin spines of nearly equal length, but becoming greatly extended anteriorly in TP. Mostly green or brown with dark blotches. TP with iridescent blue on head and fins. South coast from Seal Rocks, New South Wales to southern West Australia. Coastal to offshore reefs with kelp; juveniles shallow among broad-leafed seagrasses in exposed coastal areas; adults in kelp to about 25 m. Attains 30 cm.

Odax acroptilus Juv.

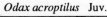

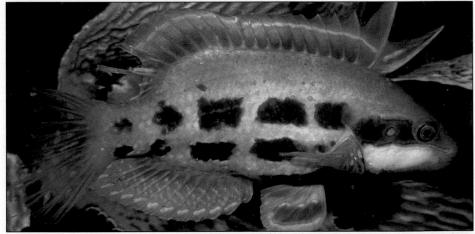

Odax acroptilus   Male ▲   Unusually coloured male ▼

PARROTFISHES
FAMILY SCARIDAE

A large tropical family with representatives in all oceans. The parrotfishes are medium-sized fishes which are characterised in two subfamilies, largely by their teeth. One group has jaws with numerous conical teeth, the other has teeth fused into beak-like plates, similar to parrots, hence their common name. In all, the family comprises nine genera and an estimated 80 species, some of which range into New South Wales. Juveniles of several species expatriate south to the Sydney area, one species as far south as Montague Island, and five are included here. No doubt more species occur in northern New South Wales or Lord Howe Island. The majority of species feed by scraping algae off dead coral rock or rubble and sand. In the process, much of the coral surface is crushed and digested. They produce vast quantities of sand in this way which often is released during displays and while swimming over reef crests. As these fishes occur abundantly on coral reefs, often feeding in densely packed large schools, they are an important component in the reef-building process. Most species have different-coloured stages as juvenile, IP and TP. The latter has usually a mixture of brilliant contrasting colours, though green is usually dominant. They are of commercial importance in tropical seas.

SEAGRASS PARROTFISH
Leptoscarus vaigiensis (Quoy and Gaimard, 1824)

D X-IX,10. A III,9. P 13. V I,5. LL 25. Large cycloid scales cover body, cheek; single row below eye; elongate scales onto caudal fin. Lateral line continuous, almost straight to end of dorsal fin, then over next lower scales along caudal peduncle. Teeth fused into dental plates; upper jaw encloses lower jaw when mouth closed. Dull species which exhibits no change in sex. Widespread tropical Indo-Pacific from west and south Pacific to east Africa and Red Sea. In Australia, south to Sydney and Rottnest Island. Coastal seagrass beds in small to large aggregations. Juveniles in Sydney Harbour occur in seagrasses close to the heads. Attains 35 cm. Monotypic genus; only representative here of subfamily Sparisomatinae.

Leptoscarus vaigiensis

CHAMELEON PARROTFISH
Scarus chameleon Choat and Randall, 1986

D IX,10. A III,9. P 14. V I,5. 17-19+4-6.
Large cycloid scales cover body, upper head,
extend by long scales in two vertical rows
onto caudal fin; three scale-rows on cheek.
Lateral line interrupted by one scale vertically
below end of dorsal fin. Teeth totally fused to
form beak-like plates with slightly irregular
margins. Colour of juvenile typical for a
number of species; usually brownish in broad
bands, capable of quick changes. Only TP is
readily identified in the field. Widespread
west Pacific from northern New South Wales
and Lord Howe Island to southern Japan and
Micronesia. Juveniles south to Sydney where
they occur on shallow rocky reefs with sparse
kelp growth. Adults on inner and outer reefs
along drop-offs to about 20 m. Attains 27 cm.
This genus of subfamily Scarinae contains
about 60 species. Many juveniles occur in
mixed species in small aggregations and look
very similar. Such small groups are often
observed in Sydney Harbour and specimens
need to be collected for a positive identification. No doubt more species than included
here expatriate to Sydney Harbour.

Scarus chameleon Juv.

BLUNT-HEAD PARROTFISH
Scarus microrhinos Rüppell, 1828

D IX,10. A III,9. P 16. V I,5. 17-19+4-6.
Large cycloid scales cover body, upper head,
extend by long scales in two vertical rows
onto caudal fin; three scale-rows on cheek.
Lateral line interrupted by one scale vertically
below end of dorsal fin. Teeth totally fused to
form beak-like plates with slightly irregular
margins. Juvenile has very dark stripes. Large
males hump-headed, caudal fin tips extended.
Widespread west Pacific species, replaced by
similar species in Indian Ocean. Juveniles
south to Sydney Harbour, usually in aggregations of mixed species; black stripes readily
identify them. Mainly occurs on outer reefs,
in lagoons and along to edge of deep drop-
offs. Large species; attains 55 cm.

Scarus microrhinos Juv.

BLUE-BARRED PARROTFISH
Scarus ghobban Forsskål, 1775

D IX,10. A III,9. P 15. V I,5. 17-19+4-6. Large cycloid scales cover body, upper head, extend by long scales in two vertical rows onto caudal fin; three scale-rows on cheek. Lateral line interrupted by one scale vertically below end of dorsal fin. Teeth totally fused to form beak-like plates with slightly irregular margins. Juveniles similar in colour to other pale-brown banded species, but vertical bars usually faintly visible, becoming more obvious with increasing size. Very widespread, tropical Indo-Pacific from Americas coasts to east Africa and Red Sea. In the west Pacific at least south to Sydney where specimens up to 30 cm not uncommon during summer. Coastal reefs, harbours, often in silty conditions. Large species; to at least 75 cm.

Scarus ghobban Juv.

Scarus ghobban   Male ▲ Initial phase ▼

BLACK-VEINED PARROTFISH
Scarus rubroviolaceus (Bleeker, 1849)

D IX,10. A III,9. P 15. V I,5. 17-19+4-6. Large cycloid scales cover body, upper head, extend by long scales in two vertical rows onto caudal fin; three scale-rows on cheek. Lateral line interrupted by one scale vertically below end of dorsal fin. Teeth totally fused to form beak-like plates with slightly irregular margins. Juvenile similar in colour to other pale-brown banded species, but has two somewhat indistinct dark spots on outer posterior scales of caudal fin, pale area heading dorsal fin. Very widespread, tropical Indo-Pacific from eastern Pacific to east Africa and Red Sea. In the west Pacific south to Montague Island, the most southern record for any scarid. The most common scarids in Sydney Harbour as small juveniles, but unable to survive winter cold. Adults venture into deep water to more than 40 m. Attains 55 cm.

Scarus rubroviolaceus Juv.

Scarus rubroviolaceus   Male ▲ Initial phase ▼

BANDFISHES
FAMILY CEPOLIDAE

A little-known family of small fishes which are widely distributed along continental margins of the western Pacific, Indian Ocean and eastern Atlantic. The family comprises at least four genera and about 20 species. A study of the Australian species is needed. The bandfishes are similar, eel-shaped fishes with a tapering body, and dorsal and anal fins along almost the entire length seemingly continuous with the pointed caudal fin. They have a rounded goby-like head with a large mouth and large eyes. Most species have identical colours, usually red or pink. They live primarily in muddy or fine sand substrates in self-made burrows, in a depth range of 20-500 m, and feed on zooplankton. Bandfishes come out of their burrows into currents, hovering vertically and looking upward for food. They return to their burrow by swimming backwards. One species is included here, but more possibly occur in our range.

BANDFISH
Cepola australis Ogilby, 1899

D 57-60. A 48-55. P 16. V I,5. Scales very tiny; lateral line close along dorsal fin base. Dorsal and anal fins lack spines, are continuous in outline with caudal fin. Head broadly rounded; mouth large with small slender teeth. Eyes large, facing forward. Pink to red, varying with depth. Originally described from Sydney Harbour but recorded from various other locations from Queensland to South Australia, however other species may be involved. Fish in photograph is from Sydney Harbour, where the species can be found in deep tidal channels in muddy burrows. Sometimes in small aggregations of fishes, each with its own burrow. Attains about 25 cm.

Cepola australis   Adult ▲   Emerging from burrow ▼

JAWFISHES
FAMILY OPISTOGNATHIDAE

A family of small burrowing species, many of which are undescribed, comprising three genera and an estimated 70 species. Jawfishes are distributed in all tropical waters but the east Pacific, and only only species ranges to south-eastern coastal waters. They are somewhat odd-looking fishes with large eyes placed high and forward on the head, a large mouth used for incubating eggs, and an elongate body. The burrows are usually vertically in the sand, and are reinforced with small rocks or coral pieces. If you look down the burrow it looks somewhat like a wishing-well. These curious fishes are given a great variety of common names, including Missing Links, Pugs, Harlequins, Grinners, Smilers, and Monkeyfish. Some have an ornate dorsal fin used for signalling or display. The dorsal and anal fins are long-based and large, and the ventral fins are peculiar in having the outer two rays unbranched. The lateral line is high on the body and terminates at about the middle of the dorsal fin. Jawfishes are usually found with their head just out of their burrow, watching for food (zooplankton) floating past. They retreat into their burrows tail first.

SMILER
Opistognathus jacksoniensis (Macleay, 1881)

D X,16. A III,14-15. C 13. P 18. V I,5. LSR 80. Body slender with tiny scales. Lateral line close along dorsal fin base. Head large with huge eyes. Large gaping mouth; row of small canines in each jaw. Fin spines slender; dorsal fin continuous, spinous section about equal in length to soft-rayed section. Anal fin similar to and opposite soft-rayed section of dorsal fin. Caudal and pectoral fins of similar size, rounded. Uncertain distribution with many species in Queensland; this species probably from Sydney Harbour to southern Queensland. Sand and rubble flats near reefs; 20-30 m, but probably deeper as well. Large genus comprising about 60 species distributed mostly in tropical reefs.

Opistognathus jacksoniensis   Frontal view of head ▲   Side view of head ▼

GRUBFISHES
FAMILY PINGUIPEDIDAE

A moderately large family comprising about four genera and more than 60 species. The grubfishes are small slender fishes also known as weevers or sand-smelts. The long-based dorsal fin is headed by four or five short spines and the anal fin consists of soft rays headed by a feeble spine. Scales are moderately small and ctenoid, and the lateral line is continuous. Eyes are large and placed dorsally on the head. Many occur in very deep water and are only known from trawls but they are also well represented in the shallows. Many species are found in tropical seas, and several in warm-temperate seas. The reef dwellers are typically found on sand or rubble patches where they perch themselves on their ventral fins during stops. Grubfishes are very active during the day, quickly dashing about or darting under rocks for cover. Some species make burrows or use those made by other creatures. There is little change in colour during growth, and the differences between sexes are slight. Some species pair and often the only difference between sexes is the markings on the lower lips. Only a single genus, *Parapercis*, is recognised in the Indo-Pacific, five species of which are included here. Only two of these are southern species. The other three range from the tropics south to the Sydney area or further as adults. They feed on a variety of small invertebrates and fishes; a few species have adapted to plankton as prey and may swim well above the substrate. Most species are small, ranging from about 15-25 cm as adults, but a New Zealand species attains 60 cm. NOTE: The feeble first spine of the anal fin is included in the soft ray count.

BARRED GRUBFISH
Parapercis allporti (Günther, 1876)

D V,21. A 18-19. P 19-22. V I,5. LL 58-60. Body elongate, slightly compressed, covered by moderately small ctenoid scales which extend onto cheeks to below centre of eyes. Eyes very large, placed dorsally, close together. Snout pointed; mouth of moderate size, reaching to below eyes; band of pointed teeth anteriorly in jaws, bordered by longer curved canines at front and along each side. Dorsal fin continuous; spines noticeably shorter than soft rays, fully connected by membrane. Variable pale to dark red; seven to nine dark bands which alternate in width. South-eastern Australia from New South Wales to Tasmania and South Australia. Usually deep; adults in 45-200 m; young occasionally relatively shallow on coastal reefs. Largest of the Australian species, reaching 33 cm.

Parapercis allporti   Frontal view ▲   Side view ▼

Parapercis nebulosa   Adult ▼ Juv. ▲

PINK-BANDED GRUBFISH
Parapercis nebulosa (Quoy and Gaimard, 1852)

D V,22. A 19. P 16-17. V I,5. LL 68-76. Body elongate, slightly compressed, covered by moderately small ctenoid scales which extend onto cheeks to below centre of eyes.

Eyes of moderate size, placed dorsally. Snout pointed; mouth of moderate size, reaching near and below eyes; band of pointed teeth anteriorly in jaws, bordered by longer curved canines at front and along each side. Dorsal fin continuous with rounded spinous section, connected by low membrane. Variable pale pink with brown to reddish blotched bands. Tropical Australian waters; adults reach south to latitude of about Sydney. Coastal bays, estuaries, often silty muddy habitat with weeds or soft corals. Attains 25 cm.

Parapercis cylindrica ▼

SHARP-NOSE GRUBFISH
Parapercis cylindrica (Bloch, 1797)

D V,21-22. A 18. P 17-18. V I,5. LL 57-60. Body elongate, slightly compressed, covered by moderately small ctenoid scales which extend onto cheeks to below centre of eyes. Eyes of moderate size, placed dorsally. Snout pointed; mouth of moderate size, reaching near and below eyes; band of pointed teeth anteriorly in jaws, bordered by longer curved canines at front and along each side. Dorsal fin in two parts, short rounded spinous section followed closely by long soft-rayed section. Distinct species with little variation in colour. Widespread tropical west Pacific ranging to southern Japan and central New South Wales. Shallow sheltered coastal bays and clear-water estuaries on rubble reef to about 15 m. Attains 15 cm

Parapercis ramsayi ▼

SPOTTED GRUBFISH
Parapercis ramsayi Steindachner, 1884

D IV,24-25. A 20. P 16-17. V I,5. LL 65-67. Body elongate, slightly compressed, covered by moderately small ctenoid scales which do not extend onto head. Eyes of moderate size, placed dorsally. Snout moderately pointed; mouth large, reaching to below eyes; band of pointed teeth anteriorly in jaws, bordered by longer curved canines at front and along each side. Dorsal fin continuous with low subequal spinous section, fully connected by membrane. Slightly variable in colour; usually pale on white sand, dark on muddy substrates. Juveniles with distinct ocellus on caudal peduncle. Southern Australian waters from New South Wales to Western Australia, but not known from southern Victoria or Tasmania. Sheltered coastal reefs and estuaries, shallow to at least 80 m. Particularly common in about 50 m off Sydney. Attains 20 cm.

WHITE-STREAKED GRUBFISH
Parapercis stricticeps (De Vis, 1884)

D V,22. A 19. P 16-17. V I,5. LL 58-66
Body elongate, slightly compressed, covered by moderately small ctenoid scales which extend onto cheeks to below centre of eyes. Eyes of moderate size, placed dorsally. Snout pointed; mouth of moderate size, reaching near to below eyes; band of pointed teeth anteriorly in jaws, bordered by longer curved canines at front and along each side. Dorsal fin in two parts, short rounded spinous section followed closely by long soft-rayed section. Distinct species with little variation in colour, but several similar species occur elsewhere. Only known from eastern Australia from central New South Wales to Queensland; possibly in New Caledonia. Rocky estuaries in clear water, shallow to about 20 m. Attains 18 cm.

SANDFISHES
FAMILY PERCOPHIDAE

A small family, represented in all major oceans but mostly in tropical and very deep waters, and comprising about six genera and an estimated 20 species, some of which are undescribed. It is to be expected that there are several more species, as some are very small as adults. They are elongate fishes with depressed heads and close-set eyes placed dorsally, and are usually smallish, some only reaching 25 mm fully grown. Scales are moderately large, the mouth is large and the jaws have fine teeth. The dorsal fin is in two parts, a short-based spinous section and a long-based soft-rayed section. Many sandfishes are usually buried with only the eyes exposed, although some tropical species can be found above the sand at times. Body colourations are similar to the sand in which they bury, though some tropical species exhibit colourful fins and males often possess elongated rays in certain fins for display purposes. Only one species is known from southern waters and is restricted to this area.

BROAD SANDFISH
Enigmapercis reducta Whitley, 1936

D 11,18. A 24. C 9. P 16. V I,5. LL 37.
Body elongate, slightly depressed anteriorly, compressed posteriorly; covered with large cycloid scales which extend over most of head. Eyes moderately large, close-set on top of head. Mouth large, reaching to below eyes; lower jaw slightly longest; narrow row of fine teeth in each jaw and on palatines and vomer. Dorsal fins widely separate; first small, rounded, short-based; second long-based, taller. Anal fin similar to and opposite second dorsal fin. Pectoral fins moderately large, ventral fins placed posteriorly to them. Pale colours, matching type of sand in which they bury. Only known from southern Australian waters from central New South Wales to South Australia, including Bass Strait. Usually buried in the upper parts of wave-formed sand in clear sand estuaries and coastal bays; shallow to at least 130 m. Attains 9 cm. Also known as Reduced Grubfish.

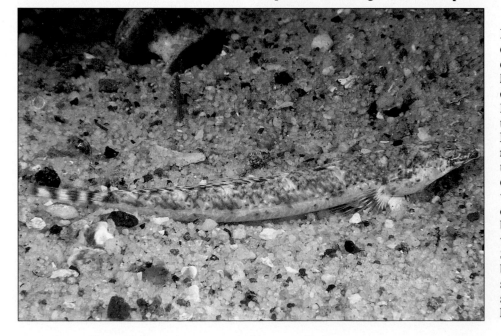

SAND DIVERS
FAMILY CREEDIIDAE

A small family comprising seven genera and 14 recognised species, known from inshore waters of the Indian and Pacific oceans. Sand divers are usually small fishes with slender to eel-shaped bodies which have large scales, though these sometimes only partly cover the body. The dorsal and anal fins are long-based and consist of soft rays only. The snout is sharply pointed and fleshy, and the upper jaw overlaps the lower jaw which bears a series of small barbels. They completely bury themselves in sand leaving only their eyes are exposed, and are almost impossible to find except by disturbing the sand so they come out to rebury elsewhere. They usually bury in specific places in relation to reefs, and often occur in large aggregations. Aquarium-kept specimens have fed on mysids, but underwater observations on *Limnichthys* suggest that they are planktivorous. Plankton appears unlikely to be an suitable diet for a sand-dweller but they seem to be able to spot their prey from some distance away and take it with great speed. Of the three species included here, one is rarely seen as it is primarily a deepwater species, but it is common and well known from literature.

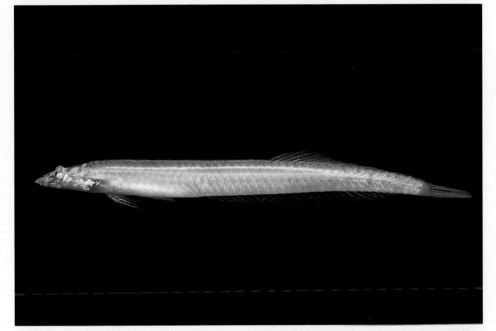

SLENDER SAND-DIVER
Creedia haswelli (Ramsay, 1881)

D 13-14. A 24-28. C 11. P 8-9. V I,4. LL 42-43. Body very elongate, slightly compressed, covered by large cycloid scales which do not extend onto head. Snout pointed; eyes small, facing upward; mouth large; minute sharp teeth in both jaws. Long-based anal fin originates well ahead of opposite and shorter dorsal fin. Caudal fin large; pectoral fins angular; ventral fins short, adapted to burying in sand. Little colouration; sandy above, translucent below; fins transparent. Known from the south coast only, Newcastle to Cape Leeuwin (Western Australia), including north-eastern Tasmania. Coastal waters in 27-55 m, but recorded to 200 m. Mostly known from trawls; seems very common in some areas, although not yet observed underwater by the author. Attains 7.5 cm.

HALF-SCALED SAND-DIVER
Creedia partimsquamigera Nelson, 1983

D 14-16. A 25-28. C 11 (9 branched). P 12-13. V I,4. LL 44-47. Body very elongate, slightly compressed; posteriorly covered by large cycloid scales which do not extend anteriorly to dorsal fin except on lateral line. Snout pointed; eyes small, facing upward; mouth large; minute sharp teeth in both jaws. Long-based anal fin originates well ahead of opposite and shorter dorsal fin. Caudal fin large; pectoral fins angular; ventral fins short, adapted to burying in sand. Little colouration as shown in photograph; sandy above, translucent below; fins transparent. Only known from nine specimens collected by the author, in search of the Slender Sand-Diver, off Sydney beaches in 10-15 m. Clean sand areas in the vicinity of rocky reefs. Buries deep in sand; captured fish taken by scooping large quantities of sand where the fish buried. Largest specimens measured just over 70 mm.

TOMMY FISH
Limnichthys fasciatus Waite, 1904

D 24-27. A 27-29. C 10. P 11-13. V I,5. LL 40-41. Body very elongate, slightly compressed, covered by large cycloid scales which do not extend onto head. Snout pointed; eyes small, facing upward; mouth large; minute sharp teeth in both jaws. Long-based anal fin originates well ahead of opposite and shorter dorsal fin. Caudal fin large; pectoral fins angular; ventral fins short, adapted to burying in sand. Body darkest above, distinctly marked with dark blotches in banded pattern; fins translucent. Widespread in southern waters, extending to northern New Zealand, Kermadec Islands; similar species in Japan. Coastal reefs, usually in shallow sandy patches near boulder reefs, congregating in small to large aggregations. Attains 60 mm.

PYGMY STARGAZERS
FAMILY LEPTOSCOPIDAE

A small and little-known family of fishes restricted to temperate Australian and New Zealand waters. Presently three genera and five species are recognised. Three of the species are from Australian waters, but at least two more from south-western waters can not be identified and probably represent new species. They are small sand-dwelling fishes which bury just below the surface with their eyes extended just above. They have slender bodies which taper posteriorly, large cycloid scales, and a blunt head. Their eyes are small and placed dorsally, the mouth is wide and fringed with cirri, and there are narrow bands of small teeth in each jaw. Pygmy stargazers have a single long-based dorsal fin and the anal fin is comprised of soft rays only. The unusually shaped ventral fins are placed forward and laterally for the purpose of burying. Australian species occur in very shallow depths along beaches and sandy bays, feeding primarily on small crustaceans such as mysids and amphipods. The New Zealand species *Leptoscopus macropygus* (Richardson) was originally reported from Port Jackson, but this appears to be a locality error.

FLATHEAD PYGMY-STARGAZER
Lesueurina platycephala Fowler, 1907

D 32-36. A 36-37. C 10. P 17-21. V I,5. LL 46-49. Body elongate, depressed anteriorly, tapering to small caudal peduncle; covered with large cycloid scales which extend over most of head. Lateral line runs mid-laterally with smooth curve from origin downwards. Head moderately large, flattened above; eyes small, placed dorsally. Mouth broad, angled upward; a series of cirri along both lips; narrow band of small, slender, pointed teeth small in each jaw. Anal fin similar to and opposite long-based dorsal fin, overlapping slightly at both ends. Ventral fins placed well in advance of large pectoral fins. Pale below, sandy colour on top; matches sand types in colour and pattern. Widespread in southern waters from southern Queensland to Western Australia, including Tasmania, however it may involve several species. Lives typically in turbulent sandy beach zones in less than 1 m. Cirri on lips enable it to breathe without sand entering mouth. Attains 11 cm.

ROBUST PYGMY-STARGAZER
Crapatalus munroi Last and Edgar, 1987

D 36-38. A 36-37. C 10. P 21-23. LL 46-49. Body elongate, tapering from large bulbous head to small caudal peduncle; covered with large cycloid scales which extend over most of head and pectoral fin bases. Lateral line runs mid-laterally with smooth curve from origin downwards. Head moderately large, flattened above; eyes small, placed dorsally. Mouth broad, angled upward; a series of cirri along both lips; narrow band of small, slender, pointed teeth in each jaw. Anal fin similar to and opposite long-based dorsal fin, overlapping slightly at both ends. Ventral fins placed well in advance of of large pectoral fins. Pale below, sandy colour on top; matches sand types in colour and pattern. Only known from southern Victoria and Tasmania. Usually in shallow quiet waters in light-coloured sand in about 2-18 m. Attains 12 cm.

SLENDER PYGMY-STARGAZER
Crapatalus sp

D 35-36. A 38. C 10. P 20-21. LL 44. Body elongate, tapering from large bulbous head to small caudal peduncle; covered with large cycloid scales which extend over most of head and pectoral fin bases. Lateral line runs mid-laterally with smooth curve from origin downwards. Head moderately large, flattened above; eyes moderately large, placed dorsally. Mouth broad, angled upward; a series of cirri along both lips; narrow band of small, slender, pointed teeth in each jaw. Anal fin similar to and opposite long-based dorsal fin, overlapping slightly at both ends. Ventral fins placed well in advance of large pectoral fins. Pale below, sandy colour on top; matches sand types in colour and pattern. Only known from southern New South Wales, but probably more widespread; remarkably similar species found in south-west Australia. Protected coastal bays, usually in small aggregations in 3-6 m. Largest known specimen 10 cm, but possibly gets larger.

STARGAZERS
FAMILY URANOSCOPIDAE

An interesting family of medium-sized fished found in all oceans, comprising eight genera and about 30 species. Althought the majority lives in depths well beyond present scuba diving techniques, some species live in remarkably shallow waters, virtually just below the intertidal zone. They have large heavy bodies, but bury with ease in the sand or mud by pumping water around them from their gill-openings. They are predators which position themselves in strategic places where there is likely to be traffic of the particular fish species on which they prey. Some species have a bait, consisting of a long tentacle which can be wriggled like a worm, inside the mouth. The head is massive and possesses large spines. The mouth is protrusible, sucking up the prey swiftly, and the jaws bear small teeth. When buried, stargazers are well anchored and on the rare occasion a fisherman hooks one, the excitement of a potentially large catch is quickly doused on landing the fish. Only a single species occurs in the shallows on south-eastern coasts.

EASTERN STARGAZER
Kathetostoma laeve (Bloch and Schneider, 1801)

D 16-17. A 14-15. C 11-13. P 18-20. V I,5. LL absent. Head large, squarish, followed by tapering, proportionally small body. Eyes placed dorsally, can be erected. Mouth large, vertical; widely spaced canines in lower jaw; upper jaw with band of fine teeth and row of depressible inner canines; lips with series of fleshy papillae. Scales absent. Dorsal and anal fins long-based, comprising soft rays only. Pectoral fins very large; ventral fins rather fleshy, placed forward, both used when burying in the substrate. Adults dull grey or brown; young with distinct, almost banded black pattern. Restricted to south-eastern waters; replaced by a similar species in the south-west. Shallow bays to at least 60 m. Reasonably common, although not often seen; large specimens may be aggressive, are known to bite divers on night dives. Attains 75 cm.

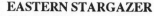
Kathetostoma laeve Lateral view ▲ Frontal view of head ▼

Kathetostoma laeve Juv.

THORNFISHES
FAMILY BOVICHTIDAE

A small family of southern origin comprising four genera and seven species distributed in the temperate waters of the southern hemisphere, with related families in Antarctic waters. Some very different forms exist within the family, and of the two Australian genera and three species, one species lacks scales on the body and also has a long spine on the opercle. They are relatively slender fishes and have large close-set eyes placed dorsally. The dorsal fin is in two parts, a short-based spinous section, followed closely by a long-based soft-rayed section. The anal fin is long-based and in some species comprises soft rays only. The caudal fin is either rounded or truncate. The scaled species have a depressed head and superficially resemble the flatheads (Platycephalidae). One of these species enters fresh water and commonly inhabits the lower reaches of rivers and streams. The second scaled species was recently discovered in collecting surveys in the Bass Strait region, but is very cryptic, only known from a few specimens, and is not included here. The two species included here are both common in coastal waters of south-eastern Australia.

THORNFISH
Bovichtus angustifrons Regan, 1913

D VIII,18-19. A 18. C 13-14. P 15-16. V I,5. LL 00. Scales absent; body elongate, tapering to narrow caudal peduncle. Lateral line consists of a series of papillae from gill opening to tail base. Head large, slightly compressed with pointed snout. Mouth reaches to below eyes; bands of small teeth in each jaw. Eyes very large, close together, placed dorsally. Large spine at upper edge of opercle. All fins large; dorsal fin in two parts, spinous section about half length of closely following soft-rayed section. Pectoral fins broadly rounded, reaching anus. Caudal fin rounded.

Variable pale brown with light and dark brown to red spots and blotches. South-east coast from southern New South Wales to the eastern Great Australian Bight, including Tasmania. Similar species in New Zealand. Shallow rocky reefs, including rock pools and under jetties on pylons. Attains 28 cm. Also known as Dragonet. Due to a type-locality error, *B. variegatus*, the name of a New Zealand species, was wrongly applied in Australia.

Bovichtus angustifrons   Adult ▼   Juv. ▲

CONGOLLI
Pseudaphritis urvillii (Valenciennes, 1831)

D VII-VIII,19-22. A II,21-22. C 14. P 18. V I,5. LL 59-65. Body elongate, compressed posteriorly, covered with moderate-sized ctenoid scales which extend onto head. Head rather large, depressed; snout rounded. Mouth large, reaching well below eyes; bands of villiform teeth in each jaw. Small spine at corner of opercle. Eyes moderately large, placed dorsally, close-set. Lateral line almost straight, follows contour of back. Fins moderately large; dorsal fins distinctly separate. Caudal fin truncate. Variable grey to brown above, pale below; large dark blotches form irregular bars. South-east coast from southern New South Wales to the eastern Great Australian Bight, including Tasmania. Estuarine species which migrates far inland up rivers. Feeds on various crustaceans, worms, small fish, insects. Attains 36 cm. Also known as Tupong.

THREEFINS
FAMILY TRIPTERYGIIDAE

A very large family of small fishes, comprising an estimated 20 genera and 150 species. Most of those in tropical waters are undescribed. The majority occur in tropical waters of all oceans and the numbers of species becomes progressively less toward temperate seas. These fishes feature three usually separate dorsal fins, hence their common name. Other features include reduced ventral fins with a single embedded spine and two or three segmented rays, large ctenoid or small cycloid scales, and an anal fin which is longer than any section of the dorsal fin and has one, two or no spines. They are small; only a few species exceed 10 cm as adults. Colouration often varies between sexes and individuals in different habitats, as they are usually well camouflaged to match surroundings. Most species live in shallow reef habitats, often on ceilings of caves or on vertical surfaces, including jetty pylons. They feed primarily on small crustaceans. The Australian south coast species are highly diverse with several monotypic genera. NOTE: The lateral line sometimes consists of two parts, an upper section (ULL) and a midline section (LLL). The latter consists mostly of intermittently spaced notched scales posteriorly, and the count given includes all scales along that line from above pectoral base.

TASSELLED THREEFIN
Apopterygion alta Kuiter, 1986

D III,XIII-XIV,9-11. A II,20-21. C 13. P 14-15. V I,2. ULL 23-25. LLL 33. Body almost cylindrical, covered with ctenoid scales; cycloid scales on abdomen. Head with some deeply embedded ctenoid scales dorsally; small patch of scales on upper opercle. Simple tentacles above eyes and on anterior nostril. Mouth large; bands of pointed teeth in jaws, outer row widely spaced and enlarged. Upper lateral line with pored scales, almost straight from origin to below about

Apopterygion alta ▲

Norfolkia incisa ▼

centre of third dorsal fin. Lower lateral line slowly curves from origin, descending to mid-body line with intermittently spaced notched scales which become a series posteriorly; one or three additional notched scales on caudal fin. Dorsal fins in three distinctly separate parts; first very short-based, each spine with bilobate leafy appendages at tips. Pectoral fins large; ventral fin slender. Colour variable, greyish-brown with red; mostly red in deepwater habitats. Only known from the Bass Strait region, including Port Phillip Bay and northern Tasmania. Occurs in 5-80 m, usually on sponges; only known species to occur so deep. Attains 65 mm.

NOTCHED THREEFIN
Norfolkia incisa Kuiter, 1986

D III,XII-XIII,9-11. A II,18-19. C 13. P 14-16. V I,2. ULL 21-24. LLL 29. Body almost cylindrical, covered with ctenoid scales which are large on body, small on abdomen; small naked area immediately behind ventral fins. Head with small ctenoid scales dorsally and on most of sides. Round to multilobate fleshy tentacle above eye; leafy tentacle on anterior nostril. Mouth large; bands of pointed teeth in jaws, outer row widely spaced and enlarged. Upper lateral line with pored scales, almost straight from origin to below third dorsal fin. Lower lateral line from origin with slow curve descending to mid-body line with intermittently spaced notched scales; poorly developed anteriorly with a few pores below upper lateral line; one or three additional notched scales on caudal fin. Dorsal fins in three separate parts, first with deeply incised membranes. Pectoral fin very large; middle rays reach near and below end of second dorsal fin. Grey or brown with six to seven darker bars on sides. South coast species, known from Wilson's Promontory to the Recherche Archipelago. Rocky reefs in caves, usually on ceilings, in 10-30 m. Attains 40 mm.

COMMON THREEFIN
Norfolkia clarkei (Morton, 1888)

D III-IV,XII-XV,10-12. A II,19-21. C 13. P 15-16. V I,2. ULL 25-30. LLL 33-36. Body almost cylindrical, covered with ctenoid scales which are large on body, small on abdomen; small naked area immediately behind ventral fins. Head with small ctenoid scales dorsally and on most of sides. Round to multilobate fleshy tentacle above eye; simple lobate tentacle on anterior nostril. Mouth large; bands of pointed teeth in jaws, outer row widely spaced and enlarged. Upper lateral line with

Norfolkia clarkei Adult ▼ Juv. ▲

Brachynectes fasciatus ▼

Trianectes bucephalus ▼

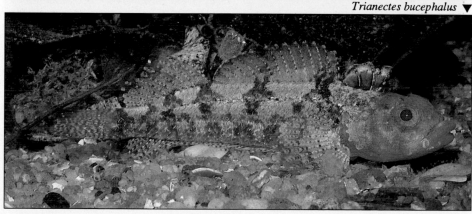

pored scales, almost straight from origin to below third dorsal fin. Lower lateral line slowly curves from origin, descending to mid-body line with intermittently spaced notched scales; poorly developed anteriorly in some populations with a few pores below upper lateral line; one or three additional notched scales on caudal fin. Dorsal fins in three parts, usually united at their bases, occasionally nearly completely between first and second; first fin with distinctly shorter spines. Pectoral fins large; middle rays reach almost to mid-body. Extremely variable from brown to almost black or pale yellow to orange, usually with seven darker bars, depending on habitat. Widespread in southern waters from New South Wales to Western Australia and Tasmania. Some variation in meristics with higher counts; larger adult size in cooler water. Shallow rocky reefs, including shallow estuaries under jetties, and coastal reefs to about 30 m. Attains 80 mm.

WEEDY THREEFIN
Brachynectes fasciatus Scott, 1957

D III,X,12-13. A II,18-19. C 13. P 13-14. V I,2-3. ULL 10-12. LLL 30. Body moderately compressed, covered with large ctenoid scales. Head without scales; large, heavily frilled fleshy tentacles above eyes; long leafy tentacles on anterior nostrils. Mouth large; bands of pointed teeth in jaws, outer row widely spaced and enlarged. Upper lateral line with pored scales, almost straight from origin to below end of second dorsal fin. Lower lateral line slowly curves from origin, descending to mid-body line with intermittently spaced notched scales; poorly developed anteriorly with a few pores below upper lateral line; one or three additional notched scales on caudal fin. Dorsal fins in three distinctly separate parts of similar height. Pectoral fins large; middle rays reach below centre of second dorsal fin. Brown or purplish with dark blotches; fins with wavy lines. Widespread along the south coast, including Tasmania. Among seagrass and dense algae growth in shallow coastal bays and estuaries. Attains 45 mm.

Brachynectes fasciatus Juv.

BIG-HEAD THREEFIN
Trianectes bucephalus McCulloch and Waite, 1918

D III,XIV-XV,11-12. A II,21. C 13. P 15-16. V I,2. ULL 27-28. LLL 33. Body almost cylindrical, covered with large ctenoid scales. Head broad, slightly depressed, without scales; large eyes, small rounded fleshy tentacles above; simple lobate tentacle on anterior nostril. Mouth large; bands of pointed teeth in jaws, outer row widely spaced and enlarged. Upper lateral line with pored scales, almost straight from origin to below end of second dorsal fin. Lower lateral line slowly curves from origin, descending to mid-body line with intermittently spaced notched scales; poorly developed anteriorly with a few pores below upper lateral line; one or two additional notched scales on caudal fin. Dorsal fins in three distinct separate parts of similar height. Pectoral fins large; middle rays reach below end of second dorsal fin. Variably greenish or brown with purple and yellow above or on head, and darker blotches. South coast from eastern Victoria and northern Tasmania to the eastern Great Australian Bight. Rocky reefs, often under loose flat rocks on top of solid reef; in the open at night. Shallow protected coastal waters. Attains 75 mm.

JUMPING JOEY
Lepidoblennius haplodactylus
Steindachner, 1867

D III,XIII-XIV,11-12. A 20-21. C 13. P 15. V I,3. LL 44-60. Body slightly compressed, covered with small cycloid scales except ventrally on belly; narrow band of scales along dorsal fins. Head naked with steep profile. Mouth large; bands of conical teeth, outer rows widely spaced, enlarged with flattened tips. Moderate-sized eyes placed dorsally. Lateral line descends from origin to mid-body line, continues to caudal fin. Dorsal fin in three sections; first and second fully joined by membrane; third immediately behind second. Anal fin long-based; membranes deeply incised, almost to base. Pectoral fins large; middle rays reach near and below end of second dorsal fin. Greenish-yellowish grey; brown blotches on back, irregular small pale spots. Restricted to the east coast from Byron Bay to Western Port Bay. Mainly occupies tide pools and mudflats, sometimes emerging onto rock faces as water levels drop. Attains 12 cm.

Lepidoblennis haplodactylus ▲

Lepidoblennis marmoratus ▼

JUMPING BLENNY
Lepidoblennius marmoratus (Macleay, 1878)

D III,XIV-XV,10-12. A 21-23. C 13. P 15. V I,3. LL 33-44. Body slightly compressed, covered with moderate-sized ctenoid scales except ventrally on belly. Head naked with steep profile. Mouth large; bands of conical teeth, outer rows widely spaced, enlarged with flattened tips. Moderate-sized eyes placed dorsally. Lateral line descends from origin to mid-body line, continues to caudal fin. Dorsal fin in three sections; first and second fully joined by membrane; third immediately behind second. Anal fin long-based; membranes deeply incised, almost to base. Pectoral fins large; middle rays reach near and below end of second dorsal fin. Greenish-grey above, pale below; dark blotches on upper sides. Confined to south-western coast, from western Bass Strait to south-west Australia. Shallow inshore reefs and rock pools in turbulent zones. Attains 12 cm.

Enneapterygius annulatus Male ▲ Female ▼

RING-SCALE THREEFIN
Enneapterygius annulatus (Ramsay and Ogilby, 1887)

D III,XII-XIII,10-11. A 19-20. P 16. C 13. V 2. ULL 16-17. LLL 32-34. Body slightly compressed, covered with moderate-sized ctenoid scales except ventrally on belly. Head naked with pointed profile. Eyes large, placed dorsally. Upper lateral line with tubed scales from origin, almost straight to below end of second dorsal fin. Lower lateral line descends from origin to mid-body line, continues to caudal fin with notched scales in a long series posteriorly. Dorsal fin in three distinct separate sections; first spine in first section longest, elongate and exceeding length of first spine of second dorsal fin in males. Pectoral fins large; middle rays reach near and below end of second dorsal fin. Variable colours; male orange, lower part of head black, first dorsal fin white; female rather plain with some dark mottling, several pale saddles in upper half of body. Queensland to central New South Wales in estuaries and harbours; commonly on pylons; seems to prefer silty habitat of upper regions. Attains about 50 mm.

BLACK-CHEEK THREEFIN
Enneapterygius rufopileus (Waite, 1904)

D III,XII-XIII,10-11. A 19-20. P 14-16. C 13. V 2. ULL 16-17. LLL 32-34. Body slightly compressed, covered with moderate-sized ctenoid scales except ventrally on belly. Head naked with pointed profile. Eyes large, placed dorsally. Upper lateral line with tubed scales from origin, almost straight to below end of second dorsal fin. Lower lateral line descends from origin to mid-body line, continues to caudal fin with notched scales in a long series posteriorly. Dorsal fin in three distinct separate sections; first spine in first section longest, extended but not exceeding length of first spine of second dorsal fin in males. Pectoral fins large; middle rays reach near and below end of second dorsal fin. Variable colours; male similar to female; displaying male turns red with two pale saddle-like markings, black on lower head, first and second dorsal fins black. Female plain greenish-grey; black bar on caudal peduncle can be turned on or off at will. Central New South Wales to Queensland, and Lord Howe Island. Coastal reefs, rockpools; to about 10 m. Attains 45 mm.

Enneapterygius rufopileus   Male ▲ Female ▼

WEEDFISHES
FAMILY CLINIDAE

A large family, comprising at least 20 genera and an estimated 100 species, most of which occur in warm-temperate seas of the southern hemisphere. They are particularly well represented in Australia and South Africa with about 40 species each. In Australia, the majority of species occur in the vegetation rich areas along the south coast. The clinids in Australia include the snake-blennies in four genera, distinguished by their slender bodies. The remaining weedfishes are poorly known. Three genera are presently recognised and a great number of species remain undescribed. Most of the weedfishes are placed in *Heteroclinus* but there are several distinct groups which in future may be divided into several genera. There are many similar and closely related species, and most fishes within a species have different colour-forms which relate to the habitat in which they live. Of these secretive fishes, a few live under rocks but most associate with seagrasses and algaes and are extremely well camouflaged. They feature small cycloid scales, often deeply embedded, a continuous or divided dorsal fin with several first spines separate but more or less joined by a membrane to the rest, and they are viviparous (give birth to live young). Most species occur in shallow coastal regions, including rock pools and estuaries, feeding on various invertebrates among weeds. There are many small species, about 10 cm long, but the largest attains about 40 cm.

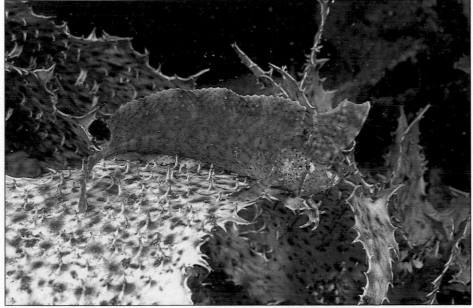

Golden Weedfish (*Cristiceps aurantiacus*)

CRESTED WEEDFISH
Cristiceps australis Valenciennes, 1836

D III+XXVI-XXIX,6-8. A II,24-26. C 9-11. P 10-11. V I,3. LL 14-21+32-34. Body very compressed, particularly posteriorly, covered with tiny cycloid scales. Anterior section of lateral line has scale on each pore; posterior section has scales between pores. Simple elongated tentacle above each eye. Nasal tentacles with two to four slender lobes. All fins have moderately long elements. Dorsal fin divided; first section elevated anteriorly, with three long spines; following membrane to near base of second part, long-based spinous section with short-based soft-rayed section confluent posteriorly. Anal fin similar to and opposite dorsal fin from anus. Large caudal fin on stalk-like skinny caudal peduncle. Ventral fin rays thick, finger-like, almost reaching anus. Extremely variable in colour and patterns; usually matches various types of weed colours; some diffused banding. Widespread southern waters, from southern Queensland to west coast at similar latitude, and Tasmania. Commonly found anywhere with weeds, from subtidal to about 30 m. Attains 18 cm; doubtfully larger but reported to 31 cm. Australian-New Zealand genus comprising three species, all included here.

SILVER-SIDED WEEDFISH
Cristiceps argyropleura Kner, 1865

D III+XXVII-XXIX,6-8. A II,22-24. C 9-11. P 11. V I,3. LL 16-20+28-32. Body very compressed, particularly posteriorly, covered with tiny cycloid scales. Anterior section of lateral line has scale on each pore; posterior section has scales between pores. Simple elongated tentacle above each eye. Nasal tentacles with two to four slender lobes. All fins have moderately long elements. Dorsal fin in two sections; first spinous, elevated anteriorly, short-based with three long spines, first spine longest; following membrane attached to second part, long-based spinous section with short-based soft-rayed section confluent posteriorly. Anal fin similar to and opposite dorsal fin from anus. Large caudal fin on stalk-like skinny caudal peduncle. Ventral fin rays thick, finger-like, reaching about halfway to anus. Variable from almost black to yellow-brown; adults with silvery-white blotches in series anteriorly on sides. Eastern Australia, New South Wales to the Bass Strait region. Mostly found in kelp (*Ecklonia spp*) to depths of 60 m. Attains 18 cm.

GOLDEN WEEDFISH
Cristiceps aurantiacus Castelnau, 1879

D III+XXVIII-XXX,6-8. A II,24-26. C 9-11. P 11. V I,3. LL 14-21+32-34. Body very

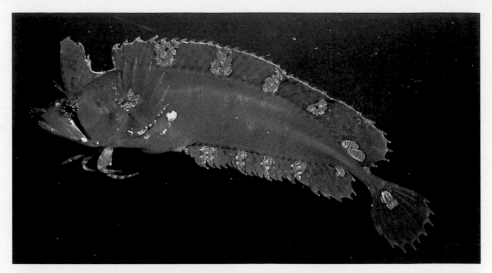

Cristiceps argyropleura ▲   *Cristiceps aurantiacus* ▼

compressed, particularly posteriorly, covered with tiny cycloid scales. Anterior section of lateral line has scale on each pore; posterior section has scales between pores. Simple elongated tentacle above each eye. Nasal tentacles with two to four slender lobes. All fins have moderately long elements. Dorsal fin divided; first section elevated anteriorly, originating in front of eyes, with three long spines; following membrane attached to base of second part, long-based spinous section with short-based soft-rayed section confluent posteriorly. Anal fin similar to and opposite dorsal fin from anus. Large caudal fin on stalk-like skinny caudal peduncle. Ventral fin rays thick, finger-like, almost reaching anus. Usually yellow to orange, sometimes with pinkish touches. New South Wales, probably eastern Victoria, and also New Zealand. Mostly in kelp beds, sometimes with loose weeds on sand; coastal bays in 2-20 m. Attains 18 cm.

COLEMAN'S WEEDFISH
Heteroclinus sp 1

D III+XXV,3. A II,18-19. C 10. P 13. V I,3. LL 19-24+24-26. Body very compressed, particularly posteriorly, covered with tiny cycloid scales. Anterior section of lateral line has scale on each pore; posterior section variably present, has scales between pores. Elongated rounded tentacle above each eye. Nasal tentacles simple, rounded. Dorsal fin in two parts; first part elevated; following membrane to near base of second part, long-based spinous section with short-based soft-rayed section confluent posteriorly. Anal fin similar to and opposite dorsal fin from anus. Ventral fin rays thick, finger-like. Brown to reddish-brown; silvery spots on head, sides. Southern waters from southern New South Wales to Kangaroo Island and Bass Straight region. Usually in large red algae beds on rock faces in about 5-15 m. Attains 10 cm. This genus presently home for about 25 species, 20 of which occur on the south coast; 16 from eastern waters are included here, several of which are undescribed.

Heteroclinus heptaeolus Brown colour-form ▲ Green colour-form ▼

SEVEN-BAR WEEDFISH
Heteroclinus heptaeolus (Ogilby, 1885)

D III+XXVI-XXVIII,3. A II,18-21. C 10-12. P 11-13. V I,3. LL 20-26+22-23. Body very compressed, particularly posteriorly, covered with tiny cycloid scales. Anterior section of lateral line has scale on each pore; posterior section has scales between pores. Short broad tentacle above each eye. Nasal tentacles small, weakly lobed. Fins with moderately long elements. Dorsal fin divided; first section has three spines; following membrane to near base of second part, long-based spinous section with short-based soft-rayed section confluent posteriorly. Anal fin similar to and opposite dorsal fin from anus. Ventral fin rays thick, finger-like. Variable brown or green; series of dark blotches dorsally and midlaterally. Widespread south coast from Seal Rocks, New South Wales, and similar latitude on the west coast, to Tasmania. Commonly occurs in shallow weedy areas in either green or brown weeds. Attains 10 cm.

WILSON'S WEEDFISH
Heteroclinus wilsoni (Lucas, 1891)

D III+XXVI-XXVIII,3. A II,20-22. C 10-12. P 12. V I,3. LL 22-26+25-31. Body very compressed, particularly posteriorly; becomes deep-bodied with age; covered with tiny cycloid scales. Anterior section of lateral line has scale on each pore; posterior section has scales between pores. Broad long bilobate tentacle above each eye. Nasal tentacles small, weakly lobed. Fins with moderately long elements. Dorsal fin divided; first section has three spines; following membrane to near base of second part, long-based spinous section with short-based soft-rayed section confluent posteriorly. Anal fin similar to and opposite dorsal fin from anus. Ventral fin rays thick, finger-like. Extremely variable; any weed colour, with or without distinct body patterns of large blotching and banding. Stripe below eye diagnostic. Southern New South Wales and Tasmania to South Australia. Rocky kelp and weed reefs from intertidal to 20 m. Attains 14 cm.

Heteroclinus wilsoni   Juv., close-up of head

Heteroclinus wilsoni ▲

Heteroclinus nasutus   Extremes of colour variation ▲ ▼

Heteroclinus eckloniae ▼

LARGE-NOSE WEEDFISH
Heteroclinus nasutus (Günther, 1861)

D III+XXVII-XXXI,3-4. A II,18-23. C 10-12. P 12-13. V I,3. LL 20-26+20-27. Body very compressed, particularly posteriorly, covered with tiny cycloid scales. Anterior section of lateral line has scale on each pore; posterior section has scales between pores. Long slender tentacle above each eye. Nasal tentacles large, multilobate. Dorsal fin in two parts; first section low; following membrane to near base of second part, long-based spinous section with short-based soft-rayed section confluent posteriorly. Anal fin similar to and opposite dorsal fin from anus. Ventral fin rays thick, finger-like. Uniformly light brown to greenish; some pale mottling, usually a distinct dark stripe through eye, white on snout. East coast from central New South Wales to Port Phillip Bay. Shallow algae rock to about 10 m; coastal rocky outcrops. Attains 9 cm.

KELP WEEDFISH
Heteroclinus eckloniae (McKay, 1970)

D III+XXVI-XXVIII,5-7. A II,22-24. C 11-14. P 13. V I,3. LL 17-23+23-30. Body very compressed, particularly posteriorly, covered with tiny cycloid scales. Anterior section of lateral line has scale on each pore; posterior section has scales between pores. Long slender tentacle above each eye. Nasal tentacles large, multilobate. Dorsal fin in two parts; first section slightly elevated; following membrane to near base of second part, long-based spinous section with short-based soft-rayed section confluent posteriorly. Anal fin similar to and opposite dorsal fin from anus. Ventral fin rays thick, finger-like. Yellowish-brown, indistinct banding; usually a series of black spots low in dorsal fin. Entire south coast and northern Tasmania. Shallow coastal algae and kelp reefs. Attains 11 cm.

BANDED WEEDFISH
Heteroclinus fasciatus (Macleay, 1881)

D III+XXVI-XXVIII,3. A II,18-21. C 10-12. P 11-13. V I,3. LL 20-26+22-23. Body very compressed, particularly posteriorly, covered with tiny cycloid scales. Anterior section of lateral line has scale on each pore; posterior section has scales between pores. Short broad tentacle above each eye. Nasal tentacles small, weakly lobed. Dorsal fin in two parts; first section low; following membrane to base of second part, long-based spinous section with short-based soft-rayed section confluent posteriorly. Anal fin similar to and opposite dorsal fin from anus. Ventral fin rays thick, finger-like. Variably banded, olive or greyish with dark bands or saddles; usually a series of pale round spots midlaterally. Eastcoast from southern Queensland to Bermagui. Shallow algae reefs, rockpools. Attains 65 mm.

WHITELEGG'S WEEDFISH
Heteroclinus whiteleggi (Ogilby, 1894)

D III+XXVII-XXVIII,3-4. A II,19-22. C 10-12. P 11-13. V I,3. LL 20-26+22-23. Body very compressed, particularly posteriorly, covered with tiny cycloid scales. Anterior section of lateral line has scale on each pore; posterior section has scales between pores. Short broaded tentacle above each eye. Nasal tentacles small, weakly lobed. Dorsal fin in two parts; first section low; high following membrane connects, often high, to second part, long-based spinous section with short-based soft-rayed section confluent posteriorly. Anal fin similar to and opposite dorsal fin from anus. Ventral fin rays thick, finger-like. Dark brown to pinkish, black narrow bands; usually a series of elongate white blotches midlaterally along sides. New South Wales, south to Jervis Bay. Rocky, low algae covered reef with mixed weedy and encrusted algaes. Shallow coastal bays. Attains 10 cm.

COMMON WEEDFISH
Heteroclinus perspicillatus (Valenciennes, 1836)

D III+XXXI-XXXIV,3-5. A II,22-26. C 10-12. P 12-14. V I,3. LL 14-26+0-25. Body very compressed, particularly posteriorly, covered with tiny cycloid scales. Anterior section of lateral line has scale on each pore; posterior section variably present, scales between pores. Eye tentacles short, broad, leaf-like with long slender lobes at edge. Nasal tentacles small, weakly lobed. Dorsal fin in two parts; first section low, slightly elevated; following membrane to basal half of second part, long-based spinous section with short-based soft-rayed section confluent posteriorly. Anal fin similar to and opposite dorsal fin from anus. Ventral fin rays thick, finger-like. Highly variable; usually greyish or greenish, large dark blotches arranged in vertical bands; usually a distinct shoulder spot. South coast from Cape Conran to South Australia and Tasmania. Rocky reef on sand, with sparse algae growth or weeds; often under rocks. Attains 20 cm.

Heteroclinus whiteleggi ▲

H. perspicillatus ▲   Close-up of head ▼

ADELAIDE'S WEEDFISH
Heteroclinus adelaidae Castelnau, 1873

D III+XXVIII-XXXIII,2-4. A II,21-25. C 11. P 10-13. V I,2. LL 18-27+0-8. Body very compressed, particularly posteriorly, covered with tiny cycloid scales. Anterior section of lateral line has scale on each pore; posterior section short, intermittently present, scales between pores. Small leafy tentacle above each eye. Nasal tentacles small, sometimes weakly lobed. Dorsal fin in two parts; first section elevated; following membrane to base of second part, long-based spinous section with short-based soft-rayed section confluent posteriorly. Anal fin similar to and opposite dorsal fin from anus. Ventral fin rays thick, finger-like; third inner ray rudimentary. Greyish with speckles, vertical broad banding, to almost black; broad greyish band sometimes along middle of sides. South coast, Bass Straight area to Shark Bay, and Tasmania. Seagrass beds, weedy reefs, often in silty areas to about 15 m. Attains 9 cm.

KUITER'S WEEDFISH
Heteroclinus sp 2

D III+XXIX-XXXI,2-4. A II,21-24. C 10-11. P 12-13. V I,2. LL 19-25+0-15. Body very compressed, particularly posteriorly, covered with tiny cycloid scales. Anterior section of lateral line has scale on each pore; posterior section variably present, scales between pores. Short rounded tentacle above each eye. Nasal tentacles slender, leaf-shaped. Dorsal fin continuous or in two parts; first part elevated; following membrane connecting high or fully to base of second part, long-based spinous section with short-based soft-rayed section confluent posteriorly. Anal fin similar to and opposite dorsal fin from anus. Ventral fin rays thick, finger-like; third inner ray rudimentary. Variable grey or brown with irregular vertical bands; males often dark brown to black with distinct white band along sides. Only known from Victoria and south-west coast. Low rocky reef on sand with sparse vegetation; usually in clear coastal waters in 3-20 m. Attains 7 cm.

Heteroclinus sp 2 Male displaying to female ▲   *Heteroclinus macrophthalmus* ▼

TASSELLED WEEDFISH
Heteroclinus macrophthalmus Hoese, 1976

D III+XXIX-XXXI,4-5. A II,25-27. C 11. P 12-13. V I,2. LL 25-27+13-24. Body very compressed, particularly posteriorly, covered with tiny cycloid scales. Anterior section of lateral line has scale on each pore; posterior section variably short, scales between pores. Broad leaf-like tentacle with filamentous lobes at tip above each eye. Nasal tentacles short with slender lobes. Dorsal fin in two parts; first part elevated, prominent tassels at tips of spines; following membrane connecting to base of second part, long-based spinous section, free single elongate flaps at tips of spines, with short-based soft-rayed section confluent posteriorly. Anal fin similar to and opposite dorsal fin from anus. Ventral fin rays long, slender; third inner ray rudimentary. Pale greenish to tan; silvery stripe along sides, variably broken in long sections; thin vertical dark banding below. Recorded from selected places along entire south coast and northern Tasmania. Shallow seagrass beds and dense algae reefs to 18 m. Attains 10 cm.

LONG-TAIL WEEDFISH
Heteroclinus sp 3

D III+XXV-XXVI,3. A II,17-19. C 10-12. P 12-13. V I,3. LL 18-23+25-31. Body very compressed, particularly posteriorly, covered with tiny cycloid scales. Anterior section of lateral line has scale on each pore; posterior section has scales between pores. No tentacles above eyes. Nasal tentacles bilobate, small. Fins have moderately long elements. Dorsal fin divided; first section low; following membrane to near or connected to base of second part, long-based spinous section with short-based soft-rayed section confluent posteriorly. Anal fin similar to and opposite dorsal fin from anus. Ventral fin rays thick, finger-like. Caudal fin large on slender caudal peduncle. Brownish or greenish with distinct pattern. East coast, central New South Wales to northern Tasmania and Port Phillip Bay. Coastal reefs in tall string-kelp and dense, tall zostera beds; 1-5 m. Attains 14 cm.

WHITLEY'S WEEDFISH
Heteroclinus sp 4

D III+XXIII-XXV,2-3. A II,15-18. C 8-10. P 11-12. V I,3. LL 17-25+22-28. Body very compressed, particularly posteriorly, covered with tiny cycloid scales. Anterior section of lateral line has scale on each pore; posterior section has scales between pores. Low, broadly rounded tentacle above eyes. Nasal tentacles small, rounded with pointed tip. Fins have moderately long elements. Dorsal fin divided; first section slightly elevated; following membrane to near or connected to base of second part, long-based spinous section with short-based soft-rayed section confluent posteriorly. Anal fin similar to and opposite dorsal fin from anus. Ventral fin rays thick, finger-like; short inner ray. Caudal fin large on slender caudal peduncle. Variable from green to purplish or reddish-brown, usually with longitudunal dark stripes. Southern waters from central New South Wales to the south-west, but apparently absent in Victoria. Rocky reefs with short but dense green or brown algae; also in *Codium*; to about 10 m. Attains 9 cm.

ROSY WEEDFISH
Heteroclinus roseus (Günther, 1861)

D III+XXIV-XXVII,3-5. A II,19-22. C 9-11. P 11-13. V I,3. LL 19-25+20-29. Body very compressed, particularly posteriorly, covered with tiny cycloid scales. Anterior section of lateral line has scale on each pore; posterior section has scales between pores. Elongate, laterally lobed simple tentacle above

Heteroclinus sp 4 ▲   *Heteroclinus roseus* ▼

eyes. Nasal tentacles with several elongated lobes. Fins have moderately long elements. Dorsal fin divided; first section slightly elevated; following membrane to base of second part, long-based spinous section with shallowly incised membranes anteriorly and short-based soft-rayed section confluent posteriorly. Anal fin similar to and opposite dorsal fin from anus. Ventral fin rays thick, finger-like. Caudal fin large on slender caudal peduncle. Usually brown to reddish-brown; vertical dark broken bands form marbled pattern. Diagnostic markings at pectoral fin bases. Widely distributed in southern waters from central New South Wales, Lord Howe and Norfolk Islands, Tasmania to Shark Bay. Also recorded from Japan but this population probably represents an undescribed species. Mostly in brown and red algaes on rocky reefs; intertidal to 35 m.

SHARP-NOSE WEEDFISH
Heteroclinus tristis (Klunzinger, 1872)

D III+XXVIII-XXX,3-5. A II,23-25. C 9-11. P 10-12. V I,3. LL 20-27+26-32. Body very compressed, particularly posteriorly, covered with tiny cycloid scales. Anterior section of lateral line has scale on each pore; posterior section has scales between pores. Elongate simple or bilobate tentacle above eyes. Nasal tentacles have small flap. Fins have long elements. Dorsal fin divided; first section highly elevated; following membrane to near base of second part, long-based spinous section with short-based soft-rayed section confluent posteriorly. Anal fin similar to and opposite dorsal fin from anus. Ventral fin rays thick, finger-like. Caudal fin large on slender caudal peduncle. Pale greenish to brownish; figure-8 like dark spots along upper and lower sides. South-east coast, from the Sydney area to South Australia and Tasmania. Shallow, low reef on sand with sparse tall weeds in seagrass areas; feeds mostly on weed shrimps. Attains 30 cm.

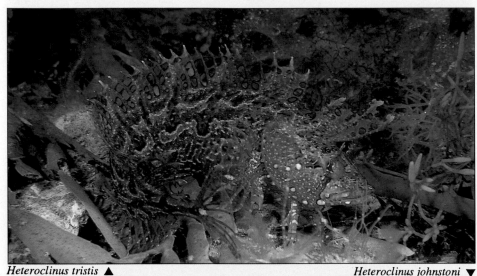

Heteroclinus tristis ▲

Heteroclinus johnstoni ▼

Heteroclinus marmoratus ▼

JOHNSTON'S WEEDFISH
Heteroclinus johnstoni (Saville-Kent, 1886)

D III+XXXI-XXXIV,5-6. A II,25-27. C 10-12. P 14-16. V I,3. LL 20-29+26-32. Body very compressed, particularly posteriorly, covered with tiny cycloid scales. Anterior section of lateral line has scale on each pore; posterior section has scales between pores. Broad, irregular-shaped multilobate tentacle above each eye. Nasal tentacles long with star-like arrangement of long lobes. Fins have long elements. Dorsal fin divided; first section slightly elevated; following membrane to base of second part, long-based spinous section with short-based soft-rayed section confluent posteriorly. Anal fin similar to and opposite dorsal fin from anus. Ventral fin rays thick, finger-like. Caudal fin large on slender caudal peduncle. Juveniles distinctly banded; adults have a series of ocellus-like spots in each dark band along upper sides. South coast from Bass Strait region and Tasmania to South Australia. Low reef on sand with tall vegetation, from intertidal to 50 m. Attains 40 cm.

Heterclinus johnstoni Juv., close-up of head

SLENDER WEEDFISH
Heteroclinus marmoratus (Klunzinger, 1872)

D III+XXXV-XXXIX,6. A II,27-29. C 12. P 12-14. V I,3. LL 14-22+0-6. Body compressed, particularly posteriorly at caudal peduncle, covered with tiny cycloid scales. Anterior section of lateral line has scale on each pore; posterior section short or absent, scales between pores. Young have elongate simple tentacle above each eye; sometimes absent in adults. Nasal tentacles tubed with small flap. Single long-based dorsal fin has long spinous part confluent with posterior soft-rayed part. Anal fin similar to and opposite dorsal fin from anus. Ventral fin placed below dorsal fin origin. Highly variable from black with some white blotches, to pale grey or brown with marbled or banded patterns. Recorded from Victoria and Tasmania; probably more widespread. Secretive, under rocks in weedy, sandy areas. Attains 14 cm. *H. puellarum* Scott, 1955, appears to be synonym based on juveniles.

VARIABLE SNAKE-BLENNY
Ophiclinus ningulus George and Springer, 1980

D XLIV-XLVI,1. A II,28-30. C 13. P 11-12. V I;2. Body elongate, compressed, with tiny cycloid scales. Lateral line consists of a series of 12 to15 pores; following pitch-like depressions, from above opercle, not associated with scales. Anterior nostril simply tubed. Fins low, of uniform heights. Single long-based dorsal fin from above posterior opercle to caudal fin, joined by membrane. Anal fin similar to and opposite dorsal fin from anus; joined by notched membrane to caudal fin. Ventral fin small; rays thick, finger-like. Variable from plain pale yellowish-brown to distinctly mottled or spotted paterns to almost brown-black. Known from entire south coast and northern Tasmania. Reef areas; most common in sponge areas from 5-20 m. Attains 75 mm. This genus, confined to south coast waters, comprises six species.

FROSTED SNAKE-BLENNY
Ophiclinus gabrieli Waite, 1906

D LII-LV,1. A II,33-36. C 13-15. P 11-12. V I,2. Body elongate, compressed, with tiny cycloid scales. Lateral line consists of a series of 12 to 16 pores; following pitch-like depressions, from above opercle, not associated with scales. Anterior nostril simply tubed. Fins low, of uniform heights. Single long-based dorsal fin from above posterior opercle to caudal fin, joined by membrane. Anal fin similar to and opposite dorsal fin from anus; joined by slightly notched membrane to caudal fin. Ventral fin small; rays thick, finger-like. Dark brown to almost black, white mottling and blotches posteriorly. Eastern south coast to Kangaroo Island and northern Tasmania. In seagrass areas, commonly amongst blackened dead *Amphibolus* seagrass leaves in collective areas in Western Port. Attains 16 cm.

BLACK-BACK SNAKE-BLENNY
Ophiclinus gracilis Waite, 1906

D XLIV-XLIX,1. A II,27-31. C 13-14. P 11-13. V I,2. Body elongate, compressed, with tiny cycloid scales. Lateral line consists of a series of 15 to 20 pores; following pitch-like depressions, from above opercle, not associated with scales. Anterior nostril simply tubed. Fins low, of uniform heights. Single long-based dorsal fin from above posterior opercle to caudal fin, joined by membrane. Anal fin similar to and opposite dorsal fin from anus; joined by notched membrane to caudal fin. Ventral fin small; rays thick, finger-like. Usually pale, dark broad stripe through eye continuing along upper sides to caudal fin; sometimes all dark, a few pale spots in series midlaterally along entire body. Wide-spread in southern waters from Sydney to Rottnest Island, including Tasmania. Silty environments, commonly among rotting vegetation in Port Phillip Bay. Attains 10 cm.

Ophiclinus ningulus Extremes of colour variation ▲ ▼

Ophiclinus gabrieli ▼

Ophiclinus gracilis ▼

VARIEGATED SNAKE-BLENNY
Ophiclinops varius (McCulloch and Waite, 1918)

D XL-XLV,1. A II,27-29. C 12-14. P 6-10. V I,2. Body elongate, compressed, with tiny cycloid scales. Lateral line consists of a series of two to three pores; following pitch-like depressions, from above opercle, not associated with scales. Anterior nostril simply tubed. Fins low, of uniform heights. Single long-based dorsal fin from above posterior opercle to caudal fin, broadly joined by membrane. Anal fin similar to and opposite dorsal fin from anus; joined by broad membrane to caudal fin. Ventral fin small; rays thick, finger-like. Variable black with frosty white patterns. Entire south coast and northern Tasmania. Secretive; in *Amphibolus* seagrass areas with dropped leaves and other organic litter on sand; extremely well camouflaged. Only attains 50 mm. This genus comprises three species, only known from the south coast.

SAND CRAWLER
Sticharium dorsale Günther, 1867

D XXXVI-XLIII,1. A II,33-39. C 13. P 8-11. V I,2. Body elongate, compressed, with tiny cycloid scales. Lateral line consisting of a series of 32 to 42 pores; following pitch-like depressions, from above opercle, not associated with scales. Eyes dorsally near tip of snout. Fins low, of uniform heights. Single long-based dorsal fin from above anus to caudal fin, joined by membrane. Anal fin similar to, opposite, and with slightly longer rays than dorsal fin; joined by membrane to caudal fin. Ventral and pectoral fins small; rays thick, finger-like, curved inwards. Pale, sandy dorsally, brownish sides. Shallow coastal estuaries; buries in sandy patches in seagrass areas. Pursues mysids along sand surface in crawling fashion, using unusually shaped pectoral and ventral fins, with just eyes exposed. Although difficult to see, specimens easily found by following distinct waving trail they leave behind. Reported from entire south coast; occur commonly in Port Phillip Bay. Attains 95 mm. This genus comprises two species, both confined to southern waters.

Sticharium dorsale ▲

DUSKY CRAWLER
Stichareum clarkae George and Springer, 1980

D XXXVIII-LXI,1. A II,35-37. C 13. P 8-11. V I,2. Body elongate, compressed, with tiny cycloid scales. Lateral line consists of a series of 36 to 42 pores; following pitch-like depressions, from above opercle, not associated with scales. Eyes dorsally near tip of snout. Fins low, of uniform heights. Single long-based dorsal fin from above anus to caudal fin, joined by membrane. Anal fin similar to and opposite dorsal fin with slightly longer rays, joined by membrane to caudal fin. Ventral and pectoral fins small, rays thick, finger-like, curved inwards. Pale, sandy dorsally, with brownish to blackish sides. Southern waters, from Montague Island to Cape Naturaliste. Shallow coastal outcrops with somewhat sheltered sandy bays. At Montague Island on sheltered coastal side where torn-loose encrusted algae accumulates near rocks and mixes with sand, in which they bury. Depth about 5-10 m. Attains 80 mm.

Sticharium clarkae ▼

EEL BLENNY
Peronedys anguillaris Steindachner, 1884

D LXXVI-LXXXIV,2-4. A II,55-62. C 13. P 3-4 VI,2. Body very elongate, slightly compressed, tapers almost to point; scales tiny, cycloid. Lateral line consists of a series of 9 to 15 pores with following pitch-like depressions, from above opercle, not associated with scales. Eyes dorsally near tip of snout. Fins low, of uniform heights. Single long-based dorsal fin from above anus to caudal fin, broadly joined by membrane. Anal fin similar to, opposite, and with slightly longer rays than dorsal fin; broadly joined by membrane to caudal fin. Ventral and pectoral fins minute. Black dorsally; pale but distinct longitudinal lines over sides of head, body. Distribution disjunct; only known from Moreton Bay and South Australia. Seems very habitat specific; lives primarily in still estuaries where living seagrasses are based on decaying ones; found among latter. Because of habitat requirements, can be expected at estuaries of Flinders Island, Corners Inlet. Attains 13 cm.

BLENNIES
BLENNIIDAE

A very large family of usually very small species, with more than 50 genera and well over 300 species presently considered to belong here. Most species are distributed in tropical seas and the number of species rapidly reduces toward temperate seas. They feature a slimy skin rather than scales, and teeth consist of a comb-like arrangement in each jaw, often with greatly enlarged canines in certain species. Most are very slender fishes, and some are eel-like. A long-based continuous dorsal fin consisting of flexible spines and soft rays covers the body from head to caudal fin, with a similar anal fin opposite, posterior to the anus. The caudal fin is mostly truncate, often with extended tips which are sometimes greatly produced with long filaments. Various species mimic other species within the family, some which are known to possess a toxin serving as models. Others mimic different fishes, probably the best known being the blenny mimic of the Cleaner Wrasse (Labridae). Blennies are primarily benthic fishes, but some specialised species feed on zooplankton. Others attack other fishes well above the substrate, feeding on their external parts. They approach with trickery, such as mimicking a cleaner wrasse. In south-eastern waters the majority of species in this family are tropical expatriates, floating down as larvae with the southern moving currents that originate in the tropical coral reefs. Of the 13 species included here, only three are common local species. The remainder are from tropical waters, and one is probably a visitor from New Zealand waters. The bottom-dwelling species feed on a mixed diet of algae and invertebrates, those living in intertidal zones feed primarily on algae, and those living deeper primarily on invertebrates.

Oyster Blenny (*Omobranchus anolius*)

OYSTER BLENNY
Omobranchus anolius (Valenciennes, 1836)

D XI-XIII,17-19. A II,19-22. C 12-13. P 13. V I,2. Body compressed. Snout has steep profile; males have large fleshy crest; eyes small, placed high above end of mouth. Single row of close-set slender teeth in each jaw, recurving canines at corner. Single long-based dorsal fin; males have greatly produced

Omobranchus anolius　Male ▼　Juv. ▲

filamentous rays posteriorly. Ventral fins long, slender, headed by embedded spine. Pectoral fins rounded; middle rays longest. Brownish to greenish; females with some black spotting, males with blue. Unusual distribution along the east coast, from the Gulf of Carpenteria to the Spencer Gulf. Commonly observed in New South Wales in estuaries with oyster shells, however occurs secretively in large tubeworm encrustations in the intertidal zone in Port Phillip Bay. Attains 75 mm. Primarily tropical genus of the Indo-Pacific comprising 19 small species.

HORNED BLENNY
Parablennius intermedius (Ogilby, 1915)

D XII,16-17. A II,18-20. C 13. P 14. V I,3. Body compressed, tapers to caudal fin. Head broad, bulbous in large individuals; snout has

steep profile; eyes small, placed high above end of mouth; multilobate fleshy tentacles above each eye, large and filamentous in males. Mouth broad; single row of close-set slender teeth in each jaw, recurving canines at corner. Single long-based dorsal fin with slight notch over posterior spines. Anal fin similar to and opposite soft-rayed dorsal section. Caudal fin rounded; rays similar length rays to dorsal fin rays. Middle rays of ventral fins long, slender; fins headed by embedded spine. Pectoral fins rounded; middle rays longest. Variable, from pale to dark grey-brown; series of moderate-sized spots along upper sides. Common east coast species; ranges from Queensland to southern New South Wales. Intertidal to about 10 m; from estuaries to coastal bays, often on jetty pylons. Attains 12 cm.

Parablennius intermedius　Juv.

Parablennius intermedius　Male ▼

Parablennius tasmaniensis　Male ▼

TASMANIAN BLENNY
Parablennius tasmanianus (Richardson, 1849)

D XII,16-19. A II,19-20. C 13. P 14. V I,3. Body compressed, tapers to caudal fin. Head broad, bulbous in large individuals; snout has steep profile; eyes small, placed high above end of mouth; multilobate fleshy tentacles above each eye, large and filamentous in males. Single row of close-set slender teeth in each jaw, recurving canines at corner. Single, long-based dorsal fin with slight notch over posterior spines. Anal fin similar to and opposite soft-rayed dorsal section. Caudal fin rounded; rays similar length rays to dorsal fin rays. Middle rays of ventral fins long, slender; fins headed by embedded spine. Pectoral fins rounded; middle rays longest. Variable pale to ash-grey; young with moderate-sized dark blotches along sides; adults finely spotted. South coast species ranging commonly from east Victoria and Tasmania to eastern South Australia. Rock pools, shallow estuaries, commonly under jetties along tops of pylons. Attains 13 cm.

Parablennius tasmaniensis　Juv.

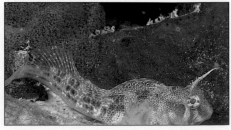

CRESTED BLENNY
Parablennius laticlavius (Griffin, 1926)

D XII,16-18. A II,18-19. C 13. P 14. V I,3. Body compressed, tapers to caudal fin. Head broad, bulbous in large individuals; snout has steep profile; eyes small, placed high above end of mouth; multilobate fleshy tentacles above each eye, large and filamentous in males. Single row of close-set slender teeth in each jaw, recurving canines at corner. Single, long-based dorsal fin with slight notch over posterior spines. Anal fin similar to and opposite soft-rayed dorsal section. Caudal fin rounded; rays similar length rays to dorsal fin rays. Middle rays of ventral fins long, slender; fins headed by embedded spine. Pectoral fins rounded; middle rays longest. Pale below, yellowish above; distinct broad, dark, black to red band along upper sides. Common northern New Zealand species, occasionally sighted in New South Wales (Seal Rocks). Clear coastal reefs in Australia, on vertical rock faces with narrow cracks and sea-urchins in 1-3 m; in somewhat turbulent spots. Attains 8 cm (New Zealand).

PEACOCK BLENNY
Istiblennius meleagris (Valenciennes, 1836)

D XII-XIII,19-20. A II,19-20. C 11. P 14. V I,3. Body compressed, tapers gradually to caudal fin. Short blunt snout; gill opening to isthmus; males with low crest. Mouth broad, low. Eyes placed high, anteriorly; large multilobate fleshy tentacles above. Single long-based dorsal fin; deep notch almost divides spinous and soft-rayed sections; rays much shorter than spines. Anal fin opposite soft-rayed dorsal section; rays short, about half length of dorsal fin rays. Caudal fin truncate, rounded corners. Middle rays of ventral fins long, slender; fins headed by embedded spine. Pectoral fins rounded. Greyish-brown with diffused darker bands and irregular rows of small ocelli. Tropical eastern Australia, south to the Sydney area. Shallow, mainly intertidal; often exposed when water level drops with retreat of waves. Rock pools, estuaries. Attains 12 cm.

BROWN SABRETOOTH BLENNY
Petroscirtes lupus (De Vis, 1886)

D XI,19-21. A II,18-20. C 11. P 13-15. V I,3. Body compressed, tapers gradually to caudal fin. Bluntly downward-pointing snout; moderate-sized mouth; lower jaw hangs well out exposing pair of long recurving canines anteriorly. Eyes placed high; gill-opening restricted, completely above pectoral fin base. Single long-based dorsal fin; second spine elongate in males. Anal fin similar to and opposite soft-rayed dorsal section. Caudal fin truncate, outer rays slightly elongate. Middle rays of ventral fins longest, slender; fins headed

Istiblennius meleagris ▲   *Petroscirtes lupus* Male guarding eggs ▼

by embedded spine. Pectoral fins rounded. Variable, usually brownish with broad lateral stripe consisting of a series of dark blotches with lighter interspaces. Only known from the east coast, Queensland to southern New South Wales, and New Caledonia. Shallow quiet coastal bays and estuaries in vegetated rocky reefs. Juveniles in floating weeds. Eggs typically laid in empty shells, guarded by male for about three weeks. Males usually stay in shell fanning eggs, only come out if food is close. Hatching larvae swim to surface, in captivity to artificial lights. Genus comprises 10 similar species variously distributed in the tropical Indo-Pacific; two commonly occur in New South Wales.

YELLOW SABRETOOTH BLENNY
Petroscirtes fallax Smith-Vaniz, 1976

D XI,18-20. A II,18-20. C 11. P 13-15. V I,3. Body compressed, tapers gradually to caudal fin. Bluntly downward-pointing snout; moderate-sized mouth; lower jaw hangs well out exposing pair of long recurving canines anteriorly. Eyes placed high; gill-opening restricted, completely above pectoral fin base. Single long-based dorsal fin; second spine slightly elongate in males. Anal fin similar to and opposite soft-rayed dorsal section. Caudal fin truncate; outer rays slightly elongate in large adults. Middle rays of ventral fins longest, slender; fins headed by embedded spine. Pectoral fins rounded. Yellow above, white below; two longitudinal dark stripes. East coast only, from central Queensland to southern New South Wales. Sheltered coastal bays and estuaries. Usually swims near substrate in pairs in algae reef habitat; 3-15 m. Juveniles in weeds, seagrass. Attains 10 cm.

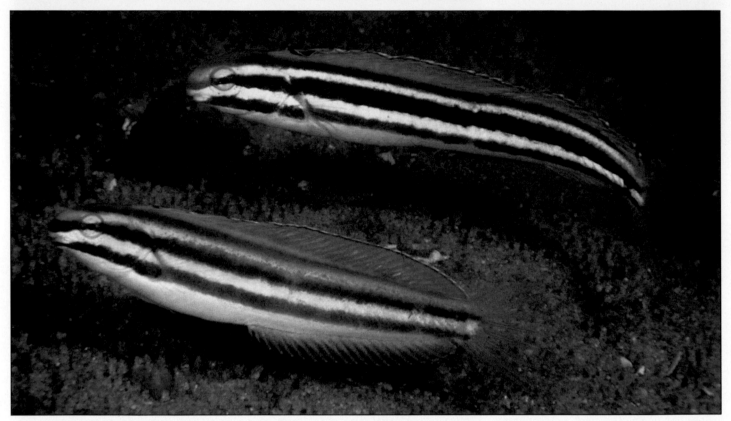

HIT AND RUN BLENNY
Plagiotremus tapeinosoma (Bleeker, 1857)

D VII-IX,34-39. A II,28-33. C 11. P 11-13. V I,3. Body compressed. Pointed conical snout; small mouth placed well back to below anterior edge of eye; lower jaw hangs well out. Eyes placed high; gill-opening restricted, completely above pectoral fin base. Single very long-based dorsal fin. Anal fin similar to and opposite posterior soft-rayed dorsal section. Caudal fin truncate; outer rays slightly elongate in adults. Middle rays of ventral fins longest, slender; fins headed by embedded spine. Pectoral fins rounded. Greenish above, white below; longitudinal band consists of close-set dark blotches. Widespread tropical Indo-Pacific, ranging to subtropical waters, including southern New South Wales and northern New Zealand. Coastal reefs, along rock walls, often in pairs mixing with similar-sized mid-water swimming fishes; 2-20 m. Attains 10 cm. Also known as Mimic Blenny. Often swims with similar-looking fishes, however mimicry is not convincing. Feeds on pieces of skin and fins from other fishes, striking fast and from behind as prey has just passed; quickly dives for cover when pursued by annoyed victim. Genus comprises 10 species distributed in various parts of the tropical Indo-Pacific.

TUBE-WORM BLENNY
Plagiotremus rhinorhynchos (Bleeker, 1852)

D X-XII,31-37. A II,29-33. C 11. P 11-13. V I,3. Body compressed. Short, pointed conical snout; small mouth placed well back to below anterior edge of eye; lower jaw hangs well out. Eyes placed high; gill-opening restricted, completely above pectoral fin base. Single very long-based dorsal fin. Anal fin similar to and opposite posterior soft-rayed dorsal section. Caudal fin truncate; outer rays slightly elongate in adults. Middle rays of ventral fins longest, slender; fins headed by embedded spine. Pectoral fins rounded. Variable, orange to almost black; pale greenish to bright blue longitudinal stripes. Widespread tropical Indo-Pacific, ranging to subtropical waters. Commonly expatriates on the east coast to southern New South Wales. Coastal and estuarine rocky reefs, often in small aggregations with other similar-sized schooling fishes, in 3-20 m. Uses empty tube-worm tubes for shelter, nest. Attains 12 cm.

P. rhinorhynchos   Male displaying to female

FALSE HARP-TAIL
Plagiotremus laudandus (Whitley, 1961)

D VII-X,27-30. A II,22-24. C 11. P 11-13. V I,3. Body compressed. Short blunt rounded snout; small mouth placed well back to below anterior edge of eye; lower jaw hangs well out. Eyes placed high; gill-opening restricted, completely above pectoral fin base. Single very long-based dorsal fin. Anal fin similar to and opposite posterior soft-rayed dorsal section. Caudal fin truncate; outer rays slightly elongate, very long in adults. Middle rays of ventral fins longest, slender; fins headed by embedded spine. Pectoral fins small, rounded. Various colour forms associated with mimicry of *Meiacanthus atrodorsalis*, which has various geographical variations. Widespread tropical Indo-Pacific; juveniles expatriate south to the Sydney area. Coastal reef slopes and rocky drop-offs in 5-30 m. Attains 65 mm.

EYELASH HARP-TAIL
Meiacanthus atrodorsalis (Guenther, 1877)

D III-VI,25-28. A II,15-18. C 11-13. P 13-15. V I,3. Body compressed. Mouth horizontal; lower jaw has pair of grooved enlarged canines with toxic glands at their base. Gill-opening restricted, completely above pectoral fin base. Single very long-based dorsal fin. Anal fin similar to and opposite posterior soft-rayed dorsal section. Caudal fin truncate; outer rays slightly elongate, to very long in adults. Middle rays of ventral fins longest, slender; fins headed by embedded spine. Pectoral fins rounded. Widespread tropical west Pacific from southern Japan to Australia; south as juveniles to the Sydney area. Coastal reefs along low vertical sides in 5-20 m. Attains 10 cm. This genus comprises 16 small tropical Indo-Pacific species, only one of which ranges to New South Wales. Southern Queensland species, *M. lineatus*, probably occurs in northern New South Wales. Their peaceful aquarium behaviour suggests that their possibly venomous bite is for defensive purposes only; they serve as model to other blennies which gain this advantage as bluff.

LANCE BLENNY
Aspidontus dussumieri (Valenciennes, 1836)

D IX-XI,28-34. A II,25-30. C 11. P 13-15. V I,3. Body compressed. Snout broadly rounded, small mouth horizontal from tip. Gill-opening restricted, completely above pectoral fin base. Single very long-based dorsal fin. Anal fin similar to and opposite posterior soft-rayed dorsal section. Caudal fin truncate; outer rays slightly elongate in adults; some geographical variations have long filaments centrally as well. Middle rays of ventral fins longest, slender; fins headed by embedded spine. Pectoral fins rounded. Usually brownish or yellowish above, pale below; dark band from snout to caudal fin. Very widespread tropical Indo-Pacific, ranging broadly into subtropical zones; on the east coast to southern New South Wales. Coastal, protected bays, usually staying close to the substrate; quickly retreats into empty tube-worm holes (backwards). Attains 12 cm. This genus comprises only two species, both widespread in the tropical Indo-Pacific.

FALSE CLEANERFISH
Aspidontus taeniatus Quoy and Gaimard, 1834

D X-XII,26-29. A II,25-28. C 11. P 13-15. V I,3. Body compressed. Snout broadly pointed, small mouth below posterior to tip. Eyes moderately large; gill-opening restricted, completely above pectoral fin base. Single very long-based dorsal fin. Anal fin similar to and opposite posterior soft-rayed dorsal section. Caudal fin broadly rounded. Ventral fins very small; middle rays longest and slender; fins headed by embedded spine. Pectoral fins small, rounded. Pale blue; black stripe increases from narrow at tip of snout to broad at end of caudal fin. Very widespread tropical Indo-Pacific, ranging well south in New South Wales as adult. Perfect copy of the Cleaner Wrasses *Labroides dimidiatus*. Feeds by biting unsuspecting prey, taking mainly bits of fin; more experienced fishes learn to recognise the imposter and often chase it. Attains 10 cm.

Aspidontus dussumieri ▲   *Aspidontus taeniatus* ▼

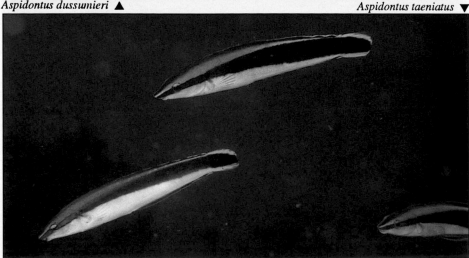

DRAGONETS
FAMILY CALLIONYMIDAE

A large family comprising at least nine genera and about 125 species, however some authors divide species over more genera than others, and numerous small species in the tropics may represent new species. These fishes have elongate, usually depressed bodies and broad spiny heads. Instead of scales, they have a tough slimy skin which is tastes bad and has a strong odour, giving some species the common name stinkfish. The mouth is greatly protrusible, extending out at a downward angle, and the jaws have villiform teeth. The gill opening is restricted to a small pore at a level just above the pectoral fin base. The preopercle spine usually armed with hooks or antrorse spines. The dragonets are sexually dimorphic; males are sometimes very colourful and usually have greatly produced fin rays or entire fins. The dorsal fin has separate short-based spinous and long-based soft-rayed sections, usually with tall rays. The anal fin is similar to and opposite the second dorsal fin. The caudal fin is large, fan-like and often greatly produced in males. The ventral fins are very large, widely separated from each other, and almost joined with the pectoral fins. Dragonets are benthic and many are buried in sand for most of the time. The reef dwellers hug the substrate closely, virtually skipping along with fins touching the bottom at all times. During spawning, the pair (occasionally an extra male joins in) rise slowly from the substrate with ventral fins together to spawn. Eggs float and the larvae are planktonic. Adults range from very shallow depths to 400 m, depending on the genus or species, and mostly occur in sandy habitats. A few small species are typical reef dwellers which, unlike most, do not bury in the substrate. The species are primarily distributed in all tropical seas, ranging to warm-temperate zones, and are usually of no commercial value.

Some species are thought to have toxin in their skin. Dragonets are mostly small species, ranging from just 35 mm to about 35 cm.

PAINTED STINKFISH
Eocallionymus papilio (Günther, 1864)

D IV,7. A 6-7. C 10. P 18-20. V I,5. Body elongate; head short, broad, depressed; caudal peduncle long. Preopercle spine has up-curving tip, one hook on inner edge. Distinct lateral line, straight along upper sides, descending to mid-body line below posterior part of second dorsal fin, continuing to caudal fin. Tall second dorsal fin centrally placed; short-based first dorsal fin just anterior. Anal fin similar and slightly posterior to second dorsal fin. Caudal fin large, fan-like. Ventral fins large, reaching as far as more posteriorly placed pectoral fins. Soft rays variably branched, partly or to base, often depending on geographical populations and size. Colours highly variable, especially between east and south coast populations, including fin patterns. Apart from males, mostly sandy-coloured with complicated patterns of diffused spots and bars (see photographs). Single wide-ranging species presently recognised from the east and south coast, ranging from southern Queensland to south-western Australia. Possibly comprises several species. Coastal reefs, estuaries, from sheltered to turbulent reefs; from intertidal to at least 50 m.

Eocallionymus papilio ▲ Displaying male ▼

COMMON STINKFISH
Foetorepus calauropomus (Richardson, 1844)

D IV,8. A 7. C 10. P 17-21. V I,5. Body elongate; head moderately large, broad, depressed. Large males develop strongly convex hump-like snout in front of eyes. Preopercle spine long with up-curving tip, one hook on inner edge. Distinct lateral line, straight along upper sides, descending to mid-body line below anterior part of second dorsal fin, continuing over very long caudal peduncle to caudal fin. Tall second dorsal fin centrally placed; short-based first dorsal fin just anterior. Anal fin similar and slightly posterior to second dorsal fin. Caudal fin large, fan-like; greatly produced in males. Ventral fins large, reaching as far as more posteriorly placed pectoral fins. Soft rays variably branched, partly or to base, often depending on geographical populations and size. Colours highly variable with depth; some geographical variations; sandy colour to bright red with blotchy markings. New South Wales fishes have blue scribbles and spots all over; males have ornamental fins. Single widespread species recognised from southern Queensland to all southern states, and also New Zealand; at least two distinct forms, east coast south to Bermagui, and south coast. Various habitats from shallow seagrass beds to deep offshore in sponge areas, in 1-100 m. Attains 30 cm. Second, smaller species, *F. phasis* (Günther, 1880), has similar range but occurs in depths in excess of 100 m. Several other species in Japan.

Male, south coast form ▲   Male, east coast form ▼

Female, east coast form ▼

SPOTTED SAND-DRAGONET
Repomucenus calcaratus (Macleay, 1881)

D IV,9. A 9. C 10. P 18-21. V I,5. Body elongate, depressed; head short, broad, depressed; caudal peduncle slender. Preopercle spine has up-curving tip, three hooks on inner edge, antrorse spine as base. Distinct lateral line, straight along upper sides, descending to mid-body line below anterior part of second dorsal fin, continuing to caudal fin. Tall second dorsal fin centrally placed; short-based first dorsal fin just anterior. Anal fin similar and slightly posterior to second dorsal fin. Caudal fin large, fan-like; elongated in males. Ventral and pectoral fins large, about equal in length; ventral fin almost reaches anal fin. Plain sandy-coloured; distinct pattern in first dorsal fin. Southern Queensland and New South Wales; one record from South Australia possibly a misidentification of similar west coast species, *R. goodladi* (Whitley, 1944). Coastal bays on sand flats near reefs, in 5-100 m. Attains 20 cm. Genus has numerous similar species; Australian species not well-known.

Repomucenus calcaratus ▲

Repomucenus limiceps ▼

Synchiropus ocellatus ▼

ROUGH-HEAD DRAGONET
Repomucenus limiceps (Ogilby, 1908)

D IV,9. A 9. C 10. P 18-20. V I,5. Body elongate, depressed; head short, broad, depressed; caudal peduncle slender. Preopercle spine has up-curving tip, two hooks on inner edge, antrorse spine as base. Distinct lateral line, straight along upper sides, descending to mid-body line below anterior part of second dorsal fin, continuing to caudal fin. Tall second dorsal fin centrally placed; short-based first dorsal fin just anterior; males have greatly extended filaments on first two spines. Anal fin similar and slightly posterior to second dorsal fin. Caudal fin large, fan-like; elongated in males. Ventral and pectoral fins large, about equal in length; ventral fin almost reaches anal fin. Plain sandy; distinctly coloured first dorsal fin. Central Queensland to northern New South Wales; uncertain distribution in latter. Coastal and sandy estuaries along seagrass and reef margins, usually in small aggregations; shallow to about 100 m. Attains 25 cm; usually much smaller.

MARBLED DRAGONET
Synchiropus ocellatus (Pallas, 1770)

D IV,8-9. A 7-8. C 10. P 18-23. V I,5. Body moderately elongate, slightly depressed; head short, broad, depressed. Preopercle spine has up-curving tip, one hook on inner edge. Distinct lateral line, straight along upper sides to caudal fin. Tall second dorsal fin centrally placed; short-based first dorsal fin just anterior; first dorsal fin in males very large, taller than second fin. Anal fin similar and slightly posterior (by one ray) to second dorsal fin. Caudal fin large, fan-like. Ventral fin very large, rounded, reaches well onto anal fin; pectoral fin reaches as far, but placed posteriorly. Broadly distributed species of the tropical west Pacific from central New South Wales to southern Japan; juveniles south to Sydney area. Shallow coral reef flats and rocky areas from about 1-50 m. Sheltered coastal bays and inner reefs. Attains 65 mm. Tropical Indo-Pacific genus of very small fishes, some very beautiful and in demand as aquarium specimens. Of about 25 species, only this one ranges to more southern waters.

GOBIES
FAMILY GOBIIDAE

The largest family of marine fishes, comprising over 200 genera and an estimated 1,500 species worldwide. The majority of species are tropical, and their numbers rapidly decrease in subtropical to temperate zones. Gobiidae is a highly diverse family and several subfamilies are variously recognised by authors. The ventral fins are usually characteristic for certain groups; in most species they are united into a cup-shape, while in others they are partly united, or just separate. Sensory canals and pores are restricted to the head, and the various systems may be diagnostic for a genus or species. Scales vary from ctenoid to cycloid, from moderately large to tiny, and may be absent in part or altogether. A lateral line is absent. The head is usually small and bluntly rounded, the eyes moderate-sized to large, the mouth slightly to very oblique with various rows of teeth in the jaws, and the outer row of teeth is usually enlarged. The gill opening extends to various heights, usually to about eye-level, and there are six branchiostegals. The preopercle margin is occasionally serrate or with a large spine. Fins spines are flexible. The dorsal fin is usually in two parts, separate or variably united by a membrane: the first part is spinous with six spines, the last of which is often separated by an extra space; the second part is headed by one spine followed by branched soft rays, the last usually branched to its base. The anal fin is similar to and opposite the second dorsal fin. The caudal fin is usually rounded, and often elongate in its centre. Primarily benthic marine fishes, gobies are usually in touch with the substrate; a few readily hover above. Many of the sand gobies bury in the sand at night, while others use burrows. Some live in brackish water and enter the lower reaches of streams, and a few are totally adapted to fresh water. About 350 species are known from Australian waters, and although they have pelagic larval stages, a relatively few tropical species settle in more southern waters, probably due to habitat requirements. Of the 44 species included here, most can be regarded as local to the area where they live. No doubt many more species occur in northern New South Wales, especially in the coral reefs, and others may range intermittently further south.

Sailfin Goby (*Nesogobius pulchellus*)

FLATHEAD GOBY
Callogobius depressus (Ramsay and Ogilby, 1886)

D VI+I,10-12. A I,9-10. C 17. P 16-18. V I,5. LSR 33-44. Scales ctenoid posterior-

Callogobius depressus   Adult ▼ Juv. ▲

Callogobius mucosus ▼

Istigobius decoratus ▼

most on side of body, more pronounced in adults; otherwise cycloid, extending dorsally to orbitals; no scales on cheeks, opercle. Head greatly depressed; eyes dorsally elevated; mouth steeply oblique. Gill openings to upper pectoral base level. Fins have flexible spines. Dorsal fins just separate; first with five spines close-set and sixth double-spaced with following membrane to body; second with one spine followed by soft rays. Anal fin similar to, slightly shorter based than and opposite second dorsal fin. Caudal fin rounded with pointed centre in large adults. Pectoral fins rounded. Ventral fins fused into cup-shaped disc. Pale sandy; dark banding in young becomes diffused in adults. Widespread south-east coast, from New South Wales to South Australia, including Tasmania. Shallow rocky reefs, including estuaries; secretive, under rocks or in narrow ledges. Attains 14 cm. Large genus comprising about 30 species, variously distributed in the tropical Indo-Pacific, two of which are found in southern waters.

SCULPTURED GOBY
Callogobius mucosus (Günther, 1872)

D VI+I,10-12. A I,8-9. C 17. P 15-18. V I,5. LSR 30-36. Scales ctenoid posterior-most on side of body, more pronounced in adults; otherwise cycloid, extending dorsally to orbitals; no scales on cheeks, opercle. Head moderately depressed; eyes dorsally elevated; mouth steeply oblique. Gill openings to upper pectoral base level. Fins have flexible spines. Dorsal fins just separate; first with five spines close-set and sixth double-spaced with following membrane to body; second with one spine, followed by soft rays. Anal fin similar to, slightly shorter based than and opposite second dorsal fin. Caudal fin rounded; centre pointed in large adults. Pectoral fins rounded. Ventral fins fused into cup-shaped disc. Pale grey to dark brown with broad dark bands; often has longitudinal thin lines along scale rows. Widely distributed along the south coast from southern New South Wales to southern Western Australia, including Tasmania. Coastal reefs and estuaries; secretive, under rocks or in narrow ledges. Attains 11 cm.

DECORATED SAND-GOBY
Istigobius decoratus (Herre, 1927)

D VI+I,10-11. A I,9-10. C 17-18. V I,5. P17-19. LSR 29-33. Scales cycloid anteriorly, becoming ctenoid posteriorly, extending dorsally to orbitals; no scales on cheeks, opercle. Head slightly depressed; eyes dorsally elevated. Gill openings to upper pectoral base level. Fins with flexible spines. Dorsal fins divided; first with five spines close-set and sixth double-spaced with following membrane to body; second with one spine, followed by deeply branched soft rays. Anal fin almost mirrors second dorsal fin, and opposite. Caudal fin rounded. Pectoral and ventral fins rounded, almost reaching anus. Pale, sandy colour with series of spots and dashes. Widespread tropical Indo-Pacific, from central New South Wales to Taiwan, and to east Africa and Red Sea. Offshore reefs on clean sand in 1-20 m. Attains 12 cm. Small genus comprising 10 similar species, almost identical except in colour; series of alternating spots and dashes diagnostic for genus.

Istigobius hoesei   Male ▲   Initial phase ▼

SLOTH GOBY
Istigobius hoesei Murdy and McEachran, 1982

D VI+I,10-11. A I,9-10. C 17-18. V I,5. P17-19. LSR 29-33. Scales cycloid anteriorly, becoming ctenoid posteriorly, extending dorsally to orbitals; no scales on cheeks, opercle. Head slightly depressed; eyes dorsally elevated. Gill openings to upper pectoral base level. Fins with flexible spines. Dorsal fins divided; first with five spines close-set and sixth double-spaced with following membrane to body; second with one spine, followed by deeply branched soft rays. Anal fin almost mirrors second dorsal fin, and opposite. Caudal fin rounded. Pectoral and ventral fins rounded, almost reaching anus. Pale, sandy colour with series of spots and dashes. Primarily only known from the Sydney area; possibly in New Caledonia and Solomon Islands. Harbours, bays, sheltered coastal areas, in 3-20 m. Attains 10 cm.

TRIDENT GOBY
Tridentiger trigonocephalus (Gill, 1958)

D VI+I,12. A I,10. C 17. P 18-22. V I,5. LSR 45-55. Scales cycloid anterior-most, becoming mostly ctenoid on body, extending dorsally to orbitals; no scales on cheeks, opercle. Head moderately depressed; eyes positioned dorsally near front of head; mouth oblique. Gill openings to upper pectoral base level. Fins with flexible spines. Dorsal fins divided; first with five spines close-set and sixth double-spaced with following membrane to body; second with one spine, followed by soft rays. Anal fin similar to, slightly shorter based than, and opposite second dorsal fin. Caudal fin rounded. Pectoral and ventral fins rounded, almost reaching anus; upper rays of pectoral fin almost free from membranes. Young with distinct longitudinal parallel stripes, becoming diffused by banded patterns in adults. Japanese species which has become established in various major harbours around the world; known in Australia from Sydney, Melbourne and Perth; Melbourne populations fluctuate greatly and without new recruitment, apparently from ships, they would probably not sustain over a long time. Upper reaches of harbours, rocky reef, mud areas. Attains 12 cm. Genus, comprising four species, originally belonged in northern west-Pacific. Several other species of gobies, and representatives of other families typically of northern hemisphere, have been found in Sydney Harbour.

Tridentiger trigonocephalus ▼

Tridentiger trigonocephalus   Juv.

PADANG FRILL-GOBY
Bathygobius padangensis (Bleeker, 1851)

D VI+I,9. A I,8. C 17. P 18-20. V I,5. LSR 33-35. Scales cycloid anterior-most, becoming mostly ctenoid on body, extending dorsally to orbitals; no scales on cheeks, opercle. Head slightly depressed, with dorsally elevated eyes. Gill openings to upper pectoral base level. Fins with flexible spines. Dorsal fins divided; first with five spines close-set and sixth double-spaced with following membrane to body; second with one spine, followed by deeply branched soft rays. Anal fin similar to, slightly shorter based than, and opposite second dorsal fin. Caudal fin rounded. Pectoral and ventral fins rounded, almost reaching anus; upper rays of pectoral fin almost free from membranes, seemingly frayed. Wide-spread tropical west Pacific; commonly south to Sydney in New South Wales. Shallow reefs and rock pools. Attains 85 mm. Tropical Indo-Pacific genus comprising about 25 species, two of which are commonly found in New South Wales.

FRAYED-FIN GOBY
Bathygobius kreffti (Steindachner, 1866)

D VI+I,10. A I,9. C 17. P 16-17. V I,5. LSR 31-34. Scales cycloid anterior-most, becoming mostly ctenoid on body, extending dorsally to orbitals; no scales on cheeks, opercle. Head slightly depressed; eyes dorsally elevated. Gill openings to upper pectoral base level. Fins with flexible spines. Dorsal fins divided; first with five spines close-set and sixth double-spaced with following membrane to body; second with one spine, followed by deeply branched soft rays. Anal fin similar to, slightly shorter based than, and opposite second dorsal fin. Caudal fin rounded. Pectoral and ventral fins rounded, almost reaching anus; upper rays of pectoral fin almost free from membranes, seemingly frayed. Mostly dark brownish-grey with darker blotching to virtually all dark. Disjunct distribution; known from New South Wales, southern Queensland, but also upper Spencer Gulf in South Australia. Shallow seagrass beds, rocky estuaries. Attains 90 mm.

EYE-BAR SAND-GOBY
Gnatholepis scapulostigma (Herre, 1953)

D VI+I,11. A I,10-11. C 17-18. V I,5. P 17. LSR 29-30. Scales finely ctenoid on body and dorsally on head; partly cycloid on pectoral bases; cycloid on upper cheek, opercle. Eyes dorsally elevated on head. Gill openings to upper pectoral base level. Fins with flexible spines. Dorsal fins divided; first with five spines close-set and sixth double-spaced with

following membrane to body; second with one spine, followed by deeply branched soft rays. Anal fin almost mirrors second dorsal fin, and opposite. Caudal fin rounded. Pectoral and ventral fins rounded, almost reaching anus. Pale, sandy colour with series of small spots and dashes; large specimens often with

distinct shoulder-spot. Widespread tropical Indo-Pacific, to central New South Wales. Lagoons, inner reefs, harbours. Rubble habitat with some algae growth, to about 10 m. Attains 65 mm. Tropical genus with about five species; only one species known from New South Wales.

Bathygobius padangensis   Male ▲   Initial phase ▼

Bathygobius kreffti ▼

Gnatholepis scapulostigma ▼

TAMAR RIVER GOBY
Favonigobius tamarensis (Johnston, 1883)

D VI+I,8. A I,8. C 17. P 17-19. V I,5. LSR 30-35. Scales cycloid on belly, becoming mostly ctenoid on body; head naked. Head slightly depressed, cheeks bulbous, eyes dorsally elevated. Gill openings to upper pectoral base level. Fins with flexible spines. Dorsal fins divided; first with five spines close-set and sixth double-spaced with following membrane to body; second with one spine, followed by deeply branched soft rays. Anal fin similar to, slightly shorter based than, and opposite second dorsal fin. Caudal fin rounded. Pectoral fins reaching near anal fin origin; ventral fins rounded, almost reaching anus. Presently recognised as wide-ranging south coast species, including Tasmania, however occurs in several some-what distinct geographical variations. Primarily in upper reaches of estuaries, entering fresh water, occasionally well upstream. On sand, usually in small aggregations. Attains 11 cm. Provisionally included in this genus, which comprises about 10 species, six of which are found in Australia; similar sand-dwelling species, three of which are included here.

Favonigobius tamarensis   East coast form ▲   South coast form ▼

Favonigobius lateralis   East coast form ▲   South coast form ▼

LONG-FINNED GOBY
Favonigobius lateralis (Macleay, 1881)

D VI+I,9. A I,9. C 17. P 15-17. V I,5. LSR 25-31. Scales cycloid on belly, becoming mostly ctenoid on body; head naked. Head slightly depressed, cheeks bulbous, eyes dorsally elevated. Gill openings to upper pectoral base level. Fins with flexible spines. Dorsal fins divided; first with five spines close-set, first spine often elongated, and sixth double-spaced with following membrane to body; second fin with one spine, followed by deeply branched soft rays. Anal fin similar to, slightly shorter based than, and opposite second dorsal fin. Caudal fin rounded. Pectoral fins reach near anal fin origin; ventral fins rounded, almost reaching anus. Widespread along south coast from central Queensland to Shark Bay, including Tasmania; some geographical variations. Shallow sandy estuaries, often near seagrass beds. Attains 9 cm.

EXQUISITE SAND-GOBY
Favonigobius exquisites Whitley, 1950

D VI+I,9. A I,9. C 17. P 15-17. V I,5. LSR 25-31. Scales cycloid on belly, becoming mostly ctenoid on body; head naked. Head slightly depressed, cheeks bulbous, eyes dorsally elevated. Gill openings to upper pectoral base level. Fins with flexible spines. Dorsal fins divided; first with five spines close-set, second spine often elongated, and sixth double-spaced with following membrane to body; second fin with one spine, followed by deeply branched soft rays. Anal fin similar to, slightly shorter based than, and opposite second dorsal fin. Caudal fin rounded. Pectoral fins reaching near anal fin origin; ventral fins rounded, almost reaching anus. Distinguished by red spots in dorsal fins. New South Wales coastal bays and sandy estuaries, sometimes in seagrass. Attains 90 mm.

GIRDLED GOBY
Nesogobius sp 1

D VI-VIII+I,8-9. A I,7-9. C 13. P 17-21. V I,5. LSR 37-49. Scales cycloid on belly, becoming mostly ctenoid on body, extended dorsally on head to orbitals. Head slightly depressed, eyes dorsally elevated, mouth slightly oblique. Gill openings extend well above upper pectoral base level. Fins with flexible spines. Dorsal fins divided; first rounded with five spines close-set and sixth double-spaced with following membrane to body; second fin clearly separate, headed by one spine followed by branched soft rays. Anal fin similar to, slightly shorter based than, and opposite second dorsal fin. Caudal, pectoral and ventral fins rounded. Sandy above, white below; distinct vertical bars. Very common Victorian and Tasmanian species, ranging to South Australia. Shallow sand flats in bays and estuaries, rarely deeper than a few metres. Attains 9 cm. Little-known southern Australian genus comprising about 10 species, most of which are undescribed.

THREADFIN SAND-GOBY
Nesogobius sp 2

D VI+I,8-9. A I,7-9. C 13. P 17-19. V I,5. LSR 26-30. Scales cycloid on belly, becoming mostly ctenoid on body; none on head or ventrally on belly. Head slightly depressed; eyes close-set, dorsally elevated; mouth slightly oblique. Gill openings extend well above upper pectoral base level. Fins with flexible spines. Dorsal fins divided, tall; first with five spines close-set and sixth double-spaced with following membrane to body; second fin closely follows first, headed by one spine, followed by branched soft rays; last ray greatly elongated in males. Anal fin similar to, slightly shorter-based than, and opposite second dorsal fin. Caudal, pectoral and ventral fins rounded. Sandy above, pale below; shiny blue dashes along mid-sides. South coast from Victoria and Tasmania to South Australia. Coastal bays and estuaries, just beyond seagrass beds on clean sand in 7-55 m. Attains 6 cm.

Nesogobius sp 1 ▲   *Nesogobius sp 2* Displaying male ▼

Nesogobius sp 2 Juv.

349

SICKLEFIN SAND-GOBY
Nesogobius sp 3

D VI,10. A 10. C 13. P 17-18. V I,5. LSR 27-33. Scales cycloid on belly, becoming mostly ctenoid on body; none on midline of belly, head. Head slightly depressed; eyes close-set, dorsally elevated; mouth slightly oblique. Gill openings extend well above upper pectoral base level. Fins with flexible spines. Dorsal fins divided; first tall in males, rounded, with five spines close-set and sixth double-spaced with long following membrane to body; second fin clearly separate, entirely soft-rayed, greatly elevated anteriorly in males. In females, anal fin similar to, slightly shorter based than, and opposite second dorsal fin. Caudal, pectoral and ventral fins rounded. Sandy above, pale below; shiny blue dashes along mid-sides. Male with dark spot between fifth and sixth dorsal fin spines. Uncertain distribution; probably south coast from Victoria and Tasmania to Kangaroo Island. Shallow sandy seagrass areas, usually in small aggregations. Attains 60 mm.

OPALESCENT SAND-GOBY
Nesogobius sp 4

D VI,9-10. A 8-10. C 13. P 16-18. V I,5. LSR 23-28. Scales cycloid on belly, becoming mostly ctenoid on body; none on midline of belly and head. Head slightly depressed; eyes close-set, dorsally elevated; mouth slightly oblique. Gill openings extend well above upper pectoral base level. Fins with flexible spines. Dorsal fins divided; first tall in males, rounded, with five spines close-set and sixth double-spaced with long following membrane to body; second fin clearly separate, entirely soft-rayed. Anal fin similar to, slightly shorter based than, and opposite second dorsal fin. Caudal, pectoral and ventral fins rounded. Sandy above, pale below; shiny blue dashes along mid-sides. Female with dark spot between fifth and sixth dorsal fin spines. Dorsal fin plain whitish in male. Presently only known from Port Phillip Bay and southern Tasmania; probably more widespread. Coastal, sandy estuaries in sparse seagrass or near seagrass beds; 3-10 m. Attains 40 mm.

Nesogobius sp 4   Male ▲ Female ▼

PALE SAND-GOBY
Nesogobius sp 5

D VI,9. A 9. C 13. P 17-18. V I,5. LSR 26-28. Scales cycloid on belly, becoming mostly ctenoid on body; none on midline of belly, head. Head slightly depressed; eyes slightly elevated, close-set; mouth slightly oblique. Gill openings extend well above upper pectoral base level. Fins with flexible spines. Dorsal fins divided; first taller in males, rounded, with five spines close-set and sixth double-spaced with long following membrane to body; second fin clearly separate, entirely soft-rayed. Anal fin similar to, slightly shorter based than, and opposite second dorsal fin. Caudal, pectoral and ventral fins rounded. Sandy above, pale below; pale blue dashes along mid-sides. Male has plain whitish dorsal fin with black anterior spine, black spot anteriorly at base. Presently only known from a few specimens collected on sandy rubble substrate under Rye Pier, Port Phillip Bay, in 3-4 m. Attains 35 mm.

Nesogobius sp 5   Male ▲ Female ▼

Nesogobius sp 6 ▼

TWIN-BAR SAND-GOBY
Nesogobius sp 6

D VII,8-11. A 8-10. C 13. P 16-20. V I,5. LSR 25-30. Scales cycloid on belly, becoming mostly ctenoid on body, extended dorsally on head to orbitals; usually not on midline of head or belly. Head slightly depressed; eyes dorsally elevated, close-set; mouth slightly oblique. Gill openings extend well above upper pectoral base level. Fins with flexible spines. Dorsal fins divided; first tall in males, rounded, with five spines close-set and sixth double-spaced with long following membrane to body; second fin clearly separate, entirely soft-rayed. Anal fin similar to, slightly shorter based than, and opposite second dorsal fin. Caudal, pectoral and ventral fins rounded. Usually moderately dark brown or greenish; cheek usually very dark. South coast, ranging from southern New South Wales to Kangaroo Island, including Tasmania. Primarily in estuaries in mixed seagrass and reef habitat. Attains 4.5 cm. NOTE: Easily confused with next species, however lacks spines in second dorsal and anal fins.

SAILFIN GOBY
Nesogobius pulchellus (Castelnau, 1872)

D VII+1,9-11. A I,8-10. C 13. P 16-20. V I,5. LSR 23-28. Scales cycloid on belly, becoming mostly ctenoid on body; none on midline of belly, head. Head slightly depressed; eyes dorsally elevated, close-set; mouth slightly oblique. Gill openings extend well above upper pectoral base level. Fins with flexible spines. Dorsal fins divided; first tall in males, rounded, with five spines close-set and sixth double-spaced with long following membrane to body; second fin clearly separate, headed by one spine followed by soft rays. Anal fin similar to, slightly shorter based than, and opposite second dorsal fin. Caudal, pectoral and ventral fins rounded. Highly variable; sandy above, pale below; shiny blue dashes along mid-sides. Often with dark patches, depending on habitat. Widespread from Sydney to Perth and Tasmania. Commonly found in seagrass areas, but also rocky reefs to 20 m. Some geographical variation; southern-most specimens grow larger, usually feature higher meristic values. Attains 70 mm; usually to 50 mm.

Nesogobius pulchellus ▲

Nesogobius sp 7 ▼

GROOVE-CHEEK GOBY
Nesogobius sp 7

D VII+1,9-12. A I,9-10. C 13. P 18-20. V I,5. LSR 24-27. Scales cycloid on belly, becoming mostly ctenoid on body; none on midline of belly, head. Head slightly depressed; eyes dorsally elevated, close-set; mouth slightly oblique. Gill openings extend well above upper pectoral base level. Shallow groove behind preopercle. Fins with flexible spines. Dorsal fins divided; first rounded, with five spines close-set and sixth double-spaced with long following membrane to body; second fin headed by one spine, remainder soft-rayed. Anal fin similar to, slightly shorter based than, and opposite second dorsal fin. Caudal, pectoral and ventral fins rounded. Sandy above with pale blue longitudinal line and spotting; pale below. Widespread south coast, from Sydney to Perth; unknown from Tasmanian waters. Coastal sandy bays, entering estuaries, usually in 10-30 m, along edges of reefs. Attains 85 mm.

SPECKLED SAND-GOBY
Nesogobius sp 8

D VI,9-10. A 8-9. C 13. P 17-19. V I,5. LSR 22-25. Scales cycloid on belly, becoming mostly ctenoid on body; none on midline of belly, head. Head slightly depressed; eyes slightly elevated, close-set; mouth slightly oblique. Gill openings extend well above upper pectoral base level. Fins with flexible spines. Dorsal fins divided; first rounded, with five spines close-set and sixth double-spaced with long following membrane to body; second fin clearly separate, entirely soft-rayed. Anal fin similar to, slightly shorter based than, and opposite second dorsal fin. Caudal, pectoral and ventral fins rounded. Sandy-coloured; numerous small pale and orange spots all over. Southern New South Wales to Tasmania and Port Phillip Bay. Shallow sandy areas, semi-exposed to surge, in 2-15 m. Attains 55 mm.

Nesogobius sp 8 ▼

LOW SAND-GOBY
Nesogobius sp 9

D VI,9. A 9. C 13. P 20-21. V I,5. LSR 28. Scales cycloid on belly, becoming mostly ctenoid on body; none on midline of belly, head. Head slightly depressed; eyes dorsally elevated, close-set; mouth slightly oblique. Gill openings extend well above upper pectoral base level. Fins with flexible spines. Dorsal fins divided; first tall in males, rounded, with five spines close-set and sixth double-spaced with long following membrane to body; second fin clearly separate, entirely soft-rayed. Anal fin similar to, slightly shorter based than, and opposite second dorsal fin. Caudal, pectoral and ventral fins rounded. Sandy above, pale below; some vertical bars, both pale and dark, about four to five of the latter on posterior half of body. Only known from head region of Port Phillip Bay, in 5-30 m. On rubble sand among rocky reef; somewhat unsual within genus, flattening its body on the sand rather than resting on ventral fins. Attains 45 mm.

ORANGE-SPOTTED SAND-GOBY
Nesogobius hinsbyi (McCulloch and Ogilby, 1919)

D VIII-IX+1,9-10. A I,9-10. C 13. P 17-20. V I,5. LSR 40-51. Scales cycloid on belly, becoming mostly ctenoid on body; none on midline of belly, head. Head slightly depressed; eyes dorsally elevated, close-set; mouth slightly oblique. Gill openings extend well above upper pectoral base level. Fins with flexible spines. Dorsal fins divided; first tall in males, rounded, with five spines close-set and sixth double-spaced with long following membrane to body; second fin headed by one spine, remainder soft-rayed. Anal fin similar to, slightly shorter based than, and opposite second dorsal fin. Caudal, pectoral and ventral fins rounded. Sandy above, pale below; some dark vertical bars and orange or brown spots. Only known from Port Phillip Bay and southern Tasmania. Rubble-sand or soft bottom habitat in 5-60 m. Attains 75 mm.

BANDED REEF-GOBY
Priolepis cincta (Regan, 1908)

D VI+I,10-11. A I,8-10. C 13. P 17-19. V I,5. LSR 30-33. Scales cycloid on belly, becoming mostly ctenoid on body, extending above head to orbitals. Head slightly depressed; eyes dorsally elevated, close-set; mouth oblique. Gill openings extend well above upper pectoral base level. Fins with flexible spines. Dorsal fins divided; first rounded, with five spines close-set and sixth double-

Nesogobius hinsbyi ▲

Priolepis cincta ▼

spaced with long following membrane to body; second fin clearly separate, headed by one spine, remainder soft-rayed. Anal fin similar to, slightly shorter based than, and opposite second dorsal fin. Caudal, pectoral and ventral fins rounded. Pale to yellow with distinct broad darker bands. Widespread tropical Indo-Pacific; local populations south to Sydney Harbour. Secretive, in caves, coastal reefs and estuaries; shallow to at least 30 m. Sydney population comprises some of the largest specimens, about 70 mm. Tropical genus, comprising about 15 species, three of which are included here.

353

HALF-BANDED REEF-GOBY
Priolepis semidoliata (Valenciennes, 1837)

D VI+I,8-10. A I,7-9. C 13. P 17. V I,5. LSR 27. Scales cycloid on belly, becoming mostly ctenoid on body; none on head. Head slightly depressed; eyes elevated, close-set; mouth oblique. Gill openings extend well above upper pectoral base level. Fins with flexible spines. Dorsal fins divided; first rounded, with five spines close-set and sixth double-spaced with long following membrane to body; second fin clearly separate, headed by one spine, remainder soft-rayed. Anal fin similar to, slightly shorter based than, and opposite second dorsal fin. Caudal, pectoral and ventral fins rounded. Pale, mostly yellowish, broad darker saddles anteriorly. Widespread west Pacific, from southern Japan to Sydney. Rocky ocean reefs in 10-30 m; secretive, in narrow ledges, back of small caves. Attains 35 mm.

ORANGE REEF-GOBY
Priolepis nuchifasciata (Günther, 1874)

D VI+I,9-10. A I,7-8. C 13. P 17. V I,5. LSR 27. Body moderately slender; depth not uniform, considerably less posteriorly to caudal peduncle. Scales cycloid on belly, becoming mostly ctenoid on body; no scales on head or dorsally from broadly above pectoral fin bases to narrow area along second dorsal fin. Head slightly depressed; eyes dorsally elevated, close-set; mouth oblique. Gill openings extend well above upper pectoral base level. Fins with flexible spines. Dorsal fins united by low membrane; first fin rounded, with five spines close-set and sixth double-spaced, usually one and occasionally two long filaments on second and third spines; second headed by one spine, remainder soft-rayed. Anal fin similar to, slightly shorter based than, and opposite second dorsal fin. Caudal, pectoral and ventral fins rounded. Distinguished by orange to red colouration. Queensland to central New South Wales. Rocky estuary reefs, in small caves, usually upside down in pairs. Attains 40 mm.

ORANGE-SPECKLED PYGMY-GOBY
Trimma necopina Whitley, 1959

D VI+I,9-10. A I,8-9. C 13. P 17-19. V I,5. LSR 21-23. Scales cycloid on belly, becoming mostly ctenoid on body; none predorsally and on head. Head slightly depressed; eyes dorsally elevated, close-set; mouth oblique. Gill openings extend well above upper pectoral base level. Fins with flexible spines. Dorsal fins divided; first rounded, with five spines close-set and sixth double-spaced with following membrane to body, second spine

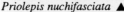

Priolepis nuchifasciata ▲   *Trimma necopina* ▼

often filamentous; second fin just separate, headed by one spine, remainder soft-rayed. Anal fin similar to, slightly shorter based than, and opposite second dorsal fin. Caudal and pectoral fins rounded. Ventral fins partly connect about halfway down their length. Distinguished by bright orange to red spots.

East coast, Queensland and south to central New South Wales. Inner reefs and harbours, shallow rocky reefs in caves or under rocks. Attains 40 mm. Large genus with many similar species. This species was until recently regarded as identical to *T. macrophthalma* from Japan.

STARRY GOBY
Asterropteryx semipunctatus Rüppell, 1828

D VI+I,9-10. A I,8-9. C 17. P 16-18. V I,5. LSR 23-25. Ctenoid scales cover body and head dorsally; cycloid scales on upper cheek, opercle. Head bluntly pointed; eyes dorsally elevated, close-set; mouth oblique. Gill openings extend to upper pectoral base level. Preopercle low, with a series of three to five small spines on posterior margin. Fins with flexible spines. Dorsal fins divided; first rounded, with five spines close-set and sixth double-spaced with following membrane to body, third spine often filamentous, reaching caudal fin; second fin headed by one spine, remainder soft-rayed. Anal fin similar to, slightly shorter based than, and opposite second dorsal fin. Caudal and pectoral fins rounded. Ventral fins separate, just connected at bases. Grey to almost black with evenly spaced tiny bright blue spots all over. Widespread tropical Indo-Pacific, south to Sydney Harbour. Inner reefs and coastal estuaries, on rubbly reef. Attains 65 mm. Small tropical genus comprising about five species, some of which are undescribed. Only one ranges to New South Wales.

AFELEI'S FRINGEFIN GOBY
Eviota afelei Jordan and Seale, 1906

D VI+I,8-9. A I,6-8. C 17. P 14-17. V I,4-5. LSR 23-25. Scales cover body except anteriorly to ventral fin; none on head. Head slightly compressed; eyes slightly elevated, close-set; mouth oblique. Gill openings extend to upper pectoral base level. Fins with flexible spines. Dorsal fins divided; first rounded, with five spines close-set and sixth double-spaced with following membrane to body; second fin headed by one spine, remainder soft-rayed. Anal fin similar to, slightly shorter based than, and opposite second dorsal fin. Caudal and pectoral fins rounded. Ventral fins separate, just connected at bases; fringe-like, branched, fifth ray very small or absent. Pale greenish with large reddish blotches. Widespread tropical west Pacific, south to Sydney. Shallow rock faces with low algae or coral. Attains 22 mm. Large genus, primarily tropical, comprising about 65 species. Usually tiny; largest about 30 mm. Several species known from Sydney Harbour; two common species are included here.

HAIRFIN PYGMY-GOBY
Eviota prasites Jordan and Seale, 1906

D VI+I,8-9. A I,6-7. C 17. P 14-16. V I,4-5. LSR 21-23. Ctenoid scales cover body except anteriorly to ventral fin; none on head. Head slightly compressed; eyes slightly elevated, close-set; mouth oblique. Gill openings extend to upper pectoral base level. Fins with flexible spines. Dorsal fins divided; first rounded, with five spines close-set and sixth double-spaced with following membrane to body, often with hair-like filament on second spine; second fin headed by one spine, remainder soft-rayed. Anal fin similar to, slightly shorter based than, and opposite second dorsal fin. Caudal and pectoral fins rounded. Ventral fins separate, just connected at bases; fringe-like, branched, fifth ray very small or absent. Widespread tropical west Pacific, south to Sydney. On rubble slopes next to coral or rock, in 5-25 m. Attains 25 mm.

Asterropteryx semipunctatus ▲

Eviota afelei ▼

Eviota prasites ▼

MANY-HOST CLING-GOBY
Pleurosicya mossambica Smith, 1959

D V-VI+I,6-8. A I,7-9. C 11. P 16-20. V I,5. LSR 20-27. Anterior half of body broad ventrally, triangular cross-section. Scales large, ctenoid on most of body, dorsally on head to orbitals; absent on belly and sometimes mid-dorsally on head. Head slightly compressed; dorsal eyes with narrow interorbital; snout pointed, mouth slightly oblique. Gill openings extend to upper pectoral base level. Fins with flexible spines. Dorsal fins divided, somewhat angular; first with five spines close-set and sixth, if present, double-spaced with following membrane to body; second fin headed by one spine, remainder soft-rayed. Anal fin of similar base length to and opposite second dorsal fin. Caudal and pectoral fins rounded. Ventral fins fully joined, disc-shaped with thickly branched rays. Highly variable in colour depending on host; often semi-transparent. Widespread tropical Indo-Pacific, south to Sydney Harbour. Lives on soft corals, sponges, stony corals, numerous other invertebrates, also algae. Found in Sydney Harbour on several different sponges and tunicates. Attains 25 mm. Widespread tropical Indo-Pacific genus with 16 species. The only other species known from New South Wales, a single specimen in Sydney Harbour, is *P. bilobata*.

LOKI WHIP-GOBY
Bryaninops loki Larson, 1985

D VI+I,7-9. A I,6-8. C 15-17. P 14-15. LSR 33-53. Ctenoid scales cover body, except predorsal or anterior to ventral fin; none on head. Head cross-section about square; eyes close-set dorsally; mouth oblique. Gill openings extend to upper pectoral base level. Fins mostly small with flexible spines. Dorsal fins separate; first triangular, with five spines close-set and sixth double-spaced with following membrane to body; second fin headed by one spine, remainder soft-rayed. Anal fin similar to and mirrors opposite second dorsal fin. Caudal fin truncate. Pectoral fins rounded. Ventral fin fleshy, cup-like. Transparent; reddish brown inside. Widespread tropical Indo-Pacific, south to Montague Island. Only known to live on seawhips and gorgonian corals. Attains 30 mm. Widespread tropical Indo-Pacific genus with nine known species, all of which are tiny and strongly associated with corals; only one species known from New South Wales.

Pleurosicya mossambica   On sponge, Sydney Harbour ▲   On ascidian, Sydney Harbour ▼

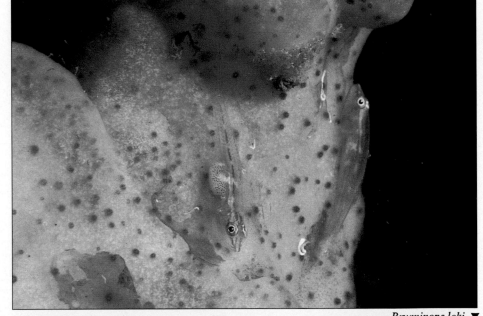

Bryaninops loki ▼

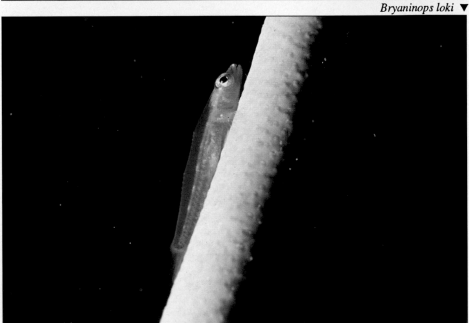

Bryaninops loki   Juv.

356

WHITE-BAR GOBY
Amblygobius phalaena (Valenciennes, 1837)

D VI+I,14. A I,14. C 17. P 19-20. V I,5. LSR 55-58. Scales small, mostly ctenoid on body, extending dorsally to orbitals, dorsally on opercle. Head slightly depressed; mouth almost horizontal. Gill openings to upper pectoral base level. Fins with flexible spines. Dorsal fins divided; first angular with five spines close-set and sixth double-spaced with following membrane to body; second with one spine followed by soft rays. Anal fin similar to, slightly shorter based than, and opposite second dorsal fin. Caudal, pectoral and ventral fins rounded. Variable pale to dark; alternating light and dark banding; spot in first dorsal fin usually distinct; often one or more spots in caudal fin. Widespread tropical west Pacific; in New South Wales south to Sydney Harbour. Coastal reef flats and seagrass areas, entering estuaries to upper reaches. Attains 10 cm. Tropical Indo-Pacific genus comprising about 15 species, some of which have colouful stripes. Only one species known from New South Wales.

Amblygobius phalaena Juv.

LARGE-MOUTH GOBY
Redigobius macrostoma (Günther, 1861)

D VI+I,7. A I,6. C 17. P 16-18. V I,5. LSR 28-30. Anterior-most scales cycloid, becoming mostly ctenoid on body, extending dorsally on head to orbitals, opercle. Head compressed; eyes dorso-laterally; interorbital about eye-diameter. Mouth varies in angle and size, becoming very oblique and large in older males. Fins with flexible spines. Dorsal fins divided; first triangular with five spines close-set and sixth double-spaced with following membrane to body; second with one spine followed by soft rays. Anal fin similar to, slightly shorter based than, and opposite second dorsal fin. Caudal and pectoral fins rounded. Ventral fin fused into cup-shaped disc. Variable pale to dark brownish with irregular spotting and dark bars; distinct spot in first dorsal fin. Southern Queensland to Victoria, west to Glenelg River, and north-eastern Tasmania. Estuaries and harbours, entering lower reaches of freshwater streams. Usually on rocky reefs or pylons in small aggregations. Attains 50 mm. Indo-Pacific genus comprising about 15 species, mostly found in tropical mangroves and rivers. Only one species found on the south coast.

Redigobius macrostoma ▲ Yawning specimen ▼

357

Pseudogobius olorum   Eastern form ▲   Western form ▼

Mugilogobius paludis   Male ▲   Female ▼

BLUE-SPOT GOBY
Pseudogobius olorum (Sauvage, 1880)

D VI+I,7-9. A I,7-8. C 16. P 14-17. V I,5. LSR 26-29 (east coast), 30-32 (west coast). Scales cycloid anterior-most, becoming mostly ctenoid on body, extending dorsally to orbitals, opercle; sometimes a few on cheeks. Head with bulbous cheeks, rounded snout, dorsally elevated eyes. Gill openings to upper pectoral base level. Fins with flexible spines. Dorsal fins separate; first low with five spines close-set and sixth double-spaced with following membrane to body; second with one spine followed by deeply branched soft rays. Anal fin similar to, slightly shorter based than, and opposite second dorsal fin. Caudal and pectoral fins rounded. Ventral fin fused into cup-shaped disc. Greyish-brown, pale below; irregular darker blotches; blue spot in first dorsal fin more or less distinct. Eastern population from southern Queensland to western Victoria, including Tasmania; western population from western Victoria to western Australia. Coastal estuaries, usually in muddy upper reaches with rocks or seagrasses. Attains 60 mm in the west, 45 mm in the east. Tropical Indo-Pacific genus; about 10 species in Australia. Southern populations may represent two species, in which case the east coast form appears to be undescribed.

MANGROVE GOBY
Mugilogobius paludis (Whitley, 1930)

D VI+I,9-10. A I,9-10. C 16. P 16. V I,5. LSR 47-55. Scales mostly cycloid; small ctenoid patches below pectoral fin, caudal peduncle; none before ventrals, only on opercle on head. Head with bulbous cheeks, rounded snout, dorsally elevated eyes. Gill openings to upper pectoral base level. Fins with flexible spines. Dorsal fins separate; first low with five spines close-set and sixth double-spaced with following membrane to body; second with one spine, followed by deeply branched soft rays. Anal fin similar to, slightly shorter based than, and opposite second dorsal fin. Caudal and pectoral fins rounded. Ventral fin fused into cup-shaped disc. Grey to brown; males almost black. Known from southern Queensland to South Australia, apparently not in Tasmania. Intertidal in mangroves; enters lower reaches of freshwater streams. Attains 60 mm. Large tropical Indo-Pacific genus, comprising perhaps 40 species, usually in mangroves.

OYSTER GOBY
Cristatogobius gobioides (Ogilby, 1886)

D VI+I,12. A I,12. C 17. P 16. V I,5. LSR 100 (approximately). Tiny cycloid scales on body only, becoming deeply embedded predorsally. High dermal ridge from interorbital to dorsal fin. Head with bulbous cheeks, rounded snout; eyes forward, dorsally elevated. Mouth oblique. Gill openings to upper pectoral base level. Fins with flexible spines. Dorsal fins divided; first low with five spines close-set and sixth double-spaced with following membrane to base of second fin, which is long-based, headed by one spine followed by soft rays. Anal fin similar to, slightly shorter based than, and opposite second dorsal fin. Caudal and pectoral fins rounded. Ventral fin fused into cup-shaped disc. Grey to brown; males almost black with bright red spots, blue markings. Known from southern Queensland to central New South Wales. Estuaries and harbours, very shallow oyster zones, usually under rocks or nearby on mud. Attains 10 cm. Small tropical west Pacific genus comprising primarily brackish water species. Only one species known from New South Wales.

MARINE GOBY
Tasmanogobius gloveri Hoese, 1991

D VI,13-14. A I,12-14. C 17. P 19-21. V I,5. LSR 38-47. Ctenoid scales cover body only; thin anteriorly over belly, absent dorsally over broad area from centres of pectoral bases to base of second dorsal fin. Head with rounded snout, dorsally elevated eyes. Mouth oblique. Gill openings to upper pectoral base level. Fins with flexible spines. Dorsal fins divided; first low with five spines close-set and sixth double-spaced with following membrane to base of second fin, which is headed by one spine followed by soft rays. Anal fin similar to, slightly shorter based than, and opposite second dorsal fin. Caudal and pectoral fins rounded. Ventral fin fused into cup-shaped disc. Pale grey to brown; distinct broad longitudinal bands along upper sides. Known from Port Phillip Bay to Kangaroo Island, and Tasmania. Shallow estuaries on silty sand or mud, usually in burrows under rocks. Attains 65 mm. Small genus comprising three species, all of which are restricted to the south-east coast; two of these found primarily in upper reaches of estuaries and fresh water.

BRIDLED GOBY
Arenigobius bifrenatus (Kner, 1865)

D VI+I,10. A I,10. C 17. P 16-18. V I,5. LSR 35-42. Scales moderately small; ctenoid on sides; cycloid on belly and predorsally, below first dorsal fin to upper pectoral fin base. Head slightly compressed, snout rounded, eyes dorsally elevated, mouth oblique. Gill openings to upper pectoral base level. Fins with flexible spines. Dorsal fins divided; first rounded with five spines close-set and sixth double-spaced with following membrane to base of second fin, which is long-based and headed by one spine followed by soft rays. Anal fin similar to, slightly shorter based than, and opposite second dorsal fin. Caudal and pectoral fins rounded, pointed in large males. Ventral fins fused into cup-shaped disc. Grey to greenish; several dark longitudinal stripes from head. South coast, ranging to southern Queensland, south-western Australia and Tasmania. Muddy coastal areas to upper estuaries, rocky reefs, in seagrass beds and mangroves. Attains 15 cm. Primarily a tropical Indo-Pacific genus, comprising about 20 species, two of which are found on the south coast.

Cristagobius gobioides ▲

Tasmanogobius gloveri ▼

Arenigobius bifrenatus Male ▼

Arenigobius bifrenatus Juvs.

HALF-BRIDLED GOBY
Arenigobius frenatus (Günther, 1861)

D VI+I,10-11. A I,10. C 17. P 17-19. V I,5. LSR 28-35. Scales moderately small; ctenoid on sides, cycloid on belly and predorsally, below first dorsal fin to upper pectoral fin base; none on head. Head slightly compressed, snout rounded, eyes dorsally elevated, mouth oblique. Gill openings to upper pectoral base level. Fins with flexible spines. Dorsal fins divided; first rounded with five spines close-set and sixth double-spaced with following membrane to base of second fin, which is long-based, headed by one spine followed by soft rays. Anal fin similar to, slightly shorter based than, and opposite second dorsal fin. Caudal and pectoral fins rounded. Ventral fins fused into cup-shaped disc. Grey to brown with fine spotting and dark saddles. East coast from northern Queensland to north-eastern Tasmania and Western Port. Upper estuaries, in seagrass beds, mangroves. Attains 11 cm.

Arenigobius frenatus   Male ▼ Juv. ▲

BLACK-LINED SLEEPER-GOBY
Valenciennea helsdingeni (Bleeker, 1858)

D VI+I,11. A I,11. C 15. P 22-24. V I,5. LSR 110-140. Tiny ctenoid scales extend to upper margin of operculum; none on midline

Valenciennea helsdingeni   Adults ▼ Juv. ▲

of nape, head. Head slightly compressed, snout rounded, eyes dorsal, mouth slightly oblique. Gill openings to well above pectoral bases. Fins with flexible spines. Dorsal fins divided; first rounded with five spines close-set and sixth double-spaced with following membrane to base of second fin, which is long-based, headed by one spine followed by soft rays. Anal fin similar to, slightly shorter based than, and opposite second dorsal fin. Caudal fin rounded in juveniles, developing long filaments on outer corners. Ventral fins separate, rudimentary connection at their bases. Distinctly marked; parallel longitudinal stripes, spot in first dorsal fin. Very widespread tropical Indo-Pacific, ranging into temperate zones as adults; particularly large adults south to Montague Island. Shallow coastal estuaries, to deep offshore reef slopes, usually in pairs hovering just above the bottom. Feed by taking a mouthful of sand which is filtered through the gills for small invertebrates, typical behaviour for the genus. Attains 25 cm at Montague Island; usually to about 18 cm in equatorial waters. Tropical Indo-Pacific genus comprising 15 species, several of which expatriate south to the Sydney area; five species are included here.

RED-LINED SLEEPER-GOBY
Valenciennea sp

D VI+I,15-16. A I,16. C 15. P 20-22. V I,5. LSR 80-100. Tiny ctenoid scales extend to upper margin of operculum; none on midline on nape, head. Head slightly compressed, snout rounded, eyes dorsal, mouth slightly oblique. Gill openings to well above pectoral bases. Fins with flexible spines, but first dorsal more sturdy. Dorsal fins divided; first rounded with five spines close-set and sixth double-spaced with following membrane to base of second fin, which is long-based, headed by one spine followed by soft rays. Anal fin similar to, slightly shorter based than, and opposite second dorsal fin. Caudal fin rounded in juveniles, developing into lanceolate long fin. Ventral fins separate, rudimentary connection at their bases. Distinctly marked with parallel red longitudinal lines. East coast from central Queensland to central New South Wales. Similar species on the west coast, also undescribed; both closely related to *V. immaculata* Ni Yong, 1981, from China seas. Coastal estuaries and inner reefs, in 3-30 m, usually in pairs; juveniles in small aggregations. Common in Sydney Harbour. Attains 14 cm.

ORANGE-SPOTTED SLEEPER-GOBY
Valenciennea puellaris (Tomiyama, 1955)

D VI+I,12. A I,12. C 15. P 19-21. V I,5. LSR 85-92. Tiny ctenoid scales extend to upper margin of operculum; none on midline on nape, head. Head slightly compressed, snout rounded, dorsally placed eyes, slightly oblique mouth. Gill openings to well above pectoral bases. Fins with flexible spines. Dorsal fins divided, first rounded with five spines close-set and sixth double-spaced with following membrane to base of second fin, third spine filamentous, second fin long-based headed by one spine, followed by soft rays. Anal fin similar, slightly shorter based than, and opposite second dorsal fin. Ventral fins separate with rudimentary connection at their bases. Distinct species, pale with large orange spots. Widespread west Pacific, juveniles south to Sydney Harbour. Coastal reef slopes and inner reefs, usually in rubble zones, juveniles in small aggregations, adults in pairs. Attains 20 cm.

Valenciennea sp   Males in territorial dispute ▲   Pair ▼

Valenciennea puellaris ▼

Valenciennea puellaris Juv.

GOLDEN-HEAD SLEEPER-GOBY
Valenciennea strigata (Brousonet, 1782)

D VI+I,17-19. A I,16-19. C 15. P 21-23. V I,5. LSR 100-120. Tiny ctenoid scales extend to upper margin of operculum; none on midline on nape, head. Head slightly compressed, snout rounded, eyes dorsal, mouth slightly oblique. Gill openings to well above pectoral bases. Fins with flexible spines. Dorsal fins divided; first rounded with five spines close-set and sixth double-spaced with following membrane to base of second fin, second and third spine filamentous; second fin long-based, headed by one spine followed by soft rays. Anal fin similar to, slightly shorter based than, and opposite second dorsal fin. Ventral fins separate, rudimentary connection at their bases. Distinctly coloured; golden head, blue stripe on cheek, but yellow may be absent in some equatorial areas. Widespread tropical Indo-Pacific; most commonly encountered expatriate of this genus in Sydney. Coastal and inner reefs, shallow flats to moderately deep slopes; juveniles in small aggregations; adults usually in pairs. Attains 18 cm.

Valenciennea strigata Juv.

Valenciennea strigata ▲

Valenciennea longipinnis ▼

TEARDROP SLEEPER-GOBY
Valenciennea longipinnis (Lay and Bennett, 1839)

D VI+I,12. A I,12-13. C 15. P 20-22. V I,5. LSR 80-110. Scales tiny, ctenoid, extend to upper margin of operculum; none on midline on nape, head. Head slightly compressed; snout rounded; eyed dorsally placed; mouth slightly oblique. Gill openings to well above pectoral bases. Fins with flexible spines. Dorsal fins divided; first rounded with five spines close-set and sixth double-spaced with following membrane to base of second fin, second and third spine filamentous; second fin long-based, headed by one spine, followed by soft rays. Anal fin similar, slightly shorter based, opposite second dorsal fin. Ventral fins separate with rudimentary connection at their bases. Little variation; slightly darker in silty habitats. Widespread tropical west Pacific; south to Sydney Harbour as adults, but the least observed species of this genus in that area. Attains 15 cm.

GLASS GOBY
Gobiopterus semivestitus (Munro, 1949)

D V,7-10. A 11-13. C 17. P 14-15. LSR 16-18. Large ctenoid scales cover only posterior half of body. Eyes set laterally; mouth greatly oblique, almost reaching upper level of eye. Gill openings extend to upper pectoral base level. Fins mostly small with flexible spines. Dorsal fins separate; first minute; second soft-rayed with very short base. Anal fin similar to and mirrors opposite second dorsal fin. Caudal rounded to truncate. Pectoral fins rounded, reaching to anal fin origin. Ventral fins minute. Transparent, sparse pigmentation. South-east coast, Queensland to South Australia; not known from Tasmania. Quiet coastal estuaries, enters fresh water; usually in small to large schools. Attains 25 mm. Photographs show extremes of variation. Tropical genus with about 10 similar small species.

Gobiopterus semivestitus ▼

Gobiopterus semivestitus Variation

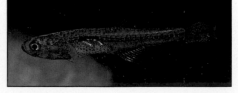

DART GOBIES
FAMILY MICRODESMIDAE

A moderately large family of gobioid fishes, primarily tropical Indo-Pacific, with only one representative in the west Atlantic. The family comprises about 12 genera and an estimated 45 species placed in two subfamilies: Microdesminae (wormfishes), which are not included here, and Ptereleotrinae (dartfishes), the approximately 35 species of which are well represented with eight species in southeastern Australian waters. However, only one is considered a local species, the remainder being tropical species which range intermittently to southern New South Wales. The dartfishes are mostly small, slender, torpedo-shaped fishes. They have a compressed body, the width of which is nearly half the depth, a small head with large eyes, and feature prominent dorsal and anal fins. The mouth is small and strongly oblique, with rows of recurving canines anteriorly, followed by small conical or villiform teeth in jaws. The dorsal fin is in two parts, usually divided at the base or partly connected by a membrane. The first part is short-based

and spinous, often featuring extended rays in males, and the second part is long-based and headed by one spine with following soft rays. The caudal fin is moderately large and varies from round to lunate, often with extended tips or long filaments. The pectoral fin is small and rounded, and the ventral fin short-based and moderately long. Spines are slender and flexible. Scales are tiny, mostly embedded and primarily cycloid but weak cirri may be present posteriorly. The head is naked. The lateral line is absent, there are five branchiostegal rays, and the gill openings are lateral, broadly attached to isthmus. The dart gobies are benthic fishes, but hover freely above the substrate, feeding primarily on zooplankton, either schooling or in pairs. They use burrows for refuge, mostly made by other fishes, and often force themselves in as unwanted guests. A large school may try to get into a single hole at once, creating an occasional problem. They hover mostly in a stationary place above the substrate but quickly dart into a hole when

worried by something, hence their common name.

THREAD-TAIL DART-GOBY
Ptereleotris hanae (Jordan and Snyder, 1901)

D VI+I,24-26. A I,22-25. C 13. P 21-24. V I,4. Body compressed, depth almost uniform over entire length; caudal peduncle slightly less deep. Mouth oblique; small fleshy barbel on chin. Dorsal fin in two parts; first spinous, sail-like, followed closely by long-based second fin headed by one spine, rays about subequal. Anal fin similar to and opposite second dorsal fin, originating slightly posterior. Caudal fin rounded until adult, developing long thread-like filaments with age. Pectoral and ventral fins rounded. Somewhat variable in ground colour; pale greenish-grey to blue-green. Widespread west Pacific; on the east coast south to Sydney. Coastal reefs and estuaries in 5-50 m. Juveniles in small schools; adults mostly in pairs but often numerous pairs in close vicinity of each other; sandy slopes adjacent to reefs. Quite common in Sydney Harbour, but always deep in muddy channels, hence very difficult to sight. Attains 11 cm, plus filaments. Distinct genus with about 15 tropical Indo-Pacific species, six of which expatriate to New South Wales central coastal waters.

Ptereleotris hanae Adult ▼

Juveniles ▲

GREEN-EYE DART-GOBY
Ptereleotris microlepis (Bleeker, 1856)

D VI+I,25-29. A I,24-27: C 13. P 21-24. V I,4. Body compressed, depth almost uniform over entire length; caudal peduncle slightly less deep. Mouth oblique; fleshy barbel on chin reduced to fleshy part of ridge anteriorly. Dorsal fin in two parts; first spinous, rather low, followed closely by long-based second fin headed by one spine, rays about subequal. Anal fin similar to and opposite second dorsal fin, originating slightly posterior. Caudal fin rounded to truncate until adult, when tips become extended. Pectoral fins rounded, ventral fins slender. Pale blue or greenish. Small dark vertical bar along preopercle edge diagnostic for this species. Widespread tropical west Pacific from central New South Wales to southern Japan. Primarily in estuaries and lagoons, or quite coastal bays, in somewhat silty habitat. Usually in small aggregations in shallows, about 1 m to at least 25 m. Attains 12 cm.

LYRE-TAIL DART-GOBY
Ptereleotris monoptera Randall and Hoese, 1985

D VI+I,35-39. A I,33-37. C 13. P 23-25. V I,4. Body compressed, depth almost uniform over entire length; caudal peduncle slightly less deep. Mouth oblique; no fleshy barbel on chin. Dorsal fins united by membrane; first dorsal fin spinous, low, continued by long-based second fin headed by one spine, rays about subequal. Anal fin similar to and opposite second dorsal fin, originating slightly posterior. Caudal fin truncate until adult, when it becomes strongly lunate. Pectoral fins rounded; ventral fins short-based, elongate. Greenish-blue to bright blue; anal fin pinkish. Continuous dorsal fin and lunate tail are diagnostic features. Widepread west Pacific, ranging well into subtropical regions. Adults found as far south as Montague Island. Coastal to clear oceanic drop-offs in 3-50 m. Usually schooling in large numbers; often separated specimens join with other species in the genus. Attains 12 cm, including caudal fin tips.

ARROW GOBY
Ptereleotris evides (Jordan and Hubbs, 1925)

D VI+I,23-26. A I,23-26. C 13. P 21-24. V I,4. Body compressed, depth almost uniform over entire length; caudal peduncle slightly less deep. Mouth oblique; no fleshy barbel on chin. Dorsal fin divided into two parts; first dorsal fin spinous, small, sail-like, followed closely by long-based tall second fin headed by one spine, rays about subequal. Anal fin similar to and opposite second dorsal fin,

Ptereleotris monoptera ▲

Ptereleotris evides   Adult ▲   Juvs. ▼

originating slightly posterior. Caudal fin rounded until adult, when it becomes strongly emarginate with rounded corners. Pectoral fins rounded; ventral fins short-based, slightly elongated. Pale anteriorly, blue-grey posteriorly; distinguished by similar-coloured second dorsal and anal fins which highlight posterior part of body and would easily confuse a predator. Widespread tropical west Pacific; juveniles south to Montague Island. Coastal reef flats to deep drop-offs. Juveniles in small schools; adults usually in pairs. Attains 12 cm.

TAIL-SPOT DART-GOBY
Ptereleotris heteroptera (Bleeker, 1855)

D VI+I,29-33. A I,27-30. C 13. P 21-24. VI,4. Body compressed, depth almost uniform over entire length; caudal peduncle slightly less deep. Mouth oblique; no fleshy barbel on chin. Dorsal fin divided in two parts; first spinous, small, sail-like, followed closely by long-based second fin headed by one spine, rays about subequal. Anal fin similar to and opposite second dorsal fin, originating slightly posterior. Caudal fin rounded until adult, when it becomes slightly emarginate with rounded corners. Pectoral fins rounded; ventral fins short-based, slightly elongated. Adults usually pale sky-blue; juveniles vary from brownish to bright blue. Distinct dark blotch on caudal fin at all stages readily identifies species of this genus. Widespread tropical Indo-Pacific; juveniles to the Sydney area. Shallow reef flats to deep reefs, usually on sand patches or fringing reefs to about 50 m. Usually in pairs or small aggregations. Attains 10 cm.

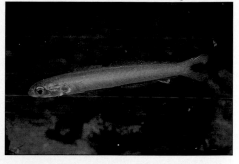

Ptereleotris heteroptera Juv.

ZEBRA DART-GOBY
Ptereleotris zebra (Fowler, 1938)

D VI+I,27-29. A I,25-28. C 13. P 23-26. VI,4. Body compressed, depth almost uniform over entire length; caudal peduncle slightly less deep. Mouth oblique; prominent fleshy barbel on chin, extended longitudinally by skin, forming narrow keel when extended forward. Dorsal fin divided in two parts; first spinous, small, sail-like, followed closely by long-based tall second fin headed by one spine, rays about subequal. Anal fin similar to and opposite second dorsal fin, originating slightly posterior. Caudal fin rounded until adult, when it becomes slightly emarginate with rounded corners. Pectoral fins rounded, ventral fins short-based. Distinctly marked; pink bars on greenish body. Widespread tropical Indo-Pacific; juveniles south to Sydney. Shallow reef flats on outer reefs, usually in large schools, in about 3-10 m. Sydney juveniles in turbulent shallow zones along rocky outcrops in about 2-4 m. Attains 12 cm.

Ptereleotris zebra Juv.

PORT HACKING DART-GOBY
Parioglossus marginalis Rennis and Hoese, 1985

D VI+I,16-18. A I,17-18. C 13. P 17-19. V I,4. LSR 90-105. Body compressed, depth almost uniform over entire length; caudal peduncle slightly less deep. Mouth oblique, almost vertical; no fleshy barbel on chin. Dorsal fin divided in two parts; first spinous, small, sail-like, followed closely by long-based second fin headed by one spine, rays about subequal. Anal fin similar to and opposite second dorsal fin, originating slightly posterior. Caudal fin rounded until adult, when it becomes strongly emarginate with pointed corners. Pectoral fins rounded; ventral fins short-based, slightly elongated. Pale brownish, lighter below; broad undefined dark band from head to end of caudal fin; distinct blue spotting on cheeks. New South Wales, upper reaches of harbours and est- uaries, in small to large aggregations. Attains 45 mm. Tropical west Pacific genus comprising about 10 small species, one of which occurs in New South Wales.

RED FIRE-GOBY
Nemateleotris magnifica Fowler, 1938

D VI+I,28-32. A I,27-30. C 17. P 19-20. V I,4. Body compressed, depth almost uniform over entire length; caudal peduncle slightly less deep. Mouth oblique; no fleshy barbel on chin. Dorsal fin in two parts connented by low membrane; first spinous, first spine greatly elongated, followed closely by long-based, moderately tall second fin headed by one spine, rays about subequal. Anal fin similar to and opposite second dorsal fin, originating slightly posterior. Caudal and pectoral fins rounded; ventral fins short-based, slightly elongated. Very pale anteriorly, gradually becoming bright red posteriorly from below second dorsal fin. Widespread tropical west Pacific from northern New South Wales to Japan. As shallow as 6 m in equatorial waters but in Australia usually in 25 m or more; pairs or small aggregations along reef edges below drop-offs. In New South Wales adults occur off Coffs Harbour. Attains 75 mm. Small tropical west Pacific genus comprising three similar species popular with aquarists.

GUDGEONS
FAMILY ELEOTRIDIDAE

A very large family with 40 genera and about 300 species worldwide, of which 30 genera and 250 species are found in the tropical Indo-Pacific. Few, however, have adapted to temperate zones, and only two are found in marine environments on the south coast. The majority live in estuaries and fresh water, and only a few are truly marine species. They are very much goby-like, but are readily recognised by the widely separated ventral fins. The two genera included here are completely different from each other, one being primarily marine and goby-like, the other more typical to its family in primarily living in brackish water. The latter enters freshwater streams a long way inland, but is also found in pure marine habitats. Several more small species occur in south-eastern waters, but are confined to brackish or fresh water, and some of them are undescribed. In general, the gudgeons are small fishes, rarely exceeding 20 cm. They have two dorsal fins, the first with up to 10 spines. The second dorsal fin is headed by a single spine, is rather short-based, and is usually less than caudal peduncle length. The body and head are mostly covered with either ctenoid or cycloid scales. There is no lateral line, no sensory pores, and canals are usually restricted to the head. The mouth is usually moderately large with several rows of mostly small conical teeth in the jaws. The gudgeons are benthic fishes and very specific to the habitats in which they occur, usually in large numbers. They are mostly found in estuarine, brackish, and muddy habitats. Colours are usually dull, brownish to very dark. Slightly sexually dimorphic, the males usually "turn on" colours when excited by either a female or competitive male.

Thalasseleotris adela   Female depositing eggs ▲   Male fertilising eggs ▼

MARINE GUDGEON
Thalasseleotris adela Hoese and Larson, 1987

D VI+I,9-10. A I,8-9. C 13-15. P 17-21. V I,5. LSR 22-27. Body short, stocky, caudal peduncle moderately long. Body covered mostly with large ctenoid scales, cycloid on belly, absent preventrally and broadly above pectoral fin bases, the area tapering to below end of first dorsal fin. Head large, slightly depressed; eyes large, close-set, slightly elevated dorsally, placed forward; snout short, raised; mouth moderately small, oblique, rows of minute sharp conical in jaws. Gill opening restricted to pectoral fin base. Fins with flexible spines. Dorsal fins divided or separate; first rounded, last spine with larger interspace and following membrane to body or base of second fin, which is headed by one spine with following branched soft rays. Anal fin similar to, slightly shorter based than, and opposite second dorsal fin. Caudal fin large, rounded; pectoral fins of similar size to caudal fins, with long base. Ventral fins clearly separate, long, about reaching anus. Variable colour, very pale to dark brown, plain or indistinct darker patches. Widespread southern waters, from Sydney to Rottnest Island, including Tasmania. Secretive, rocky reefs in coastal bays and estuaries, often silty habitat, in 1-25 m, usually in pairs. Monotypic genus.

Thalasseleotris adela   Egg development

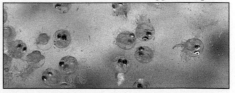

FLATHEAD GUDGEON
Philypnodon grandiceps (Krefft, 1864)

D VI-VIII+I,8-10. A I,8-9. C 15. P 16-20. V I,5. LSR 33-44. Body slender, deepest posteriorly, tapering to caudal peduncle. Body covered mostly with small finely ctenoid scales, cycloid on belly, extended dorsally on head to interorbitals. Head large, becoming greatly depressed in adults; eyes moderately small, dorsal, slightly elevated in juveniles; interorbital increases with age. Mouth slightly oblique, usually reaching to below posterior part of eye. Gill opening restricted to pectoral fin base. Fins with flexible spines. Dorsal fins separate; first rounded, last spine with larger interspace and following membrane to body; second fin headed by one spine with following branched soft rays. Anal fin similar to, slightly shorter based than, and opposite second dorsal fin. Caudal fin moderately large, rounded; pectoral fins of similar size to caudal fins. Ventral fins clearly separate, small, reaching halfway to anus. Variable colour, very pale to dark brown, plain or indistinct darker patches. Widespread southern waters, ranging to

Queensland and south Australia, and northern Tasmania. Marine, usually brackish, and fresh water, ranging far inland on the Murray. Still

waters with rocks or weeds. Attains 10 cm. Second known species in this genus, included here, appears to be undescribed,

Philypnodon sp   Male ▲ Female ▼

DWARF FLATHEAD GUDGEON
Philypnodon sp

D VI-VIII+I,8-10. A I,8-9. C 15. P 16-20. V I,5. LSR 33-44. Body slender, deepest posteriorly, tapering to long caudal peduncle. Body covered mostly with small finely ctenoid scales, cycloid on belly, extended dorsally on head to interorbitals. Head large, becoming greatly depressed in adults; eyes large, elevated dorsally, placed forward. Mouth slightly oblique, usually reaching to below eye in females, past eye in males. Gill opening restricted to pectoral fin base. Fins with flexible spines. Dorsal fins separate; first rounded, last spine with larger interspace and following membrane to body; second headed by one spine with following branched soft rays. Anal fin similar to, slightly shorter based than, and opposite second dorsal fin. Caudal fin moderately large, rounded; pectoral fins of similar size to caudal fins. Ventral fins clearly separate, small, reaching about halfway to anus. Variable colour, yellowish to dark brownish-grey with irregular dark bars; usually a dark vertical bar on pectoral fin base. Known from southern Queensland to South Australia; apparently absent from Tasmania. Brackish water, moving well inland. Attains 50 mm.

SURGEONFISHES
FAMILY ACANTHURIDAE

A large circumtropical family, comprising three subfamilies. The Acanthurinae is largest, comprising four genera and about 50 species. They feature a single movable spine, venomous in some species, on each side of the caudal peduncle. The Nasinae comprises about 15 species usually placed in a single genus, featuring one or two bony plates with spines on each side of the caudal peduncle. The more temperate Prionurinae comprises only a few species, featuring a series of bony peduncular plates. In general, the surgeonfishes are medium-sized fishes with ovate to oblong and compressed bodies, and tiny ctenoid scales. They have a single dorsal fin, long-based without a notch, a long-based anal fin, and the caudal fin is usually lunate in adults, sometimes with greatly produced tips. The pectoral fins are angular and moderately large. The mouth is rather small with small numerous teeth, adapted for various ways of feeding, depending on the genus. Some graze on algaes or feed on zooplankton, or both, and some filter food from the substrate by digesting sand. The planktivores school, often in great numbers, whilst benthic feeders either school or pair. The reef-dwelling species are sometimes very colourful and juveniles may differ greatly from adults in colour as well as shape. The spines are often surrounded by bright colours to serve as a warning. The pelagic postlarvae are transparent and have elongated venomous fin spines. They may reach a moderately large size before settling; specimens in the Sydney area are about 40-50 mm. On the south-east coast the majority of species are tropical expatriates, with Montague Island usually the most southern limit. Only two species in the subfamily Prionurinae are true local species, ranging on the east coast south to central and southern New South Wales.

Convict Surgeon (*Acanthurus triostegus*)

SAWTAIL
Prionurus microlepidotus Lacepède, 1804

D VIII,21-22. A III,20-21. P 16. V I,5. Body greatly compressed, very deep in young,

Prionurus microlepidotus Adult ▼ Juv. ▲

elongating with age; scales tiny, skin leather-like. Lateral line very distinct, following dorsal profile. Series of five to seven keeled plates along posterior sides and over caudal peduncle, accentuated by black colouring around each keel. Series of incisor-like teeth in each jaw. Dorsal and anal fins headed by very short spine. Caudal fin truncate. Pectoral fins large, bluntly pointed, upper rays longest. Mostly grey to almost black, caudal peduncle pale. Colour can change quickly; males intermittently show pale blotches on sides. East coast from southern New South Wales to central Queensland, including Lord Howe Island. Similar species, *P. scalprus* Valenciennes, in Japan. Coastal reefs and rocky estuaries, sometimes in large schools, feeding on benthic algae and in turbulent zones on floating weeds. Attains 50 cm. Small Pacific

genus comprising about five species, distributed over the cooler areas, one of which is found in the east Pacific, two in Australia, both included here.

SPOTTED SAWTAIL
Prionurus maculatus Ogilby, 1887

D IX,24-26. A III,23-25. P 17-18. V I,5. Body greatly compressed, very deep in young, slightly elongating with age; scales tiny, skin leather-like. Lateral line very distinct, following dorsal profile. Series of keeled plates, usually three, along posterior sides and over caudal peduncle, accentuated by black plates and pale blue keels. Series of incisor-like teeth in each jaw. Dorsal and anal fins headed by very short spine. Caudal fin truncate. Pectoral fins large, bluntly pointed, upper rays longest. Mostly grey to almost black; juveniles with vertical narrow yellow stripes on sides, yellow spots on upper sides and in dorsal fin, lines breaking up into spots with age. Fin margins blue. East coast from central New South Wales to southern Queensland, including Lord Howe Island. Sheltered coastal bays and rocky estuaries, usually shallow in small aggregations, feeding on benthic and suspended algae. Attains 40 cm.

BLUE-SPINE UNICORNFISH
Naso unicornis (Forsskål, 1775)

D VI,27-30. A II,27-30. P 17-18. V I,3. Body greatly compressed, scales tiny, skin leather-like. Lateral line indistinct in adults, following dorsal profile. Pair of keeled plates along midline on each side of caudal peduncle; keels knife-like with forward-curving tips, accentuated by blue colour. Adults with bony horn projecting horizontally at eye level. Series of incisor-like teeth in each jaw. Caudal fin truncate with filamentous lobes in adults. Mostly grey to olivaceus, sometimes with broad grey bands anteriorly on sides. Blue caudal peduncle plates readily identify this species, including juveniles. Widespread tropical Indo-Pacific; juveniles south to central New South Wales. Shallow reef flats to about 30 m. Juveniles in sheltered coastal bays, feeding on benthic algaes. Attains 70 cm. Tropical Indo-Pacific genus comprising about 15 species, several of which expatriate to New South Wales waters, two of which are included here.

Prionurus maculatus ▼

Naso unicornis ▼

Naso unicornis Juv.

SPOTTED UNICORNFISH
Naso brevirostris (Valenciennes, 1835)

D VI,27-29. A II,27-30. P 16-17. V I,3. Body greatly compressed, scales tiny, skin leather-like. Lateral line indistinct in adults, following dorsal profile. Pair of keeled plates along midline on each side of caudal peduncle; keels small, not particularly obvious, especially in juveniles. Adults with long bony horn projecting horizontally at eye level, extending well in front of mouth. Series of incisor-like teeth in each jaw. Caudal fin truncate with rounded corners, without filamentous lobes in adults. Greenish-grey to brownish, variable with small spots or thin vertical lines. Juveniles with white ring around caudal peduncle, a feature shared by several other species. Widespread tropical Indo-Pacific; juveniles south to the Sydney area. Young feed on benthic algae; adults usually feed along drop-offs on zooplankton. Attains 50 cm. Similar juveniles in New South Wales probably *N. annulatus, N. tuberosus*.

Naso brevirostris Juv.

BLUE SURGEON
Paracanthurus hepatus (Linnaeus, 1766)

D IX,19-20. A III,18-19. P 16. V I,3. Body greatly compressed, scales tiny, skin leather-like, head scales as small plates. Movable spine folds into shallow groove on midline on each side of caudal peduncle. Fin spines strong, venomous. Caudal fin truncate, corners slightly extended in adults. Series of incisor-like teeth in each jaw. Distinct colouration readily identifies this species; low ventral fin count separates it from all other acanthurids. Widespread tropical Indo-Pacific; on the east coast south to the Solitary Islands. Clear outer reefs, usually in schools feeding above the substrate on zooplankton, ready to dive among branching corals when approached. Adults also feed on benthic algae. Attains 30 cm. Monotypic genus.

Paracanthurus hepatus ▲

ORANGE-BLOTCH SURGEON
Acanthurus olivaceus Forster, 1801

D IX,23-25. A III,22-24. P 16-17. V I,5. Body greatly compressed, scales tiny, skin leather-like. Sharp movable spine folds into groove on midline on each side of caudal peduncle. Series of incisor-like teeth in each jaw. Caudal fin lunate, corners greatly extended in adults. Readily identified by colouration; some variation between individuals from pale yellow to almost black; changes may occur quickly. Widespread tropical Indo-Pacific; juveniles commonly to central New South Wales. Benthic feeder, grazing algaes on rocks and sand among shallow reefs. Usually in small aggregations. Attains 35 cm. Largest genus, comprising about 40 species, represented in all major tropical seas. Large number of juveniles

Acanthurus olivaceus Adult ▲ Juv. ▼

expatriate to New South Wales waters; only the regular species included here.

MIMIC SURGEONFISH
Acanthurus pyroferus Kittlitz, 1834

D VIII,27-28. A III,24-26. P 16. V I,5. Body greatly compressed, scales tiny, skin leather-like. Sharp movable spine folds into groove on midline on each side of caudal peduncle. Snout slightly produced; series of

Acanthurus pyroferus   Adult ▼ Juv. ▲

incisor-like teeth in each jaw. Caudal fin rounded in small juveniles, lunate with greatly extended corners in adults. Adults distinctly coloured; juveniles with three forms in New South Wales, mimicking *Centropyge bicolor, C. heraldi* and non-mimic (?) form which is yellow with orange scribbles all over and posterior margins of dorsal, anal and caudal fins brilliantly blue. Mimics other species elsewhere. Widespread west Pacific; replaced by similar species in Indian Ocean. Juveniles south to Montague Island (mimic of *C. heraldi* which is not known from New South Wales). Usually solitary in shallow coastal waters, grazing algae on rocks or sand. Attains 20 cm. Surgeon mimic gains some freedom out in the

open from predators, which have learned not to hunt pygmy angelfishes because they cleverly and quickly move about, giving predators little chance to strike; after many misses they may look for easier prey.

PALE SURGEONFISH
Acanthurus mata Cuvier, 1829

D IX,24-26. A III,23-24. P 16-17. V I,5. Body greatly compressed, scales tiny, skin leather-like. Sharp movable spine folds into groove on midline on each side of caudal peduncle. Series of incisor-like teeth in each jaw. Caudal fin truncate in small juveniles to strongly lunate in adults. Variable in colour from pale grey to bluish, with thin lines; juveniles can change quickly from almost black to pale grey. Widespread tropical Indo-Pacific; juveniles commonly to the Sydney area. Adults feed mid-water on zooplankton; juveniles feed on benthic algae, often in rocky estuaries such as Sydney Harbour, occurring in small aggregations. Attains 45 cm.

Acanthurus mata   Juv.

Acanthurus mata ▼

PENCILLED SURGEON
Acanthurus dussumieri Valenciennes, 1835

D IX,25-27. A III,24-26. P 16-17. V I,5. Body greatly compressed, scales tiny, skin leather-like. Large, sharp movable spine folds into groove on midline on each side of caudal peduncle. Head profile evenly convex, strongly in adults. Series of incisor-like teeth in each jaw. Caudal fin lunate, corners slightly extended in adults. Adults distinctly marked with black opercle membrane, white caudal peduncle spine. Juveniles almost black with broad pale yellow band on caudal fin, distinct blue margin on anal fin. Widespread tropical Indo-Pacific; juveniles commonly to central New South Wales. Adults usually deep, recorded to about 130 m. Juveniles in New South Wales often at rocky reefs at estuary entrances or protected coastal reefs. Benthic feeder, usually grazing algae on rocks or sand. Attains 50 cm.

Acanthurus dussumieri   Juv.

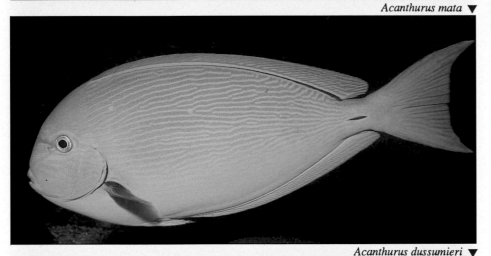

Acanthurus dussumieri ▼

LINED SURGEON
Acanthurus lineatus (Linnaeus, 1758)

D IX,27-29. A III,25-28. P 16. V I,5. Body greatly compressed, scales tiny, skin leather-like. Sharp, venomous movable spine folds into groove on midline on each side of caudal peduncle. Head profile strongly convex. A series of incisor-like teeth in each jaw. Caudal fin lunate, corners greatly extended in adults. Species easily identified by its colour pattern, even as small juveniles. Widespread tropical Indo-Pacific; juveniles south to central New South Wales. Usually very shallow, schooling over reef crests with gutters, rarely deeper than 6 m. Juveniles in the Sydney area usually in shallow interdital zones, coastal protected boulder reefs, often in small aggregations. Shy species in Australia but aggressive towards divers in other areas. Attains 35 cm.

Acanthurus lineatus Juv.

DUSKY SURGEON
Acanthurus nigrofuscus (Forsskål, 1775)

D IX,24-27. A III,22-24. P 16-17. V I,5. Body greatly compressed, scales tiny, skin leather-like. Sharp movable spine folds into groove on midline on each side of caudal peduncle. Head profile greatly convex in front of eye. Series of incisor-like teeth in each jaw. Caudal fin lunate, corners greatly extended in adults. Posterior parts of dorsal and anal fins elongated in adults. Variable, usually pale bluish-grey with violet fins which appear blue in natural light underwater, even at shallow depths. Best identified by spotted face and dark spots posteriorly at dorsal and anal fin bases. Widespread tropical Indo-Pacific; juveniles south to central New South Wales. Reef flats and slopes to about 15 m. Juveniles in the Sydney area in protected coastal bays. on rocky reefs. Small species; attains 20 cm.

Acanthurus nigrofuscus ▲   *Acanthurus triostegus* ▼

Acanthurus nigrofuscus Juv.

CONVICT SURGEON
Acanthurus triostegus (Linnaeus, 1758)

D IX,22-26. A III,19-22. P 15-16. V I,5. Body greatly compressed, scales tiny, skin leather-like. Small but sharp movable spine folds into groove on midline on each side of caudal peduncle. Head profile convex in front of eyes, snout slightly protruding. Series of incisor-like teeth in each jaw. Caudal fin slightly emarginate, corners not extended in adults. Distinct species with little variation from juvenile to adult. Widespread tropical Indo-Pacific. Juveniles often in tidal pools, commonly south to the Sydney area. Algae grazer, which in some areas occurs in massive

A. triostegus Juv., with *A. olivaceus* ▼

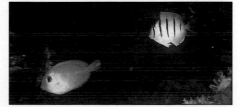

numbers, completely overwelming aggressive damsels which often vigorously defend such areas. Small species; attains 26 cm.

TWO-SPOT BRISTLETOOTH
Ctenochaetus binotatus Randall, 1955

D VIII,24-27. A III,22-25. P 15-16. V I,5. Body greatly compressed, scales tiny, skin leather-like. Sharp movable spine folds into groove on midline on each side of caudal peduncle. Snout slightly protruding. Series of numerous slender, incurving, movable teeth in each jaw. Caudal fin lunate, corners slightly extended in adults. Juveniles distinguished by yellow tail, distinct dark spots posteriorly at dorsal and anal fin bases. Adults easily confused with other species. Widespread tropical Indo-Pacific; regularly occurs in Sydney Harbour as juvenile. Attains 20 cm. Of the six species, three range to the New South Wales coast as juveniles, however *C. striatus* and *C. strigosus* rarely encountered.

Ctenochaetus binotatus   Adult ▼   Juv. ▲

SAILFIN SURGEON
Zebrasoma veliferum (Bloch, 1797)

D IV,29-33. A III,23-26. P 15-17. V I,5. Body greatly compressed, scales tiny, skin leather-like. Sharp movable spine folds into groove on midline on each side of caudal peduncle. Snout protruding. Series of incisor-like teeth in each jaw. Caudal fin truncate. Dorsal and anal fins greatly elevated, sail-like, broadly rounded; total height greater than total length in juveniles; height somewhat reduced in adults. Distinctly coloured with broad bands. Widespread tropical Indo-Pacific; replaced by similar species in the Indian Ocean. Juveniles south to the Sydney area. Coastal, often in silty areas. Juveniles in Sydney area usually well up in Sydney Harbour areas. Attains 40 cm. Only representative of genus, which comprises six species variously distributed in the tropical Indo-Pacific.

Zebrasoma veliferum   Adult ▼   Juv. ▲

LEFT-EYED FLOUNDERS
FAMILY BOTHIDAE

A very large family with 15 genera and 90 species in the Indo-Pacific alone. They are mostly moderately deep-bodied fishes, extremely compressed, with eyes on the left side of the head. The ocular side is pigmented to match their surroundings, is extremely well camouflaged, and is used as the top side. The blind side, unpigmented, is used as the underside. Scales are mostly ctenoid, and in some species the ctenii are very elongate. The lateral line is absent or poorly developed on the blind side. As a family, it is recognised as being distinct, apart from having eyes on left side, by the presence of pectoral fins and a caudal fin free from the dorsal and anal fins. The left-eyed flounders are primarily a tropical family, and the number of species rapidly decreases towards temperate zones. They are relatively poorly represented in southern waters, with only five species included here, one of which is a tropical expatriate, and a second just ranges south to the Sydney area. The larval stage swims upright, has an eye on each side, and is initially bilaterally symmetrical. It changes at various stages depending on the genus and reaches different sizes before settling on the substrate. Some species settle when in excess of 10 cm. As with all flatfishes, once settled they are typically benthic, spending much of the time buried in the substrate with just their eyes exposed. Most species are active on dawn or dusk, a few are nocturnal, and a very few are diurnal. All are carnivorous, feeding on various benthic invertebrates and small fishes. As many species attain a reasonable size and are excellent to eat, they constitute an important food source in many areas.

BASS STRAIT FLOUNDER
Arnoglossus bassensis Norman, 1926

D 96-99. A 73-78. C 15. P 10. V 6. LL 86-92. Body extremely compressed, covered with tiny cycloid scales on both sides, weakly ctenoid on ocular sides in some individuals; scales extend over all of head on both sides. Lateral line on ocular side only, straight with curve over pectoral fin. Eyes elevated closely above each other on left side; mouth oblique; small pointed teeth in each jaw. Caudal fin clearly separate from dorsal and anal fins. Dorsal fin origin above anterior nostril; anal fin origin below posterior part of head. Left ventral fin free. Left pectoral fin slightly longer than pectoral on blind side. Sandy-coloured with large blackish blotches along midline on ocular side. Blind side white. Known from southern New South Wales to eastern Tasmania and western Victoria. Sandy habitat in about 10-70 m; commonly in estuaries. Attains 25 cm. Genus comprises about 25 species worldwide, of which about seven are found in Australia, usually small (from 10-25 cm), of little commercial importance.

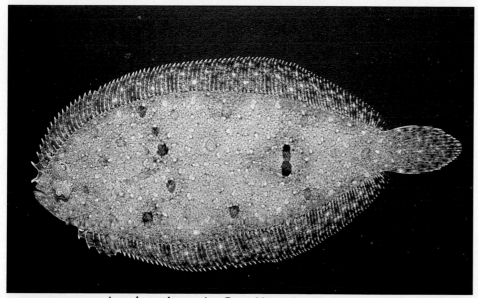

Arnoglossus bassensis   Coastal bay colouration ▲   Estuarine colouration ▼

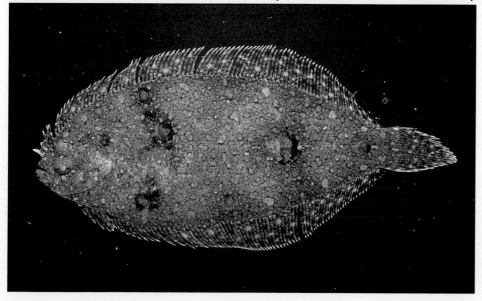

MÜLLER'S FLOUNDER
Arnoglossus muelleri (Klunzinger, 1872)

D 89-97. A 69-75. C 15. P 10-12. V 6. LL 68-72. Body extremely compressed, covered with scales on both sides, ctenoid on ocular side, cycloid on blind size; scales extend over all of head on both sides. Lateral line on ocular side only, straight with curve over pectoral fin. Eyes elevated closely above each other on left side; mouth oblique; small pointed teeth in each jaw. Caudal fin clearly separate from dorsal and anal fins. Dorsal fin origin above anterior nostril; anal fin origin below posterior part of head. Left ventral fin free. Left pectoral fin slightly longer than pectoral on blind side. Sandy-coloured; some dark blotches and numerous moderate-sized pale spots all over. South coast, from eastern Tasmania, Bass Strait to Albany. Coastal waters, rarely entering estuaries, except near ocean side; in about 5-200 m. Attains 21 cm.

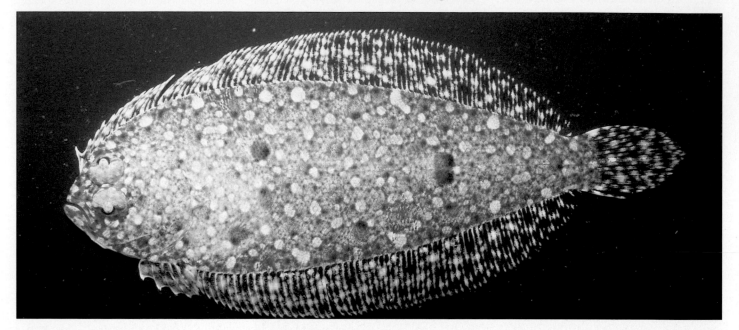

SPINY-HEAD FLOUNDER
Engyprosopon spiniceps (Macleay, 1881)

D 79-82. A 58-60. C 17. P 10. V 6. LL 40. Body extremely compressed, covered with large cycloid scales on both sides, weakly ctenoid on ocular sides in some individuals; scales extend over all of head on both sides; tiny scales over median fin rays on ocular side. Lateral line on ocular side only, straight with curve over pectoral fin. Eyes elevated above each other on left side, lower at snout-tip level. Mouth oblique; small pointed teeth in each jaw. Caudal fin clearly separate from dorsal and anal fins. Dorsal fin origin above anterior nostril; anal fin origin below posterior edge of eyes. Left ventral fin free, below head. Left pectoral fin slightly longer than pectoral on blind side. Sandy-coloured with dark blotches and moderate-sized pale spots on ocular side. Plain on blind side. East coast, Queensland to central New South Wales. Harbours and coastal bays in dark, somewhat silty sand habitat in 3-30 m. Attains 15 cm. This genus comprises about 10 similar small, large-scaled species, one of which is included here.

LEOPARD FLOUNDER
Bothus pantherinus (Rüppell, 1830)

D 86-93. A 65-72. C 16. P 9-12. V 6. LL 82-87. Body extremely compressed, covered with small ctenoid scales on ocular side, cycloid on blind side; scales extend over all of head on both sides. Lateral line on ocular side only, straight with curve over pectoral fin. Eyes with tentacles, elevated on left side, lower eye at snout tip level, upper slightly posteriorly above. Mouth oblique. Caudal fin clearly separate from dorsal and anal fins. Dorsal fin origin above anterior nostril; anal fin origin below posterior part of head. Left ventral fin free. Left pectoral fin with greatly extended filamentous rays, reaching caudal fin in males; pectoral fin on blind side with less rays, usually by two. Ocular side variable; usually sandy-coloured with various sized spots and blotches, some blue-grey; usually several dark blotches along lateral line. Widespread tropical Indo-Pacific, ranging to subtropical zones, south to central New South Wales and Lord Howe Island. Shallow reef flats in sand patches, to about 100 m. Attains 30 cm.

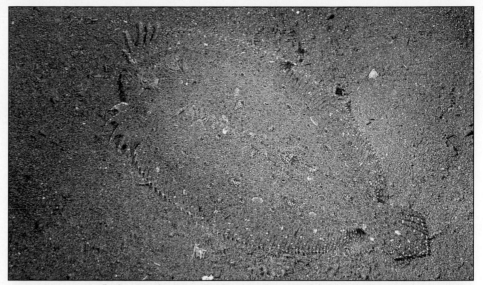

Bothus pantherinus   Dark colour form ▲ Male displaying on brown sand ▼

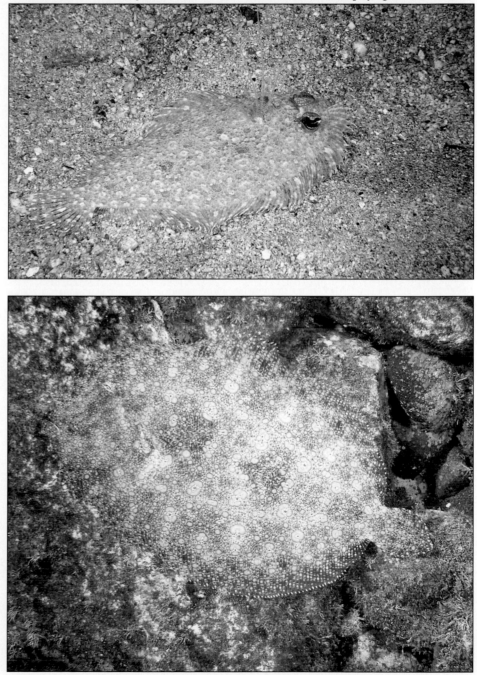

PEACOCK FLOUNDER
Bothus mancus (Brousonet, 1782)

D 96-104. A 74-81. C 16. P 10-13. V 6. LL 76-90. Body extremely compressed, covered with small ctenoid scales on ocular side, cycloid on blind side; scales extend over all of head on both sides. Lateral line on ocular side only, straight with curve over pectoral fin. Eyes elevated on left side; lower eye just below snout tip level, upper posteriorly above; interorbital width more than twice eye diameter. Mouth oblique. Caudal fin clearly separate from dorsal and anal fins. Dorsal fin origin near tip of snout; anal fin origin below posterior part of head. Left ventral fin free, below head. Left pectoral large with greatly extended filamentous rays, reaching caudal fin in males; pectoral fin on blind side with equal number of rays. Ocular side pale sandy colour with blue patterns. Widespread tropical Indo-Pacific, ranging to subtropical zones, on the east coast to central New South Wales and Lord Howe Island. Shallow reefs and lagoons, on sand but often in rocky areas; to 85 m. Attains 45 cm.

RIGHT-EYED FLOUNDERS
FAMILY PLEURONECTIDAE

A large family of small to medium-sized fishes, comprising about 45 genera and over 100 species. Many are of commercial importance. They are particularly well represented in Japan with about 40 species, nearly all of which are commercially important. The right-eyed flounders are elongate to very deep-bodied fishes with both eyes on right side (except one species in Japan and a few known mutant specimens with eyes on left side). The left side is unpigmented and used as the underside. The ocular side is usually sandy-coloured with various spotting and used as the top side. Scales are very small, mostly ctenoid, and weaker or cycloid on the blind side. The lateral line is distinct, almost straight from the upper gill opening to the caudal fin. The head is small, and the preopercle margin free and obvious. Eyes are small, close together and directly above each other. The snout is elongated and sometimes greatly extended into a rostral hook over the lower jaw. Fins consist entirely of soft rays, usually in very high numbers. Median fins surround the body, and in some genera the head, completely, and in some species have greatly produced rays anteriorly. The pectoral fin on the ocular side is normally developed, while the one on the blind side is often smaller. Ventral fins are free or joined to the anal fin, and are often large with more rays on the right. Pelagic larvae are often relatively large (about 45 mm SL), transparent with an eye on each side, and swim upright. Some *Ammotretis* larvae placed in an aquarium settled on the bottom with pigment forming quickly, and the left eye migrated through the head to the right side. In various genera the eye migrates over the head. They are benthic fishes, usually buried below the sand with their eyes exposed, feeding on a large variety of invertebrates or small fishes. They can be found in every sandy marine habitat from intertidal to deep offshore. The majority in Australia occur in relatively shallow waters, but a few exceptions are known from trawls to 600 m. About 12 species are found in Australia, most in temperate waters, and five are included here.

GREENBACK FLOUNDER
Rhombosolea tapirina Günther, 1862

D 56-63. A 40-50. C 18. P 10-13. V 6. LL 72-83. Body very compressed; very small cycloid scales cover both sides, extend over head to snout. Lateral line distinct, almost straight, slightly curved over pectoral fin. Eyes elevated closely above each other on right side. Caudal peduncle distinct. Dorsal fin origin near tip of snout, ending clear of caudal fin. Anal fin similar to and opposite posterior two-thirds of dorsal fin, extended anteriorly by right ventral fin with broad membrane; left ventral fin absent. Pectoral fin on blind side has fleshy tubercle at tip of first ray. Blind side white; ocular side variable from grey to greenish-brown. Widespread south coast, from southern New South Wales to southern Western Australia, most abundant in Tasmania; also New Zealand. Muddy and sandy bays; young estuarine, often in lower reaches of rivers, very shallow; adults from 5-100 m. Active species during the day, often crawling around above sand using the tips of fins, resting on pectoral fin which has supporting fleshy tip. Attains 40 cm, but recorded to 45 cm, which may apply to New Zealand populations.

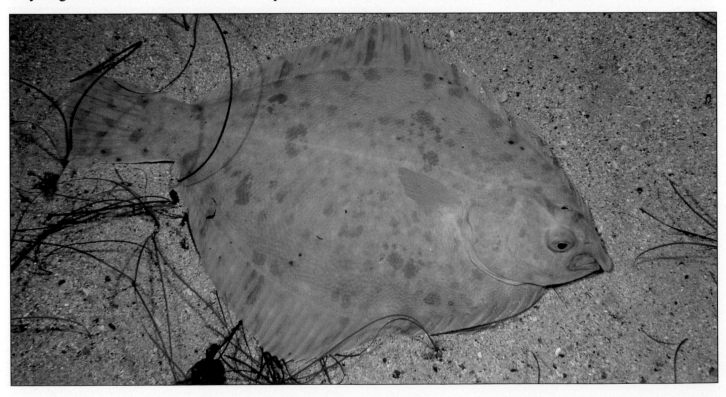

SPOTTED FLOUNDER
Ammotretis lituratus (Richardson, 1843)

D 77-82. A 54-58. C 18. P 10-11. V-right 9-10. V-left 6. LL about 78. Body very compressed, covered with very small ctenoid scales on ocular side, cycloid scales on blind side; scales extend over head to snout on both sides. Lateral line indistinct, almost straight, slightly curved over pectoral fin. Eyes elevated closely above each other on right side. Snout produced, hook-like. Caudal peduncle distinct. Dorsal fin origin on tip of snout, ending clear of caudal fin. Anal fin similar to and opposite posterior two-thirds of dorsal fin, extended anteriorly by right ventral fin with broad but shallow membrane; left ventral fin small. Pectoral fin on blind side has fleshy tubercle at tip of first ray. Blind side white; ocular side variable pale sandy with evenly spaced reddish spots. Only known from Victoria, Tasmania and South Australia. Mainly coastal, rarely entering estuaries; from surf beaches to at least 80 m. Attains 25 cm. Australian temperate genus, sole-like in appearance, comprising five species, three of which are included here.

LONG-SNOUT FLOUNDER
Ammotretis rostratus Günther, 1862

D 78-86. A 51-56. C 18. P 9-13. V-right 7. V-left 3-4. LL 78-88. Body very compressed; very small cycloid scales cover both sides, extend over head to snout. Lateral line indistinct, almost straight, slightly curved over pectoral fin. Eyes elevated closely above each other on right side. Snout produced, hook-like. Caudal peduncle distinct. Dorsal fin origin on tip of snout, ending clear of caudal fin. Anal fin similar to and opposite posterior three-quarters of dorsal fin, extended anteriorly by right ventral fin with broad but shallow membrane; left ventral fin small. No fleshy tubercle at tip of first pectoral fin ray on blind side. Blind side white; ocular grey or brown with small and large spots. Widespread southern waters from Sydney to south-western Australia, including Tasmania; particularly common in Port Phillip Bay; replaced by *A. brevipinnis* in western parts. Shallow estuaries, including lower reaches of rivers, and offshore to 80 m. Attains 35 cm.

Ammotretis rostratus　Sandy habitat colouration ▲　Muddy habitat colouration ▼

ELONGATED FLOUNDER
Ammotretis elongatus McCulloch, 1914

D 72-79. A 49-54. C 18. P 8-10. V-right 12-14. V-left 3-4. LL 88-92. Body very compressed, covered with very small weakly ctenoid scales on ocular side, cycloid scales on blind side; scales extend over head to snout on both sides. Lateral line indistinct, almost straight. Eyes elevated closely above each other on right side. Snout produced, hook-like. Caudal peduncle distinct. Dorsal fin origin on tip of snout, ending clear of caudal fin; extended rays over head with incised membranes, depth of incised membranes as continuation of following height of fin. Anal fin similar to and opposite dorsal fin, posterior to head, extended anteriorly by right ventral fin with broad but shallow membrane; left ventral fin small. Right ventral fin with extended rays, similar to anterior part of dorsal fin. Pectoral fin small on blind side; no fleshy tubercle at tip of first ray. Blind side white; ocular side very pale with fine spotting. South coast from Bass Strait to south Western Australia. Shallow coastal bays, primarily in very pale, almost white sand habitat, from intertidal to about 5 m; occasionally trawled in deeper, still relatively shallow waters. Attains 22 cm. Some geographical variations, possibly covering more than one species.

DERWENT FLOUNDER
Taratretis derwentensis Last, 1978

D 70-80. A 51-59. C 18. P 7-11. V-right 7. V-left 5-6. LL 75-83. Body very compressed, covered with very small ctenoid scales on ocular side, weakly ctenoid scales on blind side; scales extend over head to snout on both sides. Lateral line indistinct, almost straight, slightly curved over pectoral fin. Eyes elevated closely above each other on right side. Caudal peduncle distinct. Dorsal fin origin on tip of snout, at level between eyes, ending clear of caudal fin. Anal fin similar to and opposite posterior two-thirds of dorsal fin, extended anteriorly by right ventral fin with broad membrane; left ventral fin small. No fleshy tubercle at tip of first pectoral fin ray. Blind side white; ocular side pale sandy with pale blue spots. East coast from southern New South Wales to southern Tasmania. Clean fine sand, protected coastal waters in shallow depths to 50 m. Attains 12 cm.

SOLES
FAMILY SOLEIDAE

A large family of small fishes, comprising about 30 genera and more than 100 species. However, it is presently poorly defined and in need of revision. The soles are elongate to deep-bodied fishes with both eyes on the right side. The left side is unpigmented and used as the underside. The right side is used as the top side and has striped or spotted patterns. The scales are small, either cycloid or ctenoid, and the lateral line is distinct. The head is small, the preopercle edge concealed, the eyes very small, and the snout mostly elongated over the mouth and usually with teeth in both jaws, on the blind side only. There are often numerous papillae on the blind side of the head. The fins consist entirely of soft rays, almost surrounding the body outline except the head ventrally. Pectoral fins are present in some species only, variously differing between sides, or rudimentary on the ocular side. Some species are known to possess toxin in small sacs which can be released to deter predators. Soles are benthic fishes, and usually bury in fine sand or mud. They feed on small invertebrates and fishes, and sometimes congregate in large numbers. Of the six species included here, one is a tropical expatriate, but other species may range south on occasion.

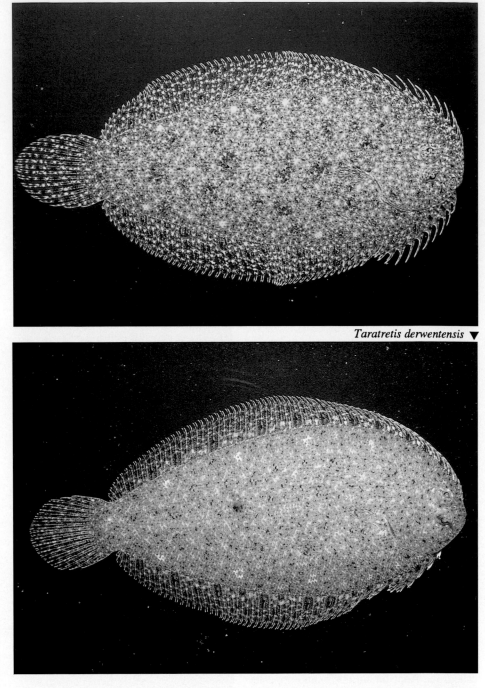

Taratretis derwentensis ▼

388

SMALL-HEAD SOLE
Aesopia microcephala (Günther, 1862)

D 77-79. A 65-75. C 16. P-right 11. V 4. LL 83-90. Body very compressed; small ctenoid scales cover both sides, fully extend over head on ocular side, over median fin rays and pectoral fin rays to about one-third of margin. Lateral line distinct, straight from above gill opening to caudal fin. Eyes elevated on right side, directly above each other; lower eye directly posterior to mouth; blind side and front of snout densely covered with papillae. Nostrils on ocular side with long tube. Ventral fins separate. Pectoral fin on ocular side with several relatively long, narrow, leaf-like rays to gill opening by membrane. Variable, grey to brown; distinct pattern of broad dark bands, blue fin margins. Juveniles thought to be of this species white with black and orange margins, mimic of known flatworm species. Only known from New South Wales. Estuaries, harbours, usually buried in muddy habitat in 3-20 m. Moves with undulating body when disturbed, reminiscent of distasteful flatworm, thus possibly deterring predators. Attains 22 cm. Little-known genus; possibly four species.

Aesopia microcephala   Disturbed specimen, moving slowly, simulating flatworm ▲ Adult ▼

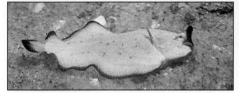

Aesopia microcephala   Juv.

MANY-BAND SOLE
Zebrias scalaris Gomon, 1987

D 75-82. A 60-69. C 18. P 6-7. V 4. LL 74-86. Body very compressed; small ctenoid scales cover both sides, fully extend over head and, on ocular side, over median fin rays close to margins. Lateral line distinct, straight from above gill opening to caudal fin. Eyes elevated on right side, closely above each other, separated by narrow scaly interorbital; upper eye slightly anterior to lower; lower eye directly posterior to mouth. Blind side of head and front of snout densely covered with papillae. Nostrils on ocular side with moderately long tube. Caudal fin broadly connected by membranes to dorsal and anal fins. Ventral fins separate. Pectoral fin rudimentary, attached to gill opening by membrane; length of rays less than half eye diameter. Distinct colouration, pale with dark bands, interspaces of similar width. East coast only, from southern Queensland to eastern Bass Strait. Harbours and coastal waters, in 20-60 m. Attains 20 cm. Previously known as *Z. fasciatus* however this name was already used for another species. Similar species *Z. penescalaris* Gomon, 1987, occurs on the south-west coast. This Indo-Pacific genus comprises about seven similarly banded species.

Zebrias scalaris   Papillae on underside of head

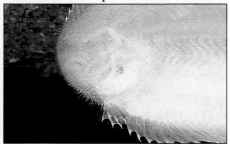

PEACOCK SOLE
Pardachirus pavoninus (Lacepède, 1802)

D 63-71. A 49-54. C 18. P 0. V 5. LL 83-90. Body very compressed; small finely ctenoid scales cover both sides, fully extend over head and, on ocular side, over median fin rays. Lateral line distinct, straight from above gill opening to caudal fin. Eyes elevated on right side, closely above each other, separated by narrow scaly interorbital; lower eye directly posterior to mouth; blind side and front of snout with papillae and some long filaments. Nostrils on ocular side with short tube. Ventral fins usually separate, occasionally joined to anal fin. Pectoral fins absent. Series of toxin glands along dorsal and anal fin bases, their pores visible. Widespread tropical west Pacific from southern Japan to northern New South Wales; recorded further south. Coastal mud or sand flats, usually buried, in 3-40 m. Attains 22 cm. Genus contains about five species, all of which possess a series of toxin glans between rays along dorsal and anal fin bases. When disturbed they release milky toxin which appears from almost entire outline of body and seems to stun predators.

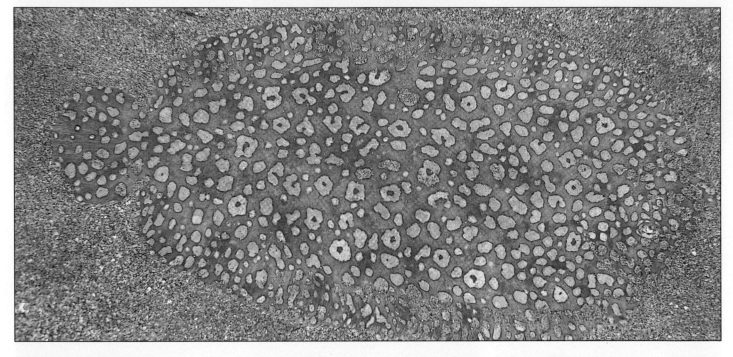

SOUTHERN PEACOCK SOLE
Pardachirus hedleyi Ogilby, 1916

D 65-74. A 50-55. C 18. P 0. V 5. LL 82-95. Body very compressed; small ctenoid scales cover both sides, fully extend over head and, on ocular side, over median fin rays. Lateral line distinct, straight from above gill opening to caudal fin. Eyes elevated on right side, closely above each other, separated by narrow scaly interorbital; lower eye directly posterior to mouth; blind side and front of snout with papillae and some long filaments. Nostrils on ocular side with short tube. Ventral fins free, not joined to anal fin. Pectoral fins absent. Series of toxin glands along dorsal and anal fin bases, their pores visible. Pale brown, usually sandy-coloured matching habitat; mixed pale and dark eye-sized spots. East coast from southern Queensland to southern New South Wales. Usually in clean sand habitat, in sheltered coastal waters, in 3-20 m. Attains 15 cm.

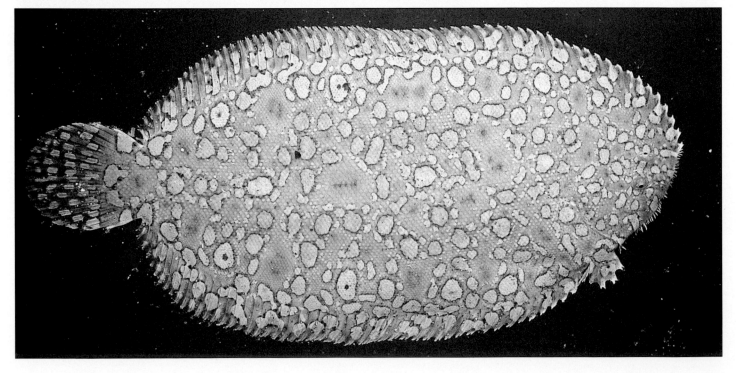

PEPPERED SOLE
Aseraggodes sp

D 65-71. A 47-53. C 18. P 0. V 5. LL 59-70. Body very compressed; very small ctenoid scales cover both sides, fully extend over head and, on ocular side, over median fin rays. Lateral line distinct with fleshy cirri, and straight from above gill opening to caudal fin. Eyes elevated on right side, closely above each other, separated by narrow scaly interorbital; lower eye directly posterior to mouth; blind side and front on snout with papillae, an enlarged series anteriorly. Nostrils on ocular side with short tube. Ventral fins usually separate, well free of anal fin. Pectoral fins absent. Sandy-coloured, usually speckled with dark and light spots. Only known from coastal New South Wales, central to southern areas, usually in protected coastal bays in clean sand. Shallow from 3-15 m. Attains 10 cm. Similar species on the south coast, two more at Lord Howe Island; this species appears to be undescribed. Pacific genus, several species in Japanese and Australian waters, comprising at least 10 species.

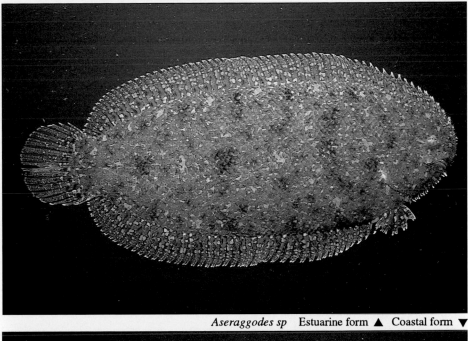

Aseraggodes sp   Estuarine form ▲   Coastal form ▼

BLACK SOLE
Synaptura nigra Macleay, 1880

D 56-62. A 44-52. C 14. P 5-7. V 5. LL 71-80. Body very compressed; small ctenoid scales cover both sides, fully extend over head and, on ocular side, over median fin rays to fin margins and pectoral fin base. Lateral line distinct, straight from above gill opening to caudal fin. Eyes very small, elevated on right side, closely above each other, separated by eye-sized scaly interorbital; lower eye directly posterior to mouth; blind side and front of snout with papillae and some long filaments. Nostrils on ocular side with short tube. Caudal fin broadly connected by membranes to dorsal and anal fins. Ventral fins separate, free from anal fin. Pectoral fins well developed but small on both sides. Blackish to pale brown; white on blind side. East coast, from southern Queensland to Wilson's Promontory. Estuaries and shallow coastal bays, in very fine sand or mud. Attains 35 cm. Single species in Australia, one of the largest; although very slimy, excellent to eat. Small Indo-Pacific genus; probably four species.

Synaptura nigra   Coastal form ▼

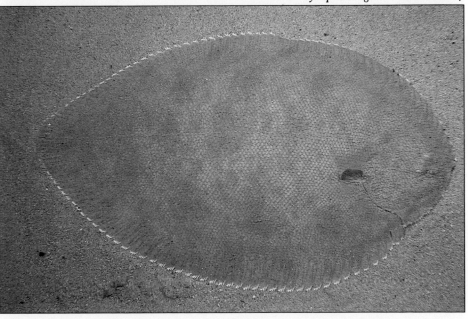

PUFFERFISHES AND FILEFISHES

ORDER
TETRAODONTIFORMES

Represented by about 10 families, six of which have representatives in southern coastal waters. They can be determined with Key 30.

TRIGGERFISHES

FAMILY BALISTIDAE

A moderately large, primarily Indo-Pacific and tropical family comprising 12 genera and about 40 species which occur worldwide. Triggerfishes are small to medium-sized fishes with ovate and compressed bodies, covered by tiny to moderate-sized hard plate-like scales, often enlarged near the gill openings. They sometimes have longitudinal ridges, tubercles or small spines posteriorly. The dorsal fin is in two parts, the first with three spines, of which the first is stout and lockable into an upright position by the second spine; the third spine is small. The remaining fins consist entirely of soft rays. The second dorsal and anal fins are large, similar and opposite. The caudal fin is moderately large and occurs in various shapes from round to deeply lunate with produced tips. The pectoral fin is usually small and paddle-like. The ventral fin is rudimentary,

1.	A single short-based dorsal fin posteriorly placed	2
	Second dorsal fin long-based, posteriorly placed	5
2.	Body hard, encased by bony plates	3
	Body soft, with or without spines	4
3.	Dorsal and anal fins not enclosed by rigid part	ARACANIDAE (p. 411)
	Dorsal and anal fins enclosed by rigid part	OSTRACIIDAE (p. 413)
4.	Skin with numerous large spines; undivided tooth plate in each jaw	DIODONTIDAE (p. 423)
	Skin smooth or finely spined; tooth plates and jaws divided in two halves in centre	TETRAODONTIDAE (p. 416)
5.	First dorsal fin with one prominent spine; body covered with tiny spinuled scales; jaws with four to six frontal teeth	MONACANTHIDAE (p. 397)
	First dorsal fin with two prominent spines; body covered with hard plate-like bony scales; jaws with eight frontal teeth	BALISTIDAE (p. 392)

KEY 30: *The Pufferfishes and Filefishes*

encased with small scales, and obvious. It protrudes from the posterior end of the ventral flap which is expandable out from the body, to a great extent in some species. The head is moderate-sized to large with eyes positioned high and posteriorly, just anterior to the pectoral fins. The mouth is small with large, very strong teeth. Each of the jaws has eight long, protruding close-set incisiform teeth, followed by

an inner row of six or more small teeth in the upper jaw. The gill opening consists of a small vertical slit, anterior to and immediately above the pectoral fin. Most species are distinctly coloured and readily identified. They have pelagic larvae, a few are completely pelagic, and some as juveniles only, and these generally look dull and show little variation with growth. Benthic juveniles are distinctly coloured and usually differ greatly from adults. There is virtually no difference between the sexes. Males of some species are known to make nests and guard eggs vigorously, often attacking divers who venture into their territory. Most species are solitary, however nesting sites may consist of numerous males, each with a large territory. Only pelagic species school. Included here are those which occur as adults in northern New South Wales with expatriates ranging well south, comprising five genera and nine species. The Oceanic Triggerfish, *Canthidermis maculatus* (Bloch, 1786), also ranges south to New South Wales, occurring offshore with weeds.

Clown Triggerfish (*Balistoides conspicillum*)   Small juvenile, about 40 mm, Seal Rocks, NSW

CLOWN TRIGGERFISH
Balistoides conspicillum (Bloch and
Schneider, 1801)

D III,25-27. A 20-23. C 12. P 14-15.
LSR 39-50. Body compressed; scales relatively large, enlarged posteriorly with gill opening; adults with longitudinal rows of small antrorse spines or tubercles posteriorly, extending over short caudal peduncle. Head with tiny scales; longitudinal groove anterior to eye, bluntly pointed snout; upper and lower profile slightly convex. Dorsal fin spines of moderate size, third well developed; second dorsal fin over posterior third of body; anal fin similar and opposite. Caudal fin round in juveniles to almost truncate in adults. Distinctly coloured; readily identified by large round white spots. Widespread tropical Indo-Pacific, ranging south into New South Wales as adults; juveniles south to Sydney. Adults primarily along deep drop-offs, swimming about openly. Juveniles secretive, in caves, in 5-50 m. Attains 30 cm. Only other member of genus more tropical.

Balistoides conspicillum Large adult

YELLOW-SPOTTED TRIGGERFISH
Pseudobalistes fuscus (Bloch and
Schneider, 1801)

D III,24-27. A 20-24. C 12. P 15. LSR 35-46. Body compressed; scales relatively large, enlarged posteriorly with gill opening; adults without spines or tubercles. Head with tiny scales; longitudinal groove anterior to eye, bluntly pointed snout; upper and lower profile slightly convex. Dorsal fin spines of moderate size, third well developed; second dorsal fin over posterior half of body, elevated anteriorly in adults; anal fin similar and opposite. Caudal fin slightly round to truncate in juveniles; produced lobes at corners in adults. Adults blue-grey with small to moderate yellow spots; very small juveniles pale with alternating black and white saddles on back. Widespread tropical Indo-Pacific. Juveniles commonly south to the Sydney area. Deep reef outcrops, frequently over sand to feed on benthic invertebrates, blowing the sand to expose prey. Juveniles in coastal, often muddy outcrops, in 3-50 m. Attains 55 cm. Sometimes called Blue Triggerfish. Genus comprises Pacific species, two of which are included here.

Pseudobalistes fuscus Small juv.

Pseudobalistes fuscus Young adult

YELLOW-MARGIN TRIGGERFISH
Pseudobalistes flavomarginatus (Rüppell, 1829)

D III,24-27. A 22-24. C 12. P 15. LSR 28-33. Body compressed; scales relatively large, enlarged posteriorly with gill opening; adults without spines or tubercles. Head with tiny scales; longitudinal groove anterior to eye, bluntly pointed snout; upper and lower profile slightly convex. Dorsal fin spines of moderate size, third well developed; second dorsal fin over posterior half of body, slightly elevated anteriorly in adults; anal fin similar and opposite. Caudal fin slightly round to truncate in juveniles; produced lobes at corners in adults. Juveniles creamy coloured, several black saddles on back, small black spots on sides; change to greenish-grey as adults with yellow outline of posterior fins prominent. Widespread tropical Pacific; in New South Wales juveniles occasionally south to the Sydney area. Coastal reef slopes, in 2-50 m; large juveniles often in small aggregations with outcrops on mud slopes. Attains 60 cm.

P. flavomarginatus Large adult ▼ Small juv. ▲

HALF-MOON TRIGGERFISH
Sufflamen chrysopterus (Bloch and Schneider, 1801)

D III,26-28. A 23-26. C 12. P 13-15. LSR 41-47. Body compressed; scales relatively small, enlarged posteriorly with gill opening; longitudinal series of small spines posteriorly on sides from below middle of second dorsal fin. Head with small scales, cheek scales larger than body scales; longitudinal groove anterior to eye, bluntly pointed snout; upper and lower profile slightly convex. Dorsal fin spines of moderate size, third well developed; second dorsal fin over posterior half of body, slightly elevated anteriorly in adults; anal fin similar and opposite. Caudal fin slightly round to truncate from juvenile to adult. Juvenile most distinct with yellow back, pale lower half; adults with distinct tail pattern. Widespread tropical Indo-Pacific; juveniles commonly expatriate south along the New South Wales coast. Adults on shallow reef flats to about 20 m. Juveniles in the Sydney area on shallow semi-protected ocean reefs in 3-10 m. Attains 30 cm. Sydney juveniles known as Yellow-Backed Triggerfish. Genus comprises five species, three of which are included here.

Sufflamen chrysopterus Small juv.

Sufflamen chrysopterus Large adult

BRIDLED TRIGGERFISH
Sufflamen fraenatus (Latreille, 1804)

D III,27-31. A 24-28. C 12. P 14-16. LSR 43-54. Body compressed; scales relative-

S. fraenatus   Large adult ▼   Small juv. ▲

ly small, enlarged posteriorly with gill opening; longitudinal series of small spines posteriorly on sides from below middle of second dorsal fin. Head with small scales, cheek scales larger than body scales; longitudinal groove anterior to eye, bluntly pointed snout; upper and lower profile slightly convex. Dorsal fin spines of moderate size, third well developed; second dorsal fin over posterior half of body, slightly elevated anteriorly in adults; anal fin similar and opposite. Caudal fin slightly round to truncate from juvenile to adult. Brownish; juveniles with darker, striated upper half; adults with yellow stripe from mouth to pectoral fin base. Widespread tropical Indo-Pacific, uncommon in equatorial waters; commonly south to Seal Rocks, New South Wales, where juveniles attain large size. Usually fairly deep, 30-150 m; juveniles as shallow as 5 m. Attains 35 cm.

BOOMERANG TRIGGERFISH
Sufflamen bursa (Bloch and Schneider, 1801)

D III,27-30. A 25-27. C 12. P 13-15. LSR 43-50. Body compressed; scales relatively small, enlarged posteriorly with gill opening; longitudinal series of small spines posteriorly on sides from below middle of second dorsal fin. Head with small scales, cheek scales larger than body scales; longitudinal groove anterior to eye, bluntly pointed snout; upper and lower profile slightly convex. Dorsal fin spines of moderate size, third well developed; second dorsal fin over posterior half of body, slightly elevated anteriorly in adults; anal fin similar and opposite. Caudal fin slightly round to truncate from juvenile to adult. Juvenile similar to adult; vertical 'V' from pectoral fin base is diagnostic. Widespread tropical Indo-Pacific, common as adults in northern New South Wales, but juveniles not known further south. Primarily along outer reef slopes and crests, in 3-90 m; juveniles in surge zones. Attains 30 cm.

Sufflamen bursa ▼

HAWAIIAN TRIGGERFISH
Rhinecanthus aculeatus (Linnaeus, 1758)

D III,23-26. A 21-23. C 12. P 13-15. LSR 32-39. Body compressed; scales relatively small, enlarged posteriorly with gill opening; longitudinal series of small spines posteriorly on sides of caudal peduncle. Head with small scales, cheek scales larger than body scales, no groove anterior to eye, bluntly pointed snout; upper and lower profile slightly convex. Dorsal fin spines of moderate size, third very small; second dorsal fin over posterior half of body, not elevated anteriorly in adults; anal fin similar and opposite. Caudal fin slightly round to truncate from juvenile to adult. Little change from juvenile to adult; body pattern readily identifies the species. Widespread tropical Indo-Pacific. Common shallow reef fish, usually just below the intertidal zone; juveniles in shallow, often surge prone reef flats. In the Sydney area usually in about 1 m with low tides, among small boulders in coastal bays. Attains 25 cm. Tropical Indo-Pacific genus comprising seven species, two of which range to central New South Wales.

Rhinecanthus aculeatus ▼

WEDGE-TAIL TRIGGERFISH
Rhinecanthus rectangulus (Bloch and Schneider, 1801)

D III,22-25. A 20-22. C 12. P 14-15. LSR 41-47. Body compressed; scales relatively small, enlarged posteriorly with gill opening; longitudinal series of small spines posteriorly on sides of caudal peduncle. Head with small scales, cheek scales larger than body scales, no groove anterior to eye, bluntly pointed snout; upper and lower profile slightly convex. Dorsal fin spines of moderate size, third very small; second dorsal fin over posterior half of body, not elevated anteriorly in adults; anal fin similar and opposite. Caudal fin slightly round to truncate from juvenile to adult. Little change from juvenile to adult; body pattern readily identifies the species. Widespread tropical Indo-Pacific. Common shallow reef fish, usually just below intertidal zone; juveniles in shallow, often surge prone reef flats. In the Sydney area usually in about 1 m with low tides, among small boulders in coastal bays. Attains 25 cm.

Rhinecanthus rectangulus   Small juv., 30 mm

STARRY TRIGGERFISH
Abalistes stellatus (Lacepède, 1798)

D III,25-27. A 24-26. C 12. P 13-16. LSR 33-41. Body very compressed; scales relatively small, enlarged posteriorly with gill opening; caudal peduncle long, depressed, broader than deep. Head with small scales, deep groove anterior to eye, bluntly pointed snout; upper and lower profile slightly convex.

Dorsal fin spines of moderate size, third well developed; second dorsal fin over posterior half of body, not elevated anteriorly in adults; anal fin similar and opposite. Caudal fin slightly round to truncate from juvenile to adult, with extended tips in large individuals. Little change from juvenile to adult; saddle pattern most distinct in juveniles, but body pattern readily identifies the species. Widespread tropical Indo-Pacific. Adults over sand staying loosely in touch with reefs. Juveniles in muddy habitats with reef outcrops. Sydney juveniles usually on silty muddy slopes in 10 m or more. Attains 25 cm. Monotypic genus.

Abalistes stellatus   Juv.

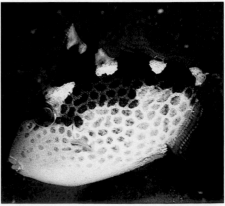

LEATHERJACKETS
FAMILY MONACANTHIDAE

A large family of small to medium-sized fishes, comprising about 30 genera and an estimated 100 species, found in all major oceans. Particularly well represented in Australia with 27 genera and almost 60 species. Japan and South Africa have about 16 species each. Many species change in shape with age. Juveniles may be almost circular and very compressed, while the large adults are very elongate. The body is covered by tiny prickly scales which form a tough leathery or velvet-like skin, and only in some species are the scales visible to the naked eye. A prominent and separate first dorsal fin spine is an obvious feature in most species. This spine is often very long, or armed with series of downward directed barbs on its edges, and is usually followed by a second, much smaller embedded spine and narrow membrane. In nearly all species the spine is lockable in an upright position, and often fits into a shallow to deep groove when folded back. A few species can inflate the abdomen in a manner similar to pufferfishes, or extend the chest area outwards, greatly in some species. In most genera there is a rudimentary ventral fin consisting of enlarged scales forming a prickly knob. Many of these features change with size and age. Most species are sexually dimorphic. Males often become brilliantly coloured and develop enlarged spines or patches of bristles on the caudal peduncle. The head is moderately large and the prominent eyes are set high, usually just below the first dorsal fin spine. The mouth is small and terminal with large, prominent teeth. The gill opening consists of a vertical slit, just anterior to and above the pectoral fin base. Fins are of moderate size, the dorsal and anal fins long-based, and the pectoral and caudal fins mostly rounded and often fan-like. The species range greatly in size, from about 10 cm to 1 m. The leatherjackets are some of the best-known fishes in southern waters, occurring commonly, and are often abundant on reefs. The tropical, usually small species, are mostly called file-fishes. The leatherjackets are well represented in southern waters, and 16 genera with 27 species are included here.

Toothbrush Leatherjacket
(*Acanthaluterus vittiger*)

MIMIC FILEFISH
Paraluteres prionurus (Bleeker, 1851)

D II,25-28. A 22-25. C 12. P 11-12. Body compressed, extended by very deep caudal peduncle. Ventral flap indistinct, moderate-sized in males, without ventral fin rudiment. Dorsal spine moderately small, followed by triangular membrane, nearly reaching second dorsal fin. Dorsal and anal fins long-based, similar, opposite. Caudal fin fan-like. Males develop a series of recurving spines on sides of caudal peduncle. Distinctly coloured with black saddles; males have some additional orange and blue. Widespread tropical Indo-Pacific; replaced by similar species in the Red Sea. Juveniles expatriate well south in New South Wales. Shallow protected reefs to about 25 m; openly about, often in small aggregations. Mimics *Canthigaster valentini*, a poisonous puffer, in colour and shape in great detail; shares same habitat. Differs in having first dorsal fin, long-based second dorsal and anal fins. Small species; attains 10 cm. Second species in genus Red Sea endemic.

Paraluteres prionurus Displaying male ▲

Paraluteres prionurus Juvs,

BRIGHT-EYE FILEFISH
Pervagor alternans (Ogilby, 1899)

D II,31-34. A 27-31. C 12. P 12-13. Body compressed, covered densely with small spinules which become relatively long posteriorly in adults. Ventral fin rudiment movable, of moderate size, prominently barbed. Snout profile concave above and below. Caudal peduncle short, deep, highly compressed. Strong first dorsal spine situated above eye; has series of prominent lateral barbs, narrow membrane reaching near second dorsal fin; folds down into narrow groove. Pectoral fins small, fan-like, with small gill opening just above base. Known from eastern Australia, south to Bermagui, New Caledonia, and in the northern Hemisphere from the Marshall Islands. Secretive, in sheltered rocky reefs, often deep in ledges, in 3-20 m. Attains 15 cm. Genus of eight small species distributed in various parts of the tropical Indo-Pacific.

EAR-SPOT FILEFISH
Pervagor janthinosoma (Bleeker, 1854)

D II,29-34. A 26-30. C 12. P 10-13. Body compressed, covered densely with small

Pervagor alternans ▲ 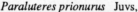 *Pervagor janthinosoma* ▼

spinules which become relatively long posteriorly in adults. Ventral fin rudiment movable, of moderate size, prominently barbed. Snout profile concave above and below. Caudal peduncle short, deep, highly compressed. Strong first dorsal spine situated above eye; has series of prominent lateral barbs, narrow membrane reaching near second dorsal fin; folds down into narrow groove.

Pectoral fins small, fan-like, with small gill opening just above base. Variable from pale green to dark brown; caudal fin usually orange; distinct vertical black blotch above pectoral fin base. Widespread tropical Indo-Pacific to east Africa, Japan and Samoa. Shallow reef flats and, in New South Wales, rocky estuaries; secretive, among boulders, to about 15 m. Attains 13 cm.

HONEYCOMB LEATHERJACKET
Cantherhinus pardalis (Rüppell, 1837)

D II,32-36. A 29-32. C 12. P 12-15. Body compressed, covered densely with minute spinules giving velvet texture. Ventral fin rudiment fixed, small; ventral flap greatly extendable. Snout profile concave above and below. Caudal peduncle short, moderately deep, highly compressed; males with dense patch of enlarged spinules on sides. Strong first dorsal spine situated above eye; anterior surface rounded, lateral edges irregular, narrow membrane reaches near second dorsal fin; folds down into moderately deep groove. Pectoral fins small, fan-like, with small gill opening just above and anterior to base. Highly variable, can quickly change colour; usually has hexagonal network on sides and some light and dark blotching. Widespread tropical to subtropical Indo-Pacific, ranging south to the Sydney area as adults. Rocky reef with weedy habitat; young commonly in floating weeds. Attains 20 cm. Primarily tropical genus comprising eight species, including two from the Atlantic.

Cantherhinus pardalis ▲

LARGE-SCALE LEATHERJACKET
Cantheschenia grandisquamis Hutchins, 1977

D II,38-40. A 34-36. C 12. P 12-13. Body compressed, covered with visible scales, set with minute spinules giving velvet texture. Ventral fin rudiment fixed, small; ventral flap moderately extendable. Snout profile concave above and below. Caudal peduncle short, moderately deep, highly compressed; two series of two or occasionally three small recurving spines on sides. Large first dorsal spine has two rows of minute recurving spines on anterior surface, one row along each side; followed by tiny embedded second spine. Eyes moderately small, directly below dorsal spine. Pectoral fins small, fan-like, with small gill opening just above and anterior to base. Distinctly coloured species; blue spots on chin, orange mark in caudal fin. East coast from central Queensland to Bass Point as adults. Primarily in large coastal estuaries in kelp beds and weed zones, shallow to about 15 m. Attains 36 cm. Second species in genus is trawled in southern waters.

Cantheschenia grandisquamis ▼

DUSKY LEATHERJACKET
Paramonacanthus otisensis Whitley, 1931

D II,24-30. A 24-30. C 12. P 11-14. Body compressed, males more elongate than females; densely covered with minute spinules giving velvet texture. Ventral fin rudiment movable, small; ventral flap moderately extendable. Snout profile concave above and below. Caudal peduncle short, not deep, highly compressed. Strong first dorsal spine situated above eyes, lateral edges with downward directed barbs; groove to receive spine absent. Pectoral fins small, fan-like, with small gill opening just above and anterior to base. Dorsal and anal fins elevated anteriorly in males. Caudal fin with moderately long filaments on upper and middle rays in adults. Pale grey or yellow to brown with variable dark markings. Tropical eastern Australia, south to the Sydney area. Weedy habitat, usually in harbours, in 5-20 m. Attains 14 cm. Genus of small fishes, comprising about 10 species.

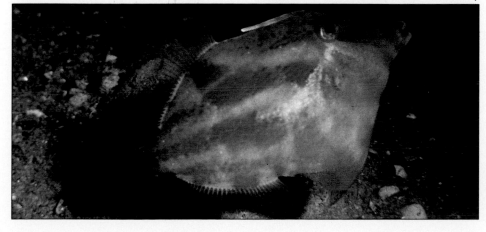

Paramonacanthus otisensis Pale variation ▲ Dark variation ▼

FAN-BELLY LEATHERJACKET
Monacanthus chinensis (Osbeck, 1765)

D II,28-34. A 27-34. C 12: P 12-13. Body very deep, compressed, densely covered with minute spinules giving velvet texture. Ventral fin rudiment movable, moderately long, well back from end of large, greatly extendable ventral flap. Snout with concave profile above. Caudal peduncle short, not deep, highly compressed. Strong first dorsal spine situated above eye, lateral edges with downward directed barbs, groove to recieve spine absent. Pectoral fins small, fan-like, with small gill opening just above and anterior to base. Anterior halves of second dorsal and anal fins elevated. Long filament on upper corner of caudal fin in large individuals. Brownish grey with darker blotching. West Pacific, as far south as Western Port, Victoria, and north to Japan. Two separate northern and southern hemisphere populations may represent good species as meristics seem to differ too much (both included in above count; northern hemisphere populations lower by 2-3 in dorsal and anal fins, 12 in pectoral fin rays). Frequently in deep muddy estuaries and inshore reefs, in 5-50 m, but occasionally trawled much deeper. Attains 40 cm.

WEEDY FILEFISH
Chaetoderma penicilligera (Cuvier, 1817)

D II,25-26. A 23-24. C 12. P 13-14. Body strongly compressed, covered moderately to heavily with dermal filaments. Ventral fin rudiment movable, moderately long. Ventral flap large, moderately extendable. Snout profile concave above and below. Caudal peduncle short, shallow, compressed. Small first dorsal spine situated high above eye; groove to receive spine absent. Numerous large, densely branched dermal flaps outline general profile of body, including spines. Pectoral fins small, fan-like, with small gill opening just above and anterior to base. Caudal fin rounded, becoming pointed in centre in large individuals. Widespread tropical west Pacific, south to Sydney. Secretive, in weed areas, extremely well camouflaged. Attains 18 cm. Monotypic genus.

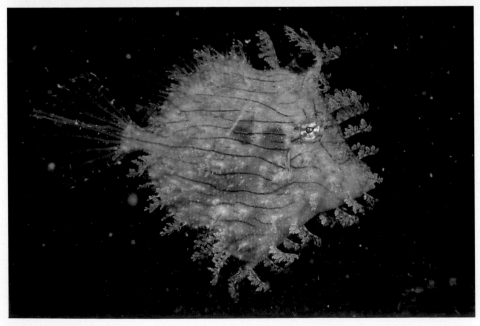

ROUGH LEATHERJACKET
Scobinichthys granulatus (Shaw, 1790)

D II,26-31. A 26-29. C 12. P 11-12. Body moderately long in males, oblong and moderately deep in females; very compressed, ventral flap rather large. Caudal peduncle shallow. Gill opening a small slit anteriorly just above pectoral fin base. Scales with large centrally placed multipointed spinule, forming rough skin. Prominent first dorsal spine above eyes, moderate-sized barbs along sides, folds down into moderately deep groove. Soft-rayed second dorsal fin slightly elevated anteriorly; anal fin similar and opposite. Pectoral fins small, rounded. Rudimentary ventral fin obvious, fixed at end of pelvis. Variable in colour; most useful pattern is large series of squarish blotches along midline, most obvious in juveniles. Southern half of Australia from southern Queensland to similar latitude in Western Australia. Weedy habitat to about 30 m. Attains 30 cm. Monotypic genus restricted to southern waters.

S. granulatus Young adult ▲ Small juv. ▼

HORSESHOE LEATHERJACKET
Meuschenia hippocrepis (Quoy and Gaimard, 1824)

D II,34-37. A 32-35. C 12. P 12-13. Body moderately long in males, oblong and moderately deep in females; very compressed, ventral flap small. Caudal peduncle shallow. Gill opening a small slit anteriorly just above pectoral fin base. Scales small with numerous spinules, skin velvety to touch. Two pairs of entrorse enlarged spines on sides of caudal peduncle, preceded by patch of densely set bristles in males. Prominent first dorsal spine above eyes, moderate-sized barbs along sides, folds down onto shallow groove. Pectoral fins small, rounded. Caudal fin convex; concave in males. Rudimentary ventral fin obvious, fixed at end of pelvis. Variably green to grey with spotted areas, yellow to orange areas on sides; males become blue on sides, feature horse-shoe shaped marking in centre. Primarily south coast, widespread from Wilson's Promontory to Houtman Abrolhos, including northern Tasmania. Common on coastal reefs and deep rocky estuary reefs, often in large aggregations in kelp areas. Attains 60 cm. Important genus in southern waters, comprising the larger commercial species; all eight species are included here.

Scobinichthys granulatus Large male ▲

Meuschenia hippocrepis Male ▼

Meuschenia hippocrepis Juv.

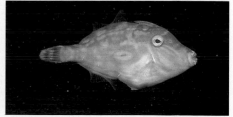

SIX-SPINE LEATHERJACKET
Meuschenia freycineti (Quoy and Gaimard, 1824)

D II,32-38. A 31-36. C 12. P 11-14. Body moderately long in males, oblong and moderately deep in females; very compressed, ventral flap small. Caudal peduncle shallow. Gill opening a small slit anteriorly just above pectoral fin base. Scales small with numerous minute spinules, skin smooth to touch. Usually three spines on sides of caudal peduncle, but sometimes two or four, entrorse and enlarged, preceded by patch of densely set bristles in males. Prominent first dorsal spine above eyes, moderate-sized barbs along sides, folds down onto shallow groove. Pectoral fins small, rounded. Caudal fin convex, concave in males. Rudimentary ventral fin obvious, fixed at end of pelvis. Females pale greenish with or without broad longitudinal bands; males mostly blue with intermittent yellow blotch; some geographical variations. East coast population from northern New South Wales to eastern Victoria; south coast population from Wilson's Promontory to western Australia, including Tasmania. East coast form more colourful, somewhat shallower in body depth. Shallow estuaries to offshore reefs to at least 50 m. Attains about 50 cm on the east coast, about 60 cm on the south coast.

Female, south coast form ▲   Male, south coast form ▼

Male, east coast form ▼

SOUTHERN LEATHERJACKET
Meuschenia australis (Donovan, 1824)

D II,33-37. A 31-36. C 12. P 12-14. Body moderately long in males, oblong and moderately deep in females; very compressed, ventral flap small. Caudal peduncle shallow. Gill opening a small slit anteriorly just above pectoral fin base. Scales small with numerous spinules, skin velvety to touch. No spines on sides of caudal peduncle. Prominent first dorsal spine above eyes, moderate-sized barbs along sides, folds down onto shallow groove. Pectoral fins small, rounded. Caudal fin convex, concave in males. Rudimentary ventral fin obvious, fixed at end of pelvis. Greenish to yellowish-brown; female has broad dark longitudinal bands. Primarily a Tasmanian species ranging to the Australian mainland, known from most of the Bass Straight area including Port Phillip Bay. Coastal kelp-covered reefs, from 5 m to at least 30 m. Attains 32 cm. Also known as Brown-Striped Leatherjacket.

Meuschenia australis   Female ▲ Male ▼

BLUE-LINED LEATHERJACKET
Meuschenia galii (Waite, 1905)

D II,32-36. A 31-34. C 12. P 12. Body moderately long in males, oblong and moderately deep in females; very compressed, ventral flap small. Caudal peduncle shallow. Gill opening a small slit anteriorly just above pectoral fin base. Scales small with numerous tiny spinules, skin smooth to touch. No spines on sides of caudal peduncle. Prominent first dorsal spine above eyes, moderate-sized barbs along sides, folds down onto a shallow groove. Pectoral fins small, rounded. Caudal fin convex, concave in males. Rudimentary ventral fin obvious, fixed at end of pelvis. Greenish-brown with variably blue and yellow lines or spots; distinct caudal fin pattern. Primarily common in south-western Australia, but extended to Wilson's Promontory, reasonably common in Port Phillip Bay near the heads. Rocky, algae-covered reefs, shallow, about 3-30 m. Attains 40 cm.

Meuschenia galii   Male ▲ Female ▼

YELLOW-FINNED LEATHERJACKET
Meuschenia trachylepis (Günther, 1870)

D II,33-39. A 31-35. C 12. P 12. Body moderately deep, slightly more elongate in males; very compressed, ventral flap moderate, with small but obvious ventral fin rudiment. Caudal peduncle moderately shallow, compressed, usually two pairs of spines on sides, large and recurving on males. Gill opening a small slit anteriorly just above pectoral fin base. Scales small, defined, with numerous tiny spinules; skin velvety to touch. Prominent first dorsal spine above eyes, moderate-sized barbs along sides, folds down onto shallow groove. Pectoral fins small, rounded. Caudal fin round, becoming almost truncate in males. Variable, best separated from other species by patch of scribbles centrally on body and by caudal fin pattern. East coast from southern Queensland to eastern Victoria. Mostly on clear-water reefs, enters rocky estuaries, in 10-40 m; juveniles secretive, with kelp. Attains 40 cm.

Meuschenia trachylepis Male ▼ Juvs ▲

YELLOW-STRIPE LEATHERJACKET
Meuschenia flavolineata Hutchins, 1977

D II,33-37. A 31-35. C 12. P 11-12. Body moderately deep, slightly more elongate in males; very compressed, ventral flap moderate, with small but obvious ventral fin rudiment. Caudal peduncle moderately shallow, compressed, usually two pairs of spines on sides, large and recurving on males. Gill opening a small slit anteriorly just above pectoral fin base. Scales small with numerous tiny spinules, skin velvety to touch. Prominent first dorsal spine above eyes, moderate-sized barbs along front and sides, folds down onto shallow groove. Pectoral fins small, rounded. Dark brown to black; male has bright orange blotch covering caudal peduncle spines, which in female is more yellow; female also has yellow in caudal fin. Widespread southern waters, central New South Wales to similar latitude on west coast, including northern Tasmania. Coastal kelp reefs to about 30 m; juveniles in estuaries. Attains 30 cm.

Meuschenia flavolineata Male ▲ Female ▼

Meuschenia flavolineata Juv.

STARS AND STRIPES LEATHERJACKET
Meuschenia venusta Hutchins, 1977

D II,34. A 31-33. C 12. P 12-13. Body moderately deep, slightly more elongate in males; very compressed, ventral flap moderate, with small but obvious ventral fin rudiment. Caudal peduncle moderately shallow, compressed, without spines. Gill opening a small slit anteriorly just above pectoral fin base. Scales small with strong central spinules, skin rough to touch. Prominent first dorsal spine above eyes, tiny barbs along sides, folds down onto shallow groove. Pectoral fins small, rounded. Caudal fin round to almost truncate. Variable brown to white, usually distinctly marked with bands of spots. Widespread south coast from Sydney to Shark Bay; not yet known from Tasmania. Mostly on deep coastal reefs, in excess of 20 m, in sponge areas; young with kelp. Attains 21 cm.

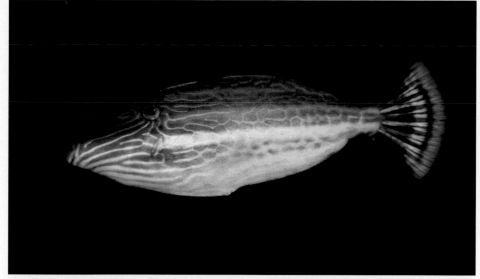

Meuschenia venusta   Male ▲ Female ▼

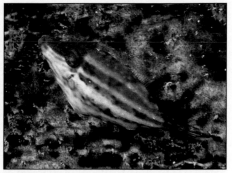

Meuschenia venusta Juv.

VELVET LEATHERJACKET
Meuschenia scaber (Forster, 1801)

D II,32-38. A 31-36. C 12. P 12-14. Body moderately deep, very compressed; ventral flap moderate, with small but obvious ventral fin rudiment. Caudal peduncle moderately shallow, compressed, without spines on sides. Gill opening a small slit anteriorly just above pectoral fin base. Scales small with numerous tiny spinules, skin velvety to touch. Prominent first dorsal spine above eyes, moderate-sized barbs along sides, folds down onto shallow groove. Pectorals fin small, rounded. Caudal fin rounded, fan-like in adults. Variable, pale to dark brown, often with large blotching. Male usually plain, has additional vertical stripe near margin of caudal fin. Widespread south coast from Sydney to Cape Naturaliste (Western Australia), and to southern Tasmania. Separate population in New Zealand from where it was described. Usually deep, schooling above reef outcrops in 20-200 m. Feeds on bottom invertebrates, but also often seen feeding mid-water on zooplankton; likes to bite divers' fingers. Attains 30 cm. The New Zealand fish attains 45 cm; differs in colour, noticeably the bright yellow pectoral fin.

Meuschenia scaber ▼

Meuschenia scaber Juv.

BRIDLED LEATHERJACKET
Acanthaluteres spilomelanurus (Quoy and Gaimard, 1824)

D II,27-34. A 26-32. C 12. P 10-11. Body very compressed. Ventral flap moderately large with minute, indistinct ventral fin rudiment. Caudal peduncle moderately shallow, elongate, compressed, without spines or bristles on sides. Gill opening a small slit anteriorly just above pectoral fin base. Scales small with numerous tiny spinules, skin velvety to touch. Prominent first dorsal spine above eyes, four-edged with moderate-sized barbs along each edge, folds down into deep groove. Pectoral fins small, rounded. Caudal fin rounded, fan-like in adults. Males have distinct blue lines, females brownish with pale spotting. Small juveniles green with white longitudinal band. Widespread south coast from Sydney to Perth, including Tasmania. Primarily in estuaries, schooling over seagrass beds and in sargassum weed areas. Attains 14 cm. Australian genus comprising three species.

Acanthaluteres spilomelanurus　Young Male ▲　Male (top) and female (bottom) ▼

406

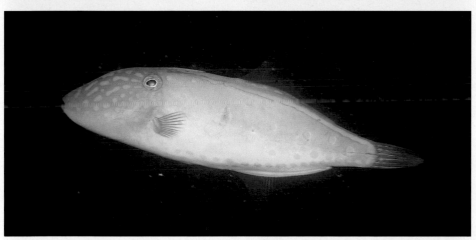

Acanthaluteres vittiger Male ▲ Female ▼

Thamnaconus degeni Male ▲ Female ▼

TOOTHBRUSH LEATHERJACKET
Acanthaluteres vittiger (Castelnau, 1873)

D II,30-35. A 27-34. C 12. P 11-13. Body very compressed. Ventral flap moderately large with small, prominent ventral fin rudiment. Caudal peduncle moderately shallow, compressed, just anterior to caudal peduncle; males with patch of bristles on sides. Gill opening a small slit anteriorly just above pectoral fin base. Scales small with numerous tiny spinules, skin coarse to touch. Prominent first dorsal spine above eyes, four-edged with moderate-sized barbs along each edge, folds down into deep groove. Pectoral fins small, rounded. Caudal fin rounded, fan-like in adults. Highly variable; males from yellow to grey with bright blue lines and spots; females and young pale brown or greenish with small and large spots and blotches, mixed dark and light. Widespread south coast from central New South Wales to Jurien Bay (Western Australia), and Tasmania; particularly abundant in the southernmost areas. Various habitats from seagrass beds to offshore reefs with weeds or kelp, to about 40 m. Attains 32 cm.

BLUE-FINNED LEATHERJACKET
Thamnaconus degeni (Regan, 1903)

D II,33-38. A 32-37. C 12. P 12-14. Body very compressed, very elongate in large males. Ventral flap small with small but obvious ventral fin rudiment. Caudal peduncle moderately shallow, compressed, without spines or bristles on sides. Gill opening a small slit anteriorly just above pectoral fin base. Scales small with numerous tiny spinules, skin velvety to touch. Prominent slender first dorsal spine above eyes, with small to minute barbs, folds down onto shallow groove. Pectoral fins small, rounded. Brown to grey; males distincly marked with iridescent blue spots and lines. Fins pale blue. South coast from Wilson's Promontory to the Great Australian Bight, including Tasmania. Deep-water species, usually on reef outcrops and shipwrecks in 15-70 m; juveniles shallow in seagrass. Attains 29 cm. Indo-Pacific genus, comprising 13 species, variously distributed throughout.

407

CHINAMAN LEATHERJACKET
Nelusetta ayraudi (Quoy and Gaimard, 1824)

D II,30-35. A 30-33. C 12. P 12-14. Body very compressed, males slightly deeper-bodied than females. Ventral flap small with minute, indistinct ventral fin rudiment. Caudal peduncle moderately shallow, elongate, com-

pressed, without spines or bristles on sides. Gill opening a small slit anteriorly just above pectoral fin base. Scales small with numerous tiny spinules, skin velvety to touch. Prominent short flattened first dorsal spine above eyes, moderate-sized barbs along each edge, folds down onto shallow groove. Pectoral fins very small, rounded. Caudal fin rounded, fan-like in adults. Juveniles with distinct longitudinal bands; adults plain brownish-yellow to reddish-brown. Southern half of Australia, from southern Queensland to North West Cape, except Tasmania. Also known from northern New Zealand. Adults rarely observed by divers, deep on outcrop reefs to 360 m. Juveniles school in estuaries; specimens up to about 50 cm occur in Port Phillip Bay, usually with shipwrecks. Attains 70 cm. Monotypic genus.

Nelusetta ayraudi   Young adult ▼ Juv. ▲

Pseudalutarius nasicornis   Initial colour-form ▼

Aluterus scriptus ▼

RHINOCEROS FILEFISH
Pseudalutarius nasicornis (Temminck and Schlegel, 1850)

D II,43-50. A 41-46. C 12. P 11. Body very elongate, slightly deepening with age, very compressed. Ventral flap and ventral fin rudiment absent. Caudal peduncle relatively deep, compressed, without spines or bristles on sides. Gill opening a small slit anteriorly just above pectoral fin base. Scales tiny, skin velvety to touch. Very long, slender first dorsal spine well anterior to eyes near tip of snout. Pectoral fins small, rounded. Broad dark longitudinal bands along sides, more pronounced in juveniles. Widespread tropical Indo-Pacific, ranging to subtropical zones, on the east coast south to Sydney. Shallow coastal reefs and estuaries with seagrasses, soft coral in tropical waters. Secretive, often positioned vertically with head down, behind weeds or seapens. Attains 18 cm. Monotypic genus.

P. nasicornis   Male (left) and female (right)

SCRIBBLED LEATHERJACKET
Aluterus scriptus (Linnaeus, 1758)

D II,43-49. A 46-52. C 12. P 13-15. Body very compressed. Ventral flap small, not very extendable. Caudal peduncle moderately deep, compressed, without spines or bristles on sides. Gill opening a small slit anteriorly just above pectoral fin base. Scales tiny, skin velvety to touch. Slender first dorsal spine above eyes, folds down onto concave smooth area. Pectoral fins small, rounded. Caudal fin rounded, very large in adults. Small juveniles yellow with black spots, becoming ornamented with bright blue with age. Circumtropical, ranging intermittently into subtropical zones. Juveniles pelagic, up to large size, with floating weeds; adults on coastal reefs, usually in more than 20 m. Attains 1 m, including large tail; largest species in the family. The other species in this genus, *A. monoceros*, has similar distribution, ranges to New South Wales waters; totally pelagic, usually occurs well offshore; greyish-blue, caudal fin truncate.

BLACK REEF-LEATHERJACKET
Eubalichthys bucephalus (Whitley, 1931)

D II,36-39. A 35-37. C 12. P 12-14. Body very compressed. Ventral flap moderately small with minute, indistinct ventral fin rudiment. Caudal peduncle moderately shallow, elongate, compressed, without spines or bristles on sides. Gill opening a small slit anteriorly just above pectoral fin base. Scales small with numerous tiny spinules, skin velvety to coarse to touch. Prominent first dorsal spine above eyes has small barbs, folds down onto shallow groove. Pectoral fins small, rounded. Brown to black, conspicuous eyes. Southern Australia, from central New South Wales to Houtman Abrolhos, not known from Tasmania. Mainly offshore reefs, in 10-250 m, but usually rather deep. Often in pairs, secretively moving about in and out of holes among boulders. Attains 40 cm. Australian genus with six species.

GUNN'S LEATHERJACKET
Eubalichthys gunnii (Günther, 1870)

D II,33-37. A 32-36. C 12. P 12-15. Body round, very deep in small juveniles to elongate, moderately deep in adults, very compressed. Ventral flap moderately small with minute, indistinct ventral fin rudiment. Caudal peduncle compressed, without spines or bristles on sides. Gill opening a small slit anteriorly just above pectoral fin base. Scales small with numerous tiny spinules, skin velvety to coarse to touch. Prominent first dorsal spine above eyes has small barbs, folds down onto shallow groove. Pectoral fin small, rounded. Dark yellow-brown to black with reticulating lines. South coast from Wilson's Promontory to South Australia and Tasmania. Coastal reefs, primarily deepwater outcrops, juveniles in estuaries; range from 5-150 m as juveniles to adults respectively. Attains 60 cm.

E. gunnii   Large juv, ▲   Small juv. ▼

409

MOSAIC LEATHERJACKET
Eubalichthys mosaicus (Ramsay and Ogilby, 1886)

D II,36-39. A 35-37. C 12. P 12-14. Body circular, very deep in small juveniles to elongate, moderately deep in adults, very compressed. Ventral flap moderately small with minute, indistinct ventral fin rudiment. Caudal peduncle compressed, without spines or bristles on sides. Gill opening a small slit anteriorly just above pectoral fin base. Scales minute, skin smooth to touch. Prominent first dorsal spine above eyes, has small barbs which fade with age, folds down onto shallow groove. Pectoral fin small, rounded. Yellow or brown-orange, blotched with blue in mosaic pattern, becoming more blue with age; males darker with indistinct whitish vertical bands. Widespread southern half of Australia from the latitude of southern Queensland. Juveniles commonly in estuaries under jetties, adults on deep coastal reefs. Attains 60 cm.

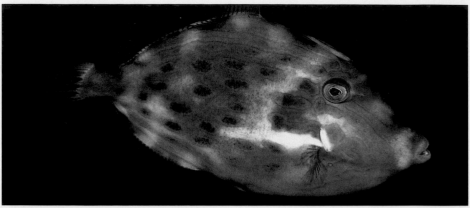

Eubalichthys mosaicus Male ▲ Female ▼

Eubalichthys mosaicus Juv.

PYGMY LEATHERJACKET
Brachaluteres jacksonianus (Quoy and Gaimard, 1824)

D II,24-28. A 22-27. C 12. P 10-12. Body about circular, very compressed. Ventral flap very large without ventral fin rudiment, abdomen expendable by inflating. Caudal peduncle moderately deep, without spines or bristles on sides. Gill opening a small slit anteriorly just above pectoral fin base. Scales small with numerous tiny spinules, skin velvety to coarse to touch, body spongy. Prominent but short, smooth first dorsal spine above eyes, folds down over concave smooth area. Pectoral fin small, rounded. Caudal fin large, rounded. Variable from pale yellowish-brown to green-brown, sometimes dusky, with small spots or ocelli. Some geographical variants. Widespread southern waters from southern Queensland to Lancelin (Western Australia) and commonly in Tasmania. From very shallow seagrass beds to deeper weed habitats in coastal bays. Attains 9 cm. West Pacific genus comprising four species, two of which are Australian.

B. jacksonianus S coast juv., unusual dark form

Brachaluteres jacksonianus Adults, east coast ▲ Adult, south coast ▼

TEMPERATE BOXFISHES
FAMILY ARACANIDAE

A small family of primarily temperate Indo-Pacific species, comprising six genera and 11 species, the majority of which occur in Australian waters. Only one species each is known from Japan and South Africa. Like the tropical boxfishes, the body is protected by a hard-shelled carapace which does not enclose the dorsal and anal fins. It is movable at the gills and is made up of rows of alternating triangular plates, forming large hexagonal and square patterns over the sides. The caudal peduncle is variably covered with separate plates, and in some species these intermittently form rings. All genera have a ventral ridge and, except one, a dorsal ridge. In addition, two more ridges on each side are often very pronounced and spines

are usually present over the plates and ridges. Small juveniles are almost as round as a marble, changing to a more elongate shape with age, but many species are ovate and slightly compressed. The eyes are moderately small and placed high and forward at an angle facing laterally and forward. Dorsal and anal fins are of moderate size and are about opposite, usually posterior-most over the caudal peduncle. The caudal peduncle is usually short and the caudal fin of moderate size. A skin toxin is present which is released under stress and can kill other fish and even the temperate boxfishes themselves if they are kept confined. Compared to tropical boxfishes, however, the temperate boxfishes are less troublesome for aquarists. The species

are sexually dimorphic with males gaudily coloured with bold yellow and blue markings. In addition, the spines are often greatly reduced. This has led to different names for the sexes, however males derive from females and some species have changed sex in captivity. Most species live deep and only a few are observed by divers. In New South Wales, only one species is commonly observed by divers and other species which occur in shallow waters on Australia's south coast are occasionally trawled off the southern part of the state. Of the six species occurring in south-eastern waters, only three are observed in shallow depths and are included here.

Aracana aurita Male ▲ Female ▼

SHAW'S COWFISH
Aracana aurita (Shaw, 1798)

D 10-11. A 10-11. C 11-12. P 11-12. Body very robust, about pentagonal in cross-section; deep keel in adults. Juveniles smooth, rounded; develop ridges and spines with growth which become very large in some females, but usually reduce in males with age. Usually a double series of large spines over back, starting above eyes. Some spines along lateral ridges. Head profile has pointed snout which steepens in males. Moderate-sized triangular plates form very large hexagonal patterns. Dorsal and anal fins short-based, opposite. Pectoral fins fan-shaped. Caudal fin truncate with rounded corners in large adults. Small juveniles almost black, developing striped pattern with light and brown areas. Males have bright blue and yellow stripes and spots. Widespread south coast, including Tasmania. Adults trawled regularly in southern New South Wales, juveniles occasionally in the shallows. Rocky reefs, usually fairly deep, including estuaries, from about 10-160 m. Attains 20 cm. Genus comprises two species, both included here.

Aracana aurita Small juv.

411

ORNATE COWFISH
Aracana ornata Gray, 1838

D 10-11. A 10. C 11. P 10. Body very robust, about pentagonal in cross section; deep keel in adults. Juveniles smooth, rounded; develop ridges and spines with growth which become very large in some females, but usually reduce in males with age. Usually a double series of large spines over back, starting above eyes. Some spines along lateral ridges. Head profile has pointed snout which steepens in males, which develop large hump in front of eyes. Moderate-sized triangular plates form very large hexagonal patterns, becoming indistinct in large adults; covered with small tubercles. Dorsal and anal fins short-based, opposite. Pectoral fin fan-shaped. Caudal fin truncate with rounded corners in large adults. Small juveniles almost black, developing striped pattern with light and brown areas. Males have bright blue and orange stripes and spots. Widespread south coast, including Tasmania, from Wilson's Promontory to Esperance. Trawl reports from southern New South Wales need verification. Shallow coastal bays, mainly in seagrass beds, sometimes abundant. Attains 15 cm.

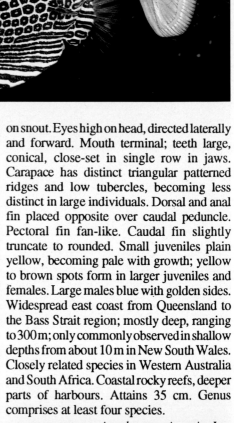

Aracana ornata Male ▼ Female ▲

EASTERN SMOOTH BOXFISH
Anoplocapros inermis (Fraser-Brunner, 1935)

D 10-11. A 10-11. C 11. P 12. Large adults oval, deep, slightly compressed; sides curved, pronounced keel-like ridges on dorsal and ventral midlines. Sides with two more indistinct ridges, longitudinal from over eyes and just below pectoral fin base. Juveniles almost spherical, smooth. Dorsal profile convex over eyes; males develop small hump on snout. Eyes high on head, directed laterally and forward. Mouth terminal; teeth large, conical, close-set in single row in jaws. Carapace has distinct triangular patterned ridges and low tubercles, becoming less distinct in large individuals. Dorsal and anal fin placed opposite over caudal peduncle. Pectoral fin fan-like. Caudal fin slightly truncate to rounded. Small juveniles plain yellow, becoming pale with growth; yellow to brown spots form in larger juveniles and females. Large males blue with golden sides. Widespread east coast from Queensland to the Bass Strait region; mostly deep, ranging to 300 m; only commonly observed in shallow depths from about 10 m in New South Wales. Closely related species in Western Australia and South Africa. Coastal rocky reefs, deeper parts of harbours. Attains 35 cm. Genus comprises at least four species.

Anoplocapros inermis Male ▲ Female ▼

Anoplocapros inermis Juv.

TROPICAL BOXFISHES
FAMILY OSTRACIIDAE

This family comprises some unusual species, known as box or trunkfishes and cowfishes, in six genera and 20 species distributed in all major tropical oceans. The body is largely covered with well-defined hexagonal bony plates fused into a ridged case with holes for the moving parts, the fins, caudal peduncle, mouth, eyes and gills. The genera differ primarily in cross-section shapes, with flat to rounded bellies, tapering above slightly to almost a square, or a broad triangle with a dorsal ridge. The surfaces are smooth but some species have prominent spines above the eyes or on the back. The mouth is small and set low, with fleshy lips and a single row of flattened conical or incisiform teeth in each jaw. Eyes are large and placed high, facing laterally. The slit-like gill opening is just anterior to the pectoral fin base. Fins consist entirely of soft rays and ventral fins are absent. Pectoral, dorsal and anal fins are of a similar size, and rounded or slightly angular. The anal fin is positioned posterior-most in the carapace, with the dorsal fin anteriorly above. The caudal fin is large and truncate to rounded, with a long caudal peduncle. The body is covered with a toxic mucus which deters predators but the toxin is also released when under stress, killing other fish or even the boxfishes themselves if they are kept confined. They are mostly shallow-water species found on sheltered reefs and estuaries, feeding on a variety of invertebrates. Some species are sexually dimorphic with colourful males. Several species range well beyond their breeding grounds with pelagic larvae taken by the current. On the east coast, six species range to New South Wales, and one of these to eastern Victoria.

LONGHORN COWFISH
Lactoria cornuta (Linnaeus, 1758)

D 8-9. A 8-9. P 10-11. C 9-10. Body short in juveniles, cube-like when just settled, elongate in large adults. Horn-like spines develop quickly after settling, very large in adults, projecting forward from above each eye to well beyond snout; spines of similiar size project backwards from end of each ventro-lateral ridge. Carapace cross-section almost square with low median dorsal ridge; flat ventrally. Head profile very steep, almost square to ventral part; mouth at angle. Eyes placed high and forward on sides. Dorsal fin placed well ahead of anal fins. Caudal fin increases in length with age, reaching almost body length. Green to brown, some blue markings. Widespread tropical Indo-Pacific; juveniles south to the Sydney area. Mostly in sandy lagoons, feeding on sand invertebrates exposed by blowing sand away. Attains 50 cm, including large tail. Genus has three species, all included here.

Lactoria cornuta   Adult ▼   Juv. ▲

413

ROUND-BELLY COWFISH
Lactoria diaphana (Bloch and Schneider, 1801)

D 9. A 9. P 10-11. C 10. Body short in juveniles, cube-like when just settled, elongate in large adults. Horn-like spines develop quickly after settling; prominent, sharp, about eye size; pair projects forward from above eyes, another pair projects backwards from end of ventro-lateral ridges, single spine central on back. Cross-section of carapace four-sided with concave sides, deeply convex ventral part, small median ridge on flat dorsal part. Dorsal profile straight from eyes to caudal fin; ventral profile deeply rounded, particularly in juveniles. Head profile moderately steep. Eyes placed high and forward on sides. Dorsal fin place well in advance of anal fin. Caudal fin elongates with age. Green to brown, some dark markings. Widespread tropical Indo-Pacific; juveniles south to Lakes Entrance, Victoria. Rocky, algae-rich reefs to about 30 m. Juveniles may have prolonged pelagic stage in some areas; specimens as small as about 15 mm were found on the bottom in New South Wales. Attains 30 cm.

Lactoria diaphana Juv.

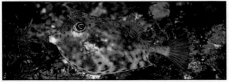

THORNY-BACK COWFISH
Lactoria fornasini (Bianconi, 1846)

D 9. A 9. P 11-12. C 10. Body short in juveniles, cube-like when just settled, slightly more elongate as large adults. Horn-like spines develop quickly after settling; prominent, about eye size, sharp; pair projects forward from above eyes, another pair projects backwards from end of ventro-lateral ridges, single spine central on back. Cross-section of carapace four-sided with concave sides; ventrally broad, slightly convex; moderate-sized median ridge on flat dorsal part. Head profile moderately steep. Eyes placed high and forward on sides. Dorsal fin placed well in advance of anal fin. Caudal fin elongates with age. Green to brown, blue spots and scribbles. Widespread tropical Indo-Pacific; adults commonly south to the Sydney area. Rocky reef and estuaries, usually in mixed sponge and weed habitats. Attains 20 cm.

TURRETFISH
Tetrosomus concatenatus (Bloch, 1786)

D 9. A 9. P 11. C 10. Body short in juveniles, somewhat pyramid-like when just settled, with extended ridges and recurving spines which reduce with age. Cross-section of carapace triangular, sides almost flat, additional short ridge with spines over each eye. Spines reduce with age, ridges become less defined. Head profile moderately steep, snout slightly pointed, mouth low. Eyes placed high and forward on sides. Dorsal fin placed well in advance of anal fin. Caudal fin slightly elongates with age. Green to brown, dark outlines on some plates, increasing blue spotting with age. Widespread tropical Indo-Pacific; adults south to latitude of Sydney. Coastal estuaries in rubble in seagrass beds and sponge habitat. Shallow protected bays to at least 30 m. Genus comprises two wide-ranging species, however only one known from New South Wales.

Lactoria fornasini ▲

Tetrosomus concatenatus Adult ▲ Juv. ▼

414

YELLOW BOXFISH
Ostracion cubicus Linnaeus, 1758

D 8-9. A 9. P 10-11. C 10-12. Small juveniles cube-shaped, elongate with growth to moderately elongate. Cross-section about square with rounded corners, adults broader ventrally. Body smooth, head profile concave anteriorly, snout moderately long. Dorsal fin slightly in advance of anal fin, both set posteriorly. Caudal fin rounded, increases proportionally in size with age; caudal peduncle becomes long and thick. Small juveniles bright yellow with black spots, sometimes called dice-fish; darken with age, spots may change to black-edged white ocelli; some geographical variations. Widespread tropical Indo-Pacific. Juveniles commonly well south in New South Wales, brought down with warm currents; in narrow ledges usually with sea-urchins, sometimes in small aggregations. Adults swim openly over reefs, often in small loose aggregations. Attains 45 cm. Largest genus; nine species, two of which range south.

Ostracion cubicus Small juv. *O. cubicus* Large adult ▲ Large juv. ▼

BLACK BOXFISH
Ostracion meleagris Shaw, 1796

D 9. A 9. P 10-11. C 10. Small juveniles cube-shaped, elongate with growth to moderately elongate. Cross-section about square with rounded corners. Body smooth, head profile straight anteriorly, snout moderately long. Dorsal fin slightly in advance of anal fin, both set posteriorly. Caudal peduncle long; caudal fin moderate-sized in adults. Juveniles jet black with white spots which reduce in size and become more numerous with age. Males derive from females, become distinctly coloured with blue and orange spotted sides. Widespread tropical Indo-Pacific with several geographical variations; juveniles known in New South Wales south to the Sydney area. Secretive, on shallow coral reefs, usually several together and one visible. Juveniles in the Sydney area usually among large boulders in coastal bays. Attains 20 cm.

Ostracion meleagris Juv.

Ostracion meleagris Male ▼

PUFFERFISHES
FAMILY TETRAODONTIDAE

A large family comprising about 20 genera and at least 100 species. The family consists of several distinct groups and subfamilies including the sharp-nosed puffers or tobies, Canthigasterinae, and the short-nosed species, Tetraodontinae. The latter comprises the large species as well as a great variety of small coastal species. Their common name comes from their ability to inflate themselves to almost balloon proportions in order to deter predators. In addition, many species are prickly and when inflated become even more hazardous to consume. All species are poisonous in either internal organs or skin toxins, so overall the message should be clear – "leave me alone". Some species are clearly marked to advertise their likely fatal properties and some totally unrelated species have taken advantage of this by copying the image (mimicking) of pufferfishes in both shape and colouration to bluff potential predators with their looks. The pufferfishes have a small beak-like mouth, fused teeth divided in front, a tough and often prickly skin, and fins which consist entirely of soft rays. Dorsal and anal fins are about opposite, placed posteriorly, are small to large and paddle-shaped or angular. The caudal fin is usually large and round. Pectoral fins are moderately large and rounded. Ventral fins are absent. The gill openings are small and just in front of the pectoral fin bases. Pufferfishes are globally distributed in tropical to temperate seas. A few species have adapted fully to fresh water and numerous species are estuarine, tolerating low salinities. The family is well represented in southern waters with 12 temperate and eight tropical species ranging to central New South Wales.

Smooth Toadfish (*Tetractenos glaber*)
Buried specimen about to take off

SADDLED PUFFER
Canthigaster valentini (Bleeker, 1853)

D 9. A 9. P 16-17. C 11. Body moderately compressed. Snout long, pointed, conical; mouth small with strong convex dental plates; eyes placed high, well back. Caudal peduncle

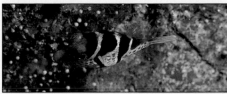

Canthigaster valentini   Adult ▼ Juv. ▲

strongly compressed, tapering to caudal fin. Movable ridge over back and belly, raised vertically. Fins rounded in juveniles; caudal fin almost truncate in large adults; dorsal and anal fins small. Colour distinct; black saddles typical for this species; males have blue lines radiating from eyes. Widespread tropical Indo-Pacific; juveniles well south in New South Wales. Sheltered reefs, shallow to about 20 m, often in pairs. Attains 10 cm. Large genus comprising about 25 small species, usually not exceeding 15 cm, commonly called sharp-nosed puffers. Few characters, general morphology virtually the same for each species; colour patterns best means to identify species. Juveniles differ slightly from adults in having bolder markings; there are slight geographical variations. Primarily tropical genus with expatriates ranging to temperate zones. Of the six species included here, only one is a true local species.

CROWNED PUFFER
Canthigaster coronata (Vaillant and Sauvage, 1875)

D 9-10. A 9-10. P 16-17. C 11. Body moderately compressed. Snout long, pointed, conical; mouth small with strong convex dental plates; eyes placed high, well back. Caudal peduncle strongly compressed, tapering to caudal fin. Movable ridge over back and belly, raised vertically. Fins rounded in juveniles; caudal fin almost truncate in large adults; dorsal and anal fins small. Colour distinct with black saddles; ornamental edging with orange and blue typical for this species. Widespread tropical Pacific, ranging well south to Montague Island; replaced by similar species in Indian Ocean. Usually fairly deep, rarely less than 10 m, common at about 30 m. Attains 14 cm.

Canthigaster coronata   Newly settled juv.

Canthigaster coronata ▼

Canthigaster amboinensis ▼

AMBON PUFFER
Canthigaster amboinensis (Bleeker, 1865)

D 10-12. A 10-11. P 16-17. C 11. Body moderately compressed. Snout long, pointed, conical; mouth small with strong convex dental plates; eyes placed high, well back. Caudal peduncle strongly compressed, tapering to caudal fin. Movable ridge over back and belly, raised vertically. Fins rounded in juveniles; caudal fin almost truncate in large adults; dorsal and anal fins small. Combination of spots and lines identifies this species; in addition, the usually 12 dorsal and 11 anal fin rays helps separation from similar species. Widespread tropical Indo-Pacific from eastern Indian Ocean to eastern Pacific, juveniles south to Sydney. Shallow, often just below surge zones. Attains 12 cm.

Canthigaster amboinensis   Juv.

WHITE-SPOTTED PUFFER
Canthigaster janthinoptera (Bleeker, 1855)

D 9-10. A 9-10. P 16-18. C 11. Body moderately compressed. Snout long, pointed, conical; mouth small with strong convex dental plates; eyes placed high, well back. Caudal peduncle strongly compressed, tapering to caudal fin. Movable ridge over back and belly, raised vertically. Fins rounded in juveniles; caudal fin almost truncate in large adults; dorsal and anal fins small. Of the several similar species, this species best separated by combination of large white spots in juveniles, becoming dense in adults, and stripes radiating from eyes. Widespread tropical west Pacific to east Africa. Secretive, moving close to substrate, usually deeper than 10 m; juveniles often in sponges in the Sydney area. Attains 80 mm.

Canthigaster janthinoptera   Adult ▼   Juv. ▲

BENNETT'S PUFFER
Canthigaster bennetti (Bleeker, 1854)

D 9-11. A 8-10. P 14-16. C 11. Body moderately compressed. Snout long, pointed, conical; mouth small with strong convex dental plates; eyes placed high, well back. Caudal peduncle strongly compressed, tapering to caudal fin. Movable ridge over back and belly, raised vertically. Fins rounded in juveniles; caudal fin almost truncate in large adults; dorsal and anal fins small. Colour variable with habitat, greenish in weedy areas. Widespread tropical west Pacific to east Africa. Juveniles south to Montague Island. Various habitats, from shallow weedy lagoons, to deeper offshore rocky reefs, to at least 30 m; commonly swims in pairs. Attains 90 mm.

Canthigaster bennetti ▼

Canthigaster callisterna ▼

CLOWN TOBY
Canthigaster callisterna (Ogilby, 1889)

D 11. A 10-11. P 17-18. C 11. Body moderately compressed. Snout long, pointed, conical; mouth small with strong convex dental plates; eyes placed high, well back. Caudal peduncle strongly compressed, tapering to caudal fin. Movable ridge over back and belly, raised vertically. Fins rounded in juveniles; caudal fin almost truncate in large adults; dorsal and anal fins small. Easily identifiable by double black stripes. Restricted to New South Wales and New Zealand waters, including Lord Howe and Norfolk Islands. Very similar species in Japan at similar latitudes. Coastal to offshore reefs, often in pairs, usually between 10-40 m. Largest species (together with *C. rivulata* from Japan), attaining 25 cm.

Canthigaster callisterna   Juv.

BRUSH-TAIL TOADFISH
Torquigener squamicauda (Ogilby, 1911)

D 9-10. A 7-8. P 13-17. C 11. Body thick, rounded above, flattened with distinct lateral skin-folds below; tapers posteriorly to narrow caudal peduncle. Teeth fused, beak-like with medial groove. Chin prominent. Eyes elongate, dorsally and posteriorly placed, facing laterally. Gill opening small, just anterior to pectoral fin base. Lateral line usually distinct, circling eye; branches over pectoral fin, along body to caudal fin with upper and lower connections. Body densely set with well-developed two-rooted small spines. Upper rounded part of pectoral fins longest. Dorsal and anal fins angular. Caudal fin truncate. Identifiable by black lateral stripe. Eastern Australia from central Queensland to just south of Sydney. Mainly in clear estuaries in shallow depths over sand, sometimes in small aggregations. Attains 15 cm. Large genus with 12 Australian species, four of which are included here.

WEEPING TOADO
Torquigener pleurogramma (Regan, 1903)

D 9-11. A 8-11. P 14-17. C 11. Body thick, rounded above, flattened with distinct lateral skin-folds below; tapers posteriorly to narrow caudal peduncle. Teeth fused, beak-like with medial groove. Chin prominent. Eyes elongate, dorsally and posteriorly placed, facing laterally. Gill opening small, just anterior to pectoral fin base. Lateral line usually distinct, circling eye; branches over pectoral fin, along body to caudal fin with upper and lower connections. Body densely set with well-developed two-rooted small spines. Upper rounded part of pectoral fins longest. Dorsal and anal fins angular. Caudal fin truncate. Mostly pale with distinct stripe; thin vertical stripes on cheeks. Widely distributed along southern half of Australia, including Lord Howe Island, except Tasmania and Bass Strait area. Sheltered coastal bays, usually in small to large schools over sand. Attains 20 cm.

SPINELESS TOADFISH
Torquigener perlevis (Ogilby, 1908)

D 9-10. A 6-7. P 15-17. C 11. Body thick, rounded above, flattened with distinct lateral skin-folds below; tapers posteriorly to narrow caudal peduncle. Teeth fused, beak-like with medial groove. Chin very prominent. Eyes elongate, dorsally and posteriorly placed, facing laterally. Gill opening small, just anterior to pectoral fin base. Lateral line usually distinct, circling eye; branches over pectoral fin, along body to caudal fin with upper and lower connections. Small embedded spines over sides of body. Upper rounded part of

pectoral fins longest. Dorsal and anal fins angular. Caudal fin truncate. Pale with brownish-yellow; best separated from other species by lack of obvious skin-spines, very prominent chin. Known from Gulf of Carpenteria to central New South Wales. Shallow, sandy estuaries in small aggregations; recorded to 53 m. Attains 20 cm.

Torquigener squamicauda   Resting on the substrate ▲   Photographed in Sydney Harbour ▼

Torquigener pleurogramma ▼

Torquigener perlevis ▼

419

ANDERSON'S TOADFISH
Torquigener andersoni Hardy, 1983

D 9-10. A 7-8. P 15-16. C 11. Body thick, rounded above, flattened with distinct lateral skin-folds below; tapers posteriorly to narrow caudal peduncle. Teeth fused, beak-like with medial groove. Chin prominent. Eyes elongate, dorsally and posteriorly placed, facing laterally. Gill opening small, just anterior to pectoral fin base. Lateral line usually distinct, circling eye; branches over pectoral fin, along body to caudal fin with upper and lower connections. Body densely set with well-developed two-rooted small spines. Upper rounded part of pectoral fins longest. Dorsal and anal fins angular. Caudal fin truncate. Pale, yellowish-brown, pale spotting. Only known from Jervis Bay and Bermagui, but appears to be more tropical, as Bermagui specimens were dying, washed up on beaches with a cold current from the south. Attains 16 cm.

Torquigener andersoni ▲   *Reicheltia halsteadi* ▼

HALSTEAD'S TOADFISH
Reicheltia halsteadi (Whitley, 1957)

D 9-10. A 7-8. P 14-16. C 11. Body thick, rounded above, flattened with distinct lateral skin-folds below; tapers posteriorly to narrow caudal peduncle. Teeth fused, beak-like with medial groove. No obvious chin. Eyes elongate, dorsally and posteriorly placed, facing laterally. Gill opening small, just anterior to pectoral fin base. Lateral line indistinct. Body spines absent from sides. Pectoral fins large, upper rounded part longest. Dorsal and anal fins angular. Caudal fin moderately long, truncate. Pale, sandy-coloured, however eyes bright green. Only known from Queensland to southern New South Wales. Only observed solitary, on sand just beyond turbulent zone off surf beaches. Attains 16 cm.

Tetractenos hamiltoni   Day colouration ▲   Night colouration ▼

COMMON TOADFISH
Tetractenos hamiltoni (Gray and Richardson, 1843)

D 8-10. A 6-8. P 15-17. C 11. Body thick, rounded above, flattened with distinct lateral skin-folds below; tapers posteriorly to narrow caudal peduncle. Teeth fused, beak-like with medial groove. Chin weakly developed. Eyes elongate, dorsally and posteriorly placed, facing laterally. Gill opening small, just anterior to pectoral fin base. Lateral line usually distinct, branches over pectoral fin, along body to caudal fin with upper and lower connections. Body densely set with small spines. Pectoral fins large, upper rounded part longest. Dorsal and anal fins angular. Caudal fin moderately long, truncate. Sandy-coloured, darker above. East coast from Townsville to southern New South Wales. Schooling species, primarily in shallow estuaries, often buried in sand with only eyes exposed. Attains 14 cm.

SMOOTH TOADFISH
Tetractenos glaber (Freminville, 1813)

D 9-11. A 7-9. P 15-18. C 11. Body elongate, thick, rounded above, flattened with distinct lateral skin-folds below; tapers posteriorly to narrow caudal peduncle. Teeth fused, beak-like with medial groove. Chin weakly developed. Eyes elongate, dorsally and posteriorly placed, facing laterally. Gill opening small, just anterior to pectoral fin base. Lateral line usually distinct, branches over pectoral fin, along body to caudal fin with upper and lower connections. Body densely set with minute spines embedded in skin giving smooth texture. Pectoral fins large, upper rounded part longest. Dorsal and anal fins angular. Caudal fin truncate. Sandy above with black blotches. South-east coast from Moreton Bay to Kangaroo Island, including Tasmania. Coastal bays on sandy flats, often in very large schools, entering fresh water in estuaries. Attains at least 15 cm.

BARRED TOADFISH
Contusus richei (Freminville, 1813)

D 9-11. A 8-10. P 14-17. C 11. Body robust, rounded above and below; tapers posteriorly to narrow, moderately long caudal peduncle. Teeth fused, beak-like with medial groove. Chin weakly developed. Eyes elongate, dorsally and posteriorly placed, facing laterally. Gill opening small, just anterior to pectoral fin base. Lateral line indistinct, angled from top of head to caudal fin. Body densely set with small spines. Pectoral fins large, upper rounded part longest. Dorsal and anal fins angular. Caudal fin rounded. Pale, greyish above, broad dark patches in irregular bands. Mainly known from the south coast from the Wilson's Promontory area to Ceduna, the top of the Great Australian Bight, including Tasmania; also recorded from New Zealand waters. Shallow water, mainly in estuaries, sometimes extremely common, but extending to 50 m. Attains 22 cm.

PRICKLY TOADFISH
Contusus brevicaudus Hardy, 1981

D 9-11. A 8-9. P 13-15. C 11. Body thick, rounded above and below; tapers posteriorly to narrow, moderately long caudal peduncle. Teeth fused, beak-like with medial groove. Chin weakly developed. Eyes elongate, dorsally and posteriorly placed, facing laterally. Gill opening small, just anterior to pectoral fin base. Lateral line indistinct, angled from top of head to caudal fin. Body densely set with small spines. Pectoral fins large, upper rounded part longest. Dorsal and anal fins angular. Caudal fin rounded. Pale, greyish or yellowish above, larger and darker blotches in upper half. Known from Jervis Bay to Rottnest Island, including northern and eastern coasts of Tasmania. Nocturnal; usually observed in estuaries to about 20 m. Attains 25 cm.

Tetractenos glaber Night photograph ▲

Contusus richei ▲   *Contusus brevicaudus* ▼

RINGED TOADFISH
Omegophora armilla (Waite and McCulloch, 1915)

D 11-13. A 9-11. P 20-23. C 11. Body rather bulky, thick, rounded above and below; tapers posteriorly to narrow, moderately long caudal peduncle. Teeth fused, beak-like with medial groove. Chin weakly developed. Eyes elongate, dorsally and posteriorly placed, facing laterally. Gill opening small, just anterior to pectoral fin base. Lateral line indistinct, angled from top of head to caudal fin. Body densely set with small spines. Pectoral fins smallish, upper rounded part longest. Dorsal and anal fins angular. Caudal fin rounded. Brown or grey above; usually has distinct black circle around pectoral fin base. Primarily known from south-western Australia, but range extends as far as Botany Bay and northern Tasmania. In Victoria, usually in more than 20 m, but much shallower in south-western Australia; recorded to 146 m. Attains 25 cm.

MAINSTAY PUFFER
Arothron firmamentum (Temminck and Schlegel, 1850)

D 13-15. A 8-9. P 15-17. C 11. Body latrally compressed, tapers posteriorly to narrow, moderately long caudal peduncle. Teeth fused, beak-like with medial groove. Chin weakly developed. Eyes elongate, dorsally and posteriorly placed, facing laterally. Gill opening small, just anterior to pectoral fin base. Lateral line indistinct, angled from top of head to caudal fin. Body densely set with small spines. Pectoral fins large, upper rounded part longest. Dorsal and anal fins angular. Caudal fin slightly rounded. Mostly dark, sometimes lighter below; numerous small pale spots in adults. Spots variable and usually larger in juveniles, sometimes joining into irregular lines. Primarily pelagic, 10-180 m, but occasionally observed inshore on reefs; specimens are frequently washed up after storms. Widespread in south-eastern waters of Australia and also New Zealand; separate population in Japan from where it was originally described. Slight colour differences between northern and southern hemisphere populations; they may represent separate species, in which case *gillbanksi* would be correct name for southern hemisphere species. Attains 43 cm in Australia, 35 cm in Japan.

STARRY TOADFISH
Arothron stellatus (Bloch and Schneider, 1801)

D 10-12. A 10-11. P 17-19. C 11. Body thick, rounded above and below; tapers posteriorly to thick, moderately long caudal peduncle. Teeth fused, beak-like with medial

A. firmamentum ▲   Several hundred specimens in dense school near West King Island, NZ ▼

Photograph: John Calcott

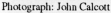

Arothron stellatus ▼

groove. Eyes elongate, dorsally and posteriorly placed, facing laterally. Gill opening small, just anterior to pectoral fin base. Lateral line indistinct, angled from top of head to caudal fin. Pectoral fins large, upper rounded part longest. Dorsal and anal fins angular. Caudal fin truncate. Variable with growth; juveniles have distinct black banding over belly; adults primarily have small black spots everywhere except belly. Very widespread in the tropical Indo-Pacific; in New South Wales, large adults range to the Sydney area. Sheltered reefs in shallow to deep water; known to 58 m. Large species; adults easily attain more than 1 m.

STARS AND STRIPES TOADFISH
Arothron hispidus (Linnaeus, 1758)

D 10-11. A 10-11. P 17-19. C 11. Body thick, rounded above and below; tapers posteriorly to thick, moderately long caudal peduncle. Teeth fused, beak-like with medial groove. Eyes elongate, dorsally and posteriorly placed, facing laterally. Gill opening small, just anterior to pectoral fin base. Lateral line indistinct, angled from top of head to caudal fin. Pectoral fins large, upper rounded part longest. Dorsal and anal fins angular. Caudal fin truncate. Mostly dark with small white spots. Widespread tropical Indo-Pacific. Adults south to Seal Rocks, New South Wales. Shallow coastal protected bays to at least 50 m. Attains 50 cm.

NARROW-LINED PUFFER
Arothron manillensis (Proce, 1822)

D 9-11. A 9-10. P 16-19. C 11. Body thick, rounded above and below; tapers posteriorly to thick, moderately long caudal peduncle. Teeth fused, beak-like with medial groove. Eyes elongate, dorsally and posteriorly placed, facing laterally. Gill opening small, just anterior to pectoral fin base. Lateral line indistinct, angled from top of head to caudal fin. Pectoral fins large, upper rounded part longest. Dorsal and anal fins angular. Caudal fin truncate. Variable dark grey to yellowish with few to many longitudinal lines. West Pacific from New South Wales to southern Japan. Estuaries, shallow lagoons, in 1-5 m. Overlaps with the elsewhere occurring, closely related *A. immaculatus*. Attains 30 cm.

PORCUPINEFISHES
FAMILY DIODONTIDAE

A small family of medium-sized fishes, comprising six or seven genera and about 20 species. Porcupinefishes occur primarily in tropical waters of the major oceans, but some range to temperate zones. They are similar to pufferfishes in their ability to inflate themselves to considerable size but, in addition, have large spines which point outwards when they are inflated. The spines are modified scales and may be rigid, movable or both, depending on the genus. Teeth are totally fused into beak-like jaws. Other features include prominent eyes, large, mostly rounded paddle-like fins consisting entirely of soft rays, and the absence of ventral fins. The gill opening is small, slit-like

Arothron manillensis ▼

and just anterior to the pectoral fin base. An inconspicuous lateral line is present. All species have pelagic juveniles and one species is fully pelagic. Adults are benthic and occur on shallow sheltered reefs or deeper offshore, ranging to depths of more than 300 m. Most species appear to be nocturnal, usually sheltering in caves during the day, and feed on a variety of invertebrates including hard-shelled species. Although reputed to be poisonous, some species are eaten by islanders in the Pacific with no obvious ill effects. Of the five species included here, only two are of southern origin.

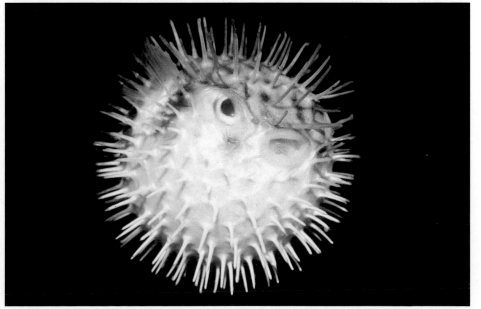

Globe Fish (*Diodon nichthemerus*)   Fully inflated; well protected by surrounding sharp spines

THREE-BAR PORCUPINEFISH
Dicotylichthys punctulatus Kaup, 1855

D 12-13. A 12. P 20-21. C'9. Body short, oblong in adults, rounded, covered with spines except snout and caudal peduncle. Spines round; short, non-erectable on upper sides and back; increase in length to moderately long, three-rooted and erectile on belly and head. Head broad, snout short, eyes lateral with broad interorbital; mouth broad, slightly less than interorbital width. Pectoral fins large, posterior edge almost straight, upper rays longest. Dorsal and anal fins rounded, placed posteriorly, opposite and of similar size. Caudal fin also of similar size, rounded. Greenish or bluish-grey above, light below; three dark bars evenly spaced on anterior half of sides, distinct black spots between spines. East coast from Queensland; strays occasionally wash up in the Bass Strait area. Shallow protected coastal reefs to offshore reefs, to about 50 m. Usually in large rocky ledges during the day, sometimes in small, loose aggregations. Attains 43 cm.

AUSTRALIAN BURRFISH
Allomycterus pilatus Whitley, 1931

D 12-13. A 12. P 20-21. C 9. Body rounded, covered with spines except snout, caudal peduncle. Spines blade-like, fixed with tripod-like bases, short anteriorly and ventrally, increasingly larger dorsally and posteriorly; largest spine about equal to eye diameter. Head broad, snout short, eyes lateral with broad interorbital; mouth broad, slightly less than interorbital width. Posterior edge of pectoral fins shallow, notched; upper pectoral rays longest. Dorsal and anal fins rounded, placed posteriorly, opposite and of similar size. Caudal fin also of similar size, rounded. Greenish-grey above, the rest pale; some black eye-sized spots on upper and middle parts of body; deepwater specimens with large yellow blotches on sides. Widespread southern waters, from the Sydney area to Western Australia and Tasmania. Occurs primarily in deep water, where sometimes trawled in great quantities in 70-180 m, but occasionaly found in shallow estuaries; recorded depth range 5-320 m. Attains nearly 50 cm.

Allomycterus pilatus Shallow-water form ▲ Deepwater form; trawled specimen ▼

GLOBE FISH
Diodon nichthemerus Cuvier, 1818

D 12-13. A 12-14. P 19-21. C 9. Body rounded, covered with spines except snout, caudal peduncle. Spines long, narrow, erectile, each with a pair of opposite basal roots; many spines equal or longer than eye-diameter. Head broad, snout short, eyes lateral with broad interorbital; mouth broad, slightly less than interorbital width. Posterior edge of pectoral fins shallow, notched; upper pectoral rays longest. Dorsal and anal fins rounded, short-based, opposite and of similar size; placed posteriorly, virtually over caudal peduncle. Caudal fin also of similar size, rounded. Greyish above with yellow or greenish tinge; pale below; four dark bars on side, but often indistinct in large adults. Southern Australia from central New South Wales to similar latitude in Western Australia, and Tasmania. Common in southern shallow bays, often in small aggregations; may be active during overcast days as well as nights. Known to about 50 m. Attains 28 cm.

Diodon nichthemerus ▲

Diodon holocanthus ▼

FINE-SPOTTED PORCUPINEFISH
Diodon holocanthus Linnaeus, 1758

D 13-15. A 13-15. P 21-24. C 9. Body rounded, covered with spines except snout, caudal peduncle. Spines long, narrow, erectile, each with a pair of opposite basal roots; many spines equal or longer than eye-diameter, longest on forehead; some variation between populations. Head broad, snout short, eyes lateral with broad interorbital; mouth broad, slightly less than interorbital width. Posterior edge of pectoral fins shallow, notched; upper pectoral rays longest. Dorsal and anal fin rounded, short-based, opposite and of similar size; placed posteriorly, virtually over caudal peduncle. Caudal fin also of similar size, rounded. Pale, brownish; juveniles have pupil-sized black spots on belly; adults have large dark blotches dorsally including interorbital bar, numerous small spots all-over. Circum-tropical distribution, ranging on the east coast south to central New South Wales. Sheltered bays and estuaries, but also known from trawls to about 100 m. Attains 30 cm.

BLOTCHED PORCUPINEFISH
Diodon liturosus Shaw, 1804

D 14-16. A 14-16. P 21-25. C 9. Body rounded, covered with spines except snout, caudal peduncle. Spines moderate-sized, narrow, erectile, each with a pair of opposite basal roots; short tri-base spine above gill opening; longest spines above pectoral fins. Head broad, snout short, eyes lateral with broad interorbital; mouth broad, slightly less than interorbital width. Posterior edge of pectoral fins shallow, notched; upper pectoral rays longest. Dorsal and anal fin rounded, short-based, opposite and of similar size; placed posteriorly, virtually over caudal peduncle. Caudal fin also of similar size, rounded. Greyish-brown, distinct pale-outlined black blotches dorsally, black bar below eyes. Widespread tropical Indo-Pacific from southern Africa to southern Japan and Society Islands; on Australia's east coast to central New South Wales. Usually fairly deep on coastal reefs, in ledges during the day. Attains 45 cm.

Diodon liturosus ▼

GLOSSARY

Abdomen: belly.

Acute: sharply pointed.

Adipose: fatty tissue.

Adipose eyelid: transparent tissue, covering or partly covering eye, usually streamlining with head.

Adipose fin: usually a small second dorsal fin lacking rays.

Allopatric: living in separate geographical areas.

Anterior: towards front or head.

Antrorse: turned forward.

Anal: behind anus.

Anus: external opening of intestine.

Axil: angular region on body at base of pectoral fin.

Barbel: a fleshy tentacle-like extension, usually near the mouth.

Benthic: living close to or on the bottom.

Bucklers: bony plates along fin bases of belly.

Canine: long conical tooth.

Carapace: hard outer shell covering body.

Carnivore: consumer of animal-matter .

Caudal: of or pertaining to the tail.

Cirri: tiny barbels or spines.

Claspers: male organs to transmit sperm.

Compressed: flattened on sides.

Corselet: a densely scaled area in tuna-like fishes.

Crenulate: edges scalloped.

Ctenoid: term used for scales with spiny edges or surface.

Cuspidate: teeth with projecting points.

Cycloid: term used for scales which are generally smooth.

Deciduous: loosely attached, usually scales.

Demersal: living on the bottom.

Denticles: tooth-like structures.

Depressed: flattened dorsally.

Diurnal: active during the day.

Dorsal: of or pertaining to the back.

Emarginate: margin slightly hollowed (fins).

Esca: bait-like portion of a luring apparatus (anglerfishes).

Finlet: small fin-like structures, usually in series in scombroids, following dorsal fins.

Fusiform: spindle-shaped and tapering to both ends.

Gill arch: bony part supporting filamentous respiration parts.

Gills: lungs function or respiration chambers.

Gill opening: exhaust for water flow through gills.

Gill slits: term used for the gill openings of sharks and rays because of their shape.

Gill rakers: series of bony projections on inner curves of gill arches, often functioning as filters..

Herbivore: consumer of vegetable matter.

Illicium: rod-like portion of a luring apparatus (anglerfishes).

Incisiform: applies to teeth with flattened cutting edges.

Interorbital: between eyes on top of head.

Jugular: position of ventral fins in the throat region.

Keel: reinforcing ridge, usually laterally on caudal peduncle in fast pelagics, compromising between streamlining and strength.

Lanceolate: spear-shaped or broadly pointed.

Lateral: of or pertaining to the side.

Lateral line: a sensory canal system along sides to detect pressure changes, ranging from a series of simple tubes to complicated pressure cells in a broad wide band, and often penetrating through scales in tubes or cut-outs (notched).

Leptocephalus: larval stage of eels.

Lunate: crescent moon shaped.

Medial: in the middle, usually along dorsal- and ventral-most edges.

Medial fins: fins along medial edges, thus dorsal, caudal and anal fins.

Meristics: countable features.

Mimicry: the act of an organism purposely resembling another.

Molariform: bluntly rounded grinding shaped (teeth).

Monotypic: containing a single species.

Nape: upper part of head over and behind eyes.

Nasal: of the nostril.

Nictitating membrane: cleaning or protecting eyelid.

Nocturnal: active at night.

Ocellus: a marking simulating the image of an eye.

Omnivore: consumer of both animal and vegetable matter .

Opercle: upper bony edge of the gill cover.

Operculum: gill cover, containing opercle and preopercle bones.

Origin: starting point, beginning of a longitudinal part at the head end.

Oviparous: egg producing, hatching externally from female afterwards .

Ovoviviparous: egg producing, hatching inside female or at birth.

Paired fins: refers to pectoral and ventral fins, usually opposite and mirroring one another.

Palate: roof of the mouth.

Palatine: bone in each side of the palate.

Papilla: fleshy projection.

Pectoral fin: uppermost of paired fins; usually on sides, immediately following gill openings.

Peduncle: body part between anal and caudal fins.

Pelagic: oceanic, belonging to the open sea.

Phytoplankton: plant life in plankton.

Planktivore: animal with a diet consisting of plankton matter.

Plankton: organisms drifting freely in the currents.

Posterior: towards rear end or tail.

Postlarva: larva after absorbtion of yolk.

Precaudal pit: small indentation in caudal peduncle just in front of fin.

Prehensile: adaption for holding on by wrapping, body or tail.

Preopercle: front part of the operculum, an angled bone distantly below and behind the eye.

Principal rays: number of fin rays, including all branched and segmented rays (excluding procurrent or simple rays).

Protrusible: usually applied to mouth with extendable jaws.

Radii: grooves in scales, crossing growth rings.

Retrorse: curving backwards.

Rostrum: bony projecting snout.

Rudimentary: reduced part without obvious function.

Scute: bony scale with a keel-like ridge or spine.

Segmented ray: fin rays showing cross striations.

Serrate: edged in saw-like spines or notches.

Spiracle: opening behind eye, leading to gill and mouth cavity, in most sharks and rays.

Sympatric: living in the same area.

Synonym: different names given to the same species.

Tholichthys: pelagic stage of a butterflyfish.

Thoracic: of or pertaining to the chest region.

Thorax: chest.

Tricuspid: having three cusps or points (teeth).

Truncate: used for caudal fin with mostly straight vertical edge.

Tubercle: short blunt pimple-like spine.

Ventral: of or pertaining to the underside.

Ventral fins: lower-most paired fins along underside.

Villiform: numerous small slender projections, brush-like, often used for teeth.

Viviparous: giving birth to live young, usually free-swimming.

Vomer: front bone in the roof of the mouth.

Zooplankton: animal organisms in plankton

INDEX